GLOBAL ANTI-TERRORISM LAW AND POLICY

All indications are that the prevention of terrorism will be one of the major tasks of governments and regional and international organizations for some time to come. In response to the globalized nature of terrorism, anti-terrorism law and policy have become matters of global concern. Anti-terrorism law crosses boundaries between states and between domestic, regional and international law. It also crosses traditional disciplinary boundaries between administrative, constitutional, criminal, immigration and military law, and the law of war. This collection is designed to contribute to the growing field of comparative and international studies of anti-terrorism law and policy. A particular feature of this collection is the combination of chapters that focus on a particular country or region in the Americas, Europe, Africa and Asia, and overarching thematic chapters that take a comparative approach to particular aspects of anti-terrorism law and policy, including international, constitutional, immigration, privacy, maritime, aviation, and financial law.

VICTOR V. RAMRAJ is an Associate Professor at the Faculty of Law, National University of Singapore (NUS). His main areas of teaching and research are anti-terrorism law and policy, legal theory, criminal law and theory, and constitutional law. Before joining the NUS Faculty of Law in 1998, he served as a judicial law clerk at the Federal Court of Appeal in Ottawa and as a litigation lawyer in Toronto. He has published widely in anti-terrorism law, criminal law and constitutional law.

MICHAEL HOR is a Professor at the Faculty of Law, National University of Singapore. He is a former Magistrate of the Subordinate Court of Singapore and has been Chief Editor of the *Singapore Journal of Legal Studies*. He is a Member of the Criminal Practice Committee of the Law Society of Singapore.

KENT ROACH is a Professor of Law at the University of Toronto. He has appeared before the Canadian Senate and Indonesia's working group on anti-terrorism law. He co-taught an innovative seminar at the University of Toronto on Comparative Anti-Terrorism Law and Policy, and has been a special lecturer at the National University of Singapore, the University of Siena and New York University on comparative anti-terrorism law. He has written eight books and over eighty articles published in a wide variety of countries.

GLOBAL ANTI-TERRORISM LAW AND POLICY

Edited by

VICTOR V. RAMRAJ, MICHAEL HOR

AND KENT ROACH

CAMBRIDGE
UNIVERSITY PRESS

CAMBRIDGE UNIVERSITY PRESS
Cambridge, New York, Melbourne, Madrid, Cape Town, Singapore, São Paulo

CAMBRIDGE UNIVERSITY PRESS
The Edinburgh Building, Cambridge, CB2 2RU, UK

Published in the United States of America by Cambridge University Press, New York

www.cambridge.org
Information on this title: www.cambridge.org/9780521851251

© Cambridge University Press 2005

First published 2005

Printed in the United Kingdom at the University Press, Cambridge

A catalogue record for this book is available from the British Library

ISBN-13 978-0-521-85125-1 hardback
ISBN-10 0-521-85125-4 hardback

CONTENTS

v

CONTRIBUTORS

WILLIAM C. BANKS, Laura J. and L. Douglas Meredith Professor, Syracuse University College of Law; Professor of Public Administration, Maxwell School of Citizenship and Public Affairs, Syracuse University

ROBERT C. BECKMAN, Associate Professor, Faculty of Law, National University of Singapore

ALEJANDRO D. CARRIÓ, Visiting Professor of Law, Louisiana State University and Professor of Law at Palermo University

KEVIN E. DAVIS, Professor of Law, New York University School of Law

LAURA K. DONOHUE, Center for International Security and Cooperation, Stanford Institute for International Studies, Stanford University

DAVID DYZENHAUS, Professor of Law and Philosophy, University of Toronto

MARK FENWICK, Associate Professor, Faculty of Law, University of Kyushu

HELEN FENWICK, Professor in Law, Human Rights Centre, Department of Law, University of Durham

OREN GROSS, Julius E. Davis Professor of Law and Director, Center for Legal Studies, University of Minnesota Law School

COLIN HARVEY, Professor of Human Rights Law, School of Law, Queen's University Belfast

MICHAEL HOR, Professor, Faculty of Law, National University of Singapore

HIKMAHANTO JUWANA, Dean and Professor of Law, University of Indonesia

C.L. LIM, Associate Professor, Faculty of Law, National University of Singapore

JÖRG MONAR, Professor of Contemporary Studies and Jean Monnet Professor, Sussex European Institute, University of Sussex

GAVIN PHILLIPSON, Senior Lecturer in Law, Human Rights Centre, Department of Law, University of Durham

C.H. POWELL, Senior Lecturer, Faculty of Law, University of Cape Town

VICTOR V. RAMRAJ, Associate Professor, Faculty of Law, National University of Singapore

KENT ROACH, Professor of Law, University of Toronto

H. HARRY L. ROQUE, JR., Assistant Professor, University of the Philippines College of Law

ALAN KHEE-JIN TAN, Associate Professor, Faculty of Law, National University of Singapore

TAN HSIEN LI, Ph.D. Candidate, Faculty of Law, National University of Singapore and Associate Researcher, Singapore Institute of International Affairs

SIMON S. C. TAY, Associate Professor, Faculty of Law, National University of Singapore and Chairman of the Singapore Institute of International Affairs

V. VIJAYAKUMAR, Professor of Law, National Law School of India University

LYNN WELCHMAN, Senior Lecturer in Islamic and Middle Eastern Law, Department of Law, SOAS, University of London

GEORGE WILLIAMS, Anthony Mason Professor and Director, Gilbert + Tobin Centre of Public Law, Faculty of Law, University of New South Wales

MARY W. S. WONG, Professor of Law, Franklin Pierce Law Centre, *formerly* Associate Professor of Law, Singapore Management University

SIMON N. M. YOUNG, Assistant Professor, Faculty of Law, University of Hong Kong

ACKNOWLEDGEMENTS

We owe an enormous debt of gratitude to R. Rueban Balasubramaniam, Sandra A. Booysen, Meyghan McCrea, Ng Pei Suin, Paul Tan, Paul Seah, and especially to Tecla Mapota, Abhinav Bhatt and Elizabeth Chua for their hard work on and dedication to this project. We are grateful to the Faculties of Law at the National University of Singapore and University of Toronto and their respective Deans, Tan Cheng Han and Ronald J. Daniels, for funding that allowed the editors to work together over a number of years in preparing this volume and this introduction. We are also extremely grateful to the National University of Singapore for providing the generous grant which made this book and the symposium that inspired it possible.

Introduction

VICTOR V. RAMRAJ, MICHAEL HOR AND KENT ROACH

I. Global anti-terrorism law and policy

The terrorist attacks of 11 September 2001 and subsequent attacks in many other parts of the world have resulted in an increased emphasis at the international, regional and national levels on anti-terrorism efforts. All indications are that the prevention of terrorism will be one of the major tasks of domestic governments and regional and international organizations for some time. Anti-terrorism law and policy has become a matter of global concern.

It is important that academics bring their critical and comparative insights to the global development of anti-terrorism law and policy. This will be a challenging task because anti-terrorism law crosses boundaries between states and between domestic, regional and international law. It also crosses traditional disciplinary boundaries between administrative, constitutional, criminal, immigration, military law and the law of war. In addition, insights from a broad range of disciplines including history, international affairs, military studies, philosophy, religion and politics will assist in understanding the development of anti-terrorism law and policy.

This book is designed to contribute to the growing field of comparative and international studies of anti-terrorism law and policy. The chapters in this book are revised versions of papers presented at a major international research symposium in Singapore in June 2004 that brought together leading legal academics from around the world to examine and compare anti-terrorism laws and policies in many of the major jurisdictions.

A particular feature of this book is the combination of chapters that focus on a particular country or region and overarching thematic chapters that take an overtly comparative approach by examining particular aspects of anti-terrorism law and policy.

Part One adopts various theoretical perspectives on anti-terrorism law and policy. The chapters in this Part examine distinctions between illegitimate terrorism and legitimate anti-terrorism, the definition of terrorism, and the role of risk perception and of legality in anti-terrorism efforts.

Part Two engages in a comparative study of anti-terrorism measures including the criminal law, laws against the financing of terrorism, immigration and asylum laws, laws involving technology and the regulation of aviation and maritime security.

Part Three discusses anti-terrorism law and policy in the strategically important and theoretical complex region of Asia. Various papers examine the evolution of anti-terrorism law and policy in Malaysia and Singapore, Indonesia, the Philippines, Japan, India and Hong Kong.

Part Four looks at the often neglected role of regional organizations in inspiring and coordinating anti-terrorism efforts. The organizations examined are ASEAN and the European Union.

Part Five examines anti-terrorism law and policy in the West with chapters on the United Kingdom, the United States and Canada. A final chapter examines both Australia and New Zealand. These last two jurisdictions could have been included in the Asian group, but seem to fit more naturally with the other western nations.

Finally, Part Six attempts to complete the world tour with chapters on the important regions of Africa, the Middle East and Latin America. No doubt other countries should have been included but there are limits to what is already a large volume. We have attempted to be as comprehensive and inclusive as we could given limits on time and space, but we are well aware that we are only starting to scratch the surface. Many other thematic topics, jurisdictions and disciplinary perspectives could usefully have been added to this collection. We see this as a preliminary point of departure for a generation of scholarship and debate about anti-terrorism law and policy.

II. Defining terrorism

Terrorism is an emotionally charged, morally laden and political contentious concept, which has nevertheless emerged as a critical and unavoidable feature of the legal landscape both internationally and domestically. As with any attempt to articulate the meaning of a contentious term, the mention of 'terrorism' evokes a range of images. Yet the emergence of terrorism as a crucial legal and political concept has forced the issue, challenging us to articulate a definition that in most cases has profound implications for the way in which individuals, businesses, communities, states, and regional and international organizations conduct their affairs.

The first step in defining terrorism consists in distinguishing terrorism from what it is not. Whatever terrorism is in its contemporary legal use, it is conceptually distinct from: (a) legitimate state responses or *counter*-terrorism, (b) national liberation struggles, and (c) ordinary criminal offences. And yet, on each of these counts, the attempt to define terrorism is fraught with difficulties. One important problem is that terrorism and counter-terrorism are indistinguishable in as much as they involve violence and fear, seek a broader audience, are purposive and instrumental, and affect non-combatants (see Chapter 2). Thus, to distinguish *legitimate* state responses from terrorist attacks is more difficult than it might first appear, and might well involve a closer look at what states do and choose not do – at the range of responses available to states and the ways in which they *refrain* from acting in the face of an act of political violence.

The uncertain distinction between terrorism and counter-terrorism has serious implications for the definition of terrorism under international law. While there is some agreement in international law in defining terrorism for specific purposes (such as stopping the flow of funds to terrorism groups – see Chapter 9), the attempt to formulate a comprehensive definition of terrorism is stymied by long-standing concerns over the legitimate use of political violence by national liberation movements.[1] Given the political difficulties involved in finding a comprehensive international definition (see Chapter 3), terrorism is defined at the domestic level with varying degrees of success.

But at the domestic level, the definition of terrorism is plagued by another concern. Once the ordinary criminal law is seen as inadequate for dealing with the perceived threat of terrorism, the tendency of legislators has been to create new super-criminal offences under the banner of terrorism. But this means that the new terrorist offences have to be distinguished from ordinary crimes and the way in which this is done often invites controversy. For example, the United Kingdom's influential Terrorism Act 2000 defines terrorism as requiring proof of religious or political motives. The political or religious motive approach has been followed with some variations in other jurisdictions including Australia (Chapter 24), Canada (Chapter 23), Hong Kong (Chapter 18) and New Zealand (Chapter 24), but has been resisted in others including the United States (Chapter 22), Indonesia (Chapter 14), and many countries in the Middle East (Chapter 26), which define terrorism primarily by reference to the nature of the harm caused.

III. The interplay between international, regional and domestic law and structures

One of the challenges of the study of global anti-terrorism law and policy is the important interplay between international, regional and domestic sources of law. There have been a number of important conventions on specific forms of terrorism at the international and regional levels, but, as discussed above, a

---

[1] This has important implications in the Philippines, for instance, where the government is involved in armed conflict with two groups which claim to be exercising the right to self-determination: see Chapter 15.

universal definition of terrorism has so far proved impossible to achieve. On 28 September 2001 the United Nations Security Council issued Resolution 1373 calling on all member states to criminalize terrorists acts and financing, planning, preparation and support for terrorism. This resolution, however, did not define what was terrorism, leaving that crucial, difficult and some might argue impossible task to each national state.

Security Council Resolution 1373 was unprecedented in part because it set forth in detail an anti-terrorism agenda for all member states and because it was issued under the mandatory provisions of Chapter VII of the United Nations Charter and as such bound all member states. It also created a new Counter-Terrorism Committee of the United Nations and called on all states to report to this new Committee no later than ninety days after the resolution was issued. In many countries this facilitated a rush to legislate new anti-terrorism laws, including the United Kingdom which already had tough anti-terrorism laws on the books (see Chapter 21). The country reports to the new Counter-Terrorism Committee provide a unique source of information about how nations are responding to terrorism.[2] At the same time, however, the resolution can be criticized for its relative inattention to international human rights norms and standards.[3] Indeed, it is not clear how this process relates to other rights-based activities at the United Nations. At both the international and domestic level, it can be argued that the imperative of security has, temporally at least, assumed a greater importance than respect for human rights.

The dominant role of the most powerful countries and of the executive in formulating Security Council Resolution 1373 has interesting parallels to the dominant role that the executive has played with respect to security issues at the domestic level (see Chapter 25). One of the starkest examples of executive domination has been the executive compilation of lists of terrorists and terrorist organizations, both domestically and internationally. In some cases, these lists can be subject to judicial review at the domestic level, but in all cases they provide an alternative to the traditional principles of the presumption of innocence and the adjudication of guilt for a specific offence in court.

Although the United Nations has played a very important role in encouraging and shaping anti-terrorism laws throughout the world, the

---

[2] See the Counter-Terrorism Committee's website at www.un.org/Docs/sc/committees/1373/reports.html.

[3] The only reference in the original resolution to human rights standards is found in paragraph 3(f) that calls on states to 'take appropriate measures in conformity with the relevant provisions of national and international law, including international standards of human rights, before granting refugee status, for the purpose of ensuring that the asylum-seeker has not planned, facilitated or participated in the commission of terrorist acts'.

role of regional organizations and regional instruments should not be ignored. This collection includes a chapter on the important role that the European Union has played in coordinating and structuring anti-terrorism efforts in members states (see Chapter 20) and the less robust role played by ASEAN (see Chapter 19). The role of regional instruments such as the Arab Convention on the Suppression of Terrorism should also not be ignored (see Chapter 26). Regional bodies and instruments can be an important mediating force between the international and the domestic. In the future, students of comparative anti-terrorism law and policy will have to be attentive to the complex interplay between international, regional and domestic laws and structures.

IV. Fairness, emergencies and the rule of law

State concerns about international terrorism have given rise to important questions of practice and principle concerning the emergence in many countries of a new broad anti-terrorism regime or the revitalization in other countries of older anti-terrorism measures. In Singapore and Malaysia few amendments to the anti-terrorism regime were needed in light of pre-existing internal security legislation dating back to the days of the communist insurgency of the 1950s and 1960s during the British colonial period (see Chapter 13). Steps have been taken under these existing laws to detain without trial suspected terrorists and, some might say, several non-terrorist suspects as well. In neighbouring Indonesia, the newly emerging democracy in the world's most populous Muslim nation, concern about the abrogation of human rights and a return to a not-yet-distant era of authoritarian rule, has so far resisted the imposition of harsh new security laws. The courts have been strict about state incursions into human rights, such as the retroactive application of anti-terrorism laws, including the death penalty (see Chapter 14).

In other countries mostly in the developed West, especially the United Kingdom (see Chapter 21) and the United States (see Chapter 22), governments have been quick to construct a complex anti-terrorism regime, amending the existing regimes of, for example, criminal law and procedure, immigration law, administrative law, aviation and maritime law, and financial law, in response to the perceived new threat of international terrorism. A particularly striking feature of anti-terrorism efforts in many of these regimes is how, despite the many amendments to the formal criminal law, governments have instead relied on alternatives to the criminal law, and in particular immigration law, which often has lower standards of proof than the criminal law. This raises important questions concerning fairness towards non-citizens including refugees seeking asylum (see Chapter 8). Indeed, claims of political and other forms of persecution made by immigrants and especially asylum seekers who in turn may be suspected as terrorists take us back full circle to the difficult process of defining what constitutes terrorism, particularly in societies in conflict and failed states.

The breadth of many anti-terrorism regimes and the vigour with which they are being enforced give rise to fundamental normative questions about the constitutional order and their implications for the role of the legislative, executive and judicial branches of government. We might question whether fundamental changes to the legal order are needed or justified in the first place. One of the important theoretical questions arising from the changing legal landscape is the extent to which the rule of law can and should be preserved. This volume features an important debate on this issue between Oren Gross and David Dyzenhaus. Building on his extra-legal measures model,[4] and the work of Dicey, Gross argues that Acts of Indemnity issued by the legislature after state officials have responded in an illegal fashion to an emergency such as terrorism can preserve legality by authorizing and constraining such illegal actions (see Chapter 5). Dyzenhaus, also drawing on Dicey, argues in favour of keeping state actions within the bounds of legality without *ex post* authorization of illegal acts. Drawing on common law principles of administrative law, Dyzenhaus proposes a 'Legality model' according to which, in times of emergency, governments adapt to the new circumstances by creating imaginative institutions with the necessary expertise to review national security decisions. While these institutions might not conform strictly to a formal conception of the separation of powers, the right sort of institution would be able to preserve legality while remaining sensitive to the special circumstances of terrorism that affect national security.

Whether and to what extent the judiciary should play a role in imposing normative constraints on the executive and legislative branches in times of crisis is an important issue. The literature on the psychology of risk perception suggests that public perception of risk may well be distorted after high-profile disasters, with such public fear having an influence on the formulation of anti-terrorism policy in the legislature and the executive branches of government. Either the judiciary or a specialized, independent administrative tribunal may well have a role to play in compelling the other branches of government to justify normatively and publicly any restrictive measure they seek to impose in the name of risk-prevention (see Chapter 6). But whether the courts are ready in practice to use their powers to constrain executive power is, however, another matter. This is so not only in Singapore and Malaysia, where judges might perceive a price to pay for asserting themselves 'against a determined government, especially if the spectre of legislative and constitutional amendment is not very far off' (see Chapter 13), but equally in the United States and the United Kingdom. Even after the United States

---

[4] 'Chaos and Rules: Should Responses to Violent Crises Always be Constitutional?' (2003) 112 *Yale Law Journal* 1011.

Supreme Court's decisions in *Hamdi* v. *Rumsfeld*[5] and *Rasul* v. *Bush*,[6] which insisted on judicial review of any detention of enemy combatants, it is 'as likely as not that the limited judicial role required by the *Rasul* and *Hamdi* decisions will be played out ... with little if any inconvenience to the government' (see Chapter 22). Similarly, while in the United Kingdom the courts 'have managed to achieve some amelioration of the scheme through the Human Rights Act ... the prospects for any general curtailment of the draconian legislative scheme ... seem remote indeed' (see Chapter 21).

As with other emergencies, the prospect of terrorist attacks forces us to take a closer look at our assumptions about fundamental values, legality and the role of the branches of government in a crisis. We are forced to consider to what extent we are prepared to subject anti-terrorism measures to judicially imposed normative side-constraints on state power, even if by doing so we reduce the effectiveness of our anti-terrorism policies. To answer this question, we need to consider whether the anti-terrorism agenda is effective in the first place.

V. How effective is the anti-terrorism agenda?

Those who study global anti-terrorism law and policy should be concerned not only with normative questions of fairness, but also more empirical questions concerning the effectiveness of anti-terrorism policy. Indeed, normative and positive analysis may complement each other should it prove to be the case that some of the most problematic anti-terrorism strategies – such as the use of torture and other extra-judicial means or the use of crude stereotypes or profiles based on race, religion or national origins – may be ineffective in stopping terrorism. Indeed, the hypothesis that violent overreaction to terrorism may spawn more terrorism should be closely examined.

Security Resolution 1373 placed much emphasis on laws against the financing of terrorism, and international, regional and domestic jurisdictions have devoted much effort to compiling lists of terrorists who cannot be financially supported and to broad laws against the financing of terrorism (see Chapter 9). The effectiveness of these interventions, however, remains an open question. The American 9/11 commission for example found that the costs of the attacks were less than half a million US dollars and expressed considerable scepticism about the ability to stop terrorists by stopping their financing.[7] This book includes chapters outlining steps that have been taken at various levels since 9/11 to improve aviation (Chapter 12) and maritime (Chapter 11) security. The strategies to protect aircraft and ports often rely on

---

[5] 124 S Ct 2633 (2004).   [6] 124 S Ct 2686 (2004).
[7] National Commission on Terrorist Attacks Upon the United States, *The 9/11 Commission Report* (New York: Norton, 2004) at 12.3.

administrative and licensing measures that are softer or less coercive than the use of criminal or immigration law or military force. Technology can play an important role in anti-terrorism law and policy by, for example, increasing the ability to screen material on aircraft and ships for hazardous substances. At the same time, the use of technology to facilitate surveillance presents serious risks to privacy (see Chapter 10).

After initially stressing the use of criminal or immigration law as the prime instruments to be used against terrorism, Canada released a new national security policy in 2004 that takes an all-risk approach that seeks to address not only the threats of terrorism including bio-terrorism and terrorism directed at critical infrastructures, but also diseases such as SARS and the disruptions of essential services by man-made or natural disasters (see Chapter 23). Even the American 9/11 Commission has recommended a softer 'hearts and minds' strategy and a strategy to prevent failed states as part of its anti-terrorism recommendations.[8] Two chapters in this book (Chapters 2 and 7) raise the issue of what would constitute a comprehensive approach to terrorism and security issues as an alternative to the use of coercive force. It remains to be seen whether a comprehensive all-risk approach to human security will result in a more rational allocation of resources and restrain some of the excesses and failures that may be associated with interventions that place all of their energies on detecting and detaining suspected terrorists.

VI. Convergence, divergence and context in anti-terrorism law and policy

It is understandable that the many lawyers that have contributed to this volume should focus on the analysis of law and legal institutions. That should not, however, be allowed to tempt us to underestimate the often decisive political and historical forces that are at play. At the level of regional cooperation in anti-terrorism initiatives, there is a striking contrast between the highly advanced discourse in Europe over the details of regional law and institutions devoted to the enterprise (see Chapter 20), and the growing accumulation of non-binding declarations of intent in Southeast Asia (see Chapter 19). In anti-terrorism as in other areas, historical reasons appear to explain the degree to which the nations of Europe trust each other, and the manner in which the nations of Southeast Asia jealously guard their national sovereignty.[9]

---

[8] *The 9/11 Commission* at 12.3 or pp. 361–98.
[9] Simplistically, European unity was forged in the fires of (at least) two catastrophic wars, while Southeast Asia bears the legacy of being colonized by different colonial powers, with the result that nations in the region have historically very little to do with each other.

Exclusive attention to legal and institutional design in anti-terrorism efforts will also fail to capture the fascinating, but troubling experience of countries like Argentina (see Chapter 27) and the Philippines (see Chapter 15) where the complicity of governmental elements in acts of terrorism reveal far more basic problems, such as the establishment of a sufficiently orderly and corruption-free government. Here it will be more fruitful to talk about how 'rule by law' may be installed, rather than how the 'rule of law' might constrain governmental excesses in the fight against terrorism.

The widely perceived 'anti-Islamic' flavour of anti-terrorism efforts since 9/11 is a serious problem anywhere, but nowhere does it influence public affairs more strongly than it does in Muslim or Muslim majority jurisdictions. In Indonesia (see Chapter 14) and the Middle East (see Chapter 26) there is a popular sentiment that many governments are being pressured by the United States to enact anti-Islamic legislation in the name of anti-terrorism. The results can be both surprising and alarming. Some governments at times appear to 'allow' real terrorists to escape the full force of the law, while at other times they use anti-terrorism legislation against mere political opponents, labelled 'extremist' for this purpose. Anti-terrorism law and policy may frequently be shaped at international and regional levels, but it also often has particular domestic uses that can only be fully understood by those familiar with local context and history.

This volume can only scratch the surface of what is really going on with anti-terrorism law and policy around the globe. In the Philippines, where the lack of institutional capacity to deal with terrorism is the most prominent issue, the alternative of importing US troops to do the work has sparked off an intense political controversy stemming from the historical experience of the Philippines being a US colony, and of the subsequent location of major US military bases there (see Chapter 15). Calls for Japan to be more pro-active in the 'war against terrorism' is snagged by the nation's professed total and perpetual renunciation of military solutions in international relations, a legacy of Japan's aggression and subsequent defeat in the Second World War (see Chapter 16). For better or for worse, attempts in Hong Kong to enact security legislation foundered, perhaps more out of a desire not to be dictated to by China, than because of human rights concerns (see Chapter 18). In many countries such as India and Pakistan, post-September 11 developments in anti-terrorism policy can only be fully understood in the context of past historical concerns and current geo-political realities (see Chapter 17).

In talking about regional and national peculiarities, care ought to be taken not to go to the other extreme of dismissing the common challenges and similarities in anti-terrorism law and policies throughout the world. Indeed, the indefinite detention of suspected terrorists under immigration laws and military orders in countries such as the United Kingdom, the United States and Canada calls into question any thesis that suggests that western responses to terrorism will necessarily reflect a more individualistic and libertarian culture than those found in the east and the south. This volume will have served its purpose if it gives some insight into the extent to which nations can usefully learn from each other, or simply talk to each other, about the problem of terrorism, a phenomenon which, however it may be defined, is common to all.[10]

---

[10] The chapters in this book were last revised between September and November 2004 and thus do not reflect changes in the law after that period. However, some of the important recent developments through June 2005 that bear directly on the chapters in this book are discussed in the Postscript (Chapter 28).

PART ONE

Theoretical Perspectives on Anti-Terrorism Law and Policy

2

Terrorism and the counter-terrorist discourse

I. Introduction

Nearly every essay on the subject of terrorism makes an apologetic nod to the difficulties of defining the term. Despite frequent mentions of 'state terrorism' as a form of many types of *terrorisms*, relatively few works then go on to discuss state terror, and those that do treat it as independent of non-state terror, state-sponsored terror or counter-terrorist policy. This chapter in some sense is little different, in that it too addresses definitional considerations. It departs from other works, however, in important ways. It adopts a Weberian mode of definition: that is, the elements discussed that constitute what is meant by 'counter-terrorism' or 'terrorism' are included not because I claim to have reached any great truth or resolved a discussion that is centuries old, but rather because I am writing about liberal, democratic states' response to what they *perceive* to be terrorist challenge. Thus, while I take Annamarie Oliverio's point well, that to have amassed a number of definitions and isolated common elements – as though truth were dependent on a majoritarian decision – distorts academic inquiry, I nevertheless find it helpful to describe the rules by which certain types of challenge become categorized. My contention is that once a challenge to a liberal, democratic state has been labelled as 'terrorist', certain responses follow. My purpose is to point out the associated risks. And my aim is to present a model of counter-terrorism that avoids the pitfalls of liberal states' past responses.

This chapter also departs from others in its evaluation of state counter-measures. It suggests that counter-terrorism, terrorism and state terrorism are not necessarily distinct phenomena. There is a relationship between them, often within the same state, and frequently within liberal, democratic regimes. Some scholars argue that state measures may be ineffectual or counter-productive.[1] But the list of individuals writing in the counter-terrorist field who suggest that liberal, democratic states' counter-terrorist

Special thanks to the Carnegie Corporation of New York for providing support for the research conducted in this chapter.

[1] See, e.g., Nadine Gurr and Benjamin Cole, *The New Face of Terrorism: Threats from Weapons of Mass Destruction* (New York, I. B. Tauris, 2000), at 232.

policies cross into state terrorism, or are anything but a *response* to a non-state, or state-sponsored challenge, are few.

This trend sits uneasily with the evidence: the United Kingdom, United States, Israel and Turkey, all liberal democracies, have been called on to defend their use of torture and 'inhuman and degrading' treatment. Controversial 'shoot to kill' policies and the disappearance of those labelled enemies of the state mark both the late twentieth and early twenty-first century treatment of terrorist challenge. Israel, the United Kingdom, Turkey, the United States and the Republic of Ireland have conducted sudden wide sweeps in which individuals have been held, incommunicado and indefinitely, with little information on their whereabouts made available. And Israel, the United States and Turkey have all openly used assassination and military measures leading to the death of thousands of unarmed civilians as a means of addressing terrorist challenge.

This is not to say that all counter-terrorist actions undertaken by these states amount to state terrorism. But rather than examining counter-terrorism separately from the phenomenon of terrorism, or including state terrorism in a broad definition or understanding of the term and then moving to case studies wherein 'terrorism from above' or 'terrorism from below' become manifest, I leave the door open to looking at state responses as themselves linked to the evolution of a terrorist discourse.[2]

One consequence in looking at links between state measures and challenges to the state is to distribute responsibility for the challenge itself. This conflicts with the aim of those in authoritative positions, whose ability to uphold their obligation to the citizenry has just been called into question. Because of this, and because such political violence is such an anathema to the principles of a liberal, democratic state, counter-terrorism is narrowly regarded as the state's response to a specific act or series of actions levied against it. Egregious state measures are then excused on the basis that their end is justified, that they apply only to the guilty, that they are present only for a temporary amount of time, or that the state faces extraordinary danger and is simply defending itself. The first three claims fail. The fourth, although frequently invoked as a consequence of the possible threat faced, is accurate in only an extremely select number of cases. Even then, it is not a blanket excuse for the adoption of extreme measures. Rather, it gives rise to an important debate regarding absolute and inalienable rights in the context of a liberal, democratic state. Together and singly, these four claims do not negate the actual circumstances surrounding counter-terrorist provisions: many aggressive as well as seemingly benign provisions contribute to grievances which become manifest in this type of violence and, more

---

[2] For a distinction between terrorism from above and terrorism from below, see Walter Laqueur, *Terrorism* (Boston, Little, Brown and Company, 1977), ch. 1.

importantly, for support for this type of violence. 'Counter-terrorist' actions may thus end up forming the basis for a response to what others perceive as a 'terrorist' act.[3]

Beyond spurring a violent response, state counter-terrorist measures, both in form and function, serve alternatively to undermine and reinforce state political legitimacy. State measures thus answer the challenge posed by non-state violence: whether the protections afforded to the individual within the liberal, democratic state will be upheld. On the one hand, this entails the right to life and property, which places a correlative duty on the government to ensure that these rights are not violated. In a liberal, democratic state it is on the basis of the protection of life and property that individuals leave a state of nature and enter into a social compact. On the other hand, this entails the protection of basic freedoms.

With these considerations in mind, what exactly is meant, in the United States, the United Kingdom, and elsewhere, by the term 'terrorism'? In the following discussion I argue first that counter-terrorism often shares many of the same qualities as terrorist acts themselves. This becomes particularly true as the state adopts a national security approach. In this way counter-terrorism can be understood not as a distinct phenomenon, but as a mirror image with many of the same consequences and implications demonstrated by acts of terror. Counter-terrorism and terrorism also share the same array of targets. And both are emotive, blatantly infused with moral meaning, and carry heavy religious overtones. This chapter addresses the issue of moral equivalence raised by this analysis. It concludes by challenging an assumption that undergirds the counter-terrorism world: that counter-terrorism is what states *do*. In contrast, the chapter asserts that of equal, and perhaps greater importance, is what states neglect – or choose *not* to do.

II. Defining the terms

Disagreement dogs the best efforts to come to a common definition of 'terrorism'. The Western inter-disciplinary debate in academia privileges the orientation of each field, with legal definitions focused on the criminal

---

[3] For instance, in 1988 the US military shot down an Iranian civilian aircraft over the Persian gulf. Although the United States claimed it was an unintended attack, the loss of 290 civilians led to international charges of terrorism against the United States. More recently, in December 2001 and January 2002, Gallup conducted a survey of 10,000 people in several Islamic countries including Jordan, Kuwait, Lebanon, Morocco, Saudi Arabia, Iran, Pakistan, Indonesia and Turkey. 66 per cent of those polled suggested that the 9/11 attacks lacked legitimacy. But a larger majority, 76 per cent, suggested the US military response to the attacks was unjustifiable. William Schneider, 'Reciprocal Hostility', *National Journal*, 9 March 2002.

nature of the acts, political constructs focused on governmental concerns such as the military or political aspects, and psychological definitions emphasizing motivation and the impact of the acts. These debates share some common elements, but few sufficiently address the deeply subjective nature of labelling an act 'terrorist'. The locus of this subjectivity is the designation of the injured party as innocent and violence as unjust. In the absence of a common, identical understanding of ethics, history and politics, however, no normative solution is possible. I return to this point in a moment. For now, a brief discussion of the term in its historical setting will demonstrate its highly manipulable qualities and lay the groundwork for a broad understanding of elements common to many interpretations of acts of terror.

A. Placement of terrorism in history

The word 'terrorism' derives from the Latin *terrere*, 'to frighten, to terrify; to scare away; to deter'. Its ancient root mirrors its antediluvian use as a means to obtain – and to maintain – power. The building of Ancient Egypt, Greece, and Rome depended upon it. From the Archaic to the Ptolemaic age, political upheaval and ruthless state action punctuated Egyptian history. In *Anabasis*, Xenophon recognized how psychological warfare could be used to great effect. And the Julio-Claudian dynasty – Tiberius, Caligula, Claudius, and Nero – employed terrorist techniques to subdue the population and counter political opposition.

Not only did states wield terror, but small bands used terrorism to pursue political and religious goals. The Sicarii of the first century, for example, sought to drive the Romans out of Palestine. They took over the fortress at Masada and attacked nearby villages, killing thousands of unarmed men, women and children. Many of the words we use to describe violence derive from such entities: the Zealots targeted Romans; the Assassins fought the Ottoman Seljuq Empire; and the Thugs assassinated travelers to pay homage to the Hindu goddess, Kali.

Despite the similarity of the ruthless actions of ancient emperors to those of later despots, and the Zealots, Assassins, and Thugs to neoteric non-state actors, the term 'terrorist' was not used until relatively recently to describe political violence. In the eighteenth century the term entered into common parlance – notably, in relation to the state, or what has come to be termed, 'terrorism from above'. Maximilien Robespierre's Jacobin party imposed its Reign of Terror, in which mass executions and extensive use of the guillotine paralyzed the population.

France was not alone in using terror to subdue the people. The Spanish Inquisition punished heresy with torture and death. England, Germany, Portugal and Italy at times depended on fear to secure their colonies. The

United States at its founding initiated a campaign that drove the number of Native Americans from between six and ten million in 1776 to less than 250,000 by 1900.[4] In the early- to mid-twentieth century totalitarian states, such as the Soviet Union under Stalin and Hitler's Germany, persecuted and killed civilians for political ends.

As previously alluded, academics frequently distinguish between terrorism from above and terrorism from below. In the nineteenth century, the Klu Klux Klan engaged in a widespread system of intimidation.[5] Attacks by one sub-state group on another, though, constitute just one type of terror from below. Non-state actors also attack states or leaders of states. In the early twentieth century a wave of anarchism swept the globe, with murders of prominent political leaders in the United States, Europe and Russia. Nationalist rebel groups such as the Irish Republican Brotherhood, precursors to the Irish Republican Army in Northern Ireland, religious groups, such as the Islamic al-Jihad in Egypt, and ideologically motivated organizations such as Sendero Luminoso in Peru provide further examples of terror from below. These groups contested those in control of state power.

Upon examination, however, the distinction between terror from above and terror from below quickly blurs. Decolonization and the advent of the Cold War led to an explosion in nationalist and ideologically-based terrorism, often fought through proxy groups by states with enormous power.[6] They supplied money, training, and weapons to rebel groups. In Nicaragua the United States supported the Contras against the Soviet-backed Sandanista regime. The Contras murdered, raped, mutilated, and kidnapped innocent civilians. In the 1960s the Central Intelligence Agency trained Cuban exiles to overthrow of Fidel Castro. In Mozambique, the US funded Resistência Nacional Moçambicana (RENAMO) against the Soviet-backed Frente de Libertaçâo de Moçambique (FRELIMO). In Rhodesia the Soviets subsidized the Zimbabwe African Peoples' Union (ZAPU) in opposition to Chinese support for the Zimbabwe African National Union (ZANU). More recently, the United States allied itself with the Northern Alliance in Afghanistan, a group responsible for the rape and murder of civilians and the death after capture of hundreds, perhaps thousands, of Taliban fighters.

---

[4] Miki Vohryzek-Bolden, Gayle Olson-Raymer, Jeffrey O. Whamond, *Domestic Terrorism and Incident Management: Issues and Tactics* (Springfield, Charles C. Thomas, 2001), 40–3.

[5] See 'History' at http://www.britannica.com/original?content_id=1447&pager.offset=2 for mention of the Klu Klux Klan and some of the other examples noted in the previous paragraphs.

[6] The following examples draw from the discussion in Noam Chomsky, 'International Terrorism: Image and Reality' in Alexander George, ed., *Western State Terrorism* (New York, Routledge, 1991), 12–38.

The lines are equally blurred when we consider the many 'governments in exile' that mark the twentieth century.

B. Problems with existing definitions

Some might disagree with the examples I have given of terrorism. It is one feature of the term that gray area marks not just the edges, but the very centre of what is considered a terrorist act. Despite numerous attempts largely spearheaded by Western liberal, democratic countries, to gain international agreement on the definition of terrorism, significantly different views exist. For instance, at the International Conference on Terrorism called by the Organization of the Islamic Conference in Geneva in June 1987, Ayatullah Shaykh Muhammad 'Ali Taskhiri, provided the following definition: 'Terrorism is an act carried out to achieve an inhuman and corrupt [mufsid] objective, and involving threat to security of any kind, and violation of rights acknowledged by religion and mankind.'[7] Taskhiri accused the United States of being the 'mother of international terrorism'. He writes:

> It is indeed comical that the United States of America, which is the mother of international terrorism, and the author of all the circumstances of oppression and subjection of peoples, by strengthening dictatorial regimes and supporting occupation of territories and savage attacks on civilian areas, etc. should seek to convene symposia on combating 'terrorism', i.e. any act that conflicts with its imperialist interests ... The real cure of terrorism – acts of individual terrorism in particular – consists, in our view, in removing the conditions that have brought it about.[8]

Taskhiri's definition includes air and sea piracy, colonialist operations, dictatorial acts against people, and all military methods contrary to human practice (such as the use of chemical weapons, the shelling of civilian popu-lated areas, the destruction of homes and the displacement of civilians). It considers all actions that undermine the international or any one national economy, adversely impact the poor and deprived, and impose debt on countries unable to burden them, to be terrorist. His definition covers any act that crushes the attempts of individuals to accomplish self-determination, and any imposition of 'disgraceful pacts'. It includes all types of pollution of geographical, cultural and informational environments. He writes, 'Indeed, intellectual terrorism may be one of the most dangerous types of terrorism.'

---

[7] Ayatullah Shaykh Muhammad 'Ali Taskhiri, 'Towards a definition of terrorism', Al-Tawhid, Vol. V No. 1 (Muharram 1408 AH/1987 CE), available at http://www.al-islam.org/al-tawhid/definition-terrorism.htm.
[8] Ibid.

I offer this concept of terrorism to illustrate the breadth of views on terrorism within the intellectual discourse. Taskhiri's definition also helps to explain support generated from socio-economic and political realities for the reaction to be perceived as violence. And it underscores the diverse manner in which terrorist actions become thus designated. In this chapter, however, I limit my understanding of what constitutes 'terrorism' more narrowly to the observed phenomena within five regions: the United States, United Kingdom, Ireland, Israel and Turkey. Within these geographically defined areas, numerous attempts have been made to define what is meant by terrorism. Many government and academic definitions share elements of, yet substantially differ from, Taskhiri's definition. And, like Taskhiri's definition, these contain faults. Where simplistic definitions have fallen short, more complex (but not necessarily more robust) have sought to take their place. These too, however, are fraught with difficulty.[9]

States, for instance, define terrorism in a manner that reflects the power bias. Since Edmund Burke's scathing condemnation of the French Revolution, the dominant interpretation of *terror* and *terrorism* has been violence thrust on society by radical elements bent on destroying the status quo: 'Thousands of those Hell-hounds called Terrorists, whom they had shut up in Prison on their last Revolution, as the Satellites of Tyranny, are let loose on the people.'[10] A term wielded by individuals with a vested interest in not just maintaining but expanding state power, the term terrorism, and countering this terrorism, has thus become embedded in the state domain – an entity with a vested interest in resisting a radically altered social and political order.

---

[9] A minimalist definition might read: 'the use, or threat of use, of violence against non-combatants in pursuance of a political end'. This definition is close to that the British Government used from 1974 until 2001. Britain's Prevention of Terrorism (Temporary Provisions) Act (PTA), defines terrorism as, 'the use of violence for political ends' and 'any use of violence for the purpose of putting the public, or any section of the public in fear'. But this deceptively simple definition quickly falls apart. Some definitions are so broad as to be almost nonsensical. In 2001 the United Kingdom replaced the Prevention of Terrorism (Temporary Provisions) Act, with the Terrorism Act. This legislation saw a new, energized terrorist definition, which became a focal point for discussions in parliament and in the media. Five subsections elaborate the meaning of the term. 'Terrorism' can mean the threat of, as well as the use of, an action listed in the subsections, that occurs anywhere in the world or impacts anyone, any property, or any government in the world: see Prevention of Terrorism (Temporary Provisions) Act 1989, c. 4, and Anti-terrorism Crime and Security Act 2001, c. 24.

[10] Letter to the Earl Fitzwilliam, Christmas 1795. First printed by Bishop King, from Burke's Manuscript, in vol. V. of the 4th ed. of Burke's works, 1812. Argument Part I, Lord Auckland's Pamphlet criticized, 3.4.72, located online as of 22 August 2002 at http://www.econlib.org/library/LFBooks/Burke/brkSWv3c4.html.

Even when definitions of terrorism *allow for* state terrorism, state actions in this area tend to be seen through the prism of war or national self-defence, not terror, such as the allied carpet-bombing of civilians in the Second World War, the United States' use of the atomic bomb on Hiroshima and Nagasaki, or the American use of more than seven million tons of bombs on Vietnam, Cambodia and Laos.[11] Even state support of insurgent groups, such as US aid to the Contras or Soviet training provided to ZAPU, while seen by other states and non-state actors as state-sponsored terrorism, again escape classification within those societies as terrorist violence. Individuals in society who try to draw attention to these as instances of state terrorism are seen as radical. It somehow flies in the face of convention to call something that a 'legitimate' government does, 'illegitimate.'

Although the state in many ways controls the application of the term, it is not immediately clear to which organizations, groups, or individuals states will apply this designation. The term frequently becomes subservient to geopolitical concerns.[12] As Michael Stohl writes, 'great power use and the threat of the use of force is normally described as coercive diplomacy and not as a form of terrorism' – despite the fact that it often involves 'the threat and often the use of violence for what would be described as terroristic purposes were it not great powers who were pursuing the very same tactic'.[13] He notes that even the term 'great power' only applies to members of an exclusive club. Yet it is 'great powers' that have the resources to engage in widespread terror.[14]

Because of dependence on geopolitical concerns, the term frequently carries with it a shifting designation. Yitzhak Shamir led Lehi, the 'Stern' gang, as a member of which Ya'akov Eliav arranged for seventy letter bombs to be sent to all members of the British Cabinet, heads of the Tory opposition and several military commanders. Irgun and the Stern gang committed numerous other atrocities. Shamir himself assassinated Jews suspected of collaborating with Britain. Menachem Begin, also a member of these avowedly terrorist organizations, went on to become Prime Minister. Yassar Arafat, the Founder of Fatah Revolutionary Council, in 1967 became chairperson of the Palestinian Liberation Organization (PLO) Executive

---

[11] Commager, 1985, 77, cited in Oliverio, *The State of Terror*, at 58.
[12] E.g., former Secretary of State George Schultz, in *The Challenge to Democracies*, writes, 'It is not a coincidence that most acts of terrorism occur in areas of importance to the West. More than 80 per cent of the world's terrorist attacks in 1983 occurred in West Europe, Latin America, and the Middle East.' Schultz's assertion clearly presents a chicken and egg issue: these events were deemed terrorist because they mattered to the United States. Steven Anzovin, ed., *Terrorism* (New York, H. W. Wilson Company, 1986), 54, 58.
[13] Michael Stohl in Alex P. Schmid and Albert J. Jongman, *Political Terrorism: A New Guide to Actors, Authors, Concepts, Data Bases, Theories, and Literature* (New York, North-Holland, 1988).
[14] Chomsky, 'International Terrorism', 12–38.

Committee. From the beginning he made no secret of his use of violence.[15] Yet over fifty governments recognized the PLO during the 1970s and 1980s.[16] This shifting designation is not singular to the Middle East. In Northern Ireland Martin McGuinness, former member of the IRA's Army Council, became the Minister for Education. Gerry Adams, previously commander of the Belfast Brigade, without renouncing violence, became a Member of Parliament. The United States initially welcomed Fidel Castro, as a response to what the country perceived as Batista's dictatorship in Cuba. When Castro paid a visit to then Vice President Richard Nixon, however, Nixon became convinced that he was a communist and in 1960 the US began plotting to reduce Castro's authority and charisma. After two mafia hit men failed to assassinate Castro, the United States attempted the ill-fated Bay of Pigs invasion.

Perhaps in reflection of the revolutionary origins of many states, successful political violence tends to be interpreted not as terrorist action, but according to nationalist histories. The leaders of the 1916 Easter Uprising in Dublin were patriots, leading Revolutionists in the United States became the 'Founding Fathers', the Stern gang translated into *Lehi*, *Lohamei Herut Israel* or Fighters for the Freedom of Israel, and Mustafa Kemal became Atatürk – the Father of the Turks. Their causes were just, their means a last resort. They were not terrorists, although they, and the states thus created, then had to face terrorism: Thomas Jefferson battled the Barbary Coast pirates, the PLO emerged as a force in Israel, and the Kurdistan Workers' Party (PKK) dominated the south-eastern territory of modern-day Turkey.

It is precisely groups like these that now form the basis for David Rappoport's much acclaimed 'wave theory' of terrorism. But this, and other theories which tabulate 'terrorist' incidents, or which group together terrorist movements and seek to compare them over time as marking different ages, represent less than half-truths. It brings to mind images of Plato's *Allegory of the Cave*, with chained individuals facing the wall and understanding the shadows as though the images were the bodies passing behind them. Terrorism can be seen in the shadow on the wall: a silhouette of a gun, discharged into the body of a man who crumples before us. But, beyond missing the full picture of those engaged in the campaign, the story of how the gun was delivered into the shooter's hands, the claim (valid or not) which gave rise to the shooting, and the nature of the structure to which the shooter

---

[15] See film footage: Arafat addressing UN, 18:50–19:20, 22:34–23:10, *Palestine 1890–1990* (Films for the Humanities and Sciences), United Nations.

[16] Aharon Yariv, 'A Strategy to Counter Palestinian Terrorism', in Merari, ed., *On Terrorism and Combating Terrorism* (1985), 1. Evidence continues to come forward in relation to his involvement in arms running and terrorist operations. See William Saffire, 'Arafat's Implausible Denials', *New York Times*, 10 January 2002.

is subject took place away from the mouth of the cave. All of these are beyond the story as related by the shadows. To look, then, at the wall of the cave and to try to discern patterns without acknowledging the corporal bodies behind us, and the more powerful structures and norms away from the mouth of the cave that influence behaviour, conveys only a small portion of the truth.

C. Essential qualities of acts of 'terrorism' and reflection in acts of 'counter-terrorism'

Just because a term is controversial, or subject to geopolitical concerns, does not mean that the phenomenon itself cannot be subjected to examination. In the five regions under consideration, seven qualities appear to form a necessary basis for an act to be considered terrorist.[17] What makes these elements important is that many of them are shared by counter-terrorist measures – and this is increasingly true as states adopt a national security approach. Recognizing these constituents contributes to an understanding of the dynamics that mark the terrorist – and counter-terrorist – dialogue.

First, the most obvious quality is that terrorist acts include violence. While I recognize the disagreement over this term, I use it here to mean causing significant physical or psychological harm. Notably, the 'otherness' implicit in the term 'violence' reinforces the 'otherness' of the application of the term 'terrorist'. Violence, like terrorism, is what *other* people do.

Counter-terrorism, too, reflects this otherness and often seeks physical and psychological harm. This is increasingly true as states adopt a national security approach, which is then used to justify the adoption of more and more aggressive provisions. Measures such as assassination, torture, military campaigns and missile attacks are, at their core, acts of extreme violence. But states, and state supporters, do not openly discuss them in this manner.

---

[17] My discussion of the definitional elements also draws from Schmid and Jongman. In their study of over one hundred definitions, the authors found that most include elements of violence or force and emphasize the political aspects of such acts. Fear and the threat of more actions, the psychological effect, and victim-target differentiation are also common. Definitions often reference the purposive nature of the acts, the use of terrorism as a strategy or tactic, and its extra-normal quality – that is, its tendency to violate existing, accepted rules. Its coercive nature is matched by its tendency to seek and attract publicity. To achieve maximum effectiveness, it involves a sense of unpredictability and indiscriminateness. Many definitions reference civilians, neutrals, or outsiders as victims and underscore the role of such actions as in order to intimidate. Some emphasis is placed on the clandestine nature of the perpetrator and the symbolic aspect of the action. Terrorism may also be defined by the criminal nature of the acts themselves. See Schmid and Jongman, *Political Terrorism*.

Instead, they are 'countermeasures', or pre-emptive operations, justified as 'necessary'. The guilt of the individuals affected is generally pre-determined by intelligence not made available to the population at large. In contrast, the term 'violence' is reserved to those who engage in the act of terrorism – to which the state actions supposedly respond. This sense of the 'other' bearing the unacceptable moral quality reflects in the application of both terrorism and counter-terrorism.

Second, to consider an act terrorist, fear must be present. This fear depends on the threat of future, unpredictable actions. The credibility of this threat is established by specific acts, and implicit in the threat is that future acts might occur, might possibly be larger, or possibly even less discriminate. This quality stems from the unknown, covert nature of terrorism. When non-state terrorist acts occur, a wide range of organizations may try to claim responsibility. Because of the covert nature of terrorism, those that engage in it must exhibit a pattern that clearly relates to the perpetrators' political programme. In other words, by establishing a pattern, individuals and organizations develop a signature, making future attacks more effective. Effectiveness is grounded in the certainty that a particular individual, group or organization engaged in the act, and that it could engage in similar or more extreme acts in the future. This breeds terror.

Like the quality of violence, counter-terrorism also incorporates an element of fear. And like violence, it becomes an essential element of counter-terrorism as the state adopts a national security approach. The government depends upon fear engendered in the target population to prevent sympathizers from aiding and abetting the actors posing a challenge, and to dissuade those participating in violence from remaining loyal to the original organization or cause. It seeks to head off the copycat effect that violent acts sometimes generate. And it tries, through its use of fear, to uphold the state's authority and ability to impose order on society.

Third, terrorism generates fear in a broader audience than the immediate, physical target. It is a form of armed propaganda. As media and technology advance and the distribution of media becomes more widespread, it may well become easier for terrorism to achieve its aim, making it more effective and more likely. If it works, people will use it. This broader audience is almost ensured by human nature itself. When a bomb goes off, people want to know why. If someone is killed, the immediate question is what happened. In answering this question, the very aims of terrorist organizations become public, bringing attention to their goals – which is why they engage in this act in the first place.

Looking more broadly at counter-terrorism, it quickly becomes apparent that state measures too are directed at a broader audience. State officials frequently target not only those immediately engaged in violence. They also target their possible community of support, possible state sponsors, other individuals and organizations who might engage in similar acts but for different reasons, the world community, and their own populations who have been targeted by an act of terror. Counter-terrorism becomes a way of saying that the state will not tolerate a certain type of challenge. Simultaneously, the state reasserts its right to sovereign control of its territory. And it is an attempt again to build state political legitimacy when it has just been found wanting in its ability to protect the population's right to life and property. Because counter-terrorism is so often thought of as a *response*, however, and not as part of an *ongoing dialogue*, this element is often masked.

Fourth, an act of terrorism is purposive. It is not accidental. It is mindful of goals, actions and the effect of these actions on each of the target areas. This aspect of the term addresses the intent of actions we or others might – or might not – deem terrorist. It combines with the concept of non-combatant, so that acts during war in which unintentional casualties result might not be considered terrorist, whereas the deliberate killing or targeting of non-combatants might be deemed terrorist.

Counter-terrorism too exhibits qualities of purposefulness. The state must act and be seen to act to protect the life and property of the citizens. Political leaders become eager to distinguish themselves through their deliberate response to the challenge posed. This quality is so important in the counter-terrorist discourse that the perception which dominates is that if a state does not purposefully act following a terrorist event, its credibility suffers greatly, and it opens itself to a proliferation of additional attacks. It is thus perceived as critical in 'good' counter-terrorist policy and emphasized by the state.

Fifth is the political nature of the act of terrorism. It is concerned with authoritative direction and control. In this capacity it targets or relates to the elites who control the current structures and institutions or the population that resists the current keepers of state power. Thus, it may be focused on instituting change or on maintaining the *status quo*.

Counter-terrorism, like terrorism, is ultimately about political power. It is the state reasserting its claim over the coercive mechanisms of government. There is thus an internal reinforcement of the use of power following an event: it is at once both a visible response and a use of the very power that has been called into question by the act itself.

Sixth, perhaps most important, for an act to be considered terrorist, it must be levied on what individuals ascribing the nomenclature consider to be non-combatants. This, more than anything, grounds the moral opprobrium that accompanies use of the term. By calling an act terrorist, it is *always* a way of denying the legitimacy of the act itself against a particular set of victims. The nexus of this delegitimation is the interception between illegitimate violence and illegitimate targets. An individual may agree with the cause that has driven a terrorist to act, and even the individual as a representative of a particular group – but disagreement with the legitimacy of the target and nature of the act underlies use of the term. Three observations follow.

The first is that, in the case of anti-state terrorism, those engaged in the violence frequently deny that the immediate victims lack culpability; they are *not* seen as non-combatants. This is an important aspect of an act of terror, for it recognizes that all groups and individuals who engage in this behavior are subject to limits. There must be some sort of justification offered for *why* these particular people, *why* this particular place, *why* at this particular time. These are the questions immediately asked by humanity, questions that groups and individuals are under pressure to answer. Regardless of the breadth of individuals included in what terrorists consider to be 'legitimate' targets, what is critical is that for terrorist organizations to obtain support, *people otherwise considered 'non-combatants' must be re-defined as 'combatants' by those engaged in violence.*

Terrorist organizations have constituents. This did not change on 9/11: al Qaeda had to make frequent media releases following the attacks to justify their actions. Public commentary on both sides of the Atlantic often emphasizes that Jenkins' assertion[18] that terrorists want a lot of people watching, not a lot of people dead no longer holds true. But what is lost in this assertion is that the shift is possible only with an elaborate justification moving victims into combatant status. Within the United States virtually no one buys al Qaeda's claims. But outside the US, where communities provide al Qaeda with refuge and resources, such claims provide a valuable opportunity to discredit the terrorist organization. There are multiple ways to do this: for instance, by offering convincing justification within the attackers' own religious doctrine that establishes the victims as illegitimate targets, by denying the grievance exists, by limiting the number of people responsible for the grievance to exclude the victims, by offering justification for the presence of the grievance and pointing out other ways the grievance can be changed, by distinguishing the grievance from the organization's true aims, or by eliminating the grievance. Any one of these solutions undermines the claim that the class of individuals targeted constitutes legitimate targets.

For nationalist, separatist movements, combatant status is equally important. And it can be countered further through the very structure of the state. Take, for instance, the claim that a particular group lacks the ability to change the political structure. Such organizations may announce that agents of the state from which they are disenfranchised (metaphorically, if not literally) are 'legitimate targets'. Yet in a democratic state, the government ostensibly reflects the voice of the people – including those engaged in violence. Agency is thus ascribed broadly, derived from the very freedoms

---

[18] Brian Michael Jenkins, 'The Future Course of Terrorism', *The Futurist*, July–Aug. 1987, available at http://www.wfs.org/jenkins.htm.

that define citizenship. The reality, of course, is that in a representative democracy, such as Britain, America, Israel, Ireland or Turkey, citizens are removed from policy decisions. State structures may not allow minority positions to surface, or public policy negotiations to grant concessions to minority groups. And the plurality of issues considered by the multiple representatives for whom one votes may be in tension with each other and the aims of certain organizations. Nevertheless, adopting a strategy that emphasizes the political, non-violent routes open to an organization undermines claims to broader 'combatant' status for civil servants and politicians: it is the terrorist who elects government officials. By collapsing the distinction through political structures that ensure inclusion and through an effective counter-terrorist media campaign, efforts to distinguish a legitimate 'combatant' group can be undermined.

The second observation relates to the changing designation of 'combatants' by the terrorist organization. Such shifts, *considered in relation to each other and not to an absolute base line*, reveal much about the strength of the terrorist movement. A latent conservatism acts on most non-state organizations that engage in terrorism. Whether or not this relates to the importance of human life as ascribed by most religions and cultures, the result of this conservatism is that changes to the list of 'combatants' reveals the strength of a movement, group or individual. That is, when an organization or movement is at its strongest, it can afford a more select target base to pursue its aims. For most organizations, this approach will offset the negative repercussions caused by less discriminate violence. As organizations become weaker, however, less discriminate violence ensues, and broader claims as to the 'combatant' status of civilian targets are made.[19] The weakness may stem from diminished resources available to the organization, from the 'hardening' of targets by the state, or from the state successfully undermining previously stated grievances (such as through the approaches highlighted above). Regardless of *why* it is occurring, expanded combatant lists do seem to indicate *that* the organization has lost strength.

The third observation is that the more obvious the status of the victims as non-combatant, and the greater the number of non-combatants injured or killed in the attack, the greater the public emotional fervour that greets actual instances of violence. This in turn drives a particular sort of response to each attack. The level of acceptance for measures with a direct impact on individual rights, such as those common in a national security approach, increases commensurate to the devastation. I return to this point in the later discussion of the targets of the attack.

[19] See, e.g., results of regression equations cited in Laura K. Donohue, Master's Dissertation, *State and Paramilitary Strategies and Tactics in Northern Ireland 1972–1992* (University of Ulster, Magee College, 1993).

Like terrorism, counter-terrorism also claims to apply only to those directly responsible for the violence – a form of 'terrorist combatant'. But the counter-terrorist claim also fails. The reasons are twofold: first, it is extremely hard to distinguish who is a terrorist and who is not. So measures such as widespread detention, the alteration of judicial structures, the suspension of due process, increased powers of surveillance, strictures on the media, house and village demolition, assassination and torture become applied across entire communities, if not society itself. Second, counter-terrorist measures also seep into other areas of law and become instruments of other special interests. As the 'war on drugs', criminal processes, and other state interests begin to apply the counter-terrorist provisions, the audience subject to the strictures extends far beyond the immediate combatant target.

Seventh, terrorist acts, like counter-terrorism, bear an instrumental aspect. They are meant to achieve something else. At least three purposes are necessarily present in this instrumental aspect: the actor intends to obtain or maintain power and affect a certain outcome, to disrupt an otherwise normal course of events, and, most importantly, to induce fear. The instrumental aspect is the reason why individuals, organizations or states engage in the act in question. The specific act may seek to disrupt, erode institutions, increase pressure, force capitulation, destroy confidence or erode resistance. The purposive quality is not constant. Nor is it limited to one quality, as some of the literature suggests. Terrorism and counter-terrorism reflect a multiplicity of purposes, many of which are related. They bear a complex relationship to each other: the immediate purpose evokes further actions and reactions that play into the hands of those engaged in violence.

For instance, the purpose of terrorism might be to provoke the state, causing further radicalization of the population and immobilizing state forces, as advocated by Mao Tse Tung. The purpose of a terrorist act may relate primarily to individuals either inside or outside the group, organization or network responsible. An act intended to punish an individual for cooperating with the 'enemy' serves the purpose of intimidating others from engaging in similar actions and establishing discipline within the organization. Numerous examples exist. A Taliban Information Ministry official, Abdul Hanan Himat, told Reuters in Kabul that Abdul Haq's execution 'happened on the basis of the verdict of the Ulema that anyone who assists the United States is liable to be killed'.[20] Haq's death followed the attack on 9 September 2001 on Ahmad Shah Masood, another leader opposed to Taliban rule. Thus, while the primary purpose of terrorism is to terrorize, in meeting this purpose further aims may be accomplished.

---

[20] http://dailynews.yahoo.com/h/nm/20011026/ts/attack_dc_570.html.

Here I draw a distinction between non-state challenges and state actions. Unlike many terrorist organizations, by definition liberal, democratic states do not terrorize their own supporters through physical or emotional violence. One could effectively argue that if they do, the regime has lost its right to be considered a liberal democracy. Because such actions have not been used against the majority or against a sizable minority, however, this has led some to assume that liberal, democratic states do not use terrorism. It would be more accurate to say, though, that terroristic state actions are directed toward the 'other' in society, or the 'other' geographically, in claimed defence of the state citizenry. There are exceptions to this rule – but most of these derive from mistakenly putting individuals into the 'other' or 'enemy' category who otherwise might support the state. This does not mean that there are no controls over the citizens – rather, informal, and essentially non-violent mechanisms, such as leverage from 'patriotism', public shaming, and presenting an inflated threat based on secret evidence, may be used to ensure loyalty. For states that engage in terrorism, the purpose of such acts may be, as Picard writes, to repress dissent, promote international policies, or to spread fear to pre-empt opposition.[21] State terror toward another state, when openly claimed by the state in question, is generally seen as an act of war.

D. Terrorist and counter-terrorist targets

To understand both the intended and unintended consequences of an action – whether taken by a non-state actor or a state – it is helpful to understand the targets involved in a terrorist act. There are four: the immediate target of the act, the symbolic target of the act, the target audience and the target of demands.[22] These four targets often also characterize counter-terrorist acts.

In the first area, the individuals harmed by the violence, the physical space and buildings involved, and the conduct of operations affected by the attack may constitute the immediate target. Using the attacks on 11 September 2001 as an example, the employees at work in the World Trade Center, the buildings themselves, and the immediate economic impact of the attacks provided the immediate targets in New York City. Counter-terrorism too has an immediate target: the individual incarcerated, the paper or subject banned from publication, the country attacked present the immediate target of state action.

In the second area, the symbolic targets may include the group that the individuals represented, a greater concept to which the action is meant to draw attention, a wider group of physical buildings, structures, or places of which the immediate site is one member, a timing element – remembering

---

[21] Robert G. Picard, *Media Portrayals of Terrorism: Functions and Meaning of News Coverage* (Ames, Iowa State University Press, 1993).
[22] See also Schmid and Jongman, *Political Terrorism*.

a past event, marking a day, or coinciding with simultaneous events, and a means of delivery symbolic of the grievance to which a solution is being sought. The people who died symbolized Americans broadly and capitalists more specifically. The building symbolized globalization – global trade and financial flows. The failure of the 1993 attack to topple the towers, and Yousef's previous comments that he wanted the job to be finished, created additional symbolism – the completion of a job begun previously. It has also been speculated that the day of the attack (9/11), the month in which it occurred (eighty years since the ending of the Caliphate), or the concurrent sentencing of individuals found complicit in the 1993 attack influenced the timing. The use of high technology in the form of a jet liner – itself a symbol of globalization and modernity – further marked the attacks.

For counter-terrorism, the target too may bear symbolic qualities. This is particularly true of retributive techniques, such as house and village demolition, which are meant to demonstrate state power over those who would seek to diminish it. Attempts to capture or kill specific individuals or groups of individuals may be referred to in heavily symbolic language: good versus evil, justice versus injustice, one ethnic or religious group in domination of another. An individual apprehended might serve as a wider example of how the state will treat perpetrators of the crime.

The third area, the target audience, may include a deity with whose will the perpetrators claim they are acting in compliance. The perpetrator may also seek to demonstrate something to himself or herself, and to the perpetrator's family. The wider community of the perpetrator, neutrals and the enemy might also be part of the target audience. Finally, elites or decision-makers, in the international arena as well as in a specific state or organization, might also be targeted. Instructions found in a suitcase belonging to Mohamed Atta, suspected hijacker on American Airlines Flight 11, as well as in wreckage from United Airlines Flight 93, which crashed in Pennsylvania, and in Dulles International Airport in a car driven by Nawaf Alhazmi, one of the suspected hijackers on American Airlines Flight 77, which crashed into the Pentagon, instructed the hijackers to recall the battle of 'the Prophet against the infidels'. The document told the hijackers to say, upon entering the plane, 'Oh God, open all doors for me. Oh God who answers prayers and answers those who ask you, I am asking you for your help. ... There is no God, but God'.[23] The note emphasized the importance of proving to oneself the ability to face challenges and to act in accordance with God's will: 'Remind yourself that in this night you will face many challenges. But you have to face them and understand it 100 percent', and 'When you have washed for prayer, angels will ask God to forgive you and angels will pray for you.' The note instructed, 'Train yourself, explain to yourself, convince yourself

---

[23] http://www5.cnn.com/2001/US/09/28/inv.document.terrorism/index.html.

and urge yourself to carry out the mission.'[24] The families and communities of the suspected hijackers formed a greater community, to whom their devotion would be made clear. They sought the attention of the world audience – captured by news media throughout the world as the event unfolded – the American public, and the United States' political and economic elite.

Counter-terrorism also targets a wider audience. The citizens, the security forces, groups targeted by terrorist violence, international elites, and the world community all form different audiences the state seeks to influence with its actions.

The fourth area, the target of demands, includes the specific areas in which change is to be accomplished. This may be in the realm of political, social, economic or military policy. Perpetrators may also have ideological goals that the action targets. While denying responsibility for the actual operation, the targets of demand issued by bin Laden subsequent to the attacks outlined three objectives: the withdrawal of the United States from Arabia, the ending of sanctions on Iraq, and the cessation of support for Israel in its treatment of Palestinians and occupation of Palestinian land. The fulfilment of these demands would create space for bin Laden and his followers to develop an Islamic state. For this, control over the regional economic, political and military power is essential. Perhaps an even more stringent claim was the ideological rejection of the 'West'.

States too include a target of demands in their actions. The primary demand is the cessation of violence and any organized activity that threatens the state. There may be additional demands, such as the ending of support for the cause espoused by those engaged in terrorist behaviour, or the accountability of financial institutions for funds distributed through the financial network and related to the groups opposing the state. These four target areas constitute the targets of attention.

E. Additional qualities shared by terrorism and counter-terrorism

Three additional, essential (intrinsic) qualities of the terms 'terrorist' and 'counter-terrorist' influence how people use the terms and regard individuals to whom they are applied. First, the terms are emotive. 'Terrorism' brings to mind images of indiscriminate violence – images that are certainly encouraged by some forms of terrorism. From the spate of anthrax mailings in autumn 2001 to the gas chambers of the Third Reich, the concept of indiscriminate violence levied on innocents evokes horror in the soul of humanity. This gives rise to indignation that humans would dare to use such violence. The emotive quality of the term 'counter-terrorism' turns on this indignation. It is an emotional answer to a violent, unacceptable challenge.

[24] Ibid.

Second, terrorism and counter-terrorism discourse is often blatantly infused with moral meaning. Using both terms becomes a way to express moral opprobrium. Luigi Bonanate suggests that 'deciding whether an action is terrorist ... is more the result of a verdict than the establishing of a fact; the formulating of a social judgment rather than the description of a set of phenomena'.[25] J. Bowyer Bell points out that the term is essentially a litmus test for closely held beliefs. He suggests that even a brief conversation quickly reveals others' world views, their interpretation of the nature of man and their view of the future. This moral meaning, however, does not entail a subjective quality. To call it such suggests that morality is intrinsically subjective, denying a normative quality to moral action. Rather, the claim of either states or sub-state organizations relies upon two conditions: the legitimacy of the claims and the actors as executors of those claims, and the force to demand compliance with those who reject the legitimacy of the assertion.

Third, the moral import intoned by both states and non-state actors in the commission of and response to acts of violence brings with it heavy religious overtones. Martyrdom, for instance, plays a central role in many terrorist acts. Osama bin Laden's asceticism recalls the Prophet. And millennial cults may contemplate their own obliteration with an eye towards rewards in the afterlife. The religious element is not limited to religious organizations. For instance, Che Guevara's life and, indeed, his death, took on mythological, martyr-like qualities. On 9 October 1967, after eleven months' fighting in Bolivia, security forces wounded, surrounded and captured Che Guevara. At Barrientos' order the security forces executed him. The following day twenty journalists flew to Vallegrande for a press conference. There, the state displayed his body at the local hospital where, presumably to identify him, his eyes were left open. With a burgeoning reputation as the liberator of the oppressed masses, and the prone manner in which he was displayed, he became a transcendental, Christ-like figure – despite his clear ideological allegiance to an atheist doctrine.[26] Mkonto we Sizwe, fighting in South Africa for an anti-apartheid, Communist state, used an altered version of the Lord's Prayer to energize the movement.[27] Nationalist-separatist organizations also draw on these concepts of martyrdom: Bobby Sands, a convicted IRA member, died on hunger strike in prison in Northern Ireland. After weeks without food, unshaven, and clad only in a blanket, wall paintings depicted him as

---

[25] Luigi Bonanate, 'Some Unanticipated Consequences of Terrorism' (1979) 16(3) *Journal of Peace Research* at 197, cited in Schmid and Jongman, *Political Terrorism*, at 7, note 12.

[26] Film footage: Guevara in final repose, 00:30, 02:50–03:12, 07:50–08:05, 08:27–09:00, 13:50–14:10 from *El Día que me quieras*, Directed by Leandro Katz. First Run Carus Films.

[27] *Witness to Apartheid* (Long Version), California Newsreel, 630 Natoma Street; San Francisco, CA 94103.

Jesus. Because of this mythological, martyrdom-like quality, terrorists may welcome death. In Turkey, for instance, Abdullah Ocalan, the leader of the PKK, commented, 'I've always said that my death will bring more change than my life. Death does not mean very much to me.'[28]

Political leaders deeply embedded in the counter-terrorist discourse also revert to moral and religious paradigms to describe and to justify state actions. Within hours of the 9/11 attacks, President Bush seized on the state's inevitable response as a modern day 'crusade'. Osama bin Laden became 'The Evil One'. And at the first meeting of his homeland security team, Bush stated: 'Our job now is to find the evil ones and bring them to justice'.[29] British Prime Minister Tony Blair announced: 'We have to set about at every single level, in every way that we can, dismantling the apparatus of terror, and eradicating the evil of mass terrorism in our world'.[30]

This moral quality is important, because it contributes to the tendency of counter-terrorist measures to remain in place long after the immediate threat has receded.[31] The moral opprobrium also means that it becomes a way to increase or emphasize rejection of other forms of violence, by labelling them 'terrorist'. In the US, for example, a number of states have introduced counter-terrorist measures that range from gang terrorism, narco-terrorism, abortion-clinic terrorism, and school terrorism to eco-terrorism, terroristic offences, and terrorism using weapons of mass destruction.

III. Distinguishing terrorism and counter-terrorism

If counter-terrorism does share so many qualities with terrorism, then what *distinguishes* terrorism from counter-terrorism? The first and most obvious answer would be that not all acts of counter-terrorism include violence: airport security, while perhaps intended to induce fear into those considering acts of terror, does not usually use violence to accomplish these aims. Similarly, a propaganda campaign might not involve any direct physical or psychological violence, yet it might be central to a state's counter-terrorist strategy. However, the same could be said of many acts that states want to call terrorism: the Provisional IRA's involvement in money laundering or tax fraud, for instance, for the most part does not involve direct violence. Identity theft is similarly central to terrorist organizations' ability to operate.

---

[28] *Good Kurds, Bad Kurds.* Produced and directed by Kevin McKiernan.
[29] 'Bush: Visa policies to get tighter', 29 October 2001, available at http://www.cnn.com/2001/US/10/29/inv.task.force/index.html.
[30] Ibid. See also http://www.whitehouse.gov/news/releases/2001/09/20010920-7.html.
[31] See Laura K. Donohue, *Counterterrorist Law and Emergency Powers in the United Kingdom 1922–2000* (Dublin, Irish Academic Press, 2000), ch. 6.

Certainly these acts are criminal; but the United Kingdom, United States and other countries target these acts as part of their overall counter-terrorist strategy. While it is an element common to our broad understanding of terrorism, not all 'terrorist' acts necessarily involve violence.

One way to approach this phenomenon is to distinguish between types of action and to suggest that terrorist groups engage in both crime and terror. An effective counter-terrorist strategy would address both. A much more difficult question presents itself, however, if the light is turned back on the state: within the realm of counter-terrorism, it appears that states engage in countermeasures that fall short of terrorism, and in others that fully enter into that realm. But it is politically inconceivable, within a state, to call such actions terrorist. To do so is to undermine state political legitimacy, forcing the state off its moral high ground. So states do whatever is possible to prevent this from occurring. Is there a more effective way to talk about such actions? In one sense, it matters little if we call state actions that stop short of violence 'countercrime' or 'heffalump'. By failing to distinguish between actions that cross into the realm of terrorism and those that do not, we lose our ability to consider the impact of such actions and anticipate further threats. I do not here suggest that, as a general rule, the state should never pursue these more extreme avenues. But in doing so it must be clear as to the path it treads and the relationship between its decision and the violence it faces.

A second answer in seeking to distinguish counter-terrorism from terrorism might zero in on the 'fear factor': not all acts of counter-terrorism depend to the same extent on fear to accomplish state aims. When states cross into these regions, as they are prone to do when countermeasures are justified through appeal to reason of state, then state actions themselves cross into the realm of terrorism. This is the heart of state action as first mover in generating increased dissent and fomenting violence against its institutions and citizenry. It is when the state engages in violence and the manufacturing of fear that the application of the measures to non-combatants, the elements of policy that reach a broader audience, the purposive and instrumental qualities in the discourse, and the political nature of the dialogue lock the state into, essentially, a terrorist discourse.

The problem with distinguishing the acts based on fear goes beyond the issue raised above (namely, that neither do all acts of terror rest on fear, but distinguishing them raises complications in relation to the state). Fear, perhaps more than any other element, is deeply dependent on subjectivity. Thus, while a state may not intend fear to be the centrepiece of a particular counter-action, the very nature of the terrorism realm introduces it. Almost all security measures are meant to create fear of capture or prevention in the mind of the potential terrorist. They may also create increased anxiety in the population. Because of the security nature of counter-terrorist provisions, it is hard to envisage a measure that does not involve some element of fear. This ties back to the emotive nature of the term itself. Even in setting the future state agenda in this realm, fear permeates the dialogue.

Critically, this is not to say that terrorism and counter-terrorism do not have other features that differ; but, rather, when the seven essential qualities of an act of terrorism are shared by an act of counter-terrorism, the line between the two fades, with similar consequences borne by both entities in relation to their domestic and international legitimacy.

If, then, such actions are indistinguishable in their execution and effect, the stark issue with which we are faced is one of moral equivalence: *is* there a difference between a liberal, democratic state engaging in these actions and a non-state actor doing so? That is to say, is there something about statehood that legitimates control over certain types of coercion that are illegitimate in their exercise by anyone but the state? Here, it seems clear that there are a number of areas where the majority of the population would grant a state unique powers: such as the ability to levy taxes, to control traffic, to adjudicate disputes, and to restrict the freedoms of those found guilty of infringing the law. Certainly, not all citizens agree with these powers: the United States, for instance, is peppered with militia organizations who virulently oppose the collection of taxes. And many of these powers have limits. Excessive taxes, after all, sparked the American Revolution. But for the most part, individuals' approaches to these issues revolve on where they place the bounds within which state action, writ large, is deemed acceptable. Communal defence, and protection of the *politai*, arguably, is at the core of the state's purpose. The Hobbesian claim, that individuals leave a state of nature and enter into society precisely for protection, emphasizes the necessity of the state answering challenges to this security with countermeasures.

Complementing the concept of defence of the state in general, and the population in particular, is the idea of defence writ-large: as long as counter-terrorism is thought of as a response, and never a first-mover, then the use of force under its guise may enjoy a greater level of support than violence employed by non-state organizations. Immediate questions of morality aside, at what point does the type of force employed generate *more* violence? At such a point it ceases merely to be defensive.

An additional question that lays siege to the concern with moral equivalence centres on the political structure of the state: is there a difference between a liberal, democratic state using terrorist techniques to respond to terrorism, and a dictatorship using the same means? While we may observe that the former political structure, at least in form, enjoys a representative characteristic, this still does not bring us to the crux of the matter. What is the line between absolute rights and negotiable ones? And under what circumstances are certain rights alienable? These questions plague liberal democratic states locked in conflict with terrorist challenge. Their answer lies beyond this chapter's remit.

IV. Concluding remarks

Three assumptions dominate the counter-terrorism discourse: that terrorism is a phenomenon distinct from counter-terrorism, that the nature of the latter is that it responds to the first and is not a first mover, and that counter-terrorism is what states actually *do*. These assumptions are important: the first two give the state political legitimacy and obtain for it the moral high ground. The last one shapes what is evaluated in determining a state's effectiveness in responding to the threat.

In this chapter I have argued that, contrary to the first assumption, the definition, targets, and additional characteristics of terrorism and counter-terrorism are intimately connected. In each of the five regions – the US, UK, Ireland, Israel and Turkey – there is a close relationship between the types of actions taken by state and non-state actors. Both incorporate violence, fear and a broader audience. They are purposive, political and (although denied in each case by the actor) affect non-combatants. And they are instrumental. Their targets range from the immediate and symbolic to a broader audience and demands. In addition, such actions are emotive and carry strong moral and religious overtones. While not all counter-terrorism involves violence, neither does all terrorism.

As for the second assumption, I have asserted that counter-terrorism is not just a response. It serves alternately to undermine and reinforce state legitimacy. This, in turn, influences how non-state actors frame their grievances, how the target populations respond and how the world community perceives the conflict. It is thus linked not just to the response of the non-state actors but to the resources available to a state to counter such threats in the future.

I now address the third assumption and suggest that counter-terrorism includes not just what states *do*, but what they choose *not* to do. This seems an obvious point, but it is almost universally missed in a state's response to terrorism. The immediate impetus is to do *something*, and then to evaluate how effective the introduction and use of that particular law, or those particular surveillance techniques, or that particular missile launch was in accomplishing the immediate aim. Yet there is a whole range of measures available if not morally, then practically, to the state. But when measures are either omitted, or consciously rejected, by an executive, legislative or regulatory body, minimal effort is made to evaluate the effect of *not* including such measures in the overall strategy. On the contrary, after the next attack, the immediate assumption is that it is because these and other measures were *not* introduced, violence occurred. And so whatever measures can be conceived – even if previously rejected for very strong reasons – become quickly integrated into the state's counter-terrorism arsenal.

While the contrary of these assertions pervades the counter-terrorist discourse – namely, terrorism and counter-terrorism are two separate phenomenon, the latter being always a response to the former, and the latter involving what states choose to do – a more accurate analysis would overturn such assumptions and begin the dialogue at the question raised, but not fully answered within this chapter's bounds: in a liberal, democratic state, how does one address the issue of moral equivalence in drawing the line between absolute and alienable rights?

3

The question of a generic definition of terrorism under general international law

C. L. LIM

I. Treaty law and custom

Recent interest in the utility or propriety of a generic definition of terrorism has been driven by larger issues, such as the need to build international solidarity in the war against terrorism, and the opposing need felt by some of guarding any such possible definition of terrorism from any undue weightage likely to be given to the unilateral beliefs of any one state, and particularly the meaning likely to be or already given to that term in the foreign policy of any one state. Talk of the need to define terrorism comprehensively under international law cannot be divorced from such over-riding political concerns which, together with some old diplomatic obstacles, continue to plague the ongoing negotiations towards a Comprehensive Convention on Terrorism. The initiative for a comprehensive treaty definition of terrorism was a response to calls beginning in the 1990s for a departure from a regime of variegated subject-specific treaties which I shall discuss further below. The initiative had come originally from India,[1] and negotiations are currently ongoing. United Nations General Assembly resolution 51/210 of 17 December 1996 had established an Ad Hoc Committee which, together with the United Nations' Sixth (Legal) Committee, is currently tasked with negotiations on the Draft Comprehensive Convention.[2] I feel any success here would, however, be mainly symbolic. In this chapter I have chosen to take what I consider a more pragmatic approach than if I had chosen to focus on the status of the negotiations on the Draft Comprehensive Convention.

---

[1] United Nations General Assembly, Fifty-Fifth Session, Sixth Committee, Agenda Item 166 (Measures to Eliminate Terrorism), Working Document Submitted by India (document of 28 August 2000, on file).

[2] See Martin Reichard, Universal Conventions Against Terrorism: Progress and Weaknesses, Part II, Seminar under Professor Hanspeter Neuhold, University of Vienna, Summer of 2002, 18–19 (available on the German language website of *Juridicum Online*). For the latest available text of the Draft Convention, see Report of the Ad Hoc Committee established by United Nations General Assembly Resolution 51/210 of 17 December 1996, Sixth Session (28 January–1 February 2002), General Assembly, Official Records, Fifty-Seventh Session, Supplement No. 37 (A/57/37), Annex I A/57/37.

I want to focus instead on the question of whether a customary or general international law definition of terrorism already exists, and if so, what that customary definition looks like.

This is because any real legal guidance that international law can give today lies at least as much in international custom as it could in a comprehensive international treaty definition that may soon become available. This is due partly to a time-lag that would normally occur between having a completed treaty text and having widespread participation in the new treaty regime. It is also due to the fact that much of the 'new comprehensive definition' would either not be that new, or if it turned out to be so could therefore prove a long way yet from achieving the necessary combination of (1) having a precise formulation that would necessarily prove useful, and (2) at the same time, attracting the necessary widespread participation of states to make such a comprehensive regime a success.[3]

II. Some old political difficulties

A. State-sponsored terrorism

Political controversy over what terrorism might be taken to mean in the eyes of the international community is hardly new. It has for long been bound up not only with terror brought about by non-state actors, but with the spectre of state-sponsored terrorism. According to Professor Brownlie, state-sponsored terrorism is governed mainly, if not exclusively, by the available categories of international legal thought such as the prohibition of the use of force in international relations, the doctrine of imputability in establishing state responsibility for the acts of individuals, the self-defence doctrine and so on. He argues that:

> There is no category of the 'law of terrorism' and the problems must be characterized in accordance with the applicable sectors of public international law: jurisdiction, international criminal justice, state responsibility, and so forth.[4]

However true this may be in so far as international law has not yet evolved to encompass an agreed definition of what terrorism is, the various subject-specific rules of international law which focus on individual criminal responsibility for different acts of terror such as hijacking, terrorist financing, and so

---

[3] The twin issues of participation and precision are dimensions of consideration which, in my view, mark out the achievement of 'hard' international law from what could merely amount to symbolism. See Chin Lim and Olufemi Elias, 'The Role of Treaties in the Contemporary International Legal Order' (1997) 66 *Nordic Journal of International Law/ Acta Scandinavica Juris Gentium* 1.

[4] Ian Brownlie, *Principles of Public International Law* (Oxford University Press, 2004), 713.

on, can neither be insulated from nor absorbed wholly by the currently existing public international law rules which may be brought to bear on state-sponsored terrorism. As we will see from the views expressed by several states during the negotiations leading up to the Rome Statute below, these states view terrorism as a distinct crime under international law which imposes *individual* criminal responsibility for state-sponsored terrorism.

In this sense, dealing with state-sponsored terrorism is different from the situation which the International Court of Justice had to deal with, for example, in the *Nicaragua Case*. There, Nicaragua had brought a claim against the United States for alleged covert support given by the Central Intelligence Agency to armed insurgents operating in Nicaraguan territory in response to the Sandinista Government's covert support of the Farabundo Marti National Liberation Front in El Salvador. At issue there were the *inter-state* international law rules pertaining to breach of the United States' legal responsibilities owed to Nicaragua by allegedly financing, supplying, equipping, arming, training and providing strategic guidance to Nicaraguan rebels seeking to overthrow the Sandinista Government.[5] In short, *Nicaragua* was about *state* responsibility.

On the other hand, Professor V. S. Mani has argued recently that what we call 'terrorism' today is, in fact, very much *state-sponsored* terrorism as a result of the prohibition in Article 2(4) of the United Nations Charter of the use of force in international relations, which would nonetheless attract *individual* responsibility for such acts. Our legal imagination may currently be seized by the figure of Osama bin Laden, and we might be startled that by the late twentieth century the only superpower in the world was required to 'go to war' with a mere individual, but that does not change the fact that, for the most part, terrorism is linked to some form of state sponsorship.[6] In 1945,

---

[5] *Nicaragua Case (Nicaragua v. United States) (Merits)*, I.C.J. reports (1986), 14. See Hilaire McCoubrey and Nigel D. White, *International Organizations and Civil Wars* (Aldershot, Dartmouth, 1995), 10–13.

[6] Indeed, one difficulty with the United States missile attacks on targets in Sudan and Afghanistan in 1998 is precisely that the United States had imputed responsibility to the Sudanese Government and the de facto Taliban regime in Afghanistan on the basis of the United States' unilateral findings of fact. According to President Clinton, he 'ordered this action ... because we have convincing evidence these groups played the key role in the Embassy bombings in Kenya and Tanzania ... because these groups have executed terrorist attacks against Americans in the past ...', amongst other reasons. In a further statement, President Clinton said: 'The United States does not take this action lightly. Afghanistan and Sudan have been warned for years to stop harboring and supporting these terrorist groups. But countries that persistently host terrorists have no right to safe havens.' Both passages are reproduced in Sean D. Murphy, 'Contemporary Practice of the United States Relating to International Law' (1999) 93 *American Journal of International Law* 161 at 161–2. The circumstances of the post-9/11 campaign in Afghanistan are arguably different for the purposes of international law.

the Charter of the United Nations came into being. One significant change the Charter sought to effect is to outlaw the use of armed solutions to international disputes, and so successful was that message and the need to demonstrate fidelity to the Charter that the countries of the world that would otherwise have been prompted to seek armed solutions could no longer do so without (1) a Security Council resolution under Chapter VII of the Charter, or (2) a justification based on unilateral or collective self-defence.[7] As a result, Mani argues, states were given every incentive to mask armed solutions to international issues through state-sponsored terrorism.[8]

The difference between Professor Mani's and Professor Brownlie's views is one which has marked the debates in the Ad Hoc Committee tasked with the negotiation and conclusion of the Draft Comprehensive Convention. Even if we do not agree with Mani that any definition of terrorism must also define *individual* responsibility for *state-sponsored* terrorism, the growing phenomenon of state-sponsored terrorism has become a powerful focal-point for advocating the plight of the Palestinian people. In a world in which we have learned to view some states as 'pariah' or 'rogue' states, calling Israel a 'terrorist state' serves to highlight the Palestinian cause, and to stigmatize the perceived moral wrongdoer all at the same time. To demonstrate the logic of this, the same accusation has been directed the other way too, at the 'Palestinian terrorists and their masters'.[9] In this way, the question of terrorism and what it means has become caught up in the complexities of the Middle-Eastern question, with any possible solution tied seemingly to a solution to the Middle-Eastern question itself.[10] But that does not mean that the political intensity that surrounds the matter is not real, or that state decision-makers can never be guilty of terrorism under international law.

B. Immunity of state armed forces

A second obstacle therefore in the negotiations on the Draft Convention belies the persistent connection between state-sponsored terrorism and individual responsibility. This second obstacle concerns the question of the

---

[7] The literature is voluminous, but see, for example, Hilaire McCoubrey and Nigel D. White, *International Law and Armed Conflict* (Aldershot, Dartmouth, 1992), Part I. One other possible exception is the controversial justification of humanitarian intervention, which if it does constitute a valid exception could justify the unilateral use of force for that purpose.

[8] V. S. Mani, 'International Terrorism and the Quest for Legal Controls', manuscript courtesy of Professor Mani (on file).

[9] Professor Robert Jensen, in his letter to the press, quoting the new Israeli Defence Minister, *Houston Chronicle*, 9 March 2001 (on file).

[10] For a concise treatment of the complex history of the Middle East peace process, see, for example, Henry Kissinger, *Does America Need a Foreign Policy?* (New York, Simon & Schuster, 2001), 166 *ff.*

immunity of state armed forces from the eventual scope of any comprehensive treaty. Clearly, this difficulty and the difficulty regarding state-sponsored terrorism are linked. Some states are wary that their own decision-makers or members of their armed forces could be prosecuted for either terrorism or aggression. While this issue continues to be debated in the negotiations on the Draft Convention, we already have a good sense of the matter by looking at the outcome of the negotiations establishing the Rome Statute of the International Criminal Court.

In the Rome context, the United States had failed to make the initiation of prosecutions before the ICC dependent on Security Council sanction. According to the 'Singapore compromise' which was adopted instead in what is currently Article 16 of the Rome Statute, the *discontinuance* of prosecution became dependent on the absence of an exercise of veto power by one of the 'Permanent Five' Members,[11] as opposed to making the *initiation* of prosecution potentially hostage to the veto power of P-5 Members as had originally been proposed in the International Law Commission's Draft Statute.[12] It is this factor, together with related disagreement over the definition of international aggression,[13] which has caused the current notable lack of full participation in the Rome Statute. Currently, the same issue has also arisen in the separate context of the negotiations towards a Comprehensive Convention on Terrorism.

C. National liberation movements

A third long-standing obstacle concerns the differences, if any, between legitimate struggles for national liberation and terrorism. This too has plagued the negotiations on the Draft Comprehensive Convention. What the United Nations brought with it in the latter half of the previous century was a new doctrine that was to revolutionize the composition of the international community. Self-determination brought about decolonization, and much of the impetus for decolonization came from the newly independent countries themselves in the 1960s and 1970s. This was to bring with it an era of grave doctrinal difficulties for international lawyers as to where the line should be drawn between legitimate efforts towards national liberation through armed struggle under the doctrine of self-determination on the one hand, and sheer

---

[11] Article 27 of the Charter of the United Nations, 26 June 1945, as subsequently amended by the General Assembly on 17 December 1963.

[12] Lionel Yee, 'The International Criminal Court and the Security Council: Articles 13(b) and 16', in Roy S. Lee (ed.), *The International Criminal Court: The Making of the Rome Statute* (Hague, Kluwer, 1999), 143, 150 *ff.*

[13] For which, see Sir Franklin Berman, 'The International Criminal Court and the Use of Force by States' (2000) 4 *Singapore Journal of International and Comparative Law* 479.

violence on the other. Attempts to contain the scope of the doctrine to the former Western colonies in Asia and Africa have had a mixed success. There was and continues to be a fuzziness around the edges as to who the beneficiaries might be of the emancipatory promise of the doctrine of self-determination.[14] For example, should it be the Israeli or Palestinian peoples?

United Nations General Assembly Resolutions 1514(XV) and 2625(XXV) speak inclusively of the entitlement of 'all peoples' to self-determination.[15] In the search for a principled solution, some Western scholars have sought to narrow down the scope of these proclamations by equating them with a right to democratic self-government which, howsoever then defined, would at least immunize democratic states against internal and irredentist claims to self-determination.[16] This could arguably preclude the claims of, for example, the IRA in Northern Ireland and ETA in Spain. Others such as the East Timorese people, whose plight has been well-known for decades, were, however, simply left to hostile political forces. In the eyes of some newly decolonized states, there was thereby a grave moral responsibility to assist certain struggles of national liberation, and which others could arguably characterize as mere state-sponsored terrorism. And so the trouble began. Even in the last ten years, the fresh independence of Timor-Lesté has carried some of the baggage of the past into the new millennium. No-one seriously suggests that there was ever a satisfactory answer to the question of self-determination. In an international community giving pride of place to the pursuit of state interests, questions of national liberation, self-determination, and the horrific instrumentality of terrorism as a tool, albeit an evil one, presented novel and inconvenient questions that stalled progress on a comprehensive and acceptable definition of international terror.

For example, General Assembly Resolution 42/159 of 7 December 1987 which had referred to the legitimacy of national liberation movements of 'peoples under colonial and racist regimes and other forms of alien domination' and which declared that nothing in the resolution itself should be taken to deny 'the right to self-determination, freedom and independence' received

---

[14] The best treatment is still Michla Pomerance, *Self-Determination in Law and Practice* (Hague, Nijhoff, 1982), 14–23. See also Antonio Cassese, *Self-Determination of Peoples: A Legal Appraisal* (Cambridge, Grotius/CUP, 1995), 141–58.

[15] These are the key instruments of the United Nations decolonization process of the 1960s and 1970s; United Nations General Assembly resolution 1514(XV), 14 December 1960, para 2; United Nations General Assembly resolution 2625(XXV), 24 October 1970, Annex. Earlier resolutions had been more circumspect and cautious in approach towards the issue of decolonization and were derided by many newly independent countries for not recognizing that colonial peoples had an 'immediate' right to self-determination, something which resolution 1514 finally recognized.

[16] Thomas M. Franck, 'The Emerging Right to Democratic Governance' (1992) 86 *American Journal of International Law* 46, 52–63.

the votes of 153 states. However, two states, the United States and Israel, voted against it precisely because of such language.[17] Thus, the issue of terrorism was never very far away from the friendships, alliances and calculations of *realpolitik* that are so much a dominant feature of United Nations voting practice.

In sum, the question of having a *generic* legal definition of international terrorism has become so heavily politicized that, even as an international lawyer, I sometimes feel that the question patently does not deserve the kind of serious attention it has evoked.

III. A short history of international lawmaking to combat international terrorism

A. A short history of lawmaking

The League of Nations had sought to bring two conventions on terrorism to life as far back as 1937, but with no success.[18] The proposed 1937 definition of terrorism had sought to include:

> All criminal acts directed against a State and intended or calculated to create a state of terror in the minds of particular persons or a group of persons or the general public.[19]

During that early conference:

> ... many states still viewed any development of international criminal jurisdiction as a serious abrogation of their sovereign criminal jurisdiction. The protagonists of international criminal jurisdiction, on their part, differed among themselves on the modality through which to achieve their ideal. One argument has been that without a substantive 'international criminal law' relating to terrorism, i.e., a law making individuals

---

[17] Jensen, above note 9.

[18] A diplomatic conference was convened in Geneva on 1 November 1937, which thirty-six countries attended. The conference opened for signature on 16 November 1937 and the Convention on the Prevention and Punishment of Terrorism and the Convention of an International Criminal Court were presented for signature, with the aim that participation in the former would be a precondition for participation in the latter. The former Convention was signed by twenty states, but was ratified by India on 1 January 1941; V. S. Mani, 'Future Strategies in the War Against Terrorism and the Proliferation of Weapons of Mass Destruction: An Indian Perception', manuscript courtesy of Professor Mani (on file).

[19] While the texts of these conventions are not widely available, this definition is reproduced on the website of the United Nations Office on Drugs and Crime. For the texts of the two conventions, see Convention on the Prevention and Punishment of Terrorism, 16 November 1937, League of Nations O.J. 23 (1938) and Convention of an International Criminal Court, opened for signature, Geneva, 16 November 1937 reprinted in Manley O. Hudson, (1935–1937) 7 *International Legislation* 862, 878 respectively.

criminally liable directly on the international plane, one cannot conceive of an international enforcement mechanism for suppression of terrorism in general and of an international criminal court in particular. The counter-argument, however, was that the best way to develop the law was by establishing at least a tribunal which would be instrumental in evolving the law.[20]

B. The age of national liberation movements

Unfortunately, it was not until the controversies surrounding the question of self-determination had become full-blown that the matter was subsequently placed on the agenda of the United Nations General Assembly in 1972. A thirty-five-member Ad Hoc Committee on Terrorism was set up, but its work was predictably impeded by the following sort of sentiment, expressed by the erstwhile Soviet Union, that:

> It is unacceptable to give a broad interpretation to the term 'international terrorism' and to extend it to cover national liberation movements or acts committed in resisting an aggressor in occupied territories.[21]

In March 1977, the Committee met again but was subsequently dissolved due to lack of progress in December of that year.[22]
One commonly referred to 'definition' today is simply that adopted by the United Nations General Assembly in 1996 in resolution 51/210 mentioned earlier:

> ... criminal acts intended or calculated to provoke a state of terror in the general public, a group of persons or particular persons for political purposes are in any circumstance unjustifiable, whatever the considerations of a political, philosophical, ideological, racial, ethnic, religious or other nature that may be invoked to justify them.

No-one suggests that this is a legal definition in the true sense.

C. Focusing on the methods of terror instead

Since the 1970s and more so from the 1980s onwards, international law-makers have been preoccupied not with a comprehensive definition of terrorism, but with *several* definitions of terrorism. Through painful experience,

---

[20] Mani, 'Future Strategies'.
[21] Quoted in Neil Haffrey, 'The United Nations and International Efforts to Deal with Terrorism', *Pew Case Studies in International Affairs, Case 313* (1998), 2; and in Martin A. Kalis, 'A New Approach to International Terrorism' (2001) 10 *International Affairs Review* 80, note 12.
[22] Kalis, 'A New Approach to International Terrorism'.

they have been content with incomplete definitions whenever there was sufficient international agreement in selective areas, focusing on known methods of terror instead. International lawyers have come to understand that we do tend to be better acquainted with the methods of terror barring the use of commercial aircraft as deadly projectiles, rather than the terror itself. There have been significant successes.

For international law-makers, what terrorism is has counted for less than what terrorists do. Terrorists, in their view, kidnap notable public figures, such as diplomats and other 'internationally protected' persons, and are generally prone to hostage taking to publicize and gain whatever leverage they perceive that might afford in furthering their cause. They hijack commercial aircraft for the same purposes. They transport plastic explosives across international borders and transfer monetary funds across international boundaries to further their activities. International lawyers and international law have focused on these very specific activities and a total of twelve multilateral conventions delimited likewise in scope have emerged (for which, see the Annex in this paper).[23] Speaking in the Sixth Committee of the United Nations General Assembly, the United States Representative (Mr Rosenstock) noted the link between achieving progress in setting international standards to combat terrorism and the need to focus on specific terrorist conduct. The benefit of such an approach is that it serves to decouple the matter at hand from the difficulty of achieving progress on a comprehensive, what I here call a 'generic', definition of terrorism that would be widely acceptable to all states.[24]

D. The 1970 Hague Convention and its progeny

So far as these multilateral conventions are concerned, most have adopted the 1970 Hague Convention for the Suppression of Unlawful Seizure of Aircraft as a model (hereafter, the 'Hague model'). Three distinct features of the Hague model are noteworthy.

1. 'Piggy-backing' on domestic law and enforcement

While these multilateral treaties and conventions are international legal instruments in their nature, they have not, generally speaking, sought international enforcement machinery to ensure the policing and enforcement of their terms. There is good reason for this, aside from the fact that these

---

[23] For an excellent treatment, see David Freestone, 'International Cooperation against Terrorism and the Development of International Law Principles of Jurisdiction' in Rosalyn Higgins and Maurice Flory, *Terrorism and International Law* (London, Routledge, 1997), 43.

[24] United Nations General Assembly, Press Release, GA/L/3169, 15 November 2000.

treaties are focused on the apprehension of terrorist fugitives across international borders, and are consequently focused on individuals and not states. International lawmakers are fully aware that one of the greatest obstacles in the enactment of any novel norm-setting treaty regime, and one of the standard objections raised in multilateral negotiations, is that of the cost of a surveillance, enforcement or adjudicative machinery. The simplest way around that practical problem has been to devolve such surveillance, enforcement and adjudicatory activities to the state parties themselves. Where the conduct called into question is not the conduct of the party to a treaty (such as in the case of human rights treaties), such an approach which piggy-backs on domestic law and enforcement tends to work relatively well.

These conduct-specific multilateral conventions following the Hague model, such as the 1971 Montreal Convention, the 1973 Internationally Protected Persons Convention, the 1979 Hostages Convention, the 1980 Physical Protection of Nuclear Material Convention and its 1988 Protocol, the 1988 IMO Convention and the Continental Shelf Platforms Protocol, the 1997 Terrorist Bombings Convention, and the 1999 Suppression of Terrorist Financing Convention have done so, more specifically, by generally imposing obligations that states are required to implement domestically. These will be in the form of the enactment of new domestic laws and enforcement machinery.

2. Focus on jurisdictional rules

Secondly, these treaties typically expand the jurisdiction of states parties and streamline the jurisdictional rules that would apply to delimit the competence of the states parties with a view towards dealing with particular terrorist acts in a concerted and coordinated fashion.[25]

3. The 'no safe haven' principle

Thirdly, they employ a common device to ensure that the states parties either prosecute or extradite those alleged to have been involved in terrorist activity to some other state party. The logic of the 'prosecute or extradite' doctrine is that it matters less who should try a terrorist than that the global terrorist should be tried by some state party (commonly referred to, therefore, as the 'no safe haven' principle).

In this way, the international rules in these multilateral conventions have been most concerned (1) with having domestic legal systems provide for certain offences as specifically international 'terrorist' offences, even though these offences may already fall to be defined by some pre-existing domestic penal offence, (2) that the individual state into whose custody the terrorist is

---

[25] Freestone, 'International Cooperation', 49 ff.

committed will usually have jurisdiction over such persons, and (3) that the state will either prosecute such persons under its own (domestic) laws or extradite that person to another state party which would also have the necessary domestic law to deal with the offence.

Putting these treaty rules aside, however, what impact have they had on the development of general, or customary, international law?

IV. The incompleteness of current international law

Of course, the absence of a comprehensive treaty definition of terrorism had its shortcomings, not least of which was the missed opportunity here of stimulating more comprehensive legal doctrine under general or customary international law, existing alongside such a comprehensive treaty definition. The emergence of parallel customary rules, arising alongside treaty rules, has long been recognized in international law doctrine.[26] Such 'parallel custom' could typically arise where the treaty rule merely codifies a pre-existing customary rule, where the practice of states during the diplomatic conference itself is evidence of a newly emergent rule, or where non-parties to a treaty were subsequently to take a treaty rule as a guide to their own conduct, thereby generating a customary rule applying to themselves and which mirrors a treaty rule applying between other states, or indeed by some combination of these various methods or some other means.

A. The Lockerbie example

In short, the way international lawmaking has 'got around' the political difficulties posed by such obstacles as the 'Middle-Eastern Question' and the national liberation/self-determination issue is by seeking incomplete definitions of global terrorism instead, and here, international lawmakers have also relied on the support of domestic penal laws and domestic enforcement machinery. Such 'incomplete' or 'scattered' regimes were always bound to be tested should the larger political factors that ordinarily would impede a more comprehensive legal approach come into play.

The most dramatic example of this sort of shortcoming was the Lockerbie affair. Under the 1971 Montreal Convention (for the Suppression of Unlawful Acts Against the Safety of Civil Aviation), Libya which was a party to that convention was required either to prosecute or extradite two accused Libyan

---

[26] *North Sea Continental Shelf Cases (FRG v. Denmark/FRG v. The Netherlands) (Merits)*, I.C.J. Reports (1969), 3, paras. 70–2. See further O. A. Elias and C. L. Lim, *The Paradox of Consensualism in International Law* (Hague, Kluwer, 1998), 24–6 arguing on the basis of a passage from the *Nicaragua Case* that what is sought to prove custom (*opinio juris*) is not qualitatively different from state consent to a rule.

persons who were said to be responsible for the tragedy. The Libyan Code of Criminal Procedures and the Libyan Constitution, however, prevent the extradition of Libyan nationals, and thus Libya argued that it could only comply with the Protocol by prosecuting these persons under Libyan domestic law, but not by extraditing them to the United States or the United Kingdom. The United States and the United Kingdom objected since these terrorists were (they argued) in fact Libyan agents. Libya denied that they were.

At bottom, the 1971 Montreal Convention was required here to deal with something which (arguably) it was never equipped to deal with; namely, state-sponsored terrorism – the Achilles' heel of the patchwork of international treaties on terrorism. While they resulted because of their success in getting around the issue of state-sponsored terrorism, they would also fail when what is at issue is state-sponsored terrorism of one sort or another.

The United States and the United Kingdom subsequently moved a number of Security Council resolutions in 1992 and 1993 in an effort to impose economic sanctions on Libya and to force Libya to comply with their demand to have these persons handed over for trial and punishment outside Libya.[27] Libya, in turn, sought the assistance of the International Court of Justice, pleading its rights under the Montreal Convention. Libya argued that once it had decided to prosecute and punish these persons, its obligations under the Protocol would have been fulfilled, and that this in turn would grant it an immunity against what the United States and the United Kingdom had sought in having sanctions brought against Libya through the collective security mechanism of the United Nations.

Some international lawyers saw this as a historic legal opportunity for the World Court to exercise an inherent power of judicial review over Security Council action,[28] but the Court has yet to oblige in any real manner.[29] However, that was not the only issue which the Court avoided. One interesting but neglected feature of the Court's judgment was that it also avoided having to deal with state-sponsored terrorism, leaving that question to the Security Council by default.

---

[27] Security Council resolution 731, UN doc. S/RES/731 (1992); Security Council resolution 748, UN doc. S/RES/748 (1992); Security Council resolution 883, UN doc. S/RES/883 (1993).

[28] Thomas M. Franck, 'The Powers of Appreciation: Who is the Ultimate Guardian of UN Legality?' (1992) 86 *American Journal of International Law* 519.

[29] See, however, the Joint Declaration issued by Judges Bedjaoui, Ranjeva and Koroma, postponing treatment of this issue to the Merits stage. For this pre-litigational skirmish in which the United States and the United Kingdom sought (unsuccessfully) to get the case brought by Libya thrown out, see C. L. Lim and O. A. Elias, 'Sanctions Without Law? The Lockerbie Case (Preliminary Objections)' (1999) 4 *Austrian Review of International and European Law* 204. However, the case will not now proceed to the merits phase: ICJ Press Release 2003/29, 10 September 2003.

B. Proving a customary law regime

Arguably, the Court *could* have backed the emergence of a general rule of international law penalizing international state-sponsored terrorism. It could have said, further, that such a general rule, being a customary rule, was also a *jus cogens* rule; in other words, a customary or general rule from which no derogation is permissible. It could have found that the acts committed there did not only amount to a crime under general international law, but also amounted to a crime that could not have been contracted out of by way of a treaty such as the Montreal Protocol.[30]

The United States in its oral arguments before the Court in that case had perhaps come close to urging this. According to the United States:

> ... the Convention is just one piece of a large tapestry of laws and international instruments designed to create multiple opportunities to bring accused terrorists to justice ...[31]

But the United States chose ultimately to rest its case on the terms of the Montreal Convention:

> The Montreal Convention, by its terms, does not displace other laws and instruments, nor does it eliminate the United States' right through peaceful, diplomatic means to promote Libya's surrender for trial of these persons.[32]

A further complication that we should note is that the bombing had not occurred in United States territory, but in fact in British airspace, and therefore some further basis for the United States' claim to jurisdiction would thereby have been required.[33] Calling the bombing of commercial aircraft an international crime from which no derogation was permitted would have supplied that necessary title to extraterritorial jurisdiction, for it would have been tantamount to saying that universal jurisdiction over such accused persons is granted to all states under customary law, and not just the state over whose airspace the tragedy was caused. Why then did the United States choose not to plead this argument?

One answer may be that the existence of new categories of international crime would ordinarily be very hard to establish in practice. Without speculating too much about the actual thinking underlying the litigation

---

[30] Article 53 of the Vienna Convention on the Law of Treaties, 23 May 1969, recognizes the existence of such customary rules as rules from which even negotiated treaty rights and obligations cannot derogate.
[31] US Oral Pleadings, para 1.20 (Andrews).
[32] US Oral Pleadings, paras 2.7 ff. (Murphy).
[33] While international law does not prohibit extraterritorial jurisdiction, it would prohibit interference with the domestic jurisdiction of another state.

strategy of the United States, another answer could also be that such a customary rule has simply not evolved at the present time, and perhaps the United States knew that (see the *Tel-Oren* case, discussed immediately below). That said, *if anything* could have qualified as a terrorist act amounting to an international crime from which no treaty derogation is permitted, it would have been the long-standing method of commercial aircraft terrorism.

V. The impact of such 'incompleteness' on domestic courts (in 'making' international law)

A. *International terrorism before state courts*

It is not so surprising then that domestic courts have not themselves ventured where the World Court has feared to tread. That is perhaps one 'link' which we may draw between the comparatively hesitant practice of domestic courts in formulating appropriate rules and principles to deal with terrorism, and the incompleteness of international law in this area.

Two notable cases have arisen before domestic courts which have invited these courts to push ahead, and to recognize that general or customary international law may have something to say about what international terrorism is. There was one well-known case before the Court of Appeals of the District of Columbia in 1984, and another recent case before the French Court of Cassation. Both involved Mr Qaddafi. The United States court in *Tel-Oren v. Libyan Arab Republic* had considered that international terrorism did not (at least in 1984) grant universal jurisdiction as there was insufficient evidence of an internationally agreed definition of terrorism under customary international law.[34] In the second case, the French prosecutor sought to annul charges brought against Mr Qaddafi on the basis that Mr Qaddafi enjoys Head of State immunity. It is not clear that the French Court of Cassation, which agreed with the prosecutor, had based its decision on the absence of a sufficiently deep international consensus on the crime of international terrorism under customary international law, but the relatively sparse reasoning does suggest this. The prosecutor had argued that there is no established 'terrorism' exception to Head of State immunity, and therefore Mr Qaddafi was immune from French justice.[35] Had a

---

[34] 726 F 2d 774 (D. C. Cir. 1984).

[35] For an account of the case and criticism that at least in respect of a terrorist bombing of a commercial aircraft, there is already sufficient practice to show that such acts have become recognized as an international crime, and would thereby form an exception to the Head of State immunity rule, see Salvatore Zappala, 'Do Heads of State Enjoy Immunity from Jurisdiction for International Crimes? The *Gaddhafi* Case before the French *Cour de Cassation*' (2001) 12 *European Journal of International Law* 595.

customary rule against terrorism been found, it would have made any state competent to try a person alleged to have committed terrorism without any express treaty rule granting such jurisdictional competence, or as in the French case, it could have created an exception to Head of State immunity where such persons are implicated in the commission of terrorist acts.

B. Should state courts be timorous?

There are very few instances in which what is required to establish a rule of general or customary international law could be found in the behaviour of domestic courts. Typically, state practice is tantamount to diplomatic practice. However, in the case of extraterritorial penal jurisdiction, and in the area of Head of State and similar immunities from jurisdiction, what would count is precisely what state courts do, and not what the Foreign Offices or State Departments of the various countries do. Proof of international custom before domestic courts could provide much needed proof that such a general rule also exists under international law. Thus, a movement on the part of domestic courts and judges to recognize terrorism as a crime under general international law in their own courtrooms would go a long way towards establishing a generic, customary, legal definition of global terrorism.[36]

The difficulty here is that while domestic courts may thereby be inclined to be timorous in the face of having to apply an uncertain international definition, the evolution of such an international definition by way of substantive domestic court practice would be impeded in turn. In the absence of a comprehensive treaty definition, it is within the possibility of such a mature body of domestic jurisprudence that, alternatively, a workable and realistic generic definition of terrorism could thereby emerge on the international plane, coupled with the potential for the several disparate terror treaty regimes on hijacking, kidnapping, maritime terror, plastic explosives, terrorist money-laundering, and so on to spawn parallel customary rules and principles which may be brought to bear beyond the parties to the individual treaties.

What I have suggested here is not a firm prediction, but simply one realistic appraisal of the true prospects for a generic definition. Does this mean that, in short, I have merely confirmed the marginal value of international standards to how domestic tribunals should go about dealing with international terror when confronted with it? Is there nothing more that international law, lawmakers and lawyers can do to help?

---

[36] Elias and Lim, *The Paradox of Consensualism*, 85–92.

VI. Three roads that lead to Rome

At the risk of being unduly selective, there are three proposals on the international plane that deserve special mention in this regard, putting aside the negotiations on the Draft Comprehensive Convention. They each would seek the benefit of 'piggy-backing' instead on the recent establishment of the International Criminal Court, albeit in different ways. I have already hinted that there are several linkages between the current negotiations towards a Comprehensive Convention on Terrorism and the Rome process. Turning the matter around, I ask in the following discussion if Rome could instead (or also) provide a solution to the terrorism question.

A. The Schmid/Lador-Lederer proposal: equating terrorism with the present list of crimes against humanity

According to the first proposal which appears to have received support within the United Nations Office on Drugs and Crime (UNODC):

Act of Terrorism = Peacetime Equivalent of War Crime

We are told that this 'short legal' definition as it is called by UNODC was originally proposed by the terrorism expert, A. P. Schmid in 1992 to the United Nations Crime Branch.[37] One problem in respect of the Schmid proposal is that it does not appear to add in a practical fashion to the war against terrorism by defining terrorism as a war crime. Surely if terrorism is tantamount to a war crime, terrorists could simply be prosecuted as war criminals. Moreover, war crimes represent one of the longest standing species of international crime that would grant universal jurisdiction to all states.

Viewed in this way, the Schmid proposal is tantamount to saying that it is unnecessary to deal with terrorism as anything other than an 'ordinary' war crime, except that such treatment would apply regardless of the existence of a state of war (i.e. also during peacetime).

But it is important to notice the 'inner logic' of this proposal, for it gets around a famous 1982 dissent by Professor L. C. Green and Dr J. J. Lador-Lederer to proposals made by the International Law Association's Committee on Terrorism towards a Draft Single Convention on the Legal Control of Terrorism. That objection was bound up with the 'national liberation' issue already referred to. According to the ILA's Committee on Terrorism:

---

[37] See the website of the United Nations Office of Drugs and Crime.

> ... surely, the humanitarian law requiring states to cooperate in the suppression of war crimes should apply to acts outside the armed conflict classification or by persons not entitled to soldiers' privileges.[38]

According to the two dissenting members of the committee, however:

> ... we fear that the proposed definition would in fact provide a loophole whereby some acts of terrorism would be excluded, while some groups of individuals claiming to be 'soldiers engaged in an international armed conflict' and having issued a declaration in accordance with Protocol I of 1977 or having been recognized as a national liberation movement by this or that group of states would be able to protect themselves on this spurious ground.[39]

In other words, the dissenting members (Green and Lador-Lederer) had objected to the 'war link' proposed by the ILA Committee for the protection that could thereby be afforded under the laws of war.

In any case, a 'war crime in peacetime' is itself a known category – for the drafters of the Nuremberg Charter, 'war crimes in peacetime' are what we now call 'crimes against humanity' (a category separate from 'war crimes'). The Schmid proposal is, in effect then, to treat terrorism according to the current list of crimes against humanity.

If this understanding of the Schmid proposal is correct, it is therefore not a new proposal, and is instead perhaps the longest standing proposal towards a generic definition of terrorism. An earlier statement of this view lies in a proposal by Dr J. J. Lador-Lederer himself. As we noted above Dr Lador-Lederer had earlier dissented from the Fourth Interim Report of the ILA Committee on the basis that terrorism should be dealt with wholly separately from the war context. Explaining his position further, Dr Lador-Lederer said in a conference held at Central Michigan University in 1983 that:

> I reject any approach which relates the issue in any way to the law of armed conflict ... The method I would favour is criminalization of terrorism – 'considering terrorism to be of the nature of crimes against humanity, it is a crime against mankind as a whole' (Preamble to my draft) – believing that penal law is that legal system which is closest to the protection of human rights.[40]

---

[38] Fourth Interim Report of the Committee on Terrorism, presented to the Sixtieth Conference of the International Law Association, Montreal, 1982, para 20.

[39] Ibid., Appendix I (*Dissenting Statement by Professor L. C. Green and Dr J. Lador-Lederer*), para 13. For the background legal issues concerning the extension of humanitarian disciplines to wars of national liberation, see Heather A. Wilson, *International Law and the Use of Force by National Liberation Movements* (Oxford, Clarendon, 1988), 162–85.

[40] J. J. Lador-Lederer, 'Defining "Terrorism" – A Comment', in Henry Hyunwook Han (ed.), *Terrorism, Political Violence and World Order* (Lanham, University Press of America, 1984), 5–6.

We will see that the Schmid /Lador-Lederer proposal, however, faces similar problems to those faced by a further, second proposal. The second proposal (below) is *not to equate terrorism with the list of crimes against humanity currently available, but simply to include terrorism in that list.*

I shall try to show below that, whichever proposal we adopt, lawyers especially have an acute sense that the development of legal doctrine by analogy is seldom a straightforward process, and often hard doctrinal choices would still have to be made when called upon actually to apply a legal doctrine by analogy only.

B. *Professor Cassese's proposal: terrorism as a crime against humanity*

The second proposal, which was recently brought up by Professor Cassese is in turn based on an earlier proposal put forward by Algeria, India, Sri Lanka and Turkey during the negotiations of the Rome Statute of the ICC.[41] Numerous other states, including the United States, had objected to the proposal of these four states. The reasons given by the objecting states was that to include terrorism as a crime against humanity would nonetheless result in a vaguely defined offence, that this would politicize terrorist trials, and that there was no need to grant jurisdiction to an international tribunal where domestic courts could do a better job in adjudicating terrorist cases.[42] In addition, several developing countries also raised the long-standing objection based on the need to accommodate genuine struggles for self-determination, and a further proposal by India, Sri Lanka and Turkey was subsequently rejected.[43]

As we have seen, the proposal to include terrorism as a distinct crime against humanity does not necessarily equate terrorist crimes with the list of crimes against humanity currently available, unlike what the Schmid /Lador-Lederer proposal seems to suggest. Strictly speaking Professor Cassese's proposal faces a slightly different problem – what then does terrorism mean, even if we take it to be a kind of crime against humanity? It appears to beg the question.

Yet perhaps the differences between the Schmid/Lador-Lederer proposal and Professor Cassese's proposal are not as pronounced as that. Clearly, we could best answer Cassese's difficulty by looking at how a crime against

---

[41] A/CONF.183/C.1/L 27.

[42] Antonio Cassese, 'Terrorism is also Disrupting some Crucial Legal Categories of International Law'; paper posted on the European Journal of International Law's Discussion Forum ('The Attack on the World Trade Centre: Legal Responses') (on file). See also Herman von Hebel and Darryl Robinson, 'Crimes within the Jurisdiction of the Court', in Lee (ed.), *The International Criminal Court*, 79, 85–7.

[43] A/CONF.183/C.1/ L 27/Rev 1.

humanity *is* currently defined. But here we run into a further set of unresolved questions, not insurmountable in themselves but unresolved.

In the *Tadic* case before the International Criminal Tribunal for the Former Yugoslavia (hereafter, 'the ICTY'), the Appeals Chamber had taken the view there that:

> It is by now a settled rule of customary international law that crimes against humanity do not require a connection to international armed conflict. Indeed, as the Prosecutor points out, *customary international law may not require a connection between crimes against humanity and any conflict at all.* Thus, by requiring that crimes against humanity be committed in either internal or international armed conflict, the Security Council may have defined the crime in Article 5 [of the Statute of the ICTY] more narrowly than necessary under customary international law.[44]

What the Appeal Chamber suggests in the passage above is that a parallel but not fully identical customary norm exists to Article 5 of the Statute of the ICTY.

In these sorts of cases, the parallel customary rule need not always be identical to the treaty rule in question.[45] It is noteworthy that in the *Nicaragua Case*, the International Court of Justice concluded that the customary law on self-defence was not wholly identical with the (treaty) self-defence rule in the Charter of the United Nations.[46]

However, Article 5 of the Statute of the ICTY provides (instead) that:

> The International Tribunal shall have the power to prosecute persons responsible for the following crimes *when committed in armed conflict, whether international or internal in character,* and directed against any civilian population:
>
> (a) murder;
> (b) extermination;
> (c) enslavement;
> (d) deportation;
> (e) imprisonment;
> (f) torture;
> (g) rape;
> (h) persecutions on political, racial and religious grounds;
> (i) other inhumane acts.[47]

---

[44] *Prosecutor* v. *Dusko Tadic* (Cassese, President; Li, Deschenes, Abi-Saab and Sidhwa), ICTY Appeals Chamber, 2 October 1995, para 141 (emphasis added).

[45] *Nicaragua Case (Nicaragua* v. *United States) (Merits)*, I.C.J. reports (1986), 14, paras 185–6.

[46] Ibid., para 200. [47] Emphasis added.

Article 5 differs in turn from the earlier 'original' definition at Nuremberg whereby 'crimes against humanity' were simply defined in Article 6(c) of the Nuremberg Charter by reference to, and was parasitic upon, the other 'crimes' under international law (e.g. 'crimes against peace' and 'war crimes'). The Nuremberg Charter first defines crimes against peace and war crimes in Articles 6(a) and (b), then stipulates that:[48]

> Leaders, organizers, instigators and accomplices participating in the formulation or execution of a common plan or conspiracy to commit any of the foregoing crimes are responsible for all acts performed by any persons in execution of such plan.

The aim here was, importantly, to include the Final Solution within the ambit of the postwar Nuremberg trials where the policy which the Final Solution represented comprised also the persecution of German nationals in Nazi Germany prior to the war itself, during peacetime. Consequently, the drafting intent underlying Article 6(c) was to expand the scope of war crimes to peacetime by linking such 'peacetime offences' to the war itself.[49]

In any event, the approach taken in Article 3 of the Statute of the International Criminal Tribunal for Rwanda (hereafter, the ICTR), coming in the wake of the ICTY and the *Tadic* decision, was simply to speak of crimes:

> ... when committed as part of a widespread or systematic attack against any civilian population on national, political, ethnic, racial or religious grounds ...

The problem, in short, is that there is a multiplicity of overlapping treaty definitions today, each individual definition of which could exert some influence still on any judgment made on what the customary law definition of crimes against humanity (and terrorism) should look like. For example, the drafting language of Article 7(1) of the Rome Statute of the International Criminal Court omits mention of the words 'on national, political, ethnic, racial or religious grounds' (in the ICTR definition above) and contains instead the additional words 'with knowledge of the attack':

> ... when committed as part of a widespread or systematic attack directed against any civilian population, *with knowledge of the attack* ...[50]

Moreover, this ICC definition contains a 'longer' list of specific offences which are included within and thereby comprise a part of the notion of crimes against

---

[48] Charter of the International Military Tribunal, annexed to the London Agreement for the Prosecution and Punishment of the Major War Criminals of the European Axis, 1945.

[49] See further Bradley F. Smith, *The Road to Nuremberg* (NY, Basic Books, 1981), at 48–74; Hersch Lauterpacht, *International Law and Human Rights* (London, Stevens, 1950), 36.

[50] Emphasis added.

humanity.[51] Which if any of the three definitions discussed above would be the likely basis of a definition of the customary prohibition of crimes against humanity? This sort of problem was highlighted by the Austrian delegation in the negotiations leading up to the Rome Statute, and caused the following saving clause in Article 22(3) to be inserted in the Rome Statute:

> This Article shall not affect the characterization of any conduct as criminal under international law independently of this statute.[52]

A further problem that would have to be resolved is that the divergent definitions above are also dependent on the tapestry of interwoven and interlocking provisions in the treaty instruments within which each definition arises. Picking one definition and not another would nonetheless leave unanswered which 'treaty tapestry' would apply. Take Article 7(2)(a) of the Rome Statute, for example. Article 7(2)(a), which defines 'armed attack against civilians' in Article 7(1), suggests that a single act of one of the listed offences above could in principle suffice to constitute an international crime provided it is coupled with an unspecified number and combination of commissions of (an)other listed offence(s) so as together to constitute a 'systematic' attack.[53] Should this be true of a customary definition?

---

[51] The list in Article 7(1) of the Rome Statute specifies:

(a) Murder;
(b) Extermination;
(c) Enslavement;
(d) Deportation or forcible transfer of population;
(e) Imprisonment or other severe deprivation of physical liberty in violation of fundamental rules of international law;
(f) Torture;
(g) Rape, sexual slavery, enforced prostitution, forced pregnancy, enforced sterilization, or any other form of sexual violence of comparable gravity;
(h) Persecution against any identifiable group or collectivity on political, racial, national, ethnic, cultural, religious, gender as defined in paragraph 3, or other grounds that are universally recognized as impermissible under international law, in connection with any act referred to in this paragraph or any crime within the jurisdiction of the Court;
(i) Enforced disappearance of persons;
(j) The crime of apartheid;
(k) Other inhumane acts of a similar character intentionally causing great suffering, or serious injury to body or to mental or physical health.

[52] Per Saland, 'International Criminal Law Principles', in Lee (ed.), *The International Criminal Court*, 189, 195.

[53] Article 7(1) states, in the relevant part that:
For the purpose of paragraph 1:
a. 'Attack directed against any civilian population' means a course of conduct involving the *multiple commission of acts referred to in paragraph 1* against any civilian population,

There are further examples of this problem. Article 7 of the Statute of the ICTR states, for example, in paragraph 4 that:

> The fact that an accused person acted pursuant to an order of a Government or of a superior shall not relieve him of criminal responsibility, but may be considered in mitigation of punishment if the International Tribunal determines that justice so requires.

Paragraph 4 is identical to paragraph 4 of Article 7 of the Statute of the ICTY. In contrast, Article 33 of the Rome Statute is cast in altogether different terms:

> 1. The fact that a crime within the jurisdiction of the Court has been committed by a person pursuant to an order of a Government or of a superior, whether military or civilian, shall not relieve that person of criminal responsibility unless:
>   (a) The person was under a legal obligation to obey orders of the Government or the superior in question;
>   (b) The person did not know that the order was unlawful; and
>   (c) The order was not manifestly unlawful.
> 2. For the purposes of this article, orders to commit genocide or crimes against humanity are manifestly unlawful.

My point is not that all these details (which the Schmid/Lador-Lederer proposal also faces with the customary definition of war crimes) are insurmountable, but that there is a more direct, indeed more intellectually honest, approach which we will now turn to.

C. The 'treaty crimes' issue in Rome: terrorism as a crime to be defined by future treaty negotiation

The true value of Professor Cassese's proposal lies in its suitability as a starting-point for *international negotiations* on a generic definition of terrorism. Provided such a definition could also absorb whatever past consensus has already been achieved in the form of the several treaty regimes already in place on hijacking, hostage taking, and so on, there is no reason in principle why crimes against humanity could not become a component, even an important component, of a generic definition of international terrorism. This brings us to a (third) broader approach that was adopted by some delegations in the negotiations leading up to the Rome Statute.

These delegations sought to include terrorism within the jurisdiction of the ICC at some point in the future *when* an appropriate definition can be

pursuant to or in furtherance of a State or organizational policy to commit such attack (emphasis added).

agreed upon by the state parties to the Rome Statute (i.e. *a definition by further negotiation*).

As von Hebel and Robinson point out, the question of including terrorism within the jurisdiction of the ICC is bound up with the broader proposal to include a list of other 'treaty crimes' in the Rome Statute; principally 'drug trafficking', 'crimes against United Nations and associated personnel', and 'crimes involving the illicit traffic in narcotic drugs'.[54] As Wilmshurst has also noted,[55] Article 20(e) of the International Law Commission's 1994 Draft Statute had earlier referred to 'crimes, established under or pursuant to the treaty provisions list in the Annex, which, having regard to the conduct alleged, constitute exceptionally serious crimes of international concern'. Of the fourteen treaties listed in the Annex, six were concerned with terrorist offences from hijacking to hostage-taking, amongst others.[56]

Professor Wilson of the American University, Washington D.C. reports however that:

> The major concern of the delegates appeared to be that such crimes, while defined by treaty, have not been uniformly subscribed to or recognized, and their exclusion from 'core crimes' of the ICC might facilitate the acceptance of jurisdiction of the Court by States that are not parties to the treaties in question. The view was also expressed that the drafters had failed to include other important treaty-based offenses such as crimes against the environment.[57]

---

[54] The inclusion of measures to combat the drug trade was due to public pressure that was, at the time, brought to bear on the negotiations.

[55] Elizabeth Wilmshurst, 'Jurisdiction of the Court' in Lee (ed.), *International Criminal Court*, 127, note 10.

[56] Draft Statute for an International Criminal Court, Report of the International Law Commission on the work of its forty-sixth session, 2 May–22 July 1994, Chapter II.B.I. United Nations General Assembly Official Records, Forty-ninth Session, Supplement No. 10, A/49/10 (1994), 29–140. Principally, unlawful seizure of aircraft defined under the 1970 Hague Convention; hostage-taking and related crimes defined under the 1979 Hostages Convention, piracy under the 1988 IMO Convention, and treaty definitions of apartheid and crimes against diplomatic personnel; discussed in Richard J. Wilson, 'A Permanent International Criminal Court: Impunity Loses Another Round', paper presented by Professor Wilson at the International Conference on 'Impunity and its Effects on Democratic Processes', Santiago de Chile, 14 December 1996 (available on the world-wide web).

[57] Wilson, ibid. See also Kai Ambos, 'Establishing an International Criminal Court and an International Criminal Code: Observations from an International Criminal Law Viewpoint' (1996) 7 *European Journal of International Law* 519, 527: 'There are crimes which are virtually unrecognized by the state community in spite of their codification in international treaties, for example mercenarism. Or there are treaty crimes, whose wrongfulness is less than that of other non-treaty crimes, which are nevertheless recognized by customary international law. In spite of this fact, these non-treaty crimes do not – according to the treaty approach – fall within the jurisdiction of an ICC.'

Nonetheless, these 'treaty crimes' (so-called by the International Law Commission)[58] were eventually included in the list of negotiating items following a February 1997 (Rome) Preparatory Committee Decision to do so, with the caveat that their inclusion was without prejudice to the question as to whether they would ultimately be included in the Rome Statute.[59] On 14 July 1998, during the subsequent Rome Conference, the delegations that had originally proposed the inclusion of terrorism within the list of crimes suggested that the same compromise should be made as had been struck over an appropriate definition of the crime of aggression. Specifically, this was to list the crime in the Statute but to leave its precise definition for another day prior to which the ICC would not be able to exercise jurisdiction over that specific crime. In negotiating terms this was a neat device by which to keep the issue firmly on the negotiating table. But there was scant support for this proposal.

As things turned out, the delegation from Turkey only succeeded in ensuring the inclusion of a resolution in the Final Act of the Rome Conference, recommending that a future Review Conference should reconsider achieving an acceptable definition of terrorism with a view to its inclusion in the Rome Statute and in order that terrorism should fall to be considered as a crime within the jurisdiction of the ICC.[60]

VII. Conclusion

We have seen how the original ILC Draft Statute contained a list of treaty crimes, based on the sorts of terrorist acts identified in the earlier subject-specific treaties. From this viewpoint, the definition of terrorism is as straightforward as it is merely the sum total of all the available subject-specific definitions. These various subject-specific treaties remain the most reliable sources of international law today as to what terrorism looks like. Beyond these treaties there arises the question of what a general customary law definition would look like, and whether these treaty rules may have stimulated broad acceptance by states of parallel customary rules since these treaties have arguably resulted from the *opinio juris communitatis* of a not insignificant number of states.[61] But beyond these subject-specific rules that are focused only on some well-known methods of terror, the two

---

[58] Defined by the International Law Commission as 'crimes established under or pursuant to the treaty provision of an international treaty which, having regard to the conduct alleged, constitute exceptionally serious crimes of international concern'; ILC Commentary to Article 20 of its Draft Statute, ibid., 70 and 147–157.

[59] Decisions Taken by the Preparatory Committee at its session held from 11 to 21 February 1997, A/AC.249/1997/L.5 (1997).

[60] Final Act of the Conference, Resolution E, A/CONF.183/C.1/L.76/Add. 14, 8.

[61] See also Freestone, 'International Cooperation', 60.

pronouncements by the American and French courts and the traditional differences between states on the international plane count against the existence of a more comprehensive definition of what terrorism is under customary international law.

The end result, in terms of what international law is today, is a body of international rules that will tell you that someone who traffics in plastic explosives, or blows up a fixed platform on a continental shelf, or who blows up or hijacks an airplane, or takes hostages is a terrorist in the eyes of international law, and that certain states that are party to certain treaties could claim jurisdiction over such persons, and would prosecute or extradite these persons. One could even argue that some of these treaty rules are customary rules. But beyond that international law has nothing to say, for example, about whether an ordinary murderer convicted under domestic penal law also becomes a terrorist because of the political or other motivation he has in committing murder.[62] International law is silent on the question of what terrorism is, generally speaking.

[62] For some domestic legal systems in respect of which offence categories under international law would become common law offences too, that international law may call such a person a terrorist and may define terrorism as an international crime would prove crucial in so far as a court would not otherwise have the offence category under its domestic penal law or even if it already does, may nonetheless not be entitled to extraterritorial jurisdiction should the offending act have been committed abroad. In other countries, even within the common law family, common law offences may not be possible because only statutory offences are recognized. In Singapore, which is shy of common law extraterritoriality, it is an open question whether the Singapore courts could assert jurisdictional competence over universal crimes outside of specific statutory provision, such as the Penal Code provisions on piracy *iure gentium* and slavery, or offences provided for in pursuance of one of the subject-specific terrorism treaties to which Singapore is party. See further C. L. Lim, 'Singapore Crimes Abroad', (2001) *Singapore Journal of Legal Studies* 494, note 118, and the discussion of common law extraterritoriality therein. There is also an apparent loophole in respect of genocide which I raised there. Singapore is a party to the Convention on the Prevention and Punishment of the Crime of Genocide, 9 December 1948 but there appears no specific offence of genocide in Singapore's statute books. This could lead to difficulties were a person accused of having committed genocide were to arrive on Singapore's shores. For the debate in Parliament on this between Nominated Member, Associate Professor Simon Tay and the Honourable Minister for Law, Professor S. Jayakumar, see the Singapore Parliamentary Reports, Vol. 73, Sess. 9 (13 March 2001), cols. 928–32. For some complex but interesting developments in customary international law in respect of genocide, see Guglielmo Verdirame, 'The Genocide Definition in the Jurisprudence of the *Ad Hoc* Tribunals' (2000) 49 *International and Comparative Law Quarterly* 578. So far as the post 9/11 war against terrorism is concerned, Singapore has also enacted parent legislation under which the Minister may, under direction from the United Nations Security Council, provide for extraterritorial penal offences under Singapore's United Nations Act, on which see C. L. Lim, 'Executive Lawmaking in Compliance of International Treaty' (2002) *Singapore Journal of Legal Studies* 73.

Admittedly, there are some plausible proposals that we have seen towards the question of a generic customary definition. These would link any customary law definition of terrorism to Rome in some way, either by linking a definition of international terrorism with war crimes or crimes against humanity, or simply by advocating that any definition of international terrorism should occur in the context of a review of the Rome Statute. The link to Rome is as it should be, for even in the League era the question of a convention on terrorism was linked, as we have seen, to the creation of an international criminal court. However, I do not find any approach which might rely on summing the political will of states to negotiate a comprehensive definition with an end in sight particularly promising in the short term. Not because a Draft Comprehensive Convention on Terrorism might not result, indeed it is expected to come into being, but because the old political problems stretching back to 1937 and which we have since also witnessed in countless General Assembly debates are all still there. The existence of these 'old problems' suggests that such a convention could have more of a symbolic role than a real one. I do not wish to be overly cynical, but treaty lawmakers know that if a treaty is what their political masters and others really want, you just need to give them something they can call a treaty and leave it at that. So far as efforts on the international plane are concerned, a strategy of avoiding the old political pitfalls seems therefore more attractive, making the regime of subject-specific treaties more attractive than talk of replacing or augmenting these treaties which we already have and which work quite well with a comprehensive treaty definition of terrorism. According to this view, it is not as important to decide what a terrorist looks like as it is to decide what methods used by terrorists need to be dealt with, and how we might wish to do so.

In practical terms, the most promising path towards a useful, as opposed merely to a symbolic, comprehensive international definition of terrorism also lies in leaving terrorism largely to be defined by domestic law – by domestic courts, domestic legislative activity, or both. Each state must currently push ahead according to its own lights. But there are clear fairness-based difficulties with the construction by domestic courts of offences and defences from such an amorphous body of material evidence of the applicable customary rules. At the best of times, the reception of customary law into domestic law by way of the exercise of judicial powers is haphazard, but where the liberty of the individual is concerned, to do so risks politicizing any trial to a degree that may simply be considered unacceptable under the constitutions and legal cultures of a whole host of democratic nations. This could suggest that some states might consider themselves better advised if the legislative branch were to step into the void instead – both to 'transform' available customary standards into domestic law via legislation, and to progressively fill in the gaps where the customary rule is still in its infancy or remains relatively ill-developed. In due course, should there arise sufficient similarities in legislative activity, sufficient borrowing and adaptation of legislative approaches, this could pave the way for eventual harmonization. If this happens, instead of the previous approach of having treaties that required domestic legal reception of new categories of international crime such as hijacking and so on, domestic legislative activity could drive the international lawmaking process instead, bottom-up so to speak. Approaching the matter in this bottom-up fashion could also have the ancillary advantage of ensuring both greater rule-precision and a greater breadth of state participation. International lawmakers could simply engage in a process of codification by seeking out clear commonalities in comparative legislative activity, coupled with a measure of progressive development through gap filling, rather than quibble over an appropriate starting point for international legislation. Roughly speaking, this is the position that many states have taken, including Singapore.[63]

Annex

Multilateral Conventions in chronological order

Convention on Offences and Certain Other Acts Committed on Board Aircraft, signed at Tokyo on 14 September 1963.

Convention for the Suppression of Unlawful Seizure of Aircraft, signed at the Hague on 16 December 1970.

Convention for the Suppression of Unlawful Acts against the Safety of Civil Aviation, signed at Montreal on 23 September 1971.

Convention on the Prevention and Punishment of Crimes against Internationally Protected Persons, including Diplomatic Agents, adopted by the General Assembly of the United Nations on 14 December 1973.

International Convention against the Taking of Hostages, adopted by the General Assembly of the United Nations on 17 December 1979

Convention on the Physical Protection of Nuclear Material, signed at Vienna on 3 March 1980.

Protocol on the Suppression of Unlawful Acts of Violence at Airports Serving International Civil Aviation, supplementary to the Convention for the Suppression of Unlawful Acts against the Safety of Civil Aviation, signed at Montreal on 24 February 1988.

---

[63] As Singapore's Minister for Foreign Affairs and Law put it during the 57th Session of the United Nations General Assembly: 'where international consensus has not yet consolidated over situations posing serious and immediate threats, the lack of international consensus in itself cannot be an excuse for inaction. This would be an abdication of individual and collective responsibility'; Professor S. Jayakumar, Address to the 57th Session of the United Nations General Assembly, New York, 13 September 2002 (on file).

Convention for the Suppression of Unlawful Acts against the Safety of Maritime Navigation, done at Rome on 10 March 1988.

Protocol for the Suppression of Unlawful Acts against the Safety of Fixed Platforms Located on the Continental Shelf, done at Rome on 10 March 1988.

Convention on the Marking of Plastic Explosives for the Purpose of Detection, signed at Montreal on 1 March 1991.

International Convention for the Suppression of Terrorist Bombings, adopted by the General Assembly of the United Nations on 15 December 1997.

International Convention for the Suppression of the Financing of Terrorism, adopted by the General Assembly of the United Nations on 9 December 1999.

4

The state of emergency in legal theory

DAVID DYZENHAUS

'There are times of tumult or invasion when for the sake of legality itself the rules of law must be broken. ... The Ministry must break the law and trust for protection to an Act of Indemnity. A statute of this kind is ... the last and supreme exercise of Parliamentary sovereignty. It legalises illegality. ... [It] ... combine[s] the maintenance of law and the authority of the Houses of Parliament with the free exercise of that kind of discretionary power or prerogative which, under some shape or other, must at critical junctures be wielded by the executive government of every civilized country'. A. V. Dicey[1]

I. Introduction

Dicey says that in an emergency situation public officials might find themselves compelled to act outside the law and Parliament might then indemnify them. But an Act of Indemnity does not make what the officials did legal – Parliament has 'legalised illegality'. Rather, it places them in a zone uncontrolled by law – a legal black hole, to use the current term. His point is that political power can be exercised in a brute fashion, permitting those who wield it to break free of the constraints of constitutionality and legality.

It might, Dicey thinks, be at times justified to do this because without illegal action the state and thus law itself might have been overthrown. But it would be far better if Parliament were to delegate in advance the resources to public officials to deal with the emergency. In addition, the resources would not be power uncontrolled by law, equivalent to the prerogative. Dicey was not only enthusiastic about taming the prerogative by subjecting it to statutory control.[2] He also said that it would be erroneous to suppose that a

I thank Geneviève Cartier, Michael Hor, Rayner Thwaites, Victor V. Ramraj and, especially, Tom Hickman and Kent Roach, for comments on a draft, as well as the participants in the 'Comparative Anti-Terrorism Law & Policy Symposium' for critical discussion.

[1] *Introduction to the Study of the Law of the Constitution* (10th edn, London, Macmillan, 1959), 412–13.
[2] Ibid., 64.

prospective legislative response to an emergency merely substitutes the 'despotism of Parliament for the prerogative of the Crown ... the fact that the most arbitrary powers of the English executive must always be exercised under Act of Parliament places the government, even when armed with the widest authority, under the supervision, so to speak, of the courts'. And judges would exercise a control on executive action informed by their understanding of the 'general spirit of the common law'. In England, 'Parliamentary sovereignty has favoured the rule of law ... the supremacy of the law of the land both calls forth the exertion of Parliamentary sovereignty, and leads to its being exercised in a spirit of legality'.[3]

Dicey distinguishes clearly between two legal responses to an emergency. In the first, the response is the after-the-fact recognition that officials made an excusable decision to act outside of the law because it was necessary to act and the law did not provide them with the right resources. In the second, Parliament in advance gives to officials resources to deal with emergencies in accordance with the rule of law. Dicey prefers the second option, although he thinks we should be aware that officials might have to react to an emergency situation before Parliament can respond. In sum, Dicey's model for dealing with emergencies relies on legislative solutions that preserve the rule of law.[4] In the face of an ongoing emergency, he would insist on the prospective legislative response.

I argue that Dicey was right. My foil is Oren Gross's recent article 'Chaos and Rules',[5] which suggests that the situation Dicey depicts in the epigraph should be the general model for dealing with a state of emergency, particularly an ongoing one.[6] My argument is that one should not extract a prescriptive model from the matter-of-fact judgment of necessity which Dicey sketches. I first set out the main components of Gross's argument. I then show how Gross, despite his awareness of the contours of debate, finds himself trapped by some of the same assumptions which produce those

---

[3] Ibid., 413–24.

[4] John Ferejohn and Pasquale Pasquino, in 'The Law of the Exception: A Typology of Emergency Powers' (2004) 2 *International Journal of Constitutional Law* 210, 237–9, disagree, against textual evidence. They also go astray in supposing that the legislative normalization of the exception is driven by the need for democratic legitimation. This claim is true in part of democratic societies, but the more fundamental driving force is the need for rule-of-law legitimation, which is why one sees the same move made in non-democratic societies. Since the driving force is rule-of-law legitimation, the kind of dualism they sketch is not, for Dicey, the preferable legal response.

[5] 'Chaos and Rules: Should Responses to Violent Crises Always be Constitutional?' (2003) 112 *Yale Law Journal* 1011.

[6] At the symposium, Gross suggested that his model is tied to what he called catastrophic situations and is thus not, as I claim, general. On rereading 'Chaos and Rules', I do not find this limitation and if the model were so to be limited, it would, for reasons I give below, cease to be a model.

contours. His model turns out to be highly unstable in theory and the likely result is that in practice his model turns into something distant from, even opposite to, his intentions.

Gross recognizes that the legal responses after 9/11 are not to a state of emergency, classically conceived. Rather, prompted by the allegation that terrorism is here to stay, these responses seek to deal with the emergency not as temporary external threat, but as an internal, permanent problem. The standard reaction, which Gross wishes to resist, is that the normal legal order has to be changed to deal with the fact that the exceptional situation has become permanent.

Gross is wrong to resist this reaction so resolutely. There is something to it, although it goes wrong in supposing that we are confronted with a completely new reality. The reality is rather one which legal order has always had to confront, in sometimes banal, sometimes dramatic ways. That confrontation might require imaginative experiments in institutional design, but only a legal theory not trapped by the standard assumptions of much of contemporary legal thought can explore such possibilities. For such experiments are inhibited by a failure to recognize the second problem, a failure which plagues Gross and much of contemporary legal theory. It arises from the grip of a formal doctrine of the separation of powers and my argument is that only if the grip is loosened can the first problem be addressed.

II. Chaos and rules

Gross sketches two traditional models used to respond to emergency situations. The first is the 'Business as Usual' model, which holds that the legal order as it stands has the resources to deal with the state of emergency and so no substantive change in the law is required. The second model is one of 'Accommodation', which argues for some significant changes to the existing order so as to accommodate security considerations, while keeping the ordinary system intact as far as possible. The principal criticism of the Business as Usual model is that it is naïve or even hypocritical, as it either ignores or hides the necessities of the exercise of government power in an emergency. The Accommodation model, in contrast, risks undermining the ordinary system because it imports the measures devised to deal with the emergency.[7]

Gross argues that two basic assumptions dominate debates about the state of emergency and thus underpin the models. The first is the assumption of separation between the normal and the exceptional which is 'defined by the belief in our ability to separate emergencies and crises from normalcy,

---

[7] Gross, 'Chaos and Rules', 1021–2. Gross finds several different models within the Accommodation camp, but for the sake of simplicity I talk about one model.

counter-terrorism measures from ordinary legal rules and norms'.[8] This assumption makes it easier for us to accept expanded government powers and extraordinary measures, since we suppose both that once the threat has gone, so we can return to normal, and that the powers and measures will be deployed against the enemy, not us. The second assumption is of constitutionality: 'whatever responses are made to the challenges of a particular exigency, such responses are to be found and limited within the confines of the constitution'.[9] Gross supports the critiques of both models and he also calls into question both assumptions.

The assumption of separation between the normal and the exceptional ignores the way in which emergency government has become the norm, a trend which has only gathered strength since the widely copied US response to 9/11. And the assumption of constitutionality, whether made by claiming business as usual or that the accommodation conforms to constitutional values, risks undermining the legal order.

Thus Gross proposes the 'Extra-Legal Measures model'. This model tells public officials that they may respond extra-legally when they 'believe that such action is necessary for protecting the nation and the public in the face of calamity, provided that they openly and publicly acknowledge the nature of their actions'.[10] Gross claims that this model preserves the 'fundamental principles and tenets' of the constitutional order.[11] In addition, public officials will have to disclose the nature of their activities and hope for 'direct or indirect *ex post* ratification', either through the courts, the executive or the legislature. The process involved will promote both popular deliberation and individual accountability, while the uncertain outcomes will provide a brake on public officials' temptation to rush into action.[12]

To persuade us to accept the Extra-Legal Measures model, Gross suggests that we should agree on three points: '(1) Emergencies call for extraordinary governmental responses, (2) constitutional arguments have not greatly constrained any government faced with the need to respond to such emergencies, and (3) there is a strong probability that measures used by the government in emergencies will eventually seep into the legal system after the emergency has ended.'[13] The model, in his view, recognizes the force of all three points. But by rejecting the naivety of the Business as Usual model while requiring that exceptional government responses happen outside the law, it greatly diminishes the probability of seepage.

---

[8] Ibid., 1022. Two ideas that do considerable work in this chapter share a term, 'the assumption of separation between the normal and the exceptional' and 'the formal doctrine of the separation of powers'. I try to avoid confusion by giving 'the assumption of separation' its full description each time – 'the assumption of separation between the normal and the exceptional'.

[9] Ibid., 1023.   [10] Ibid.   [11] Ibid., 1023–4.   [12] Ibid.   [13] Ibid., 1097.

Gross find the intellectual roots of his model in John Locke's theory of the prerogative, where prerogative is defined as '*nothing but the Power of doing publick good without a Rule*'. For Locke, the prerogative is the 'power to act according to discretion for the publick good, without the prescription of the Law and sometimes even against it'.[14] As Gross understands Locke, he is providing a functional test for use of the prerogative power – the test of the public good. Locke supposes that it is within the subjective discretion of the executive to decide both when the exercise of this power is required and how it is to be exercised. The functionality of the test – whether the powers were in fact exercised in accordance with the public good – resides in popular acquiescence in the measures – the tacit approval of the public evidenced in its failure to rebel. If advance public trust in government is shaken by the exercise of the prerogative powers, after the fact the public will revolt.[15]

The Extra-Legal Measures model adopts Locke's understanding of the need for and nature of the prerogative. It differs in its requirement of 'explicit, particular and *ex post* ratification'.[16] This requirement both puts public officials at risk and makes them accountable, because their exercise of power will be subject to public scrutiny and deliberation – to an assessment of whether their actions were necessary to secure the public good. This requirement, Gross claims, will also prevent illegal official action from breeding a culture of lawlessness that one might suppose would ensue if citizens were to take such action as an example.[17]

Gross recognises that his model, like the other two, rests on the false assumption of separation between the normal and the exceptional, perhaps even more so.[18] But he claims that its appeal lies in its 'open recognition of the assumption's limitations and in an attendant endeavor to minimize the actual reliance on it' through requiring openly illegal and thus potentially costly official responses.[19] His model thus preserves the distinction between the normal and the exceptional situation while permitting the state to address the exception subject to after-the-fact legal controls.

Gross is aware that Locke is not his only intellectual precursor. His model also echoes the claims of fascist legal theorist Carl Schmitt about the inapplicability of legal norms to exceptional situations.[20] Gross agrees with Schmitt that a pre-existing legal norm cannot be successfully applied to an exceptional situation. But it fails to follow, Gross thinks, that no norms apply or that law has no role to play.[21] Political norms of accountability, transparency and the good of

---

[14] John Locke, *Two Treatises on Government*, P. Laslett (ed.) (Cambridge University Press, 1988), 375.
[15] Gross, 'Chaos and Rules', 1104.   [16] Ibid., 1105.   [17] Ibid., 1117 and 1126–33.
[18] Ibid., 1133.   [19] Ibid.
[20] I rely here on my discussions of Schmitt in *Legality and Legitimacy: Carl Schmitt, Hans Kelsen and Hermann Heller in Weimar* (Oxford, Clarendon Press, 1997).
[21] Gross, 1120–1.

democratic deliberation govern the decision to act outside the law. And when it comes to the question of the appropriate consequences of illegal action, law has a role to play since officials will be pardoned, indemnified, punished, and so on. So Gross distinguishes himself from Schmitt as he distinguishes himself from Locke – through the substance of his functional test.

Any agreement with Schmitt is perilous. Gross is therefore keen to point out that Schmitt's theory of the exception is not normatively sound; it has only 'certain descriptive validity'.[22] But Schmitt did not present himself as a normative theorist. He claimed to provide a descriptive account of the problems of liberalism and its attempt to constrain politics through law and of the consequences that followed inevitably from the description. It is consistent to hold both that Schmitt's self-presentation was disingenuous since his account of the state of exception is premised on certain normative commitments and that, if one adopts his account, he is right about the consequences which will follow. The question then arises about whether one can adopt his account and avoid its normative commitments.

Consider an example taken from Schmitt's own career. On 30 June 1934, the 'Night of the Long Knives', Hitler purged the Nazi movement of those elements he considered undermined his hold on power and murdered rivals from the conservative but non-Nazi right, including people to whom Schmitt was close. He then had his Cabinet accept a draft Law for the Emergency Defence of the State: 'The measures taken on 30 June and 1 and 2 July for the suppression of high treasonable and state treasonable attacks are, as emergency defence of the state, legal.' This law was declared by the Minister of Justice to confirm existing law.[23]

While the world outside Germany was shocked by these murders as well as by their retrospective validation, within Germany there was widespread and vociferous approval.[24] Schmitt joined in by quickly publishing one of his most notorious essays, 'Der Führer schützt das Recht',[25] in which he praised

---

[22] Ibid., 1121, note 474, referring to Oren Gross, 'The Normless and Exceptionless Exception: Carl Schmitt's Theory of Emergency Powers and the "Norm-Exception" Dichotomy' (2000) 21 *Cardozo Law Review* 1825.

[23] The Enabling Act of 1933 – the 'Act for the Removal of Distress from People and Reich' – effectively gave legislative power including power to override the Weimar Constitution to the executive. It was rammed through a cowed Reichstag, in an atmosphere of complete demoralization caused by Nazi acts of terror; only the 94 socialists who were able to reach the forum opposed it. For incisive analysis of the law's significance in the decline of legality in Germany, see Peter L. Lindseth, 'The Paradox of Parliamentary Supremacy: Delegation, Democracy, and Dictatorship in Germany and France, 1920s-1950s' (2004) 113 *Yale Law Journal* 1341 at 1371.

[24] See Ian Kershaw, *Hitler, 1889–1936: Hubris* (London, Penguin, 1998), 505–22, especially 517–22.

[25] Schmitt, 'Der Führer schützt das Recht' in Schmitt, *Positionen und Begriffe im Kampf mit Weimar-Genf-Versailles 1923–1939* (Berlin, Duncker & Humblot, 1988), 199.

Hitler's retrospective validation of the murders. No doubt Schmitt was fearful because of his ties to some of the victims and eager to begin a new career as chief legal philosopher of the Nazis. But he was also theoretically committed to the position of approval of Hitler's acts, if not to the sycophantic tone in which he expressed that commitment, the product of his own functional test.

For Hitler had done everything that Schmitt positively required of a leader. He had distinguished between friend and enemy, which Schmitt argued is the mark of the 'political',[26] had established himself decisively as the sovereign – the supreme source and judge of all right and law – and had done away with the liberal and parliamentary fictions of Weimar. Most important, he had through his personal representation of the German people as a substantive homogeneous unit, brought about the 'democratic' identity of the people (*Volk*), which Schmitt prized above all else. Moreover, there could be no doubt about the popular acclaim, the resounding '*Ja*' that greeted Hitler's vision of an orderly Germany.[27]

How does the substance of Schmitt's test differ from Gross's? Hitler acted in a way that he thought, at least initially, was outside of the law to bring Germany from a state of exception into normality. He sought and procured legal validation for what he did after the fact and justified himself to the Reichstag and to the German people; both responded positively. Moreover, the basis for the legal validation of his act depended on a statute enacted by the German Parliament after he had been elected leader of Germany at a time when at least the vestiges of Weimar's parliamentary democracy were in place. It might then seem that Gross can distinguish his test from Schmitt's only by appealing to substance – through the claim that the Extra-Legal Measures model has a legitimate place if, and only if, as he says, the community is 'worth saving'; a 'despotic, authoritarian, and oppressive society is not worth the effort'.[28]

But then the test for the legitimacy of the model is primarily substance, the character of the political regime, rather than the formal indicia of action outside the law followed by the officials seeking vindication from the public, from politicians, and from the law. What was wrong with the Night of the Long Knives stemmed from the obnoxious character of the regime which Hitler was seeking to stabilize, not with the steps he took.[29] But there are two major problems with this view.

---

[26] Carl Schmitt, *The Concept of the Political* (New Jersey: Rutgers University Press, 1987), translated by George Schwab).

[27] Carl Schmitt, *Verfassungslehre* (Berlin, Duncker & Humblot, 1989).

[28] Gross, 'Chaos and Rules', 1115.

[29] At the symposium, Gross suggested that the dangers of a Night of the Long Knives were very remote in Western societies and in any case such dangers cannot be forestalled by law. But the events of that night were made possible in part by the gradual decline in respect for

First, consider a distinction between a society that is just according to
Western standards and a society that is not just because it is neither democratic nor liberal, but is still 'well-ordered' because it can plausibly claim to
abide by the rule of law.[30] It is not clear to me that Gross's model has a place in
such societies, because they are neither liberal nor democratic. If right, this is
a severe problem for his model since such well-ordered societies are plausibly
in the front line of the fight against terrorism.

Second, there was something wrong with the steps Hitler took beyond the
fact that they were taken to stabilise an obnoxious regime. These steps are
considered to make a mockery of legality or the rule of law. The worry here is
not the one Gross depicts of officials' acting outside the law, thus setting a
precedent for other officials and for ordinary citizens. It is that if the law is
used to give the officials the cloak of legality, legal form is used to cover the
substantive damage to the rule of law. Public officials are supposed to be
accountable to the law, an accountability that becomes most urgent when
they exercise the kind of coercive powers associated with dealing with emergencies. If the law to which they are accountable is not the law that exists at
the time of their actions, but a law which after the fact declares their actions to
be legal, then they are not accountable at all. One is left with the façade not the
substance of the rule of law. This criticism applies to all societies which can
genuinely claim to abide by the rule of law and one of the main marks of a
well-ordered society is that it is entitled to such a claim.

Moreover, Gross, in my view, vastly overestimates what he calls the
'process-oriented' aspect of his model – its promotion of deliberation
among the public and among officials.[31] The atmosphere of public fear that
attends emergencies is not conducive to deliberation and leads to easy
acceptance of official action that is claimed to be necessitous. If the

legality: see Dyzenhaus, *Legality*, ch 1. This kind of decline is well illustrated in Justice
Thomas's dissent in *Hamdi* v. *Rumsfeld* 124 S Ct 2633 (2004). Thomas uses an interesting
analogy in his argument that the President can do as he pleases during an emergency and
so does not have to accord a hearing to a citizen indefinitely detained as an 'enemy
combatant'. He mentions, at 2684, a CIA missile strike in Yemen in which a US citizen was
apparently killed and says that no 'additional process' would be required for the citizen.
'The result here', he says, 'should be the same'. On the basis of this analogy, the executive is
permitted to assassinate its perceived enemies both within and outside the US. This
thought is the product of a mind-set which has led to both abuse and torture by the US
and the employing of other nations to do its torturing by proxy. Whether the courts will
prevent this decline still remains to be seen. But it is difficult to measure the effectiveness
of their stand unless they make it; and it is a counsel of self-fulfilling despair to say they
should not because it will make no difference.

[30] This distinction is inspired by John Rawls, *The Law of Peoples* (Cambridge, Harvard
University Press, 1999), 62–8. But my idea of a decent society is much thinner than
Rawls's as it is confined to respect for the rule of law. For an exploration of the idea of the
rule of law in the societies I have in mind, see Hor, Chapter 13, in this volume.

[31] Gross, 'Chaos and Rules', 1129.

Extra-Legal Measures model were public, as it must be if it is to promote deliberation, the expectation would be generated of after-the-fact validation of illegal official acts. In an atmosphere of fear that expectation would likely be met rather easily, especially when the threat is, or is claimed to be, a constant one and the government successfully manipulates public opinion.

Finally, Gross recognizes that his model relies, perhaps even more heavily than the other two, on the false assumption of separation between the normal and the exceptional situation. His antidote, once again, is accountability through raising the potential costs of official action. But an acknowledgement of the falsity of the assumption plays directly into Schmitt's hands. All Schmitt needs for almost complete induction into his camp is that one accepts first that legal norms cannot apply to exceptional situations and second that there is no clear demarcation between the normal and the exceptional. With those two elements in place, his definition of sovereignty is incontestable: 'Sovereign is he who decides on the state of exception'.[32] This definition asserts that in abnormal times the sovereign is legally uncontrolled. But Schmitt's thought goes further. Not only is the sovereign legally uncontrolled in the state of emergency; the quality of being sovereign, he who *is* the sovereign, is revealed in the answer to the question of who gets to decide *that* there is a state of emergency.

In this respect, Gross might go even further than Schmitt. He appears to give the power to determine that there is an emergency to any public official who is prepared to take the risk that he will not receive after-the-fact legal validation for his illegal acts. Schmitt would have thought this model is indicative of the fundamental problems he claimed to have exposed in what is referred to these days as liberal legalism – the liberal claim about the legitimacy of government under the rule of law. The model, that is, seeks to respond to exceptional situations but finds itself doing so in ways that fissure the state apparatus. It establishes a multitude of potential sovereigns, thus rendering itself more vulnerable and open to capture by interest groups.

My critique of Gross shows the importance of contesting the very assumption of separation between the normal and the exceptional. I will argue that banishing the exception from legal order has to be, as Schmitt claimed, the ideal of liberal legal order, but that where he went wrong is in thinking that this dream can never be realized by a liberal legal order. Put differently, I argue that the way to do away with the assumption is to reverse Schmitt and collapse the exceptional into the normal, which requires holding fast to the other assumption Gross sketches – the assumption of constitutionality. Moreover, while the model suggested by this argument might seem to partake of elements of the other two models, it represents a superior approach, not accommodation in Gross's sense of a compromise of the rule of law, but

---

[32] Carl Schmitt, *Political Theology: Four Chapters on the Concept of Sovereignty*, George Schwab, trans. (Cambridge, MIT Press, 1988), 5.

experiments in institutional design fully consistent with the rule of law. The linchpin of my argument is that we must loosen the grip that a formal doctrine of the separation of powers appears to have on legal theory.

According to this doctrine, the legislature has a monopoly on lawmaking, judges a monopoly on interpretation of the law, while the executive or administration both implements the law and makes determinations about policy within the area of discretion delegated by the legislatures to public officials. I argue below that this formal doctrine should be discarded in favour of a view, the Legality model, that regards the separation of powers as instrumental to the values of the rule of law or legality. Once that is done, one can conceive of imaginative responses to emergencies which preserve the rule of law without the risks Gross associates with the Accommodation model.

III. The norm and the exception

In Schmitt's first publication, *Gesetz und Urteil*, he examined the relationship between statutory law and judgment.[33] His concern was the problem of what now would be described as gaps in the law – those occasions on which a judge has to decide a matter but the law is indeterminate, so the judge has to exercise a quasi-legislative discretion to fill the gap. Schmitt did not think there was a normative solution. The lack of stability in legal order created by inability of law to provide a solution can be cured sociologically, by conceiving of the judge as an empirical type.[34] Schmitt means that as long as judges are legally well-trained solid sorts, who come from a class of men with fairly set views, their exercise of discretion will be both predictable and safe.

In sum, the legal order does not contain the resources to deal with the problem of indeterminacy. But this problem is containable on two conditions. First, there is the legal positivist assumption that the law generally provides determinate answers, so that the number of cases to be resolved by discretion is relatively small compared to the number that do not become cases at all because the law is clear. In terms introduced later by H. L. A. Hart, this condition can be expressed by saying that the legal order will be stable as long as the 'core' of 'settled' law is larger than the 'penumbra' of 'doubt' about what law requires.[35] And in the distinction between area of stable core and unstable penumbra, we can see the assumption of separation between the normal and the exceptional at

---

[33] *Gesetz und Urteil: Eine Untersuchung zum Problem der Rechtspraxis* (Munich, C. H. Beck, 1969, first pub. 1912). See my 'Holmes and Carl Schmitt: An Unlikely Pair', (1997) 63 *Brooklyn Law Review* 165, 180–6.

[34] Schmitt, *Gesetz und Urteil*, 71: 'A judge's decision can today be taken for correct when we can predict that another judge would have decided the matter in exactly the same way.'

[35] H. L. A. Hart, 'Positivism and the Separation of Law and Morals' in *Essays in Jurisprudence and Philosophy* (Oxford, Clarendon Press, 1983), 49, 62–72.

work. Second, and Schmitt's own contribution, the judges charged with resolving penumbral cases are a homogeneous bunch with the right sorts of views. Schmitt seems then to combine a legal positivist diagnosis of the relationship between law and judgment with what we would think of today as a conservative legal realist response to the diagnosis. But the work is interesting as a lens both into the way Schmitt's political and legal theory developed and into the lack of resources contemporary legal theory has to offer when it comes to states of emergency. For the moment of uncertainty or indeterminacy is a kind of mini state of emergency for a positivist theory of law. It is an emergency because, by positivist stipulation, it is not resolvable by law. It is mini because it is containable: order can be secured as long as the core of law is large enough and as long as judges are of the right sort. But if the boundary between core and penumbra cannot be sharply drawn, the core seems to disappear; and the state of emergency becomes uncontainable and generally pervasive. Here it is important to see that Schmitt does not think that his solution to the problem of the gap is merely a matter of sociological prediction. He still thinks it is important for judges to adopt what he calls the 'postulate of legal determinacy' and that they are a 'learned professional' group.[36] If these two elements are in place, he thinks that adjudication can still be conceived as a distinctively legal enterprise because judges orient themselves around the legal value of together achieving legal determinacy.

Schmitt's later work gives up on this hope. The distinction between core and penumbra, and thus the stability of legal order, is not sustainable because of inherent qualities of law, nor is it sufficient to keep things trundling along that there is a homogeneous group of judges. The distinction is sustainable if and only if there is a substantively homogeneous population whose identity as a people is represented by a sovereign, who can then fill the role of guardian of the constitution. Liberalism wishes to displace the political necessity of determining the basis for such identity onto the law and the rule of law. But law cannot carry this burden. Rule of law patriotism, so to speak, is not patriotism at all without the right sort of substantive basis in place, in which case it is not law but its basis onto which patriotism will latch. It is, on Schmitt's view, no surprise, when liberal legal orders are faced with a crisis such as 9/11, that political theories of the sort espoused by Samuel Huntington come to the fore, as these seek to express, perhaps in veiled terms, the kind of identity required for a serious response to the crisis.

One can of course call into question the very terms in which this problem is framed. Ronald Dworkin, in the best known critique of legal positivism of the last forty years, argues that positivism goes wrong in conceptualizing law as a model of rules of determinate content, where the question of what the rules of

---

[36] Schmitt, *Gesetz und Urteil*, 86.

a system are is settled by other rules relating to their origin or pedigree.[37] It
follows from this model that, when a rule does not supply a determinate
answer to a question, the judge has to exercise discretion. But, as Dworkin
argued, law is not just a matter of rules; it also contains principles which are
moral as well as legal. Such principles have to be assigned weight by the judge
when they are relevant to a dispute about the law. So Dworkin's first challenge
to positivism advanced the view that in penumbral or 'hard' cases, judges are
under a legal duty to decide the case by resort to principles already immanent
in the law. Dworkin's theory of interpretation holds that there is in principle
one right answer in all such cases, an answer fully determined by law.[38]

Dworkin's second challenge was to the positivist view that the idea of legal
order as consisting of determinate rules is not threatened by the concession
that there is a penumbra of uncertainty. As we have seen, there is supposed to
be no threat because the core is in fact much larger than the penumbra and
this provides the certainty that makes legal order possible. But Dworkin
argued there is no core in the positivist sense. What appears to be the
core is the product of interpretation in just the way that decisions in the
penumbra are. The core is merely an area of provisional agreement as to
interpretation.[39]

Dworkin's second challenge makes the first more radical. If there is no
clear boundary between core and penumbra, so that the core does not so
much diminish in size as disappear, then legal order as positivists understand
it implodes. If all questions about what law is are interpretative in this sense,
there is no such thing as law. More precisely, there is no such thing as law in
the positivist sense of a set of rules whose content can be determined without
resort to moral argument. From the positivist perspective, the problem which
they acknowledged as occurring only at the margins of legal order now
appears throughout.

Now in one respect Dworkin's critique of legal positivism looks quite
similar to that to be found in Schmitt's later work, as both want to contest
the distinction between core and penumbra. The difference between them lies
in Dworkin's optimism that one can do without that distinction and still hold
the edifice together through the principles immanent in the law, while
Schmitt thinks that the basis has to be found outside of the law, in the identity

---

[37] Ronald Dworkin, *Taking Rights Seriously* (London, Duckworth, 1978).
[38] Hart dealt with this challenge by claiming that the choice between principles could not be
settled by the law but only by a legally unconstrained act of judicial choice or discretion.
Put differently, he claimed that the more Dworkin showed that the adjudication of hard
cases involves a decision based on legal principles, the better the evidence for the positivist
thesis about judicial discretion. In my view, this claim is fatal to legal positivism, for
reasons I explore in 'The Genealogy of Legal Positivism' (2004) 24 *Oxford Journal of Legal
Studies*, 39.
[39] Ronald Dworkin, *Law's Empire* (London, Fontana, 1986).

of the people. Further, Schmitt argues that the liberal principles which for Dworkin make up the normative basis of the law are corrosive of identity. The basis of identity will be substantive in the negative sense of being anti-liberal and in Schmitt's ideal legal order, that basis will be given determinate expression by the sovereign in his code of law. Schmitt is not then a critic of positivism's model of law, only of positivism's naivety about the political conditions that have to be in place before a relatively large core of determinate law can be sustained.

Schmitt no less than liberal legal thinkers wishes to banish the exception from the political and legal order. He differs from liberals only in thinking that once substantive homogeneity has been successfully established within a state, the exception will not disappear but be displaced to international relations which he, like Hobbes, conceives of as inherently unstable – a state of nature. For Schmitt, the instability of the international realm is beneficial. It is through the contrast with the political identities of other states and the constant threat of conflict with them that the internal identity of any particular people is preserved. So not only the exception but politics itself is banished from the internal legal order.

From this we can see that for Schmitt, as for positivists, the idea of separation between legal normality and extra-legal state of exception is important. But for Schmitt, separation is not strictly speaking an assumption but a distinction between internal and external – between the inside and the outside of law – which has to be brought about by establishing the right sort of political conditions. And once separation is seen as an ideal state rather than as an assumption about the way the world works, one can appreciate that for Schmitt it is not separation, however conceived, that is the real issue. Rather, it is the assumption of constitutionality. Dworkin, in contrast, accepts the assumption of constitutionality. His model of law is not perturbed by Schmitt's thoughts about the separation between the normal and the exceptional, since separation, on Dworkin's view, is a symptom of positivist thought. Where Dworkin goes wrong, along with Gross, is in adhering to the different idea of separation, the idea that the best way to understand legal order is in terms of a formal doctrine of the separation of powers between the legislature, the judiciary and the executive.

I now argue that once we loosen the grip of that doctrine, we can also qualify Gross's central claims as follows: (1) emergencies call for governmental responses that cannot be accommodated by the formal doctrine, (2) constitutional arguments premised on that formal doctrine have not greatly constrained any government faced with emergencies, and (3) there is a strong probability that if we hang on to that formal doctrine, emergency measures will eventually seep into the legal system. But then one should give up the formal doctrine, so that legislative responses to emergencies can be controlled by the rule of law.

IV. Constitutionality and the separation of powers

Dworkin's model of law is a Business as Usual model, in which public officials who act to deal with emergency situations should be held accountable to law, where law includes the constitutional values of which judges are the exclusive guardians. And that is because Dworkin operates with a rather formal understanding of the separation of powers, in which the legislature makes policy decisions, public officials implement those decisions, and judges make sure that both legislation and official actions are limited by constitutional principle.

If it is the case that imaginative legal solutions to emergency situations cannot operate within the constraints of this model, then Gross has to be right that it follows that such solutions are outside the reach of the rule of law. His worry about the effects of using law to give cover to official acts to deal with genuine emergency situations, especially when the emergency is or is alleged to be permanent, would be fully justified.

It follows that Gross accepts the Business as Usual model with all its assumptions except for the claim that it can cope with emergencies. And because he thinks that that model governs the normal situation but that something different is required for emergencies, he must adopt the assumption of separation between the normal and the exceptional, despite his keen awareness of its problems. He ends up with a highly unstable combination of: a model of Business as Usual for the ordinary situation; a model of Schmittian positivism for the exception or emergency; and a kind of deliberative democratic model as the after-the-fact cure for the ills of the intervening Schmittian positivism.

His position is unstable because he accepts the assumption of constitutionality for the ordinary situation, while rejecting that assumption for the exception, a rejection which depends on the admittedly false (for Schmittian reasons) assumption of separation between the norm and the exception. Moreover, the instability is not confined to the fact that Gross accepts a model for dealing with the exception whose presuppositions are supposed to implode the model he adopts for dealing with the normal situation. Schmittian positivism regards as a charade the kind of deliberative democratic process Gross envisages as triggered by extra-legal official action, one which either serves as an excuse for postponing an effective executive decision or as political camouflage for the decision the executive has already made.

It is helpful to note that for Dicey, the ordinary situation of administrative law, in which an administrative official is delegated authority by the legislature, is a site of arbitrary power. Dicey advocated abolishing legislative delegations of authority to administrative officials, since such delegations introduced pockets of lawlessness – mini exceptions – into the ordinary legal order. The decision to create the administrative state need not and should not be taken, precisely because these pockets of lawlessness will damage the integrity of the legal order as a whole.[40] Such delegations he viewed in much the same way as he depicted the legalization of illegality when officials were given after-the-fact legislative indemnification, the only difference being that the former were not retrospective but prospective indemnifications of illegality.

The idea that the delegated discretionary power of public officials is not subject to the rule of law, that it is 'unfettered' or that the officials are a 'law unto themselves' within the limits clearly stated in the statute, has important affinities with the Lockean idea of the prerogative as a legally uncontrolled space. But Dicey was not only enthusiastic about taming the prerogative by subjecting it to statutory control.[41] As we have seen, when it came to emergencies, he moved away from the position he took in regard to delegations of ordinary executive authority to one which seemed to countenance that delegated authority could be thought of as subject to the rule of law. There is thus a tension between Dicey's claim that the emergency situation should be dealt with by legislative delegation of authority controlled by the rule of law and his more famous argument against the delegation of discretion to public officials because that delegation creates pockets of arbitrary power.

Perhaps part of the explanation lies in the fact that Dicey's hostility to the administrative state as a site of lawlessness was motivated by his adherence to a laissez-faire political philosophy. But it was also motivated by an incomprehension about how such a state could ever be subject to the rule of law. And that incomprehension had much to do with his views about the separation of powers, where the legislature has a monopoly on lawmaking, and judges on interpretation.[42] He thus held the same view of the separation of powers as that presupposed by a Business as Usual model.

However, in common law countries, there is now in place a highly developed rule-of-law system for administrative officials, including controls of reasonableness, independence, impartiality, and often a requirement to give reasons. Ultimately, there is the check of judicial review, accompanied by the understanding that administrative officials have an expertise in their area of decision-making which generalist judges lack. That understanding is captured in tests indicating that judges will not normally overturn decisions on a correctness standard, on the basis of mere disagreement with the merits of the

---

[40] I am indebted here to Geneviève Cartier's lucid discussion in Chapter 1 of her SJD thesis, 'Re-conceiving Administrative Discretion: From Discretion as Power to Discretion as Dialogue'.

[41] Dicey, *Law of the Constitution*, 64.

[42] In *Lectures on the Relation Between Law & Public Opinion in England during the Nineteenth Century* (London, Macmillan, 1920), Dicey in an Appendix discussed what he calls 'Judge-Made Law', 483–94, in which he is willing to talk about 'judicial legislation'. But Dicey seems to mean by this phrase the kind of creative interpretation of law which Dworkin's theory of adjudication advocates.

decision. Rather, they will declare decisions invalid only if they are unreasonable. In addition, influenced by the fact that most of the prerogative powers have been incorporated into statutory regimes, judges in the common law world have become increasingly willing to think of exercises of such powers as subject to the rule of law and so have asserted, at least at the level of abstract principle, their authority to review such exercises.[43]

To create this understanding of judicial review, judges had to move away from the formal doctrine of the separation of powers which required that any administrative decision involving interpretation of the law had to be reviewed on a correctness standard. At the same time, judges had to develop a sense that rule-of-law standards should be tailored to particular administrative contexts.

If we are to take seriously Gross's Extra-Legal Measures model, we have also to take seriously his point of agreement with Schmitt – that legal norms cannot apply to exceptional situations. But that means that the history of gradual legislative and judicial colonization of the prerogative, as well the creation of the common law understanding of the rule of law governing public officials, are mistakes. Gross's view must be that these are situations of discretion where the attempt to use law to deal with the exception results in variants of the Accommodation model, thus damaging law's integrity in the normal situations where its writ properly runs. But, as I have suggested, this recognition is premised on a conception of law as a system of rules. If one's conception of law is different – the test of law's integrity is its compliance with immanent principles – then law's writ is not confined in this way.

I do not want, however, to suggest that a conception of law as a matter of principle is immune to damage through the wrong kind of institutional experiment. Whether law is conceived as a matter of rules or principles, it is dangerous to permit governments the luxury of claiming that they govern in accordance with the rule of law when in fact law provides them with a formal façade that serves only to cover abuse of power. But in liberal democracies and beyond, it has become almost unthinkable for governments to govern outside of the framework of the rule of law. In addition, the allegedly permanent nature of the terrorist threat makes, in my view, a legislative response inevitable. Finally, and most importantly, it is desirable, as Dicey argued, that the response be a legal one, which means that one should experiment only in so far as experimentation is constitutionally justifiable.[44]

---

[43] Nevertheless, that a power is or was at one stage a prerogative power often looms large in judges' approach to statutory interpretation, especially when officials are given broad discretionary powers to make security or immigration determinations. And as we know, these two areas – immigration and security – frequently overlap, which can serve to increase judicial wariness about review.

[44] See Michael Ignatieff, *The Lesser Evil: Political Ethics in an Age of Terror* (Princeton University Press, 2004).

One must then hold the assumption of constitutionality in place, which is to be done by treating, with Schmitt, the separation between the normal and the exceptional not as an assumption but as a conclusion which has to be argued for. If there were no model for experiment controlled by legality, no Legality model, it would seem that the inevitability of experiment, or what Gross calls accommodation, would leave us in a highly uncomfortable position. But, as I have indicated, there is ample evidence of the right sort of experiment – the development of the common law of judicial review in the last forty or so years. Since security issues will be dealt with by delegating authority to public officials, one should look to the common law of judicial review for ideas about how such authority can remain subject to the rule of law. In the next section, I briefly examine one manifestation of such a model – the Special Immigration Appeals Commission (SIAC), a creation of the legislature in the United Kingdom.

V. SIAC and the separation of powers

Before 1997 those subject to deportation from the UK on national security grounds were statutorily deprived of the right of appeal that individuals subject to deportation on other grounds enjoyed. Their only recourse was to an executive committee, which gave advice to the responsible minister. In *Chahal v. UK*,[45] the European Court of Human Rights rejected the government's argument that national security grounds are inherently incapable of being tested in a court of law and held that the advisory panel was not a 'court' before which the legality of one's detention could be challenged, as required by Article 5(4) of the European Convention of Human Rights.

The government responded with a statute establishing SIAC, a three-person panel of which one member had to have held high judicial office, the second had to have been the chief adjudicator or a legally qualified member of the Immigration Appeals Tribunal, while the third would ordinarily be someone with experience of national security matters. The statute gave the individual, who would have had the right to appeal against a deportation order but for the fact that national security was involved, a right to appeal to SIAC. It gave SIAC itself the authority to review the Secretary of State's decision on the law and the facts as well as the question whether the discretion should have been exercised differently. There was a further appeal to the Court of Appeal on 'any question of law material to' SIAC's determination. In addition, the statute provided for a special advocate who could represent the appellant if parts of the proceedings before SIAC took place in closed session because it was considered necessary to keep

---

[45] (1996) 23 EHRR 413.

information confidential. SIAC's decision is based on both the closed and the open session though its reasons do not disclose information from the closed sessions.

SIAC seems a workable answer to concerns about the sensitivity of security issues and the need to hold public officials accountable to the rule of law. It is seized of jurisdiction through a statutory right of appeal and it has the explicit authority and the necessary expertise to review security decisions, thus ensuring that the decisions of the security services are accountable to the law. And this is in large part because when SIAC reviews it has before it the information on which the executive and the security services act, which is fully tested even if it is highly confidential. Moreover, it is important to see that in contrast to the Extra-Legal Measures model, SIAC builds reason-giving requirements and deliberation about those requirements into the legal process. Put in the more abstract terms of this chapter, SIAC is a remarkable exercise in imaginative institutional design to address security concerns. It internalizes the exception to the rule of law that had been created by the removal of the right to appeal and does so in such a way that preserves legality at the same time as taking into account the special circumstances of the security services.

At least, SIAC would have seemed to be the answer, were it not for the fact that the House of Lords has responded to SIAC in a way which shows that judges care less about the rule of law than about their place in the hierarchy of legal order, in which case the creation of such a body might be seen as an occasion for judicial jealousy.[46]

In *Secretary of State for the Home Department v. Rehman*,[47] the Court, to preserve its sense of role, refused to concede to SIAC the capacity to be a more effective enforcer of the rule of law than a generalist court.[48] The Court first interpreted the legislation as giving courts some review authority, though one which clearly undersells the resources of the common law: courts can review only if decisions are manifestly absurd. The Court then cut down SIAC's authority to fit the Court's parsimonious understanding of its own role.

While this decision is in part motivated by political concerns, the customary judicial spinelessness in security, it is officially presented in Lord Hoffmann's infamous judgment as required by the formal doctrine of the separation of powers. This stance is astonishing given that he and another judge on this bench, Lord Steyn, are responsible for articulating a principle of legality in ordinary administrative law which requires that all executive acts

---

[46] As a result, the lay member of SIAC who provided the expertise on security, Sir Brian Barder, resigned making public his reasons. For the full account, see his article in the (2004) 26 *London Review of Books*, issue of 18 March, 40–1.

[47] [2002] 1 All ER 123.

[48] See Lord Hoffmann ibid, especially, 139, para 49.

be demonstrated to be justifiable in law, where law is assumed to include fundamental values.[49] These two judges thus find that in some cases they are driven to constitutional bedrock, which is full of values and principles, while in others they find that the constitution amounts only to a very formal understanding of the separation of powers.[50]

I want to emphasize two points. First, the Court ignored the exercise of institutional imagination which had gone into making SIAC an effective enforcer of the rule of law in security matters. Because a generalist court cannot be effective in such matters, it was unwilling to concede that an administrative panel could have a special role as guardian of constitutional values. Second, in reverting to the formal understanding of the separation of powers, one which is inconsistent with developments in the common law of judicial review, the judges introduced a rather glaring inconsistency into English public law. The lesson to be learned is that an adequate response to emergencies, especially in light of the way emergencies are now regarded as in a sense normal, must start from a premise other than one that adopts the formal doctrine of the separation of powers.

VI. Responding through the rule of law

As should now be clear from my argument, following Dicey, I hold the view that governments which have the luxury of time to craft a response to emergency situations should do so in a way that complies with the rule of law. The issue is not accommodation in Gross's sense of compromises which undermine the integrity of the rule of law. Rather, it is about imagination in institutional design, experiments which seek to address both the concerns of the rule of law and security. The Legality model is not then about accommodation, nor is it the Business as Usual model if that model requires adopting the formal doctrine of the separation of powers that gets in the way of such experiments.

The Legality model does, however, preserve the assumption of constitutionality in that it insists that the values of the rule of law are not to be compromised. It also preserves the idea of a separation between the exceptional and the normal. It holds that to the extent that political power can be

---

[49] Thus in *R v. Secretary of State for the Home Department, ex p Pierson* [1997] 3 WLR 492, at 518, Lord Steyn said that 'Parliament does not legislate in a vacuum' but 'for a European liberal democracy founded on the principles and traditions of the common law'. Compare *R v. Secretary of State, ex p Simms* [1999] 3 All ER 400, at 412, *per* Lord Hoffmann: 'In the absence of express language or necessary implication to the contrary, the courts therefore presume that even the most general words were intended to be subject to the basic rights of the individual.'

[50] Lord Steyn has since made public a radical change in his thinking; see 'Guantanamo Bay: the Legal Black Hole' (2004) 53 *International and Comparative Law Quarterly* 1.

successfully subjected to the discipline of the rule of law, it should. But, as in Schmitt, the idea functions not as an assumption but as an ideal; at most it is a regulative assumption, an assumption one adopts for political reasons because it will regulate practice in the best possible way. One assumes its truth to bring the legal order closer to the ideals which underpin it.

It does not follow, however, that all possible acts by public officials should be subject to the rule of law. Torture is absolutely prohibited by international law and by the domestic laws of many states for good reasons having to do with our understanding of ourselves as human beings and the fact that even the prudential reasons for torture are so dubious. But the humanitarian reasons are so strong that no decent regime could permit torture. So if officials consider that they have to torture to avoid a catastrophe – the ticking bomb situation – such an act must happen extra-legally, more or less the position of the Israeli Supreme Court. All a court should say is that if officials are going to torture they should expect to be criminally charged and may try a defence of necessity.[51] But in saying that, a court is not adopting Gross's Extra-Legal Measures model. It is simply recognizing, as Dicey did, that in some situations where officials act outside of the law they merit after-the-fact recognition that they made an excusable decision because it was necessary to act and the law did not provide them with the resources they needed. The twist with torture is that a decent regime is precluded from providing prospective legal resources to legalize what would otherwise be illegal. Torture is, in other words, 'unlegalizable'.

What falls into this category of the unlegalizable is, of course, controversial. Does preventive detention fall into this category, or trials which fall far short of the standards prescribed for criminal justice? Take for example the division in the United States Supreme Court in *Hamdi* v. *Rumsfeld*.[52] Only Justice Thomas accepted in his dissent the blank cheque position that the Congressional authorization to the executive to wage war on terrorism – to use 'all necessary and appropriate force' – included the power to detain indefinitely people deemed by the executive to be 'enemy combatants'. Only he accepted the government's main argument – that the executive had a blank cheque even without that Congressional authorization since Article II of the Constitution provides that the President is 'Commander in Chief of the Armed Forces'. And only he put

---

[51] See Judgment of the Supreme Court of Israel, sitting as the High Court of Justice, 6 September 1999, concerning the Legality of the General Security Services' Interrogation Methods. The Court did indicate the possibility that the Legislature might enact a statute that put in place prior authorization to torture, modelled on the defence of necessity. But my sense is that this indication was a dare which the Court thought the Legislature could not afford to take up and if it did there would be grounds for invalidation. See my 'With the Benefit of Hindsight: Dilemmas of Legality in the Face of Injustice' in Emilios Christodoulidis and Scott Veitch (eds.), *Lethe's Law: Justice, Law and Ethics in Reconciliation* (Oxford, Hart Publishing, 2001), 65 at 86–9.

[52] 124 S Ct 2633 (2004). See also Roach, Chapter 7 in this volume.

forward a basically Schmittian argument to the effect that the executive needs the authority to respond to exceptional situations unconstrained by legality. Justice O'Connor for the plurality of the Court held that the detentions were authorized by implication but that the detainees were entitled to some due process. The only way they could be deprived of review altogether would be if Congress were to suspend habeas corpus.[53] Since they had had no access to review, the case was remanded and the plurality outlined the process to which the detainees were entitled. The detainees had to be given notice of the factual basis for the classification and a 'fair opportunity to rebut the Government's factual assertion before a neutral decisionmaker'.[54]

However, the fact that the plurality did not require express authorization for detentions is deeply troubling.[55] Moreover, while they rejected as too deferential a 'some evidence' rule,[56] the rule accepted by the House of Lords in *Rehman*, their understanding of appropriate due process included a military tribunal, which could rely on hearsay evidence and require the detainee to accept the onus of rebutting a presumption in favour of the government. Moreover, they suggested that the kind of cost benefit analysis for fair procedures, developed by the Supreme Court in *Mathews* v. *Eldridge*,[57] would be suitable for testing the appropriateness of the procedures. Not only is *Mathews* widely regarded as weakening the rights-protecting approach to deprivation of important interests outlined in the earlier decision in *Goldberg* v. *Kelly*,[58] but, as Justice Scalia pointed out in dissent in *Hamdi*, *Mathews* was about the withdrawal of disability benefits, not the interest in protection against arbitrary deprivations of liberty.[59]

In contrast, Justice Souter with Justice Ginsburg argued that any detention of a citizen had to be 'pursuant to an Act of Congress', a requirement of the Non-Detention Act, which had been enacted to rule out a repetition of the wartime detention of Japanese Americans. Justice Souter still wished to give practical effect to the majority's view which rejected the government's position, so he went on to agree with the plurality that the detainees should be entitled to due process. However, he doubted the appropriateness of a reverse onus and was wary of litigation before a military tribunal.[60]

Justice Scalia, joined by Justice Stevens, argued that there was no authorization for the detentions. The only possible authorization resided in an explicit Congressional suspension of habeas corpus. Failing that, the detainees

---

[53] *Hamdi*, Plurality at 2644–7.   [54] Ibid. at 2648.
[55] Here the plurality follows the majority in *R* v. *Halliday* [1917] AC 260 (HL) and thus the even more infamous majority in *Liversidge* v. *Anderson* [1942] AC 206. For discussion of both, see my 'Intimations of Legality Amid the Clash of Arms' (2004) 2 *International Journal of Constitutional Law*, 244. On *Halliday*, see David Foxton, 'R v Halliday Ex Parte Zadig in Retrospect' (2003) 119 *Law Quarterly Review* 455.
[56] *Hamdi*, Plurality, at 2651.   [57] 424 US 319 (1976).   [58] 397 US 254 (1970).
[59] *Hamdi*, at 2672.   [60] *Hamdi*, at 2660.

should be released or charged with criminal offences. Scalia's dissent is closest to Gross's Extra-Legal Measures model, because it draws a clear line between full constitutional protection and action outside of the law. It thus has the virtue of requiring the government openly to declare that it will not govern by the rule of law and such a declaration can promote political accountability.[61] But his dissent also shares much with Thomas, in that he is prepared to countenance the government writing itself a blank cheque, as long as it can persuade Congress to certify it. Moreover, in *Rasul v. Bush*,[62] released on the same day as *Hamdi*, where the majority found that US Federal Courts do have jurisdiction over detainees at Guantanamo Bay, Scalia showed in dissent that he is not at all perturbed by the idea of legal black holes, zones of official illegality, as long as they are (in his view) properly created.[63]

While this advance legalization of illegality is contrary to Gross's Extra-Legal Measures model, it is what I think the model amounts to in practice, if it is to be anything more than after-the-fact legal recognition that officials made an excusable decision to act outside of the law. My point here is different from the one made earlier about the theoretical instability of the model because of the way it falls into the trap Schmitt sets for liberalism, a trap sprung by seeking to address the exception through either the Business as Usual or the Accommodation models. It is that in an era when the rule of law has a currency such that at least lip service to its ideals is required, governments will generally seek to use vaguely framed statutes prospectively to indemnify official illegality. Governments will prefer to use vague authorizations in the hope that judges will not intervene to curb executive arbitrariness. But judges who do so intervene can force governments to come clean in their legislation in a way which increases political accountability and which might permit judges to find the explicit authorizations unconstitutional.

I do not wish to underestimate the importance of forcing governments to come clean. Nor do I want judges to do what Justice Thomas's dissent in *Hamdi* did when, in as fine an example of judicial spinelessness as one could find, he handed to government the cloak of the rule of law by deeming illegality to be legal. I also do not want to underestimate the perils of the

---

[61] Dyzenhaus, 'Intimations of Legality'.
[62] *Rasul* v. *Bush* 124 S Ct 2686 (2004).
[63] Dicey argued that an Act suspending habeas corpus suspends legal remedies for detainees until it is lifted, but an Act of Indemnity must follow the lifting of the suspension if the officials are to be protected against legal action by the detainees: Dicey, *Law of the Constitution*, 233–37. So the suspension does not quite create a legal black hole; it only renders legal remedies temporally ineffective. At 237, Dicey explains somewhat enigmatically his remark in the epigraph that an Act of Indemnity maintains the authority of Parliament. Such an Act is an 'exercise of arbitrary sovereign power' but its enactment by a parliamentary assembly 'maintains in no small degree the real no less than the apparent supremacy of law'.

sliding scale of due process or legality which the plurality in *Hamdi* with Souter and Ginsburg contemplated. Their approach, which seems closer to my Legality model, seeks to preserve the rule of law. But it risks preserving the rule of law in a way that, like Thomas's dissent, legitimates the government while it does more or less what it likes. However, the risk of this result is much greater for the plurality than it is for Souter's and Ginsburg's opinion.

My main point is only that the world of legality is more messy than the Extra-Legal Measures model supposes, even abstracting from the situation of responses after 9/11. In ordinary administrative law, there are issues about how best to protect liberty interests when decisions are made by administrative bodies like parole boards, prison disciplinary panels, and tribunals which make mental health determinations. And I offered SIAC as an example of a body which could successfully preserve legality in an area where otherwise none might exist. With the caveat mentioned above about the category of the unlegalizable, I do think it is worthwhile running the risk of preserving legality through institutional experiments. However, judges must insist, as Souter and Ginsberg did in *Hamdi*, that there is both an absolutely explicit legislative mandate for such experiments and that the experiments be conducted in accordance with the Legality model.

Further, when it comes to the category of the unlegalizable, I think it would be helpful to revisit the idea of an Act or Bill of Attainder. As the author of the Note in 1962 in the *Yale Law Journal* explains, the term Act or Bill of Attainder comes from the practice in sixteenth, seventeenth and eighteenth century England of using statutes to sentence 'to death, without a conviction in the ordinary course of judicial trial, named or described persons or groups'.[64] In addition, the term came to be used for 'bills of pains and penalties', statutes that imposed sanctions less than capital.[65] Both sorts of statute were aimed at revolutionaries and were considered offensive to the spirit of the common law because they attempted to bypass the courts by establishing a system of either legislative or administrative conviction and punishment.

One way of understanding the offence is in terms of an idea of the separation of powers, where the judiciary has the role of determining in an open trial both guilt and appropriate punishment. As T. R. S Allan argues in the leading theoretical treatment of the rule of law, the substance of the argument against bills of attainder pertains to the fact that the statute in issue offends the constitutional guarantee, written or unwritten, of an independent judiciary presiding in open court over determinations of guilt and punishment. A bill of attainder, he says, is just 'the paradigmatic example of legislation whose violation of the principles of equality and due process

---

[64] Note, 72 *Yale Law Journal* (1962) 330.   [65] Ibid., 331.

contravenes the rule of law'.[66] The repugnance of the common law tradition to such statutes is born of the idea that while the legislature can enact into law its understandings of subversion and other offences, the rule of law requires both that that offence be framed generally and that anyone accused of such an offence be tried in a court of law. The argument is a deeply normative one. But it is not so much about the separation of powers, as about the reasons for the separation of powers – the constitutional role of the judges is to see to it that the fundamental values of legal order are preserved, by whatever means are most appropriate. When statutes seek to legalize activity contrary to these fundamental values, to legalize the unlegalisable, they lack legal authority. Judges may then refuse to enforce such statutes even without explicit constitutional authority to do so.

Those with authority, including those at the very top of the hierarchy of legal order, must understand these values, so that they can take part in the common project of their realization. On this view, the separation of powers is instrumental to realizing the legal order's ideals. If to ensure the integrity of legal order, it is necessary to imagine institutions for the enforcement of legality that go against the grain of received views about the separation of powers, one should not let those views stand in the way of enforcing legality.

Moreover, this claim applies to all societies that assert they are governed by the rule of law. Earlier, I mentioned the distinction between liberal democratic societies and well-ordered societies, the point being that well-ordered societies, while neither fully liberal nor democratic, share with liberal democratic societies the commitment to the rule of law. I suggested further that Gross's Extra-Legal Measures model had no place in a well ordered society because its legitimacy seems to depend on protecting liberal democracy. In contrast, the model I have sketched in this chapter applies to such a society as long as its assertion has some basis to it, that is, as long as it does not pay mere lip service to the rule of law. As long as there is such a basis, those subject to the law will be able to hold public officials to account, their accountability not being just to the positive law but also to the values of legality.[67]

---

[66] T. R. S. Allan, *Constitutional Justice: A Liberal Theory of the Rule of Law* (Oxford University Press, 2001), 148.

[67] At the symposium, several people expressed concern that while an institution such as SIAC might work well in the United Kingdom, it has the potential to be a mere fig-leaf for the executive in well ordered societies. Everything depends, they suggested, on the character of those who staff the institution. My response, which owes much to conversations with Kristen Rundle, is that one should not neglect the way in which the design of institutions shapes perception of agency. To appoint a person to an internal, advisory committee with the task of hearing appeals against detention orders is to ensure that those on the committee are likely to rubber stamp executive decisions. But give those same people the powers of SIAC and they might be forced into an understanding of their role far different from the rubber stamp.

It is important to stress this last point lest one think that my claim that the separation of powers has to be understood as instrumental to the substantive values of legality means instrumental to whatever values the powerful decide to implement through law. If that thought were right, then, for example, the legislature could simply decree that communal values are the values to which judges should have regard when it came to imposing the rule of law on public officials. The thought is not right, however.

There are other ways of attempting to place officials in a black hole than the legislature certifying the blank cheque to officials or indemnifying them after the fact. One is the general privative clause which seeks to exclude judicial review. Another is what I like to call a substantive privative clause, a provision which does not exclude review in general but review on particular grounds, for example, natural justice or reasonableness. I am not here concerned with the appropriate judicial response to these provisions, only with the characterization of them – that they place officials in an extra-legal space or black hole. When it comes to well-ordered societies, which might have a strong orientation to communal values, my claim is that their commitment to the rule of law will be tested by the extent to which they are prepared to refrain from allowing communal values to take precedence over the values of legality. Extra-legal space can also be created by permitting certain communal values, for example Schmittian values to do with the alleged moral identity of the nation, a large role in interpreting the law. In this case, officials become accountable to those values, which means really to their sense of what the values require. In other words, they are no longer accountable. Thus, a commitment to the rule of law is also a commitment to abiding by values of fairness, reasonableness and equality before the law. Abiding by those values, the values of the Legality model, provides a basis for a society to claim some legitimacy even if one supposes that to be fully legitimate, a society should also be both democratic and liberal. But to have that legitimacy, the society must not opt for the Extra-Legal Measures model in its dealings with either emergencies or terror.

5

Stability and flexibility: a Dicey business

OREN GROSS

The chief restraint upon those who command the physical forces of the country . . . must be their responsibility to the political judgments of their contemporaries and to the moral judgments of history.[1]

I. Introduction

A significant part of the life of the law has been attempts to balance the competing values of stability and flexibility. In some areas greater weight may be accorded to flexibility while in others stability is particularly valued. In some areas the balance between stability and flexibility will be stable, in others it will require frequent re-calibration.

The rule of law has long been identified as one of the most fundamental tenets of a democratic regime, as 'the soul of the modern state'.[2] The terms 'rule of law', 'constitutionalism', 'individual rights', 'democracy' and 'liberalism' are frequently mentioned as integral parts of a unified whole. Despite lack of consensus as to its precise content and scope, the rule of law has been connected to notions of generality, clarity, certainty, predictability and stability of rules. At the same time, general legal rules must also be flexible enough to adapt to unforeseen circumstances and developments. When such developments take place over time there may be a sufficient lag to allow for changing the rules so as to accommodate the new realities. Constitutional amendment provisions offer one example. A power to amend may be necessary to allow adaptations to sustained pressures for change. At the same time, the tension between the demands of stability and flexibility becomes almost unbearable when there is not enough time to adapt the laws to the changing circumstances and when immediate 'specific' action is deemed necessary. Emergencies present the challenge of enabling government to confront the crisis by, if necessary, using special emergency powers and greater flexibility of operation while, at the same time, ensuring that such powers and flexibility do not get out of control and allow government to impose long-term

[1] *Korematsu v. United States*, 323 US 214, 248 (1944) (Jackson J, dissenting).
[2] Roberto Mangabeira Unger, *Law in Modern Society* 192 (New York, Free Press, 1976).

limitations on individual rights and liberties or modify the nature of the
relevant constitutional regime. How then should the legal system deal with
the need to allow the authorities to respond effectively to a given crisis while
minimizing the risks of overreaction both in the short and the long term?
David Dyzenhaus begins his excellent contribution to this volume by
reference to A. V. Dicey's treatment of the challenge of balancing stability
and flexibility in the context of emergencies and grave crises. Dyzenhaus
reads Dicey as suggesting that 'it would be far better if Parliament could
have delegated in advance the resources to public officials to deal with the
emergency' than leave those officials to act outside the law with the possibility
of a subsequent Act of Indemnity. Put differently:

> Dicey thus distinguishes very clearly between two legal responses to an
> emergency situation. In the first, the response is the after-the-fact recogni-
> tion that officials made an excusable decision to act outside of the law
> because it was necessary that they act and the law did not provide them with
> the resources they needed. In the second, Parliament in advance gives to
> officials resources to deal with emergencies in accordance with the rule of
> law. Dicey prefers the second option ... one that relies on legislative
> solutions that preserve the rule of law.[3]

Dyzenhaus takes a similar position in order to develop his own model of
legality which is based on 'experiments in institutional design'.[4] He argues
that such experiments carry the promise of dealing with crises and exigencies
in a manner that is fully consistent with the rule of law, i.e. without forcing
public officials to act outside the law.

This chapter will not attempt to address all of the issues raised by
Dyzenhaus's sophisticated argument. Rather, I will focus on his critique of
my Extra-Legal Measures model and leave a fuller discussion of his own
model of legality for another day. As noted above, Dyzenhaus invokes
Dicey's discussion of the legal responses to 'times of tumult or invasion' in
building his model of legality and argues that Dicey's approach to the
fundamental dilemma of stability and flexibility in times of crisis was
right.[5] Part I follows Dyzenhaus's lead and examines Dicey's solutions to
the problem of emergencies. I suggest that Dicey does present two ways
of responding to emergency situations, but that he sees both as two sides of
the same coin. Thus, the two solutions are complementary allowing the use
of one when the other may be unavailable or undesirable. I then tie Dicey's
analysis with John Locke's theory of the prerogative, suggesting that
Dicey's recognition of the possibility of public officials acting outside the law
answers a significant problem with Locke's theory. Part II focuses on a closer

---

[3] David Dyzenhaus, Chapter 4, in this volume.
[4] Ibid. at 67.   [5] Ibid. at 65.

examination of the *ex post* ratification component of the Extra-Legal Measures model. Once again, it does so by using Dicey's discussion of the Act of Indemnity, which is a particular case of *ex post* ratification. This Part seeks to demonstrate that Dyzenhaus's critique of the Extra-Legal Measures model as placing public officials in a 'legal black hole ... a zone uncontrolled by law' misses some of the essential components of the Extra-Legal Measures model.

A brief summary of the Extra-Legal Measures model may be in order.[6] The basic assertion of the model is that there may be circumstances where the appropriate method of tackling grave dangers and threats may entail going outside the constitutional order, at times even violating otherwise accepted constitutional principles, rules and norms. The model is built around three essential components: official disobedience, disclosure and *ex post* ratification. The model calls upon public officials having to deal with catastrophic cases to consider the possibility of acting outside the legal order while openly acknowledging their actions and the extra-legal nature of such actions. If a public official determines that a particular case necessitates her deviation from a relevant legal rule, she may choose to depart from the rule. At the same time, not only does the basic rule continue to apply to other situations (that is, it is not cancelled or terminated), it is not even overridden in the concrete case at hand. Thus, rule departure constitutes, under all circumstances and all conditions, a violation of the relevant legal rule. However, whether the actor will be punished for her violation remains a separate question. Society retains the role of making the final determination whether the actor ought to be punished and rebuked, or rewarded and commended for her actions. It should be up to society as a whole, 'the people', to decide how to respond *ex post* to extra-legal actions taken by government officials in response to extreme exigencies. The people may decide to hold the actor accountable for the wrongfulness of her actions, or may approve them retrospectively. Until the extra-legal action is ratified *ex post*, and, as explained below, even after it is so ratified, the official does not know what the personal consequences of violating the rule are going to be.

A final point regarding the 'generality' of the model seems to be in need of some clarification. Dyzenhaus questions the extent to which the Extra-Legal Measures model is designed as a general model for dealing with states of emergency.[7] In *Chaos and Rules*, I suggested that,

> The proposed Extra-Legal Measures model does not seek to do away with the traditional discourse over emergency powers. It does not claim to

---

[6] For a fuller discussion of the model see Oren Gross, 'Chaos and Rules: Should Responses to Violent Crises Always Be Constitutional?' (2003) 112 *Yale Law Journal* 1011, 1096–133.
[7] Dyzenhaus, Chapter 4.

exclude the constitutional models of emergency powers. It is a model for truly extraordinary occasions. There may be circumstances when it would be appropriate to go outside the legal order, at times even violating otherwise accepted constitutional dictates, when responding to emergency situations. Yet, even in circumstances where use of the model is inappropriate, and where the constitutional models may supply an answer to the particular predicament, we must recognize the limitations of each of these alternatives and its long-term implications.[8]

Part I starts by suggesting that Dicey would agree with this statement.

II. Dicey's 'spirit of legality'

A. 'Aid from Parliament'

In his celebrated *Introduction to the Study of the Law of the Constitution*,[9] A. V. Dicey addresses the challenge of balancing stability and flexibility. His basic approach views executive discretion with much suspicion treating it as leading to use of arbitrary powers. Rather than face the prerogative of the Crown, Dicey reminds us that 'the supremacy of the law of the land both calls forth the exertion of Parliamentary sovereignty, and leads to its being exercised in a spirit of legality'.[10] At the same time, he acknowledges that 'the rigidity of the law constantly hampers (and sometimes with great injury to the public) the action of the executive'.[11] Specifically, he concedes that 'under the complex conditions of modern life no government can in times of disorder, or of war, keep the peace at home, or perform its duties towards foreign powers, without occasional use of arbitrary authority'.[12] How are we supposed, then, to meet the challenge of the need to authorize occasional use of arbitrary (i.e. discretionary) authority while maintaining limitations and checks on the use of such power and ensuring that it is confined in some sense? Dicey offers us two complementary solutions. First is for the executive to obtain from Parliament 'the discretionary authority which is denied to the Crown by the law of the land', i.e. by recourse to 'exceptional legislation'.[13] While exigencies call for the exercise by the executive of discretionary power such power must be governed by statute. The executive must obtain 'aid from Parliament' in fashioning the discretionary powers with which to meet, and successfully repel, crises and emergencies.[14] The fact that executive emergency powers are derived from, and based on, statutes reaffirms parliamentary supremacy even in times of grave threats to the nation, while at the same

---

[8] Gross, 'Chaos and Rules', at 1134.

[9] A. V. Dicey, *Introduction to the Study of the Law of the Constitution* (8th edn., Liberty Classics reprint, 1982). Throughout this chapter I refer to the 8th edition of Dicey's work since that was the last edition that he himself prepared.

[10] Ibid. at 273.   [11] Ibid. at 271.   [12] Ibid.   [13] Ibid.   [14] Ibid. at 272.

time, it acts to limit and confine the scope of such powers. They may be
discretionary. They may be extraordinary. But they are never unlimited and
as such they are always open to review by the courts.[15]

What form should 'aid from Parliament' take? The obvious response
suggested by Dicey is the passage of 'exceptional legislation' that would
enable the executive to exercise discretionary powers.[16] Such legislation
may seek to adapt existing laws so as to make them more sensitive to the
needs of dealing with crises,[17] or it may, but need not, take the format of
stand-alone legislation: emergency provisions may be included in specific
'emergency' legislation, but they may also be incorporated into an ordinary
piece of legislation while retaining their specific emergency features.[18] The
special legislation may introduce institutional and structural modifications
to the existing legal system that are deemed essential for crisis management.
Most significantly for the purposes of this chapter, such exceptional legislation will be enacted *ex ante*, i.e. prior to the exercise of the relevant powers by
the executive. It may be introduced either on an ad hoc (i.e. to meet a
concrete exigency) or on a permanent (e.g., as a constitutional scheme set
for dealing with 'emergencies') basis.[19] Once put in place it serves as the legal
background against which executive emergency powers will be exercised, and
against which their legality and eventual legitimacy will be measured and
evaluated.

Yet, Dicey also recognizes that ex ante special legislation does not 'exhaust
the instances in which the rigidity of the law necessitates the intervention of
Parliament'.[20] Rather, 'there are times of tumult or invasion when for the sake
of legality itself the rules of law must be broken. The course which the
government must then take is clear. *The Ministry must break the law and
trust for protection to an Act of Indemnity.*'[21] By enacting such an Act of
Indemnity Parliament 'legalizes illegality' and asserts its sovereignty and
supremacy.[22] Here, again, the executive must obtain aid from Parliament.

---

[15] Ibid. at 273.

[16] Dicey gives here the example of an Alien Act, Foreign Enlistment Act and Extradition Acts.
Ibid. at 272.

[17] See, e.g., William J. Stuntz, 'Local Policing After the Terror' (2002) 111 *Yale Law Journal*
2137, 2139 (noting that some anti-terrorism legislation is not targeted, in that additional
governmental powers are not limited to the fight against terrorism but are rather general);
ibid. at 2162.

[18] Gross, 'Chaos and Rules' at 1065–6.

[19] See Oren Gross, 'Providing for the Unexpected: Constitutional Emergency Provisions'
(2003) 33 *Isr. YB Hum. Rts.* 13.

[20] Dicey, *Law of the Constitution* at 272.

[21] Ibid. at 272 (emphasis added).

[22] Ibid. at 10–11 (arguing that Acts of Indemnity 'being as it were the legalisation of illegality
are the highest exertion and crowning proof of sovereign power [by Parliament]'); see also
ibid. at 142.

But whereas the exceptional legislation discussed above calls for such legislative aid to be accorded *ex ante*, legislative Acts of Indemnity give an after-the-fact, retrospective, *ex post* aid to the executive.

What are we to make of Dicey's 'aid of Parliament' approach? He would certainly reject claims of inherent executive powers to deal with emergencies, regarding them as certain to undermine parliamentary sovereignty and supremacy, by leading to practically unfettered discretion and authority in the hands of the executive branch of government.[23]

Significantly, Dicey also rejects what he calls 'the doctrine of political expediency', namely the view that 'during an invasion, a general, a mayor, a magistrate, or indeed any loyal citizen, is legally justified in doing any act, even though *prima facie* a tort or a crime, as to which he can prove to the satisfaction of a jury that he did it for the public service in good faith, and for reasonable and probable cause'.[24] For Dicey, then, necessity does not, in and of itself, make legal that which in other circumstances would have been illegal. Even where public officials perform illegal actions to preserve and protect the nation, that alone does not make their actions legal. This is a significant point that must be considered in light of the tradition of the prerogative power which is most famously associated with John Locke.

B. John Locke's theory of the prerogative power

Locke's theory of the prerogative power is significant not only because of its intellectual potency, but also because it has greatly influenced many of the Founding Fathers of the United States and their contemporaries. For Locke, the prerogative power vested in the executive branch of government[25] is *'nothing but the power of doing public good without a rule'*.[26] It is the power 'to act according to discretion, for the public good, *without the prescription of the law, and sometimes even against it'*.[27] Put somewhat differently 'prerogative can be nothing, but the people's permitting their rulers, to do several things of their own free choice, where the law was silent, and sometimes too *against the direct letter of the law*, for the public good; and their acquiescing in

---

[23] On the concept of inherent executive powers under the US Constitution see, for example, Laurence H. Tribe, *American Constitutional Law* (2nd ed., New York, Foundation Press, 1988), 676; William C. Banks and Alejandro D. Carrió, 'Presidential Systems in Stress: Emergency Powers in Argentina and the United States', (1993) 15 *Mich. J. Int'l L.* 1, 42–6; Henry P. Monaghan, 'The Protective Power of the Presidency', (1993) 93 *Colum. L. Rev.* 1.

[24] Dicey, *Law of the Constitution*, at 412.

[25] 'Where the legislative and executive power are in distinct hands . . . there the good of the society requires, that several things should be left to the discretion of him, that has the executive power'. John Locke, *The Second Treatise of Government* in Mark Goldie (ed.), *Two Treatises of Government* (London, Everyman, 1993) (first pub. 1690), para 159.

[26] Ibid. para 166 (emphasis added).   [27] Ibid. para 160 (emphasis added).

it when so done'.[28] Locke considers such power as necessary in order to deal with situations when strict and rigid observation of the laws may lead to grave social harm.[29]

Locke offers a functional litmus test for evaluating whether the prerogative power has been appropriately used in any given case. He focuses on the purpose behind the exercise of the prerogative, i.e. whether it was directed at promoting the public good.[30] Government cannot have any legitimate ends apart from promoting the good of the community. Governmental power used for any purpose other than the public good is properly regarded as tyrannical[31] and may justify, under certain circumstances, an uprising to restore the people's rights and to limit the government's resort to such arbitrary power.[32]

Locke puts much faith in human reason and rationality as mitigating and limiting factors on the exercise of prerogative power.[33] His theory of the prerogative reveals a substantial degree of trust in government in general, and particularly in times of emergency. He gives the executive the benefit of the doubt: if there are allegations that the ruler's use of the prerogative power has not been for the purpose of promoting the public good, but rather was in the service of the ruler's own interests and purposes the people have no remedy available from any 'judge on earth'. Their sole recourse is 'to appeal to heaven' or, when the majority of the people feels wronged, to revolt against the oppressive ruler.[34] This is a tall order indeed.[35] On the other hand, if it

---

[28] Ibid. para 164 (emphasis added).

[29] Ibid. paras 159–60. Locke suggests that it is 'fit that the laws themselves should in some cases give way to the executive power, or rather to this fundamental law of nature and government, viz. that as much as may be, all the members of the society are to be preserved'. Ibid. para 159. Explaining his reasons for vesting the prerogative power with the executive, Locke argues that the legislature cannot anticipate in advance and regulate by statute all that may be, at any point in the future, beneficial to society, and that lawmaking power may be too slow to adapt adequately to exigencies and necessities of the times.

[30] Ibid. para 161 ('But if there comes to be a question between the executive power and the people, about a thing claimed as a prerogative; the tendency of the exercise of such prerogative to the good or hurt of the people, will easily decide that question'); see also ibid. paras 163, 164, 168.

[31] Ibid. para 199 ('*tyranny is the exercise of power beyond right*, which nobody can have a right to. And this is making use of the power any one has in his hands; not for the good of those, who are under it, but for his own private separate advantage'); see also ibid. 202 ('*Wherever law ends, tyranny begins*, if the Law be transgressed to another's harm').

[32] Ibid. paras 203–209.   [33] Ibid. paras 163–64.   [34] Ibid. para 168.

[35] Locke recognizes that the right of the people to revolt against a ruler who abuses her powers will likely be exercised on rare occasions, for 'revolutions happen not upon every little mismanagement in public affairs. Great mistakes in the ruling part, many wrong and inconvenient laws, and all the slips of human frailty will be born by the people, without mutiny or murmur.' Ibid. para 225; see also ibid. paras 223, 230.

appears that the ruler used his prerogative power in an appropriate manner the evaluation of his actions is straightforward: '*prerogative* can be nothing, but *the people's permitting their rulers*, to do several things of their own free choice, where the law was silent, and sometimes too against the direct letter of the law, for the public good; *and their acquiescing in it when so done*'.[36] In other words, when the ruler applies his prerogative power for the public good, such action is considered the right thing to do. An appropriate exercise of the prerogative power is legitimate per se and *ex ante* due to the implicit acquiescence of the public to any such exercise (albeit not necessarily to the specific use of the prerogative power in the circumstances of any particular crisis). There is no need for any further public involvement.

This is where Dicey's discussion of the Act of Indemnity departs from, and improves on, the Lockean model of the prerogative. Whereas Locke seems to put his trust in an implicit, general, *ex ante* public acquiescence in the exercise of an executive power to act outside the law, Dicey, as we already saw, insists that an explicit, particular, *ex post* legislative ratification of the same must be awarded. While the Extra-Legal Measures model takes a further step by not pegging ratification to an act of the legislature, it retains Dicey's insistence that extra-legal actions cannot be justified merely by reference to the motives of the actors, laudable as these may be. Rather a separate and independent *ex post* ratification must take place in order for the extra-legal action to be justified or excused.

There may be another important distinction between Locke's discussion of the prerogative and Dicey's recognition of the possibility of an executive power to act outside the law. One possible reading of Locke draws distinctions between what is 'extra-legal' and that which is 'extra-constitutional.' According to this reading, while Locke may be willing to recognize governmental actions that run contrary to positive law, i.e. extra-*legal* actions, he does not consider the prerogative to be an extra-*constitutional* power. Rather, he sees it as an integral part of the broader constitutional scheme.[37] That constitutional order, which enjoys a higher normative value than any particular set of positive laws, acknowledges the possibility of extra-legal governmental action in times of emergency and necessity. Thus, the prerogative power ought to be considered as a concrete (extreme to be sure) example of the 'political power' – that power 'which every man, having in the state of nature, has given up into the hands of the society, and therein to the governors, whom the society hath set over itself, with this express or tacit trust, that it shall be employed for their good, and the preservation of their

---

[36] Ibid. para 164 (emphasis added).

[37] See, e.g., Carl J. Friedrich, *Constitutional Reason of State: The Survival of the Constitutional Order* (Providence, Brown University Press, 1957) 110, 111 (1957) (Locke's theory of prerogative power not as an extra-legal power but rather as a power inherent in the constitutional order, i.e. as a legal, albeit exceptional, power).

property'[38] – as distinguished from 'despotical power'.[39] Locke's warning
that exercise of the prerogative power by the good, even 'godlike', prince will
serve as a precedent for the application of similar powers by a lesser ruler
'managing the government with different thoughts',[40] may also suggest that
he considers the prerogative power to be functioning within the boundaries
of the constitutional system rather than outside these boundaries. If it were
not so, could the implementation of extra-constitutional powers establish a
precedent for the future and coat with a cover of legality and legitimacy the
actions of a less worthy prince?[41]

This understanding of the prerogative power leads, in turn, to an apparent
dilemma: is there any point in identifying the prerogative power as a *constitutional* power, when the substantive content of that power permits violation of constitutional norms?[42] Specifically, if the power of prerogative
permits actions that are against the direct letter of the law, what prevents
the wielder of that power from exercising it in violation of the prescribed legal
limitations on the use of that very power, turning it into an unlimited power,
constrained neither by legal norms nor by principles and rules of the constitutional order?[43]

III. Acts of indemnity and *ex post* ratification of extra-legal actions by public officials

An Act of Indemnity may be one method of *ex post* ratification. More
generally, such ratification may be formal or informal, legal as well as social
or political.[44] Legal modes of ratification include, for example, the exercise of
prosecutorial discretion not to bring criminal charges against the public
officials who acted in violation of the law, jury nullification where criminal
charges are brought, executive pardoning or clemency where criminal proceedings result in conviction, and governmental indemnification of state
agents who are found liable for damages. Political and social ratification is
also possible.

---

[38] Locke, *The Second Treatise of Government*, para 171.   [39] Ibid. para 172.

[40] Ibid. para 166. Locke warns that so perilous may such consequences be that upon this is
founded that saying, that 'the reigns of good princes have been always most dangerous to
the liberties of their people'. Ibid.

[41] Gross, 'Chaos and Rules', at 1094–5.

[42] Friedrich, *Constitutional Reason of State* at 83.

[43] See, e.g., Sotirios A. Barber, *On What the Constitution Means* (Baltimore, Johns Hopkins
University Press, 1984), 188–90; Joseph M. Bessette and Jeffrey Tulis, 'The Constitution,
Politics, and the Presidency' in Bessette and Tulis (eds.), *The Presidency in the
Constitutional Order* (Baton Rouge, Louisiana State University Press, 1981), 3, 24–5.

[44] Oren Gross, 'Are Torture Warrants Warranted? Pragmatic Absolutism and Official
Disobedience' (2004) 88 *Minn. L. Rev.* 1481; Gross, 'Chaos and Rules', at 1111–15.

Does *ex post* ratification render legal that which previously had been illegal, or does it excuse the acting official from liability for her extra-legal actions without making such actions legal? Much would depend on the nature of the ratification. The answer to such questions would be made on a case-by-case basis. Sticking with Dicey, this Part focuses on Acts of Indemnity as a method of *ex post* ratification. It should be noted, however, that the Extra-Legal Measures model goes beyond Dicey's approach in so far as it does not necessitate the 'aid of Parliament' to the executive. Whereas Dicey discusses the Act of Indemnity as reflecting, *ex post*, the supremacy and sovereignty of Parliament, the Extra-Legal Measures model is more open to the possibility of *ex post* ratification taking place outside the legislature.

An Act of Indemnity, Dicey suggests, 'legalises illegality'.[45] Dyzenhaus argues that Dicey's notion of the Act of Indemnity places public officials in a 'legal black hole' in as much as it allows 'political power [to be exercised] in a brute fashion (the last and supreme exercise of Parliamentary sovereignty) *permitting those who wield it* to break free of the constraints of constitutionality and legality'.[46] Rather than make what the acting officials did legal, the Act of Indemnity places them in a 'zone uncontrolled by law'.[47] Compelling as this statement may seem at first blush, it is problematic on several levels.

First, Acts of Indemnity may do one of two things: they may shelter the acting public official from civil or criminal responsibility for her violations of the law while holding that her actions were, and remain, illegal. Alternatively they may seek to exculpate the actor from any legal responsibility for her actions by making such actions, retrospectively, lawful. Dyzenhaus seems to suggest that Dicey opts for the former interpretation, i.e. that Acts of Indemnity deny otherwise available legal remedies for certain violations of the law. That is certainly a plausible understanding of the nature and function of the Acts, but it is not Dicey's. In explaining his own view of Acts of Indemnity and their effects, Dicey is quite clear: 'Acts of Indemnity . . . are retrospective statutes which free persons who have broken the law from responsibility for its breach, and *thus make lawful acts which when they were committed were unlawful*'.[48] He rejects Frederick Pollock's suggestion that an Act of Indemnity is merely 'a measure of prudence and grace. Its office is not to justify unlawful acts ex post facto, but to quiet doubts, to provide compensation for innocent persons in respect of damage inevitably caused by

---

[45] Dicey, *Law of the Constitution*, at 10–11, 142.
[46] Dyzenhaus, Chapter 4 at 65 (emphasis added).
[47] Ibid.
[48] Dicey, *Law of the Constitution*, at 142 (emphasis added). See also ibid. at 10 ('An Act of Indemnity is a statute, the object of which is to make legal transactions which when they took place were illegal, or to free individuals to whom the statute applies from liability for having broken the law').

justifiable acts which would not have supported a legal claim',[49] calling it a 'very inadequate description of an Act of Indemnity'.[50] This surely fits with Dicey's overall argument for the supremacy of law since an 'Act of Indemnity, again, though it is the legalisation of illegality, is also ... itself a law ... It is no doubt an exercise of arbitrary sovereign power; but where the legal sovereign is a Parliamentary assembly, even acts of state assume the form of regular legislation.'[51] Thus, by 'making lawful acts which when they were committed were unlawful', the Act of Indemnity ensures that all actions by public officials are done under a legislative framework and are not, at the end of the day, to be found outside the law.

Second, if by 'it' (as in 'those who wield *it*') Dyzenhaus refers to political power then it seems to me that he fails to distinguish between the actions of public officials that are taken outside the law and the subsequent acts of Parliament. For the exercise of the political power in a way that amounts to 'the last and supreme exercise of Parliamentary sovereignty', i.e. the enact-ment of an Act of Indemnity, is carried out by Parliament whereas those who are permitted 'to break free of the constraints of constitutionality and legality' are surely those public officials who may find themselves compelled to act extra-legally when dealing with an emergency. But then again those public officials are not those who wield 'it', i.e. the political power to pass an Act of Indemnity and thus express the 'last and supreme exercise of Parliamentary sovereignty'. This may seem as no more than a hair-splitting exercise and an overly pedantic reading. However, I suggest that the view that Dyzenhaus expresses in the passage quoted above – namely that *ex post* ratification of extra-legal acts of public officials, such as done by way of Acts of Indemnity, empowers public officials to 'break free of the constraints of constitutionality and legality' – misses some of the essential components of the Extra-Legal Measures model precisely because it does not pay sufficient attention to the distinction between the extra-legal action (the act of official disobedience) and the possibility (but not certainty) of a subsequent, *ex post*, ratification of such actions by the legislature or, under the Extra-Legal Measures model, the people.

One of several themes running through Dyzenhaus's argument is that the Extra-Legal Measures model does not offer any meaningful method to main-tain constitutional and legal constraints over public officials. Does not that model merely amount (or, perhaps more appropriately, descend) to legit-imating the exercise of 'brute' power uncontrolled by law? If we accept the possibility, in extreme cases, of certain governmental actions that are extra-legal, can there be any constitutional or legal limitations on such govern-mental exercise of power? Extra-legal power can only mean an unlimited

---

[49] Frederick Pollock, 'What is Martial Law?' (1902) 70 *L. Q. Rev.* 152, 157.
[50] Dicey, *Law of the Constitution* at 414.   [51] Ibid. at 145.

power, constrained neither by any legal norms nor by principles and rules of the constitutional order!

I have defended the Extra-Legal Measures model elsewhere.[52] What I wish to do here is to address the charge regarding the perceived freedom of the constraints of constitutionality and legality, which the model seems to offer to public officials. I do so by using as my starting base Dicey's own arguments in support of the use of Acts of Indemnity.

To make the argument clearer let me rephrase the challenge to the Extra-Legal Measures model in the concrete context of Acts of Indemnity: if the effect of Acts of Indemnity is, indeed, to legalize illegality and if, as Dicey openly acknowledges, the expectation of the executive that such Acts will be passed by Parliament 'has not been disappointed' as a matter of history and experience,[53] what limits remain on the exercise of powers by the government and its agents? After all, public officials will always, so it seems, be able to act outside the law, without legal and constitutional shackles on their actions, and be secure in the knowledge that an Act of Parliament shielding them from all responsibility and making their actions lawful is forthcoming.

Dicey is aware of this critical challenge. 'Still,' he argues, 'there are one or two considerations which limit the practical importance that can fairly be given to an expected Act of Indemnity. The relief to be obtained from it is *prospective and uncertain.*'[54] I suggest that the uncertainty of the prospective relief may not only slow down the rush to act extra-legally in the first place, but it also facilitates meaningful limitations on such actions once they are taken and provide important benchmarks against which to evaluate such actions *ex post*. To acknowledge the possibility of extra-legal action is not the same thing as accepting willy-nilly limitless powers and authority in the hands of state agents.

In a democratic society, where values of constitutionalism, accountability, the rule of law, and individual rights, freedoms and liberties are firmly entrenched and traditionally respected, we can expect that the public would be circumspect about governmental attempts to justify or excuse illegal actions even if taken, arguably, to promote the general good. That being the case, 'any suspicion on the part of the public, that officials had grossly abused their powers, might make it difficult to obtain a Parliamentary indemnity for things done'.[55] The Act of Indemnity may never be enacted.

---

[52] Gross, 'Chaos and Rules', at 1118–34.
[53] Dicey, *Law of the Constitution*, at 144 (noting that an Act suspending the Habeas Corpus Act 'has constantly been followed by an Act of Indemnity'); see also *Mitchell* v. *Clark*, 110 US 633, 640 (1884) (noting that Acts of Indemnity are 'passed by all governments when the occasion requires it').
[54] Dicey, *Law of the Constitution*, at 144–5 (emphasis added).
[55] Ibid. at 145.

The separation between extra-legal actions taken by public officials in catastrophic cases and subsequent public ratification – for example by way of the passage of an Act of Indemnity – creates a 'prudent obfuscation'[56] that introduces a significant element of uncertainty to the decision-making calculus of public officials and raises both the individual and national costs of pursuing an extra-legal course of action.

With the need to obtain *ex post* ratification, the public official who decides to act extra-legally undertakes a significant risk because of the uncertain prospects for subsequent ratification. The public may, for example, disagree after the fact with the acting official's assessment of the situation and the need to act extra-legally. Ratification would be sought *ex post*, when more information about the particular case at hand may be available to the public, and possibly after the particular danger has been eliminated. Under such circumstances, it is possible that calm and rationality, rather than heightened emotions, would govern public discourse, emphasizing the risk for the official in acting first and seeking approval later. The public may also determine that the extra-legal actions violated values and principles that are too important to be encroached upon, as a matter of principle or in the circumstances of the particular case. The greater the moral and legal interests and values infringed upon, the less certain the actor can be of securing ratification.

What, then, about Dicey's, and Dyzenhaus's,[57] observation that as a matter of practice the expectation of the executive that Parliament will pass an Act of Indemnity 'has not been disappointed'? Does not that eliminate any uncertainty on the part of the public officials or at least create a significant risk of under-deterrence?

Even if we accept that there exists a good chance that *ex post* ratification will be forthcoming, there are still significant costs to acting extra-legally. For starters, there is still a certain degree of anxiety that ratification will not, in fact, follow. More significantly, ratification may not be comprehensive or fully corrective. As Dicey notes: 'As regards ... the protection to be derived from the Act by men who have been guilty of irregular, illegal, oppressive, or cruel conduct, *everything depends on the terms of the Act of Indemnity*.'[58]

---

[56] Dan M. Kahan, 'Ignorance of Law Is an Excuse – But Only for the Virtuous' (1997) 96 *Mich. L. Rev.* 127, 139–41 (discussing 'prudent obfuscation' as a means to respond to the penal law's persistent incompleteness). Kahan discusses the use of vague terms in criminal laws, giving courts 'the flexibility to adapt the law to innovative forms of crime *ex post*'. Ibid. at 139.

[57] Dyzenhaus, Chapter 4, at 72–3 ('If the Extra-Legal Measures model were public, as it must be if it is to promote deliberation, the expectation would be generated of after-the-fact validation of illegal official acts. In an atmosphere of fear that expectation would likely be met rather easily, especially when the threat is, or is claimed to be, a constant one and the government successfully manipulates public opinion.')

[58] Dicey, *Law of the Constitution*, at 145 (emphasis added).

Subsequent ratification may shield the actor against criminal charges, but not bar the possibility of civil proceedings. It may also not shield the actor from liability for all of her actions.[59]

In addition, if an Act of Indemnity is enacted, then

> The fact that the most arbitrary powers of the English executive must always be exercised under Act of Parliament places the government, even when armed with the widest authority, under the supervision, so to speak, of the courts. Powers, however extraordinary ... are never really unlimited, for they are confined by the words of the Act itself, and, what is more, by the interpretation put upon the statute by the judges.[60]

The fact that the courts will be called to deal with an *ex post* ratification in the form of an Act of Indemnity may also make judicial supervision over the exercise of emergency powers by government officials more meaningful and robust. In times of emergency courts, both domestic and international, assume a highly deferential attitude when called upon to review governmental actions and decisions.[61] The courts' apparent inability to protect

---

[59] Ibid. at 145. Similarly, when ratification comes in the form of an executive pardon or clemency, it eliminates the criminal penalty that was imposed on the individual actor, but it neither removes the ordeal of criminal prosecution nor the condemnation associated with criminal conviction. See Leon Sheleff, 'On Criminal Homicide and Legal Self Defense' (1997) 6 PLILIM 89, 111–12; Yale Kamisar, 'Physician Assisted Suicide: The Problems Presented by the Compelling, Heartwrenching Case' (1998) 88 *J. Crim. L. & Criminology* 1121, 1143–4 (reliance on mitigation of sentence fails to mitigate the 'ordeal of a criminal prosecution or the stigma of a conviction').

[60] Dicey, *Law of the Constitution* at 273.

[61] See, e.g., Thomas M. Franck, *Political Questions/Judicial Answers: Does the Rule of Law Apply to Foreign Affairs?* (Princeton University Press, 1992), 10–30; Harold Hongju Koh, *The National Security Constitution: Sharing Power After the Iran-Contra Affair* (New Haven, Yale University Press, 1990), 134–49; Christopher N. May, *In the Name of War: Judicial Review and the War Powers Since 1918*, (Cambridge, Harvard University Press, 1989), at 261–4 (speaking of 'ritualistic approval' by courts of governmental emergency measures); William H. Rehnquist, *All the Laws but One* (New York, Knopf, 1998), 221–2; Michal R. Belknap, 'The Warren Court and the Vietnam War: The Limits of Legal Liberalism' (1998) 33 *Ga. L. Rev.* 65, 66–7; Anne-Marie Slaughter Burley, 'Are Foreign Affairs Different?' (1993) 106 *Harvard Law Review* 1980, 1991–5; John Hart Ely, *War and Responsibility: Constitutional Lessons of Vietnam and Its Aftermath* (Princeton University Press, 1993), 54–60; Laurence Lustgarten and Ian Leigh, *In from the Cold: National Security and Parliamentary Democracy* (Oxford, Clarendon, 1994), 320–59; George J. Alexander, 'The Illusory Protection of Human Rights by National Courts During Periods of Emergency' (1984) 5 *Hum. Rts. L. J.* 1, 15–27. For the argument that international and regional judicial bodies are not necessarily more effective in dealing with the concept of 'emergency' than are domestic courts, see Fionnuala Ni Aolain, 'The Emergence of Diversity: Differences in Human Rights Jurisprudence' (1995) 19 *Fordham Int'l L. J.* 101; Oren Gross, 'Once More unto the Breach: The Systemic Failure of Applying the European Convention on Human Rights to Entrenched Emergencies' (1998) 23 *Yale J. Int'l L.* 437, 490–500.

individual rights while extreme violence is raging around them, compared
with their greater willingness to resume their role as guardians of human
rights and civil liberties once the crisis is over, may mean that judicial review
of Acts of Indemnity may be relatively more meaningful.[62]

When we consider international legal rules and norms, the costs and
uncertainties that are involved in acting extra-legally are increased further.
Thus, even if a particular extra-legal act is domestically ratified *ex post*, it may
be subject to a different judgment on the international plane. This may have
significant consequences both for the individual public official and her
government. Acting officials may potentially still be subject to criminal and
civil proceedings in jurisdictions other than their own. Moreover, to the
extent that the relevant extra-legal action violates the nation's international
legal obligations, especially its obligations and undertakings under the major
international human rights conventions, and is not covered by an appropriate derogation (or, indeed, it violates a non-derogable right), state agents
who engage in such acts expose their government to a range of possible
remedies under the relevant international legal instruments. Indeed by recognizing what has occurred, a domestic Act of Indemnity may facilitate international litigation.

The Extra-Legal Measures model imposes significant burdens on public
officials. They must act in the face of great uncertainty. They may still decide
to act extra-legally 'for the public good' and expect to be protected subsequently by a form of *ex post* ratification. At the same time, the model makes it
extremely costly to resort to such drastic measures, limiting their use to
exceptional exigencies. As Sanford Kadish notes, 'Would not the burden on
the official be so great that it would require circumstances of a perfectly
extraordinary character to induce the individual to take the risk of acting?
The answer is of course yes, that's the point.'[63] The more uncertain it is that
ratification will be forthcoming, the more uncertain its potential scope, and
the greater the personal risk involved in wrongly interpreting either of those
is, the greater the incentive for individual actors to conform their action to
the existing legal rules and norms and not risk acting outside them. The
burden lies squarely on the shoulders of the public officials who must act,

---

[62] See, e.g., May, *In the Name of War* at 268 (suggesting that, in light of judicial practice of
abdicating review of executive activities during an emergency, 'courts should steer a
middle course and defer review until the emergency has abated'). Chief Justice
Rehnquist also noted: 'If, in fact, courts are more prone to uphold wartime claims of
civil liberties after the war is over, may it not actually be desirable to avoid decision on
such claims during the war? ... While the body of case law might benefit from such
abstention, those who are actually deprived of their civil liberties would not. But a decision
in favor of civil liberty will stand as a precedent to regulate future actions of Congress and
the Executive branch in future wars.' Rehnquist, *All the Laws but One* at 222.
[63] Sanford H. Kadish, 'Torture, the State and the Individual' (1989) 23 *Isr. L. Rev.* 345, 355.

sometimes extra-legally, without the benefit of legal pre-approval of their actions by the courts or the legislature. Public officials have no one to hide behind. They must put themselves on the front line and act at their own peril. Their burden is composed not merely of political norms of accountability, transparency and democratic deliberation, but also of legal norms. The argument that such an approach puts public officials in a 'zone uncontrolled by law' underestimates the significance of such disincentives to step outside the legal framework and of the possibilities for external supervision, both by the public and by other branches of government, which this approach has to offer.

The limitations on the resort to extra-legal actions that the Extra-Legal Measures model offers are further strengthened by the fact that we can and should expect public officials to feel quite uneasy about possible resort to extra-legal measures, even when such actions are deemed to be for the public's benefit. The knowledge that acting in a certain way means acting unlawfully is, in and of itself, going to have a restraining effect on government agents, even while the threat of catastrophe persists. Furthermore, in order to enjoy *ex post* ratification some disclosure as to the extra-legal actions that were taken during the crisis and some justification for taking such actions in the first place are likely to be demanded (and, as noted above, disclosure and justification form critical components of the Extra-Legal Measures model). The need to give reasons *ex post* – to publicly justify or excuse, not merely explain, one's actions after the fact – may limit the government's choice of measures *ex ante*, adding another layer of restraint on governmental action.[64] In any event it emphasizes the accountability of government agents. It will also contribute to open and reasoned discourse and dialogue between the different branches of government, between the government and its domestic constituency, between the government and other governments, and between the government and non-governmental or international organizations.[65] Consider, once again, the issue of Acts of Indemnity. The legislative process that leads to the enactment of such Acts presents the legislature with a unique opportunity to review the actions of the executive branch and assess them *ex post*, relieved from the pressures of the crisis, before deciding whether to ratify them. Furthermore, the legislative process may also invoke public deliberation and force the legislative branch to take an affirmative stand on issues connected with the emergency. This may counteract the reluctance of legislatures to assume responsibility or supervise the executive in times of

---

[64] See Frederick Schauer, 'Giving Reasons' (1995) 47 *Stan. L. Rev.* 633, 656–7; see also Bessette and Tulis 'Constitution, Politics', 10.

[65] The reasons put forward by a state to justify its actions may be subject to scrutiny not only by other governments and non-governmental organizations, but also by judicial and quasi-judicial bodies such as the European Court of Human Rights, the Inter-American Court of Human Rights and the United Nations Human Rights Commission.

emergency.[66] In addition, the judiciary has a role to play in interpreting the scope of the Act of Indemnity.

I cannot end this discussion without briefly commenting on Dyzenhaus's most provocative example of the 'all bets are off' critique of the Extra-Legal Measures model, namely the story of the 'Night of the Long Knives'.[67] The gist of his critique is that the model cannot impose any limitations on actions such as those taken by Hitler and his henchmen since those were publicly acknowledged (in fact, boasted about) and received a subsequent statutory ratification through a special Act promulgated by the German Cabinet, acting under the authority of the Enabling Act of 1933 that vested the German government with legislative powers.

Yet, there is very little, if any, point in trying to bring rational discussion – to talk about the rule of law, legality and legitimacy, rights, and limitations on powers – to the experience of Nazi Germany. Dyzenhaus is absolutely correct in attributing to the Extra-Legal Measures model a substantive precondition, namely that it is applied and used in a community that is 'worth saving'. But that, surely, is a condition that ought to underlie any meaningful discussion of emergency powers.

Writing during the early days of the Cold War, Carl Friedrich, a Harvard University professor of political science, described the tension between national security and civil rights and liberties as arising 'wherever a constitutional order of the libertarian kind has been confronted with the Communist challenge, and with the Fascist response to that challenge'.[68] In other words, to what extent, if any, can violations of liberal democratic values be justified in the name of the survival of the democratic, constitutional order itself; and if they can be so justified, to what extent can a democratic, constitutional government defend the state without transforming itself into an authoritarian regime? The tension between self-preservation and defending the 'innermost self' of the democratic regime – those attributes that make the regime worth defending – presents decision-makers with tragic choices.[69] However, this tension, which is at the heart of all discussions of emergency powers, can only be captured by those who share the belief in the viability and desirability of a constitutional, liberal, democratic regime while taking cognizance of the fact that emergencies require special treatment that may deviate from the ordinary norms.

---

[66] Koh, *The National Security Constitution*, at 117–33.
[67] Dyzenhaus, Chapter 4, at 70.
[68] Friedrich, *Constitutional Reason of State*, at 13.
[69] Ibid. at 13 (noting that the survival of a constitutional order involves more than self-preservation due to the rational and spiritual content of this order); see also Pnina Lahav, 'A Barrel Without Hoops: The Impact of Counterterrorism on Israel's Legal Culture' (1998) 10 *Cardozo L. Rev.* 529, 531 (noting the 'tragic dimensions of the tension between terrorism, counterterrorism, and justice in any democratic society').

6

Terrorism, risk perception and judicial review

VICTOR V. RAMRAJ

I. Introduction

The legal response to the threat of terrorism has been driven, in large part, by public fear about future attacks and worst-case scenarios. There are, of course, many risks that ought to be taken seriously by governments. But all too often policy responses are motivated by a widespread public misperception of risk and a heightened collective sense of fear and vulnerability that call into question our ability to think clearly about policy options. In this chapter, I reconsider the role of the legislative, executive and judicial branches of government in an emergency, first by considering how misperception of risk and public fear influence policy-makers, and then by examining the role that judicial review can play in times of crisis.

One response to public fear is to respond legislatively to popular opinion, enacting strict anti-terrorism measures. As democratic as this option might first seem, it is problematic because, as empirical research shows us, social forces amplify and distort our judgments about risk, particularly in emotionally charged situations. Only on a thin, *populist* conception, could democracy be seen simply as an aggregating mechanism for mere popular opinion, rather than as a sophisticated system to promote public deliberation and ensure that public decisions are fair and informed ones. Another approach, one that recognizes the technocratic nature of lawmaking in the regulatory state and relies on the integrity of the government and its expert advisors, is to defer to the executive on matters of national security. The problem with this option is its assumption that the executive would be competent to assess the risks in question, and that it would be trustworthy and unbiased. All of these assumptions are generally suspect, perhaps even more so in an emergency.

The approach that I defend in this chapter vests policy-making power in a well-informed executive that is fully accountable to the courts (or, at the very

I am grateful to Alan Khee-Jin Tan and David Dyzenhaus for their comments on a draft and to the participants in the Comparative Anti-Terrorism Law & Policy Symposium for their provocative comments.

least, a specialized, independent tribunal), whose decisions are in turn subject to public scrutiny and debate. This option allows for a careful consideration of risks and responses in a forum in which limitations on liberty are given their due and where the effectiveness of the policy can be assessed against limitations on rights, ideally in full public view. Although this judicial review option is largely *reactive*, it is a critical institutional safeguard against policy-making motivated primarily by fear and, more broadly, contributes to an inter-branch and broader societal dialogue on anti-terrorism measures. It also positions the courts as an integral institution in a democracy, ensuring that collective decision-making takes place in a setting in which assumptions about risks are laid bare and substantive values are fully considered.

The next part of this chapter draws on the contemporary literature on perception of risk to show how misperception often leads to laws that are ill-advised from a risk-reduction perspective. In this part, I explain why populist and supposedly democratic responses are inadequate. I then consider the executive option, with particular emphasis on claims that the executive has a particular expertise on matters of national security and that, particularly in an emergency, trust in and deference to the executive are imperative. Finally, I defend judicial review against objections that the courts have neither the institutional competence nor the capacity to deal with sensitive intelligence information. In particular, I argue that both the courts and, in some cases, specialized administrative tribunals, provide a crucial institutional safeguard against policies motivated primarily by fear.

II. Risk perception and the limits of democratic populism

How much are we willing to sacrifice to ensure that something catastrophic doesn't happen? As tragic as the September 11 terrorist attacks in New York and Washington – and subsequently in places as diverse as Indonesia, Pakistan, Kenya, Turkey, Spain and Saudi Arabia – have been, the haunting thought that seems to be driving legislative responses to terrorism is that something *worse* might be in store.[1] And if something worse *is* in store, why shouldn't we do everything in our power to stop it, even if it means sacrificing our fundamental values and principles?

This way of thinking draws its persuasive power by its appeal to fear and to the way in which we perceive risk. Research on the perception of risk

---

[1] See, for example, Nicholas D. Kristol, 'Risks of a nuclear Sept. 11 are increasing' *International Herald Tribune* (11 March 2004), at 7; 'Global terrorism must be tackled, whatever the cost' *The Straits Times* (Singapore) (6 March 2004), at 22 (reporting British Prime Minister Tony Blair's view 'that governments could not "err on the side of caution" when dealing with the threat of terrorism and weapons of mass destruction' and Foreign Secretary Jack Straw's view that 'international terrorism represented a new scale of threat').

describes a broad range of phenomena which influence perception of risk.[2] I want to focus on two of these, specifically, the *psychological factors*, such as probability neglect, that bear on risk perception, and the *social amplification of risk*, both of which have direct implications for anti-terrorism law and policy.

A. The psychology of risk perception

In his recent work on risk perception in the context of terrorism, Cass Sunstein, drawing on a vast body of multi-disciplinary literature, discusses three psychological responses to acts of terrorism: the use of heuristics, the tendency to show a disproportionate fear of unfamiliar risks, and the tendency, when strong emotions are involved, to focus on the bad outcome rather than on the probability that it will occur ('probability neglect').[3] Sunstein focuses on the last phenomenon, but all three have important implications for anti-terrorism law and policy.

Consider first the use of heuristics. Sunstein explains: 'In the face of ignorance, people assess probabilities through the use of various heuristics, most notably the availability heuristic, in accordance with which probability is measured by asking whether a readily available example comes to mind.'[4] As we observed in the aftermath of the September 11 attacks, people tend to think that another such attack is especially likely, whether or not it is in fact,[5] as is shown by the dramatic drop in air travel in the months following the attacks. Second, people 'show a disproportionate fear of risks that seem unfamiliar and hard to control'.[6] As Sunstein explains, a terrorist attack can cause significant changes in private and public behaviour 'even if the magnitude of the risk does not justify those changes, and even if statistically equivalent risks occasion little or no concern'.[7] A third response is that when strong emotions are involved, people focus on 'the bad outcome itself, and they are inattentive to the fact that it is unlikely to occur'.[8] Sunstein calls this phenomenon 'probability neglect' and argues that it is highly likely to occur in the aftermath of a terrorist attack.[9]

These three responses to unfortunate and rare events such as terrorist attacks suggest that people make significant mistakes about risk, particularly in situations where strong emotions are involved. Indeed, some experts on risk perception argue more generally that our emotional responses to an activity influence our perception of the risk associated with that activity.

[2] Paul Slovic, 'Introduction and Overview,' in Paul Slovic (ed.), *The Perception of Risk* (London and Sterling, Earthscan Publications, 2000).
[3] Cass Sunstein, 'Terrorism and Probability Neglect' (2003) 26 *The Journal of Risk and Uncertainty* 121.
[4] Ibid. at 121.   [5] Ibid.   [6] Ibid.   [7] Ibid. at 122.   [8] Ibid.   [9] Ibid.

Paul Slovic uses the term 'affect heuristic' to refer to the mental short-cuts people use when they draw on their affective or emotional responses when making risk-benefit judgments and suggests that, particularly when emotions are involved, people are unlikely to find an activity to be *both* risky and highly beneficial.[10] While the research in this area raises important questions about the nature of emotions and their relation to cognition,[11] it supports the more general point that 'people's reactions to risks are often based mostly on the harms caused by the potential outcome and the vividness of that outcome rather than on the probability of its occurrence'.[12]

B. The social amplification of risk

Not only do terrorist acts have a direct impact on the way individuals think about risk, the way that information about a terrorist attack is transmitted can amplify the perception or risk on a social level. The social amplification of risk refers to the 'social structures and processes of risk experience, the resulting repercussions on individual and group perceptions, and the effects of those responses on community, society and economy'.[13] The basic claim made by risk researchers is that an unfortunate event such as an accident, discovery of pollution, sabotage, or product tampering, interacts 'with psychological, social, and cultural processes in ways that can heighten or attenuate public perception of risk and related risk behaviour'.[14] In particular, the flow of information, particularly through the media, has an important effect on our perceptions of risk and is 'a major agent of amplification'.[15] Social amplification is thus said to be influenced by the '*volume* [of information], the degree to which the information is *disputed*, the extent of *dramatization* and the *symbolic connotations* of the information'.[16] Writing before 9/11, risk researchers used events such as the nuclear reactor accident at Chernobyl in 1986 to illustrate how the dramatization of the event, together with sensational media headlines, increased the 'memorability of that accident and the perceived catastrophic potential of nuclear power'.[17] These lessons are even more poignant after September 11.

Drawing on this research and other recent work on information cascades, Sunstein demonstrates very clearly the social origins of individual belief and the

---

[10] Slovic, *The Perception of Risk*, xxxi, and in the same volume, Melissa L. Finucane, 'The Affect Heuristic in Judgments of Risks and Benefits', 413–29.
[11] Cass Sunstein, 'The Laws of Fear' (2002) 115 *Harvard Law Review* 1119 at 1140.
[12] Ibid. at 1141.
[13] Roger E. Kasperson et al., 'The Social Amplification of Risk: A Conceptual Framework', in Slovic, *The Perception of Risk*, 232–45.
[14] Ibid. at 234.   [15] Kasperson, 'Social Amplification', at 241.
[16] Ibid.   [17] Ibid. at 242.

way in which individuals 'contribute to the intensity of the very forces by which they are influenced', particularly when individuals have little first-hand information. He uses the following stylized example to illustrate his point:

> Ann is unsure whether global warming is a serious problem, but Bob, whom Ann trusts, believes that it is. Influenced by Bob's views, Ann concluded that global warming is indeed a serious problem. Carl is inclined, on his own, to discount the risk; but confronted with informational signals given by the shared views of Ann and Bob, Carl might well come to believe that global warming is indeed a serious problem. Deborah, a skeptic about global warming, would need a great deal of confidence in the correctness of her view to reject the shared belief of Ann, Bob, and Carl. The members of this little community will come to share the belief that global warming is a matter of considerable concern.[18]

Sunstein concludes that most of us 'think and fear what we do because of what we think other people think and fear'.[19] He goes on to show that reputational influences might also contribute to the social amplification of risk. In the aftermath of 9/11, he argues, a safety expert may well choose to remain silent rather than pointing out, to the detriment of his or her reputation, that new security measures at airports, by making air travel less convenient, will force more people to drive, causing a net loss of lives.[20] What is clear from the literature on the social amplification of risk, however, is that the mistakes that ordinary people are prone to make in their judgments about risks can be compounded by a range of social influences which, in the case of terrorism, may well heighten the public perception of risk.

C. Ordinary judgments about risk

Does this mean that ordinary public judgments about risk are generally misguided? Some risk experts, notably Slovic, resist this conclusion, arguing that risk 'does not exist "out there," independent of our minds and cultures'[21] and that 'there is wisdom as well as error in public attitudes and perceptions' since the layperson's 'basic conceptualization of risk is much richer than that of the experts and reflects legitimate concerns that are typically omitted from expert risk assessments'.[22] Slovic therefore concludes that risk-management efforts should involve the public and that each side, the experts and the public, 'must respect the insights and intelligence of the other'.[23]

---

[18] Sunstein, 'The Laws of Fear', at 1132.
[19] Ibid. at 1132–3. It may be, then, that the misperception of risk is compounded in that not only do we tend to misperceive risk, but we misperceive what others perceive as risks. I am grateful to David Dyzenhaus for alerting me to this point.
[20] Ibid. at 1134.   [21] Slovic, *Perception of Risk*, at xxxvi.
[22] 'Perception of Risk' in Slovic, *Perception of Risk*, at 231.   [23] Ibid.

Sunstein challenges both of these claims. As far as the subjectivity of risk is concerned, he concedes that there is uncertainty and normativity in science and in the way that risks are presented, but argues that such uncertainty and normativity does not support Slovic's broader claim that there is no objective risk.[24] We all recognize the dangers of smoking, driving under the influence of alcohol, and crossing a busy road against the traffic lights, however difficult the corresponding risks might be to quantify.[25] More important for our purposes, though, is Sunstein's claim that ordinary people do not display a 'rival rationality' and that experts are, in their area of expertise, more likely to be right.[26]

Sunstein highlights two problems with Slovic's argument. First, he challenges the methodology of Slovic's empirical studies which purport to demonstrate that ordinary people have a richer rationality. He argues, for instance, that these studies do not disprove competing and equally plausible explanations of their judgments of risk and he challenges some of the qualitative factors (such as whether a risk involves 'dread'), purportedly used by ordinary people in making judgments about risk, which Sunstein says need conceptual unpacking.[27] Second, Sunstein concedes Slovic's general point, that qualitative factors (for example, whether children are at risk and the extent to which the activity is involuntary) are important in assessing risk. But his more general argument, largely confirmed by Slovic's own work, is that ordinary people tend to err on the basic factual question of how large a risk is.[28] The use of heuristics, the tendency disproportionately to fear unfamiliar risks, and the phenomenon of probability neglect all support this general conclusion.[29]

If we are apt to make mistakes in our judgments about risk in everyday life, then we are all the more likely to make mistakes about the risks associated with terrorism. This is not to say that there is no risk associated with terrorist acts, but only to underscore that in the aftermath of high-profile terrorist attacks, the public response and level of fear will generally be heightened and our perception of the risks associated with such events will be greatly distorted. A corollary point, which has become even clearer after Richard A. Clarke's testimony before the 9/11 commission, is that where a potential

---

[24] Sunstein, 'The Laws of Fear', at 1146–7.
[25] Sunstein argues that even Slovic would have to agree that there is a 'real risk' in smoking three packs of cigarettes a day over a period of years or a small risk of getting killed by a shark while swimming at the beach in Marblehead, Massachusetts, even if these risks cannot be quantified with precision (Sunstein, 'The Laws of Fear', at 1147). Sunstein's position here is not a metaphysical argument about the objectivity of risk, but his basic position is convincing. There are, as even Slovic admits, dangers and uncertainties in life, and, argues Sunstein, 'if dangers are real, so are the risks' (ibid.).
[26] Ibid. at 1147ff.   [27] Ibid. 1147–50, 1152–5.   [28] Ibid. at 1150.
[29] Ibid. at 1150ff and text accompanying note 3, above.

danger is well out of public view, both the public and their representatives in governments are not likely to take it as seriously.[30] This tendency on the part of the public to see high-profile events as greater risks and latent, low-profile dangers as minimal risks has profound implications for policy-making in a democracy.

D. Anti-terrorism law and policy in a democracy

If a high-profile event, such as a terrorist attack, is likely to lead to a heightened public fear of terrorism, then in a populist democracy, a high-profile attack will inevitably be followed by a spate of anti-terrorism laws,[31] hastily enacted.[32] This tendency to look to the law as the solution to distressing events is not unique to the terrorism context, and has been described by criminologists as 'govern[ing] through crime',[33] as politicians have an incentive to seek heavier penalties in the wake of horrific crimes.[34] The reaction of politicians to public emotion and fear exposes a deeper flaw in the workings of modern democracies because politicians can activate, as Philip Pettit puts it, 'a politics of passion in which they appear as the only individual or the only group really concerned about the sort of horrible crime in question' and can thus let loose 'a rule of knee-jerk emotional politics that works systematically against the common good'.[35]

Recognition of the dysfunctional nature of populist democracy is, of course, not new. Political and legal theorists have long recognized and attempted to address the dangers associated with the tyranny of the majority, while some contemporary proponents of deliberative democracy attempt to conceive of democracy 'as a system for empowering the public reasons recognized among a people, rather than the will of that people considered as a collective agent'.[36] These efforts have in common their rejection of popular sovereignty and *populism* as the essence of democracy. They attempt

---

[30] 'Excerpts of Testimony from Richard Clarke, Former National Coordinator for Counterterrorism' in Steven Strasser (ed.), *The 9/11 Investigations* (New York, Public Affairs, 2004), 174–6.

[31] On the anti-terrorism legislation enacted post-September 11, see generally 'Special Feature: Terrorism, Security and Rights: Anti-Terrorism Legislation in Singapore, Britain, Malaysia, South Africa, Canada, Australia, and the United States' (2002) *Singapore Journal of Legal Studies* 1–270.

[32] Philip A. Thomas, '9/11: USA and UK' (2003) 26 *Fordham International Law Journal* 1193.

[33] Roach, Chapter 7, in this volume, and his *September 11: Consequences for Canada* (Montreal and Kingston, McGill-Queen's University Press, 2003), at 24, referring to Jonathan Simon, 'Governing Through Crime' in L. Friedman and G. Fischer (eds.), *The Crime Conundrum* (New York, Westview Press, 1997), at 174.

[34] Philip Pettit, 'Depoliticizing Democracy' (2003) 7 *Associations: Journal for Legal and Social Theory* 23 at 26.

[35] Ibid.   [36] Ibid. at 32–3.

instead to develop a more substantive vision of democracy, which includes mechanisms from constitutional constraints to other sorts of institutional 'deliberation filters',[37] such as consultative procedures and arms-length bodies, to sift out policies that are inconsistent with more enduring public values.[38]

The literature on perception of risk and the public response to terrorist acts gives us yet another reason to be suspicious of a *populist* approach to policy-making in the anti-terrorism context. It suggests that lay persons are likely to overreact in the immediate aftermath of a terrorist attack and that the legislative branch, as the institutional embodiment of popular sovereignty, is ill-suited to take the lead in policy-making in response. Whatever attempts are made to refine democracy to get past these difficulties, they necessarily involve a radical departure from populism, a rejection of the view that fact of widespread public fear is sufficient justification for anti-terrorism laws, and a search for mechanisms to transform popular opinion into informed and fully considered judgments.[39]

While the literature on perception of risk, and particularly Sunstein's work in this area, is unsupportive of a populist response to acts of terrorism, it leaves open another possibility, namely that anti-terrorism policy ought to be made largely by technocrats with the requisite expertise. It suggests deference to those who have access to the relevant information and the expertise to interpret it. In short, it leaves open the view that there ought to be an increase in and deference to the executive in times of crisis.

III. National security and executive power

Conferral of greater power on the executive can take a number of forms. For instance, in many modern legal systems, vast amounts of power have been

---

[37] Ibid. at 33.

[38] Ibid. at 33, 35. See generally, David Estlund, 'Introduction' in David Estlund (ed.), *Democracy* (Malden, Blackwell, 2002), 1–28. The National Commission on Terrorist Attacks Upon the United States, as 'an independent, bipartisan commission created by congressional legislation and the signature of President ... chartered to prepare a full and complete account of the circumstances surrounding the 11 September 2001 terrorist attacks, including preparedness for and the immediate response to the attacks [and] mandated to provide recommendations designed to guard against future attacks' (http://www.9-11commission.gov/) might be one example of such an arms-length deliberative institution. See, National Commission on Terrorist Attacks Upon the United States, *The 9/11 Commission Report* (New York, Norton, 2004).

[39] I do not dispute that the right set of institutional mechanisms might yield legislative results that better reflect informed, considered judgments rather than misperception and fear; the point I defend later in this chapter, however, is that judicial review plays an important institutional role in this regard.

conferred on the executive through delegated legislation. In the particular context of anti-terrorism policy post-9/11, an increasing amount of power has been concentrated in the executive,[40] such as the power in Canada to designate groups as 'terrorist groups' for the purpose of criminal proceedings[41] and to detain and remove non-citizens 'on the basis of secret evidence not disclosed to the deportee'.[42] But perhaps the most controversial power is that of preventive detention, when this power is available without a formal trial or is not subject to full judicial review. Such is the case under internal security legislation in Singapore and Malaysia,[43] and initially under military tribunals established in the United States post-9/11.[44]

This section considers three typical arguments in support of increased executive power: the argument (implicit in Sunstein's work) that the executive is in a better position to assess the risks associated with terrorism; the argument, sometimes based on grounds of cultural particularism, that a government that has earned the trust of the people ought to be afforded more latitude; and the argument that extraordinary circumstances call for extraordinary powers, including, in some instances, the power to act extra-legally. It will be shown that these arguments are, at the very least, overstated, and to the extent that they do justify greater executive powers, such powers ought to be accompanied by corresponding checks and balances.

A. Arguments from executive expertise

Sunstein's work on risk perception and policy-making suggests a greater role for and deference to experts in policy-making. It can be argued that when it comes to threats to national security, the executive, with the advice of the

---

[40] The concentration of counter-terrorism powers in the executive is a common theme in this volume: see, for instance, Powell, Chapter 25 (expressing concerns about 'disproportionate executive power'), and Monar, Chapter 20 (arguing that the 'EU co-operation framework has clearly contributed to the strengthening of the role of the executive branches in the fight against terrorism').

[41] Section 83.01(1) of Canada's Criminal Code (RSC 1985, c. C-46). See generally Roach, *Consequences for Canada*, at 36–38.

[42] See Roach, Chapter 23, in this volume at 512, referring to Canada's Immigration and Refugee Protection Act, SC 2001 c. 27.

[43] Internal Security Act, (Cap 143, 1985 Rev Ed Sing); Internal Security Act 1960 (Act 82, Laws of Malaysia).

[44] See *Military Order on Detention, Treatment and Trial of Non-Citizens in the War Against Terrorism* (George W. Bush, November 13/01). Note, however, that the decision of the US Supreme Court in *Rasul* v. *Bush*, 124 S Ct 2686 (2004), may well have opened the door to greater judicial oversight of executive detentions by the United States at its naval base in Guantanamo Bay, Cuba, of foreign nationals captured during the US campaign against al Qaeda and the Taliban regime in Afghanistan.

security intelligence community and other security experts within the bureaucracy, is in a much better position to assess and respond to the risk of terrorism than the public, the legislature or the judiciary. When it comes to risk assessment, experts, particularly in their area of expertise, are more likely than ordinary people to be right.[45]

But experts are not immune from error and the nature of risk assessment is hardly an exact enterprise. When, as the aftermath of September 11 and the American-led invasion of Iraq demonstrate, expert evidence is interpreted by the executive through a political lens, it is hardly surprising that serious risk-assessment mistakes result.[46] We ought therefore to be sceptical of claims that executive expertise *per se* is enough to justify our automatic deference to the executive in matters of national security. This is all the more so given the problem of transparency. In the realm of national security, executive power is itself often shielded not only from full pubic scrutiny, but from judicial scrutiny as well.[47] And expert advice, particularly advice based on secret intelligence-gathering and which forms the basis of executive judgments about risk, is even less accessible to the public. But a significant possibility of abuse of power arises when the executive and its intelligence-gathering branches are able to operate absent some form of direct oversight of their authority.[48]

B. Arguments from trust

A second, related argument concerns the need for trust. In a complex modern society, much of the business of regulation needs to be done by a professional bureaucracy and effective governance requires that the

---

[45] See above note 26.

[46] Some recent examples include the failure of American forces in Iraq, well over a year after the invasion, to discover the weapons of mass destruction that provided the ostensible justification for the invasion (see generally, 'Ex-U.N. Inspector Has Harsh Words for Bush', *The New York Times* (16 March 2004), A3, on the charge by the former chief United Nations weapons inspector, Hans Blix, that 'the Bush administration convinced itself of the existence of banned weapons based on dubious findings before invading Iraq and was not interested in hearing evidence to the contrary'); the claim prior to the invasion made by British Prime Minister Tony Blair to the effect that Iraq had the power to deploy its weapons within 45 minutes (see Patrick E. Tyler, 'Threats and Responses: An Assessment: Britain's Case: Iraqi Program to Amass Arms Is "Up and Running" ' *The New York Times* (25 September 2002), A12; and the allegation by Richard A. Clarke that the Bush adminis-tration had failed to take heed of warnings by its own intelligence experts prior to September 11 that the threat of terrorism had to be taken seriously: above, note 30.

[47] See Young, Chapter 18, criticizing the lack of consultation and transparency in the process of drafting security laws in Hong Kong.

[48] Philip B. Heymann, *Terrorism, Freedom, and Security* (Cambridge, MIT Press, 2003), 152–6.

bureaucracy be trusted by the public and by the other branches of government.[49] While constitutional checks might theoretically be available, checks on the bureaucracy must also come from an internal ethic – the professionalism and integrity of those within it, and their respect for the rules that govern them. A bureaucracy that exhibits this sort of professionalism and integrity will command the trust of the public, making external checks less important.

The argument for trust in government can be pitched at a very general level, but a cultural particularist version of this argument has also been made in Singapore. It is argued, for instance, that the Confucian idea of government by 'honourable men' (*junzi*) plays an important role in public life, in contrast with the 'Western idea that a government should be given as limited powers as possible, and should always be treated with suspicion unless proved otherwise'.[50] But the public reaction to 9/11 suggests that trust in government might be as circumstantial as it is cultural. Trust in government in the United States rose markedly in the weeks and months after 11 September 2001, with double the number of people (at 64 per cent) saying they 'trusted the government to do what is right most of the time or virtually always' than in the spring of 2000.[51]

Whether the call for trust in government is circumstantial or cultural, the more general problem here is that even a once trustworthy government can subsequently (or secretly) abuse its power and when such a change occurs, laws authorizing greater flexibility and deference are no longer able to check the abuse. Indeed, despite its reliance on the idea of government by honourable men, the Singapore government has, in recognition of the possibility of some future abuse of governmental power, created additional institutional safeguards[52] to prevent abuse. Moreover, even in a trustworthy, thoroughly professional, and competent bureaucracy, experts responsible for making policy do make normative judgments (as noted earlier) and might even

---

[49] While the plurality of the US Supreme Court in *Hamdi* v. *Rumsfeld*, 124 S Ct 2633 (2004) did not insist on explicit Congressional authority for the detention of US citizens regarded by the government as 'enemy combatants', it nevertheless acknowledged the need for judicial oversight in national security cases to prevent abuse, arguing that 'crucial as the Government's interest may be in detaining those who actually pose an immediate threat to the national security of the United States during ongoing international conflict, history and common sense teach us that an unchecked system of detention carries the potential to become a means of oppression and abuse of others who do not present that sort of threat' (at 2647).

[50] White Paper on *Shared Values* (Singapore: 2 January 1991), Cmd. 1 of 1991 at para. 41.

[51] David S. Broder, 'The Trust Factor', *The Washington Post* (3 October 2001), A31.

[52] One example is the office of the 'Elected President' which has the power to safeguard, among others, the use of government reserves: see generally Kevin Tan and Lam Peng Er (eds.), *Managing Political Change in Singapore: The Elected Presidency* (New York, Routledge, 1997).

display an 'affiliation bias',[53] holding general views that are favourable to the industry or organization with which they are affiliated.

C. Arguments from extraordinary circumstances

But even if executive expertise should ordinarily be carefully circumscribed, it might be argued that in extraordinary circumstances greater deference to the executive and its professional bureaucracy is needed. The stakes may well be so high that ordinary rules simply do not apply; constitutional rights would have to yield to security concerns as the very survival of the state is at stake. One version of this argument, advanced by Oren Gross, is that in the immediate aftermath of an emergency, the executive will often act illegally or extra-constitutionally. In these circumstances, the conduct of the executive cannot properly be judged by ordinary constitutional standards, and ought instead to be subject to democratic ratification after the fact.[54] This argument is part of a sophisticated defence of extra-legal measures; Gross argues that by containing these measures to truly exceptional circumstances, and allowing after-the-fact democratic ratification, we can avoid diluting normal constitutional principles and uphold the rule of law. A full response to this argument is provided by David Dyzenhaus in this volume,[55] but suffice it to say that whatever the merits of Gross's proposal as a way of preserving the rule of law, the idea that through popular democratic ratification we could exonerate extra-constitutional government action[56] in emergency situations is deeply problematic. The problems arising from risk perception and trust suggest that the outcome of a ratification vote would turn largely on how closely after the event the vote takes place and how emotionally charged the atmosphere remains.

IV. Judical review and anti-terrorism policy

The argument thus far suggests that we need to be cautious about conferring excessive power over anti-terrorism policy-making to the legislative and

---

[53] Nancy Kraus et al., 'Intuitive Toxicology: Expert and Lay Judgments of Chemical Risks' in Slovic, *The Perception of Risk*, 285–315 at 311 (observing that 'toxicologists working for industry see chemicals as more benign than do their counterparts in academia and government').

[54] Oren Gross, 'Chaos and Rules: Should Responses to Violent Crises Always Be Constitutional?' (2003) 112 *Yale Law Journal* 1011, at 1111–15.

[55] Chapter 4.

[56] One difficulty with Gross's argument concerns the very idea of justifying extra-constitutional measures. If we accept Gross's argument, it is not entirely clear what we are saying about the legality of illegal government conduct that is subsequently ratified. If, as Gross seems to suggest, it then becomes legally unobjectionable, his theory might then be seen as an attempt to articulate *higher order* constitutional norms as to when a government, faced with an emergency, can depart from lower order or *prima facie* constitutional norms.

executive branches. The argument is not that these branches of government should be denied a say, only that they should not have the *final* say as to what sorts of anti-terrorism policies should be adopted. The dysfunctional nature of populist democracy is especially pronounced in a fearful and emotionally charged atmosphere in which judgments about risk are likely to be distorted, resulting in ill-conceived and hastily enacted laws that unnecessarily restrict individual freedom. And, of course, executive expertise in matters of national security remains fallible. Yet arguments persist in favour of insulating the executive from judicial review in times of crisis. In particular, it may be argued that the judiciary lacks the necessary institutional competence to provide a legitimate safeguard in matters of national security and, in any event, that national security cases involve sensitive intelligence information that cannot be disclosed.

A. *Objections to judicial review*

A common argument against judicial review is that the judiciary has less knowledge and expertise than the executive with respect to national security matters. The purported institutional incompetence of the courts figured prominently in the famous wartime preventive detention case of *Liversidge* v. *Anderson*, in which the House of Lords deferred to the subjective discretion of the Secretary of State on questions of national security.[57] According to Lord Wright: 'In my judgment, a court of law could not have before it the information on which the Secretary of State acts, still less the background of statecraft and national policy which is what must determine the action which he takes on it.'[58] A similar approach can be seen in Justice Thomas's dissent in *Hamdi* v. *Rumsfeld*, on the issue of whether the courts should have the power to review the executive's decision to detain without trial a suspected 'enemy combatant'. For Justice Thomas the 'question of whether Hamdi is an enemy combatant is "of a kind for which the Judiciary has neither aptitude, facilities nor responsibility"'.[59] This sort of hands-off approach defers both to the

---

[57] [1942] AC 206 (HL). See also Lord Romer at 281: 'There are (among others) acts prejudicial to the public safety or the defence of the realm committed in a time of grave national danger and of such a nature that "by reason thereof" it is necessary to exercise control over the person suspected of committing them. Whether or not the acts of some individual appear to be of this description is a question which the Secretary of State must plainly be a better judge of than any court of law.'

[58] Ibid. at 267.

[59] 124 S Ct 2633 (2004) at 2678, quoting *Chicago & Southern Air Lines* v. *Waterman S. S. Corp.*, 333 US 103 at 111. See also 2676: 'Congress, to be sure, has a substantial and essential role in both foreign affairs and national security. But it is crucial to recognize that judicial interference in these domains destroys the purpose of vesting primary responsibility [to protect the national security and to conduct the Nation's foreign relations] in a unitary Executive'.

executive's empirical assessment of the extent of the risk and to its determination of whether that risk is sufficiently grave as to deny ordinary due process and restrict individual freedom.

The second argument against judicial review is that there are legitimate concerns about the sensitivity of intelligence information, particularly in times of crisis. For instance, in *Liversidge*, Viscount Maugham stressed the importance of protecting confidential sources,[60] while Lord Romer expressed concerns about leakage to the enemy, even in the course of an *in camera* hearing.[61] Moreover, when it comes to intelligence-gathering activities, the willingness of an intelligence agency to provide information required by an oversight body that monitors its activities 'depends on providing a very high measure of assurance that a body whose independence the public can trust will not make secret information public in the course of receiving secret reports, calling hearings, and inquiring about complaints.'[62] Similar concerns arise as to the disclosure of secret information to the courts on judicial review. These are compelling arguments against judicial review, but they are not insurmountable, once we recognize the judiciary's institutionally unique and important area of competence and consider imaginative ways of designing our institutions[63] to address these concerns.

B. The unique role of judicial review

Even allowing that the executive has a special expertise in assessing the *magnitude* of the risk of terrorism because of its privileged access to intelligence information, it still has no special expertise in measuring the risk of terrorism against state incursions on fundamental, but intangible public values, such as liberty. It is important, then, to distinguish clearly between two sorts of questions – questions about the nature and extent of the risk, in which experts may well have a special expertise, and questions about what *ought* to be done given the magnitude of the risk, which involves a normative judgment in respect of which the executive, even with its security experts, holds no special expertise.[64] Clearly, our response to normative questions will influence our answer to quantitative questions about risk, and this would be so even for

---

[60] *Liversidge* at 241. See also David Dyzenhaus, 'Intimations of Legality Amid the Clash of Arms' (2004) *International Journal of Constitutional Law* 244 at 254.

[61] Liversidge, at 280.

[62] Heymann, *Terrorism, Freedom, and Security*, at 153.

[63] I borrow this turn of phrase from Dyzenhaus, Chapter 4, in this volume.

[64] The executive might well give insufficient weight to the rights or interests of minorities, for instance, and, as Davis suggests, enforce an anti-terrorism regime irrationally or arbitrarily by using it 'against some of the most vulnerable members of society such as members of racial or ethnic minorities' (Chapter 9, in this volume, at 197).

experts.[65] But to the extent that we could hold these two sorts of judgment apart, experts would be able to assist the executive only to determine the extent of the risk; their expertise would not extend to the more complex, normative questions.

In this respect, the judiciary holds a comparative advantage over the other branches. While judges might personally be susceptible to the same social phenomena that amplify the perception of risk, they remain in a unique institutional position to distinguish empirical questions about the extent of the risk from the normative questions that hang in the balance. The courts can provide a forum in which empirical evidence is presented and policies that interfere with individual freedoms are defended and justified; they serve as an institutional safeguard against policy-making motivated primarily by public fear. But crucially, judicial review allows for a careful and sober consideration of risks and responses in a forum in which limitations on liberty are given their due and where the effectiveness of anti-terrorism policies can be assessed against its impact on fundamental freedoms.

C. Specialized administrative tribunals and the role of the courts

But even if the courts are competent in relation to the complex normative questions that arise in national security cases, and have the ability to measure security concerns against normative values, they still do not have knowledge or expertise in relation to security intelligence. And the concern about the sensitive nature of intelligence information remains unaddressed. Dyzenhaus's proposal in this volume may be useful in helping to answer these concerns. He proposes a model of legality which maintains the rule of law within an institutionally flexible system. Modern common law, he explains, provides us with the tools to recognize the importance of specialized administrative tribunals within a legal order committed to the rule of law, allowing the courts to play a more detached, supervisory role. An institution such as the Special Immigration Appeals Commission,[66] he argues, can answer many of the objections to judicial review, including concerns about institutional competence and sensitive intelligence information.[67]

Curiously, a similar conclusion was reached in Singapore from a very different starting point. In the aftermath of *Chng Suan Tze*, which (until quickly reversed by legislative and constitutional amendment) asserted the power of judicial review over preventive detention under the Internal

---

[65] Slovic, 'Trust, Emotion, Sex, Politics and Science: Surveying the Risk-assessment Battlefield' in Slovic, *The Perception of Risk*, 399–412.

[66] On the powers of and problems with SIAC, see generally in this volume: Fenwick and Phillipson (Chapter 21); Harvey (Chapter 8).

[67] Dyzenhaus, 'Intimations of Legality', at 260.

Security Act,[68] Sin Boon Ann criticized the courts for not deferring sufficiently to the executive.[69] The arguments that he made are the now familiar
ones concerning, for instance, the expertise of the executive at intelligence
gathering and the need for executive discretion.[70] Yet despite his stinging
criticism of the judiciary, Sin comes to a similar conclusion to Dyzenhaus,
arguing that what is needed is an *independent* advisory board, 'empowered to
make political judgments',[71] which could take a 'more active role in making
inquiries like reserving the right to determine whether the Minister's decision
to withhold information on grounds of national security has any valid
basis'.[72]

Dyzenhaus is right to stress the importance of imaginative institutional
design. We should not be constrained by an overly formal understanding of
the separation of powers if this means that only the courts can check executive
power in an emergency. And Sin may well be right to stress that emergencies
require a unique set of executive powers and distinct legal response.
A specialized administrative tribunal could scrutinize executive actions in a
manner that takes into account the sensitivity of intelligence information
and, if carefully constituted, can respond to concerns about institutional
competence.

For a specialized administrative tribunal to protect sensitive intelligence
information and sources while preserving legality, it must be both independent and effective. It must be able to scrutinize the executive's arguments and
have the power, as needed, to reverse executive decisions. The independence
that is required here is both institutional and substantive. It is crucial that the
reviewing body is independent in the sense that it is institutionally separate
such that the usual standards of independence (such as security of tenure and
remuneration) are present. But it is also imperative that the institution also
have a distinct institutional culture. It must be able to view the matter through
a different lens, looking not only at the magnitude of the risk, but also the
values at stake, so as to counter-balance an executive institutional culture
dominated by a security imperative with its particular understanding of
risk.[73] Subject to these caveats, a specialized administrative tribunal may well
be able to scrutinize the factual and legal basis of executive decisions in
individual cases (e.g. in the context of preventive detention) in a manner that
preserves the confidentiality of intelligence sources, with the appropriate level
of expertise in security matters.

---

[68] See Hor, Chapter 13, in this volume.
[69] 'Judges and Administrative Discretion – A Look at *Chng Suan Tze* v. *Minister of Home Affairs*' [1989] 2 MLJ ci.
[70] Ibid. at ciii, cvi.   [71] Ibid. at cvii.   [72] Ibid.
[73] See discussion of 'affiliation bias' in Kraus, 'Intuitive Toxicology', at 311.

Be that as it may, the courts still have an important role to play. This can be seen by distinguishing two ways in which the courts or tribunals can provide a check on executive power. First, as we have just seen, a specialized administrative tribunal might scrutinize the factual and legal basis of executive decisions in individual cases, with access to the sensitive intelligence information on the basis of which those decisions are made. Here, a specialized administrative tribunal plays an important role in scrutinizing the exercise of executive power in an emergency. Second, the ordinary courts can nevertheless provide a public forum for contesting the broader policy decisions of both the legislative and executive branches in as much as they purport to be weighing rights against security considerations. Neither the legislature nor the executive has an institutional expertise in rights and the courts can play an important role here in compelling the government to be forthright about its assumptions about risk.

The opinions of Justice O'Connor and Justice Souter in *Hamdi* implicitly recognize the role that specialized administrative tribunals can play in checking executive power. For instance, neither judge was satisfied with a mere declaration by the executive that Hamdi was an enemy combatant who could therefore be detained without trial, and saw a need for some form of scrutiny of the decision to detain him:

> Often the executive will argue that 'security considerations' led to a government action and request that the court be satisfied with this argument. Such a request should not be granted. 'Security considerations' are not magic words. The court must insist on learning the specific security considerations that prompted the government's actions. The court must be persuaded that these considerations actually motivated the government's actions and were not merely pretextual. Finally, the court must be convinced that the security measures adopted were the available measures least damaging to human rights.[74]

A detainee must be given a fair opportunity to contest the factual basis for the detention before the courts. But as William C. Banks observes, 'the neutral decision maker prescribed by Justice O'Connor's plurality opinion . . . could be a military commission rather than a civilian court'.[75] There are, no doubt, reasons to be cautious here, but if it is designed carefully enough within an institutional culture already committed to principles of legality, a specialized administrative tribunal may well be able to address the need for independent 'judicial' scrutiny.

While opening the door to specialized administrative tribunals, *Hamdi* also signals an important role for the *courts* by insisting that they will scrutinize

---

[74] Aharon Barak, 'Forward: A Judge on Judging: The Role of a Supreme Court in a Democracy' (2002), 116 *Harvard Law Review* 16 at 157–8.
[75] Chapter 22, in this volume, at 506.

the use of preventive detention as a general policy. By assuming this role, the courts could well demand evidence both that measures damaging to constitutional rights will be effective in reducing the risk[76] and that any restriction on rights is proportionate to the risk. By insisting on learning as much of the factual basis for a particular policy as might be disclosed without compromising confidential sources (which would be easier where a general policy, rather than an individual instance of preventive detention, is in question), the courts can force a careful examination of the gravity of the risk and the effectiveness of the proposed countermeasures, as against the other values that might be sacrificed in the hope of preventing the risk from materializing.

On this approach, the executive would have to convince the court both that the measures in question, such as the authorized use of preventive detention, were a rational response to the security threat, and that alternative measures, less restrictive of individual freedom, were insufficient. The executive might be compelled to explain, for instance, why criminal proceedings are markedly less adequate than preventive detention in preventing acts of terrorism, particularly when some terrorist suspects (such as John Walker Lindh, an American captured in Afghanistan while fighting with the Taliban) are tried in the ordinary courts. Or it might be asked to explain why the extraordinary powers it claims are needed when considered in light of the wide range of policy options at its disposal.

D. Judicial review, democracy, and the limits of law

Critics of judicial review might still object to its anti-democratic nature. However, it is crucial to distinguish between populist conceptions of democracy and other more complex notions of democracy designed to ensure fair collective decision-making or, more ambitiously, to secure substantively just laws. Judicial review may well encroach on democratic populism, but its goal is to articulate and express the wishes of the people at the level of 'the most profound values of society in its progress through history', not at the level of 'passing vogues'.[77] There is, of course, an element of judicial paternalism here, but perhaps a 'softer' and more palatable kind of paternalism than a courts-know-best variety, one that seeks only to ensure that public decisions

---

[76] Banks argues in Chapter 22 of this volume that at least some of the successful terrorism-related prosecutions in the United States post-September 11 were due not, as claimed by President Bush, to the Patriot Act and expanded investigative powers, but rather to information obtained 'in the old-fashioned way – from an anonymous letter left at a local FBI office' (at 509).

[77] As Justice Barak of the Supreme Court of Israel puts it, 'the choice is not between the wishes of the people and the wishes of the judge. The choice is between two levels of the wishes of the people. The first, basic level reflects the most profound values of society in its progress through history; the second ad hoc level reflects passing vogues' ('A Judge on Judging', at 51).

are fully informed and considered.[78] In this way, judicial review (or even the *prospect* of judicial review)[79] can serve as a check on democratic law-making to ensure that in times of heightened emotion and widespread fear, a decision to limit individual liberty is not lightly taken. The courts might not always be able to prevent excessive responses to terrorist attacks, but their willingness to scrutinize new laws may stimulate public debate and provide civil society groups with the means to ask critical questions about anti-terrorism policies.[80] They might empower concerned citizens to ask more pointed questions about the extent of the risk and remind them of the sacrifices that they are being asked to make.

One final point is in order. It is tempting to turn to the law to solve our most pressing problems. This is a tendency that we must resist. The law should function in tandem with other measures – political, diplomatic, and otherwise – to address those problems that most concern us. But while the law might not be able to solve our problems, including the threat of terrorism, it might still play an important role in ensuring that our *legal* response to particular problems is an appropriate one. Of course, even in legal systems with a long-standing tradition of judicial review, the courts have often in times of emergency deferred to the executive on matters of national security. It takes a confident judiciary with a strong culture of judicial review to challenge the concentration of power and the implementation of reactive anti-terrorism policies. So it can hardly be expected that the courts in legal systems that do not have such an institutional culture would be in any position to take on the robust, supervisory role recommended in this chapter.[81] In the absence of judicial or even specialized administrative

---

[78] See Gerald Dworkin, 'Paternalism: Some Second Thoughts' in Rolf Sartorius (ed.), *Paternalism* (Minneapolis, University of Minnesota Press, 1983), 105–111 at 107, where he defines 'soft paternalism' as the view that '(1) paternalism is sometimes justified, and (2) it is a necessary condition for such justification that the person for whom we are acting paternalistically is in some way incompetent'.

[79] See Barak, 'A Judge on Judging', at 159: The impact of the court's willingness to engage in judicial review should be measured 'not merely in the few cases brought before it, but also in the many potential cases not brought before it, since governmental authorities are aware of the court's rulings and act accordingly'.

[80] Roach, *Consequences for Canada*, at 202.

[81] On this front, I am less optimistic than Dyzenhaus (see Chapter 4, note 67) about our ability to shape perceptions of agency *simply* through the design of institutions. Having the 'right' legal framework alone does not guarantee a robust approach to judicial review. An institutional culture supportive of notions of legality and the rule of law may depend on a host of other factors including the educational background of the judges, their social status and influence, and their relationship to the political elite. So even if Dyzenhaus is right that respect for the rule of law plays an increasingly important role even in 'well-ordered societies', it may well be that the number of societies that have the deep institutional capacity to respect and enforce the rule of law is fewer than we might think. There is enough evidence in this volume alone of societies past and present whose legal institutions are weak to suggest that the law is not enough.

review, other institutions, such as civil society groups, academics, and independent experts, would have to step in to play a supervisory role. Without the firm backing of the courts, however, they would find it all the more difficult to encourage public deliberation and influence policy.

V. Conclusion

At a time when anti-terrorism policy is high on the public agenda, the literature on perception of risk serves as an important reminder that the fear inspired by terrorism might far exceed the danger it poses, especially relative to the dangers we face in everyday life. In our efforts to be vigilant, we must keep the threat of terrorism in perspective. When we step into a car or board a plane, when we buy our next meal or take medication, we live with and manage these risks. Likewise, the risks of terrorist acts need to be managed, and a level of tolerable risk must be set. The real challenge is not to eliminate the risk, but to manage and learn to live with it, confident that what might reasonably be done (and no more) is being done. We do need to be conscious of the limits of the law. But the courts can still provide an important institutional role in times of anxiety and fear to ensure that a dispassionate assessment of risk takes place and that the response to the threat of terrorism is a measured one.

PART TWO

A Comparative Study of Anti-Terrorism Measures

7

The criminal law and terrorism

KENT ROACH

Many societies instinctively and quickly reach for the criminal law as a response to terrorism. The criminal law has frequently been expanded as a direct response to acts of terrorism. In the first part of this chapter, I will provide an overview of how new criminal laws have often been produced in response to terrorism and relate this to narrative, memorial, and communicative uses of the criminal law and increased concern about the rights of victims and potential victims of crime. New anti-terrorism laws, however, are not solely based on a symbolic focus on state punishment and denunciation. They also incorporate a more modern approach that sees crime as one of the many risks of modern society. The risk of crime can only be managed by enlisting non-state actors in the crime control enterprise.

In the second part of the chapter, I will examine some of the dangers of the criminal law solution to terrorism from both instrumental and normative dimensions. The enactment of new criminal laws after acts of terrorism implies that the existing criminal law was inadequate to respond to acts of terrorism. The accuracy of such a claim, however, depends on the baseline established by the ordinary criminal law in each particular jurisdiction. In many jurisdictions, ordinary crimes with respect to attempts, conspiracy and accomplice liability for crimes such as murder and bombings could already be applied to terrorists should they be apprehended by police and intelligence officials. In such countries, criminal law reform after acts of terrorism may falsely suggest that the criminal law, as opposed to its enforcement, was to blame for the failure to stop the terrorism. Another danger is that repressive criminal laws may backfire by provoking successful due process challenges and/or widespread resentment of the law. A normative danger is the distorting influence that strong anti-terrorism laws may have on the criminal law. The incursions on criminal law principles may intensify should new criminal laws fail to stop terrorism and should other serious crimes command the same public concern as terrorism. Broad definitions of terrorism, as well as

I thank William Banks, David Dyzenhaus, Trish McMahon and Victor V. Ramraj for helpful comments on an earlier draft.

claims that tough new anti-terrorism laws are consistent with rights protection instruments, may also encourage the spread of incursions on criminal law principles beyond the terrorism context. Perhaps the ultimate corruption of the criminal law are wrongful convictions such as occurred in terrorism cases in the United Kingdom in the 1970s.

Although it is relatively easy to be critical and even cynical about reliance on criminal law as a response to terrorism, the virtues of the criminal law should not be ignored. They emerge when comparisons are made to a sometimes lawless and no-holds barred war that has, at times, been waged against terrorism. Although principles of individual responsibility, legality and due process have been stretched by many new anti-terrorism laws, these principles have also exercised an important restraining influence. In the third part of this paper, I will examine some of the restraints of the criminal law as compared to the use of war, assassination, extraordinary rendition, torture, preventive detention and immigration law. These less restrained responses are inspired by the idea that many societies cannot afford to rely on the legalities of the criminal law and its costly and public emphasis on establishing individual fault in order to incapacitate or deter suspected terrorists. The less restrained alternatives to the criminal law relate to what Oren Gross has argued is an extra-legal approach to terrorism[1] and to what Lord Steyn has called a 'black hole' approach that abandons the restraint of legality altogether.[2] Although such approaches may avoid corrupting the criminal law with attempts to accommodate the threat of terrorism, they also bring anti-terrorism policies uncomfortably close to the techniques used by terrorists. As Laura Donohue suggests in her contribution to this volume, the imposition of violence and fear without regard to guilt or innocence and in order to impress a larger audience are key features of terrorism and, regrettably, of some anti-terrorism measures.[3]

In the final part, I will begin the task of situating the criminal law in a more comprehensive and multi-faceted anti-terrorism strategy. As in the second part of this paper, there will be both instrumental and normative dimensions to my argument. Normatively, I share the uneasiness expressed by David Dyzenhaus in this volume about the less restrained and extra-legal approaches that have been used in the war against terrorism.[4] The criminal law with its emphasis on the presumption of innocence, no detention without charges being laid, proof of guilt beyond a reasonable doubt, and the right to full answer and defence is the repository of many values associated with the

---

[1] Oren Gross 'Chaos and Rules: Should Responses to Violent Crises Always Be Constitutional' (2003) 112 *Yale Law Journal* 1011.
[2] Johan Steyn, 'Guantanamo Bay: The Legal Black Hole' (2004) 53 *International and Comparative Law Quarterly*, 1.
[3] Donohue, Chapter 2, in this volume.   [4] Dyzenhaus, Chapter 4, in this volume.

rule of law. At the same time, however, a rule of law approach, especially one based on the criminal law, leaves one open to criticisms of being naïve about the threat of terrorism since 9/11. The answer in my view is to construct a comprehensive anti-terrorism policy that employs much more than the criminal law. Drawing on work in the fields of public health, technology and crime prevention, I will suggest that administrative and private sector strategies can play an important role in making it more difficult for terrorists to have access to sites and substances vulnerable to terrorism and can take steps to limit the harms of terrorism. There may also be a role for harder strategies including incapacitation of terrorists and perhaps even war. At the same time, escalating force against terrorism should be matched with corresponding systems of legality. If war must be employed, it should be war that respects the law of war. This is necessary to preserve the vital distinction between terrorism and anti-terrorism efforts and to avoid the moral danger of legal black holes in which no rules apply.

I. New criminal laws against terrorism

There is a long history of new criminal laws being enacted as a direct response to horrific acts of terrorism. For example, new criminal laws were enacted in the United Kingdom as a response to the IRA bombings in Birmingham in 1974 and in Omagh in 1998.[5] In the United States, new terrorism offences were created in reaction to the murder of Leon Klinghoffer upon the *Achille Lauro* when it was hijacked by the PLO in 1985 and in response to the bombing of the World Trade Centre in 1993 and the Oklahoma City bombing in 1995.[6] One danger of reactive legislation is that there may often be inadequate time for debate either in the legislature or in civil society about the proposed measures. For example, there was only seventeen hours of legislative debate before the draconian Prevention of Terrorism (Temporary Provisions) Act 1974 was enacted after the Birmingham bombings killed 21 and injured another 180 people. The dangers to civil liberties and general principles of criminal law and legality may be particularly great when new anti-terrorism laws are enacted as a direct and immediate response to terrible acts of terrorism.[7]

---

[5] Philip Thomas, 'Emergency Terrorist Legislation' (1998) *Journal of Civil Liberties* 240; Philip Thomas, 'September 11 and Good Governance' (2002) 53 *Northern Ireland Law Quarterly* 366.

[6] Laurie McQuade, 'Tragedy as a Catalyst for Reform: The American Way?' (1996) 11 *Connecticut Journal of International Law* 325.

[7] Note, however, that even anti-terrorist legislation that is not enacted as a quick response to terrorism and in a state of crisis or emergency may still threaten such values. See for example the United Kingdom's Terrorism Act 2000 examined in Fenwick and Phillipson, Chapter 21, in this volume.

Reactive law reform that occurs quickly after acts of terrorism often proceeds without a full understanding of why the terrorists succeeded. In the absence of such an understanding, it is often tempting to conclude that new offences and new investigative powers could prevent terrorism. There may also be a tendency to 'fight the last war' by focusing on the means used by the successful terrorists or even a particular terrorist organization. Reactive law reform in response to terrorism may not only threaten legal principles and civil liberties, but also produce high profile laws that fail to use all the policy instruments that can be used against terrorism.

Governments often experience pressure to enact new criminal laws after well publicized and shocking crimes. In North America this has led to a new memorial style of law-making where new laws are at times named after prominent victims of crime and crafted in response to the powerful narratives of horrific crimes. New criminal laws have become something of the ultimate tribute to crime victims. As David Garland has observed 'the new political imperative is that victims must be protected, their voices must be heard, their memory honoured, their anger expressed, their fears addressed'. This leads to the enactment of new criminal laws as 'retaliatory measures' designed to be cathartic denunciations of crime and 'to respond with immediate effect to public outrage'.[8] The attempt to mould laws to particular crimes places considerable strain on general and rational principles of criminal law. The nature of terrorism as a crime that targets innocent people and is designed to maximize fear in the general populace makes it particularly likely to produce reactive and emotional criminal law reform.

Reactive anti-terrorism laws fit into a pattern that Jonathan Simon has coined 'governing through crime'. Writing in the American context, Simon observed that even as crime rates decrease, media and governments have been drawn to 'crime as the preferred metaphor for all forms of social anxiety and highlighted acts of punishment or retribution as the primary way of resolving disputes of almost any kind'.[9] I have suggested elsewhere that the focus on crime has led to a 'criminalization of politics' in which criminal law reform has been offered as a symbolic and relatively cheap response to a broad range of social, economic and cultural problems.[10]

The new emphasis on the criminal sanction and retributive punishment is also tied to a sense that 'nothing works' except perhaps punishment. There is an impatience with strategies that address the broader causes and

---

[8] David Garland, *The Culture of Control: Crime and Social Order in Contemporary Society* (University of Chicago Press, 2001), at 11, 133–4.
[9] Jonathan Simon, 'Governing through Crime' in L. M. Friedman and G. Fisher (eds.), *The Crime Conundrum: Essays on Criminal Justice* (New York, Westview Press, 1997), at 173.
[10] Kent Roach, *Due Process and Victims' Rights* (University of Toronto Press, 1999), at 312–13.

determinants of crimes or that compare the harms of crime with other threats to human security such as disease and poverty. This process also fits into a retrenchment from the welfare state and increasing privatization of many services. In such an environment, criminal law becomes an even more important focus of formal state activity. It becomes the primary means for the neo-liberal state to be seen as doing something about social problems and to communicate society's disapproval of crime and its solidarity with victims.

The tendencies to use criminal law as a means both to govern and to control risks are magnified in the terrorism context. Terrorism is designed to cause maximum fear and damage to innocent victims. This is turn creates enormous pressures on governments to act. Despite having enacted a comprehensive and quite severe anti-terrorism law the year before 9/11, the United Kingdom joined countries throughout the world in enacting another new anti-terrorism law shortly after 9/11. The government entered into a formal derogation of rights under the European Convention demonstrating what Garland observed before September 11 was a decreasing concern about 'the risk of unconstrained state authorities, of arbitrary power and the violation of civil liberties' by a public that was 'decidedly risk-averse' and in 'a perpetual sense of crisis' on issues of crime.[11]

The worldwide expansion of anti-terrorism laws in the wake of September 11 was facilitated by Resolution 1373 of the United Nations Security Council which required all states to ensure that terrorist acts, including the financing of terrorism, 'are established as serious criminal offences in domestic laws and regulations and that the punishment duly reflects the seriousness of such terrorist acts'.[12] The bulk of this resolution enacted under mandatory provisions in the United Nations Charter contemplated criminalization and punishment as the primary response to terrorism.[13] It facilitated the pattern of reactive law reform by calling for countries to report back to the Counter-Terrorism Committee within ninety days on the steps taken to comply with the resolution. Some countries took this as a virtual deadline for enacting new anti-terrorism laws. Domestic criminal law reform can be shaped by international standards and bodies.

Blanket media coverage of 9/11 increased a sense of fear and anxiety that demanded both punitive measures by the state and self-protective measures by individuals. The quickest response came from the United States. The Patriot Act was introduced into Congress on 23 October 2001. It was approved by the

---

[11] Garland, *The Culture of Control*, at 12, 19.
[12] UN Security Council Resolution 1373. See Kim Lane Scheppele, 'Other People's Patriot Acts' (2004) 50 *Loyola Law Review* 89 at 91–3.
[13] The resolution placed great stress on criminalizing the financing of terrorism and also contemplated cooperative exchanges of information and immigration law reforms as secondary responses to terrorism.

House of Representatives by a vote of 357–66 and by the Senate in a 98-1 vote. It was signed into law by President Bush on 26 October 2001.[14] The Patriot Act responded to the United Nations Resolution to 'deny safe haven to those who finance, plan, support or commit terrorist attacks, or provide safe havens' with a new criminal offence that punished with up to ten years' imprisonment 'whoever harbors or conceals any person who he knows, or has reasonable grounds to believe, has committed or is about to commit' a long list of offences associated with terrorism. The crime of providing material support for terrorism, which was first created in 1996 in the wake of the first World Trade Centre and Oklahoma City bombings, was broadened to include the provision of monetary instruments and 'expert advice and assistance' to terrorists groups. The maximum penalty for this offence was increased from ten to fifteen years with the possibility of life imprisonment if death results.[15] These parts of the Patriot Act demonstrate a faith that broadening and toughening the criminal law will help stop terrorism.

The phenomenon of enacting new criminal laws as a response to acts of terrorism was not limited to the West. A new anti-terrorism law was proposed in Indonesia shortly after September 11, but met significant resistance in civil society. After the Bali bombings killed over 200 people on 12 October 2002, however, a new anti-terrorism regulation was enacted as an emergency measure on 18 October 2002. Unlike the Patriot Act, the new law was made effective with retroactive force. The 2004 bombing of the Australian embassy in Jakarta has started another round of proposed amendments to toughen the law raising concerns about human rights.[16] Another act of terrorism in the United States would have produced a similar momentum to enact a Patriot Act II. Indonesia, like the United States, employs the death penalty for the most serious acts of terrorism subject to the qualification that it would not be imposed on those who committed their crimes as juveniles. Both countries turned to instant criminal law reform in the wake of terrible terrorist attacks and relied on broader and tougher offences to prevent acts of terrorism. In both countries there was pressure on the government to be seen to be doing something about terrorism. Tough new anti-terrorism laws were enacted to denounce acts of terrorism, express solidarity with the victims and attempt to deter future acts of terrorism.

New anti-terrorism laws fit into a process of the state governing through the enactment of new criminal laws and by increasing terms of punishment. At the same time, however, the new anti-terrorism laws also incorporate a newer less state-centred approach to crime that is designed to encourage

[14] John Whitehead and Steven Aden, 'Forfeiting "Enduring Freedom" for "Homeland Security"' (2002) 51 *American University Law Review* 1081 at 1087, note 26.
[15] Patriot Act ss. 803, 805 and 810.
[16] See Hikmahanto Juwana, Chapter 14, in this volume.

corporate and private actors to take responsibility for crime. New laws against the financing of terrorism combine punitiveness on behalf of the state with newer security strategies that require individuals to play their own role in the fight against crime. Much of UN Resolution 1373 was devoted to having states enact laws aimed at those who provide terrorists with financial and others forms of support, consistent with the most recent international convention against terrorism: the 1999 Convention for the Suppression of the Financing of Terrorism. The objects of such financing laws are not so much terrorists or even their ideological supporters but third parties such as bankers and landlords.[17] Duties were placed on financial institutions and others to report dealings to the authorities. These new laws represented both an expansion of the traditional scope of anti-terrorism laws and the impact of security strategies that relied less on state imposition of punishment and more on risk management strategies throughout society.

Although they were featured in Resolution 1373 and many new anti-terrorism laws, there are also reasons to doubt the effectiveness of laws against the financing of terrorism. The 9/11 Commission stated that 'trying to starve the terrorists of money is like trying to catch one fish by draining the ocean'. It expressed doubts that the financing laws can be a 'primary weapon' against decentralized terrorist groups that can fund destructive missions such as 9/11 at a cost of about half a million.[18]

Even in the area of national security, privatization has occurred alongside the emergence of the punitive state that governs through crime. As Ulrich Beck has argued, the ability to assess the multiple risks of modern society has outstripped the ability to control such risks.[19] September 11 reaffirmed a sense that the state's experts, this time in the field of intelligence and policing, had once again failed. Part of the response has been to download some of the tasks of anti-terrorism enforcement on private actors. Patrons on the London subway are asked to be on the lookout for suspicious and abandoned packages. The Mounties in Canada have established a 24-hour toll free national security hotline asking for tips on suspicious people. Private companies that manage data volunteer or are asked by governments to provide information about high risk people. The United States has introduced a national system of colour coded risk assessments that attempt to assess risk and place both state and non-state actors on higher levels of alert. Although the state has got tougher on terrorism since 9/11, it does not have a monopoly on anti-terrorism efforts.

---

[17] See Davis, Chapter 9, in this volume.
[18] *The 9/11 Commission Report* (New York, Norton, 2004), at 12.3.
[19] Ulrich Beck, *Risk Society: Towards a New Modernity* (London, Sage Publications, 1992).

II. Instrumental and normative limits of the criminal law

The instrumental value of new criminal laws in preventing terrorism can only be determined by a careful examination of the criminal law as it existed before it was expanded in response to a successful act of terrorism. In many countries, laws against being an accessory to murder or conspiring to commit murder already existed. People alleged to have been involved in the 9/11 plot have been prosecuted under existing criminal laws in both Germany and the United States. 9/11 was much more a failure of law enforcement and intelligence coordination than a failure of the criminal law. At the same time, this does not mean that new investigative powers and more broadly defined crimes could not have some utility in terrorist investigations. My point is that the utility of such new laws is a marginal one and one that can be exaggerated by ignoring the existing laws that could apply against terrorists.

The value of formal criminal law reform in some societies cannot be discounted. The Indonesian Penal Code for example does not have a general conspiracy offence and it defines attempted crimes restrictively to require the accused to have commenced performance of the crime and that the performance was 'not completed only because of circumstances independent of the [accused's] will'.[20] In such a context, new criminal laws applying to various forms of preparation and financing of terrorism may have a significant instrumental value in the apprehension of terrorists before they strike. As the Indonesian experience of subsequent bombings demonstrates, however, formal law reform is not enough. Police, prosecutors and courts must have sufficient capabilities to investigate apprehended acts of terrorism.

In July 2004 the Indonesian Constitutional Court held in a 5:4 decision that the law making the new terrorism law retroactive to the Bali bombings violated the prohibition against retroactive punishment in the 1999 Constitution, but it was not clear whether its decision would overturn convictions already rendered under the retroactive law, including three death sentences.[21] The effectiveness of tough new anti-terrorism laws in general may be diluted by successful due process challenges. If controversial anti-terrorism laws are perceived as unjust or illegitimate by large segments of the

---

[20] Indonesian Penal Code Article 53.
[21] The majority of the Court stated that 'The non-retroactive principle is strict. Otherwise, it would open the door for certain regimes to use the laws as a tool to take revenge against political opponents. There must be no chance for it to happen' while the minority used precedents such as the Nuremberg trials to uphold the retroactive law. Various commentators indicated that the court's decision did not annul previous verdicts but meant that the regular penal code would have to be applied to subsequent prosecutions arising from the Bali bombings. 'Terror law "against constitution"' *Jakarta Post* 24 July 2004; 'Justice perturbed' *The Economist* 31 July 2004.

population, the ordinary criminal law may also be more effective in denoun-cing acts of terrorism. Reasonable people should agree that murder is murder while reasonable people can disagree about definitions of terrorism. In Indonesia, the Bali bombers could likely have been charged under the existing law relating to murder and explosives. This would have minimized the dangers of convictions being overturned on appeal because of the use of a retroactive criminal law.[22] Even in international criminal law, there might be some advantage to prosecuting catastrophic acts of terrorism such as 9/11 as crimes against humanity rather than trying to define and add crimes of terrorism to the jurisdiction of the International Criminal Court.

The danger that controversial anti-terrorism laws may undermine some of the denunciatory and communicative value of criminal law is particularly high in the many countries that have followed the British example of requir-ing proof of a political, religious or ideological cause as an essential element of new crimes of terrorism. Although designed to differentiate terrorism from ordinary crime, such an approach will require prosecutors to prove religious or political motivations for the crime. This could lend some support to claims that accused persons are being prosecuted because of their politics or religion. The new Indonesian anti-terrorism law is sensitive to this danger as it provides that terrorism should not be considered a political crime and that it does not discriminate against any particular religion.[23]

New criminal laws against terrorism often feature enhanced penalties for acts defined as terrorism. Although higher and harsher penalties may serve communicative and symbolic purposes in denouncing terrorism, their value in deterring terrorism is likely to be very marginal. A person planning a serious act of terrorism already faces relatively high maximum penalties. The marginal deterrent value of a new criminal law depends not only on the severity of punishment, but its certainty and celerity. Terrorists, especially international terrorists, may also be unfamiliar with the relevant penalties in the jurisdiction in which they plan to commit their crime and they may be prepared to die for their cause. Third parties who may provide assistance to terrorists may, however, be more amenable than suicide bombers to deterrence.

There are normative dangers when the criminal law is ratcheted up after acts of terrorism in an attempt to deter acts of terrorism. Some criminal laws may challenge basic principles of criminal law such as the requirement for a clear illegal act that is committed with fault. As in the United Kingdom, membership in a terrorist organization may be criminalized. Various forms of association or parti-cipation in a terrorist group may also be punished. The possession of instruments or documents that could be used for terrorism may also be punished. Terrorism

---

[22] Ross Clarke, 'Retrospectivity and the Constitutional Validity of the Bali Bombing and East Timor Trials' (2003) 5 *Asian Law* 128.
[23] Indonesian Anti-Terrorism Law arts. 2 and 5.

may be defined broadly to include much more than violence against civilians. Many new laws against terrorism apply to the disruption of essential public and private services including electronic systems and not all of them make adequate allowance for political protests or stoppages of work.

Alan Dershowitz has suggested that terrorists may be amenable to deterrence because of the calculated and political nature of terrorism. Even assuming the empirical accuracy of Professor Dershowitz's claim, the deterrence strategies that he proposes depend in part on collective punishment, something that he admits is 'the most immoral technique for combating terrorism'.[24] The idea of collective punishment is implicit in Dershowitz's argument that the political cause of the terrorists should be punished for acts of terrorism because 'the cause hopes and expects to benefit collectively from terrorism'.[25] The problem is that 'causes' do not commit acts of terrorism, individuals do. From the perspective of the criminal law, the punishment of the cause imposes punishment on the innocent. Although at times he seems aware of the injustice of collective punishment, Professor Dershowitz concludes that 'any effective attack calculated to reduce terrorism – especially suicide bombers – must include an element of collective responsibility and punishment for those supporting terrorism'.[26] This departs from the fundamental focus on individual responsibility under the criminal law and the idea 'that punishing the mentally innocent with a view to advancing particular objectives is fundamentally unfair. It is to use the innocent as a means to an end'.[27] Although the notion of collective guilt can influence public discourse, it is alien to legal discourse.[28]

Laws against the financing of terrorism are not aimed at terrorists or even those who may sympathize with their cause, but business people who are required, on pain of criminal conviction, to use their own resources to ensure that they are not assisting terrorists. Such systems are also encouraged by lists distributed by international, regional and domestic agencies of people who are designated as terrorists, lists that are often incorporated in the domestic law of many nations. Those listed are not generally given an opportunity to make submissions before they are listed and the provisions for removing those mistakenly added to the list may be slow and not repair the damage of being officially listed as a terrorist. The International Bar Association has criticized the UN for not providing 'for any judicial review or right of appeal to an individual or entity whose assets are incorrectly frozen'.[29] There is also a

---

[24] Alan Dershowitz, *Why Terrorism Works* (New Haven, Yale University Press, 2002), at 117.
[25] Ibid. at 174.   [26] Ibid. at 181.
[27] *R. v. Hess* [1990] 2 S. C. R. 906 at 923–4 per Wilson J.
[28] George Fletcher, *Romantics at War* (Princeton University Press, 2002).
[29] International Bar Association, *International Terrorism: Legal Challenges and Responses* (Ardsley Park, Transnational Publishers, 2003), at 126.

danger that executive listing mechanisms will spread into domestic criminal law and undermine the role of the judiciary in determining who is a terrorist.[30] Another danger is that the new laws may encourage third parties to err on the side of caution by not dealing with those that they suspect may be involved in terrorism. If this occurs, the process of punishment will have been contracted out by the state to financial institutions. The sanction will be applied not after a court has found the accused guilty beyond a reasonable doubt or even the executive has made a listing decision, but rather when a private institution decides it does not want to run the risk of association with a terrorist and possible prosecution. The sanction imposed by such third parties will not, of course, be imprisonment, but it could amount to a form of civil death in which the suspect is denied access to a wide range of essential services including banking and shelter. Although this process may not meet all definitions of state-imposed punishment, it will be one in which people suffer harm and stigma because of suspicions that they are terrorists.

There are normative dangers of distorting criminal law principles in order to facilitate the apprehension of terrorists. One danger is that extraordinary powers may be introduced and justified in the anti-terrorism context but then spread to other parts of the criminal law. Incursions on the right to silence were first made in the United Kingdom in anti-terrorism law but have now spread throughout the entire law.[31] The United States Department of Justice has proudly boasted that parts of the Patriot Act have been used against those charged with child pornography and other crimes that have nothing to do with terrorism.[32] Broad definitions of terrorism and claims that new anti-terrorism regimes are consistent with rights protection instruments may facilitate the spread of anti-terrorism law to other parts of the criminal law. In any event, anti-terrorism measures will be intensified should they not be successful in stopping other acts of terrorism. One of the reasons why a widely rumoured Patriot Act II has not yet been introduced in the United States is the fortunate absence of other acts of terrorism on American soil since 9/11. As the experience of the first part of this chapter suggests, anti-terrorism law will expand and build on its own failures.

Another danger is that changes to criminal law principles will produce a greater risk of miscarriages of justice. In the United Kingdom, a series of wrongful convictions occurred with respect to IRA bombings. Suspects were

---

[30] In Pakistan a new anti-terrorism law allows either groups or individuals to be listed as terrorists and allows for the arrest of terrorist suspects on this basis. See ibid. at 45.
[31] Oren Gross, 'Cutting Down Trees: Law-Making Under the Shadow of Great Calamities' in Ronald J. Daniels, Patrick Macklem and Kent Roach (eds.), *The Security of Freedom: Essays on Canada's Anti-Terrorism Bill* (Toronto, University of Toronto Press, 2001).
[32] United States Department of Justice, *Report From the Field: The USA Patriot Act at Work* (July 2004), at 19.

identified in part because of their nationality and political sympathies. They were mistreated in custody and did not have adequate disclosure of evidence, including dubious forensic evidence, used against them. Although there is always a risk of wrongful convictions even under the ordinary criminal law, some features of new anti-terrorism laws produce even greater risks of wrongful convictions. Some anti-terrorism laws allow restrictions on the disclosure of relevant evidence to the accused in an attempt to protect intelligence sources and other national security information. Some terrorism offences are defined in such a broad manner that they resemble both status offences and guilt by association. Other offences neglect principles of subjective fault and the presumption of innocence. Extreme interrogation techniques may increase the risk of false confessions and false intelligence.[33]

Although new criminal laws against terrorism may increase the risk of wrongful convictions, a possible safeguard is the role of the judiciary in applying such laws. Most countries have not derogated from rights protection instruments and this allows the accused to argue to the independent judiciary that aspects of the new laws violate rights. In the United States, parts of the new offence of providing material support for terrorism have been held to be unconstitutional because of the vagueness of some of the terms used. In the United Kingdom, reverse onuses imposed on the accused have been changed to evidential burdens in recognition of the accused's right to a fair trial. At the same time, judges are not entirely immune from the pressures that are placing increased emphasis on security. They may be willing to accept arguments that anti-terrorism laws are justified in part by reference to the rights of victims and potential victims and they may decide that it is a mistake to evaluate these laws only through the traditional due process optic of the balance of power between the individual accused and the state.[34] Ronald Dworkin has eloquently warned of the dangers of concluding that 'the requirements of fairness are fully satisfied, in the case of suspected terrorists, by laxer standards of criminal justice which run an increased risk of convicting innocent people'.[35] It is important that criminal law does not lose sight of its foundational principles such as the presumption of innocence and the necessity of proof of individual fault beyond a reasonable doubt. These demanding standards, however, create another risk, namely that states will find the crime model, despite its political and moral appeal, to be too weak for fighting a war against terrorism.[36] When

[33] Kent Roach and Gary Trotter, 'Miscarriages of Justice in the War Against Terror' (2005) 109 *Pennsylvania State Law Review* 967.
[34] Irwin Cotler, 'Terrorism, Security and Rights: The Dilemma of Democracies' (2002) 14 *National Journal of Constitutional Law* 13.
[35] Ronald Dworkin 'The Threat to Patriotism' *New York Review of Books* 28 Feb. 2002.
[36] For arguments that the crime model is not sufficient to deal with terrorism and new rules are required see Bruce Ackerman, 'The Emergency Constitution' (2004) 113 *Yale Law Journal* 1029. For arguments against Professor's Ackerman's proposed regime including

the state goes beyond the criminal law, however, the restraining rules become much less clear and demanding. Indeed, at times, there appears to be no rules at all.

III. Less restrained alternatives to the criminal law

Although there are many instrumental and normative dangers in reliance on the criminal law as a means to combat terrorism, the focus on individual responsibility and deserved punishment in the criminal law has many virtues, especially when compared to some of the other techniques that have been used against terrorism. Since September 11, many countries have chosen to use other instruments that, like the criminal law, rely on coercive force and detention, but do so without most of the safeguards and restraints associated with the criminal law. These less restrained alternatives to the criminal law have included wars in Afghanistan and Iraq, assassinations,[37] the use of torture and humiliation in prisons in Iraq and elsewhere, extraordinary rendition to third countries, the use of detention without judicial review at Guantanamo Bay and the use of detention with limited judicial review under immigration or internal security laws. All of these measures starkly reveal the virtues of the criminal law and the dangers of opting out of the crime model.

In his 2004 State of Union address, President George W. Bush made clear that the United States under his leadership would not rely on the criminal law in its war against terrorism. He stated:

> I know that some people question if America is really in a war at all. They view terrorism more as a crime, a problem to be solved mainly with law enforcement and indictments. After the World Trade Center was first attacked in 1993, some of the guilty were indicted and tried and convicted, and sent to prison. But the matter was not settled. The terrorists were still training and plotting in other nations, and drawing up more ambitious plans. After the chaos and carnage of September the 11th, it is not enough to serve our enemies with legal papers. The terrorists and their supporters declared war on the United States, and war is what they got.[38]

The idea that is not 'enough to serve our enemies with legal papers' is a recurring theme in American counter-terrorism policy. It is seen in President

---

its use of preventive detention, see David Cole, 'The Priority of Morality: The Emergency Constitution's Blind Spot' (2004) 113 *Yale Law Journal* 1753.

[37] Plans by both President Clinton and Bush to capture and preferably kill bin Laden before the September 11 attacks are discussed in *The 9/11 Commission Report*, chs. 3 and 4. Justice Thomas (in dissent) has expressed concern that the Supreme Court's decision in *Hamdi* v. *Rumsfeld* might have required some due process in a case such as the November 2002 use of a Hellfire missile fired from a CIA predator drone at a vehicle in Yemen believed to contain al Qaeda members including an American citizen.

[38] State of the Union Address 20 January 2004.

Bush's military order authorizing the detention and trial of people captured in Afghanistan. The order provides that the rules of evidence will not apply and purports to preclude the jurisdiction of either the domestic courts of the United States and international courts over the detainees. It is also seen in the attempts made by the United States to dispense with the requirements of due process by declaring American citizens Yaser Hamdi and Jose Padilla to be enemy combatants under the control of the military and by detaining over 600 non-citizens in Guantanamo Bay in an ultimately futile attempt to evade the habeas corpus jurisdiction of American courts.

The war against the Taliban regime in Afghanistan was in part justified by the same language of disrupting terrorist networks that is used to justify criminal laws against financing terrorism.[39] The use of the language of the criminal law can give war, and its inevitable killing of innocent people,[40] a moral legitimacy that is not deserved. The war against the Hussein regime in Iraq was also justified in part as an anti-terrorism effort. Efforts were made to link Iraq with al Qaeda and unfounded claims about weapons of mass destruction in Iraq were made in a manner that appealed to public fears about the possibility of biological, chemical or even nuclear terrorism.

Although wars are governed by laws, including criminal law pertaining to war crimes, war is a much more indiscriminate instrument of force than a criminal prosecution. Modern technology may allow more innocent lives to be spared than ever before, but so-called collateral damage is an accepted part of war. This can be contrasted with the widespread revulsion at the conviction of the innocent under the criminal law. To be sure, wrongful convictions do occur and may at some level be inevitable given widespread use of the criminal law, but they are a matter of grave concern in most criminal justice systems.

Immigration law, particularly in Western countries, has been used as perhaps the prime instrument to counter international terrorism since 9/11. It routinely employs what in criminal law would be seen as problematic status-based offences and standards of proof well below the criminal law standard of proof beyond a reasonable doubt. Although new anti-terrorism criminal laws have been influenced by concepts developed in immigration law,[41] they still provide a higher standard of fairness and due process than

---

[39] For an account of how language borrowed from the criminal law has been used to justify military action in the war against terrorism, see Note 'Responding to Terrorism: Crime, Punishment and War' (2002) 115 *Harvard Law Review* 1237.

[40] For an estimate of 100,000 additional deaths in post-invasion Iraq, most attributable to Coalition Forces, see Les Roberts et al, 'Mortality Before and After the 2003 Invasion of Iraq: Cluster Sample Survey' *Lancet* 29 Oct. 2004, at http://image.thelancet.com/extras/04art10342web.pdf

[41] Audrey Macklin 'Borderline Security' in *The Security of Freedom*; David Cole, *Enemy Aliens* (New York, New Press, 2003).

immigration laws. Although it is not a crime to be a member of a terrorist group in either the United States or Canada, it is a ground for apprehension and removal under both countries' immigration laws. Immigration law is also more accepting of preventive, investigative and indefinite detention than the criminal law.[42] The United Kingdom has derogated from fair trial rights in order to provide for indefinite detention of non-citizens suspected of involvement with terrorism who could not be deported because of concerns that they would be tortured. There are strong arguments that this law discriminates against non-citizens. Immigration proceedings in many countries are closed to the public and make use of evidence not disclosed to the accused. Western immigration laws have fulfilled some of the same roles in facilitating preventive detention without trial as the Internal Security Acts in Malaysia and Singapore.

The use of immigration law to detain and deport suspected terrorists is striking given the alternative that is available under most new anti-terrorism criminal laws of charging these people with a broad range of criminal offences relating to terrorism. Most new criminal anti-terrorism offences define support for terrorism in a broad fashion and apply extraterritorially. In the United Kingdom reliance on immigration law in the Anti-terrorism, Crime and Security Act 2001 is especially striking given the broad crimes, including crimes of membership in a terrorist group, that are available under the Terrorism Act 2000. To this end, the Newton Committee recommended that as 'a matter of urgency' the immigration law powers of indefinite detention contained in Part 4 of the 2001 Anti-terrorism Act be replaced and steps taken to rely more on criminal prosecutions against non-citizens and citizens alike.[43] The United Kingdom government has rejected this suggestion concluding that the Newton Committee did 'not offer a solution to the need to protect sensitive information whilst enabling the defendant to know the full case that has been put against him'.[44] The easiest route for Western states since 9/11 has been to proceed under immigration laws which allow preventive and indefinite detention and closed hearings based on evidence not disclosed to the non-citizen rather than attempt to prove guilt beyond a reasonable doubt in a criminal trial.

---

[42] See Roach, Chapter 23, in this volume.

[43] Lord Newton (chair) *Anti-terrorism, Crime and Security Act 2001 Review Report* 18 Dec. 2003, at para 203–5. The Newton Committee suggested that some reforms to the criminal law such as the use of a security cleared judge to assemble the case, greater incentives for plea bargains and 'a more structured disclosure process that is better designed to allow the reconciliation of the needs of national security with the rights of the accused to a fair trial' might be required. Ibid. at para. 241.

[44] Home Secretary, *Counter-terrorism Powers: Reconciling Security and Liberty in an Open Society* Feb. 2004 Part II, at para. 37.

Immigration law can tolerate a degree of over and under-inclusiveness that would not be accepted in the criminal law. Some countries have restricted their acceptance of refugee applicants for security reasons even though terrorists would only be a small percentage of such applications and most terrorists would want to avoid the scrutiny that accompanies a refugee application. Immigration law is also under-inclusive because it cannot be applied against home-grown terrorism or internationally inspired terrorism that is committed by citizens of the particular country.

The demands of the criminal law can be seen in the few 9/11 related criminal prosecutions that have been undertaken in the United States and Germany. Zacarias Moussaoui, the so-called twentieth hijacker, has been charged with a variety of existing criminal conspiracy offences under American law. The government has refused Moussaoui access to Ramzi bin al-Shibh who is in American custody and is believed to have played a key role in the attacks. The trial judge eventually ruled that the death penalty should not be applied and the matter is now the subject of appellate litigation. An appeal court has affirmed Moussaoui's right to have access to witnesses who can provide material evidence essential to his defence, but has also held that the government has acted in good faith and overturned the sanction of making the accused ineligible for the death penalty.[45] There has been speculation that should the courts require the production of key al Qaeda witnesses, the United States government may halt the criminal prosecution and declare Moussaoui, a French citizen, to be an enemy combatant subject to indefinite detention and trial before a military tribunal. The prospect of the American government opting out of a criminal prosecution to avoid a full adversarial exploration of all relevant issues in a criminal trial would demonstrate the impatience of the United States government with the idea that 'legal papers' must be served on those suspected of involvement with 9/11.

The experience in Germany with prosecutions under the criminal law illustrates in even more dramatic form the commitment of the criminal law to basic principles of legality. The conviction of Mounir el-Motasssedeq in a Hamburg court of over 3,000 counts of accessory to murder, including the accused's fifteen-year sentence, was reversed on appeal. Although noting that the accused 'is certainly far removed from being clear of suspicion', the appeal court stressed that the accused should have access to evidence of a key witness, Ramzi bin al-Shibh. The German court reasoned that 'a conflict between the security interests of the executive and the rights to defence of the accused cannot be resolved to the disadvantage of the accused'. The court defended the legality model of the criminal law over the war metaphor by stating that 'we cannot abandon the rule of law. That would be the beginning

---

[45] *United States of America* v. *Moussaoui* 22 April 2004 (4th Cir.)

of a fatal development and ultimately a victory for the terrorists . . . The fight against terrorism cannot be a wild, unjust war.'[46] This appeal court ruling followed on the heels of an acquittal of another alleged member of the Hamburg al Qaeda cell a few weeks earlier, with both courts emphasizing the importance of providing the accused access to relevant evidence.[47]

The lack of success of 9/11 criminal prosecutions reveals that even under the sway of that terrible event, criminal courts in both the United States and Germany are still drawn to the due process and legality norms associated with the criminal law. In the German criminal courts, victims of 9/11 were represented and in one case tried without success to introduce incriminating evidence. Even with respect to the initial conviction, the maximum fifteen-year sentence was criticized as too lenient given the enormity of the damage. Although the criminal law is often defended in the language of the rights of victims, the ability of the criminal law to deliver satisfying justice to victims remains very much in doubt.

The willingness of the United States government to risk criminal convictions in order to keep intelligence sources secret[48] is not novel. Even before 9/11, governments often preferred covert surveillance or infiltration of terrorist groups to criminal charges and prosecutions. Such an approach appears to be driven by utilitarian and instrumental rather than retributive demands for punishment. It is striking that even in relation to 9/11, fears about exposing intelligence sources still prevailed over the need to turn over evidence to support a criminal prosecution. At the same time, the desire for retribution and punishment arising from 9/11 has been channelled into instruments less restrained and discriminating than the criminal law. As discussed above, these measures include war, targeted killings, torture and humiliation of prisoners and the rendition of suspects to face torture. These blunt and bloody alternatives to the criminal law reveal the virtues of the criminal law in focusing on questions of individual responsibility within a due process framework, as well as the danger that the criminal law will be abandoned in the combat of a perpetual war against terrorism.

---

[46] As quoted in Jeff Sallot, 'Guilty verdict overturned in al-Qaeda suspect's case' *Globe and Mail* (Toronto) 5 March 2004, A14; Desmond Butler, 'German Judges order a Retrial for 9/11 Figure' *New York Times* 5 March 2004.

[47] Luke Harding, 'German court clears student of plotting with 9/11 terrorists' *The Guardian* 6 Feb. 2004.

[48] The US government has subsequently indicated that it is prepared to release 'unclassified summaries' of intelligence. The accused objected to the use of such documents because of concerns about how such intelligence had been obtained, raising objections from one of the victims that such arguments desecrate 'the memory of 3000 people who died, including my mother'. 'US Pledges to Share Evidence as 9/11 Retrial Begins in Germany' *New York Times* 10 Aug. 2004.

IV. Instrumental and normative dimensions of a broader anti-terrorism strategy

The criminal law should not be abandoned, but it cannot be the exclusive instrument used against terrorism. There is a need to situate the criminal law within a more comprehensive anti-terrorism strategy. Such work should account for the reality that while criminal law reform often figures prominently in public discourse and in country reports concerning compliance with Resolution 1373, the criminal law only plays a partial role in most anti-terrorism strategies. It is important to account for both the instrumental and normative dimensions of a broader anti-terrorism strategy that does not rely on the criminal law. Why from an instrumental perspective have many states not relied upon the criminal law in their actual fight against terrorism? What are the normative dangers of abandoning the criminal law as society's ultimate response to terrorism?

The full development of a comprehensive anti-terrorism policy is obviously beyond the scope of this chapter, but the project can be advanced by selective incorporation of regulatory strategies from outside the field of terrorism or crime. A promising construct for situating the criminal law in broader anti-terrorism policy can be taken from the fields of public health and science and technology.[49] In order to assess a variety of countermeasures that could reduce death and injury from traffic accidents, epidemiologist William Haddon constructed a matrix evaluating countermeasures that could be taken to minimize harm before, during and after the accident. Haddon also distinguished between countermeasures directed at the agent of harm and those directed at third parties and the larger environment. He argued that too many resources had been devoted to changing driver behaviour before the accident and that harm could be reduced by greater regulation of third parties and the environment in which the crash occurred. Thus the objects of a comprehensive traffic safety policy should not only be bad drivers, but those who constructed the roads, auto manufacturers and those who responded at the scene of the accident. Haddon argued that policy-making had to occur on the assumption that not all driver behaviour could be modified and that some accidents will occur. His contribution to the field is associated with reforms such as padded dashboards and airbags which are designed to minimize the harms of accidents.

I have argued elsewhere that the Haddon matrix can be modified to apply to terrorism.[50] Following Haddon, we should assume that at least some

---

[49] National Research Council, *Making the Nation Safer: The Role of Science and Technology in Countering Terrorism* (Washington, National Academy Press, 2002).

[50] William Haddon 'A Logical Framework for Categorizing Highway Safety Phenomena and Activity' (1972) 12 *Journal of Trauma* 193. For an application of the Haddon matrix for preventing and reducing injury to the field of terrorism, see Kent Roach, *September 11: Consequences for Canada* (Montreal, McGill-Queens University Press, 2003), at 168–74.

terrorist activity cannot be deterred and spend more resources on regulating the environment before, during and after acts of terrorism so as to minimize the harms of terrorism. Before the act of terrorism, this means better regulation of sites and substances that are attractive to terrorists. It is particularly important to take steps to ensure that potential terrorists cannot obtain access to lethal substances such as toxins, nuclear material and airplanes. The terrorist attacks that brought down two aircraft in Russia reveal that more can be done to screen passengers and baggage. Much of this type of environmental regulation may be achieved by administrative laws that may present less of a threat to values such as liberty, due process and equality than the criminal law. Some of these preventive measures may also have the advantage of making us safer from accidents involving nuclear material and toxins. The Haddon matrix approach should make us think about what can be done to minimize harm during and after an act of terrorism. Although this will be dismissed as defeatist damage control by some, it remains crucial to minimizing the harms of terrorism. Without evacuation strategies introduced after the 1993 attacks, the death toll at the World Trade Centre might have been in the tens of thousands.[51] The death toll in subsequent terrorist hostage takings in a Moscow theatre and a Beslan school might have been reduced by better preparedness and emergency response. Emergency preparedness also can assist in dealing with natural and man-made disasters.

Another instrumental concept that could inform a comprehensive anti-terrorism policy is the idea of responsive regulation advocated by John Braithwaite. The central idea of responsive regulation is a regulatory pyramid which allows for the escalation of the state's response when regulation fails. Braithwaite stresses that the behaviour of potential wrongdoers can often be best controlled not by the state, but by third parties who have greater influence over the target of regulation. Attempts at persuasion, negotiation and peaceful problem solving lie at the base of the pyramid with escalation to deterrent threats of punishment and finally to incapacitation of irrational actors.[52] It may well be that persuasion, problem solving and even deterrence can quickly be ruled out when applied to groups like al Qaeda that seem bent on death and destruction.[53] Nevertheless, it may be very valuable with respect to third parties who can influence the behaviour of terrorists. One of the dangers of a

---

[51] It took four hours to evacuate the WTC in 1993 whereas all but 2,152 of the 16,400 to 18,800 civilians in the towers were evacuated in under one hour in 2001. *The 9/11 Report* at 9.4.

[52] John Braithwaite, *Restorative Justice and Responsive Regulation* (Oxford University Press, 2002), at 31–32.

[53] Although he recognizes the potential for democratic outlets for grievances in Spain, Canada and Northern Ireland, Michael Ignatieff argues that the 'apocalyptic nihilists' of al Qaeda 'cannot be engaged politically and must instead be defeated militarily'. Michael Ignatieff, *The Lesser Evil Political Ethics in an Age of Terror* (Toronto, Penguin, 2004), at 99.

focus on war or criminal law is that softer strategies that address the causes of terrorism can be ruled out categorically. The 9/11 Commission deserves credit for recognizing that failed and repressive states and desperation and lack of education are contributing factors to terrorism that should be addressed.[54]

A pyramid approach could impose some sense of ordering to various incapacitation strategies. First order strategies may include administrative regulation designed to deny potential terrorists access to sites and substances that can be used for terrorism. Higher up the pyramid would be the use of the criminal law, preventive detention and even more forceful strategies such as war. The pyramid idea may also be helpful in making clear that techniques such as war and preventive detention should be seen as the last resort for dealing with a terrorist threat. The pyramid is not an end in itself and should be supplemented by normative analysis that imposes some legality requirements on each anti-terrorism instrument.

One danger of a pyramid approach of escalating force against terrorism is that the very act of mapping out 'how an immoral society could fight terrorism'[55] may make it easier to use and justify such means. Some techniques such as torture and targeted assassinations should not be placed on the pyramid and they should remain illegal. At the same time, a variety of questionable and unrestrained methods are being used in the war against terrorism and we ignore them at our peril. As Michael Ignatieff has argued, there needs to be more democratic debate and legal challenges to the variety of harsh anti-terrorism policies that are being employed.[56] There is a normative need to subject all anti-terrorism measures to some measure of legality.

The United States Supreme Court's June 2004 decisions in the enemy combatant and Guantanamo Bay cases reveal some of the potential and some of the pitfalls of attempts to impose systems of legality on less restrained alternatives to the criminal law. In both cases, the Bush Administration was true to its leader's conviction that it was not enough to serve its enemies with legal papers. It argued that American courts had no jurisdiction over the detainees at Guantanamo Bay and that they should defer to the executive decisions to declare American citizens enemy combatants. It was a victory for legality that this essentially lawless position only commanded support from three judges in the Guantanamo Bay case and one judge in the enemy combatant case. Six judges affirmed habeas corpus jurisdiction over Guantanamo as an area controlled by the United States and refused to accept the minority's argument that the jurisdiction did not extend to non-citizens held indefinitely off-shore.[57]

---

[54] *The 9/11 Commission Report*, at 12.2 and 12.3.
[55] Alan Dershowitz, *Why Terrorism Works*, ch. 4.   [56] Ignatieff, *The Lesser Evil*.
[57] *Rasul* v. *Bush* 124 S Ct 2686 (2004).

Four judges led by Justice O'Connor found that Yaser Hamdi, an American citizen who had been designated an enemy combatant, was entitled to a diluted version of due process designed to accommodate the state's interest in combating terrorism. They would accept a rebuttable presumption in favour of the government's evidence, use of hearsay evidence and trial before a military tribunal. Four other judges would have imposed more demanding standards of legality. Justice Souter with Justice Ginsberg refused to find authorization for Hamdi's detention in Congress's open-ended declaration of war against the terrorists, as Justice O'Connor did, and would have required the legislature to authorize forceful anti-terrorism measures. Justice Souter also expressed reservations about Justice O'Connor's dilution of due process. Justice Scalia joined by Justice Stevens also opposed Justice O'Connor's diluted due process as 'an unheard-of system in which the citizen rather than the Government bears the burden of proof, testimony is by hearsay rather than live witnesses, and the presiding officer may well be a "neutral" military officer rather than a judge and jury'. Justice Scalia argued that 'if civil rights are to be curtailed during wartime, it must be done openly and democratically'[58] through legislative suspension of habeas corpus. If Congress did not derogate from this right, Hamdi should be entitled to all of the benefits of a criminal trial. This approach affirmed the virtues of the criminal law in requiring proof of guilt of a crime beyond a reasonable doubt, but it also flirted with the possibility that the legislature through a clear suspension of habeas corpus could dispense with all pretence with legalities. Justice Scalia took a dichotomous and daring approach that rejected the pragmatic sliding scale approach taken by Justice O'Connor. There are many virtues in maintaining criminal law principles in the face of terror and insisting that the guilt of terrorists be proven beyond a reasonable doubt in a court of law.

The United States has not followed the legislative model of legality championed by Justice Souter, by refusing to make clear legislative statements concerning its treatment of combatants. It has also opted out of the criminal law or derogation of rights model championed by Justice Scalia, by not trying the combatants in the ordinary courts and not signalling to the public that it is derogating from basic norms of legality by suspending habeas corpus. Rather, it has followed Justice O'Connor's model of diluted legality through combatant status tribunals at Guanatanamo Bay that contain a presumption in favour of the government's evidence, allow hearsay, use military officers as judges and deny detainees independent counsel.[59] The fifth vote on the Supreme Court for this diluted due

---

[58] *Hamdi v. Rumsfeld* 124 S Ct 2633 (2004).
[59] In an order issued shortly after the Court's decision, combatant status review tribunals were established, to be composed of three military officers. The detainee would be

process approach could only come from Justice Thomas who was the only judge who dissented and would not have provided any relief to Yaser Hamdi.[60] The ultimate resolution of Hamdi's case is a telling warning of the danger that governments can opt out of any form of legality. Rather than attempt to justify his detention under even the minimal standards required by Justice O'Connor, the United States sent the American citizen to Saudi Arabia after having detained him for more than two years. A Department of Justice spokesperson made clear that the issue was not one of Hamdi's guilt or innocence, but of the national interest.[61] This is consistent with President Bush's views that it is not necessary to serve legal papers on the enemy in the war against terrorism.

V. Conclusion

The criminal law is no solution to terrorism and must be integrated into a larger strategy that includes creative regulation of third parties and the environment. We need hard-headed and rational strategies that protect us not only from terrorism, but from the broad range of harms and risks of modern society. To focus too narrowly on the risk of terrorism may give the political aims of the terrorists a weight that is not deserved. Indeed perhaps the greatest danger of terrorism is that it will produce an over-reaction in democracies that undermines the fabric of democracy.

At the same time, the political demand to enact new criminal laws as a response to terrible acts of terrorism seems irresistible and the criminal law will play an important role in anti-terrorism policies. It will be directed not only at terrorists but at third parties who may support terrorists. Care must be taken not to overestimate the marginal deterrent value of new anti-terrorism laws and to ensure that any violations of general principles of due process in the context of anti-terrorism law do not spread to other parts of the criminal law. At the same time, the criminal law represents important values of individual responsibility, legally authorized detention, restrained

---

represented by another military officer and have access only to unclassified and 'reasonably available' information and witnesses. The rules of evidence would not apply and 'preponderance of evidence shall be the standard used' in determining that the enemy combatant was properly detained 'but there should be a rebuttable presumption in favour of the Government's evidence'. Deputy Secretary of Defence 'Memorandum: Order Establishing Combatant Status Review Tribunals' (7 July 2004) www.defenselink.mil./news/Jul2004/d20040707review.pdf. For criticisms see Ronald Dworkin 'What the Court Really Said' *New York Review of Books* 12 Aug. 2004.

[60] Justice Thomas stressed 'the Government's interest in not fighting the war in its own courts' (*Hamdi* at 2685).

[61] 'US, Bowing to Court, to Free "Enemy Combatant"' *New York Times* 23 Sept. 2004. Hamdi will be subject to conditions including renunciation of his American citizenship and restrictions on his travel.

punishment, and due process that should not be lightly discarded in the war against terrorism.

The terrorist threat can produce distorted and unjust criminal laws, but a perhaps even greater danger is that states will be impatient and abandon the restraints of the criminal law in favour of much less restrained and less discriminating anti-terrorist measures including war, assassination, torture, preventive detention and wholesale restrictions on migration.

8

And fairness for all? Asylum, national security, and the rule of law

COLIN HARVEY

I. Introduction

Asylum, immigration and nationality law have all been used in the 'war against terrorism' in, for example, the UK, the US and Canada.[1] The heightened focus on these areas has highlighted the already draconian aspects of existing law and practice. Anti-terrorism law and policy is having a significant impact on refugees and asylum seekers.[2] There is, however, no necessary connection between national security and asylum and what tends to be neglected is that refugee law was designed precisely to regulate the 'exceptional situation' of forced migration.[3] The existence of the humanitarian institution of asylum need not raise security concerns and refugee law contains well-established mechanisms to address the issue. It is essential that the refugee regime does not become confused with, and undermined by, anti-terrorism law and policy.

Claims to the novelty of contemporary security concerns must be approached with caution. Refugee lawyers have noted for some time the 'security discourse' being constructed around the treatment of forced migration. In the UK, the government has woven migration policy into the narrative of providing security for citizens.[4] In recent years concern about asylum has reached the highest political levels and extended beyond national contexts. The UN Security

Editorial note: This chapter was written before the ruling of the House of Lords in A. v. *Secretary of State for the Home Department* [2004] UKHL 56 and should be read in the light of that judgment. See 'Postscript', Chapter 28, in this volume.

[1] Roach, Chapter 23, in this volume; Howard Adelman, 'Refugees and Border Security Post-September 11' (2002) 20 *Refuge* 5; Kate Martin, 'Preventive Detention of Immigrants and Non-Citizens in the United States since September 11th' (2002) 20 *Refuge* 23.

[2] In Britain, the terrorist threat is not confined to non-nationals. There is evidence of involvement of British nationals in 'international terrorism'.

[3] Adelman, 'Refugees and Border Security', at 11 ('there is virtually no evidence linking *global* terrorism with refugees').

[4] See Home Office 'No let up combating abuse of the asylum system' 17 December 2003, where Home Secretary David Blunkett stated: 'This Bill is part of our strategy to secure our borders and tackle abuse of the asylum system, in order to build the public confidence and trust necessary to welcome legal migration in the interests of the UK's economy.'

Council, for example, made clear after September 11 that there should be no safe havens for terrorists and that refugee status should not be 'abused' by 'perpetrators, organizers or facilitators of terrorist acts'.[5] Events demonstrate that security threats are credible, but these debates must be seen as part of a pattern of responses to migration that is not novel.[6] The pressures exerted in the national security context are simply more intense versions of the strain the asylum system is under.[7] And claims to novelty can obscure the complex reasons for flight, which often include political, social or economic factors.

The linking of asylum and terrorism in political discussions has the potential to do lasting damage to the institution of asylum. One suggestion in this chapter is that the rule of law is under threat when national security concerns assume excessive prominence in the asylum debate. When credible security threats are perceived, there is a tendency to focus on the executive as best placed to address the matter because of its greater access to information. But this argument neglects the importance of rigorous scrutiny of legal standards which regulate exceptional situations. The controversy over asylum and national security thus requires a careful examination of the role of the judiciary in this area of public policy. Do different elements emerge when security concerns are raised? Are the courts interfering excessively in government asylum policy, occasionally undermining the will of Parliament, as some politicians suggest,[8] or is judicial deference to the executive a continuing problem, as many commentators and human rights advocates argue?

This chapter suggests, with reference to decided cases, that the senior judiciary is *not* engaged in an attempt to undermine government asylum policy in the UK. The senior judiciary is aware (only too aware, at times) of its institutional and constitutional roles, but is prepared to advance incrementally the interpretation of refugee law and on occasion question executive decision-making. There are limits to what judges can, and should, do in this area. But there is a danger that when national security is raised undue deference is accorded to the executive. Some concept of due deference may be appropriate, but there are risks if it becomes too extensive and undermines the judicial role of interpreting and applying existing norms.

---

[5] UN Security Council Resolution 1373 (2001).
[6] See Prakash Shah, 'Taking the "political" out of asylum: the legal containment of refugees' political activism' in Frances Nicholson and Patrick Twomey (eds.), *Refugee Rights and Realities: Evolving International Concepts and Regimes* (Cambridge University Press, 1999), 119–135.
[7] See Reg Whitaker, 'Refugee Policy after September 11: Not Much New' (2002) 20 *Refuge* 29.
[8] Richard Rawlings talks of a 'revenge package' developed by government to address this and views asylum as a significant constitutional arena and an example of 'pressure through law': 'Review and Revenge (and Retreat)' W. G. Hart Legal Workshop, July 2004, Institute of Advanced Legal Studies.

The debate in public law is (and has long been) polarized between those who are sceptical of the judicial role and those who believe the judges do not go far enough in defence of individual rights. Those sceptical of the judicial role place their trust in the potential of Parliament to deliver more effective protection of rights. They believe that Parliament is not only best placed but has the legitimacy required to make these judgments. Those who view the majoritarian nature of parliamentary democracy with suspicion look to the courts to provide necessary restraints. But this is not an either/or choice. Some construction of the judicial role must form part of any analysis of public law which has not abandoned adjudication as a form of decision-making. One problem is that the UK government is steadily narrowing the practical scope for individuals to challenge asylum decisions. This was evident in the recent failed attempt to exclude judicial review in the asylum context. Similar objectives can, however, be achieved through a variety of other legal and policy mechanisms. Whatever theory of the judicial role is adopted it must confront a legal system that is making it increasingly difficult to contest asylum decisions. The rule of law is not only undermined through direct attempts to exclude judicial review. It may also be eroded by a creative legal and policy framework which seeks to immunize itself from effective judicial scrutiny.

An approach is needed which recognizes both the importance of parliamentary democracy, properly understood, and the robust parliamentary and judicial protection of the rights of vulnerable groups.[9] This will not be found in excessive deference to the executive in matters of asylum, particularly when national security concerns are raised, nor in attempts to place too much strain on the judicial role. But a start might be made by switching attention from the institutional question of who should decide to those arguments which deserve recognition in a constitutional democracy committed to the rule of law. When national security concerns are prominent, the existing normative framework must be interpreted and applied appropriately. This process need not be exclusively undertaken by the judiciary. In the UK, parliamentary committees, MPs, human rights and equality bodies, and NGOs all have a responsibility to argue for the values which underpin legal order; vibrant networks have emerged to challenge government policy. But criticism of judicial activism or deference suggests that some understanding of the judicial role is at work – one that needs to be positively argued for and not simply assumed. This approach places considerable emphasis on the values which underpin legal order and the arguments which best serve those values, even when national security threats arise.

[9] Rabinder Singh, 'Equality: The Neglected Virtue' [2004] EHRLR 141.

II. A conversation on limits: the rule of law as constitutional constraint

Before any attempt is made to consider asylum law, thought should be given to the rule of law and the judicial role. Even if the starting point is scepticism, it is worth reflecting on what the judicial role *should be or might be*. The rule of law is often deployed in this area, but there is not always agreement as to its meaning. Even A. V. Dicey believed that arbitrary power was necessary in times of social disturbance or disorder[10] and that 'order can hardly be maintained unless the executive can expel aliens'.[11] This was within a conception of the rule of law where arbitrary power was regarded as exceptional, but it highlights a common assumption that certain actions *must* be permissible in times of crisis if government is to function effectively. I want, in this chapter, to question the assumption that there are exceptional areas where legal order must not go, or if it does, tread very lightly. This task involves an inquiry into the meaning of and values implicit in the rule of law and the implications for governing within a legal order.

First, there is what may be termed the 'formal tradition'. Writing within this tradition, Joseph Raz notes the importance of the rule of law as a formal concept which means that legal rules must be general, prospective, open, clear and stable.[12] There is little in the description that one would wish to disagree with. In legal theory, the debate is whether legal order is devoid of substantive moral or political content. The label 'formal tradition' simplifies the issues, but it captures a shared belief in the importance of separating legal validity from moral or political views. In this 'formal tradition' the rule of law may exist in a range of democratic contexts.

Second, there are 'value-based' schools of thought. These approaches vary, but they see the rule of law as more than the mere existence of formal legal rules and processes. In popular usage the concept is often deployed in place of a substantive argument about justice, suggesting that we imbue it with political and moral ideals. When we talk about the principle of legality we appear to mean more than simply following enacted rules. Dicey famously linked the rule of law to the supremacy of regular law as opposed to arbitrary power.[13] Dicey's distrust of discretionary power has particular relevance in the asylum context, in which it is accepted that the discretion afforded by the legal framework can be exercised in a number of ways. For Dicey, no one could be punished except by law, everyone must be equal before the law

---

[10] A. V. Dicey, *Introduction to the Study of the Law of the Constitution* (8th edn., London, Macmillan, 1915), 271: 'Under the complex conditions of modern life no government can in times of disorder, or of war, keep the peace at home, or perform its duties towards foreign powers, without occasional use of arbitrary authority.'
[11] Ibid.   [12] 'The Rule of Law and its Virtues', (1977) 93 LQR 195.   [13] See note 10 above.

(in the sense that all classes of persons are subject to it) and it must be administered by the ordinary courts.[14] These core values underpin modern understandings of the rule of law, even if one accepts that law is, by nature, arguable. They are values which have particular significance for marginalized groups. One fear of extensive discretionary power, for example, is precisely that vulnerable individuals and groups will suffer as a result. How this approach is classified in legal theory is, in my view, of less interest than the values it reflects and seeks to promote. What it suggests is that the rule of law has a substantive value and is not simply a formal or procedural concept.

Finally, some prefer to view the rule of law as political rhetoric and a potential obstacle to social change. This is, of course, a crude simplification. However, it does capture a view which regards all talk of the rule of law or legality as a mask for power relations. In other words, law is arguable in nature and simply reflects power relations within wider society and should be approached from a strategic and instrumental perspective. The commitment to legal order thus becomes a tactical one and law, if useful at all, is constructed as a tool, in appropriate circumstances, to advance or impede wider political struggles. The strategic attitude towards the rule of law is often discussed in the human rights context. But accepting the arguable and political nature of law does not imply that the rule of law or the principle of legality is necessarily indeterminate.

The disagreement over the meaning of the rule of law reflects basic disputes in law and politics. My own view is that modern approaches which aim to hold on to a substantive understanding of the rule of law remain the more convincing. The rule of law is a political ideal, but one which should focus on the substance of legal argumentation and promote a culture of justification.[15] The aim should be to highlight the arguable and dynamic nature of law and its basis in distinct values.[16] It means something, in substantive political terms, to be committed to legal order, as opposed to discretionary power administered on a case-by-case basis. The rule of law, then, is essential to the construction of a democratic culture in which people are treated equally, but the debate shifts towards legal reasoning as opposed to a rigid focus on the institutions or the decision-maker. When national security is raised there is no reason in principle why judges should not be consistent and thus bring exceptional situations fully within the principle of legality.

---

[14] Ibid.

[15] David Dyzenhaus, 'The Permanence of the Temporary' in Ronald J. Daniels, et al. (eds.), *The Security of Freedom: Essays on Canada's Anti-Terrorism Bill* (University of Toronto Press, 2001), 21–37.

[16] David Dyzenhaus, 'Recrafting the Rule of Law' in Dyzenhaus (ed.), *Recrafting the Rule of Law* (Oxford, Hart Publishing, 1999), 1–12; Neil MacCormick, 'Rhetoric and the Rule of Law' in *Recrafting the Rule of Law*, at 163–77.

But how is this relevant to the debate on refugees and asylum seekers? Surely this focus on the arguable nature of law simply brings instability and uncertainty with it? These are genuine concerns and many democracies do not have a proud record on protecting the rights of asylum seekers. However, legal orders generate mechanisms to resolve disagreement on the basis of existing norms and, often, foundational constitutional norms and values. Law is arguable, but it is not indeterminate in the sense this is sometimes used. The turn to rational argumentation is convincing as a way to move beyond the current preoccupation with the decision-maker, which eventually weakens the protection of vulnerable groups and exacerbates the problem of Westminster executive dominance. I do not underestimate the importance of the legitimacy of lawmaking processes, or the significance of judges who should be reflective of the societies they serve. But the judicial role must primarily revolve around the interpretation and application of norms and standards in particular cases, without undue anxiety about the political environment. The emphasis should be on continuing conversation over the terms of asylum law within the legal constraints that protect vulnerable individuals and groups. The rule of law promotes a democratic culture of equal concern and respect and in the asylum context it advances a reasoned approach to this highly contested area.

The justification of policy must *deserve* recognition within the terms of legal argumentation, and not solely on the basis of its pedigree. In the asylum context, it is not enough for judges to defer to executive decisions on the basis that Ministers are best placed to make them. This simply shifts the responsibility to another institution to make the substantive decision the law requires. In my view, the judges are obliged to address the substance of the legal arguments, even in cases where immigration, asylum and national security collide.

Dicey emphasized the importance of ordinary courts and expressed concerns about discretionary power, but there is still value in encouraging the development of expert bodies with knowledge of particular subject areas, like immigration and asylum. These bodies may, in practice, reach better decisions than the ordinary courts and ones which accord with the culture of justification mentioned here. Respect for the rule of law or legality need not accord with established judicial hierarchies.

The strength of the approach rests on respect for the individual and the basic principles of fairness which this implies. But we need to move beyond the idea that this respect is owed to citizens mainly. This is an area where judges may well be ahead of political and legal theorists. It is still too often the case that status is used unreflectively, neglecting non-nationals. In asylum law, where extensive pressures are placed on government and public administration to deliver quick results, insistence on the importance of each individual is significant. A commitment to legalism thus has an ethical dimension.[17] But this argument in favour of legalism as a positive conception does not mean support for a particular institutional belief in the courtroom as the only forum for its vindication.

III. Securing asylum

A. The legal framework

Asylum law in the UK has developed in the last decade as a specific area of public law. Legal regulation has responded to increasing numbers of asylum seekers with a range of measures to speed up the system and deter future applications. The policy premise is that the system is being widely abused by those who are not in genuine need of protection. A 'culture of suspicion' has surrounded the system for some time, and 9/11 has simply intensified an existing process. The trends are again evident in the latest asylum legislation which includes: new criminal offences around entering the UK without a passport; factors to be considered as impacting negatively on credibility assessments; new categories of persons not eligible for support; provision of accommodation made conditional on participation in community activities; and the further erosion of appeal rights.

The law is primarily concerned with the provision of protection to asylum seekers from return to another state where there is a real risk of sufficiently serious human rights abuse. Protection exists in the form of both refugee law and human rights law. Asylum is a humanitarian institution designed to provide surrogate protection to those in real need of it. Permanent settlement in the UK may be the result of a grant of refugee status; however, the principal purpose of the legal regime is to offer protection as long as it is needed. Decision-making in asylum cases is particularly challenging because it involves judgments about future risk based on the applicant's testimony and empirical evidence about the applicant's state of origin.

There is now an extensive statutory framework and a substantial body of case law.[18] In addition, the Human Rights Act 1998 changes the human rights context and the full impact of the Act requires careful assessment over time. There are other measures of relevance. For example, the Anti-terrorism Crime and Security Act 2001 has an express section on immigration and asylum.[19] This controversial legislation increases the powers of the Home Secretary in relation to the deportation, removal and detention of 'suspected international terrorists'. Someone certified as a suspected international terrorist may be refused leave to remain, deported, or removed from the UK.

---

[17] MacCormick, ibid.
[18] Asylum and Immigration (Treatment of Claimants, Etc.) Act 2004; Nationality, Immigration and Asylum Act 2002; Immigration and Asylum Act 1999; Asylum and Immigration Act 1996; Asylum and Immigration Appeals Act 1993.
[19] Part 4.

A person may also be detained even when it is unlikely that the removal order will in fact be executed. An appeal is available to the Special Immigration Appeals Commission (SIAC) against certification. As a consequence of these measures the government had to derogate from Article 5 of the European Convention on Human Rights. Concerns have been consistently raised about this legislation and whether the indefinite detention of suspected international terrorists is a proportionate response.[20] The Act deals directly with the interpretation of the key provisions in refugee law; these are Articles 1F (exclusion clauses) and 33(2) (permissible *refoulement*) of the Refugee Convention.[21] The 2001 Act grants the Home Secretary the power to certify that a person is not protected against *refoulement* because Article 1F or Article 33(2) applies and his or her removal would be conducive to the public good. In this specific context, the exclusion clauses are applied before inclusion is considered.[22] The Act also makes clear that no balancing exercise is involved in the assessment of these provisions. Against this statutory backdrop, my aim is to focus on the role of the judges in the English asylum process and assess their response in the area of national security and public order.

National security *may* become relevant to the asylum process at different stages, but there is no necessary connection between the asylum system and national security. A link may emerge if asylum seekers, like other individuals, engage in specified actions in the asylum state or before entry. Some asylum seekers and refugees will have been politically active in their state of origin. The issue of security may arise when the exclusion clauses are being considered during the status determination process. National security is not intended to be the primary concern at this stage, but there is evidence that it does enter into the process. If a person is still awaiting determination of her claim, or is recognized as a refugee, her actions in the asylum state may trigger concern about a possible security risk. At this point her removal may be sought with reference to national security considerations. Removal in this context presents particular challenges where the individual faces a real risk of serious ill-treatment upon return. But there is no necessary impediment to prosecution under anti-terrorism or criminal laws. The legal framework thus includes provision for dealing with asylum seekers and refugees who are suspected of being involved in terrorism.

[20] See, for example, Privy Counsellor Review Committee, *Anti-terrorism, Crime and Security Act 2001 Review: Report* (18th December 2003, HC 100) 48–68; Joint Committee on Human Rights *Anti-terrorism, Crime and Security Act 2001: Statutory Review and Continuance of Part 4* (2003–04) Sixth Report, HL Paper 38, HC 381. In normal immigration law circumstances indefinite detention pending deportation would be unlawful, see *Youssef* v. *The Home Office* [2004] EWHC 1884 (QB).

[21] See James C. Hathaway and Colin Harvey, 'Framing Refugee Protection in the New World Disorder' (2001) 34 *Cornell International Law Journal* 257.

[22] See *Gurung* v. *Secretary of State for the Home Department* [2002] UKIAT 04870.

The rule of law has implications for all the institutions of government, including the executive. Parliament has debated asylum on numerous occasions, and in the last decade several legislative initiatives have been undertaken. Government policy is regularly examined in the courts. What emerges is a dynamic relationship between government, administrators, adjudicators and the courts. However, the evidence does not suggest a senior judiciary intent on undermining asylum policy. There are cases where judges have taken a firm stand on the progressive development of asylum law and the senior judiciary continues to display an acute awareness of executive policy preferences. The result is that excessive deference is sometimes accorded to the decision-maker rather than the substance of the legal argument. This result is troubling for those concerned with the effective legal protection of human rights in the UK. The managerial imperatives and concerns of the executive are important, but the principal focus should be on the legal argument and the development of refugee and asylum law in individual cases. To advance my argument I highlight three themes in asylum law: first, the contested meaning of refugee status and human rights protection; second, the treatment of asylum seekers awaiting a determination of their claim; and finally, national security.

B. Refugee status, asylum and human rights protection

Refugee status determination is the core of the asylum process. Although not strictly domestic law, the definition of 'refugee' is contained in the 1951 Convention relating to the Status of Refugees.[23] An individual is a refugee if he or she has a well-founded fear of persecution for a 'Convention reason' and is unwilling or unable to seek the protection of his or her state of origin.[24] The 1951 Convention definition is applied in domestic law in the UK and an asylum seeker can make an application for refugee status. A person who is not recognized as a refugee may still fall within the category of 'humanitarian protection' or benefit from discretionary leave. An individual also cannot be returned if doing so would be contrary to the European Convention on Human Rights. The House of Lords has attempted to establish a clear approach to the interpretation of refugee status which will facilitate asylum decision-making. It has also, on some occasions, been prepared to advance the interpretation of the definition to reflect the purpose of the law and modern legal developments in the protection of human rights.

In *R v. Secretary of State for the Home Department, ex parte Sivakumaran,*[25] a refugee case involving six Tamil asylum seekers, Lord Keith stressed that the fear (in 'well-founded fear') had to be objectively shown to be justified and

---

[23] 189 UNTS 154, entry into force: 22 April 1954.   [24] Article 1A(2).   [25] [1988] 1 AC 958.

not merely subjectively felt by the individual: 'the requirement that the applicant's fear of persecution should be well-founded means that there has to be demonstrated a reasonable degree of likelihood that he will be persecuted for a Convention reason if returned to his own country'.[26] By emphasising the 'well-founded' nature of the 'fear' the House of Lords guaranteed that, in practice, the objective element in the test would trump any subjective considerations. The focus was on the conditions in the state of origin as the principal matter in the assessment of asylum claims. The Law Lords opted for an interpretation which reflected the government's preferred view of the refugee definition, and which focused on making the interpretation of refugee status manageable.

Disagreements within states on the meaning of refugee law are typically resolved by domestic courts and tribunals. But what happens, in the context of European integration, if states disagree over the meaning of refugee law when a system is in place to transfer responsibility for the substantive assessment of claims? The issue was addressed in *R. v. Secretary of State for the Home Department, ex parte Adan*,[27] which involved two appeals to the House of Lords. In the first appeal, Adan, a citizen of Somalia, had unsuccessfully sought asylum in Germany. She then claimed asylum in the UK, but the Home Secretary determined that the Dublin Convention 1990 (a treaty designed to facilitate the transfer of responsibility for asylum claims) was applicable and Germany should take responsibility. The German authorities accepted responsibility and her claim for asylum in the UK was refused without consideration of the merits. In the second appeal, Aitseguer, an Algerian citizen, had travelled to the UK by way of France. He claimed to be at risk from an armed group in Algeria and that the government was unable to protect him. The Home Secretary determined that under the Dublin Convention 1990 Aitseguer should be returned to France. The French authorities agreed to take him back. Aitseguer challenged the decision on the basis that the Home Secretary had not taken the French position fully into account.

The problem in these cases was the conflicting interpretations of refugee law within the EU. As Lord Steyn noted, a minority of states confined protection to those who could link persecution to the state. France and Germany followed this approach, but the UK did not. Adan feared persecution in Somalia as a result of being a member of a persecuted minority clan, while Aitseguer claimed to be the target of the Groupe Islamique Armé in Algeria. The feared persecution could not be attributed directly to the state. The Home Secretary accepted that if returned both might be sent to their states of origin, due to the interpretation of the Convention applied in

---

[26] Ibid. 994. Lord Templeman followed a similar approach, at 996.   [27] [2001] 2 AC 477.

Germany and France. But the Home Secretary suggested that there were alternative forms of protection in both states for Adan and Aitseguer. An important question emerged: is there a true and 'international meaning' of the 1951 Convention, or do a range of possible interpretations exist, some of which the Home Secretary is entitled to regard as legitimate? According to Lord Steyn, the question for the Home Secretary was not whether some other form of protection might be available in France or Germany, but what the 1951 Convention required.[28]

It is difficult to view this as a case of the court stepping beyond the law to interfere with public administration. Even though the judgment had an impact on the safe third country rule, the Law Lords were not prepared to defer to the argument of the Home Secretary. Their approach was based on the fundamental value of respect for the individual and the protection of the person in the determination of asylum cases. The Law Lords accepted that disagreement over the meaning of refugee law existed, but acknowledged the unfairness and risk to the individual were the Home Secretary allowed to rely on reasonable disagreement within Europe. Refugee law has a determinate content even in the face of disagreement in the EU. The case highlights neatly how the legal system can find a determinate way out of disagreement based on respect for the value of individual human dignity and the importance of procedural fairness.

This case must now, however, be considered in the light of the Immigration and Asylum Act 1999, R. (Yogathas) v. Secretary of State for the Home Department and R. (Thangarasa) v. Secretary of State for the Home Department.[29] These cases involved the application of the safe third country rule to Germany. The House of Lords held that the Home Secretary had not acted unlawfully. The German approach was not significantly different on persecution by non-state agents and on internal relocation and there was no real risk in either case that Article 3 of the European Convention on Human Rights would be violated.[30] Lord Bingham stressed the importance of the 'anxious scrutiny test' (discussed below) but argued there were two further considerations. First, that courts should not infer that 'a friendly sovereign state which is party to the Geneva Convention will not perform the obligations it has solemnly undertaken'.[31] Only significant differences, in his view, should be allowed to prevent return in such cases. Second, he stated that the key issue was the prevention of return to places where the person will suffer persecution; in ex parte Adan the Law Lords had not reflected fully on other

---

[28] Ibid. 509.   [29] [2003] 1 AC 920 (HL).
[30] It is well-established that individuals are protected from return if contrary to Article 3. But other rights might also prevent return: R. v. Special Adjudicator, ex parte Ullah; Do v. Secretary of State for the Home Department, [2004] UKHL 26 (Article 9); and R. v. Secretary of State for the Home Department, ex parte Razgar, [2004] UKHL 27 (Article 8).
[31] Ibid. para 9.

forms of protection and German domestic law. These cases suggest an awareness of the problems faced by the Home Office in the administration of asylum. They also are evidence of a judicial retreat from *ex parte Adan* influenced by the problems experienced in trying to make this system function effectively.

Two further cases reveal the contested meaning of refugee law. In the first case, *Horvath* v. *Secretary of State for the Home Department*,[32] the appellant was a member of the Roma community and a citizen of the Republic of Slovakia. He left Slovakia with his family and came to the UK to claim asylum. He argued that he feared persecution from skinhead groups which targeted Roma and that the Slovak police had failed to provide adequate protection. The issue for the House of Lords was the failure of the state to provide protection. What was the link to the persecution feared? For Lord Hope, the purpose of the 1951 Convention was to offer surrogate protection when an individual no longer enjoyed the protection of his state of origin. This purpose had implications for the interpretation of the word 'persecution'. Since the failure of state protection was central to the entire system of refugee law, the word 'persecution' implied 'a failure by the state to make protection available against the ill-treatment or violence which the person suffers at the hands of his persecutors'.[33] The case is a useful example of the government's concerns about asylum policy entering fully into the assessment of the interpretation of refugee status. Rather than decide on the meaning of 'persecution', as a distinct concept, the Law Lords were more focused on the availability of protection in the state of origin. The case also reveals an unwillingness to accept that treatment in other European states might generate a valid refugee claim. In particular, the House of Lords relied heavily on an argument about the surrogate nature of refugee protection in its assessment of the meaning of the term 'persecution'. The assumption is that sufficient protection is available in other European states.

The decision in *Horvath* can be contrasted with *R.* v. *Immigration Appeal Tribunal, ex parte Shah and Islam and others* v. *Secretary of State for the Home Department*.[34] The appellants were two Pakistani women who had been forced from their homes by their husbands and risked being falsely accused of adultery. They argued that they would be unprotected by the state if sent back and that they ran the risk of criminal proceedings for sexual immorality. They sought asylum in the UK on the basis that they had a well-founded fear of persecution as a result of membership in a particular social group, within the terms of the 1951 Convention. The issue before the House of Lords was the precise meaning to be given to 'membership in a particular social group'. A majority of the House of Lords concluded that the phrase could be applied

---

[32] [2000] 1 AC 489 (HL).   [33] Ibid. 497.   [34] [1999] 2 All ER 545 (HL).

to groups which might be regarded as coming within the Convention's anti-discriminatory objectives. This meant it applied to those groups which shared a common immutable characteristic, and were discriminated against in matters of fundamental human rights. In certain circumstances women could constitute such a group if they lived in societies like Pakistan. Unlike *Horvath*, the majority in the House of Lords was here prepared to be generous in the interpretation of refugee law, and in its assessment of the conditions in Pakistan.

Although *Shah/Islam* might appear to extend the applicability of refugee law widely, the Law Lords were careful to stress the particular circumstances of the cases. The exercise of a more purposive interpretation within refugee law thus promotes at best incremental advances. The Law Lords were influenced by arguments about what a modern interpretation of refugee status should be in the light of ongoing developments in human rights law. In this construction the 1951 Convention is viewed as a 'living instrument'.[35]

C. Fair treatment

The second main area of dispute in asylum policy is the treatment of asylum seekers while awaiting a decision and the decision-making process itself. Disagreement between some members of the judiciary and the executive is evident from the case law.[36] In *R. v. Secretary of State for the Home Department, ex parte Saadi*,[37] Saadi and four other asylum seekers argued that their detention at Oakington detention centre was unlawful, with reference to Article 5 of the European Convention on Human Rights.[38] A fast-track procedure had been introduced at the centre in 2000, whereby asylum seekers could be detained for seven days if it was felt that their claims could be determined quickly. Saadi and others challenged their detention. The House of Lords concluded that their compulsory detention could not be said to have been arbitrary or disproportionate; in fact, the process was highly structured and tightly managed. This structure would be disrupted if asylum seekers were able to live wherever they wished. A balance had to be struck between the deprivation of liberty and the need for speedy decisions to prevent long

---

[35] *Sepet and another* v. *Secretary of State for the Home Department* [2003] UKHL 15. The Convention should be viewed as a living instrument: 'While its meaning does not change over time its application will' (at para 4).

[36] See *R.* v. *Secretary of State for the Home Department, ex parte Joint Council for the Welfare of Immigrants* [1997] 1 WLR 275 (CA).

[37] [2002] UKHL 41. See also *ZL and VL* v. *Secretary of State for the Home Department and Lord Chancellor's Department* [2003] EWCA Civ 25; *R. (Refugee Legal Centre)* v. *Secretary of State for the Home Department* [2004] EWHC 684 (Admin).

[38] Article 5 guarantees the right to liberty and the security of the person subject to listed limitations.

delays. Conditions at Oakington were reasonable and the periods of detention were not excessive, so on balance the detention at Oakington was reasonable and proportionate. The judgment demonstrated a willingness to defer to the overall objectives of asylum policy and judicial 'understanding' of the concerns of public administration and the overall management of the asylum process. The first instance judgment (in the appellants' favour) had triggered an angry reaction from the Home Secretary. The result, however, was based on an interpretation of the limitations to Article 5 which suggested that the deprivation of liberty could be justified.

The Home Secretary was also unimpressed with the first instance decision of Mr Justice Collins in *R. (Q and others) v. Secretary of State for the Home Department*.[39] Section 55 of the Nationality, Immigration and Asylum Act 2002 prohibits the provision of support to the destitute,[40] but allows the Home Secretary to offer support if it is necessary to prevent a breach of Convention rights.[41] To meet government targets on the reduction of the number of asylum claims, the Home Secretary embarked on a policy of refusing welfare support to asylum seekers who did not make a claim 'as soon as reasonably practicable' upon entering the UK. The question was the level of destitution to which an individual had to fall before his or her suffering or humiliation reached the minimum level of severity required to amount to inhuman and degrading treatment under Article 3 of the European Convention on Human Rights. The precise meaning of the Act was unclear, and the problem was left to the courts to resolve.

All the applicants were asylum seekers who were refused support because they had not made their claims as soon as reasonably practicable upon entering the UK. The applicants challenged the lawfulness of the decision and argued that their human rights were violated because the refusal to offer support meant they had no way of gaining access to food and shelter. Mr Justice Collins held that the policy was unlawful. He found flaws in the decision-making process relating to a general failure to consider each case on its merits. He concluded that there was a real risk of a violation of Article 3 (prohibition on torture or inhuman or degrading treatment or punishment) and Article 8(1) (the right to privacy) of the European Convention on the basis that a person would be left destitute once benefits were refused. He also held that there had been a violation of Article 6 (right to a fair trial) with respect to the flawed procedures for challenging the initial refusal of support. The Court of Appeal, in rejecting the appeal, clarified the meaning of the

---

[39] [2003] EWHC 195 (Admin).
[40] Section 55(1). See Mayor of London *Destitution by Design-Withdrawal of support from in-country asylum applicants: an impact assessment for London* (Greater London Authority, 2004).
[41] Section 55(5).

relevant provisions of the 2002 Act with reference, in particular, to Article 3.[42] But the more significant aspect of the judgment related to the assessment of the overall fairness of the procedures. The court held that the process was unfair for a range of reasons including: the flaws in the interview process; the fact that the purpose of the interview was not fully explained; that the Home Secretary had not taken into account the state of mind of the individuals involved; and the use of standard form questionnaires.

The Home Secretary opted not to appeal and on 17 December 2003 announced a change in the approach to the 'as soon as reasonably practicable' test. Applicants who could give a credible explanation within three days of arrival would normally be considered to be eligible for support. Problems continued and in *R. (Limbuela)* v. *Secretary of State for the Home Department* the Court of Appeal held (Lord Justice Laws dissenting) that the Home Secretary had wrongly declined to provide support to asylum seekers under s. 55(5) of the 2002 Act.[43] The Court of Appeal provided in this case some further clarity on the meaning of the test to be applied. The Home Secretary was given permission to appeal to the House of Lords. Following this decision the Home Office eventually opted to change its approach.

The importance of these cases rests in the strict scrutiny of the procedures applied and the emphasis, at first instance and in the Court of Appeal, on the importance of a proper assessment of each individual case. This aspect of the application of the rule of law is sometimes neglected, but in a climate of hostility towards asylum seekers, the stress on fair procedures, and the precise factors which need to be incorporated, is valuable. Here the judges fulfil an important role in ensuring procedural fairness and that equality before the law has meaning in practice for each individual. The stress on fairness is essential in the face of an asylum process which is under severe pressure from the executive to deliver quick results.

The importance of procedural fairness and fundamental rights was stressed more recently in *R. (Anufrijeva)* v. *Secretary of State for the Home Department*.[44] The majority of the House of Lords held that constitutional principle required an administrative decision which was adverse to be communicated before it could have the character of a determination with legal effect. General statutory words could not override fundamental rights and would be presumed to be subject to them. The European Convention on Human Rights was not an exhaustive statement of fundamental rights and 'fairness is the guiding principle of our public law'.[45] But the discourse of human rights has long been apparent in administrative law. For instance, in *Bugdaycay* v. *Secretary of State for the Home Department*,[46] the House of Lords

---

[42] *R. (Q)* v. *Secretary of State for the Home Department* [2003] EWCA Civ 364.
[43] [2004] EWCA Civ 540.   [44] [2004] 1 AC 604.   [45] Ibid. para 30.
[46] [1987] AC 514 (HL).

had to consider the 1951 Convention (although not the definition of refugee status) for the first time. In respect of one of the appellants, Musisi, the issue was whether there was a safe country (Kenya) to which he could be returned. After stating the limitations on the role of the court in judicial review proceedings Lord Bridge noted: 'The most fundamental of all human rights is the individual's right to life and when an administrative decision under challenge is said to be one which may put the applicant's life at risk, the basis of the decision must surely call for the most anxious scrutiny.'[47] Lord Bridge concluded that the Secretary of State's decision to place faith in the Kenyan authorities was misplaced.[48] As Nicholas Blake notes, the introduction of the 'anxious scrutiny' test in this case resulted in a sharp rise in judicial review applications and effectively assisted in the eventual creation of a comprehensive appeals system.[49] The judgment recognized – well before the Human Rights Act 1998 – that where fundamental rights are at risk (in this instance the right to life), the courts, in judicial review proceedings, should examine the decision-making process very closely to ensure that there is no unfairness to the individual.

D. Making the principle of legality matter: national security, terrorism and the asylum process

It is important to understand the judicial role in asylum cases generally. But the principal aim of this chapter is to explore the judicial role when national security is raised, and it is to that issue that I now turn. The institution of asylum and the law of refugee status both contain express provision for excluding certain persons from protection.[50] When it comes to deciding whether certain persons are undeserving of protection, judicial deference to the executive is particularly marked. This trend is not confined to asylum and immigration law. When a credible security threat exists there is a temptation to defer to the expertise and knowledge available to the executive. But as has often been stated, this is precisely when judicial vigilance is most required.

---

[47] Ibid. 531.

[48] Ibid. 533. Following a similar approach Lord Templeman stated: 'In my opinion where the result of a flawed decision may imperil life or liberty a special responsibility lies on the court in the examination of the decision-making process' (at 537).

[49] See Nicholas Blake, 'Judicial Review of Expulsion Decisions: Reflections on the UK Experience' in David Dyzenhaus (ed.), The Unity of Public Law (Oxford, Hart Publishing, 2004), 225–52.

[50] Universal Declaration of Human Rights 1948 Article 14(2); Convention relating to the Status of Refugees 1951 Article 1F. See also Articles 32 and 33. In the UK see IND Asylum Policy Unit Notice 1/2003 'Humanitarian Protection and Discretionary Leave', making clear that those who commit serious crimes, and terrorists or others who raise a threat to national security will be excluded from Humanitarian Protection, even if they cannot be removed. They will usually be granted discretionary leave.

Non-nationals are particularly vulnerable at such times and judges have a
significant role in interpreting and applying the law to ensure that there are
no exceptions to the presuppositions of legal order.

The first case of interest concerns the ongoing debate about the scope of the
exclusion clauses in refugee law. The UNHCR has recently provided updated
guidance on their interpretation and application.[51] It suggests that the primary
purpose of these clauses 'is to deprive those guilty of heinous acts, and serious
common crimes, of international refugee protection and to ensure that such
persons do not abuse the institution of asylum to avoid being held legally
accountable for their acts'.[52] The guidelines also address the issue of terrorism:

> Despite the lack of an ... agreed definition of *terrorism*, acts commonly
> considered to be terrorist in nature are likely to fall within the exclusion
> clauses even though Art. 1F is not to be equated with a simple anti-
> terrorism provision. Consideration of the exclusion clauses is, however,
> often unnecessary as suspected terrorists may not be eligible for refugee
> status in the first place, their fear being of legitimate prosecution as
> opposed to persecution for Convention reasons.[53]

The UNHCR's view is that each case requires individual consideration and
the fact that someone may be on a list of terrorist suspects might trigger
assessment under the exclusion clauses but should not in itself justify exclusion.[54] In addition, it suggests that the exclusion decision should in principle
be addressed within the regular status determination process.[55]

The Law Lords have addressed the issue of exclusion in *T* v. *Home
Secretary.*[56] The appellant, an Algerian citizen whose claim for asylum in
the UK was rejected, had been involved in a bomb attack on Algiers airport in
which ten people were killed and a raid on an army barracks at which another
person was killed. The special adjudicator concluded that this brought him
within the exclusion clause in Article 1F(b)[57] because, as provided in that

---

[51] UNHCR *Guidelines on International Protection: Application of the Exclusion Clauses-
Article 1F of the 1951 Convention relating to the Status of Refugees,* 4 September 2003 UN
Doc. HCR/GIP/03/05. See also Volker Türk, 'Forced Migration and Security' (2003) 15
International Journal of Refugee Law 113; Geoff Gilbert, 'Editorial' (2004) 16 *International
Journal of Refugee Law* 1.
[52] UNHCR ibid. para 2.   [53] Ibid. para 25   [54] Ibid. para 26.   [55] Ibid. para 31.
[56] [1996] AC 742 (HL). In the UK see, *KK* v. *Secretary of State for the Home Department*
[2004] UKIAT 00101; *Secretary of State for the Home Department* v. *PK* [2004] UKIAT
00089; *Gurung* v. *Secretary of State for the Home Department* [2002] UKIAT 04870. See also
Canada v. *Ward* [1993] 2 SCR 689; *Pushpanathan* v. *Canada* [1998] 1 SCR 982; *Zrig* v.
Minister of Citizenship and Immigration (2003) FCA 178; and in the US, see *INS* v. *Aguirre-
Aguirre* (1999) 526 US 415.
[57] Article 1F provides: 'The provisions of this Convention shall not apply to a person with
respect to whom there are serious reasons for considering that: (b) he has committed a
serious non-political crime outside the country of refuge prior to his admission to that
country as a refugee.'

provision, 'there were serious reasons for considering' that he had committed serious non-political crimes. The House of Lords dismissed his appeal. However, the ruling contains extensive consideration of the meaning of 'serious non-political crime' within the context of refugee law. It demonstrated again the role of the House of Lords in resolving a disagreement over the meaning of refugee law with reference to the values the law was intended to promote. The debate in this case primarily involved the precision of the exclusion clauses rather than whether or not he should have been excluded. The Law Lords displayed a desire to advance a clear definition which could be straightforwardly applied in the process of decision-making in light of the purpose of refugee law and the values it is intended to uphold. In particular, some individuals should be excluded from refugee status because of their criminal activity outside the state of refuge.

A related issue is what to do about those who are seeking asylum from persecution arising from anti-terrorism operations in other states. While a state may seek to arrest and prosecute terrorists, there is ample evidence of human rights being abused in the process. In *R. (Sivakumar) v. Secretary of State for the Home Department* the claimant was a Tamil from Sri Lanka whose claim for asylum was rejected by the Home Secretary.[58] Article 1F was not raised. On appeal the adjudicator accepted he had been detained and tortured, but this was due to the suspicion held that he was involved in terrorism and not to his political opinions. In the House of Lords, Lord Steyn stated that 'not all means of investigating suspected terrorist acts fall outside the protection of the Convention'.[59] By suggesting that being investigated for involvement in terrorist acts took a person outside the protection of the Convention the adjudicator had got it wrong. For Lord Hutton, the proper conclusion was that the acts of torture were inflicted not solely to obtain information to tackle terrorism, but also 'by reason of the torturers' deep antagonism towards him because he was a Tamil'.[60]

Past cases reveal that when national security, immigration and asylum collide then the judges are likely to defer extensively to the views of the executive. The dominance of this trend was confirmed in *Secretary of State for the Home Department* v. *Rehman*.[61] The issue here was whether the Home Secretary could make a deportation order under the Immigration Act 1971 on the grounds that the appellant's deportation was conducive to the public good for national security reasons. The appellant, a Pakistani national, arrived in the UK in February 1993 after being given entry clearance to work as a minister of religion in Oldham. Both his parents were British citizens. The Home Secretary refused his application for indefinite leave to remain, citing information linking the appellant to an Islamic terrorist

---

[58] [2003] UKHL 14.   [59] Ibid. para 17.   [60] Ibid. para 29.   [61] [2001] UKHL 47.

organization and argued that his deportation from the UK was in the interests of national security. Rehman appealed to SIAC.[62]

The Home Secretary stated that the appellant had directly supported terrorism in the Indian subcontinent and was therefore a threat to national security. But SIAC held, to the contrary, that the term 'national security' should be narrowly defined:

> We adopt the position that a person may be said to offend against national security if he engages in, promotes, or encourages violent activity which is targeted at the United Kingdom, its system of government or its people. This includes activities directed against the overthrow or destabilisation of a foreign government if that foreign government is likely to take reprisals against the United Kingdom which affect the security of the United Kingdom or of its nationals. National security extends also to situations where United Kingdom citizens are targeted, wherever they may be.[63]

SIAC concluded that it had not been established to a high civil balance of probabilities that the appellant was likely to be a threat to national security. The Home Secretary appealed successfully to the Court of Appeal.[64]

On further appeal to the House of Lords, Lord Slynn acknowledged that the term 'in the interests of national security' could not be used to justify any reason the Home Secretary had for seeking the deportation of an individual.[65] However, he did not accept the narrow interpretation suggested by the appellant.

> I accept that there must be a real possibility of an adverse affect on the United Kingdom for what is done by the individual under inquiry but I do not accept that it has to be direct or immediate. Whether there is a real possibility is a matter which has to be weighed up by the Secretary of State and balanced against the possible injustice to that individual if a deportation order is made.[66]

Lord Slynn stressed the need for SIAC to give due weight to the assessment and conclusions of the Home Secretary in the light of his responsibilities.[67] Lord Steyn agreed, adding that 'even democracies are entitled to protect themselves, *and* the executive is the best judge of the need for international co-operation to combat terrorism and counter-terrorist strategies'.[68] He concluded by acknowledging the well-established position that issues of national security do not fall beyond the competence of the courts. But it

---

[62] SIAC was created in 1997 in response to concerns raised in *Chahal* v. *UK* (1996) 23 EHRR 413, about the procedures for challenging deportation in the national security context. *Chahal* is important for its emphasis on the absolute nature of Article 3 protection in removal cases and its rejection of the need for a balancing exercise.
[63] Note 61 above at para 2.   [64] [2000] 3 WLR 1240 (CA).   [65] Note 61 above at para 15.
[66] Ibid. para 16.   [67] Ibid. para 26.   [68] Ibid. para 28.

was 'self-evidently right that national courts must give great weight to the views of the executive on matters of national security'.[69] Lord Hoffmann continued this theme, stating that SIAC had failed to acknowledge the inherent limitations of the judicial function which flowed from the doctrine of the separation of powers and the need 'in matters of judgment and evaluation of evidence, to show proper deference to the primary decision-maker'.[70] This restraint did not limit the appellate jurisdiction of SIAC and the need for it 'flows from a common-sense recognition of the nature of the issue and the differences in the decision-making processes and responsibilities of the Home Secretary and [SIAC]'.[71] In a postscript Lord Hoffmann stated:

> I wrote this speech some three months before the recent events in New York and Washington. They are a reminder that in matters of national security, the cost of failure can be high. This seems to me to underline the need for the judicial arm of government to respect the decisions of ministers of the Crown on the question of whether support for terrorist activities in a foreign country constitutes a threat to national security ... if the people are to accept the consequences of such decisions, they must be made by persons whom the people have elected and whom they can remove.[72]

The notion that the executive must be deferred to because of its democratic legitimacy and expertise, particularly in times of crisis, raises several problems. Lord Hoffmann's comments suggest that the executive can step outside the normal application of the rule of law in times of public emergency by making its own decision about what the law is. In addition, the ruling hampered the work of SIAC. *Rehman* is an example of the senior judiciary restraining the more liberal leanings of an (admittedly flawed) expert tribunal.

As Trevor Allan suggests, the focus should be on the quality of the reasons advanced.[73] The main question should be whether the legal reasoning is worthy of support in the individual case. To defer mainly because it is an executive decision based on sweeping assessments of the national security threat is problematic. In the national security context, the rule of law is tested, both in the sense of protecting individual rights and ensuring that an effective regulatory framework exists within which to offer security. By according conclusive weight to the views of the executive, judges are not discharging their responsibility to take a view on the meaning of law. If the courts do not do this they risk abandoning one of the values of the rule of law: the defence of the person against arbitrary power. Why the House of Lords was prepared to

---

[69] Ibid. para 31.   [70] Ibid. para 49.   [71] Ibid. para 58.

[72] Ibid. para 62. Cf. *R. v. BBC, ex parte Pro Life Alliance* [2003] UKHL 23, at para 74 ff; *R. v. Secretary of State for the Home Department, ex parte Simms and O'Brien* [2000] 2 AC 115.

[73] 'Common Law Reason and the Limits of Judicial Deference' in Dyzenhaus, *Unity of Public Law*, 289–306.

insist on its approach in *Shah/Islam* and *ex parte Adan* and not in *Rehman* remains unclear from the perspective of the substantive legal arguments.

Although dealing with a different issue, similar trends are evident in *A and others* v. *Secretary of State for the Home Department*,[74] which concerned the detention of a number of individuals under the Anti-Terrorism, Crime and Security Act 2001. The Act and the Human Rights Act 1998 (Designated Derogation) Order 2001 were introduced after the terrorist attacks of September 11. The Act empowers the Home Secretary to issue a certificate if he reasonably believes that the individual's continuing presence in the UK is a risk to national security and suspects that the person is a terrorist. Suspected international terrorists may be detained. There is a right of appeal to SIAC.[75] A challenge was brought against the provisions of the 2001 Act which allow the Home Secretary to detain indefinitely foreign nationals who are suspected of links with terrorist activity or organizations, but who cannot be deported, extradited or removed from the UK. The government derogated from Article 5 of the Convention for the specific purpose of these provisions. SIAC held that the measures were discriminatory and contrary to Articles 5 and 14, as they did not apply equally to British nationals.

On appeal against the SIAC decision the Court of Appeal reached a different conclusion. Following a similar approach to *Rehman*, Lord Woolf stated:

> Decisions as to what is required in the interest of national security are self-evidently within the category of decisions in relation to which the court is required to show considerable deference to the Secretary of State because he is better qualified to make an assessment as to what action is called for.[76]

British nationals were not in the same position as foreign nationals in this context. According to Lord Woolf, the non-nationals involved in this case no longer had a right to remain, only a right not to be removed.[77] This distinguished their plight from that of nationals. He also stressed the distinction in international law between the treatment of nationals and non-nationals. Parliament was entitled to limit the measures to foreign nationals on the basis that Article 15 of the European Convention on Human Rights (ECHR) permitted measures that derogate only 'to the extent strictly required by the exigencies of the situation'. The tension between Articles 14 and 15 had, Lord Woolf argued, an important impact. The Secretary of State was obliged to derogate only to the extent necessary and widening the powers of indefinite detention would conflict with this objective.

---

[74] [2002] EWCA Civ 1502.

[75] For criticism of SIAC from a former member see Sir Brian Barder, 'The Special Immigration Appeals Commission' *London Review of Books* Vol. 26 No. 6, 18 March 2004.

[76] Note 74 above at para 40.   [77] Ibid. para 47.

While acknowledging the importance of human rights protection, the Court of Appeal also accepted that it had to accord a degree of deference to the views of the executive when national security is involved. Lord Woolf stated:

> The unfortunate fact is that the emergency which the government believes to exist justifies the taking of action which would not otherwise be acceptable. The ECHR recognises that there can be circumstances where action of this sort is fully justified. It is my conclusion here, as a matter of law, and that is what we are concerned with, that action is justified. The important point is that the courts are able to protect the rule of law.[78]

Lord Woolf's reference to the rule of law rests uneasily with other aspects of the case. What the statement reveals is a concern to ensure that the government's policy could be justified with reference to established legal norms. But the rigorous assessment in other immigration and asylum cases was not present here. It is also evident from the SIAC ruling that scope for disagreement on the content of the law existed in this case. The weight given to the views of the executive (by both SIAC and the Court of Appeal) on what was necessary in this context, and whether there was in fact an emergency which threatened the life of the nation, is revealing. Again, there is evidence that the views of the Home Secretary are being accorded excessive weight. This is an area where 'anxious scrutiny' of the reasons provided is most needed. In my view, this is not happening when national security is raised.

Suspected international terrorists have not fared much better on other aspects of their detention,[79] but this deferential trend was halted to some extent in *Secretary of State for the Home Department* v. *M*.[80] In this case SIAC allowed an appeal against an order deporting a Libyan national. M was a failed asylum seeker, but he was not removed and it came to be accepted that he could not be returned. He was certified in November 2002 as a suspected international terrorist, his deportation was sought and he was subsequently detained. M's argument was that he feared persecution on return to Libya as a result of his opposition to the Ghadafi regime. The Home Secretary believed that he had links to al Qaeda. The judgment of the Chief Justice, Lord Woolf, contained strong comment on the value of SIAC, which can perhaps be viewed in the light of the public criticism of this body.[81] Lord Woolf stressed the critical nature of the value judgement which SIAC had to make:

> While the need for society to protect itself against acts of terrorism today is self evident, it remains of the greatest importance that, in a society which

---

[78] Ibid. para 64.
[79] See *R. (A)* v. *Secretary of State for the Home Department*, [2004] HRLR 12 (Admin) (refusing on grounds of national security to review conditions imposed on journalists for an interview of suspected terrorists).
[80] [2004] EWCA Civ 324.   [81] Note 75 above.

upholds the rule of law, if a person is detained, as 'M' was detained, that
individual should have access to an independent tribunal or court which
can adjudicate upon the question of whether the detention is lawful or not.
If it is not lawful, then he has to be released.[82]

This was the first time SIAC had allowed an appeal under the 2001 Act and
thus also the first time that the Home Secretary had reason to challenge the
decision under this legislation. It also followed the resignation of Sir Brian
Barder.

Another case arising from the work of SIAC was *G v. Secretary of State for
the Home Department*.[83] The case again involved an individual who had been
certified as a suspected international terrorist. He applied to SIAC for a grant
of bail, claiming that his mental and physical health had deteriorated rapidly
as a result of detention. SIAC held that once certain conditions were met he
should as a matter of principle be granted bail. The Home Secretary appealed
against this decision. The Court of Appeal held that it had no jurisdiction to
hear the appeal since bail was not a final determination of an appeal for the
purposes of the legislation. The Home Secretary again reacted badly to the
decision[84] and the government's response was to introduce an amendment to
the Asylum Bill then going through Parliament.[85] *A, B, C and others v.
Secretary of State for the Home Department* involved an appeal against SIAC
decisions not to cancel certificates issued by the Home Secretary.[86] The Court
of Appeal held that SIAC had not erred in its approach, but the issue which
provoked considerable comment was the admissibility of evidence which may
have been gathered through the use of torture by other states. The debate on
the efficacy of SIAC continues, with a general view that criminal prosecution
would be the best course of action for those who are now detained under the
2001 Act.

Although not specifically in the national security area a case involving
public order further supports the general argument. In *R. (Farrakhan) v.
Secretary of State for the Home Department* the claimant was an African-
American US citizen who was refused entry to the UK on public order
grounds.[87] The issue was whether Article 10 of the European Convention
on Human Rights was engaged in a decision to exclude an individual to
prevent his expressing opinions in the UK. The Court of Appeal held that
Article 10 was engaged, but concluded that the exclusion was for a legitimate
aim under Article 10(2). Disagreeing with the judge at first instance the Court
of Appeal held that the Home Secretary had provided sufficient explanation

[82] Note 80 above , at para 34 (iii).   [83] [2004] EWCA Civ 265.
[84] 'Blunkett may change law over suspect's bail', *Guardian*, 23 April 2004.
[85] Mr Browne, HC Deb. 421 col. 778w, 17 May 2004. See Asylum and Immigration
(Treatment of Claimants, Etc.) Act 2004, s. 32.
[86] [2004] EWCA Civ 1123.   [87] [2002] 3 WLR 481 (CA).

for the decision. While this involves a difficult assessment, it was not evident in this case that a 'significant threat to community relations' would be the result of the visit. A different approach was evident in the case of Abu Hamza, a prominent Muslim cleric who had expressed vocal support for terrorism. In this instance, however, the individual involved was a British citizen. The Home Secretary opted to try to revoke his citizenship. Abu Hamza appealed to SIAC and while his appeal was pending his extradition to the US was sought. He was subsequently charged under anti-terrorism legislation in the UK. This case has not been resolved at the time of writing. These cases provide useful examples of the approaches adopted by the Home Secretary to deal with those (citizens and non-citizens) whose views and actions are perceived to be a threat to public order and/or national security. It displays a concern to control the political activism of both citizens and non-citizens alike.

Beyond the national security context the views of the Home Secretary, and the administrative perspective, are accorded significant weight, but they are not generally regarded as decisive. While one can understand a certain judicial unease in addressing national security matters, excessive deference to the views of the executive is inappropriate if there is a principled commitment to the consistent interpretation and application of the law. Evidence suggests that this is precisely the time when the values which underpin the rule of law need to be upheld. While the Home Secretary will have access to detailed factual information, and is the person who will face democratic accountability for the decision, the courts should not automatically defer to his or her understanding of the substantive content of the law. On this matter the Home Secretary is in no better position than a judge. This view is reinforced when one considers that human rights standards are now a secure part of domestic law in the UK in the form of the Human Rights Act 1998. The judges have a responsibility to ensure that the law, properly understood, is applied to all on an equal basis. The risk is that exceptional treatment of particular groups and particular legal subject areas will lead to further erosion of existing guarantees.

E. Talking about asylum law

The cases examined address some key areas of disagreement over the meaning of asylum law. Questions were raised over the definition of 'refugee', the management of the asylum process, the effective implementation of international agreements, as well as the matter of national security. The House of Lords has now clarified central elements of the refugee definition in an attempt to resolve disputes within the process of adjudication. The Law Lords, in my view, have not adopted an approach which can easily be reduced to a single or unified theme. On the current evidence it is not possible to be wholly dismissive or unequivocally supportive of the role of the senior judiciary. There is no simple pattern that has emerged in the cases. However, it is inaccurate to describe the judicial approach as a concerted attempt to undermine government asylum policy. When they might have been robust they have been deferential. While there have been incremental advances in doctrinal development, and in ensuring procedures are applied fairly to each individual, the senior judiciary consistently displays a measure of deference toward the executive and a rather generous understanding of the managerial problems faced by successive governments. The risk in this approach is that the value which the rule of law attaches to the protection of the individual is steadily eroded and the responsibility for applying legal standards is neglected.

On national security, decisions reveal an established trend of deference towards the government's view. This is evident in *Rehman* and *Farrakhan*. In these cases, the judges selected an approach designed to facilitate government policy and relied on deferring to the executive on the basis of its democratic mandate and/or special position with regard to the facts. The reference made to the rule of law in *A and others* by Lord Woolf reflects a rather 'thin' version of the concept. This general 'facilitative approach' goes beyond national security and is evident in the other cases examined above. *M* does not necessarily signal a major shift in approach, although the comments about the role of SIAC are significant when viewed in context.

The senior judiciary places considerable weight on the overall management implications of judicial decision-making and is inclined to defer excessively to the executive, particularly if national security is raised. Reservations expressed by politicians about judicial activism appear to have little validity. This is a cause for concern. Even in areas where a clash with the government is likely, the judges should insist on following the most persuasive legal argument in the context of the asylum case before it. Fairness to the individual and equality before the law should not be abandoned when judges are faced with difficult choices. These values are more, not less, important when national security concerns are raised or when a marginalized group is at risk. In this context, each individual relies on institutions willing to remain consistently focused on the rule of law and the values which underpin it. The defence of legality is not the exclusive preserve of the judiciary. Those who are serious about creating a culture of respect for human rights know that the principles of legal order must be reflected throughout public administration and the parliamentary system.

IV. Conclusion

In this chapter, I have attempted to place the judicial role in asylum cases within a wider conception of legal order. 'Dialogic' approaches which shift attention away from institutions and sources of power towards argumentation and justification are useful for both understanding and evaluating the existing case law. Law is arguable, but we should concentrate on the legal arguments which deserve recognition in a democracy committed to human rights, equality and the rule of law. The focus shifts to the interpretation of legal norms. Laws enacted by Parliament do not function in a legal void. This approach, however, also puts considerable stress on promoting a responsive parliamentary process which can react to and internalize arguments of principle.

The traditional values associated with the rule of law are of particular significance for refugees and asylum seekers in all cases whether national security is at issue or not. The protection against arbitrary power and the basic principles of fairness, which are built into legal order, remain important to marginalized groups. Judges, and others, have a duty to uphold the rule of law even when they risk serious public criticism and even when there is a general political climate of insecurity. The protection from arbitrary power that the concept should bring is undermined if judges refuse to engage with contested areas of public policy. Recent attempts by the government to oust judicial review in the asylum context have shown little recognition of the potential value of judicial scrutiny of the executive. Asylum policy in the UK is increasingly marked by measures which limit in practice the ability of individuals to challenge asylum decisions. While not as blatant as the deliberate exclusion of judicial review the practical impact can be similar. The rule of law may be undermined by a combination of laws and policies which make it difficult to contest the legality of administrative decision-making.

In my view, there are two problems which have arisen in asylum law when considering the judicial role. First, the judges are too often influenced by the broader policy debates on asylum and the problems the government has experienced in trying to manage the process in an efficient and effective way. These factors should not be discounted, but if they become the dominant concern there is an increased risk of unfairness in individual cases. Adjudication in asylum cases should revolve primarily around the interpretation and application of existing norms to individual cases. In a climate of hostility toward asylum seekers, the heated public policy debates on asylum should not distract judges from their constitutional role.

Second, there is a willingness to defer to the executive when rigorous scrutiny of the merits of legal arguments is required. Due deference is appropriate but more attention should be paid to the reasons offered in justification. Many arguments advanced in the national security, immigration and asylum context are simply unpersuasive. Reference to national security, public order and other such concepts should not be enough to deter judges from a close assessment of the law and its proper application.[88]

---

[88] Cf. *Abbasi and another* v. *Secretary of State for Foreign and Commonwealth Affairs and Secretary of State for the Home Department* [2002] EWCA Civ 1598, para 106: 'It is not an answer to a claim for judicial review to say that the source of the power of the Foreign Office is the prerogative. It is the subject matter that is determinative.'

This is precisely when the rule of law is most at risk. When national security also becomes a factor there is a real risk that deference to executive judgment will result in weak arguments gaining undue prominence.

Under the substantive concept of legality advanced here, adherence to the rule of law brings with it a commitment to respect the dignity of the individual. While its application is associated with the judiciary, this is not the only institution responsible for ensuring respect for the principle. In my view, the senior judiciary has on occasions demonstrated an understanding of the significance of the rule of law in asylum law. But there is no reason why arguments of principle should be confined to the courtroom. The 'dialogic' model can be easily mocked. But it does capture what should be a dynamic relationship between the courts, the executive and the legislature with the aim of internalizing arguments of principle in processes of democratic deliberation.

When national security is raised there is a danger of inadequate scrutiny of government arguments and excessive deference undermining a thorough examination of the substantive legal issues. Asylum seekers, in particular, depend on judges and decision-makers who are prepared to uphold the values which underpin legal order. These are values which are in danger in times of fear and insecurity.

9

The financial war on terrorism

I. Introduction

In the aftermath of 9/11 many facets of counter-terrorism legislation have come under intensive scrutiny. Provisions granting state officials enhanced investigative powers, greater authority to withhold information from the public and broader powers to detain people without trial have all been hotly debated around the world. In contrast, relatively little attention has been paid to the provisions aimed at controlling the financing of terrorism. Yet these provisions have the potential to affect an extremely broad range of economic activity, both legitimate and illegitimate, and for that reason are worthy of scrutiny.

This chapter is designed to provide an introduction to the legal instruments designed to counter financing of terrorism and the policy concerns that they raise. Part I describes three main types of legal provisions designed to combat the financing of terrorism (prohibitions, provisions authorizing deprivations of property and monitoring provisions), different approaches that have been taken to the design of those provisions, and the advantages and disadvantages of each approach. The central objective of this Part is to discuss the range of actors and transactions that are likely to be affected by the various legal initiatives, with particular attention to the degree of proximity to actual terrorist activity that is required and whether legitimate commercial activity is likely to be affected. Part II then examines concerns that have been raised about the manner in which these provisions are likely to be implemented and enforced. Part III discusses whether, even if reasonably well implemented and enforced, these provisions are likely to be effective in combating the financing of terrorism. The chapter concludes with a call for further research in this area.

I am grateful to GuyLaine Charles, Alan Tan Khee, Victor V. Ramraj, Mary Wong and participants in the Symposium on Comparative Anti-Terrorism Law & Policy for helpful comments upon an earlier version and to Michael Kruse and Kevin Lees for excellent research assistance.

II. The scope of legislation concerned with financing of terrorism

A. Background

Much of the recent interest in counter-terrorism legislation in general, and legislation concerned with financing of terrorism in particular, dates to 9/11. Even before that date, countries such as the United States and the United Kingdom had adopted legislation that prohibited the most significant forms of financing of terrorism. However, prior to September 2001, the international community as a whole does not appear to have been fully committed to legislating against financing of terrorism, as evidenced by the fact that the United Nations Convention for the Suppression of Terrorist Financing (Financing of Terrorism Convention) was only opened for signature in January 2000 and prior to 11 September 2001 had been ratified by only four countries. Strikingly, the Financing of Terrorism Convention now has 132 signatories and has been ratified by 117 countries.[1]

Since 2001 there has been significantly more international interest in the development of legal instruments designed to combat the financing of terrorism. In the immediate aftermath of the attacks, the United Nations Security Council passed Resolution 1373 which, among other things, bound all of the UN's member states to 'prevent and suppress the financing of terrorist acts . . . ', to implement the Financing of Terrorism Convention and to cooperate with other countries in this regard.[2] Resolution 1373 also created specific obligations for states to criminalize the financing of terrorism and to freeze the assets of entities implicated in terrorism. This Resolution builds upon a previous series of Security Council resolutions binding states to freeze the assets of individuals or entities related to al Qaeda and the Taliban, including those designated upon a list maintained by the Security Council Committee established pursuant to Resolution 1267 concerning Al Qaeda, the Taliban and associated individuals and entities (the '1267 Committee').[3] Resolution 1373 was also complemented by the efforts of other influential international organizations. For example, on 31 October 2001 the Financial Action Task Force ('FATF') released a list of eight recommendations concerning terrorist financing which, in addition to the matters referred to in Resolution 1373, also discussed monitoring provisions such as reporting of suspicious transactions.[4]

---

[1] UN Doc. A/RES/54/109 (1999), 39 I.L.M. 270, entered into force 1 April 2002. See, http://untreaty.un.org/ENGLISH/Status/Chapter_xviii/treaty11.asp.

[2] United Nations S/RES/1373 (2001).

[3] See S/RES/1526 (2004), S/RES/1455 (2003), S/RES/1452 (2002), S/RES/1390 (2002), S/RES/1388 (2002), S/RES/1363 (2001), S/RES/1333 (2000), S/RES/1267 (1999).

[4] Financial Action Task Force, *Special Recommendations on Terrorist Financing*, 31 October 2001.

The legislative provisions that have emerged from or coincided with this wave of international initiatives can be grouped into three categories: prohibitions upon various types of dealings with terrorists and their property; provisions permitting terrorists to be deprived of their property; and measures designed to make it easier for the government to monitor dealings with terrorists or their property. The following sections discuss each of these categories of provisions in turn. The final section briefly discusses the extent to which recent legislative initiatives extend pre-existing law.

B. Prohibitions

1. Overview and objectives

The legislation most obviously concerned with countering the financing of terrorism is generally designed to prohibit, upon pain of criminal sanction, activities that in some way allow resources – both property and services – to be directed toward terrorism. These provisions appear to be designed both to punish and prevent dealings with terrorists. The purely punitive objective reflects the fact that in many cases knowingly financing terrorist activity seems just as blameworthy as more direct forms of participation. As for the preventative function, there are two points to consider. The first is that, to the extent that these provisions discourage various actors from providing resources to terrorists, they cut off terrorists' access to resources that they may need in order to carry out terrorist activities. The second and perhaps less obvious point stems from the fact that, typically, provisions ostensibly concerned with the financing of terrorism actually serve to discourage a broad range of dealings with terrorists. As a result, they affect actors who have had even relatively innocuous dealings with terrorists and, in many cases, expose them to risk of criminal liability. This in turn gives law enforcement officials a great deal of leverage over those actors. Officials might be able to use that leverage to persuade those actors to assist in efforts to apprehend the actual terrorists.

The extent to which the prohibitions upon financing terrorism achieve these objectives depends upon the physical and mental elements of the conduct that they capture. In other words, they depend upon what sorts of activities are considered to be 'financing', what sorts of activities constitute the 'terrorism' whose financing is prohibited, and what mental state must accompany the physical acts that amount to financing of terrorism in order to attract liability.

2. What activities are covered?

There appears to be a reasonably strong international consensus on the core of the definition of 'financing' of terrorism. That consensus is embodied in the Financing of Terrorism Convention. The Convention's main operative articles provide that criminal liability should be imposed upon not only individuals or entities that engage in financing of terrorism but also their accomplices, leaders and co-conspirators.[5] The Convention effectively defines 'financing' to mean providing or collecting funds (defined to mean assets of all kinds) with the intention or knowledge that they will be used, in whole or in part, to carry out terrorist activity.[6] Terrorist activity is defined both by reference to a list of specific criminal acts that are commonly committed by terrorists as well as a broad principled definition. It is worth noting that the term 'provides' seems to capture not only the donation of property for use in connection with terrorism, but also the sale or lease of property for use in connection with terrorism on commercially reasonable terms.[7]

For the purposes of prohibiting financing of terrorism some countries define terrorist activity both in distinctly local terms as well as those used in the Financing of Terrorism Convention. For instance, in the United States the offence of 'providing material support to terrorists' is formulated as the provision of support or resources for use in preparation for, or in carrying out, violations of specified provisions of the US Code. Meanwhile, the offence of financing terrorism is defined as providing funds to carry out, essentially, the set of terrorist activities referred to in the Financing of Terrorism Convention.[8] Other jurisdictions do employ general definitions of terrorist activity but have modified the definition used in the Financing of Terrorism Convention. The Convention's definition essentially equates terrorism with politically motivated violence but it is not uncommon for lawmakers to limit the types of political motivations that qualify as terrorist motivations or to expand the set of acts that qualify as terrorist forms of violence.

Many jurisdictions also depart from the terms of the Financing of Terrorism Convention by employing broader definitions of the concept of financing. For instance, Canada and the UK explicitly proscribe the solicitation of funds for the purposes of terrorism.[9] Furthermore, in Canada and the UK it is an offence merely to 'use' or 'possess' property with the intention or knowledge that it will be used for terrorist purposes.[10] This language suggests that virtually nothing in the way of an overt act need be committed in order to trigger liability under these provisions, thus raising concerns that people may be punished simply for having bad thoughts.[11] In addition, many countries

---

[5] Ibid., Art. 2(5).   [6] Financing of Terrorism Convention, Art. 2(1).
[7] This point is made explicit in the UK's Terrorism Act 2000 s. 15(4): 'In this section a reference to the provision of money or other property is a reference to its being given, lent or otherwise made available, *whether or not for consideration*' (emphasis added).
[8] 18 U.S.C., ss. 2339A, 2339C.
[9] See Criminal Code, s. 83.03 and Terrorism Act 2000, s. 15(1) (referring to a person who 'invites a person to provide' financing).
[10] Criminal Code, s. 83.04(b); Terrorism Act 2000, s. 16(2).   [11] Ibid.

explicitly prohibit the provision of certain services as well as property. For instance, the US prohibition on providing 'material support or resources' expressly proscribes the provision of financial services, lodging, training and transportation.[12]

Perhaps the most significant expansion of the prohibitions set out in the Financing of Terrorism Convention is the fact that many instruments prohibit the financing of terrorists as well as the financing of terrorist activities. The most prominent examples of this approach involve prohibitions upon dealings with individuals or organizations that have been placed upon some sort of official list.[13] Targeted entities are sometimes given an opportunity to challenge their listing – either in a judicial proceeding or some other forum – and in principle this opportunity can arise either before or after the decision becomes final. However, as will be discussed below, these lists are often also used for the purpose of targeting property for freezing and forfeiture. In this context it is counter-productive to give targeted organizations advance notice of the state's intention to place them on an official list because it gives them an opportunity to transfer funds to safety before they become subject to official sanctions.[14] Perhaps as a consequence, the listing procedures created by the Security Council's 1267 Committee and under the domestic legislation of countries such as the United States, Canada and the UK typically do not provide targeted individuals or entities with prior notice.[15] Also, in the case of the 1267 Committee's listing procedure, it is not clear that listing decisions can be challenged before any sort of judicial body.[16] In other jurisdictions, however, more substantial evidence and/or a judicial finding may be required

---

[12] 18 U.S.C. s. 2339A ('In this section, the term "material support or resources" 'means currency or other financial securities, financial services, lodging, training, expert advice or assistance, safehouses, false documentation or identification, communications equipment, facilities, weapons, lethal substances, explosives, personnel, transportation, and other physical assets, except medicine or religious materials'). The Canadian legislation separately proscribes making available 'financial or other related services' and 'participating in or contributing to an activity of a terrorist group' (the latter term is defined to include providing training, skill or an expertise). See Criminal Code, ss. 83.03 and 83.18.

[13] 18 U.S.C. s. 2339B; Executive Order 13224, s. 1.

[14] Executive Order 13224, s. 10.

[15] See, for example, 1267 Committee, *Guidelines of the Committee for the Conduct of its Work* (adopted November 2002 and amended on 10 April 2003), http://www.un.org/Docs/sc/committees/1267/1267_guidelines.pdf; 8 U.S.C. s. 1189(a)(2) (procedure for designating a 'foreign terrorist organization') (held unconstitutional in *National Council of Resistance of Iran v. Department of State*, 251, F 3d 192 (D. C. Cir. 2001); Criminal Code, s. 83.05 (procedure for designating a 'listed entity'); Terrorism Act 2000, s. 3.

[16] See Jose E. Alvarez, 'Hegemonic International Law Revisited' (2003) 97 AJIL 873 at 876–7; E. Alexandra Dosman, 'For the Record: Designating "Listed Entities" for the Purposes of Terrorist Financing Offences at Canadian Law' (2004) 62(1) *U. T. Fac. L. Rev.* 1.

before steps will be taken to sanction an allegedly terrorist organization, particularly when it purports to be a charitable organization.[17]

Prohibitions upon financing of terrorists are not always limited to prohibitions upon dealings with organizations located upon official lists. For example, under Canadian law it is an offence to finance a 'terrorist group', defined as an entity that has *either* been placed on an official list *or* 'has as one of its purposes or activities facilitating or carrying out any terrorist activity'. Significantly, this definition appears to include even an individual who has expressed an intention to support terrorist activity.[18] The UK position is similar. Although the Terrorism Act 2000 only forbids the financing of 'proscribed organizations', regulations promulgated under the United Nations Act 1946 make it an offence to provide financing to 'a person who commits, attempts to commit, facilitates or participates in the commission of acts of terrorism [or their accomplices]' without a licence.[19]

There are several advantages to legislating against terrorists as opposed to terrorist activities. First, this approach makes it possible to target individuals who provide 'blank checks' to terrorists by providing financing for terrorist organizations' general purposes as opposed to specific activities. Second, dispensing with the need for proof that financing is connected to specific terrorist activities may, by reducing the burden on law enforcement agencies, make it easier to secure convictions.[20]

The principal disadvantage of the organizational approach is the danger of proscribing legitimate as well as illegitimate dealings with terrorists. This problem arises in a variety of contexts but perhaps most frequently in connection with charitable organizations with mixed purposes and activities. For example, it is not uncommon for organizations suspected of sponsoring terrorist acts to have official purposes that encompass poverty relief and peaceful political engagement. It may be difficult to establish that either the purpose or the effect of financing such an organization will be to support terrorist activity. Alternatively, it may be the case that any funds provided are likely to support both legitimate charitable activities and terrorist activities.

---

[17] Second Report of the Monitoring Group established pursuant to Resolution 1363 (2001) and extended by Resolutions 1390 (2002) and 1455 (2003), on sanctions against al Qaeda, the Taliban and individuals and entities associated with them, S/2003/1070 (*Second Report of the 1363 Monitoring Group*, para. 39).

[18] Criminal Code, ss. 83.03, 83.08. The conclusion that a single natural person can qualify as a terrorist group follows from the fact that the term 'entity' as it is used in s 83.01 is defined to include a 'person'. By contrast, the US legislation refers to 'foreign terrorist organizations' and the term organization is defined to include 'a group of persons', but does not explicitly include a mere 'person.' See 18 U.S.C. s. 2339B and 8 U.S.C. s. 1101.

[19] See Terrorism Act 2000, s. 1(5) and Terrorism (United Nations Measures) Order 2001, s. 3.

[20] *Legislation Against Terrorism: A Consultation Paper*, Cm 4178 (Stationery Office, London 1998), chapter 6.

Under these circumstances, subjecting either the organization or its supporters to the harsh sanctions contemplated by counter-terrorism legislation may be a disproportionate response to the threat they pose.

Prohibitions upon financing of terrorists rather than terrorist activity also risk capturing transactions that are legitimate in the sense that they enable terrorists to secure their human rights.[21] For example, access to legal services is guaranteed to some extent under virtually all human rights instruments. However, an unqualified ban on dealings with terrorists seems to render lawyers potentially liable for providing services to terrorists. The larger the number of proscribed types of dealings and the broader the set of terrorists with whom those dealings are proscribed, the more significant will be this concern. For example, the language of Security Council Resolution 1373, which is reflected in the domestic legislation of countries such as Canada, contains a sweeping ban upon dealings with terrorists. It is difficult to see how such legislation, if applied to its fullest extent, can be compatible with human rights norms.[22] By comparison, UK law, which covers only the provision of property and 'financial or related services' and in certain circumstances allows parties to seek a licence to engage in prohibited transactions, is less suspect.[23]

Prohibitions upon the financing of terrorists can also threaten legitimate economic activity when individuals or organizations have ambiguous purposes. This sort of ambiguity threatens to create two types of problems. First, wholly legitimate entities may be shunned by third parties concerned about violating the prohibitions. Second, some parties may be prosecuted for unwittingly supporting terrorists. The most obvious way to mitigate these concerns is by limiting the scope of organizational prohibitions to entities that have been placed upon an official list and granting entities that have been or are about to be listed an opportunity to challenge the decision. However, publicly proscribing the financing of only listed terrorists as opposed to all terrorists is only an effective tactic when lawmakers have solid prior information about both the existence of an individual or group with terrorist

---

[21] The US legislation does, however, exclude the provision of medicine or religious materials. See 18 U.S.C. s. 2339A.

[22] Security Council Resolution 1452 permits the 1267 Committee to create exceptions from the sanctions overseen by that Committee in respect of funds required to meet targeted individuals' 'basic expenses', such as expenditures upon food and medical care. However, as Jose Alvarez has pointed out, the Committee has the discretion to refuse to authorize member states to use this exception. See Alvarez, above at 877n.

[23] The Canadian Criminal Code contains a provision that allows the Solicitor-General to authorize transactions with a terrorist group. Unfortunately, however, the provision only seems to permit the Solicitor-General to provide an exemption from liability arising under one of several provisions that prohibit the financing of terrorists. See Criminal Code s. 83.09.

purposes or activities and its *nom de guerre* at any given point in time. This seems unrealistic.

The most significant concerns about the organizational approach to prohibiting financing of terrorism are probably the concerns about impacts upon legitimate economic activities. However, a second ground for concern is the idea that regimes adopting this approach risk violating notions of procedural fairness. A perfectly fair regime would give suspected terrorists notice and an entitlement to a judicial hearing, and perhaps even rights of appeal, both before and after the imposition of any prohibitions upon dealings with them. In practice, however, many legal regimes provide far fewer procedural protections to alleged terrorists. To a certain extent these departures from the procedural ideal can be justified by the need to preserve the element of surprise for law enforcement agencies and to prevent publication of confidential information. However, the virtually complete absence of procedural protections from some regimes is difficult to justify.

3. Mental elements

In addition to the physical elements described so far, the criminal laws concerned with financing of terrorism also include some sort of mental element, typically either intention or knowledge. Unfortunately, the meanings of these concepts are not wholly self-evident. For instance, does a person who provides financing to an organization possess the requisite mental element if he or she is unaware that the organization has been placed upon some sort of official list and unaware of the organization's specific terrorist activities, but are aware in a general way that it engages in terrorist activities? Suppose the financier lacks even the most general sort of knowledge about the terrorist activities? Or, what if the financier is aware of some of the terrorist activities but honestly believes that their resources will be channelled toward non-terrorist activities?

The legislation in some jurisdictions provides guidance on some of these issues. For example, the Canadian provision that makes it an offence to participate in or contribute to the activity of a terrorist group states that the offence may be committed 'whether or not ... the accused knows the specific nature of any terrorist activity that may be facilitated or carried out by a terrorist group'.[24] In many cases, however, the answers to these questions are left open by the text of the statutory provisions. So, for example, there has been litigation in the United States over whether the offence of providing material support to a foreign terrorist organization includes a requirement that the defendant be aware of the fact that the organization has been designated as a foreign terrorist organization or of the activities that led to

---

[24] Criminal Code, s. 83.18(2).

the designation. In one particular case, the Ninth Circuit rejected the US government's argument that neither form of knowledge was required.[25]

In many circumstances, the approach taken to defining the mental elements of financing offences will be at least as important in determining their practical effects as will the approach taken to defining the physical elements. This point is particularly important to keep in mind in connection with discussions of whether legislation can or should capture financing of terrorist activity or financing of terrorists. Suppose that financing a terrorist group with knowledge of its general purposes is taken to qualify as proof of an intention to finance terrorist activity. Now suppose that this determination is made in the context of a prosecution for conspiring to finance terrorist activity. This possibility suggests that a broad definition of the concepts of intention or knowledge can allow legislation that appears to capture only financing of terrorist activity to effectively capture financing of terrorists. Of course the reverse is also true. If a person is not considered to have knowingly financed a terrorist group unless he has specific knowledge of the activities that support the conclusion that the group is a terrorist one, provisions that ostensibly take an organizational approach to legislating against the financing of terrorism will be essentially vitiated.

C. Deprivation of property

1. Overview and objectives

Lawmakers concerned with financing of terrorism have not limited themselves to pursuing the individuals who participate in channelling resources to terrorists or terrorist activity. They have also crafted laws that, where physically possible, permit resources connected to terrorists or terrorist activity to be removed from the control of terrorists, whether by freezing, seizing or confiscating the property through forfeiture proceedings.

When a government freezes property, it prohibits transfer, conversion, disposition or movement of assets, although other legal rights over the property remain intact. The effects of seizure of property are similar to a freeze, but in addition the government typically takes control of the property. Freezes and seizures of property are often designed to be temporary measures.[26] By contrast, forfeiture or confiscation permanently transfers legal

---

[25] *Humanitarian Law Project* v. *United States DOJ*, 352 F 3d 382 (9th Cir. 2003).

[26] In the UK, assets can be seized for just 48 hours: Terrorism Act 2000, s. 25(4). However, authorities can obtain an order for further detention for no more than three months from the time of the initial seizure: ss. 26(1) and 26(2). It is possible to have more than one order, but the assets cannot be seized for more than two years from the time of the first order: s. 26(4). In Canada, a report is required within seven days identifying the property seized and the location of the property: Criminal Code, s. 462.32(4). Property may be

rights over the property to the government and extinguishes the rights of some or all other parties. Regardless of the nature of the deprivation contemplated, however, legislation providing for deprivation of property associated with terrorism typically has two main components: a definition of the types of property that can be targeted, and a description of the procedural steps that must be followed in order to accomplish various forms of deprivation.

To a certain extent, these provisions are designed to complement the prohibitions upon financing of terrorism discussed in the previous section by ensuring that significant economic consequences flow from violating those prohibitions. This is consistent with a global trend towards ensuring that legal mechanisms exist to deprive offenders of property that represents the instruments or proceeds of crime.[27] However, as will be shown below, not all of the provisions that permit deprivation of property are triggered by violations of the prohibitions upon financing of terrorism. Consequently, the deprivation provisions can be used in circumstances where it is inconvenient or impossible to link assets that are discovered to be under the control of terrorists to transactions with specific actors. This may be particularly helpful in combating terrorist organizations that rely heavily upon resources generated by business enterprises – either legitimate or illegitimate – operated by full-blown members of the organization.

2. Which property?

Perhaps the most interesting conceptual issue that arises in defining the types of property that can be removed from the control of terrorists is whether it is appropriate to include only property associated with terrorist activity, or whether it is important to include any and all property associated with terrorists.[28] As far as freezing property is concerned, the issue is resolved by Resolution 1373. That resolution calls upon states to freeze the property of 'persons who commit, or attempt to commit, terrorist acts or participate in or

---

detained for up to six months: s. 462.35(1). Property can be detained even longer if forfeiture proceedings have been instituted: s. 462.35(2). The period can be extended from six months upon a judge's satisfaction: s. 462.35(3). In the United States, however, the broad language of the International Emergency Economic Powers Act (IEEPA) appears to permit assets to be seized or blocked so long as the unusual and extraordinary threat exists or the US remains in armed hostilities.

[27] See generally, Guy Stessens, *Money Laundering: A New International Law Enforcement Model* (New York, Cambridge University Press, 2000), at 4–5; R. T. Naylor, 'Washout: A Critique of Follow-the-Money Methods in Crime Control Policy' (1999) 32 *Crime, L. & Soc. Change* 1.

[28] Another important issue is to what extent should the interests of third parties be affected by measures designed to deprive terrorists of property? For a general discussion of the issue of the effects of forfeiture on third parties, see Kevin E. Davis, 'The Effects of Forfeiture on Third Parties' (2003) 48 *McGill L. J.* 183.

facilitate the commission of terrorist acts; of entities owned or controlled directly or indirectly by such persons; and of persons and entities acting on behalf of, or at the direction of such persons and entities . . .'[29]

Resolution 1373 is silent on the question of what sort of property ought to be subject to forfeiture as opposed to a freeze. Here the Financing of Terrorism Convention adopts the narrow approach, instructing states to take appropriate measures for the forfeiture of only those funds 'used or allocated for the purposes of committing terrorist offenses and the proceeds derived from such offences'.[30] However, the trend seems to be for states to adopt a broader approach in their domestic legislation. For example, Canadian law allows the Attorney General to apply for an order of forfeiture not only for property that 'has been or will be used, in whole or in part, to facilitate or carry out a terrorist activity',[31] but also for 'property owned or controlled by or on behalf of a terrorist group'.[32] Likewise, British law allows for forfeiture of cash intended to be used for terrorism; proceeds of terrorism; and cash that forms the whole or part of the resources of a proscribed organization.[33] Meanwhile, some post-September 11 American legislation goes even further. The Patriot Act extends the possibility of forfeiture not just to all instruments and proceeds and all property belonging to terrorist groups or entities, but to all assets affording any person a 'source of influence' over terrorist entities.[34] Furthermore, additional Patriot Act provisions amending the International Emergency Economic Powers Act (IEEPA) allow for confiscation of *any* property of any foreign person, foreign organization or foreign country that the President or his officials have determined has 'planned, authorized, aided, or engaged' in an attack on the United States.[35]

The advantages and disadvantages of targeting property of terrorists as opposed to simply property associated with specific terrorist acts parallel the advantages and disadvantages of targeting actors who are linked to specific terrorist activities as opposed to terrorist groups. On the one hand, the organizational approach makes it possible to deprive terrorists of property that has not been allocated to specific activities but is nonetheless available for its general purposes. This approach also relieves law enforcement agents of the burden of linking property to specific terrorist activities. On the other hand, depriving actors of property that is not linked to any particular terrorist activity may be inappropriate in cases involving organizations with ambiguous or mixed purposes.

---

[29] Resolution 1373, Art. 1(c).　　[30] Financing of Terrorism Convention, Art. 8(2).
[31] Criminal Code, s. 83.14(1).　　[32] Ibid.　　[33] Terrorism Act 2000, s. 25(1).
[34] 18 U.S.C. s. 981 (a)(1)(G) (as amended by the Patriot Act, s. 806). This language is derived from the Racketeer Influenced Corrupt Organizations (RICO) implying that the draftsperson of the Patriot Act equated terrorist groups with 'criminal enterprises'.
[35] 50 U.S.C. 1702(a)(1)(C) (as amended by the Patriot Act, s. 106).

3. Procedure for effecting deprivations

As we saw above, the mental elements of the relevant offences place important practical limits upon the range of activity likely to be captured by criminal prohibitions upon financing of terrorism. Another highly significant point is that the effective range of those prohibitions is also determined by the procedural rules that govern investigations and prosecutions of such offences. Similarly, in the case of provisions directly concerned with freezing, seizing and confiscating property associated with terrorism, the practical effect of the provisions can only be assessed after taking into account a range of other legal provisions. The effective scope of the provisions that focus upon property linked to terrorist organizations is heavily determined by the substantive and procedural rules mentioned above that govern the identification of terrorist organizations. The procedure that must be followed prior to depriving a person or organization of property also places important practical safeguards upon the property likely to be affected.

In functional terms, the two most critical features of the procedural regimes at issue here are first, whether any sort of judicial hearing is required before depriving a person of his property and second, the evidentiary burden that the government must meet. Under both British and Canadian law, the pattern is that increasingly onerous procedural requirements must be satisfied in order to freeze, seize and confiscate property. Specifically, in both jurisdictions, assets can be frozen by the merely administrative act of designating an organization as a terrorist organization, whereas seizure requires satisfying a judge that there are 'reasonable grounds' for suspicion that the property is related to terrorist activities,[36] and forfeiture requires satisfying a judge on a 'balance of probabilities'.[37] This is all broadly consistent with the approach typically taken in American federal forfeiture law. For the most part the Patriot Act simply expanded that existing body of law to include terrorism offences. However, the Patriot Act also expanded executive powers through the IEEPA, giving the Department of Treasury almost *carte blanche* to confiscate a group's assets without the evidentiary and due process protections normally afforded through federal forfeiture law. As already mentioned, the trigger is an attack upon the United States by foreign nationals and the President's determination that the group or entity planned, authorized, aided or engaged in the attacks.[38] Consequently, to the extent that there is a significant difference between freezing and confiscating a person's property, the American provisions aimed at depriving terrorists of their property are that much more potent than their Commonwealth counterparts.

---

[36] Criminal Code, s. 83.13(1); Terrorism Act 2000, s. 26(3).
[37] Criminal Code, s. 83.14(5); Terrorism Act 2000, s. 28(2).
[38] 50 U.S.C. s. 1702 (as amended by the Patriot Act, s. 106).

D. Monitoring provisions

1. Overview and objectives

The prohibitions upon financing of terrorism may be the most visible components of the financial war against terrorism. Less visible but equally important are a raft of initiatives designed to make it difficult for terrorists and their affiliates to hold or transfer property anonymously and thereby facilitate detection of terrorists' activities.[39] Naturally, these provisions can also aid in enforcing prohibitions upon dealings with terrorists and in depriving terrorists of their property.

2. Reporting obligations

The least remarkable sorts of monitoring provisions are those that impose obligations upon financial institutions to report to the authorities when they have information about dealings with or the property of terrorists.[40] FATF has recommended the imposition of such reporting obligations and they can be found in all of the jurisdictions that have been mentioned so far in this chapter.[41] Canada and the United Kingdom also require individuals to report suspicious activity.[42] Future debates surrounding these provisions are likely to revolve around which actors are subject to the disclosure obligation, what circumstances should trigger a duty to report, and the extent to which those who file reports are entitled to indemnification for or exemption from any resulting liability. An important policy concern raised by these provisions is the extent to which they might deter productive but necessarily confidential dealings with terrorists. For example, Helen Fenwick and Gavin Phillipson have argued that the UK versions of these provisions might discourage investigative journalists from making contact with known terrorists.[43]

3. Other monitoring provisions

Other monitoring provisions are more remarkable because they impose new obligations upon actors dealing with the general population in the ordinary course of business rather than just those dealing with suspected terrorists or

---

[39] For an in-depth analysis of the relevant US provisions see Mariano-Florentino Cuéllar, 'The Tenuous Relationship Between the Fight Against Money Laundering and the Disruption of Criminal Finance' (2003) 92 *J. of Criminal L. & Crim.* 311.

[40] These provisions sometimes also encourage sharing of information between financial institutions. See, for example, Patriot Act, s. 314(b).

[41] Terrorism Act 2000, s. 19; Criminal Code, ss. 83.1, 83.11; 31 CFR 103; Financing of Terrorism Convention, Art. 18(1)(b).

[42] Criminal Code, s. 83.1; Terrorism Act 2000, s. 19; Proceeds of Crime Act 2002, ss. 330–2 (in the UK); Proceeds of Crime (Money Laundering) and Terrorist Financing Act, ss. 5–11 (in Canada).

[43] Chapter 21, in this volume.

involved in inherently suspicious transactions. For example, the USA Patriot
Act includes a provision requiring financial institutions to verify the identity
of any person opening an account and to maintain records of the information
used to verify the person's identity with a view to enabling a determination of
whether the person appears on any list of known or suspected terrorists or
terrorist organizations.[44] The costs of these 'know-your-customer' obligations are likely to be substantial. Although this kind of regulation can also be
justified as a response to money laundering, and has in fact been justified this way
in the United Kingdom,[45] it seems reasonably clear that the United States
would not have taken this step without the impetus provided by the terrorist
attacks.[46]

In a similar vein, FATF has recommended that the international community strive to ensure that information about both originators and recipients of
wire transfers be included in the wire transfers and remain with it throughout
the payment chain.[47] The United States has already largely implemented this
recommendation and the EU is in the process of doing so.[48] Again, given the
volume of transactions that will be affected, the costs of implementing this
initiative seem likely to be substantial and so it is not clear that it would have
been pursued in the absence of an enhanced terrorist threat.

The impact of the proposals concerning wire transfers is augmented by a
separate FATF recommendation that urges all persons or entities who engage
in the transmission of money or value be subjected to licensing and registration requirements and required to comply with FATF's recommended anti-
money laundering obligations.[49] The United States has taken a leading role in
implementing this recommendation and in encouraging other countries to
follow suit.[50] This initiative is directed at so-called alternative remittance
systems such as *hawala*. It is widely believed that al Qaeda and its associated
groups place great reliance upon such systems to transfer money.[51] However,

---

[44] 31 U.S.C. s. 5318, (as amended by Patriot Act, s. 326).
[45] See Financial Services Authority (UK), *Money Laundering Sourcebook*, section 3.1, and
'Why Do I Need to Prove My Identity?' online information sheet available at
www.fsa.gov.uk.
[46] See Federal Register, Vol. 64, No. 59, 14845–6, 29 March 1999 (Department of Treasury
and Federal Deposit Insurance Corporation jointly withdrawing proposed regulation to
institute a 'know-your-customer' obligation; the FDIC withdrawal noted that of 254, 394
submitted comments, only 105 were in support of the obligation).
[47] FATF, *Special Recommendations on Terrorist Financing*, above, Recommendation VII.
[48] Patriot Act, s. 328 and 31 CFR 103.33(f); Communication concerning a New Legal
Framework for Payments in the Internal Market, COM (2003) final, 12 Feb. 2003.
[49] FATF *Special Recommendations on Terrorist Financing*, above, Recommendation VI.
[50] 31 U.S.C. 5330; Tim Golden, '5 Months After Sanctions Against Somali Company, Scant
Proof of Qaeda Tie' *New York Times*, 13 April 2002, A10 (reporting that after the Sept. 11
attacks, the United States rapidly shut down al Barakat, Somalia's main *hawala* network).
[51] See, for example, *Second Report of the 1363 Monitoring Group*, para. 85

alternative remittance systems are also important – and less costly – methods of transferring funds for legitimate purposes, particularly for migrants or refugees attempting to remit money to family members in rural areas not served by banks. *Hawala* is particularly popular in Muslim countries.[52]

It is worth noting that monitoring provisions need not be targeted either at highly suspicious transactions or at the entire universe of ordinary business transactions. Between those polar alternatives it is possible to design intermediate measures that target only a narrow range of transactions that are unusually amenable to the purposes of terrorists. For example, it is now widely recognized that charities have played a significant role in channelling funds to al Qaeda and associated individuals and organizations, especially in Southeast Asia.[53] In an effort to facilitate the monitoring of charities' financial activities it has been proposed that charities should be required to route their transactions through established banking systems.[54] Although this measure would affect a significant volume of economic activity, it obviously would not have the same impact as a blanket requirement that all actors transact business through established banking systems.

E. Comparison to pre-existing law

One possible criticism of the newly enacted prohibitions is that they are redundant because much of the conduct at issue could be prosecuted under existing legislation imposing liability upon those who aid, abet or conspire in the commission of activities such as murder, arson, hijacking or bombing. Of course this critique is not particularly damning if the new legislation merely serves to increase legal certainty.[55] In any event, it is not clear that pre-existing legislation permitted the targeting of activities based simply on their relationship to terrorists as opposed to terrorist activities. Also, although this goes somewhat beyond the scope of the matters discussed to this point in this chapter, it is not clear that the pre-existing framework granted law enforcement agencies equally effective investigative powers and procedural flexibility, or contemplated the imposition of penalties as severe as those contained in the recently enacted legislation.

---

[52] Ibid., para. 86.   [53] *Second Report of the 1363 Monitoring Group*, ibid., paras. 57–8.
[54] Ibid., paras. 61–2.
[55] Redundant legislation that is not carefully integrated with pre-existing legislation can increase the complexity of a legal regime and thereby reduce legal certainty. This concern probably applies in some of the jurisdictions discussed in this paper (e.g., the various tools that US law enforcement agents have at their disposal to disrupt the financing of terrorism are scattered among pre-existing federal law, Patriot Act provisions, and IEEPA which all contain varying – and unclear – degrees of due process protections).

III. Implementation and enforcement

Legislation can also be overly broad in the sense that it gives law enforcement officials broad discretion to determine which types of activities are to be punished under circumstances in which that discretion is likely to be abused. Mariano-Florentino Cuéllar has recently advanced a sophisticated argument in support of the idea that law enforcement officials cannot be expected to exercise their discretion to enforce prohibitions upon financing of terrorism wisely.[56] He adopts a model of law enforcement officials' behaviour premised on the idea that law enforcement officials are generally motivated by a desire to please voters. He then assumes that voters have imperfect information about the steps that law enforcement agencies have taken to combat the financing of terrorism and their likely efficacy. Cuéllar posits that in this context voters will typically reward officials who take highly visible steps to prosecute financiers of terrorism, regardless of the actual efficacy of those steps and even if those officials have failed to take more efficacious but less visible steps to counter terrorism.

Using this model, Cuéllar predicts that law enforcement officials typically will not exercise their discretion in a manner that is designed to minimize the threat of terrorism. Rather, officials are likely to be biased against such a strategy in at least three different ways. First, they are likely to be unduly interested in cases that are relatively easy to detect because investments in detecting other types of cases are not particularly observable to voters. Second, officials are likely to prefer to bring cases against actors who are already stigmatized by voters because it will be relatively easy to persuade voters that such cases are effective means of countering terrorism. Third, officials will be inclined to bring cases against actors that they personally disfavour if voters cannot readily distinguish those actors from others who pose a greater threat.

One shortcoming of Cuéllar's model is that it assumes that voters reward officials based solely upon their perceptions of the *efforts* that the officials are making to counter terrorism. However, it seems equally plausible to assume that voters judge officials at least in part upon the *results* of their actions and accordingly officials who fail to prevent terrorist attacks can expect to be punished by voters. In countries that are highly likely to be the targets of attacks this incentive may be sufficient to ensure that officials are properly motivated to minimize the threat of terrorism. On the other hand, Cuéllar's model may have greater application in countries that are not targets of terrorism, but face pressure from targeted countries to undertake counter-terrorism activities. In those countries the government may behave in the

---

[56] 'The Mismatch Between State Capacity and State Power in the Global Attack on Criminal Finance' (2003) 22 *Berkeley J. Int'l L.* 15.

ways that Cuéllar suggests in order to please imperfectly informed foreign actors (rather than imperfectly informed voters).[57]

Even if we leave aside Cuéllar's concerns about voters' imperfect information and assume that officials are motivated to minimize the threat of terrorism, there remain grounds for concern about the manner in which they are likely to go about this task. In an ideal world officials would arguably strive not only to minimize the costs of terrorism, but also to minimize the costs that counter-terrorist initiatives impose upon innocent actors. However, as Cuéllar observes, public officials may not be equally sensitive to the interests of all actors. For instance, they may not be particularly sensitive to the interests of small minority groups who cannot attract the sympathies of members of more powerful groups. Similarly, the officials in any given jurisdiction will often be relatively insensitive to the interests of inhabitants of foreign jurisdictions. Consequently, it seems reasonable to fear that public officials will systematically tend to impose undue costs upon members of certain minority groups and inhabitants of foreign jurisdictions in the course of their counter-terrorism activities. This intuition seems to underlie minority groups' complaints about racial or ethnic profiling. It also implies that countries that are targets of terrorism will favour global adoption of monitoring provisions that are likely to be viewed as excessively costly from the perspective of countries that are not targets of terrorism.

An important challenge for the future will be to devise legal tactics capable of responding to concerns about the exercise of discretion. One approach is to challenge the constitutionality of the relevant prohibitions on the grounds of overbreadth or vagueness. This approach has been attempted with some success in the United States where a California federal court recently held that the material support provisions were 'impermissibly vague' (but not overbroad), and specifically ruled that the prohibition against 'expert advice or assistance' was not sufficiently clear.[58] An alternative approach would be to use laws designed to prevent discrimination against racial or ethnic minorities to control abuses directed at disempowered local groups. There may even be creative ways to use principles of international economic law, such as the national treatment and most favoured nation obligations contained in the GATT, to limit abuses directed at foreigners.

---

[57] For anecdotal evidence supporting this conjecture, see Salman Masood, 'Path Out Of Poverty Is Cut Short By Antiterror Snare' *New York Times*, 10 May 2004 (quoting a Macedonian government official claiming that a previous administration had killed seven economic migrants as part of an attempt to 'present themselves as participants in the war against terrorism and demonstrate Macedonia's commitment to the war on terrorism').

[58] *Humanitarian Law Project v. Ashcroft* 309 F. Supp. 2d 1185 (C. D.Cal. 2004).

IV. Potential effectiveness

Even if it is applied rationally and in good faith there are reasons to doubt that the recently upgraded legislative scheme will help law enforcement officials make any meaningful progress towards punishing or preventing terrorism.[59] First, terrorists' economic activities are often inherently difficult to detect because they involve property of relatively little value. It has been estimated that the 9/11 attacks could have been carried out on a budget of a little over $300,000, spread over several transactions.[60] Even if it is able to monitor a significant proportion of the enormous number of transactions involving such small amounts of money, it will be difficult for any law enforcement agency to use the resulting data effectively to identify illegitimate transactions.

A second ground for concern about the effectiveness of recent initiatives is the possibility of substitution between various forms of terrorist financing. Even if recent legal reforms have enhanced law enforcement authorities' ability to detect and punish certain types of dealings with terrorists, they almost certainly have not allowed them to disrupt all of the alternative channels through which terrorists may obtain resources. For example, it is now believed that al Qaeda finances itself through a combination of external funding from state actors, external funding from private individuals or organizations such as Islamic charities, funds generated internally through illicit activity such as drug trafficking and fraud, and funds generated internally through legitimate business activities such as trading in honey and tanzanite, and ownership of shipping.[61] Recent legislative initiatives and diplomatic pressure aim to deprive terrorist organizations of certain forms of external funding. But even if those efforts are completely successful, they may simply encourage organizations like al Qaeda to substitute internal funding for external funding. (In fact, this trend may already be underway; it is believed that the funding for the Madrid attacks was all obtained internally.)[62]

Alternatively, law enforcement activities may cut off access to certain forms of external funding in certain jurisdictions while allowing terrorists

---

[59] See generally, Eric J. Gouvin, 'Bringing Out the Big Guns: The USA Patriot Act, Money Laundering and The War on Terrorism' (2003) 55 *Baylor L. Rev.* 955.

[60] Paul Beckett, 'Sept. 11 Attacks Cost $ 303,672, But Few Details of Plot Surface' *Wall Street Journal*, 15 May 2002, at B4.

[61] *Second Report of the 1363 Monitoring Group*, para. 31; Judith Miller and Jeff Girth, 'Honey Trade Said to Provide Funds and Cover to bin Laden' *New York Times*, A1, 11 Oct. 2001; Robert Block and Daniel Pearl, 'Underground Trade: Much-Smuggled Gem Called Tanzanite Helps Bin Laden Supporters' *Wall Street Journal*, A1, 16 Nov. 2001; 'Peril on the sea' *The Economist*, 4 Oct. 2003.

[62] Elaine Sciolino, 'Complex Web of Madrid Plot Still Entangled' *New York Times*, A1, 12 April 2004.

to use alternative channels and/or jurisdictions. For example, even if authorities make it prohibitively risky for terrorists to transfer funds from Egypt to the United States by way of wire transfer, they may not be able to prevent them from transferring funds through a *hawaladar* from Egypt to an accomplice in Malaysia and then by ordinary wire transfer to the United States via Singapore.

Legislation designed to counter the financing of terrorism threatens to impose significant costs upon legitimate economic activities. The potential ineffectiveness of the legislation suggests that the offsetting benefits may be small. Concerns about this possible imbalance ought to be taken into account in assessing the merits of proposals to retain or amend this legislation.[63]

V. Conclusion

This chapter has attempted to outline the legislative provisions that provide the legal underpinnings of the financial war against terrorism as well as some of the concerns that they have generated. Some of the most substantial concerns have revolved around the question of whether the new legislation captures an overly broad range of conduct. Many have suggested that the legislation permits costs – financial or otherwise – to be imposed upon actors engaged in wholly legitimate activities. For example, prohibitions upon donating funds to charities with ambiguous or mixed purposes may serve to discourage donations to a broad range of charitable organizations that find it too costly to generate detailed documentation of their activities.[64] Ultimately, the costs of such regulations may be borne by the prospective beneficiaries of the charities. Similarly, the new procedures governing the opening of bank accounts and sending wire transfers have imposed enormous costs upon financial institutions and their customers, including both the financial costs of compliance and the less tangible but arguably just as significant costs represented by loss of privacy. Imposing costs upon innocent actors in this way not only seems unjust but also may serve to deter socially valuable activities and foster dangerous levels of resentment in affected communities.

A second and related concern about the new regime is that it will be enforced irrationally or arbitrarily. At the domestic level, the new regime may be used against some of the most vulnerable members of society such as members of racial or ethnic minorities. At the international level, there are

---

[63] A complicating factor in such an analysis will be that many of the costs associated with the legislation may already have been incurred and so should not be taken into account when assessing the costs of retaining the legislation.

[64] Stephanie Strom, 'Small Charities Abroad Feel Pinch of U.S. War on Terror' *New York Times*, 5 August 2003, A8. See also *Humanitarian Law Project* v. *United States DOJ*.

analogous grounds for concern that enforcement of the new regime may cause the weakest members of the international community to bear disproportionate costs. In addition, in both contexts some reason exists to believe that law enforcement agents might focus upon only the most easily detected threats and ignore targets that pose threats that are just as serious, if not more.

A third and final concern is that the financial war against terrorism is doomed to failure in light of the inherent difficulty of combating some methods of terrorist financing. The chain of domestic and international legal provisions that has been forged to combat financing of terrorism may turn out to be only as strong as its weakest link. Under these circumstances it may be difficult to justify the tremendous costs that have been incurred to create the regime.

For the time being, much of the foregoing analysis is highly speculative. Ultimately, the scope and effects of the legislative provisions concerned with financing of terrorism will depend upon how the applicable legislation is interpreted and enforced. Future research – including doctrinal studies of legislative amendments and relevant judicial decisions, empirical studies of trends in the enforcement of the legislation and its impact on targeted activities, and theoretical studies designed to identify potential improvements to existing provisions and their likely effects – will play an important role in assessing the impact of the legal framework and identifying potential improvements.

10

Terrorism and technology: policy challenges and current responses

MARY W. S. WONG

I. Introduction

The direct, immediate legislative and policy response of many governments to the September 11 terrorist attacks on the United States highlighted an increasing reliance by governments on surveillance technology. Many of these post-9/11 laws and policies have attracted controversy and public attention for their impact on privacy protections, particularly in the US, where civil liberties advocates have accused the US government of favouring security over liberty. Given the US government's continuing lead role in the fight against terrorism, its actions and the public reaction to them may provide useful lessons for other governments and lawmakers as they too seek to find an appropriate, justifiable and legitimate approach to deal with similar threats. In addition, because the US is popularly perceived by many non-Americans to be a fully-fledged democracy and a leading defender of civil liberties, the current view of many privacy advocates and watchdog groups – that post-9/11 the US government has adopted rules and mechanisms that threaten free speech and increase government secrecy – deserves closer attention. The picture that emerges from this chapter is a sobering one for governments seeking to model their policies after those of the US government. Even where a responsible and democratic government is taken to be acting in what it believes to be in the best national interest, it can nonetheless be perceived as unnecessarily secretive and possibly untrustworthy. Where broad law enforcement powers are coupled with unchecked government use of surveillance technology, it is important that a government practises, as far as that is reasonable and practicable, open dialogue and transparency with its citizenry and their advocates.

It should be noted from the outset that some major changes to US law and practice, which also carry implications for privacy (e.g., immigration controls, detentions and treatment of prisoners) are beyond the scope of this

I am grateful to Kent Roach and Victor V. Ramraj for their helpful comments on a draft of this chapter. The laws, policies and programmes described in this chapter are those as of August 2004.

chapter, which will focus largely on privacy issues raised by the increasing use of surveillance technology.[1] Specifically, post-9/11 changes to US law and policy that affect the protection of personal information and public access to information will be examined. As a point of comparison, similar legal changes in the United Kingdom, the major ally of the US in the current military campaign in Iraq, will also be examined.

II. Background

A. Post 9/11 anti-terrorism law and policy developments in the US

1. The Patriot Act

The enactment of the USA PATRIOT Act[2] in October 2001 (barely six weeks after the terrorist attacks of 9/11) and its attendant controversies highlighted several characteristics of the US government's previous counter-terrorism activities. These included the traditional distinction between the government's 'intelligence' and 'law enforcement' activities; the differences in practice and process between domestic surveillance and foreign surveillance; and the increasing difficulties arising from the existence of distinct, specific and technically complex pieces of legislation concerning potentially overlapping activities (e.g., wiretapping and computer hacking). The constitutional right to freedom of speech and freedom from unreasonable search and seizure would by their very nature come under potential threat from any proposed increase in government surveillance of its citizens and other persons, including any easing of process rules for the authorization of any surveillance activity. The changes to US surveillance, government access and investigatory powers wrought by the Patriot Act highlighted these tensions, and continuing attempts by the current US government to tweak the Act have met with challenges from civil liberties groups and privacy advocates.[3]

Essentially, the Patriot Act made a number of changes to US surveillance laws, including the wiretap statute, the pen/trap statute, the Foreign Intelligence Surveillance Act (FISA) and the Computer Fraud and Abuse

---

[1] For a more detailed analysis of other changes to US law and policy, see William C. Banks, Chapter 22, in this volume.
[2] The United and Strengthening America by Providing Appropriate Tools Required to Intercept and Obstruct Terrorism Act 2001 (Patriot Act), Pub. L. No. 107–56, 115 Stat. 272 (2001).
[3] For a fuller discussion of the provisions of and changes wrought by the Patriot Act, see Charles Doyle, 'The Patriot Act: A Legal Analysis' (RL 31377, 15 April 2002, a Congressional Research Service Report for Congress, http://www.fas.org/irp/crs/RL31377.pdf); Nathan C. Henderson, 'The PATRIOT Act's Impact on the Government's Ability to Conduct Electronic Surveillance of Ongoing Domestic Communications' 52 *Duke L. J.* 179; and Mary W. S. Wong, 'Electronic Privacy in the United States After September 11th 2001' (2002) *Sing. J.L.S.* 214.

Act (CFAA). These changes tended to increase overall the US government's ability and powers of surveillance by, for example: (1) increasing the number and type of crimes falling within the interception provisions of the wiretap statute; (2) allowing 'sneak and peek' searches (i.e., without requiring the giving of contemporaneous notice to the search subject); (3) providing for nationwide application of warrants and surveillance orders; (4) allowing roving wiretaps; (5) increasing the scope of subpoenas for the obtaining of electronic communications records; (6) lowering the standard required for FISA surveillance; and (7) removing restrictions on pen registers and trap and trace devices for telephone communications.[4] The Patriot Act did, however, preserve some judicial oversight and Congressional safeguards, particularly as regards procedures to be followed when obtaining search orders, and some of its more expansive provisions were subject to 'sunset' provisions.[5]

2. Subsequent developments

Subsequent legislative and regulatory changes could also have an impact on privacy and liberty. Unlike the Patriot Act, these changes did not all come in an omnibus package, but were more piecemeal and at least initially less obvious. These include: (1) the introduction of reforms to the Federal Bureau of Investigations (FBI) aimed primarily to transform it 'from a largely reactive law enforcement agency focused on criminal investigations into a more mobile, agile, flexible, intelligence-driven agency that can prevent acts of terrorism';[6] (2) the establishment of a new Department of Homeland Security in November 2002 (the legislative basis for which included additional government exemptions from the Freedom of Information Act); (3) the launch of the Total (later renamed Terrorist) Information Awareness (TIA) Program in 2002; (4) the development of a new air passenger screening system (CAPPS II); and (5) the issuing of various government agency guidelines dealing with surveillance, investigations and intelligence work. These guidelines include the Department of Justice's memorandum issued soon after the Patriot Act on Field Guidance on New Authorities Enacted in the

---

[4] Ibid; see also the Electronic Privacy Information Center's summary of the Patriot Act: http://www.epic.org/privacy/terrorism/usapatriot/.

[5] Additionally, a bipartisan bill, The Security and Freedom Ensured Act of 2003 (SAFE), H.R. 3352 and S. 1709, was introduced in Congress in late 2003, seeking to limit some of the Patriot Act's broader surveillance provisions.

[6] These were instituted in large part as a reaction and response to the report of the Congressional Joint Inquiry Into the Terrorist Attacks of 11 September 2001, which specifically noted that the FBI had been 'seriously deficient' in identifying, reporting on and sharing information regarding the threat of terrorist attacks in the US: see, e.g., Alfred Cumming and Todd Masse, 'FBI Intelligence Reform Since 11th September 2001: Issues and Options for Congress' (RL 32336, 4 August 2004, a report published by the Congressional Research Service: http://www.fas.org/irp/crs/RL32336.pdf).

2001 Anti-Terrorism Legislation, and the release in November 2003 of the new
Attorney-General Guidelines for FBI National Security Investigations and
Foreign Intelligence Collection.[7]

In addition to these changes, the US government had also apparently
intended to introduce new legislation that was quickly dubbed 'Patriot II'
for further increasing government investigatory and surveillance powers
beyond those already provided for in the original Patriot Act.[8] The draft of
Patriot II (or more accurately, the Domestic Security Enhancement Act) was
not prepared by Congress, and its existence was made public only through a
leak from the Justice Department in January 2003, a fact that contributed to
the growing public perception of government secrecy above legislative participation and public debate.[9] This perception was probably enhanced by the
fact that the leak of Patriot II occurred around the same time that President
Bush, in his State of the Union address in January 2003, called on Congress to
'renew' the Patriot Act even though its 'sunset' provisions are not due to be
reviewed until 2005.

Although Patriot II as drafted was quickly shelved, in part due to a storm of
criticism, elements of it found their way into subsequent, specific legislation.
This included a provision in the Intelligence Authorization Act for Fiscal Year
2004[10] which was passed in December 2003. As a piece of legislation required
annually to allocate funding for US intelligence agencies, such Acts are
usually passed without much Congressional debate.[11] The 2004 Act
authorizes the FBI to obtain financial records from a broad range of 'financial
institutions' without the need for judicial scrutiny,[12] a power that had been

---

[7] These replaced the previous Attorney-General Guidelines for FBI Foreign Intelligence
Collection and Foreign Counter-intelligence Investigations. There had previously also
been revisions to the general guidelines for FBI criminal investigations which were
reissued in May 2002 as part of a broader review.

[8] Among other matters, Patriot II would have permitted the collection of genetic information, easier access by the government investigators to credit reports, and expanded orders
under FISA; there also appeared to be no 'sunset' provisions similar to those in the Patriot
Act. For a draft of Patriot II and a section-by-section analysis of the Act, see http://
www.publicintegrity.org/report.aspx?aid = 94&sid = 200.

[9] See, e.g., the articles collected by the Center for Democracy and Technology on its website
on Patriot II: http://www.cdt.org/security/010911response.shtml.

[10] P.L. 108–177, December 2003, 117 Stat. 2599.

[11] It appears that such legislation is largely viewed as a 'must pass' bill drafted in relative
secrecy; however, this means it could be a vehicle for a quick passage of otherwise
controversial or difficult provisions: see Kim Zetter, 'Bush Grabs New Power for FBI'
Wired News, 6 January 2004, http://www.wired.com/news/privacy/0,1848,61792,00.html.

[12] 'Financial institutions' is fairly broadly defined (by means, in s. 374, of an amendment to
s. 1114 of the Right to Financial Privacy Act of 1978 (12 U.S.C. 3414)) and would include
businesses such as real estate brokers and car dealerships. In effect, this means that the FBI
need only comply with the requisite statutory requirements regarding requests and
written certification (which may be in the form of so-called 'National Security Letters'

sought under Patriot II and which is accompanied by a non-disclosure obligation on the part of the financial institution concerned. Bills have also been introduced in Congress that either echo or contain elements of Patriot II; for example, in September 2003, the Anti-Terrorism Intelligence Tools Improvement Act of 2003 was introduced in the House of Representatives. The Act, if passed, would strengthen the penalties for violating the non-disclosure provisions of various laws relating to financial privacy, allow the Attorney-General to seek a court order to compel compliance with records requests, and amend certain portions of FISA.[13]

The continuous stream of such changes contributes to a belief that overly broad executive powers are being sought in the name of national security, accompanied by a whittling down of accountability (e.g. judicial oversight) and an increased reliance on secrecy. Among the most controversial federal proposals is the use of data mining and data harvesting techniques to create and analyze data from commercial and government databases, to help to identify potential terrorists, and to facilitate information-sharing among counter-terrorism agencies.[14] The US government has also pushed for biometric identifiers to be included on new US passports issued after 2005 (this being a requirement for passports issued by countries participating in the US Visa Waiver Program as of 26 October 2005),[15] and there are some advocates for the adoption of a national ID card, as already exists in some countries.[16] In addition, the Federal Communications Commission (FCC) in response to a petition filed by the FBI and other government agencies recently proposed a rule that would subject communications over the Internet to the requirements of the Communications Assistance for Law Enforcement Act of 1994 (CALEA).[17] CALEA requires that telecommunications providers design their equipment so as to facilitate authorized wiretapping by the FBI.

Many countries outside the US have considered deploying surveillance technology such as biometrics and data mining for law enforcement and

drafted by its officers of a certain rank) in order to obtain financial records from a wide range of institutions, and would not need to obtain a court order.

[13] H.R. 3179. Hearings were held before the House Judiciary Committee in May 2004, and the bill is thus currently 'in process'. There are several other bills pending before Congress that deal with some of the powers and issues raised in Patriot II; e.g., H.R. 3037, the Anti-Terrorism Tools Enhancement Act of 2003 and H.R. 2935 and s. 1604, the Terrorist Penalties Enhancement Act of 2003.

[14] The TIA Program and CAPPS II, probably the most well-known initiatives involving data mining, are analyzed later in this chapter.

[15] This was mandated by the Enhanced Border Security and Visa Entry Reform Act of 2002, under which the original deadline was 26 October 2004. The one-year extension was approved by Congress and signed by the President in August 2005.

[16] E.g., some European countries, Australia, Hong Kong, Malaysia and Singapore.

[17] See FCC 04–187, ET Docket No. 04–295 RM-10865, 'In The Matter of Communications Assistance for Law Enforcement Act of 1994 and Broadband Access and Services, Notice of Proposed Rulemaking And Declaratory Ruling', adopted 4 August 2004.

anti-terrorist purposes, and in the wake of 9/11 some have enacted legislation enhancing government surveillance powers.[18] As mentioned previously, some countries already use national identification cards and some regularly employ video surveillance, though mainly for detecting traffic violations and crimes such as theft. But except for jurisdictions such as the EU, which has clear and specific data protection and privacy protection laws, in other jurisdictions privacy laws are vague or minimal, or contained in a diverse 'patchwork' of laws. In the US, the lack of comprehensive privacy, data protection and database laws may not be entirely alarming. This is because balance can be provided and public scrutiny ensured through its strong Constitutional tradition, the number of cases brought to its courts challenging laws and executive authority,[19] the existence of a generally strong and participative Congress and the active monitoring of government initiatives by privacy and other advocacy groups. But in countries without effective privacy laws or judicial or other oversight mechanisms to prevent abuse of executive authority the increasing use of surveillance technology is more disturbing.

Although each new law may in itself constitute a potential threat to privacy, this plethora of changes may have an overall erosive effect on privacy. For example, increased access by investigators to personal and communications data coupled with a data retention regime could mean that more information is stored, and for a longer period of time, by service providers. This information would be easily accessible to authorities in the absence of strict standards as to how and when it is to be turned over. Similarly, having few legal restrictions on data mining, harvesting and sharing, combined with an increased investment of resources in law enforcement capabilities and organizations, would facilitate profiling of persons and wider usage of personal information generally. When these legal and policy developments are seen in the light of developments in technology such as data analysis methods, biometrics and improved surveillance techniques, their potential impact on privacy appears even greater.

---

[18] In the United Kingdom, the Terrorism Act of 2000, among other things, widened the scope of police investigatory powers, including the power to detain suspects for up to seven days. Post-9/11, the Anti-Terrorism, Crime and Security Act 2001 (ATCSA) dealt with, among other things, the potentially-indefinite detention of foreign nationals suspected to be terrorists. In August 2004, the Court of Appeal rejected the appeals of several detainees who had challenged their detention under the ATCSA, alleging that the evidence on which the detentions were based had been obtained through torture of prisoners held in Guantanamo Bay. Also significant is the Regulation of Investigatory Powers Act 2000 (RIPA), discussed below, which deals with the interception of content over communications networks and access to communications data.

[19] On the privacy and free speech front, these include the Fourth Amendment cases of *Katz* v. *US*, 389 US 347 (1967); *Kyllo* v. *US*, 533 US 27 (2001); and *Bartnicki* v. *Vopper*, 532 US 514 (2001).

B. The many faces and uses of surveillance technology

The term 'surveillance technology' is very general and fairly broad, and encompasses virtually any type of device or means that enables someone to be watched and monitored. Case law and much of the early media attention on the Patriot Act focused largely on technology such as key logging devices, the FBI's 'Carnivore' software and similar 'sniffer techniques';[20] 'spycams' and video surveillance;[21] facial recognition software; and more widely used commercial technology such as 'cookies', 'web bugs' and other 'adware' that monitored an electronic user's computer and online activities. Since then, however, the use of other technology has surfaced including RFID (radio frequency identification) tags and technology, biometrics and 'smart ID' cards, data mining and data harvesting techniques, and the creation of agencies, databases and other legal mechanisms deploying these and a range of similar technology ostensibly for counter-terrorism purposes.[22] Of these, the use of data mining and harvesting techniques – largely to aid in data sharing and analysis across agencies and governments – has been highlighted by the US government as a highly useful, even necessary, tool for detecting and preventing terrorism. The US government's approach in this area, and its possible international effects, is analyzed in the next section.

Fundamentally, an act of terrorism can be seen as simply another form of criminal act, whatever the moral justifications and objections. As such, many forms of surveillance technology have been and are being used by criminals, from hackers to organized crime, for the same purposes. Similarly, it is known that terrorists use the same modern technological tools as governments, such as the Internet, computer and communications technology, to organize, communicate and perpetrate their activities.[23]

---

[20] The *Scarfo* case (Criminal No. 00–404 D.N.J.) was apparently the first case dealing with the FBI's use of 'key logging' software and technology to obtain evidence from a suspect's computer. The government opposed the court-ordered disclosure of the technology, and eventually was required to release only very limited information. In a December 2001 decision, the District Court found that the disclosure of such unclassified information provided the defence with as much information as they required. There was no further appeal as the defendant entered into a plea agreement in February 2002.

[21] These have apparently been more commonly used in Europe rather than the US. According to the Electronic Privacy Information Center (EPIC), 'in the past decade, successive UK governments have installed over 1.5 million cameras in response to terrorist bombings. While the average Londoner is estimated to have their picture recorded more than three hundred times a day, no single bomber has been caught' (see http://www.epic.org/privacy/surveillance).

[22] Such as CAPPS II, TIA and the Homeland Security Department.

[23] See, e.g., 'Countering the Changing Threat of International Terrorism', a report of the National Commission on Terrorism made pursuant to Public Law 277 (105th Congress): http://www.fas.org/irp/threat/commission.html.

Fears of cyber-attacks against critical national infrastructures are taken seriously by most governments[24] and legislation has been implemented to criminalize terrorist-related hacking and other similarly motivated cyber-attacks. For example, the United Kingdom's Terrorism Act 2000 widens the definition of terrorism to include acts that 'seriously interfere with or seriously disrupt an electronic system', where they are 'designed to influence the government or to intimidate the public' and are done 'for the purpose of advancing a political, religious or ideological cause'. Threats to critical infrastructures and increasingly vital communications equipment including the Internet had already been identified prior to 9/11. For example, in 1997 US President Clinton's Commission on Critical Infrastructure Protection had stated that 'the rapid proliferation and integration of telecommunications systems and computer systems have connected infrastructures to one another in a complex network of interdependence. This interlinkage, combined with an emerging constellation of threats, poses unprecedented national risk.'[25] Post-9/11 governments have acted swiftly to protect critical information systems and national communications infrastructure. The US government issued a formal National Strategy to Secure Cyberspace, complemented by its National Strategy for the Physical Protection of Critical Infrastructures and Key Assets.[26] The strategic objectives are stated to be the prevention of cyber-attacks against critical American infrastructures, the reduction of national vulnerability to such attacks, and the minimization of damage and recovery time from attacks. The report summarizes clearly the objectives that ought to figure most highly in any government's plan to protect against cyber-attacks of such scope.[27]

Of course, no documented act of cyber-terrorism has yet occurred, but there have been many instances of cyber-attacks in the form of unauthorized

---

[24] For an overview and assessment of the risks of cyber-terrorism and other aspects of 'information warfare', see Adam J. Elbirt, 'Information Warfare: Are You At Risk?' (2003/2004), *IEEE Technology & Society Magazine*, 22(4), 13–19: http://faculty.uml.edu/aelbirt/information_warfare_final.pdf.

[25] R. T. Marsh, 'Critical Foundations: Protecting America's Infrastructure' (President's Commission on Critical Infrastructure Protection, October 1997) at ix, see www.timeusa.com/CIAO/resource/pccip/intro.pdf.

[26] In the US government's previously-released National Strategy for Homeland Security (July 2002), the following areas were identified as 'critical infrastructure sectors', viz. food, water, agriculture, public health, emergency services, government, defence industrial base, information and communication, transport, energy, banking and finance, chemical industry, postal and shipping. Key assets were considered to be individual targets whose destruction could not only have vital consequences but also damage the nation's morale; major historical symbols and attractions are thus included in the phrase. See http://www.whitehouse.gov/homeland/book/sect3–3.pdf.

[27] The National Security to Secure Cyberspace (February 2003), http://www.fas.org/irp/threat/cyber/strategy.pdf.

hacking, computer virus and malicious code releases, and denial of service attacks. A cyber-attack 'becomes' an act of cyber-terrorism only if it is motivated by terrorist aims. Further, cyber-attacks and even acts of cyber-terrorism need not be attacks on critical infrastructures. It is thus important that any laws drafted or amended to deal with these activities are enacted with a clear understanding as to the distinctions between them.[28] It is noteworthy also that many of these acts are likely to already constitute criminal offences in the laws of many countries.

The legal response to the use of technology in terrorism-related activities must be seen in the wider context of the balance between national security and law enforcement on the one hand, and freedom of speech, access to information and government transparency on the other. In this regard, many of the US consumer/citizen and privacy advocacy groups have been collecting and making available documents and information relating to the workings of this balance post-9/11. For example, the Electronic Frontier Foundation (EFF) maintains a list of websites that have been shut down either by the US or other governments, under the banner 'Chilling Effects of Anti-Terrorism: [the] "National Security" Toll on Freedom of Expression'.[29]

III. Salient features of US law and government practice

A. The post-9/11 US government approach to data sharing and analysis

Some of the organizational and policy changes post-9/11 provide useful examples of how the US government has approached its goals of improving data sharing across agencies and facilitating counter-terrorism measures. Actions taken to implement these goals include the creation of the Terrorist Information Awareness (TIA) Program, the creation of the Department of Homeland Security, and the development of CAPPS II.

One of the most controversial issues in this context has been the US government's declared intent of using data mining and analysis tools to identify potential terrorist threats. The term 'data mining' can be misleadingly general, conjuring up as it does images of automated 'spiders' and other

---

[28] For a summary of these and a description of the various legal tools that are available (at least to the US government) to combat cyber-terrorism, see the 24 February 2004 testimony before the US Senate Committee on the Judiciary of Mr John Malcolm, Deputy Assistant Attorney-General at the US Department of Justice, titled 'Virtual Threat, Real Terror: Cyber-terrorism in the 21st Century', http://www.globalsecurity. org/security/library/congress/2004_h/040224-malcolm.htm.

[29] See http://www.eff.org/Privacy/Surveillance/Terrorism/antiterrorism_chill.html; it also maintains a 'Surveillance Monitor' listing incidents of video surveillance worldwide: http://www.eff.org/Privacy/Surveillance//surveillancemonitor.html.

search technology fanning out across databases and files to gather information; in its specific meaning, however, data mining involves the application of algorithms to data sets in order to discover predictive patterns in such data.[30] A related, if lesser known term, is 'automated data analysis', which can be applied to patterns generated by data mining. Automated data analysis uses models that predict behaviour, perform risk assessment or data association (i.e. link analysis) and other tasks; it is particularly useful as a tool for accurate identification (e.g., of a person) and for providing clues through link analysis across data sets. Although the term 'data mining' is often used generally as a single description of these and other analytical tools, it is therefore but one step in a broader 'knowledge discovery' process.[31] A stark illustration of the power and potential of such tools is the fact that link analysis could likely have identified all the 9/11 terrorists for follow-up investigation before that date, had government watch lists, airline records and other publicly-held information been analysed this way.[32]

The controversies generated by data mining and automated data analysis have little to do with the way the technology works; rather, they coalesce around two specific issues: (1) the risk of mathematical, pattern or human errors in using the technology (e.g., 'false positives') and the potential for abuse or mistaken harassment, investigation, and even prosecution due to these errors; and (2) the lack of public discussion and transparency over how, on what data, and for what specific purpose the government intends to use the technology. The latter risk itself would tend to increase the public discomfort already identified over the potential for abuse or mistaken application of the results generated by such technology. In particular, because the 'stakes are so high when fighting catastrophic terrorism that there will be a great temptation for the government to use these techniques as more than an analytical tool ... [they] will want to take action based on [the results] alone ... [including] detention, arrest or denial of a benefit'.[33] The possibility that such temptation is now very real, combined with public unease over past abuses of domestic surveillance powers by the FBI,[34] means that any government seeking to use these tools while preserving respect for civil liberties must address public concerns over potential abuses, secrecy and lack of transparency. In this respect, the US government's handling of the public outcry over its data mining plans seems particularly unfortunate.

---

[30] See Mary DeRosa, 'Data Mining and Data Analysis for Counter-Terrorism', published by the Center for Strategic and International Studies (March 2004), http://www.cdt.org/security/usapatriot/20040300csis.pdf.
[31] Ibid.   [32] Ibid., at 6–8.   [33] Ibid., at 15.
[34] E.g., as reported by the 1976 Church Committee.

1. The TIA Program

The TIA Program was established in 2002 under its original name of 'Total Information Awareness' in the new Office of Information Awareness, a division of the Defense Advanced Research Projects Agency, the main research organization of the Department of Defense (DoD). It was envisaged that a large data collection and analytical system would be developed. The resulting controversy over this program led the DoD to establish an internal oversight board and an external advisory board in an attempt to ensure 'that TIA develops and disseminates its products to track terrorists in a manner consistent with US constitutional law, US statutory law, and American values related to privacy'.[35] While acknowledging that TIA intended to develop technology including language and pattern recognition tools, the DoD seemed defensive in stating that TIA was not intending to 'create a gigantic database', 'has not ever collected or gathered and is not now collecting or gathering any intelligence information [and] has never collected, and has no plan or intent to collect privately held consumer data on US citizens'. In October 2003, Congress ended funding for the Office of Information Awareness, at least in respect of projects other than for foreign surveillance purposes. However, some of the general research planned by the Office and the TIA Program is apparently still continuing under other agencies and projects.[36]

2. The Department of Homeland Security

The original purpose of the Department of Homeland Security was to ensure 'greater accountability over critical homeland security missions and unity of purpose among the agencies responsible for them'.[37] Alongside obvious areas such as border controls and immigration procedures, the proposal identified improving the FBI's analytic capabilities, the deployment of biometrics and analytical tools, and the need to integrate information-sharing as important initiatives requiring action. In November 2002 the Homeland Security Act[38] created a new Cabinet department, to which twenty-two government agencies, including the Immigration and Naturalization Service, the Secret Service and the Customs Service, were transferred.[39] The Department may access and

---

[35] See 'Total Information Awareness (TIA) Update', a press release issued by the US Department of Defense on 7 February 2003, http://www.defenselink.mil/releases/2003/b02072003_bt060–03.html.

[36] See, e.g., the EFF's statement on the Congressional move at http://www.eff.org/Privacy/TIA/20031003_comments.php.

[37] See the US government's 'National Strategy for Homeland Security' issued in July 2002: http://www.whitehouse.gov/homeland/book/.

[38] H.R. 5005.

[39] With about 170,000 employees, the Department is also apparently one of the largest federal agencies ever created by the US government.

analyze a wide range of information, including information from law enforcement, intelligence, federal, state and local government agencies, and private sector sources. To allay privacy concerns, the Act contains some oversight provisions, including the need to appoint a Privacy Officer and to establish procedures that would limit re-dissemination of information to ensure there is no unauthorized use, ensure the security, confidentiality and integrity of information, and protect the legal rights of the information subjects. In addition, certain provisions in earlier versions of the law that had been criticized heavily by privacy and civil liberties groups did not survive into the final version.[40]

3. CAPPS II

The passenger screening program known as CAPPS II also attracted controversy. The original CAPPS, launched in 1998, was operated by the airlines through their reservations systems to identify passengers who required a higher level of scrutiny by matching the passenger's itinerary against certain behavioural rules and government watch lists. Unlike CAPPS, CAPPS II was to be managed by the Transportation Security Administration (TSA), which since November 2001 has taken over civil aviation security from the Federal Aviation Administration.[41] CAPPS II is also broader than CAPPS in its access to and analysis of a greater amount of data, including commercial databases. The main purpose is to classify air passengers into three different risk levels. A passenger making a reservation will have to provide certain personal information (her name, date of birth, address and home phone number), which is checked against various databases. The result is returned to CAPPS II as an identity authentication score, which is then checked against government databases to generate a risk assessment score for that passenger, which is encoded onto the passenger's boarding pass at the airport. Passengers deemed to be 'unacceptable' risks will be denied boarding passes and the law enforcement authorities notified; in some cases, such passengers may be taken into custody.

Implementation of CAPPS II has significant implications for privacy. Prime amongst these implications are the possibility of error and data inaccuracy, both in relation to the commercial databases that are checked initially for the passenger's identity authentication as well as the analysis and methods used to generate the risk assessment. The latter case may be particularly disturbing if the incidents or scope of error in CAPPS II are fairly high,

---

[40] These included the controversial Operation TIPS and a proposal for a national ID card. Operation TIPS was a proposal apparently by the Department of Justice to facilitate the creation of a network of informants using people whose jobs gave them access to private homes (e.g., utility workers).

[41] For an analysis of CAPPS II in the context of aviation security, see Alan K-J. Tan, Chapter 11, in this volume.

given the gravity of the possible consequences if a passenger is denied a boarding pass.

The initial announcement of CAPPS II and a broadly drafted notice about its scope and operations placed in the Federal Register in January 2003 led to a storm of controversy. In July 2003 a revised notice was placed in the Federal Register – apparently as a result of discussions with and feedback from privacy groups, legislators and the public – so that some fears of the plan's breadth was dispelled. For example, it became clearer that CAPPS II would not use a person's financial or credit information, that passenger data would be deleted shortly after travel was completed, and that the commercial data providers would not be permitted to use information provided to them by the system.

Further implementation of CAPPS II was halted pending a General Accounting Office (GAO) review of, *inter alia*, the status of CAPPS II with respect to certain developmental, operational and public acceptance issues, including privacy safeguards. The GAO report was released in February 2004,[42] and it disclosed that as of 1 January 2004, CAPPS II had met only one out of eight key issues Congress had identified; among those unmet were issues related to unauthorized access prevention, data inaccuracy and privacy concerns. Specifically, the GAO report disclosed that the TSA was still working on a system to address either identity theft or accuracy issues with the commercial and government databases to be used within CAPPS II,[43] had yet to formulate a redress system for passengers mistakenly identified as 'false positives', and had not determined the actual period for which passenger data would be retained. Although the report acknowledges that the TSA has gone some way toward meeting privacy concerns by attempting to develop processes in keeping with internationally recognized Fair Information Principles,[44] the overall impression and findings in the report seem clearly to indicate that CAPPS II had a long way to go before its development status or plans are definite enough for any determinative finding as to whether privacy concerns have been adequately addressed or not.

In July 2004 Tom Ridge, Secretary of the Department of Homeland Security, indicated publicly that CAPPS II may be dropped due to concerns

---

[42] As GAO–04–385, 'Aviation Security: Computer Assisted Passenger Prescreening System Faces Significant Implementation Challenges', http://www.epic.org/privacy/airtravel/gao-capps-rpt.pdf.

[43] It would appear that commercial data providers, although generally using accuracy testing, do not necessarily employ the same factors and processes in doing so.

[44] These relate generally to transparency as regards the collection and use of data, including maintaining accuracy and use only for disclosed or specific purposes. See, e.g., the 1980 OECD Guidelines Governing the Protection of Privacy and Transborder Flows of Personal Data, http://www.oecd.org/document/18/0,2340,en_2649_34255_1815186_1_1_1_1,00.html; and the Federal Trade Commission's Reports to Congress on online privacy in 1998, 1999 and 2000, http://www.ftc.gov/privacy/privacyinitiatives/promises_reptest.html.

over privacy and system interoperability.[45] However, he left open the possibility that another programme could be developed to replace it. It is unclear at this point what the 'new' programme will consist of;[46] however, when the broad aim and scope of CAPPS II is contrasted with the lack of clarity as regards specific privacy concerns identified by Congress, it seems clear that the US government is taking drastic steps to ensure that the events of 9/11 do not reoccur, and that these steps include developing and deploying technology like CAPPS II that will clearly, and perhaps negatively, impact on individual privacy.

Despite the fury that CAPPS II has drawn from privacy advocates, it is difficult to see how the US government could have left the issue of airline security alone, or what other system can be developed that will be more likely than the current system to help identify terrorist risks. It is beyond the scope of this paper to analyze the models and error projections or margins that such systems use, or the assertion that such a system will not help deter or detect terrorism.[47] The main privacy objections, however, seem to centre on the secrecy, the possibility of 'mission creep' and the lack of assurance (warranted, in the present circumstances) about how the system will work and how inaccuracies and mistakes can be minimized. In light of the recent revelations about American airline companies unilaterally revealing passenger data to government agencies for passenger profiling studies and airline security projects[48] (possibly in violation of the airlines' own privacy policies), it is vital that the TSA take immediate, public and substantial steps to allay public outcry and concern over the issue of privacy and airline security.

The development of CAPPS II has obvious international implications as well, since much airline travel is international in nature. Where data collection and checking of travellers from the European Union is concerned, the impact of the EU Data Protection Directive has to be considered. Although the EU and the US reached preliminary agreement in 2003 for US inspectors

---

[45] This was widely reported, having first been announced by USA Today: 'Plan to Collect Flier Data Cancelled', 14 July 2004 http://www.usatoday.com/news/washington/2004-07-14-fly-plan_x.htm.

[46] See the ACLU letter of 20 July 2004 to Secretary Ridge, 'Is CAPPS II Really Dead?' http://www.aclu.org/Privacy/Privacy.cfm?ID=16133&c=130.

[47] See, e.g., Samidh Chakrabarti and Aaron Strauss, 'Carnival Booth: An Algorithm for Defeating the Computer Assisted Passenger Screening System', a student paper published in May 2002 as part of the MIT course 'Law and Ethics on the Electronic Frontier', http://www.swiss.ai.mit.edu/6805/student-papers/spring02-papers/caps.htm.

[48] JetBlue turned over passenger data to a US defence contractor in September 2003, while Northwest Airlines admitted in January 2004 that it had revealed passenger data to NASA (having earlier denied doing so – the disclosures were so large that apparently 6000 CDs had to be used to contain the information), and most recently, in April 2004, American Airlines disclosed that it had divulged over one million passenger records to the TSA. JetBlue and Northwest are currently facing class action lawsuits in respect of such disclosures from some of their passengers.

to examine passenger records of flights originating in the EU, the European Parliament voted 276–260 in April 2004 to send the agreement to the European Court of Justice (ECJ) for its review, contending that the agreement violated the Directive. While the ECJ's decision could have been fairly significant – for example, if the US–EU agreement is found not to be in compliance with the Directive, it could limit the scope and applicability of CAPPS II or its progeny to the extent it related to flights or passengers originating in the EU – that may now be a moot point. On 14 May 2004, the European Commission (EC) adopted an 'adequacy finding' under the Data Protection Directive. The agreement was signed between the EU and the US on 28 May, thus establishing the legal framework for the transfer of passenger name record (PNR) data.

In the Annex to the EC decision, the US Bureau for Customs and Border Protection (CBP) undertakes to develop and use filters for mutually agreed terms and codes relating to so-called 'sensitive' data (specific examples given include data relating to race, ethnicity, political opinions, religious beliefs and health); until such time as the filters are deployed the CBP agreed it will not use any such data. PNR data would be accessed only by authorized personnel, for 7 days in the first instance, and by a more limited number of persons for 3.5 years thereafter. Any PNR data that has not been accessed during that 3.5 year period will be destroyed, and data that has been accessed retained for a further 8 years (except for data 'linked to a specific enforcement record', which will remain accessible till the record is archived).

To concerns that PNR data accessible to the CBP could be subject to a disclosure under the US Freedom of Information Act (FOIA), the Annex makes clear that the CBP will consider such data to be within the class of confidential information that is exempt from FOIA disclosure. Regarding disclosure to other US and foreign government agencies, the Annex states that this will be on a case-by-case basis and only to those agencies having counter-terrorism or law enforcement powers, and with the disclosed data subject to the same FOIA-exempt treatment. Finally, the Annex also contains provisions for the giving of notice, access and opportunities for rectification of PNR data on the part of passengers. It is, however, doubtful whether a similar review as that undertaken by the EU will take place in other countries, in part because not all countries have clear data protection or privacy laws.[49]

Technology already exists to protect data privacy and minimize abuse in the use of data mining technology on large databases by governments. These

---

[49] On this point, it may be of interest to note that some privacy advocates consider the EU's review process not entirely effective. For example, although the Working Party overseeing the Data Protection Directive issued an Opinion (22 June 2004) expressing disappointment that the EC took the Working Party's demands into account only 'partially', groups such as Privacy International considered the Working Party's recommendations in the Opinion fairly weak: see http://pi.gn.apc.org/article.shtml?cmd[347]=x-347-60528.

include technology to eliminate and resolve false positives; anonymizing technology (to mask specific identifying information without prejudicing the accuracy of the analysis); audit technology (to maintain a record of searches so as to 'watch the watchers'); and rule-based processing (to conduct the analysis according to clear and transparent rules, e.g., of access and scope).[50] But even with the deployment of such protective technology, there remains a need to develop and implement clear, consistent and open guidelines for government agencies, officials and data processors as to the processing, harvesting and handling of data and results. Such guidelines will help to address public concern over privacy issues while facilitating the adoption of new technology for legitimate public policy purposes.[51] Further, given the US government's recent difficulties with handling public perceptions and concerns over TIA, homeland security and CAPPS II, the need for greater openness and clear guidelines on data mining and analysis seems all the more urgent.

B. The existence of a public access right to government information in the US

The federal Freedom of Information Act of 1996[52] is particularly relevant when considering the balance between individual rights and national interests. Under the FOIA US government agencies are required to make available to the public certain information regarding its structures, procedures and statements of policy. Where the agency's records are not specifically listed as requiring publication in the Federal Register, they may be requested under the FOIA. The FOIA 'establishes a presumption that records in the possession of agencies and departments of the executive branch of the US government are accessible to the people ... Before enactment of the FOIA in 1966, the burden was on the individual to establish a right to examine these government records ... With the passage of the FOIA, the burden of proof shifted from the individual to the government ... the "need to know" standard has been replaced by a "right to know" doctrine. The government now has to justify the need for secrecy.'[53]

Consumer advocacy groups such as the Electronic Privacy Information Center (EPIC) use the FOIA to seek clarity and information regarding FBI and other government policies on privacy protection, including, most recently,

---

[50] DeRosa, 'Data Mining'.
[51] See 'Creating a Trusted Network for Homeland Security', the Second Report of the Markle Foundation Task Force on National Security in the Information Age (December 2003), http://www.markletaskforce.org.
[52] 5 USC Sec. 552.
[53] See 'A Citizen's Guide on using the Freedom of Information Act and the Privacy Act of 1974 to request Government Records', being the First Report from the House of Representatives' Committee on Government Reform and issued during the 2nd Session of the 107th Congress on 12 March 2002 as House Report 107–371.

a pending lawsuit regarding information that Northwest Airlines had disclosed several months' worth of passenger data to NASA for use in passenger profiling and data mining research.[54] Previously, in September 2003, EPIC had also filed an FOIA request seeking information from the US Transportation Security Administration (TSA) regarding CAPPS II, including information on privacy assessment reports related thereto. The TSA resisted the request, claiming the documents concerned did not fall within the ambit of the FOIA.[55]

Conceptually, it seems obvious how a legally transparent mechanism such as the FOIA helps to balance the conflict between the public/individual's right to information and the government desire in the interest of national security to keep certain information classified.[56] To the extent that laws such as the Patriot Act appear to tip the balance in favour of more secrecy and less public scrutiny, other laws such as the FOIA act as a check and balance on this trend. The challenge, however, is to ensure that such disclosure/accountability mechanisms perform that role effectively. In other words, their scope, procedures and implementation must avoid either making too much information available so that intelligence gathering, law enforcement and other legitimate and justifiable (in the context) executive activities are compromised, or making too little information available so that the citizenry/public's right to know is merely a question of lip service. While it may be axiomatic to state that a government will naturally prefer not to have its every move questioned (particularly as regards politically sensitive matters, including foreign surveillance issues) or its motives challenged (particularly where it genuinely believes it is acting in the national interest), it does not mean that every refusal to disclose information or reluctance to open its processes to public scrutiny is necessarily suspicious, malignant or damaging to the public interest. At the same time, those charged with administering or deciding on FOIA-type requests ought not to assume that the government's assertion of national security concerns will necessarily outweigh the need to make information publicly available. This remains the case even where the executive genuinely believes

---

[54] *EPIC v. National Aeronautics and Space Administration* (N.D. Cal. 2004).

[55] *EPIC v. Transportation Security Administration et al.*, Civ. No. 03–1846 (D.D.C. 2003). On 2 August 2004, the court handed down an opinion concluding that while the documents were exempted from disclosure under the FOIA's deliberative process privilege, the TSA had not met the requisite statutory burden requiring an analysis of reasonably segregable non-exempt information that would have to be released. The TSA thus has to conduct such an analysis and either release such information or refile a motion with the court addressing the segregability issue. The court's Memorandum of Opinion can be found at http://www.epic.org/privacy/airtravel/pia_order.pdf.

[56] According to EPIC, 'As the government seeks to expand its power to collect information about individuals, it increasingly hides that surveillance power behind a wall of secrecy. Congress has long recognized this tendency in the Executive Branch, and sought to limit government secrecy by creating legal obligations of openness under the FOIA and the Privacy Act of 1974' (see http://www.epic.org/open_gov/foiagallery.html).

this to be the case, and it must be borne in mind especially in today's environment where terrorist activity appears to be widespread, imminent and unceasing. There always needs to be an open, transparent and thorough examination of each request, while weighing the various and competing interests.

In this context, privacy advocates have found recently released statistics about the US government's acts in relation to the classification of secret information and the requests for surveillance orders disturbing, and indicative of a growing tendency to perform greater surveillance under conditions of lesser accountability. In the 2003 Wiretap Report issued by the Administrative Office of the US Courts, it was disclosed that applications for wiretap orders made by federal officials rose 16 per cent in 2003, with the average length of a wiretap increasing from 39 to 44 days.[57] In the 2003 Foreign Intelligence Surveillance Act (FISA) Annual Report, it was disclosed that the FISA court[58] granted 1,724 applications for secret surveillance last year, more than in any previous year and a more than 50 per cent increase from 2001. In addition, 2003 appears to be the first year where more surveillance orders were granted than federal wiretap warrants.

Outside the US the challenge may be to ensure that adequate checks and balances exist in the legal system to safeguard against government abuse of surveillance powers. Although the FOIA can be a powerful tool, in the US it exists as part of a system that also includes judicial review and other oversight mechanisms. As such, it may be said that despite the apparent growing trend of secrecy within the executive, its actions are still open to some measure of public scrutiny.

IV. The international dimension

A. Recent anti-terrorism legal and policy developments in the United Kingdom

In the wake of 9/11, several laws and programmes enhancing the government's surveillance powers were introduced into the UK which alarmed civil liberties groups.[59] In light of the UK's role as a staunch ally of the US in the fight against terrorism and its position as a leading common law jurisdiction, an examination

---

[57] See http://www.uscourts.gov/wiretap03/2003WireTap.pdf.

[58] This is a court set up especially to review applications for FISA surveillance orders. The Court has been perceived as being extremely secretive, with even its proceedings and rulings closed to the public. It is interesting to note, however, that in August 2002 the FISA Court uncharacteristically issued a public opinion in which it overruled its lower court's refusal of the government's application for a FISA order.

[59] See, e.g., the websites relating to UK privacy laws and government surveillance maintained by Privacy International (http://www.pi.greennet.org.uk/countries/uk/) and the Foundation for Information Policy Research (http://www.fipr.org/surveillance.html).

of some of these changes to the UK's laws and their impact provides an interesting parallel to the changes to US law and policy already described. As the changes in the UK were fairly complex and relatively broad, this part will focus only on those amendments that have an actual or potential impact on privacy.[60] In the main, these were changes to the UK's statutory laws (including secondary legislation) that concerned the acquisition (through interceptions) of the actual contents of telephone, postal and electronic communications, as well as the persons to whom, and purposes for which, access to data relating to such communications (e.g., location and traffic data) could be granted.

Under the Regulation of Investigatory Powers Act 2000 (RIPA), interception of communications 'in the course of their transmission' through either a postal service or telecommunication system may be conducted upon the issuing of a warrant by the Secretary of State. A warrant may be issued only if the Secretary believes it is 'necessary' to fulfil one of three identified purposes, and that the interception being authorized is 'proportionate' to the reason for seeking the warrant. The specific purposes for which a warrant may be necessary are that interception is 'in the interests of national security', for the purpose of 'preventing or detecting serious crime', or for 'safeguarding the economic well-being of the United Kingdom'.[61] It is not entirely clear what factors would govern the determination of what is 'necessary' and 'proportionate', and the fact that it is the Secretary of State rather than a judge who determines the issuing of a warrant has led to the criticism that the powers of interception conferred by RIPA are overly broad.[62]

The legal framework governing access to communications data by public authorities has been described as 'diffuse' and lacking a coherent supervisory legal framework.[63] Limited access rights by public authorities had been conferred by a variety of specific statutes, while oversight is generally provided by the Data Protection Act 1998 and the Human Rights Act 1998. The introduction of Codes of Practice under RIPA and the Anti-Terrorism, Crime and Security Act 2001(ATCSA) added complexity to the situation, and created some confusion as to the potential 'disparity of purpose' between the data retention requirements under the ATCSA and the ability under RIPA for public authorities to access such data. The complexity of the situation and increased public concern over the UK government's actions in the name of national security were heightened by the government's proposal in June 2002 to increase the type and number of public authorities who could access data

---

[60] See Helen Fenwick and Gavin Phillipson, Chapter 21, in this volume.
[61] Section 5, RIPA. RIPA also contains provisions detailing the procedure for obtaining a warrant, the contents of a warrant, its duration and renewal.
[62] Paul T. Dougan, 'Cybercrime and Human Rights' http://www.strath.ac.uk/Other/ staffclub/web2law/cybercrime%20and%20human%20rights.pdf, 44–7.
[63] See the Privy Counsellors' 2003 Report on the ATCSA, below note 81, at 93–7.

retained by communications service providers. The controversy and protest that this proposal (dubbed the 'snoopers' charter') attracted led to the withdrawal of the draft Order later the same month.

Although the pre-9/11 RIPA raised some privacy advocates' hackles, the quick passage and scope, post-9/11, of ACTSA proved even more controversial, leading to increased media attention to the UK government's plans for data retention and surveillance, thus contributing to a growing public backlash. ATCSA's data retention provisions covered data relating to mobile text messages as well as web activity, and applied to communications service providers. In this respect, and as required by the ATCSA, a Draft Voluntary Code of Practice on Retention of Communications Data and a Draft Retention of Communications Data (Code of Practice) Order 2003 was laid before the UK Parliament in September 2003.

In its review of the draft Code, the Joint Committee on Human Rights of both UK Houses of Parliament expressed concern over certain matters relating both to the scope and operation of the Code and the Order. These included, *inter alia*, (a) the need to ensure that they were compatible with the human rights protection provisions of the European Convention on Human Rights (ECHR),[64] which requires any invasion thereof to be both 'necessary' and 'proportionate'; (b) the possibility of overlap with RIPA where access to the data retained was concerned;[65] and (c) the short period of time made available to Parliament to consider these proposals.[66] Nonetheless, a revised 'snoopers' charter' that the Home Office claimed cut down on the number of public authorities who could access communications data retained by communications service providers and tightened procedural safeguards for such access was passed by Parliament in November 2003.[67] In January 2004, a negotiated Voluntary Code of Practice under ATCSA also

---

[64] See in particular Article 8 (the right to private life). In the UK, the implementation of the ECHR by the Human Rights Act 1998, however, seems to obligate public authorities only to act compatibly with Convention rights. In this respect, the Joint Committee was concerned with the potential lack of adequate safeguards for proper data retention on the part of communications service providers, since the government was of the view that these did not constitute public authorities: see pp. 7–16 of its Report on the Draft Voluntary Code of Practice on Retention of Communications Data Under Part 11 of the Anti-Terrorism, Crime and Security Act of 2001, Sixteenth Report of Session 2002–03, HL Paper 181 and HC Paper 1272, 11 November 2003 (http://pi.gn.apc.org/issues/terrorism/library/ukjrcretentionreport.pdf).

[65] Particularly in view of the fact that, at the time the Code was under review by the Joint Committee, a Draft Regulation of Investigatory Powers (Communications Data) Order had been presented to Parliament under RIPA; the Order would have expanded the number and type of bodies who could gain lawful access to communications data. See ibid. at p. 14.

[66] See Report on the Draft Voluntary Code of Practice, 17.

[67] The Regulation of Investigatory Powers (Communications Data) Order 2003, which came into force in January 2004.

came into force. The Code specifies different retention periods of between four and twelve months for different types of data, and contains several assurances as to the legitimacy of data retention.[68] Under ATCSA, the Home Secretary will have until December 2005 to assess the effectiveness of the Code, after which he has the power (through secondary legislation) to impose a mandatory code if the voluntary Code is found ineffective.

The fact that the UK government chose to issue five proposed statutory instruments within a single week in 2003, each dealing with particular aspects of RIPA or the ATCSA,[69] most likely contributed to a growing public perception that the government was expanding its surveillance powers not merely to combat terrorism, but also to enhance its investigatory powers in other areas as well. It is thus somewhat disconcerting that the UK government nonetheless went ahead with an even more controversial proposal: the introduction of a national ID card.[70]

The proposal has been scrutinized by Parliamentarians. In July 2004, the House of Commons Home Affairs Committee released its Identity Cards report,[71] which listed an array of concerns over privacy issues and the possible over-breadth of the ID card scheme, while concluding that it could significantly assist in tackling terrorism, identity theft and criminal activity more generally, and would support other aims such as improving citizens' access to public services. However, it noted that the scheme in the draft Bill would confer on the government 'powers to register a wide range of information not obviously related to establishing identity and ... wider access to the database than is justified by the fight against organised crime and terrorism'. The Committee thought it 'unacceptable to leave to secondary legislation questions over the degree of access to the database, especially since the purposes of the Bill need to be made less broad' and stated its opinion that the scheme would 'undoubtedly represent a significant change in the relationship between the state and the individual in this country'. Finally, the Report

---

[68] E.g., 'service providers are entitled to rely heavily on the fact that the Secretary of State and Parliament will have concluded that the retention of communications data for the periods specified in the Code is necessary in order to safeguard national security'.

[69] Including the Draft Codes and Order mentioned above. The other proposals were the Regulation of Investigatory Powers (Directed Surveillance and Covert Human Intelligence Sources) Order 2003 (which restricted the purposes for which public authorities could conduct directed surveillance) and the Regulation of Investigatory Powers (Intrusive Surveillance) Order 2003 (which dealt with intrusive surveillance of prisoners by the Northern Ireland prison service).

[70] See, e.g., the *Guardian* newspaper's 'Big Brother' special report, http://www.guardian. co.uk/bigbrother/privacy/0,12377,783005,00.html; the statement by the Foundation for Information Policy Research, 'ID Card Scheme An Expensive Flop', April 26, 2004 (http:// www.fipr.org/press/040426id.html); and the comments on 'National ID Cards' by Privacy International (http://pi.gn.apc.org).

[71] HC 130–1 (http://pi.gn.apc.org/issues/idcard/uk/ukhomeaffairsreportt29_07_04.pdf).

recommended that 'the test should be whether the measures needed to install and operate an effective identity card system are proportionate to the benefits such a system would bring and to the problems to be tackled and whether such a scheme is the most effective means of doing so'.

In February 2004, the Home Office issued a discussion paper on 'Counter-Terrorism: Reconciling Security and Liberty in an Open Society'.[72] The discussion paper outlines the government's response to the Privy Counsellors' critical review of the ATCSA in December 2003,[73] in particular, as regards its recommendations on immigration, detention and terrorist financing. The paper also addressed concerns over the lack of adequate safeguards for, and judicial oversight of, the disclosure of personal information by one public authority to another for a wide range of criminal investigations. It clearly sets forth the UK government's view that the current oversight regime is adequate, and that the standards and requirements of the ECHR have been met.

The issuing of the discussion paper and regular public comments by the Home Secretary on the importance of public debate seem to indicate that the UK government is taking steps to address its increasingly Orwellian public image. Unfortunately, since many of these steps are reactive – even defensive – in nature, and given its various missteps in this regard (e.g. its proposal and subsequent withdrawal of the 'snoopers' charter' in 2002) as well as the ongoing push for programmes such as national ID cards, it seems certain that privacy advocates will continue to be suspicious of the UK government. Equally certainly, the media and various watchdog groups will continue to monitor the government's legislative, regulatory and other proposals.[74] The situation in the UK – in terms of the relationship between the government and privacy advocates, and the public scrutiny of the appropriate policy balance to be struck between national security and individual liberty and privacy – is thus very similar to that in the US on these issues.

Finally, a Freedom of Information Act under which an individual has a right to access information will come into force on 1 January 2005.[75] Approximately 100,000 'public authorities' are required to maintain

---

[72] CM 6147 (http://www.homeoffice.gov.uk/docs3/CT_discussion_paper.pdf).

[73] HC 100. See also Fenwick and Phillipson, Chapter 21, in this volume.

[74] One of Privacy International's annual UK Big Brother Awards (given to those who have done the most to devastate privacy and civil liberties in the UK) – the Lifetime Menace Award – was renamed the David Blunkett Lifetime Menace Award (after the then UK Home Secretary). The 2004 awards saw the greatest number of votes for Mr Blunkett, the Home Office and the national ID card scheme; however, these were apparently disqualified because of having won a number of awards in previous years.

[75] The UK Information Commissioner and the Department of Constitutional Affairs have published user-friendly, detailed guides to the Act on their websites: see, respectively, http://www.informationcommissioner.gov.uk and http://www.dca.gov.uk/foi/index.htm.

and update 'publication schemes' that will describe information that is publicly available, how such information may be obtained, and whether a fee will be charged. Almost any person, including non-citizens, has a right to find out whether the information requested is being held by the authority and, if so, to have that information disclosed to her. There are, however, certain statutory exemptions from disclosure (e.g., in the public interest).[76] Although the scope of the Act seems broad, it remains to be seen how effective it will be in providing government accountability and how frequently it will be used by individuals or advocacy groups. It does, however, provide yet another parallel with the US system and might thus serve as a useful check against the abuse of executive power.

B. The Echelon surveillance system

Any discussion of increased government surveillance must consider the confirmation by a committee of the European Parliament in July 2001 of the existence of a government-backed international communications surveillance system known as Echelon.[77] Echelon is a 'system used by the United States National Security Agency (NSA) to intercept and process international communications passing through communications satellites. It is one part of a global surveillance system that is now over 50 years old. Other parts of the same system intercept messages from the Internet, from undersea cables, from radio transmissions, from secret equipment installed inside embassies, or use orbiting satellites to monitor signals anywhere on the earth's surface. The system includes stations run by Britain, Canada, Australia and New Zealand, in addition to those operated by the United States.'[78] According to Duncan Campbell, the system was initiated under a UK–USA Agreement in 1947, which linked British and American systems, personnel and stations. The networks of Canada, Australia and New Zealand were later included. Subsequently, other countries including Norway, Denmark, Germany and Turkey also became participants in the UK–USA network.[79] The system's networks are apparently engineered along similar lines as the Internet, and are comprised of many systems, networks and applications connected across international transoceanic cables and space links. Although how Echelon

---

[76] See, e.g., the various Awareness Guidance publications prepared by the Information Commissioner's office.

[77] 'Report On The Existence Of A Global System For The Interception Of Private And Commercial Communications (ECHELON interception system)', 2001/2098(INI).

[78] See Duncan Campbell, 'Inside Echelon: the History, Structure and Function of the Global Surveillance System Known As Echelon' (2000): http://www.heise.de/tp/english/inhalt/te/6929/1.html.

[79] Campbell, ibid.

actually operates is not publicly known, it seems clear that the system is capable of a large number and volume of interceptions of electronic and other communications, and that increasingly sophisticated filtering technologies are employed to search, filter, process and analyse the information received. The privacy implications of such a system, particularly if it is a secret system, backed and long-used by democratic governments, are obvious. They are compounded so long as the governments apparently leading or participating significantly in the system do not acknowledge its existence: the US has not officially acknowledged Echelon, although Australia and New Zealand have. At the same time, there are potential advantages to such a system, such as its ability to quickly and efficiently minimize the difficulties of data sharing across governments and agencies.

Since the release of the European Parliament report and related resolution that was adopted (in September 2001), there have been many reports regarding the existence, workings or abuses either of alleged parts of the Echelon system, or of similar large-scale surveillance programmes.[80] The organizations that compile these reports and news pieces are generally privacy and civil liberties advocates; a fact which illustrates the public scrutiny role of such groups in an open society. Where governments may be justly cautious in their public disclosures and discussions, these groups can act as a useful public voice and counterbalance. There is a risk, of course, that the pro-privacy, even libertarian, stance of these groups could lead to a somewhat unilateral or one-sided perspective on the matter. If so, however, it would be up to governments to determine if, when and to what extent they ought to counter or answer what may appear to them to be the more extreme assertions about government surveillance and secrecy.

V. Summary and conclusion

The use of surveillance technology has become, and will remain, a key tool in the fight against terrorism. The challenge for governments is to use such technology in ways that further that important cause, in the name of security, but without unduly compromising the need to ensure that civil liberties are respected to the fullest extent possible. Certainly, it would be unrealistic to expect governments not to use the most advanced technology available to them. At the same time, 'countering terrorism' and 'ensuring national security' are broad and general causes. Without doubting the legitimacy of these policies in the present circumstances, it would be unfortunate if governments

---

[80] See, e.g., the pages maintained by the American Civil Liberties Union (http://archive. aclu.org/echelonwatch/), Cyber-Rights and Cyber-Liberties UK (http://www.cyber-rights. org/interception/echelon/), and the Center for Democracy & Technology (http:// www.cdt.org/wiretap/).

simply relied on those broad justifications for an entire range of executive decisions and policies that, whether individually or holistically, erode individual freedoms and threaten privacy unnecessarily. After all, 'counter-terrorist legislation must be sufficiently flexible to meet the potential threat to society, but it must also contain proper protections for the privacy and liberty of the individual and ... [be] accompanied by its own tailored safeguards, including careful monitoring and review of its use. It is important that it commands broad public support, otherwise its use risks being mistrusted and therefore less effective.'[81]

In the US, the post-9/11 policy and legislative changes are wide-ranging and seem set to continue. Since the Patriot Act first began life as a proposed Anti-Terrorism Act immediately after the 9/11 attacks, privacy advocates have publicly worried about the chilling effects that overly broad government surveillance powers could have on public access to information, free speech and other constitutional rights and civil liberties. This concern is acute when judicial oversight of executive powers seems to have been diluted. The public view in the US that this is the case has been further strengthened with the advent of the other legislative changes and new mechanisms and policies discussed in this chapter, many of which have a clear potential impact on privacy.

While legal developments outside the US have not been subject to as much public scrutiny and debate (in part because of the relatively more active privacy groups based in the US), the trend appears to parallel that in the US, i.e. to consolidate and enhance government surveillance powers, at least where national security and other fundamental public interests are at stake. This chapter has examined some of the post-9/11 measures adopted in the UK that potentially impact privacy protections there. As the US and the UK are two major common law jurisdictions as well as leaders in the international fight against terrorism, the similarities in law and policy changes in these two countries are noteworthy and potentially influential.

In light of the discussion above, governments would be well-advised to consider engaging their public in more open discussions over the necessity for and scope of surveillance that is seen to be overly invasive. This will be particularly significant in countries where privacy concerns have traditionally been important, but is no less needed in countries where that has not been the case. Although some element of secrecy is admittedly necessary due to the

---

[81] The UK Privy Counsellor Review Committee, 'The Anti-Terrorism, Crime and Security Act 2001 Review: Report', HC 100, 12 December 2003 (http://www.homeoffice.gov.uk/docs3/newton_committee_report_2003.pdf). The Committee considered two general principles to be of fundamental importance in this context: that an individual has a right to privacy and liberty, and that the government has a duty to take 'necessary' steps to protect society from terrorism.

very nature of surveillance and national security policy, governments should not fall prey to the temptation of operating from a default position of total or maximum secrecy. Similarly, individuals and privacy advocates should distinguish between policies and processes: it may be necessary at times to question the former, but where the former can be found to be justifiable and legitimate, it may be the latter that requires very close scrutiny, e.g., to minimize the possibility that the scope of proposed laws and procedures (in the name of a justified policy) are wider than necessary for the declared purpose. The fears of each 'side' can be allayed only if governments and their watchers (constructive though any criticism might be) operate from these premises and have the mutual public interest – of striking the most appropriate balance of individual and the wider public interests in a particular context and time – in mind.

Finally, it must be said that the use of surveillance technology by governments is not always or necessarily a negative. Where terrorists seek to intimidate and destroy, responsible governments are presumed to have the public good in mind when using technology. It would be irrational to deny that the use of bomb scanners, metal detectors and other search devices at airports and other major points of entry/exit into/out of a country are necessary; whether or not they are actually statistically effective, they at least succeed in assuring the public that preventive measures are being taken in the name of security, and may succeed to some extent as deterrents. Similarly, wiretapping and video surveillance can and probably does assist in crime detection. In other words, most if not all of the forms of surveillance technology identified earlier in this chapter have benign and positive uses, at least in the hands of a responsible government (acting through its law enforcement or security arms). The risks in instances where there is a clear public interest in personal or national security are therefore centred on the possibility of abuse of that technology by the government, and on the possible flaws and error rates of such technology. Such risks and attendant public concern are heightened if governments maintain an aura of non-disclosure or secrecy about either the technology or the extent to which it is used.

11

Recent developments relating to terrorism and aviation security

ALAN KHEE-JIN TAN

I. Overview

Before 11 September 2001 aviation security concerns revolved primarily around preventing aircraft hijacking and sabotage, and apprehending the perpetrators of such acts.[1] In this regard, any risk to lives was largely confined to passengers and crew on board aircraft. In response to such long-held concerns several international conventions adopted under the auspices of the International Civil Aviation Organisation (ICAO)[2] had sought to

I am grateful for the insights provided by my students in the Aviation Law and Policy course offered at the Faculty of Law, National University of Singapore, in the 2003–2004 academic year. All errors remain my own. The law and developments are reflected as at early August 2004.

[1] Other criminal acts against the safety of aviation include attacks on airports and air navigation facilities and the use of surface-to-air missiles aimed at aircraft in flight (these are known as man-portable air defence systems or MANPADS). The latter is a serious concern today, and has led to moves to secure flight pathways and airport perimeters. In the US a new Act to address this issue – the Commercial Aviation MANPADS Defense Act of 2004 (CAMDA) – is currently being debated.

[2] These conventions include the 1963 Tokyo Convention on Offenses and Certain Other Acts Committed on Board Aircraft, 20 U.S.T. 2941, 704 U.N.T.S. 219, reprinted in 58 *Am. J. Int'l L.* 566 (1959); the 1970 Hague Convention for the Suppression of Unlawful Seizure of Aircraft, 22 U.S.T. 1641, 860 U.N.T.S. 105, reprinted in 10 *I.L.M.* 133 (1971); the 1971 Montreal Convention for the Suppression of Unlawful Acts Against the Safety of Civil Aviation, 24 U.S.T. 564, 974 U.N.T.S. 177, reprinted in 10 *I.L.M.* 115 (1971); the 1988 Montreal Protocol for the Suppression of Unlawful Acts of Violence at Airports Serving International Civil Aviation, ICAO Doc. 9518, reprinted in 18 *Ann. Air & Space L.* 251 (1993) and the 1991 Montreal Convention on the Marking of Plastic Explosives for the Purpose of Detection, ICAO Doc. S/22393 & corr. 1, reprinted in 30 *I.L.M.* 721 (1991). In addition to these instruments, Annex 17 (Safeguarding International Civil Aviation against Acts of Unlawful Interference) to the 1944 Chicago Convention on Civil Aviation, 61 Stat. 1180, 15 U.N.T.S. 295, requires state parties to establish their respective national civil aviation security programmes and relevant institutions in order to regulate matters of security such as the presence of weapons, explosives or other dangerous devices on board aircraft; the inspection and screening of aircraft, passengers, baggage, cargo and mail; and the training and certification of security personnel.

establish universal jurisdiction over the perpetrators of violence against aircraft and to provide for states to prosecute or extradite these individuals.[3]

Since 9/11, however, the bigger concern has been the use of aircraft as weapons of destruction, aimed at causing massive loss of lives and property on the ground.[4] Consequently, the aviation industry has had to face a plethora of new security measures designed to prevent the occurrence of not only conventional hijacking and sabotage, but more ominously, the use of aircraft as suicide weapons against interests on land. This shift in emphasis toward preventing the use of aircraft as weapons has introduced unprecedented challenges for civil liberties as well as heightened costs and inconvenience for the air travel industry and travellers alike.[5] This chapter assesses some of these concerns and outlines the new measures that have been adopted to deal with the post-9/11 aviation security environment. It also analyzes the prospect of harmonizing security measures among countries with different perceptions of terrorism risks and the varying capacities to comply with the requisite measures.

II. Aviation security responses post-9/11

In the past three years or so, aviation security has become a priority on regulatory agendas worldwide. In the US, the Aviation and Transportation Security Act (ATSA),[6] first adopted in November 2001 placed aviation security matters within the purview of the federal government.[7] ATSA also

---

[3] A number of aviation security arrangements exist outside the ICAO regime, including the 1977 European Convention on the Suppression of Terrorism, reprinted in 15 *I.L.M.* 1272 (1976) and the 1978 Bonn Declaration on Hijacking, reprinted in 17 *I.L.M.* 1285 (1978). The academic literature on aerial terrorism is abundant – see, e.g., S. K. Agrawala, *Aircraft Hijacking and International Law* (Dobbs Ferry, NY, Oceana, 1973); Nancy D. Joyner, *Aerial Hijacking as an International Crime* (Dobbs Ferry, NY, Oceana, 1974); Edward McWhinney, *Aerial Piracy and International Terrorism: The Illegal Diversion of Aircraft and International Law* (2nd rev. ed., Dordrecht, Boston, 1987) and Rosalyn Higgins and Maurice Flory (eds.), *Terrorism and International Law* (London, Routledge, 1997).

[4] For details, see Phillip A. Karber, 'Responses to the September 11 Attacks: Re-constructing Global Aviation in an Era of the Civil Aircraft as a Weapon of Destruction' (2002) 25 *Harv. J. L. & Pub. Pol'y* 781, at 781–82, and Eric J. Miller, 'The "Cost" of Securing Domestic Air Travel' (2003) 21 *John Marshall J. Computer & Info. L.* 405, at 420.

[5] In the US alone, the estimated costs over the five-year period from 2002–2006 is US$9 billion, see Cletus C. Coughlin, Jeffery P. Cohen and Sarosh R. Khan, 'Aviation Security and Terrorism: A Review of the Economic Issues', *Federal Reserve Bank of St. Louis Review*, (Sept/Oct 2002), at 20.

[6] Pub. L. No. 107–71, 1447, 115 Stat. 597 (2001) (codified as amended in various sections of 49 U.S.C.).

[7] Hitherto, these functions were exercised by the airlines and their private contractors under Federal Aviation Administration (FAA) regulations.

established the Transportation Security Administration (TSA)[8] within the Department of Transport, giving it the authority to regulate security in all modes of transportation. In 2002 the Homeland Security Act[9] was enacted, establishing the Department of Homeland Security which assumed competence over the numerous agencies with anti-terrorism mandates, including the TSA itself. Apart from federalizing airport security functions, ATSA also imposed a whole host of new aviation security measures, including minimum job qualifications for security employees, the installation of impregnable cockpit doors and video monitors to link the cockpit and cabin, the performance of background checks on airport employees, enhanced security for airport perimeter access, the installation of explosive detection systems at airports to scan baggage and the placement of armed air marshals on board high-risk flights.

On its part the European Union responded by enacting Regulation 2320/2002 establishing common rules for civil aviation security.[10] The Regulation laid down common security standards for EU Member States and obliged them to set up their respective national civil aviation security programmes to implement the common standards.[11] Among the standards enacted or contemplated pursuant to Regulation 2320/2002 are those relating to restricted areas at airports and the screening of departing passengers and their baggage for prohibited articles. The European Council is also considering a proposal for the introduction of biometric identifiers in passports. At the same time, the EU has yet to formally include armed sky marshals in its regulatory agenda, leaving the matter to be dealt with by individual member states.

The international agency responsible for civil aviation, ICAO, has reviewed and amended its Standards and Recommended Practices (SARPs) on

---

[8] For more on the TSA, see Kent C. Krause (2002) 'Putting the Transportation Security Administration in Historical Context', 68 *J. Air L. & Com.* 233 and David Norton, 'Recent Developments in Aviation Law' (2002) 67 *J. Air L. & Com.* 1107.

[9] Pub. L. No. 107–296, 116 Stat. 2153, in force 25 November 2002.

[10] EC, Parliament and Council Regulation 2320/2002 of 16 December 2002 establishing common rules in the field of civil aviation security, [2002] O.J. L 355/1. See also Jan Wouters and Frederik Naert, 'The European Union and "September 11th"' (2003) 13 *Ind. Int'l & Comp. L. Rev.* 719. Implementing instruments enacted pursuant to Regulation 2320/2002 include Commission Regulation (EC) No. 622/2003 laying down measures for implementation of the common basic standards on aviation security, Regulation No. 1217/2003 of 4 July 2003 laying down common specifications for national civil aviation security quality control programmes and Regulation No. 1486/2003 of 22 August 2003 pertaining to the conduct of inspections to verify the effectiveness of security measures.

[11] For details, see John Balfour, 'EC Aviation Scene (No.2: 2003)' (2003) 28:2 *Air & Space L.* 106, at 111. In September 2003, the European Aviation Safety Agency (EASA) was established, see EC Regulation 1592/2002 establishing a European Aviation Safety Agency, 2002 O.J.L 240/1–21.

Aviation Security found in Annex 17 of the 1944 Chicago Convention.[12] In amending Annex 17, ICAO extended the provisions of the Annex to domestic flights and laid down new requirements on the locking of cockpit doors and other procedures aimed at preventing flight deck intrusion, the implementation of security controls such as background checks on airport personnel, increased security of passports and the standardization of airline and airport personnel identity documents.

In June 2002, ICAO approved an 'Aviation Security Plan of Action', establishing a Universal Aviation Security Audit Programme. The Programme is premised upon the conducting of 'regular, mandatory, systematic and harmonized audits' to evaluate the aviation security measures in place in member states.[13] The audits are to be conducted with a view to identifying and correcting deficiencies in the implementation of the Annex 17 SARPs. The Aviation Security Plan of Action also includes the identification, analysis and development of an effective global response to new and emerging threats, and the integration of timely measures to be taken in airports, aircraft and air traffic control systems. ICAO is also considering the proposed implementation of machine readable travel documents (MRTDs) and the adoption of a global system of biometric identification information for passports and other MRTDs.

Meanwhile, the association of airlines – the International Air Transport Association (IATA) – established the Global Aviation Security Action Group (GASAG), which initiates the harmonization of industry-wide security measures.[14] GASAG has developed industry positions on: harmonization of aviation security standards; state/public funding for enhanced security measures; background checks for persons having unescorted access to restricted areas in airports; the establishment of and effective maintenance of restricted zones at airports; new identification technologies such as biometrics; increased passenger and baggage security controls; risk assessment of passengers; and reinforced cockpit doors.

---

[12] Amendment 10 to Annex 17, see ICAO Doc. 7300/8, 8th Edition (2001). See also the Declaration of Misuse of Civil Aircraft as Weapons of Destruction and Other Terrorist Acts Involving Civil Aviation, ICAO Ass. Res. A33–1, § 7 (2001), issued in the immediate aftermath of the 9/11 incident. For comments, see Ruwantissa Abeyratne, 'The Events of 11 September 2001 – ICAO's Responses to the Security and Insurance Crises', 27:6 *Air & Space L.* 406 (2002).

[13] The audit programme is modeled on ICAO's existing safety oversight audit programme established in 1999. The expression 'mandatory' is somewhat misleading, as auditing is still contingent on state consent. For more on the security audit programme, see Anthony J. Broderick and James Loos, 'Government Aviation Safety Oversight – Trust but Verify' (2002) 67 *J. Air L. & Com.* 1035, at 1052.

[14] See IATA website at http://www.iata.org/whatwedo/security_issues.htm.

IATA's Board of Governors has also approved a set of Recommended Security Standards (RSSs),[15] containing recommendations that are to be met or exceeded by member airlines. In addition, a resolution was adopted calling on states to ensure that effective airline security programmes are in place which are in line with ICAO's Annex 17 requirements and the RSSs. IATA has also initiated a Simplified Passenger Travel (SPT) Programme based upon a travel card facilitating an individual's journey. The card will contain relevant personal data and travel history, including machine-readable biometric data and passport/visa information.

Pursuant to the numerous laws, policies and programmes adopted by states, ICAO and IATA, improved security measures are now being implemented to varying degrees of comprehensiveness around the world. The most significant of these can be divided into: (a) airborne security measures such as air marshals, armed pilots and fortified cockpit doors; and (b) ground security measures such as baggage screening, airport perimeter security, and passenger profiling and information gathering using new technology such as biometrics.[16] These measures will now be assessed.

A. Airborne security – air marshals, armed pilots and fortified cockpit doors

Under the ATSA, the Under-Secretary of Transportation Security is authorized to provide Federal air marshals on passenger flights.[17] In particular, the Under-Secretary is *obliged* to do so for flights deemed to be 'high security risks'.[18] Thousands of air marshals are now being deployed on US domestic flights, as well as on certain international flights operated by US and foreign airlines flying into and out of the US. In the EU enthusiasm for air marshals has been more muted, with a significant number of member states and their pilots' unions being strongly opposed to the measure.[19] At the same time, states like Germany, the Czech Republic, Austria and Switzerland have

---

[15] See 'IATA Recommended Security Standards,' IATA Security Manual, at http://www. iata.org/NR/ContentConnector/CS2000/Siteinterface/sites/soi/file/ IATA_Recommended_Security_Standards.pdf.

[16] In addition, it should be noted that an important revision to the 1952 Rome Convention on Damage to Third Parties on the Ground is being considered at ICAO, with a view to increasing the certainty and amount of compensation to victims of air crashes, including those resulting from acts of terrorism.

[17] ATSA, note 6 above, s. 110(c). S. 105 allows for the marshals to be armed. They may be placed on 'every passenger flight of air carriers and air transportation or interstate air transportation', 49 U.S.C. 44917(a) (2002).

[18] ATSA, ibid., s.105(a).

[19] Portugal, Denmark, Sweden, Italy and Finland, amongst others, have voiced their concerns against air marshals, while the UK and France plan on using them only in some cases.

begun providing air marshals on selected flights. Meanwhile, a proposal has been forwarded to the European Council regarding a potential EU-wide sky marshals programme, but no legislative developments have taken place since then.[20]

On its part, ICAO's Amendment 10 to Annex 17 provides that each Contracting State *shall consider*[21] (i.e. at its discretion) requests by any other State to allow the travel of armed personnel on board the aircraft of operators of the requesting State. Only after agreement by all States involved in a particular flight sector shall such personnel be allowed.[22] IATA, through a common GASAG stand, supports ICAO's position and urges all airlines to ensure that their State complies with Annex 17.[23]

The air marshals programme has some concrete benefits – primarily, it acts as a further line of defence supplementing on-the-ground baggage and passenger screenings where these might fail in detecting potential threats. However, armed air marshals are opposed by many states, airlines, and pilots' unions for their huge safety risks. The major concern is the presence of guns on board a plane: bullets may cause cabin depressurization should they puncture the windows or walls of aircraft.[24] There are also fears of accidental shootings of passengers, and of the marshal's weapon being used against himself by terrorists or any other party.[25] There have also been reports of ill-trained or over-zealous marshals holding innocent passengers at gunpoint at the slightest provocation.[26]

---

[20] EC, 'Introduction of European Union "Sky Marshals" Programme: Discussion Paper,' Proposal by the Austrian Delegation to the Council of the European Union, No. 6391/02 (19 February 2002), available online at http://register.consilium.eu.int/pdf/en/02/st06/06391en2.pdf.

[21] Annex 17, note 12 above, para. 4.6.5. Amendment 10 is also significant in that it extends, for the first time, principles governing measures designed to safeguard against acts of unlawful interference into the domestic context, see Annex 17, § 2.1.3. State parties to the Chicago Convention are henceforth obliged to comply with these principles even for domestic flights.

[22] Annex 17, note 12 above, para. 4.6.5.

[23] GASAG also sets out guidelines for the operational deployment of air marshals.

[24] Apparently, even veteran police officers 'have only an 18 to 22 per cent hit ratio in armed confrontations', see Monica G. Renna, 'Fire in the Sky: A Critical Look at Arming Pilots with Handguns' (2003) 68 *J. Air L. & Com.* 859, at 871. Thus, even if air marshals or pilots had the accuracy of a highly trained police officer, there is still a risk that bullets might go astray some 80 per cent of the time.

[25] Police statistics show that 21 per cent of officers are shot with their own weapons, see Renna, ibid.

[26] In one example in the US, an air marshal detained two passengers solely because of their appearance and the way they looked at him. It was later discovered that the air marshal had previously failed a psychological examination for the Philadelphia Police Department, see 'Air marshal in dispute failed police test', *Philadelphia Inquirer*, 2 October 2002.

In some countries, suggestions have been made for air marshals to carry stun or taser guns or those with low-velocity bullets capable of incapacitating a target but not presenting risks to passengers or the safety of the flight. Overall, many states deem it incongruous for ground security measures to diligently seek to exclude guns from planes only to allow air marshals to bring them on board at considerable risk to the flight. In addition, there are questions relating to the authority of the air marshal *vis-à-vis* the aircraft commander's, particularly when a terrorist situation calls for quick judgments. Whether the marshal's discretion overrides the aircraft commander's authority is still uncertain and is a primary reason why many pilots' unions remain opposed to air marshals.

Another legal issue concerns the liability of air marshals and their employers (whether airline or state) for accidental injuries to passengers. Under the Warsaw Convention regime,[27] an airline may, by categorizing a terrorist incident as an 'accident' under Article 17, rely on the Article 20 defence that it took 'all necessary measures' to avoid the damage or that it was 'impossible' to take such measures. If the 1999 Montreal Convention[28] is applicable, the carrier could argue under Article 21 that the passenger's injury was 'not due to the negligence or other wrongful act or omission of the carrier or its servants or agents' or was 'solely due to the negligence or other wrongful act or omission of a third party'.

Hence, the carrier's liability in situations of injury to passengers by an air marshal turns on the precise relationship between the airline and the marshal. In most states currently deploying marshals, marshals are typically members of the police force or other government agencies – government employees whose presence may be obliged by law. If so, an airline could argue that the marshals are not their 'servants or agents' but 'third parties' whose sole negligence may have caused injury to passengers, exempting the airline from liability. On the other hand, if marshals are employed by an airline, it would be more difficult for the airline to argue that the marshal is not its servant or agent.

Costs are also an issue. It is estimated that to effectively cover most flights today, the air marshal programme in the US alone would cost $20 billion per year.[29] The bulk of these costs would be passed on to the airlines and consumers, much to the resistance of industry groups like IATA. In any event, due to the massive number of flights worldwide, it will take time before

---

[27] 1929 Warsaw Convention for the Unification of Certain Rules Relating to International Carriage by Air, 137 *L.N.T.S.* 11, as amended.

[28] 1999 Montreal Convention for the Unification of Certain Rules for International Carriage by Air. The Convention entered into force in late 2003 and is now progressively gaining widespread acceptance and displacing the old Warsaw Convention (which remains in force for state parties who have not moved to the Montreal regime).

[29] John R. Lott, 'Marshals are Good, But Armed Pilots are Better' *Wall Street Journal Europe*, 2 January 2004, available at http://johnrlott.tripod.com/op-eds/ArmedMarshalsWSJE.html. For an assessment of the total costs of aviation security, see below note 101.

national authorities can recruit, train and deploy enough marshals to satisfy the security needs of commercial airlines.[30]

In the US, it has been noted that marshals are being rushed through training and relevant standards are being compromised to get more armed marshals on board flights. Some airlines have also asked whether the state should shoulder the entire costs, including the cost of the marshal's seat on board the plane. From the airline's perspective, the state should pay for all security measures since these are essentially public goods. There is also concern among airlines that some states like the US are providing security-related funding to their airlines which essentially constitutes subsidies which foreign airlines do not enjoy.

In the short term, it is unrealistic to expect uniform implementation of air marshals programmes worldwide, even if ICAO were able to craft harmonized rules for the training, emplacement and financing of air marshals. At ICAO, states are likely to scrutinize the cost-effectiveness of air marshals, the liability of air marshals for causing passenger injury, the relationship between the marshal and the aircraft commander, and whether a US-type air marshal programme is suitable for flights in other parts of the world.

Indeed, there is every reason for states to assess for themselves the particular level of risk which may necessitate the employment of air marshals on certain flight sectors. It is conceivable that many flights, particularly those which do not involve entering US airspace, may be adjudged to bear a lower risk and may thus be fully or partially exempt. Presumably there is no reason why a flight from Bangkok to Beijing should carry the same number of air marshals or be subjected to the same stringent screening procedures as, say, a flight from London to New York.

In other words, differentiated risk assessment can be recognized as an operating principle in ICAO's deliberations. In the meantime, states would simply have to be prepared for the likes of the US and the European states imposing requirements for air marshals on foreign airlines entering their airspace.[31] ICAO itself recognizes the need for flexibility and differentiation in this matter, as reflected by its Amendment 10 to Annex 17 which provides

---

[30] Karber, 'Re-constructing Global Aviation', at 794–5.

[31] On 29 December 2003 the Department of Homeland Security warned foreign carriers that they would be denied landing rights at US airports if they failed to put armed guards on flights which the US considered to be security risks. The US Department of Transport has on occasions terminated air transport services between the US and states whose airports were found to be wanting in upholding security standards. See the Foreign Airport Security Act of 1985, Pub. L. 99–83, Tit. V, Pt. B, 99 Stat. 222 which requires the FAA to assess the security procedures of foreign airports and foreign air carriers that serve the US. In order to be allowed to serve US airports, foreign airlines must adopt and implement security procedures established by the federal government. Foreign airlines are also required to maintain effective security programmes, see 49 U.S.C. 44906–7 (2002).

that states retain the discretion to meet requests by other states to allow the placement of air marshals.

As always, the challenge for ICAO is to ensure that whatever rules and standards it puts in place can be implemented in a timely and effective manner by member states. One major problem which has always afflicted ICAO is that it possesses little authority to enforce compliance with its rules and standards – the so-called 'SARPs'. This has long been a challenge for aviation safety, where the furthest ICAO has gone is to develop an audit scheme to assess the aviation safety arrangements of states and their air operators. The audits can only be conducted with the consent of the relevant state, and there is no penalty associated with non-compliance.[32] In practice, though, other states may customarily deny access to their airspace to carriers from states which they (or ICAO) have determined to have violated the relevant SARPs. This has proven to be a highly effective deterrent, particularly for air operators that cannot afford to be excluded from lucrative markets like the US.

In light of this inherent weakness in ICAO's enforcement machinery, states must continue to possess the authority to impose and enforce standards higher than ICAO's minimum standards. Thus, for air marshals, ICAO could develop minimum standards applicable to all states, for instance, in conducting risk assessments using common criteria to determine if air marshals need to be deployed on particular flight sectors. In addition, a uniform standard for the training, arming and financing of air marshals can be established, should marshals be necessary.

Beyond these minimum standards, states which feel particularly vulnerable should have the flexibility of adopting (and enforcing) more stringent and specialized standards for aircraft entering their airspace, particularly for flight sectors considered high-risk. This may include the deployment of any number of marshals thought necessary, and for extra training and specified weaponry if needed. In this manner, a differentiated system of risk assessment responding to varying perceptions of risk can be established, not only for air marshals but all other associated security measures.

Even more controversial than air marshals is the arming of pilots. In July 2002 the US enacted the Arming Pilots Against Terrorism Act (APATA)[33] as part of the Homeland Security Act measures. Under the APATA, the TSA is tasked with establishing a programme 'to select, train, deputize, equip, and supervise volunteer pilots'. Under the 'Federal Flight Deck Officer Program' (FFDOP) which was subsequently set up, pilots are to be trained to use

---

[32] Results of the audits may be published, but often in consultation with the state concerned, and sensitive information is rarely made public.
[33] H.R. 4635, 107th Cong. (2002).

firearms at a level of proficiency 'comparable to the level of proficiency required of Federal air marshals'.[34]

For the moment, the FFDOP remains a voluntary programme, and any pilot who volunteers and completes the training course is considered qualified (subject to a pre-determined maximum number of pilots who may be deputized).[35] The Act grants air carriers total immunity from liability for damages in actions filed in federal or state courts arising out of an armed pilot's use or failure to use a firearm.[36] However, the Act only partially protects the pilots themselves – an armed pilot can still be liable in cases involving gross negligence or wilful misconduct.[37]

One argument in favour of armed pilots is that there is less risk of passengers being accidentally shot, given that pilots are largely confined to cockpits. Their only responsibility would be to defend the cockpit against intrusion, a task facilitated by the requirement for hardened cockpit doors.[38] However, many countries, airlines and crew unions have strenuously opposed proposals to arm flights crews with lethal weapons or to require them to undergo training in the use of lethal force.[39] The fear is that armed pilots, like armed air marshals, introduce the risk of stray bullets being fired in the cockpit which can jeopardize electrical or navigation equipment.[40]

Arming pilots could also have detrimental consequences if a fatigued pilot's judgment is impaired by long flying shifts. The lack of sleep can negatively affect perception and reaction time and contribute to the risks of pilot error.[41] Also, it would be unwise to distract a pilot or to have his attention diverted from flying – in principle as well as in practice, a pilot should not have to choose between his duties as a pilot and his duties as a federal law enforcement officer.[42] The defence of the aircraft should properly be left to air marshals. At the same time, allowing pilots to bring guns into airports and onto aircraft runs contrary to the overall security objective, which is to prevent potential terrorists from gaining access to a weapon.[43] The economic costs of a pilot arming and training programme can also be substantial, with the costs likely to be passed on to consumers.[44]

Both ICAO and IATA have instead called for flight crews to be trained in non-lethal forms of self-defence and/or that non-lethal protective devices be

---

[34] APATA, s. 1402(a). The FFDOP has now been extended to cargo pilots and other personnel.
[35] Renna, 'Fire in the Sky', at 867.   [36] APATA, s. 2(h)(1).   [37] APATA, s. 2(h)(2).
[38] Lott, 'Marshals are Good'.
[39] See, e.g., IATA's response through GASAG and Renna, note 24 above, at 860.
[40] Bartholomew Elias, 'Arming Pilots against Terrorism: Implementation Issues for the Federal Flight Deck Officer Program', Report for Congress, Congressional Research Service, Library of Congress, Order Code RL31674 (25 March 2003), at 6.
[41] Renna, 'Fire in the Sky', at 870.   [42] Ibid., at 874.   [43] Elias, 'Arming Pilots', at 6.
[44] Miller, 'The "Cost" of Securing', at 434.

made available in the cabin area (e.g. stun guns, pepper sprays, etc.).[45] Overall, it is imperative for ICAO and IATA members to achieve some form of negotiated compromise on this issue, again flexibly allowing for differing perceptions of risks in different parts of the world.

The other major security measure enacted after 9/11 is the fortification of cockpit doors. Section 104 of ATSA authorizes the relevant government agency to require that cockpit doors have locks and can be fortified so they cannot be forced open from the passenger compartment.[46] It also requires that the door remain locked during flight and that no member of the flight crew has a key unless assigned to the flight deck.[47] Furthermore, ATSA provides the authority to take other necessary action, including modification of safety and security procedures and flight deck redesign.[48] ATSA also provides for funding to airlines to fortify their cockpit doors.[49]

ICAO, through amendments to the Chicago Convention's Annex 6, has also thrown its weight behind the fortification of cockpit doors.[50] This has been one area where it has been thought that some measure of global harmonization is desirable and viable. ICAO's cockpit door measure was largely influenced by the US provisions, with the FAA working closely with ICAO to develop the standards after they had entered into force domestically and for all foreign airlines entering the US.[51] By 1 November 2003 all passenger-carrying planes above a certain mass and carrying more than sixty passengers must be equipped with cockpit doors designed to 'resist penetration by small arms fire and grenade shrapnel, and to resist forcible intrusions by unauthorized persons . . . [and] be capable of being locked and unlocked from either pilot's station'.[52] In addition, the cockpit door is to be locked from embarkation to disembarkation.[53]

On its part, IATA has made similar recommendations and supports the employment of advanced cockpit door technology. Meanwhile, the EU has called on its member states to support the ICAO amendment to Annex 6.[54] Overall, the costs of hardening cockpit doors have been considerable. In September 2003 the TSA announced that it had reimbursed fifty-eight domestic air carriers a total of $100 million for the cost of reinforcing their cockpit doors. This was in addition to the $97 million already reimbursed by

---

[45] See, e.g., ICAO's Amendment 27 to Annex 6, para. 13.4.1.   [46] ATSA, s.104(1)(a)(1)(B).
[47] Ibid., s.104(1)(a)(1)(C), (D).   [48] Ibid., s.104(1)(a)(2).   [49] Ibid., s.118(c)(1).
[50] Amendment 27 to Annex 6. The requirement applies to aircraft heavier than 45,500 kg or seating more than 60 passengers.
[51] See William Karas and Carol Gosain, 'Recent US Regulation of Foreign Airline Practices: Impermissibly Unilateral or Not?' (2002) 16 *Air & Space L.* 4, at 6.
[52] Annex 6, Amendment 27, para. 13.2.2.   [53] Ibid., para. 13.2.3(a).
[54] Communication from the Commission, 'Co-ordinated answer by Member States to the ICAO document AN 11/1.3.16–02/23 on new protection standards for flight crew compartment doors,' Com (2002) 444(01).

the FAA earlier.[55] In the future it is likely that there will also be costs to maintain, replace and reinstall doors.[56]

B. Airport security – baggage and passenger screening

On the ground, enhanced baggage and passenger screening are the most significant new measures employed.[57] In the US, ATSA has federalized baggage, passenger, mail and cargo screening tasks.[58] All baggage, including checked-in baggage, are to be screened. ATSA also laid down a requirement for explosive detection systems (EDS) to be installed in all US airports by 31 December 2002, and for all checked baggage to be screened by these systems.[59] Employees screening baggage must be US citizens and possess a high school diploma or equivalent, or have experience deemed sufficient to perform screening duties.[60] Screeners must also have a satisfactory score on a federal selection examination and possess the basic aptitudes and physical abilities to use the screening equipment.[61]

The federalization of screening responsibilities was brought about by the belief that better-paid and better-trained personnel would produce better results,[62] and that such responsibilities could only be carried out by properly-selected US citizens. Implicit in this requirement was the belief that non-US citizens posed a greater threat to domestic security than citizens, particularly if these were illegal aliens. Predictably, the requirement has resulted in the displacement of thousands of non-citizen airport screeners in the past few years.[63] The costs of the additional screening measures have also been extremely high.[64] At the same time, the EDS machines have been shown to be

---

[55] TSA, Press Release, 'TSA Approves $100 Million to Reimburse Airlines for Reinforcing Cockpit Doors' (24 September 2003), http://www.tsa.gov/public/display?content = 0900051980056949. See also note 101 on costs.

[56] The initiative has been criticized as ineffective. In one incident, an overnight cleaning crew at Dulles Airport near Washington, D.C. apparently rammed a drinks cart into one of the new doors on a United Airlines plane, breaking the door off its hinges, see Lott, 'Marshals are Good'.

[57] See generally Jack H. Daniel III, 'Reform in Airport Security: Panic or Precaution?' (2002) 53 Mercer L. Rev. 1623, and Jamie L. Rhee, 'Rational and Constitutional Approaches to Airline Safety in the Face of Terrorist Threats' (2002) 49 DePaul L. Rev. 847.

[58] ATSA, s.110.   [59] Ibid., ss.110(b)(2) and 110(c).

[60] Ibid., s.111(a)(2). See also Francine Kerner and Margot Bester, 'The Birth of the Transportation Security Administration: A View from the Chief Counsel' (2002) Air & Space L. 20, at 22.

[61] ATSA, ss. 110 and 111.   [62] Miller, note 4 above, at n.144.

[63] See Paul S. Dempsey, 'Aviation Security: The Role of Law in the War Against Terrorism' (2003) 41 Colum. J. Int'l L. 649, at 716.

[64] For the 2005 financial year, the TSA has requested $4.8 billion to cover screening costs. The cost of an EDS machine is approximately $1 million, with between $700,000 and

error-prone, with an initial figure of 22 per cent in false-positive records.[65] This problem can lead to inconvenient delays as well as potential invasions of privacy for individuals whose bags are inaccurately singled out by the EDS.

In the EU, Reg. 2320/2002 requires all checked-in baggage to be placed in areas where only authorized persons have access,[66] and that such baggage be protected from any unauthorized interference from the time of check-in to departure.[67] If a passenger has checked in baggage but does not board the flight, such baggage will be removed from the aircraft, as had been common practice in most states even before 9/11.[68] Checked-in baggage must be screened by one of several methods, including hand search, conventional X-rays, EDS, and Trace Detection Equipment.[69]

ICAO has also laid down improved screening procedures. Pursuant to Amendment 10 to Annex 17, states are required to take action to detect weapons, explosives or other dangerous devices.[70] States are to ensure that by the year 2006 all checked-in baggage are screened at airports, and that screeners are subjected to stringent background checks and selection procedures.[71] While such requirements may easily be met by the developed states, there will presumably be difficulties for airports in developing countries. The need for flexibility is recognized by ICAO itself, which is not attempting to lay down specific standards or methods for baggage screening. Due to the unreliability of EDS measures, it may well be advisable for states to adopt the EU's practice of combining different baggage detection systems, including the use of hand searches. IATA's GASAG recommendation for countries to work together and share R&D costs to develop better EDS technology should also be taken up.

What has become more far-reaching and controversial post-9/11 has been the screening of passengers.[72] This now goes beyond conventional metal detectors and body searches to include the collection of passenger data, the employment of biometric technology and the use of data collected through various means to screen passengers through a process of profiling. In

---

$1 million needed annually for operation and maintenance. See also note 101 for a brief assessment of the total costs of aviation security.

[65] Dempsey, 'Aviation Security', at 723. [66] Annex, Part 5, s.5.1(1)(c). [67] Ibid., s.5.3(1).

[68] Ibid., s.5.1(2).

[69] For the US position, see Frank Costello, 'The New Federal Approach to Transportation: The First Three Months of the Transportation Security Act and the Transportation Security Administration' (2002) 14 DePaul Bus. L. J. 333, at 336.

[70] See generally Dempsey, 'Aviation Security', at 678.

[71] Ibid., at 678–79. On its part, IATA supports the ICAO's standards through its RSSs, particularly Recommendations 8 to 10.

[72] For screening generally, see Jonathan Miller, 'Search and Seizure of Air Passengers and Pilots: The Fourth Amendment Takes Flight' (1994) 22 Transp. L.J. 199.

particular, the TSA is now authorized to provide for the use of biometrics to identify passengers who pose a threat to aircraft security and to subject them to additional screening.[73]

Pursuant to the USA Patriot Act,[74] the Department of Homeland Security has incorporated the use of biometric technology into the US Visitor and Immigrant Status Indicator Technology Program (US-VISIT). In addition, biometric technology has been considered for use in IATA's Simplified Passenger Travel (SPT) programme, which is meant to alleviate passenger clearance at airports. Under the programme passengers can simply swipe their cards which hold relevant information in order to attain instant clearance every time they travel.[75]

Pursuant to the US-VISIT programme, the entry and exit of all non-US citizens at airports will be tracked through the use of inkless fingerprints and digital photographs. The information will be used to verify visitors' identities and to match these against 'watch lists' of known high-risk individuals.[76] In addition, the Patriot Act mandates that all countries on the Visa Waiver Program (which permits entry into the US without visas) are to issue their citizens with machine-readable travel documents (MRTDs) carrying biometric identifiers that comply with ICAO standards by 26 October 2005.[77]

---

[73] ATSA, note 6 above, s. 109(a)(7).
[74] Uniting and Strengthening America by Providing Appropriate Tools Required to Intercept and Obstruct Terrorism Act, H.R. 3162, 107th Cong., 2001, s.414(b)(1). See also the Immigration and Naturalization Service Data Management Improvement Act of 2000 (DMIA), *Public Law* 106–215 (2000), 114 Stat. 339 (codified as amended at 8 U.S.C. 1365a).
[75] See generally Ruwantissa Abeyratne, 'Attacks on America: Privacy Implications of Heightened Security Measures in the United States, Europe, and Canada' (2002) 67 *J. Air L. & Com.* 83, at 83–84. For SPT, see http://www.simplifying-travel.org/.
[76] A measure of tit-for-tat was reported by irate states like Brazil, which reacted to the US programme by announcing its own fingerprinting of US nationals entering Brazil.
[77] The original deadline was 26 October 2004. However, it has been reported in recent months that countries on the visa waiver programme (VWP), including allies like the European states, do not expect to be able to issue passports with biometric identifiers by 26 October 2004. The US House of Representatives' extension on 16 June 2004 of the deadline by one year was approved by the Bush Administration in August 2004. However, doubts remain over whether biometric identifiers can be developed in time by October 2005, see Face Recognition Passports Expected by December, http://www.cnn.com/2004/TECH/06/15/face.passport/. Meanwhile, visitors from VWP countries will continue to enjoy visa-free travel but will have to be fingerprinted and photographed from 30 September 2004 pursuant to the US-VISIT programme. All passports from VWP countries must also be machine-readable from October 2004. Note that Canada is not part of the visa waiver programme, and Canadians do not generally require visas to enter the United States.

ICAO-recommended standards for biometrics are laid out in its Technical Report on MRTDs, which drew heavily from the US experience.[78] The standards take into account such factors as global inter-operability, uniformity and technical reliability. Facial recognition was identified as the preferred globally inter-operable biometric, though states can elect to supplement this with fingerprint and/or iris recognition. On its part, the EU has yet to enact any laws concerning biometrics in MRTDs. However, it has considered a proposal on common standards for biometrics, taking into account the US deadline and the ICAO standards.[79] Thus, it is likely that some form of global harmonization in relation to biometric identification for travellers will be in place soon.

At the same time, passenger information is being actively collected in the US pursuant to ATSA.[80] Thus, all carriers operating passenger flights into the US must electronically transmit a 'passenger and crew manifest' to the relevant authority before landing in the US. ATSA permits such information to be shared with other federal agencies for the purpose of national security. The list of information required includes the date of birth of passengers and crew and the number and country of issuance of their passports. Carriers are also required to make passenger name records (PNRs) available to the Bureau of Customs and Border Protection (constituted under the Department of Homeland Security) upon request.[81]

In addition, US legislation has provided for another database system known as Advanced Passenger Information (API) as a requirement for all carriers flying into the US.[82] The API system works on the basis of each passenger's information being transmitted to immigration and customs authorities in advance of his/her actual arrival. The information would then be used to determine if the passenger should be admitted to the destination state.[83] Concurrently, TSA is required to keep a 'watchlist' of names posing an immediate threat to passenger safety in the air.

Yet another US initiative is the Computer Assisted Passenger Prescreening System (CAPPS II), authorized by ATSA.[84] This programme seeks to authenticate travellers' identities and perform risk assessments to detect individuals who may pose a terrorist-related threat, and involves asking passengers for certain information well before the flight, typically at the time of the reservation of air tickets. Individuals will be categorized or profiled according

---

[78] On 28 May 2003, ICAO adopted a global, harmonized blueprint for the integration of biometric identification information into passports.

[79] Above note 77.   [80] ATSA, s. 115(c).   [81] Ibid., s.115.

[82] See N. Banerjea-Brodeur, 'Advance passenger information leads to better border control and faster clearances', ICAO Journal, Vol. 58, Issue 7, at 30 (September 2002).

[83] Ibid.

[84] S109(3). CAPS was originally developed after the 1996 TWA crash and its revised version is now being targeted at post-9/11 concerns.

to risk levels, and those who are deemed not to be a risk will likely experience shorter waiting times at screening points. As mentioned above, IATA's 'Simplified Passenger Travel' initiative also entails screening passengers at the commencement of their journey and sharing that information electronically with service providers during subsequent trips. Frequent travellers posing no risk will experience less delay at screening points as a result.[85]

The collection of passenger information, whether through PNRs, API, CAPPS II, SPT or any other means, and the use of that information for profiling purposes, can ostensibly be an effective tool. Principally, it has the benefit of reducing wait times for passengers and frequent travellers who are deemed to be risk-free, and allows screeners to pay more attention to those thought to pose a threat. In other words, the practice facilitates the optimal allocation of scarce law enforcement resources to those populations in which crime is thought to be more likely to occur.

At the same time, however, the extent to which profiling-based methods optimize the allocation of enforcement resources is heavily dependent on the *quality* of available information on 'risky' individuals. A biometric system based on facial or retinal recognition is contingent upon records being available to facilitate a comparison, and a terrorist with no known previous record will likely not be detected. Thus, its utility is limited to identifying *known* terrorist suspects. In any event, there is still a potential for a false match rate, given that none of the face, finger or retinal scans are known to be 100 per cent perfect.[86] In addition, biometric identification and verification simply ensure that the person getting on board the plane is a rightful ticket-holder, and does not prevent would-be terrorists who are properly-ticketed (and with no known record) to board. Indeed, this method would not have prevented the 9/11 attacks, as the terrorists responsible *did* have proper tickets for those fateful flights.[87]

In the same vein, the proposed CAPPS II system is fraught with problems – there are serious concerns over its application, including who operates it and how it is operated, passengers being incorrectly denied boarding, its hasty adoption without the benefit of proper economic analysis and reservation software not being currently able to perform flagging functions. Moreover, there are concerns over the integrity of the information collected – profile data can apparently be leaked so that terrorists themselves may be able to use

[85] For more on SPT, see Abeyratne, 'Attacks on America', at 83.
[86] See also Daniel, 'Reform in Airport Security', at 1635, citing a Department of Defense study showing that this technology has a higher error rate with regard to false positives.
[87] For a discussion, see Karber, 'Re-Constructing Global Aviation', at 798, citing Traci Watson, 'US Looks at Which Tech Proposals Will Fly: Government Deluged with Ideas for Airports, Airliners' *USA Today*, at A-4, 26 November 2001.

the profiles as part of their own deceptive strategies.[88] For all these reasons, the TSA has reportedly scrapped CAPPS II, even though it appears that research is continuing into the development of alternative passenger pre-screening systems.[89]

Perhaps the biggest concern over profiling relates to invasion of privacy and the erosion of fundamental civil liberties.[90] Under the US proposal for the sharing of PNR information, sensitive personal data will be surrendered to government officials. Such information can be transmitted to other federal agencies, where it can be collated with independent information collected by these agencies to build a profile on the relevant passenger. Personal information such as travel histories and even lodging preferences and meal habits can be tracked, permitting governments to build up profiles according to racial or religious grounds. This can open the way to arbitrary discrimination, as certain individuals of particular ethnicities or religious faiths will invariably be subjected to greater scrutiny in security operations.[91] Indeed, profiling based solely on race or ethnicity has been a bane which scores of travellers have unpleasantly experienced post-9/11.[92] There are also fears that as biometrics-based identification becomes the entrenched norm, more extensive use will be made of this

---

[88] R. W. Bloom, 'Commentary on the Motivational Psychology of Terrorism against Transportation Systems: Implications for Airline Safety and Transportation Law' (1998) 25 *Transp. L. J.* 175, at 179.

[89] See 'Uncle Sam Mothballs Screening Program', washingtonpost.com, 16 July 2004, at http://www.washingtonpost.com/wp-dyn/articles/A54487–2004Jul16.html.

[90] See Wong, Chapter 10 in this volume. According to an Associated Press poll taken in August 2002, two-thirds of American respondents felt concerned that the new security measures restricted their individual liberties, see Miller, note 4 above, at 408 and Robert L. Crandall, 'Security for the Future: Let's get our airlines flying' (2002) 67 *J. Air L. & Com.* 9.

[91] Racial profiling may be permissible under the Fourth Amendment if race is one factor among several for a decision to stop a person, but not the sole basis. Racial profiling may also be challenged under the Equal Protection Clause under the Fourteenth Amendment. Under federal equal protection principles, it may be that racial profiling is generally prohibited, at least in the absence of finding that it is 'narrowly tailored' to serve a 'compelling state interest'. See generally Samuel G. Gross and Debra Livingston, 'Racial Profiling under Attack' (2002) 102 *Colum. L. R.* 1413; John Rogers, 'Note: Bombs, Borders and Boarding: Combating International Terrorism at United States Airports and the 4th Amendment' (1997) 20 *Suffolk Transnat'l L. R.* 501; and Jamie Rhee, 'Rational and Constitutional Approaches'.

[92] For more on racial profiling, see Kareem Shora, 'Guilty of Flying While Brown' (2002) 17 *Air & Space L.* 4; Ellen Baker, 'Flying While Arab – Racial Profiling and Air Travel Security' (2002) 67 *J. Air L. & Comm.* 1375; Charu A. Chandrasekhar, 'Flying While Brown: Federal Civil Rights Remedies to Post-9/11 Airline Racial Profiling of South Asians' (2003) 10 *Asian L. J.* 215; Ryan L. Bangert, 'When Airlines Profile Based on Race: Are Claims Brought Against Airlines Under State Anti-Discrimination Laws Preempted by the Airline Deregulation Act?' (2003) 68 *J. Air L. & Com.* 791; and Richard Sobel, 'The Demeaning of Identity and Personhood in National Identification Systems' (2002) 15 *Harv. J. L. & Tech.* 319, at 355.

technology beyond security-related purposes. In other words, biometric technology may slowly desensitize society's awareness of the right to privacy.

For all these reasons, the EU had been reluctant to comply with US requirements for PNRs for flights originating in Europe and bound for the US.[93] After extensive negotiations, an agreement was struck in May 2004 between the two sides, providing for the release of information on European passengers travelling to the US and the strict conditions attached to such release.[94] The conditions restrict which US government agencies can have access to the information and requires sensitive information such as race and health to be deleted immediately.[95] Overall, the Agreement ensures that the way in which PNR data is used by US authorities will not unlawfully discriminate against EU passengers and guarantees reciprocal support from the US for any potential European passenger identification system.

Within the EU, the presence of instruments like Directive 95/46 relating to the protection of the processing and movement of personal data affords some level of protection to passengers.[96] However, few countries in the world have such comprehensive laws on privacy protection for their citizens. In this regard, it would be preferable if a harmonized standard for passenger information exchange can be instituted through ICAO or IATA auspices, incorporating the types of safeguards guaranteed by the EU–US Agreement.

Airlines and passengers worldwide may have little choice but to accept that despite the potential violation of privacy rights, there appear to be few practical alternatives to data collection and profiling. Without some form of profiling, the prospect of long delays at airports is a real one, since all

---

[93] See Communication from the European Commission to the Council and Parliament on Transfer of Air Passenger Name Records (PNR) Data: A Global EU Approach, Com 2003/ 0826 final, 16 December 2003, at 4–5.

[94] See International Agreement on Passenger Name Records between the European Community and the United States, signed and entered into force 28 May 2004: see http://europa.eu.int/comm/external_relations/us/news/ip04_694.htm. The Agreement provides the legal framework under which airlines can transfer PNR data to US authorities and grants permission to US authorities to access such data held on EU territory.

[95] See Regulation (EC) No. 68/2004 of 15 January 2004 amending Commission Regulation (EC) No. 622/2003 laying down measures for the implementation of the common basic standards on aviation security.

[96] 1995 O.J.L. 281, 31. Pursuant to this Directive, the EC adopted a so-called 'adequacy finding', based on US undertakings regarding the protection of transferred data. The Agreement, note 94 above, and the 'adequacy finding' are linked, so that the former only remains in force as long as adequate data protection in the US is granted. The presence of provisions like Art. 25, para. 6 of Directive 95/46 relating to the protection of the processing and movement of personal data can be expected to afford some level of protection, even though Arts. 6, 7 and 13 of the Directive arguably allow for the processing of data for legitimate purposes and where this is necessary in the public interest, e.g. for the purpose of aviation security.

travellers would have to be searched systematically. The solution lies in effecting a balance between security risks and the right of the individual to his or her privacy. Where exactly this balance falls is, of course, a difficult question, but any assessment made must take into account the magnitude of the risks involved, the means of assessing these risks and ultimately, the weight to be attached to the risks, given the competing imperative of individual rights. At the very least, restrictions on the number and type of government agencies which can have access to passenger information and the duration and purpose for which such information should be stored are the main safeguards which can and must be imposed.

III. Harmonization of aviation security measures

In the light of efforts taken by ICAO and IATA to attain some measure of harmonization of aviation security measures, care must be taken to ensure that the measures eventually prescribed are capable of being enforced and complied with, particularly in the less developed parts of the world. In the aftermath of 9/11, many of the aviation security initiatives have arisen out of the developed states like the US and EU countries. Domestically, the US public's perception and fear of the risk of a recurrence of terrorist events on the scale of 9/11 has led to a discernible increase in the government's willingness to take strong action, particularly on the part of the executive, and commonly at the expense of civil liberties.

At the same time, it must be recognized that the dynamics of institutional intercourse in the US and the EU and its implications on civil liberties and the aviation industry may have important effects internationally. Many of the new security measures that have been imposed by the US are backed up by sanctions such as airlines' exclusion from the US market.[97] Thus, foreign airlines wishing to continue flying to, from and over US airspace have had no choice but to comply with the regulations. In addition, the US may also ban flights from foreign airports which do not maintain adequate security standards. This has the immensely powerful effect of influencing not only the compliance behaviour of foreign airlines, but of foreign airports and states as well in relation to airport security measures such as pre-departure passenger and baggage screening. Such enforcement capability makes up for the inability of bodies like ICAO and IATA to enforce compliance among states and airlines with prescribed standards.

However, while these measures have the effect of unifying regulations applicable to US-related flights, it remains doubtful whether such measures, even if adopted by ICAO for international application, can be properly and meaningfully implemented worldwide. These doubts are particularly

---

[97] Paul S. Dempsey, 'Wide Range of Air Law Instruments Work to Curb Acts of Violence Against Aviation', *ICAO Journal*, Vol. 58, Issue 7, at 30 (September 2003).

pertinent if the measures entail high compliance costs which cannot be easily borne by other states and their airlines. An example is the proposed use of biometric technology in passports and other travel documents, which will entail the use of expensive technology.[98] In the developing world, in particular, it appears unrealistic that such measures will enjoy widespread application, at least in the short to medium term.

Hence, ICAO, in its effort to craft aviation security standards that are to be enforceable globally, must be alive to the fact that a balance will have to be sought between technologically responsive regulations and realistic expectations for enforceability and compliance in many parts of the world. This challenge is certainly not new to ICAO – disparate levels of enforcement have long been observed in relation to matters such as aviation safety, as mentioned above. Yet, aviation safety has long proceeded on the premise that the *prescription* of safety standards worldwide must be uniform, as encapsulated in ICAO's SARPs. It is just that the *enforcement* of the prescribed SARPs has been replete with problems, not least because it is impossible for ICAO to demand that every state live up to its obligations under the SARPs. What this means is that differentiated enforcement may be inevitable, even if the prescribed standards are fairly uniform. Thus, from a regime-effectiveness view, it would be desirable if the legislation process can take into account the realities of differentiated enforcement from the outset, and the standards prescribed accordingly so as to maximise the chances of compliance.

In this regard the aviation industry may not be alone[99] in witnessing the gradual demise of the 'lowest common denominator' approach to

---

[98] Biometric technology is premised upon the identification of passengers using fingerprint, facial, retinal or iris records.

[99] The industry's close cousin, the maritime industry, is arguably experiencing a similar trend, in that states with higher expectations for safety, pollution and security standards are pressing for high regime standards to be enforced in ports against foreign ships. The sanctions in such cases would be denied entry or detention of sub-standard ships in ports, a practice known as 'port state control' or 'port state enforcement'. While such moves can be pursued unilaterally (in that both legislated standards and enforcement measures in port can be wholly home-driven), the developed states tend to prefer to 'up' the standards in international conventions adopted by the International Maritime Organization (IMO). Differentiated enforcement may then ensue, with the developed port states pursuing stricter enforcement of these measures while developing states are left to grapple with the complexities of stricter (and usually difficult-to-enforce) regulations. The negative effects of such a regime could be the flight of sub-standard ships and operators to the developing world, a prospect that could also happen in the aviation sector. Thus, 'good' airlines with commendable safety (and now security) records will continue to fly to the US and Western Europe, while lesser airlines may concentrate on regional flights in developing regions of the world where expectations for aviation security are lower. Empirical proof for such a phenomenon remains, of course, to be researched.

international regime formation, one characterized by the tendency to pre-
scribe standards that can ideally be met by the weakest of participants in the
decision-making process. By the same token, neither is it desirable to pre-
scribe 'maximal' standards that are so stringent that they do not afford
meaningful compliance by weaker target actors. Thus, it may be that a
more differentiated 'two-track' approach will have to be adopted – an
approach consisting of, on the one hand, minimal 'baseline' standards
applicable to all states, and beyond that, the flexibility to recognize the need
for higher standards by certain interested states.

In this regard, differentiation in measures may be contingent upon at least
two variables – the subject matter of the standard itself, and its geographical
application. Both variables are, in turn, linked to the difference in perception
of risks by different actors and the weight attached to such risks. Thus, a
particularly costly measure (such as biometric technology or air marshals)
may be less appealing to a state in a region of the world which sees little reason
to expend huge resources on what may appear to be a minimal terrorist risk.
Yet, at the same time, the state may be persuaded as to the cost-effectiveness
of a fortified cockpit door or increased baggage surveillance.

In this regard, the individual aviation security measures discussed in this
chapter should not be viewed in isolation, but as a package of numerous
alternatives that can be tailored to meet the specific demands and needs of
states. In other words, ICAO should afford the possibility of states using a
combination of measures that best reflects their specialized needs, rather than
imposing fixed standards on all states. The compliance of states with these
measures can then be taken up either by ICAO's auditing scheme, or by
individual states requiring compliance as a condition of entry into their
airspace. This flexible approach will maximize the chances of compliance
by states with the requisite standards.

IV. Conclusion

The broad themes dealt with in this chapter revolve around the strengths and
weaknesses of aviation security measures proposed and implemented, and the
best possible means to harmonize these measures given the differentiated
perception of risks in various countries. On the latter issue, the complete
harmonization of universal standards is counter-productive, as this will only
lead to chronic non-compliance among many countries. Instead, international agencies like ICAO should seek to impose a certain band of minimal
standards applicable to all actors, with the allowance for some to impose
more stringent standards, even if these had to be unilaterally enforced.

Following from this, and relating it to the first issue, it can be appreciated
that while armed marshals and pilots can act as a supplementary line of

defence against terrorism,[100] the risks of having guns on board planes may be
too high for some states to accept. This is particularly so if these states view
themselves and their airlines to be less at risk of terrorist attacks. Fortifying
cockpit doors represents a more viable solution as they entail less costs and
minimal safety risks. Thus, flight sectors which are viewed to be less terrorist-
prone should be allowed to settle for a less expensive alternative such as
fortified cockpit doors, as opposed to air marshals. In other words, the
different aviation security measures should be viewed as a coherent whole
in tailoring the response of states, with flexible combinations of such measures being prescribed for states with different needs.

As for baggage screening, the benefits of stopping dangerous items from
being brought onto the plane are clear, for flights anywhere in the world. In
this respect, the solution appears to be for countries to work together to
develop more cost-effective technologies for baggage screening. On their
part, passenger screening initiatives come at high financial as well as privacy
infringement costs.[101] For the sake of protecting privacy, a balance must be
found between the amount of information required from passengers and the
use to which government agencies put such information. Privacy protection
should ideally be extended to the citizens of all countries, not only those
which have the laws to ensure this.

Of course, it remains a worthy ideal to have all states and airlines pursue all
security measures within a harmonized regime, regardless of the particular
level of risk that exists for different countries. Such harmonization is particularly desirable for a global industry such as aviation, where the 'weakest
link' in a particular actor may have ramifications for other states. However,
the realities are such that stringent standards will be viewed as necessary by
some, but not all states, and a level of appreciation must be given to the
different perceptions of risks by different actors. Ultimately, the overriding
challenge remains for the international community to develop a regulatory

---

[100] A concept known as 'layering' in the US whereby the hope is for ground security
measures to track down any security breaches so that onboard measures are put into
use only on the rarest of occasions as a last line of defence.

[101] In terms of cost, the US government is reportedly seeking US$435 million more from the
airline industry for passenger screening, arguing that the airlines should be paying for
their share of aviation security. IATA views this as a new tax and is vigorously opposing it,
pointing out that carriers already gave the government US$2 billion every year to prevent
terrorist attacks. IATA also argues that financially struggling airlines cannot pass new
taxes onto passengers because of intense competition. Air carriers now administer a $2.50
security tax onto passenger tickets, which amounts to about $1.6 billion annually.
Airlines are also assessed $315 million every year for passenger screening, a responsibility
the federal government assumed soon after the 9/11 attacks. The airlines were given a
four-month reprieve last year from both the passenger security tax and the annual
assessment because the war in Iraq was expected to hurt their business, see the *Straits
Times* (Singapore), 1 May 2004.

regime that is not only highly effective in preventing acts of aerial terrorism, but one which is responsive to the different security needs of different actors, and which does not, in the overall scheme, unduly interfere with the efficiency and productivity of commercial aviation, impose excessive costs, create unwarranted passenger inconvenience or intrude unnecessarily into individual privacy or civil liberty.[102]

[102] Dempsey, 'Aviation Security', at 721–722.

12

International responses to combat maritime terrorism

ROBERT C. BECKMAN

I. Introduction

The terrorist attacks in the United States on 9/11 shocked not only the United States, but the entire international community. The attacks were unequivocally condemned by the United Nations Security Council and by most members of the international community. They triggered an almost immediate response led by the United States at the international level for additional measures and increased cooperation to prevent and suppress terrorist activities.

As a result of 9/11, states and international organizations were forced to completely rethink the threat of maritime terrorism. They recognized that if terrorists groups could strike powerful states using commercial aircraft, they could also strike using commercial shipping. The threat of maritime terrorism suddenly included the following: oil tankers being hijacked and used as weapons against other ships or port facilities; terrorists entering countries posing as seafarers, and weapons of mass destruction being shipped on merchant ships to terrorist organizations.

The United States recognized that the threat of maritime terrorism could not be dealt with unilaterally. International shipping is by its very nature, international, and can only be regulated through international cooperation. Since 9/11 the United States has led a two-pronged approach to obtain international cooperation to deal with the threat of maritime terrorism. First, it has worked vigorously and patiently to encourage the relevant United Nations bodies such as the UN Security Council, the International Maritime Organization (IMO) and the International Labour Organization (ILO) to take action that requires member states to impose new measures to deal with the threat of maritime terrorism. Second, the United States has used its power and influence to get cooperation from other states through bilateral agreements and the establishment of 'coalitions of the willing'. As a result, established principles of international law have been adapted and changed, and in some cases, challenged.

In this chapter, I will outline the actions and measures that have been taken and are being taken to prevent and suppress acts of terrorism against international shipping. I will discuss how the actions and measures have presented challenges to existing principles of international law, and evaluate how principles of international law have been adapted or modified to meet the challenges posed by maritime terrorism.

II. Actions to enhance port and ship security

A. IMO actions to enhance port and ship security

Following the events of 9/11, the United States initiated and led the drive at the IMO to adopt measures to strengthen maritime security on ships and in ports.[1] As a result, the IMO undertook a thorough review of measures to combat acts of violence and crime at sea. At the 22nd Assembly meeting in November 2001, it was agreed to hold a Conference on Maritime Security in December 2002 to adopt new regulations to enhance ship and port security.[2]

After a year of preparations the Conference of Contracting Governments to the International Convention for the Safety of Life at Sea 1974 was held from 9 to 13 December 2002. The Conference adopted resolutions containing a series of measures to strengthen maritime security and prevent and suppress acts of terrorism against international shipping. Many of the measures were adopted through amendments to the major IMO Convention governing the safety of ships, the 1974 International Convention for the Safety of Life at Sea (SOLAS).[3] The 2002 amendments to SOLAS entered into force on 1 July 2004.

1. Actions in December 2002 to enhance maritime security

One of the most important measures taken at the 2002 Conference was to add a new Chapter on maritime security to SOLAS. The new Chapter XI-2 is

---

[1] On 15 January 2002 the United States submitted a proposal to the 75th Session of the IMO Maritime Security Committee on measures to improve maritime security (IMO Doc MSC 75/ISWG/5/7) (text provided to author). The proposal covered the following areas: Automatic Identification Systems, Ship and Offshore Facility Security Plans, Port Facility Security Plans, Ship Security Officers, Company Security Officers, Seafarer Identification Verification and Background Check, Port Vulnerability Assessments, Port of Origin Container Examinations, Cooperation with the World Customs Organization, Information on the Ship and its Cargo and People, Means of Ship Alerting, and Ship Security Equipment.

[2] For a summary of the actions of the IMO on maritime security, see http://www.imo.org.

[3] For a summary of the measures adopted in December 2002, see http://www.imo.org/ Newsroom/mainframe.asp?topic_id = 583 &doc_id = 2689. The December 2002 amendments to the SOLAS convention are available online in the Australian Treaty Series (not yet in force), [2003] ATNIF 11, http://www.austlii.edu.au/au/other/dfat/treaties/notinforce/ 2003/11.html.

entitled 'Special Measures to Enhance Maritime Security'. Among the special measures included in Chapter XI-2 are the following.

First, flag states are required to set security levels for their ships, and port states are required to set security levels for their port facilities. Ships entering a port or in port are required to comply with the security level of the flag state or port state, whichever is higher. Second, the master of a ship is required to have information on board the ship concerning persons or organizations responsible for the employment of crew members of the ship. Third, ships constructed after 1 July 2004 are required to be provided with a Ship Security Alert System. The deadline for installing a Ship Security Alert System on ships constructed before that date depends upon the type of vessel. Fourth, it is provided that the master of a ship has the overriding authority and the responsibility to make decisions and measures with respect to the safety and security of the ship.

2. Adoption of ISPS Code

Supplementary to Chapter XI-2 is the International Ship and Port Facility Security (ISPS) Code.[4] The 2002 Amendments to SOLAS provide that shipping companies and ships must comply with the requirements of the ISPS Code. As the title suggests, the ISPS Code contains measures designed to enhance the security of ships and the security of port facilities. The ISPS Code has two parts, A and B. Part A is mandatory for the purpose of compliance with Chapter XI-2. Part B is to be used as a guide and treated as recommendatory. The following requirements are prescribed in the ISPS Code.

First, a ship is required to carry on board a Ship Security Plan approved by the flag states on the basis of a Ship Security Assessment. Second, a company operating a ship must designate a Company Security Officer (CSO) for every ship, and every ship is required to have a designated Ship Security Officer (SSO). The CSO and the SSO are required to undergo training in maritime security in accordance with the guidance given in Part B of the ISPS Code. Third, drills and exercises with respect to the Ship Security Plan are required to be carried out at appropriate intervals by all parties concerned. The CSO and appropriate shore-based personnel are also required to participate in the drills and exercises to ensure effective shore-ship coordination with respect to the Ship Security Plan. Fourth, a ship will be issued an International Ship Security Certificate (ISS Certificate) after verification that the ship complies with Chapter XI-2 and the ISPS Code. Fifth, a ship is required to act upon the security levels set by the port state or the flag state by carrying out the activities prescribed in the ISPS Code with the aim of identifying and taking preventive measures against security incidents, which are defined in

---

[4] The full text of the ISPS Code is available online in the Australian Treaty Series with the other amendments adopted in December 2002. Ibid.

Chapter XI-2 as 'any suspicious act or circumstance threatening the security of the ship'. Sixth, Port Facilities to which Chapter XI-2 applies are required to develop and maintain a Port Facility Security Plan on the basis of a Port Facility Security Assessment. These facilities are also required to designate Port Facility Security Officers who, together with appropriate port facility security personnel, are required to undergo training in maritime security in accordance with the guidance given in Part B of the ISPS Code. They are also required to conduct drills and exercises with respect to the Port Facility Security Plan.

3. Compliance and control measures by port states

Ships are subjected to Port State Control with respect to compliance with Chapter XI-2. The Port State Control inspection is limited to verifying that there is on board a valid ISS Certificate issued under the provisions of Part A of the ISPS Code. When a valid ISS Certificate cannot be produced or when there are clear grounds for believing that a ship is not in compliance with the requirements of Chapter XI-2 or Part A of the ISPS Code, certain control measures may be taken by the port state against the ship. Such control measures include inspection of the ship, delaying the ship, detention of the ship, restriction of operations including movement within the port, or expulsion of the ship from port.

In addition, a port state may require that ships provide information to ensure compliance with Chapter XI-2 prior to entry into port, including information relating to the ISS Certificate, the security level of the ship, the security level at previous port calls, and security measures taken at previous port calls.

4. Other measures to enhance maritime security on ships

The 2002 Amendments to SOLAS also contain other measures to enhance maritime security, including the following.

First, they brought forward the dates by which certain ships had to install an Automatic Identification System (AIS). The AIS enables shore facilities to automatically identify ships and obtain basic information about them. Second, the regulations require that a ship's Identification Number must be permanently marked in two places on the ship, one of which must be clearly visible. Third, ships are required to carry on board a Continuous Synopsis Record, which is intended to provide an on-board record of the history of the ship with respect to the information recorded therein.

5. Significance of the new maritime security measures

The new maritime security measures did not pose any challenge to existing rules of international law. They gave new responsibilities to port states and imposed new obligations on flag states and shipping companies, but these measures are consistent with the provisions of international law as set out in the 1982 UN Convention on the Law of the Sea (UNCLOS).

The measures adopted by the IMO were very significant in two respects. First, they expanded the IMO's traditional responsibility for maritime safety to include maritime security. Maritime security suddenly became an integral part of the responsibilities of the IMO. Second, they expanded the IMO's rule-making authority into port facilities, an area that had previously been considered a matter within the domestic jurisdiction of the port states because port facilities are within their territorial sovereignty.

The new measures required flag states, port states and shipping companies to make maritime security a major priority so that they would be able to meet the 1 July 2004 deadline for entry into force of the new measures. Some developing countries have had a very difficult time attempting to meet the deadline. The result, however, is that in most areas of the world port facilities and ships became more secure after 1 July 2004.

The new measures can also be viewed as a major victory for the United States in the field of multilateral diplomacy. The measures finally adopted by the IMO in December 2002 are very similar to those made by the United States in its proposal to the IMO in January 2002.[5] The United States used its power and influence to get almost the entire international community to agree to adopt and implement comprehensive new measures on ship security and port security, notwithstanding the fact that many might not have had the same level of concern about maritime terrorism as the United States.

B. ILO actions on seafarers' identity documents

One of the other major concerns of the United States was that there was no reliable international system for identifying seafarers who enter the United States as crew members of a ship. It was generally known that many seafarers carried false documents and that the identity systems used for seafarers in many developing countries were not secure. This was one of the issues that had been included in the United States proposal to the IMO Maritime Security Committee in January 2002,[6] but it was later decided that this matter should be dealt with by the International Labour Organization (ILO) rather than the IMO.

On 3 June 2003, at the ninety-first session of the governing body of the ILO, major revisions were made to the Seafarers' Identity Documents Convention of 1958.[7] The revisions were intended to address the continuing threat posed by maritime terrorism to the security of passengers and crews

---

[5] US Proposal, above note 1.   [6] Ibid.
[7] The text of the Revised Convention is available at: http://www.ilo.org/ilolex/cgi-lex/convde.pl?C185.

and to the national interests of states, in a manner that was consistent with the mandate of the ILO to promote decent conditions of work for seafarers.

The Seafarers' Identity Documents Convention (Revised) 2003 will come into force six months after the date on which the ratifications of two Members have been registered with the Director-General of the ILO.[8] It provides that each Member shall issue to each of its seafarer nationals a seafarer's identity document that is designed to prevent tampering and falsification while at the same time being generally accessible to governments at the lowest possible cost. The identity document must include at least one security feature such as watermarks, ultraviolet features, holograms or laser engraving. Members are also required to keep a record of identity documents in an electronic database, and to provide a focal point for responding to inquiries from the authorities of other Members. The Convention is generally seen as a move that will further improve security in the global shipping industry.

Following its adoption in June 2003 there were negotiations and discussions on the technical features and on the economic and political implications of the new convention. On 26 March 2004 the ILO adopted a new 'biometric' identity verification system which sets a new global standard. It allows for the use of a 'biometric template' for turning two seafarer's fingerprints into an internationally standardized barcode on the Seafarer's Identify Document. The new global standard will enable biometric identification of the world's seafarers.[9]

Most of the 1.2 million seafarers who handle 90 per cent of the world's trade are from developing countries, and it will be difficult for them to meet the standards for the new identify document. For example, the Philippines is one of the world's leading suppliers of the world's seafarers, and more than half of the 500,000 Filipino seafarers are officially employed overseas. The US Trade and Development Agency (USTDA) has awarded a grant of US$515,000 to the Philippines government to fund technical assistance related to the development of a seafarers' identity system that would meet the requirements of the 2003 Convention.[10]

The developments on seafarers' identity documents are another example of how the international community moved with unprecedented speed to modernize its rules and standards in response to the threat of maritime terrorism.

---

[8] The Revised Convention will come into force from 9 February 2005. The go-ahead follows ratification of the convention by Jordan and France, fulfilling the entry into force requirement of two member states supporting it.

[9] ILO Press Release, Friday 26 March 2004 (ILO/04/12).

[10] TDA Press Release, 30 September 2003, http://www.tda.gov/trade/press/Sept30_03.html.

254   ROBERT C. BECKMAN

C. US Customs Container Security Initiative (CSI)

At the same time as the United States initiated actions at the IMO and ILO to enhance maritime security, it also initiated actions outside of existing international institutions to deal with the threat of maritime terrorism. The first of its initiatives to establish coalitions of willing partners to cooperate to combat the threat of maritime terrorism was the Container Security Initiative (CSI).

In January 2002 the US Customs proposed the CSI in order to secure what it determined to be an indispensable, but vulnerable link in the chain of global trade: the sea container. The objective of the CSI is to prevent global containerized cargo from being exploited by terrorists. The fear was that sea containers could be used by terrorists to bring weapons of mass destruction (WMD), or even terrorists themselves, directly into ports in the United States.

The United States maintained that ensuring the security of the maritime trade system is essential because approximately 90 per cent of the world's cargo moves by container. Some 200 million sea cargo containers move annually among the world's top seaports, and nearly 50 per cent of the total value of all US imports arrive via sea. In 2001 US Customs processed more than 214,000 vessels and 5.7 million sea containers.[11]

The objective of the CSI is to first engage the ports that send the highest volumes of container traffic into the United States, as well as the governments in these locations, in a way that will facilitate detection of potential problems at the earliest possible opportunity. Since approximately two-thirds of all US bound sea containers pass through twenty major seaports around the globe, the United States initially focused on these twenty ports. As of August 2004, nineteen of the twenty ports have committed to joining CSI and are at various stages of implementation, and ports in several other countries have also joined the initiative.[12]

CSI consists of four core elements:

- using intelligence and automated information to identify and target containers that pose a high risk;
- using advanced detection technology to quickly pre-screen containers that pose a risk;
- using smarter, more secure containers with tamper-proof seals which alert authorities to tampering while the container is in transit;
- pre-screening those containers that pose a risk, at the port of departure before they arrive at US ports.

---

[11] US Customs Press Release, 22 February 2002, http://www.cbp.gov/xp/cgov/newsroom/press_releases/archives/legacy/2002/22002/02222002.xml.
[12] CSI in Brief, http://www.customs.gov/xp/cgov/enforcement/international_activities/csi/. This site gives detailed information on the CSI, including a list of ports, a fact sheet, etc.

Under the CSI programme a small number of officers from the US Customs and Border Protection office are deployed in foreign ports to work together with their host nation counterparts to pre-screen containers that will be shipped to the United States. The US officers assist in identifying high risk containers that will be subject to screening, but the actual screening or inspection is done by officers from the host country. The programme is reciprocal, and the United States offers participating countries the right to send their customs officers to major ports in the United States to target ocean-going cargo to be sent by sea container to their countries. Japan and Canada currently station their customs personnel in United States ports under this reciprocal arrangement.

The CSI is an example of an initiative by the United States to establish a framework for international cooperation outside of existing international institutions and international regulations. The United States used its bargaining power to persuade countries to cooperate. Given the threat of delays for ships coming to the United States from ports that were not part of the CSI, states decided that it would be in their economic interests to cooperate with the United States. Some may even have felt that it would give their ports a competitive economic advantage over rival ports that were not part of the CSI. Therefore, states were willing to accept what before 9/11 might have been regarded as an infringement of their sovereignty.

Critics of United States unilateralism can argue that the CSI is directed at protecting the United States and is pushing the risk to foreign ports. They can argue that a better approach might have been to work through established international bodies such as the IMO and International Customs Organization (ICO) to establish a system for securing containers which protects all countries, and that the CSI might undermine efforts to develop international regulations and standards through the IMO or the ICO.[13] Nevertheless, given the fact that most major ports have joined the initiative, one must conclude that it has been a success.

III. Actions to interdict suspect vessels at sea

A. Proliferation Security Initiative (PSI)

The Proliferation Security Initiative (PSI) is an initiative of the United States to establish a coalition of willing partners to respond to the growing challenge posed by the proliferation of WMD. Like the CSI, it is an attempt by the

---

[13] For a critical analysis from an Australian perspective, see Nigel Brew, 'Ripples from 9/11: the US Container Security Initiative and its Implications for Australia', Information, Analysis and Advice for the Parliament, 13 May 2003, at http://www.aph.gov.au/library/pubs/CIB/2002-03/03cib27.pdf.

United States to create a framework for international cooperation outside the international organizations and international treaties.

The PSI was announced by United States President George Bush in Poland on 31 May 2003, just prior to the G8 Summit. President Bush stated that the United States and its close allies would search planes and ships carrying suspect cargo and seize illegal weapons or missile technologies.[14] As the PSI has developed, it has been based primarily upon the development of cooperative arrangements among a coalition of participating states regarding the interdiction of ships suspected of carrying WMD and missile-related technologies.

The United States began working with ten other countries in 2003 to develop a set of principles that would identify practical steps to interdict shipments of WMD, their delivery systems or related materials flowing to or from 'state or non-state actors of proliferation concern'. The ten countries were Australia, France, Germany, Italy, Japan, the Netherlands, Poland, Portugal, Spain and the United Kingdom.[15] At a meeting in Brisbane in September 2003 the ten original participating countries agreed that North Korea and Iran were of particular proliferation concern. At that meeting the participating states also agreed to a 'Statement of Interdiction Principles'.[16] The ten original participating countries were later joined by five new participating countries – Canada, Denmark, Norway, Singapore and Turkey. At the first anniversary meeting of the PSI in May 2004 it was stated that more than 60 states had expressed support for the PSI, and that Russia had decided to join the core group of PSI participating states.[17]

1. PSI interdiction principles and the law of the sea

In the Statement of Interdiction Principles participating states agreed to take certain specific actions in support of interdiction efforts regarding cargoes of WMD, their delivery systems or related materials, to the extent their national legal authorities permit and *consistent with their obligations under international law and frameworks*. Questions have been raised as to whether some of the actions called for in the Statement of Interdiction Principles are consistent with existing rules of international law. Of particular concern was whether the principles with respect to interdiction at sea are consistent with

---

[14] Remarks by the President to the People of Poland, Wawel Royal Castle, Krakow, Poland, http://www.whitehouse.gov/news/releases/2003/05/20030531-3.html.
[15] See US State Dept web page http://www.state.gov/t/np/c10390.htm.
[16] For the full text, see http://www.state.gov/t/np/rls/fs/23764.htm.
[17] Undersecretary John R. Boulton, Press Conference on the Proliferation Security Initiative, 31 May 2004 http://www.state.gov/t/us/rm/33556.htm.

the provisions of UNCLOS. This concern is especially relevant because the United States is not a party to UNCLOS.[18]

In May 2004 the Bureau of Nonproliferation of the US State Department published 'Frequently Asked Questions' on the PSI on the Internet.[19] On 28 July 2004 the United States published a new brochure on PSI on the Internet which is intended to answer basic questions about the PSI.[20] These documents seem to be intended to help states understand the PSI and to alleviate their concerns. For example, one of the issues that has been of concern was whether the PSI would affect legitimate commerce in dual use equipment. The Frequently Asked Questions address this issue as follows:

> PSI is not aimed against legitimate commerce, dual-use or otherwise . . .
> PSI does not envision stopping and inspecting every shipment that might involve items that could be used in a WMD- or missile-related proliferation program; rather the United States intends to take action based on solid information. Legitimate dual-use commerce will very rarely be affected by PSI.

In the Interdiction Principles states agree, on their own initiative, to board and search any suspect vessels flying their flag in their internal waters or territorial seas or in areas beyond the territorial seas of any state. This is consistent with the principles governing the law of the sea. States have a right to board and search vessels in their internal waters and territorial sea which are flying their flag because the sovereignty of a state extends to its internal waters and to its territorial sea and a state's laws apply on ships flying their flag.[21]

A major concern with PSI was the circumstances under which the interdiction principles were intended to allow participating states to board and search foreign vessels in international waters.[22] Under UNCLOS, high seas principles govern jurisdiction over ships in such areas. The general principle is that ships on the high seas are subject to the exclusive jurisdiction of the flag state, except in exceptional circumstances provided for in UNCLOS or other international treaties.[23]

---

[18] As of 16 July 2004, there were 145 parties to UNCLOS, but the United States was not one of them. See http://www.un.org/Depts/los/.

[19] See http://www.state.gov/t/np/rls/fs/32725.htm.

[20] See http://www.state.gov/t/np/rls/other/34726.htm.

[21] UNCLOS, Articles 2 and 92.

[22] 'International waters' is not a term of art in the law of the sea or in UNCLOS. However, it generally refers to waters that are seaward of the territorial sea of any state, that is, outside the territorial sovereignty of any state. Thus international waters would include the exclusive economic zone as well as the high seas because under Article 58(2) of UNCLOS, the principles of jurisdiction governing vessels on the High Seas also apply in the exclusive economic zone.

[23] UNCLOS , Article 92.

If the interdiction principles are interpreted in a manner that is consistent with the principle that ships in international waters are subject to the exclusive jurisdiction of the flag state, the interdiction of ships in international waters must be premised on the principle of flag state consent. Participating states would have a right to board and search vessels flying the flag of another state only if the flag state consents to such boarding and search. The interdiction principles provide that a participating state should seriously consider giving other states consent to board and search vessels flying its flag under appropriate circumstances. This clause is consistent with the principle of flag state consent. Among states participating in the PSI it would be expected that, if one PSI state were to request permission to board and search a ship flying the flag state of another PSI state, the latter PSI state would favourably consider the request. The Frequently Asked Questions published in May 2004 make it clear that interdiction of ships in international waters will be premised on the consent of the flag state.[24]

The interdiction principles also provide that participating states should take action regarding vessels in their ports and internal waters as well as vessels entering or leaving their ports or internal waters. Participating states agree to stop and/or search vessels in their ports or internal waters when such vessels are reasonably suspected of carrying such cargoes to or from states or non-state actors of proliferation concern. Participating states also agree to enforce conditions on suspect vessels entering or leaving their ports and internal waters. Such conditions might include a requirement that such vessels be subject to boarding and search prior to entry. Although there is no provision in UNCLOS directly on this point, such actions would be consistent with principles of international law. Ports and internal waters are within the territorial sovereignty of a state, and states may impose conditions on vessels in its ports and internal waters and on vessels in its territorial sea that intend to enter its ports or internal waters.

The most controversial actions set out in the interdiction principles concern actions of coastal states with regard to vessels in their territorial sea or contiguous zone, and with regard to vessels entering or leaving their territorial sea. These are controversial because under UNCLOS the vessels of all states have a *right of innocent passage* through the territorial sea of all states.[25] Passage is innocent so long as it is not prejudicial to the peace, good order or security of

---

[24] Note 19 above. One of the answers states that: 'PSI actions will be taken consistent with existing national legal authority and international law and frameworks. This includes relevant international legal principles relating to boarding of vessels on the high seas. In the case of interdiction of vessels flying flags of convenience, the consent of the flag state would ordinarily provide a clear basis for a boarding on the high seas under international law'.

[25] UNCLOS, Articles 17–19.

the coastal state. It is difficult to argue that the mere passage of a vessel containing component parts for making weapons of mass destruction through the territorial sea of a coastal state is prejudicial to its peace, good order or security.

Furthermore, special passage rules for the vessels of all states apply in straits used for international navigation which fall within the territorial sea of the littoral states. The vessels of all states have the *right of transit passage* through straits used for international navigation, and such right cannot be impeded or suspended by the littoral states.[26] The right of transit passage is an even broader right than the right of innocent passage.

Therefore, states parties to UNCLOS are not likely to interfere with the vessels exercising the right of transit passage through a strait used for international navigation or the right of innocent passage through the territorial sea. Instead, they are likely to take the position that any action taken with respect to such vessels must be *consistent with their obligations under international law* as set out in UNCLOS. However, it would be legal for the coastal state to board and search a suspect vessel passing through its territorial sea if the flag state of the suspect vessel expressly authorized or requested such action by the coastal state.

There is one other circumstance in which it may be legal for a coastal state to board and search a suspect vessel in its contiguous zone or territorial sea. If a suspect vessel was on a route which indicated that it was intending to bring WMD into the territory of the coastal state in violation of its customs laws and regulations, such vessel would not have a right of innocent passage. It could be boarded and searched by the authorities of the coastal state in its territorial sea. Similarly, it could be boarded and searched in the contiguous zone, which is a zone adjacent to the territorial sea in which the coastal state has special powers to enforce certain of its domestic laws, including its customs laws.[27]

Unfortunately, the Frequently Asked Questions issued by the State Department do not address the difficult issues relating to interdiction by coastal states of vessels exercising the right of transit passage or the right of innocent passage.

2. PSI and the international legal system

The United States has argued that the PSI builds on efforts by the international community in existing treaties and regimes to prevent the proliferation of WMD. It has pointed out that the PSI is consistent with and a step which implements the Statement of the President of the UN Security Council in January 1992, when he stated that the proliferation of all WMD constitutes a

---

[26] UNCLOS, Article 38.   [27] UNCLOS, Article 33.

threat to international peace and security. Supporters of the PSI argue that the PSI is justified because of the threat and danger posed should WMD fall into the hands of rogue states or terrorist organizations.[28]

Critics of the United States can argue that the PSI is another example of the United States using its power to establish an international framework for creating and enforcing norms outside the framework of existing international conventions and international institutions. They point out that the existing legal regimes governing nuclear non-proliferation do not contain any provisions authorizing member states of the UN to enforce the principles of non-proliferation through the interdiction of vessels carrying WMD. They argue that the PSI is a threat to the existing international legal order because the United States and its partners are not acting within the framework of the relevant international institutions to build upon and develop existing international legal regimes to meet new problems. Instead, the PSI is an example of the United States using its influence to create a 'coalition of the willing' to act outside of existing international legal regimes and conventions.[29]

B. Bilateral ship-boarding agreements

One of the goals of the United States under the PSI is to enter into bilateral agreements with major flag states which give the United States permission to board and search vessels flying their flag when such vessels are suspected of carrying WMD.

The first such boarding agreement was signed by the United States and Liberia on 11 February 2004.[30] The boarding agreement provides the United States with authority to board vessels flying the flag of Liberia if they are suspected of carrying illicit shipments of WMD. Liberia has the world's second largest ship registry. According to the United States, this boarding agreement is an important step in further operationalizing the PSI and strengthening the mechanisms that the United States has at its disposal to interdict suspect WMD-related cargoes.

On 12 May 2004 the United States and Panama signed the bilateral Panama – United States PSI Ship-Boarding Agreement.[31] Panama is the world's largest ship registry. Now that the United States has bilateral ship-boarding agreements with the world's two largest ship registries in order to supplement the boarding

---

[28] Baker Spring, 'Harnessing the Power of Nations for Arms Control: The Proliferation Security Initiative and Coalitions of the Willing', Backgrounder, No. 1737, The Heritage Foundation, 18 March 2004.

[29] Articles critical of the PSI include 'The Proliferation Security Initiative: The Legal Challenge', Bipartisan Security Group Policy Brief, September 2003, www.gsinstitute. org/gsi/pubs/09_03_psi_brief.pdf.

[30] For a summary and the full text, see http://www.state.gov/t/np/c12387.htm.

[31] For a summary and the full text, see http://www.state.gov/t/np/c12390.htm.

arrangements it has with its coalition partners, almost 50 per cent of the total commercial ships in dead weight tonnage is subject to the rapid consent procedures for boarding, search and seizure by United States forces.[32]

The bilateral ship boarding agreements are consistent with UNCLOS. They are premised on the principle of flag state consent to the boarding of ships in international waters. They contain a procedure for obtaining expedited consent of the flag state to a request for boarding from the United States if there are reasonable grounds to suspect that a ship of the flag state is engaged in proliferation by sea. They also contain a 'tacit authorization' provision which provides that if the authorities in the flag state do not respond within two hours to a request from law enforcement officers of the other state to take appropriate measures, the law enforcement officers may proceed to board and search the suspect ship.

The ship-boarding agreements complement the special arrangements the United States has with its partners under the PSI. If the United States has arrangements containing procedures for expedited consent with its PSI partners as well as the major flag states that are not members of the PSI, it will have procedures in place which will enable it to seek the consent of flag states to board a significant percentage of the world's tonnage of vessels.

C. Proposed protocol to 1988 SUA Convention

1. The SUA Convention

The global convention which addresses the issue of maritime terrorism is the 1988 Convention for the Suppression of Unlawful Acts Against the Safety of Maritime Navigation (SUA Convention).[33] The SUA Convention was adopted in Rome on 10 March 1988 and entered into force on 1 March 1992. The IMO serves as the secretariat and depository for the Convention.

The SUA Convention and Protocol follow the scheme that was first established in the 1970 Convention for the Suppression of Unlawful Seizure of Aircraft.[34] The scheme of the 1970 Hijacking Convention has been followed in several other conventions that are commonly referred to as the 'terrorist conventions'.[35] The scheme in all of the conventions is to establish 'universal jurisdiction' among states parties to the Convention.

---

[32] US State Department, Daily Press Briefing, 12 May 2004, http://www.state.gov/r/pa/prs/dpb/2004/32428pf.htm.

[33] The text of the SUA Convention is available on the home page of the Australia Treaties Library at: http://www.austlii.edu.au/au/other/dfat/treaties/1993/10.html.

[34] The text of the 1970 Hijacking Convention is available on the Australia Treaties Library website at: http://www.austlii.edu.au/au/other/dfat/treaties/1972/16.html.

[35] The other 'terrorist conventions' following the scheme of the 1970 Hague Convention include: (1) Convention for the Suppression of Unlawful Acts against the Safety of Civil Aviation, signed at Montreal on 23 September 1971; (2) Convention on the Prevention

The SUA Convention applies to the following acts that endanger the safety of international maritime navigation:

- seizure of or exercise of control over a ship by any form of intimidation;
- violence against a person on board a ship;
- destruction of a ship or the causing of damage to a ship or to its cargo;
- placement on a ship of a device or substance which is likely to destroy or cause damage to that ship or its cargo;
- destruction of, serious damaging of, or interference with maritime navigational facilities;
- knowing communication of false information;
- injury to or murder of any person in connection with any of the preceding acts.

States parties have an obligation to make the above offences a crime under their laws when the alleged offence takes place in their territory. In addition, all states parties must establish jurisdiction over the offence when the alleged offender is 'present in their territory', even though it has no other links to the alleged offence.

States parties also have an obligation to take alleged offenders into custody *if they enter their territory*, and to either extradite them to another state party that has jurisdiction, or to turn the case over to their own authorities for prosecution in their courts. This is generally referred to as the obligation to 'extradite or prosecute'. The obligation of a state to arrest alleged offenders who enter their territory applies no matter where the offence took place.

2. United States proposal for a new protocol

In October 2001, one month after 9/11, the Legal Committee of the IMO decided to review the SUA Convention in the wake of the terrorist attack on the United States. The Legal Committee agreed to include the review of the SUA Convention as a priority item in its work programme.[36]

In April 2002 the Legal Committee agreed to establish a Correspondence Group led by the United States with the short-term aim of developing a working paper on the scope of possible amendments for consideration at the 85th session of the Committee. The longer aim was to draft the amendments and make a recommendation to the IMO Assembly that it convene an international

and Punishment of Crimes against Internationally Protected Persons, including Diplomatic Agents, adopted by the General Assembly of the United Nations on 14 December 1973; (3) International Convention against the Taking of Hostages, adopted by the General Assembly of the United Nations on 17 December 1979; (4) International Convention for the Suppression of Terrorist Bombings, adopted by the General Assembly of the United Nations on 15 December 1997; (5) International Convention for the Suppression of the Financing of Terrorism, adopted by the General Assembly of the United Nations on 9 December 1999.

[36] IMO Legal Committee, 83rd Session, 8–12 October 2001. A summary of the work of the Legal Committee is available at www.imo.org.

diplomatic conference to consider and adopt amendments to the SUA Convention.[37]

On 17 August 2002 the American delegation introduced document LEG 85/4 containing draft amendments to the SUA Convention and Protocol, together with related documents.[38] Among the most important amendments proposed by the United States are the following: (1) the addition of seven new offences into Article 3 of the SUA convention, four of which are concerned with activities taking place on the ship or directed toward the ship that involve a terrorist purpose; (2) new provisions permitting the boarding and search of a suspect ship by law enforcement officials of another when such ship is in international waters (located seaward of any state's territorial sea) and is reasonably suspected of being involved in, or reasonably believed to be the target of, acts prohibited in Article 3 of the SUA Convention.

Concern was expressed by some delegations to some of the United States proposals, especially the new provisions on the boarding and search of a suspected ship. The United States draft was described as a 'work in progress' and the discussion was described as a preliminary exchange of views. It was decided that it was premature to establish an intersessional working group, but it was decided to continue the work of the correspondence group. It was emphasized that the objective must be to develop a draft instrument which would attract wide ratification.[39]

The correspondence group has continued to work on a revised draft protocol over the past two years. It has received comments and suggestions from numerous states and organizations which participate in the work of the IMO. The two articles which have been the subject of major debate and disagreement are Article 3 *bis*, which sets out new offences to be added to the Convention, and Article 8 *bis*, which establishes new provisions for the boarding and search of suspect ships.

3. Proposed new offences on maritime terrorism

Article 3 *bis* on new offences has been through several drafts. It is intended to add new offences which bring the Convention up to date to deal with maritime terrorism in light of 9/11.

The draft in mid-2004[40] provides that there is an offence within the meaning of the Convention if a person unlawfully and intentionally commits certain acts with a particular intent or purpose. The purpose of the act, by its nature or context, must be to intimidate a population, or to compel a

---

[37] IMO Legal Committee, 84th Session, 22–26 April 2002.
[38] IMO Legal Committee, 85th Session, 21–25 October 2002.
[39] IMO Legal Committee, 86th Session, 28 April–2 May 2003.
[40] July 2004 Intersessional Meeting, draft of 28 June 2004 (text provided to author).

government or an international organization to do or to abstain from doing any act. Under draft paragraph 1(a), offences, if committed with that purpose, occur where a person:

    (i) uses against or on a ship or discharges from a ship any explosive, radio- active material or prohibited weapon in a manner that causes or is likely to cause death or serious injury or damage, or

    (ii) discharges, from a ship, oil, liquefied natural gas, or other hazardous or noxious substance in such quantity or concentration, that causes or is likely to cause death or serious injury or damage, or

    (iii) uses a ship in a manner that causes death or serious injury or damage; or

    (iv) threatens, with or without a condition, as is provided under national law, to commit an offence set forth in paragraph (i), (ii) or (iii).[41]

The most controversial of the new offences in Article 3 *bis* relate to the issue of whether the SUA Protocol should make it an offence to transport WMD or related material on board a ship if the transport of such material is done with a specific intent. Difficulties remain over how to define what cannot be transported as well as the requisite intent. The proposed draft is set out in paragraph 1(b). It includes not only the transport of WMD, but also the transport of related material, including equipment, materials or software intended to be used in the design or manufacture or delivery of a prohibited weapon. Although a specific intent is required for each subparagraph, some delegations have expressed concern that the language is too broad and inclusive.

The United States recommended the inclusion of this provision because of its concern for the proliferation of WMD or their delivery systems. Some states have objected to the inclusion of this paragraph as a matter of principle because it created offences relating to the non-proliferation of WMD or other materials that were not directly linked to terrorism. Furthermore, it makes the transport of component parts of WMD offences even though such transport does not endanger the safety of the ship or the safety of maritime navigation. Some states have stated that they do not consider the IMO to be the competent forum for dealing with non-proliferation issues and they do not consider the SUA Convention to be the proper instrument to deal with non-proliferation issues.[42]

This issue was discussed at the 88th session of the Legal Committee in April 2004. Four delegations stated that they were of the view that the Committee was acting outside the scope of the mandate given them in resolution A.924(22) by the IMO Assembly. The delegations of India and Pakistan registered formal reservations in this regard. Nevertheless, a substantial

---

[41] Article 3 *bis*, LEG 88/3, Annex 1, 13 February 2004.
[42] Report of the Legal Committee on the Work of its Eighty-Seventh Session, pages 14–20, LEG 87/17, 23 October 2003.

majority of delegations did not support this narrow reading of the mandate given by the resolution of the Assembly. The majority of delegations support the inclusion of the non-proliferation provisions, and the intersessional working group is proceeding to work to finalize with those provisions included.[43]

4. Proposed new provisions on boarding of ships

Article 8 *bis* on boarding has also been controversial because it permits the boarding and search of vessels in international waters (beyond the limits of the territorial sea) if such vessels are reasonably suspected to be involved in offences under the SUA Convention. This enforcement measure is new, as the SUA Convention contains no provisions allowing the boarding and search of vessels in international waters. The new boarding provision would create an express exception to the general principle of the law of the sea that ships on the high seas are subject to the exclusive jurisdiction of the flag state. Concerns have been expressed that such a provision would take the SUA Convention to a new level. Fears have also been expressed that the boarding and search provisions might be subject to abuse.[44]

Many states have accepted the need for such a provision, but they have insisted that it be narrowly drafted, and contain detailed safeguards to prevent abuse. As a result, Article 8 *bis* has been through numerous drafts and substantial revisions, as the United States as the head of the intersessional correspondence group has attempted to meet the concerns expressed by states. Article 8 *bis* is an attempt to balance the interests of the flag state in controlling its vessel and the interests of the boarding state in investigating acts of maritime terrorism.

The current draft provides that if law enforcement officers of a state party encounter a ship in international waters which they believe has been or is about to be involved in the commission of an offence under the Convention, they may request the flag state to authorize them to take appropriate measures, including boarding and search. The major difficulty is caused by the so-called 'flags of convenience', that is, states which register ships but do not carry out their obligations or responsibilities seriously, as it may not be possible to contact the appropriate authorities in such states within a reasonable amount of time. To deal with this problem, the draft provision provides that if the authorities in the flag state do not respond within four hours to a request from law enforcement officers to take appropriate measures, the law enforcement officers may proceed to board and search the suspect ship. This

---

[43] Report of the Legal Committee on the Work of its Eighty-Eighth Session, pages 8–15, LEG 88/13, 18 May 2004.
[44] Ibid.

provision providing for 'tacit authorization' to board and search if there is no objection within four hours has generated much discussion and debate.[45]

Article 8 *bis* has also generated much discussion on whether the current draft contains sufficient safeguards to prevent abuse, to limit the possible use of force, to provide for the safety and human rights of the passengers and crew, etc.[46]

5. Consistency of proposed SUA protocol with international law

The United States believes that the threat of maritime terrorism after 9/11 presents new dangers which demand new solutions and further development of the rules of international law. It has taken the position that its objectives can be realized through a new protocol to the SUA Convention if new offences are created and new enforcement powers are legitimized. The United States believes it is essential that its law enforcement officers have the power of interdiction to board and search vessels in international waters if persons on such vessels have been or will be involved in offences under the SUA Convention. It is attempting to convince the international community to create new exceptions to the existing rules governing the law of the sea as set out in UNCLOS. This is an example of the superpower taking a genuine multilateral approach, to work with existing international institutions to adapt and change the rules of international law to meet the threat of maritime terrorism.

Where the United States seems to be running into the most difficulty in the negotiations on the proposed new protocol to the SUA Convention is with its proposal to make the transport of WMD or their delivery systems an offence. This is because some states believe that the IMO is not the appropriate institution to deal with the enforcement of non-proliferation treaties. Given this development, it is understandable that the United States is also pursuing complementary approaches to dealing with the problem through the PSI and through the UN Security Council. Nevertheless, it appears that a majority of states at the IMO support the position of the United States for inclusion of non-proliferation offences.

If the SUA Convention were amended to provide for the boarding and search of suspect vessels on the high seas, it would be an express exception to the principle of exclusive jurisdiction of the flag state on the high seas. However, since treaties are binding only on states that have become parties to them, the United States and participating states would only be able to search vessels suspected of transporting WMD if both the boarding state and the flag state were parties to the SUA Protocol.

---

[45] Article 8 *bis*, paragraph 3, LEG 88/3, Annex I, 13 February 2004.
[46] Report of Legal Committee, above note 43.

IV. Actions at the United Nations Security Council

A. Security Council Resolution 1373 of 28 September 2001

Within days of 9/11 UN Security Council Resolution 1373 was adopted on 28 September 2001.[47] The Security Council stated in the resolution that it was acting under Chapter VII of the UN Charter and that terrorism constituted a 'threat to international peace and security'. These determinations make the resolution legally binding on all member states. Security Council Resolution 1373 sets out a comprehensive set of measures that all member states of the United Nations must take in order to prevent and suppress the financing of terrorist acts. It establishes that states have a legal obligation to refrain from providing any form of support, active or passive, to entities or persons involved in terrorist acts. Further, it calls on all states to enhance coordination of efforts on national, subregional, regional and international levels in order to strengthen a global response to the challenge of international terrorism.

B. UN Security Council Resolution 1540 of 28 April 2004

Almost two years later, after many of the other actions described in this paper had been taken, the United States returned to the UN Security Council requesting that it adopt another resolution which it believed was necessary to combat international terrorism. In September 2003 President Bush asked the UN Security Council to adopt a new anti-proliferation resolution that called upon all members of the United Nations to criminalize the proliferation of weapons of mass destruction, to enact strict controls consistent with international standards, and to secure any and all such materials within their own borders.[48]

On 28 April 2004, the UN Security Council unanimously adopted Resolution 1540 on preventing proliferation of weapons of mass destruction. Invoking its enforcement powers under Chapter VII of the UN Charter, it affirmed that the proliferation of nuclear, chemical and biological weapons constitutes a threat to international peace and security. Under the resolution all members of the United Nations are legally bound to establish domestic controls including legislative measures to prevent the proliferation of WMD, in particular for terrorist purposes.[49] The resolution calls upon all states, in

---

[47] UNSC Res 1373, 28 September 2001, S/RES/1373 (2001). The text of this resolution and other Security Council resolutions on terrorism are available at http://www.un.org/terrorism/sc.htm.

[48] Address to the UN General Assembly, 23 September 2003, http://www.whitehouse.gov/news/releases/2003/09/20030923-4.html.

[49] UN Security Council Resolution 1540, 28 April 2004, http://www.state.gov/t/np/rls/other/31990.htm.

accordance with their national legal authorities and legislation *and consistent with international law*, to take cooperative action to prevent illicit trafficking in WMD.

Significantly, however, the resolution, at the request of the delegation from China, contains no reference to interdiction.[50] Furthermore, the statements from UK and Indian delegations made it clear that the resolution did not authorize use of force or enforcement action against any state or non-state actors in the territory of another country, and that any enforcement action would require a new decision of the Security Council.[51]

The United States position is that the unanimous passage of UN SCR 1540 establishes clear international acknowledgement that cooperative arrangements such as PSI are both useful and necessary.

UN SCR 1540 has been used by the United States to support its arguments that the proposed SUA Protocol should be adopted and that it should include a provision making the transport of WMD and their delivery systems an offence. SCR 1540 calls upon all states to take cooperative action to prevent illicit trafficking in WMD that is consistent with international law. Shortly after the adoption of SCR 1540 the United States amended its report to the correspondence group to reflect the adoption of the resolution. It also submitted a White Paper on Non-Proliferation Offences to members of the intersessional group.[52]

V. Conclusion

Many measures have been taken by the international community since 9/11 to enhance maritime security. Most of the measures have been initiated and led by the United States. The United States initiated measures at the IMO and the ILO to enhance maritime security and it has been working with those institutions to establish new international rules and procedures to enhance maritime security. This can only be described as a multilateral approach to problem-solving.

At the same time, the United States has also been working on a parallel track to enhance cooperation to strengthen maritime security by establishing 'coalitions of the willing' to take measures outside of the international institutions and regimes governing those areas. Examples of this approach

---

[50] Statement of Chinese representative Wang Guangya, 22 April 2004, reprinted in Disarmament Documentation, Security Council Members Express 'Doubts' about UN Draft Resolution on Weapons of Mass Destruction, 22 April 2004, reprinted in www. acronym.org.uk/docs/0404/doc03.htm.

[51] Statements of Adam Thomson of the United Kingdom and Vijay K. Nambiar of India, ibid.

[52] White Paper on the Non-Proliferation Offences, 1 July 2004 (paper provided to author).

to international cooperation are the CSI, PSI and bilateral ship-boarding agreements.

The proposed new protocol to the SUA Convention would update the Convention to deal with threats to maritime terrorism in light of developments since 9/11. The United States has had the most difficulty obtaining international cooperation when it has attempted to use cooperative measures designed to combat maritime terrorism that include provisions containing non-proliferation offences. It seems likely that the draft protocol will eventually be adopted and will include non-proliferation offences. If the concerns of states over the definitions of the offences and over safeguards on boarding can be met a majority of states are likely to accept it. The work of the intersessional group on the new protocol has ensured that most members of the IMO are aware of its provisions and of the policy behind them.

PART THREE

Anti-Terrorism Law and Policy in Asia

13

Law and terror: Singapore stories and Malaysian dilemmas

MICHAEL HOR

I. Law and terror

It is odd to conceive of anti-terrorism law in Malaysia and Singapore as if it were something exceptional or extraordinary. The truth is that for as long as independent Malaysia and Singapore have existed,[1] and for some time before, there has been in coexistence a formidable phalanx of anti-terrorism legislation. Not only has this network of laws been retained, it has gone from strength to strength, enjoying the occasional patch to remedy governmentally perceived flaws. Measures, once thought of as temporary and confined to narrow situations, have defied temporal and contextual boundaries. Legislative and (subsequently) constitutional entrenchment of anti-terrorism law provided the framework for a pattern of executive use in contexts as varied as the post-War armed communist, and substantially Chinese, insurrection to the recent efforts of the Islamic, and substantially Malay, Jemaah Islamiyah to retaliate against the United States and its allies. It is perhaps inevitable that individuals who were adversely affected by the use of anti-terrorism legislation should call upon the courts for relief. The result is, on occasion, a heroic attempt by the judges to be faithful to governmental intent, and at the same time to demonstrate a degree of independence from the government. This, in turn, has provoked the government to respond through legislative and constitutional amendments, setting up a tense dialogue between these great institutions of state. What is perhaps not immediately obvious is the fact that successive governments in both Malaysia and Singapore have consistently held the conviction that the law does matter.[2] In times of stress the

---

[1] Malaysia gained independence from Britain in 1957; Singapore ceased being a British colony when it joined Malaysia in 1963, before becoming independent by separation from Malaysia in 1965. On Singapore, see Lee Kuan Yew, *The Singapore Story – Memoirs of Lee Kuan Yew* (Singapore, Times Editions, 1998).

[2] See Rhoderick dhu Renick Jnr, 'The Emergency Regulations of Malaya – Causes and Effect' (1965) 6 *Journal of Southeast Asian History* 1–39, 18: 'Throughout the period of the [communist] Emergency ... the British meticulously established the legal authority necessary to insure a government of laws.' This British tradition was itself meticulously followed by the independent governments of Malaysia and Singapore.

temptation to ignore or override rules and legality is strong and it is to the credit of these governments that they have not yielded. The product is a substantially coherent body of jurisprudence of anti-terrorism law from which there is much to learn about how governments and courts behave in the times of crisis.

II. Law and the communist insurrection

Without a doubt, the seminal event in anti-terrorism law in Malaysia and Singapore was the barrage of legislation put in place to deal with the armed insurrection[3] of the Communist Party of Malaya shortly after the end of the Japanese occupation in the Second World War.[4] Much has been written about the course and causes of what has come to be known as 'The Emergency'.[5] The primary motivation for the insurrection was probably a compound of anti-colonialism, Chinese rights activism and political ideology.[6] The flashpoint was the assassination of two white plantation owners in 1948. The colonial government responded with the enactment of the Emergency Regulations.[7] It provided the legal authority underpinning a comprehensive menu of counter-insurgency measures which would have been problematic by the 'normal' laws of the land. Some of these provisions came before the

---

[3] The communist movement was variously described by the British as banditry, insurgency and ultimately terrorism. For an analysis of the 'political terminology' see Phillip Deary, 'The Terminology of Terrorism: Malaya, 1948–52' (2003) 34 *Journal of Southeast Asian Studies* 231–47.

[4] It is true that exceptional laws were put in place by the British Military Administration by proclamation in the immediate post-Japanese Occupation period, but those set of laws were not used for the communist insurgency – new laws passed by the relevant legislative authority were instead passed: Renick, 'Emergency Regulations' 18.

[5] See Anthony Short, *In Pursuit of Mountain Rats* (Singapore, Cultured Lotus, 2000). The leader of the communist insurrection, Chin Peng, has published his version of the Emergency: *My Side of History* (Singapore, Media Masters, 2003).

[6] Simply, the British had collaborated with the communists, mostly ethnic Chinese, to combat the Japanese occupation. After the Japanese surrender, the British set up the Malayan Union on citizenship terms favourable to the Chinese. The Chinese, mainly recent immigrants brought in to power the colonial economy, were then slightly outnumbered by the Malays, who were in Malaya long before the Chinese. When the Malays opposed the Malayan Union, the British replaced it with the Federation of Malaya, with terms distinctly less favourable to the Chinese. The Chinese felt betrayed and those who were in the communist movement felt that something drastic had to be done. The colonial economy was, of course, the antithesis of the socialist ideal. The communist antipathy towards the colonial government was naturally extended to the native leaders whom the colonial government had groomed to take over on (what they felt was a false) independence.

[7] See Renick, 'Emergency Regulations'. Although the theatre of action was Malaya (as Peninsula Malaysia was then known), very similar legislation was enacted in Singapore attesting to the intimate link between the two British-controlled territories.

courts in the form of criminal prosecutions. Advocates of judicial independence will be pleasantly surprised to discover that, even in those troubled times, the courts were quite capable of ruling against the prosecution and in favour of the accused.

In one instance, the courts encountered the peculiar offence of consorting with or being found in the company of someone in illegal possession of arms or ammunition.[8] The Emergency Regulations had created what was essentially a crime of guilt by association. The Court of Appeal of the Federation of Malaya, in what must have been a bold decision at the height of the insurgency, declared that the prosecution had to prove that the accused knew of the illegal possession, although this was not explicitly required in the Regulations.[9] The court could, of course, do nothing about the existence of the offence, but it could, and it did, reject the prosecution's protestation that this was a crime of strict liability. Even more surprisingly, there was no legislative response, indicating governmental acquiescence in the decision. The offence remains unchanged in this respect to this day in the statute books of both Malaysia and Singapore.[10]

This respectful tolerance, if not acceptance, of judicial limitation of the Emergency Regulations was not universal. Some other judicial initiatives were met with swift and stern legislative amendments.[11] In one interesting example, the Emergency Regulations had made admissible for the first time statements made to the police in the course of investigation or custodial

---

[8] Regulation 5(1) defined the offence in these terms: 'Any person who consorts with or is found in the company of another person who is carrying or has in his possession arms or explosives [without lawful authority or excuse] in circumstances which raise a reasonable presumption that he intends to or is about to act with, or has recently acted with, such other person in a manner prejudicial to public safety or the maintenance of public order shall be ... liable to be punished with death, or with penal servitude for life and whipping'. This offence departed significantly from the usual rules on complicity, and carried three of the most severe punishments possible. In addition to the *mens rea* ruling discussed in the text, the courts also sought to tighten the other elements of the offence: *PP* v. *Wong Kwang Soon* [1948] MLJ Supp 69 ('reasonable presumption' meant 'the only reasonable presumption'); *Soo Sing* v. *PP* [1951] MLJ 143 ('consorts' meant something 'more than a casual meeting or conversation').

[9] *Si Ah Fatt* v. *PP* [1950] MLJ 161. The prosecution had pressed the strict liability construction on the court.

[10] Section 59(1), Internal Security Act, Chapter 143, 1985 Revised Edition (Singapore); Section 58, Internal Security Act 1960, 1999 Reprint (Malaysia).

[11] In another notable example, the courts had decided that the defence of duress applied to the offences under the Emergency Regulations although there was no express provision one way or the other: *Subramaniam* v. *PP* [1956] MLJ 220 (Privy Council, Malaya). The Government eventually tired of repeated pleas of duress and amended the Regulations to exclude that defence – this suspension of the defence of duress is now found in section 70, Internal Security Act (Singapore); and section 69, Internal Security Act (Malaysia).

interrogation.[12] For more than half a century, such evidence, normally confessions, was not to be adduced to incriminate the accused in a criminal
trial.[13] The redoubtable Court of Appeal of the Federation of Malaya decided that statements were nonetheless inadmissible if they had been extracted
through cross-examination – to be admissible, the police could do no more
than ask questions to clarify what the accused had said.[14] This time there
was to be no governmental submission – the Regulations were amended to
allow for the admissibility of statements elicited through question and
answer.[15] The courts in turn responded by requiring strict adherence to the
caution that was to be given to the accused,[16] but the battle was already lost.[17]
This kind of legislative intransigence was to foreshadow the future.

An interesting sequel was to change, in a fundamental way, the administration of criminal justice in both Malaysia and Singapore. The Emergency
Regulations had made police and custodial statements admissible only for the
prosecution of offences under the Regulations. Years later the government in
Singapore was to use the precedent of the Emergency Regulations in pushing
through legislation to make such statements admissible for all criminal
offences.[18] If it worked so well for Emergency offences, it would work as
well for any offence. Thus it came to be that statements made to the police,

---

[12] Regulation 33 provided that for the purpose of Emergency offences, 'any statement,
whether such statement amounts to a confession or not or is oral or in writing, made at
any time, whether before or after such person is charged and whether in the course of a
police investigation or not, by such person to or on the hearing of any police officer of or
above the rank of Inspector shall, notwithstanding anything to the contrary contained in
any written law, be admissible at his trial in evidence'.

[13] This was because of the rule excluding statements made to the police in the course of
investigation (now section 122(1), Criminal Procedure Code, Chapter 68, 1985 Revised
Edition (Singapore); the Malaysian provision was repealed in 1976 – Abdul Ghani bin
Jusoh v. PP [1981] 1 MLJ 25), and the rule excluding statements made by anyone in police
custody (now section 25, Evidence Act, Chapter 97, 1997 Revised Edition (Singapore);
section 26, Evidence Act 1950, 1999 Reprint (Malaysia)).

[14] Cheng Seng Heng v. PP [1949] MLJ 175.

[15] The phase 'whether or not wholly or partly in answer to questions' was inserted into
Regulation 33: Poon Heong v. PP [1949] MLJ 114.

[16] E.g. Liew Ching v. PP [1949] MLJ 184. The caution was to warn the accused that there was
no obligation 'to say anything or to answer any question'. The police had told the accused
that he was not obliged to say anything, but had omitted to say specifically that he need not
answer any question – the court refused to admit his statements.

[17] Presumably, it was quite easy for the police to get into the habit of reading the prescribed
caution verbatim.

[18] Speech of the Minister for Labour and Law, Singapore Legislative Assembly Debates,
2 Sept 1959, column 557 which resulted in amendments to the Criminal Procedure Code
along the lines of Regulation 33 (now section 122(5), Criminal Procedure Code). Malaysia
was to make the change in 1976 (see Abdul Ghani bin Jusoh v. PP [1981] 1 MLJ 25). The
direct descendant of Regulation 33 remains in the Internal Security Acts of both jurisdictions: s. 76 (Singapore); s. 75 (Malaysia).

originally taboo in criminal prosecutions, have become the single most important piece of evidence in most criminal trials. The exceptional had been normalized, and not just for the admissibility of police statements, but for a host of other legislation and institutions which came into being because of the Emergency.[19]

Judicial decisions on the Emergency Regulations are even more striking for what they did *not* deal with. Criminal prosecutions were, by most accounts, the poorer cousins compared with a set of Emergency measures which had little to do with the Courts. There were those, like banishment[20] and the remarkable provision for collective punishment,[21] which were entirely executive and had nothing to do with the judiciary. There were those, like detention without trial, which involved judges as members of secret review or advisory committees.[22] One perhaps need not wonder too long about why executive detention and any other executive decision was never challenged in court – amongst other things, there had been a then recent, and subsequently infamous, House of Lords decision standing in the way of any administrative action.[23]

III. Law and detention without trial

The Emergency itself was eventually to pass away,[24] but detention without trial, that crown jewel of Emergency measures, like the word of God, was to remain. In Malaysia, that power was to migrate from the Emergency

---

[19] For example, the compulsory 'identity card' in Malaysia and Singapore has its origins in The Emergency (Registration Areas) Regulations 1948 as a means of combating the insurgency, presumably in the belief that the insurgents, most of whom had taken to the jungles, would find it difficult to register and obtain one. Failure to produce an identity card was itself an offence: PP v. *Lim Kwai Thean* [1959] MLJ 179.

[20] This was possible and potent because many of the insurgents were ethnic Chinese and recent immigrants who had not been given any right to remain in Malaya.

[21] Renick ('Emergency Regulations', 26–8) recounts the incident of General Templer, the person subsequently credited with the defeat of the insurgents, punishing an entire town, through curfew and reduction of rations, because he suspected that some of its residents were holding back relevant information.

[22] Ibid. 19–20.

[23] In *Liversidge* v. *Anderson* [1942] AC 206, the House of Lords (barring a famous dissent) ruled that the courts were not to inquire into the reasonableness of war time detentions – the detaining authority's subjective satisfaction was all that was required. See R. F. V. Heuston, '*Liversidge* v. *Anderson* in Retrospect' (1970) 86 LQR 33, and the more racy A. W. B. Simpson, 'Rhetoric, Reality and Regulation 18B' [1988] *Denning Law Journal* 123. The decision continues to influence (or plague, depending on one's convictions) and perhaps even dictate the law in Malaysia and Singapore.

[24] The state of emergency declared in 1948 was officially rescinded in 1960: Short, *Mountain Rats*, 495.

Regulations into the Internal Security Act.[25] In Singapore it found its way into two separate pieces of legislation: the Preservation of Public Security Ordinance (PPSO) and the Criminal Law (Temporary Provisions) Ordinance (CL(TP)O).[26] Both were to be of limited lifespan, but the PPSO was allowed to lapse in favour of the permanent Internal Security Act (ISA),[27] and the CL(TP)O, faithfully renewed from time to time, will soon celebrate its golden anniversary.[28] Nor has the use of the power of detention abated, although the scale of operations has certainly decreased since the Emergency.[29] It was to

[25] Act No. 18 of 1960: see L. W. Athulathmudali, 'Preventive Detention in the Federation of Malaya' (1961) 3 *Journal of the International Commission of Jurists* 100, and 'Preventive Detention in Malaysia' (1965) 14 *Journal du Droit International* 543.

[26] Respectively, Ordinances 25 and 26 of 1955. See the ironic contest preceding the passing of the Ordinances between Singapore's first Chief Minister David Marshall (later to be a liberal voice) proclaiming the necessity of the legislation, and Singapore's future Prime Minister Lee Kuan Yew (then in the opposition) expressing disdain for what he labelled 'an alias for the Emergency Regulations' (at column 719): Singapore Legislative Assembly Debates, 21 Sept 1955, columns 695–755. Lee was then allied with 'communist' or at least left-wing socialist politicians, and the power of detention without trial would have been most likely to be used against them. This proved to be true. Although Marshall had misgivings about its use, his successors, including Lee (who eventually discarded his left-wing confederates), did not: see Lee Ting Hui, *The Open United Front – The Communist Struggle in Singapore 1954–1966* (Singapore, South Seas Society, 1996). The deliberate political-criminal dichotomy between detention under s. 3 of the PPSO (to prevent conduct 'prejudicial to the security of Malaya') and detention under s. 30 of the CL(TP)A (concerning 'activities of a criminal nature') has been officially maintained. See also Bernard Brown, 'Administrative Internment in Singapore' (1961) 3 *Journal of the International Commission of Jurists* 126.

[27] When Singapore, and the Bornean states of Sabah and Sarawak, merged with Malaya to constitute the Federation of Malaysia in 1963, the federal Internal Security Act was extended into Singapore: LN 231, under section 74(1), Malaysia Act 1963. The PPSO, a piece of legislation of limited lifespan, was renewed from 1955 till 1969. Between 1963 and 1969, both laws were in force with the result that for as long as Singapore was in Malaysia (1963–65) detention powers under the ISA were held by the federal government, and those under the PPSO by the state government of Singapore. When Singapore ceded from the Federation, the ISA was continued in force, and so it remains today.

[28] Chapter 67, 2000 Revised Edition. It has been renewed once every five years since 1955, and its future looks reasonably secure: see the discussion in Parliament at the last renewal: Parliamentary Debates, volume 70, 15 April 1999, columns 1215–28.

[29] In Malaysia, for example, detentions during the Emergency ran into the hundreds, and even thousands: Renick 'Emergency Regulations' 22, note 3. The largest exercise in recent years, Operation *Lalang* (graphically named after a common and virtually indestructible weed) in 1987 scored about 100 detentions, and 'operations' thereafter were of a smaller scale: see Theresa Lee, 'Malaysia and the Internal Security Act' (2001) *Singapore Journal of Legal Studies* 56, at 57–63. In Singapore, Operation 'Coldstore' in 1963 chalked up about 130 detentions (see Lee Ting Hui, *The Open United Front*, 257), while the action against the 'Marxist Conspirators' in 1987 numbered a mere 16 (see *Report of the International Commission of Jurists to Singapore, 1987*, The International Commission of Jurists, Switzerland).

survive the institution of independence constitutions in both Malaya and Singapore. Notwithstanding the inauguration of an impressive Bill of Rights, officially called 'Fundamental Liberties', in these august documents,[30] explicit provision was made for the preservation of detention without trial.[31] Like a constitutional super-hero, the power of detention without trial to combat 'subversion' was given licence to over-ride almost all of the 'Fundamental Liberties'.[32]

With the rise of administrative law in the common law world,[33] and the communist armed insurgency receding from popular memory,[34] it was only a matter of time before the courts were called upon to stand between the aggrieved detainee and the government. Early attempts in the 1960s and 1970s to persuade the judiciary to intervene were met with the resolute refusal of the judges to be drawn into what they then saw as a purely political matter. The 'subjective satisfaction' of the detaining authority was the only requirement for a legal detention – whether that satisfaction was reasonable or rational was not for the courts to embark upon.[35] Indeed, the original

---

[30] Part II, Federal Constitution of Malaysia, and Part IV, Constitution of the Republic of Singapore, 1999 Revised Edition. The 'fundamental liberties' are similar, but not identical because Singapore, with some modifications, adopted the Malaysian provisions on separation from the Federation in 1965.

[31] Articles 149 and 151 of both the Malaysian Constitution and the Singapore Constitution. Post-1965 amendments to the once very similar 'subversion' provisions have made them less so.

[32] These include due process, freedom of movement, freedom of speech, assembly and association, and, with subsequent amendment, rights to property in Malaysia, and equality rights and rights against retrospectivity and double jeopardy in Singapore.

[33] In the wake of several 'landmark' House of Lords decisions: *Ridge* v. *Baldwin* [1964] AC 40; *Padfield* v. *Minister of Agriculture* [1968] AC 997; *Anisminic* v. *Foreign Compensation Commission* [1969] 2 AC 147, culminating in *O' Reilly* v. *Mackman* [1983] 2 AC 237, an influential decision in Malaysia and Singapore.

[34] In Malaysia, the communist insurgency had long ceased even before the official rescission of emergency powers in 1960. Malaysia was however to face two other unrelated crises – the Indonesian Confrontation of 1964, and the race riots of 1969, events which presented opportunities for the use of preventive detention. In Singapore, which was never directly involved with the armed communist insurrection, the 'communist threat' was never to really resurface after Operation Coldstore in 1963. Recent accounts contest the official view (see Lee Ting Hui, *The Open United Front*; Lee Kwan Yew, *Singapore Story*) that those targeted by Coldstore were indeed communist, or that if they were, they would have contemplated unlawful attempts to achieve their political objectives: Tan Jing Quee and Jomo K S (eds.), *Comet in Our Sky – Lim Chin Siong in History* (Malaysia, Insan, 2001); Said Zahari, *Dark Clouds at Dawn – A Political Memoir* (Malaysia, Insan, 2001). Lim Chin Siong and Said Zahari were key detainees in Coldstore.

[35] In Singapore, *Re Choo Jee Jeng* [1959] MLJ 217 set the tone, declaring in respect of a PPSO detention that 'it was not open to the Court to inquire whether in fact [there were] reasonable grounds for being satisfied that the detention was necessary'. More than a

detention law in Singapore had judges sitting in Appeal Tribunals with powers to countermand a detention order. This sufficiently discomfited the Singapore judiciary into making a special request to the legislature to relieve them of this function.[36] Matters did however come to a head in the 1980s. In Malaysia the judges were finally persuaded that there were detentions that were so wrong that they had to exercise their powers of judicial review to order release. In a notable decision the Supreme Court of Malaysia[37] released a detainee who was at the centre of a bank scandal. He had been detained on the ground that the depositors, many of whom were members of the armed forces, might otherwise take to violence.[38] The judges found this piece of security reasoning so 'incredible' that they had to strike down the detention order.[39] They were, of course, keenly aware that the government would be gravely displeased with this result.[40]

decade later, in a challenge to an ISA detention, the Singapore court in *Lee Mau Seng* v. *Minister for Home Affairs* [1969–1971] SLR 508 ruled that even if the detaining authority had 'arrived at his satisfaction without exercising care, caution and a sense of responsibility and in a casual and cavalier manner or on vague, irrelevant or incorrect grounds and facts', this was 'not a justiciable issue'. *Liversidge* was invoked. It also figured prominently in the Malaysian Federal Court decision in *Karam Singh* v. *Minister of Home Affairs* [1969] 2 MLJ 129, where a bench of five judges decided that ISA detentions were purely 'a matter for the personal or subjective satisfaction of the executive authority'. See John Tan Chor-Yong, 'Habeas Corpus in Singapore' [1960] *Malaya Law Review* 323; Rowena Daw, 'Preventive Detention in Singapore – A Comment on the Case of *Lee Mau Seng*' [1972] *Malaya Law Review* 276; H. F. Rawlings, 'Habeas Corpus and Preventive Detention in Singapore and Malaysia' [1983] *Malaya Law Review* 324; Tan Yock Lin, 'Some Aspects of Executive Detention in Malaysia and Singapore' [1987] *Malaya Law Review* 237.

[36] The original PPSO was amended in 1959, reducing the Appeal Tribunals to a purely advisory role. The story is recounted in vol. 52 Parliamentary Debates, 25 Jan 1989 column 469–70, curiously by the Minister for Home Affairs in pushing through constitutional amendments to prevent the judges, newly converted to the cause of judicial review, from reclaiming that role. The Chief Justice had said in 1959 that 'it is extremely undesirable for members of the judiciary to constitute the Appeal Tribunal'. The Tribunal, renamed the 'Advisory Board', was eventually to regain some of its original powers when Singapore moved from a titular to an elected presidency. If the President concurs with the Advisory Board's recommendation to release a detainee, the wishes of the government are overridden: article 151(4), Singapore Constitution.

[37] The highest court in Malaysia, originally named the Federal Court and then the Supreme Court (in 1985 when appeals to the Privy Council were abolished), and has since 1994 reverted to its first appellation.

[38] *Re Tan Sri Raja Khalid bin Raja Harun* [1988] 1 MLJ 182.

[39] The court agreed with the trial judge, who 'thought it to be incredible that losses sustained by a public bank where the depositors also include members of the public at large could result in any organized violence by the soldiers' (at 188).

[40] About six months later, the Lord President who presided over the appeal and delivered judgment, was suspended from office and subsequently removed. It was no secret that the government had been alarmed by a string of decisions against it (see the strange contempt litigation against the Prime Minister over unflattering remarks about the judiciary – *Lim Kit Siang* v. *Dato Seri Dr Mahathir Mohamad* [1987] 1 MLJ 383). Although the formal dismissal

They sought to placate the politicians by pretending that the law had not changed.[41]

Just over a year later, the Singapore Court of Appeal delivered what is perhaps the single most important constitutional decision in the history of the nation.[42] The pretence of the Malaysian court was not lost on the Singapore judges who were quick to point out that, to have achieved the result that the court did, the test of subjective satisfaction of the detaining authority must have changed.[43] A series of detentions in 1987, twenty-seven years after the official termination of the Emergency, set the stage. The power of detention was used in the 1960s and 1970s to deal with alleged 'Communist United Front' activities – communists operating through ostensibly lawful organizations like trade unions, schools and political parties, but who would not have stopped at merely lawful activities in their attempt to wrest political control.[44] Debate continues to rage as to whether these operatives were indeed communist, or merely nationalists or socialists, and as to whether they would have resorted to unlawful and violent means had they not been detained.[45] Be that as it may, the political and social fragility of Singapore in the 1960s had for most passed into distant memory. It was in a super-stable, economic dragon context of Singapore in the late 1980s that the power of detention was again used – this time to deal with an alleged 'Marxist Conspiracy' of what was essentially a network of Catholic social workers who saw as their Christian duty the task of organizing and creating awareness about social issues such as working conditions for factory workers, foreign domestic maids, civil rights and the like.[46] This they tried to do through the

of the Lord President (*Tribunal Report on the Dismissal of Tun Salleh Abbas* [1988] 3 MLJ xxxiii) does not refer to these decisions, the proffered grounds were singularly unconvincing, leading to the speculation that these extraordinary steps were taken because the government could no longer rely on the judiciary to make the 'right' decision in a pending lawsuit in which the political future of the Prime Minister rested. Crossing swords with the government can have disastrous consequences on the judiciary. See F. A. Trindade, 'The Removal of the Malaysian Judges' (1990) 106 *Law Quarterly Review* 51.

[41] The court described the nature of judicial review as a 'subjective test', expressly rejecting the 'objective approach', but proceeded to conduct a rather objective review.

[42] *Chng Suan Tze* v. *Minister of Home Affairs* [1988] SLR 132. See Thio Li-ann, 'Trends in Constitutional Interpretation – Oppugning *Ong*, Awakening *Arumugam*?' [1997] *Sing JLS* 240; Sin Boon Ann, 'Judges and Administrative Discretion – A Look at *Chng Suan Tze* v. *Minister of Home Affairs*' [1989] 2 MLJ ci.

[43] The Court in *Chng Suan Tze* said of *Re Tan Sri Raja Khalid bin Raja Harun*: 'With respect, it seems to us that despite having said that the subjective test applied, the court in actual fact applied the objective test in evaluating and assessing the evidence.'

[44] Described in detail in Lee Ting Hui, *The Open United Front*.

[45] See Tan and Jomo, *Comet in Our Sky*, and Said Zahari, *Dark Clouds at Dawn*.

[46] The official stand is best gleaned from the speeches of ministers in parliament: e.g. those of Prime Minister Lee Kuan Yew, vol. 51 Parliamentary Debates, 27 May 1988, cols. 187–201; 1 June 1988, cols. 324–51. The view of the critics is found in the *Report of the International Commission of Jurists to Singapore*.

Catholic Church, student unions, drama groups, the Law Society, and opposition political parties – all quite legal. Their sin was that their efforts might lead
to dissatisfaction with the government, destabilization, and ultimately after a
number of years, violence, public disorder and serious harm to the economy. All
this seemed a far cry from the 'Communist United Front' of 1960s Singapore,
but the government sought valiantly to draw the analogy. Terror and mayhem, if
it was to come to pass at all, was years away – but the government felt it had to
nip it in the bud. The detainees filed for habeas corpus.

The judgment of the Court of Appeal was a study in subtle manoeuvring. It
could have simply affirmed the subjective satisfaction rule and dismissed the
claim[47] – but it did not do that. It could have departed from that rule in
favour of objective judicial review and released the detainees on the ground
that the government's fears were too remote or 'incredible', much as the
Malaysian court did[48] – that too it did not do. Instead, the court seized on a
technical defect in the state of the evidence for the 'President's satisfaction', a
condition precedent of detentions without trial.[49] There being no satisfactory
evidence of such satisfaction, the court said, the detentions were unlawful and
the detainees were ordered to be released.[50] What followed this technical
ruling was extraordinary – an elaborate, and seemingly gratuitous, discussion
of substantive judicial review of detentions without trial.[51] The court boldly
over-ruled precedents establishing the 'subjective satisfaction' school of judicial review,[52] and summoning support from all over the common law world,
declared that detentions were to be objectively reviewed. Those who were
detained irrationally would be released. That the courts had such a power, nay
a duty, was put in the form of a ringing celebration of the 'rule of law' and the
denunciation of 'arbitrary' executive power.[53] The judgment then took

---

[47] There would have been ample precedent for this course of action – see the decisions in
note 35.

[48] *Re Tan Sri Raja Khalid bin Raja Harun.*

[49] Section 8 of the ISA required the President (on Cabinet advice) to be 'satisfied' that
detention is required to prevent the detainee from 'acting in any manner prejudicial to the
security of Singapore or any part thereof or to the maintenance of public order or essential
services therein'.

[50] The degree of technicality bordered on the unreal – the affidavit filed in evidence of the
President's satisfaction had been signed by the Permanent Secretary, the wrong official.
Curiously, a similar malady had afflicted a set of detentions in the 1960s: *Lim Hock Siew* v.
Minister of the Interior and Defence [1965–68] SLR 697.

[51] The court said that the issues were 'fully argued' and that they were 'important questions
of law'.

[52] Notably, the Singapore decision in *Lee Mau Seng* and the Malaysian case of *Karam Singh.*

[53] Says the court: '[The] notion of a subjective or unfettered discretion is contrary to the rule
of law. All power has legal limits and the rule of law demands that the courts should be able
to examine the exercise of discretionary power. If therefore the executive in exercising its
discretion under an Act of Parliament has exceeded the four corners within which

another curious turn – the court attempted to assure the government that it was not trying to tell the executive what was or was not a threat to national security.[54] More surprisingly, the court refused to apply to the facts of the case the new principles of judicial review which it had painstakingly propounded and defended.[55]

Some scholars have pondered long and deep over what the court was really trying to do. Surely, the technical ground could not have been a serious one. There could have been no doubt that the President was satisfied,[56] and it would have been easy enough for the court to have given the government an opportunity to produce such evidence.[57] Indeed one of the detainees chose not to advance this argument – but had the argument foisted upon her anyway. The court must have known that a technical victory for the detainees would prove to be Pyrrhic – there would be no bar to a fresh detention order, this time accompanied by the appropriate evidence should the detainee choose to challenge it again.[58] The mystery deepens with the court propounding that while objective judicial review was the law, that exercise was not to be carried out on the facts because it was unnecessary to do so. There could have been no doubt that from any meaningful perspective, it was necessary to decide whether the detentions were indeed irrational – where a detainee is released on substantive grounds, the government would risk being in contempt of court if a fresh detention order were issued. It will

Parliament has decided it can exercise its discretion, such an exercise of discretion would be ultra vires the Act and a court of law must be able to hold it to be so' (at 156).

[54] The court suggests initially that national security situations were different: '[Where] a decision is based on considerations of national security, judicial review of that decision would be precluded. . . . [What] national security requires is to be left solely to those who are responsible for national security'. But it then reverts to normal principles of judicial review: '[It] is in our judgment clear that the scope of review of the exercise of discretion under sections 8 (detention) and 10 (revocation of suspension) of the ISA is limited to the normal judicial review principles of "illegality, irrationality or procedural impropriety"'.

[55] On apparently technical grounds: 'we find it unnecessary to consider whether the appellants or any of them have discharged the burden of proving that the exercise of the discretion by the President under s 8 and/or by the minister under s 10 is invalid . . . the reason is, as we have held, that the respondents have not discharged the initial burden, which is on them, to prove the President's satisfaction'.

[56] On the criminal standard of proof beyond reasonable doubt, there could not have been much doubt about the President's satisfaction (on Cabinet advice). There was much in the newspapers and national television; the chilling televised 'confessions' were telecast in prime time. The Permanent Secretary of the Ministry of Home Affairs had signed an affidavit, and senior officers from the Attorney-General's Chambers were in court to defend the detentions. Between the doctrine of judicial notice and circumstantial evidence, there must surely have been enough for the court to act on.

[57] The court retains a discretion to allow such evidence as was available at the time of the trial, although the discretion is to be exercised exceptionally: *Tan Puay Boon v. PP* [2003] 3 SLR 390. Allowing it in this case would not have caused appreciable delay, nor would it have affected the fairness of the proceedings.

[58] This was indeed what happened after the decision was announced.

probably never be known with any degree of certainty whether the judges were hinting to the government that if the matter came before them again, they would rule in favour of the detainees on substantive grounds. If that were indeed the implicit message of the judgment, how did the judges predict the government would react – by grudgingly accepting the release of the detainees, or by initiating massive legislative and constitutional amendments to forbid objective review? Were they being naïve in expecting governmental submission, or being subtly conspiratorial in giving the government a chance to amend the law to prevent objective review? The tone of the judgment does not lead the reader to think that the judges expected to be legislatively overruled. Not only did the court assert the power of objective review, it also strongly implied that this was as it should be.[59] The judges had not simply been led astray by foreign jurisprudence, as some speeches in the legislature were later to insinuate,[60] they were making constitutional history by staking a claim that any meaningful construction of the rule of law must carry with it the possibility of objective judicial review. Perhaps the judges half-expected the government to react strongly, but felt they had to make the constitutional point anyway, and yet leave the government with a face-saving way out through either constitutional and legislative amendment, or a 'voluntary' abandonment of the detentions.

Governmental response to the court's pronouncements was swift and sure. The detainees had, of course, to be released, to comply with the letter of the law – but fresh detention orders were prepared even before the detainees were released and served on them as they were taken for a ride outside the detention centre – a brief spell of freedom which ended with captivity when they were conveyed back to where they started from. Massive legislative and constitutional amendments, attempting to reverse the judges, were introduced and passed at the next available sitting of Parliament.[61] One of the

---

[59] See note 53.
[60] The Minister for Law, Professor S. Jayakumar said, vol. 52 Parliamentary Debates, 25 Jan 1989, cols. 466–7, that the Court of Appeal abandoned the 'long standing position' in *Lee Mau Seng* 'because of cases decided in the United Kingdom and other parts of the Commonwealth'. But surely we can *agree* with the view of someone else without that opinion being the *cause* of our own belief. There is an impressive tenacity to the rhetoric that 'subversive' movements happen only because of external influence, and never because of genuinely held indigenous beliefs. In *Singapore – A Police Background* (London: Crisp, circa 1946), Rene Onraet, one of the principal architects of anti-subversion policy in Malaya, stressed that the 'subversive activities in Malaya were due to outside influences'. Hence, the communist insurrection of the 1940s and 1950s and the 'United Front' disturbances in the 1960s and 1970s were caused by Chinese and communists outside of Singapore, the Marxist conspirators were influenced by 'Euro-Marxists' and Philippine liberation theologians, and Jemaah Islamiyah in the early 2000s was inspired by radical Islamic influences beyond Singapore.
[61] The events are recorded in *Teo Soh Lung v. Minister of Home Affairs* [1990] SLR 40 (Singapore CA).

detainees had already filed again for habeas corpus, but the application was not heard until the amendments came into force.[62] In the High Court, the application was dismissed on the ground that the amendments had restored the regime of subjective review and there was no evidence that the President or the Cabinet was not satisfied that the detention was necessary for national security.[63] It went on appeal to the Court of Appeal, constituted identically with the earlier one. The tone and tack this time were very different. The court ruled that, even if the detention was reviewed objectively, the decision to detain had passed the test of rationality. This is curious for it would have been easy enough to have made such a ruling in the earlier decision – the facts had not changed – and had it done so, all the parties concerned would have been spared much time, money and anguish. Again, it is unlikely that it will be known for certain whether and why the court changed its mind about the rationality of the detention, but there was a distinct retreat from the lofty constitutional sentiments of the earlier decision. Also striking is what the court decided not to decide.[64] It refused to decide whether the legislative and constitutional amendments had indeed succeeded in precluding objective review.[65] It also refused to decide whether, if that was the intended effect, the constitution allowed for such amendments which (might arguably) breach

[62] The fresh application for habeas corpus was made before the amendments were passed, but the new section 8D of the ISA explicitly provided that the exclusion clauses applied 'whether such proceedings have been instituted before or after the commencement' of the amendment Act. It shall never be known what would have happened if the fresh application had been given a hearing date before the amendments came into force or why the application was not fixed for hearing before that date.

[63] *Teoh Soh Lung* v. *Minister of Home Affairs* [1989] SLR 499. Chua J seemed to go out of his way to disagree with the constitutional underpinnings of *Chng Suan Tze* (see above note 53): 'A reaffirmation of principles laid down by the courts [in earlier decisions such as *Lee Mau Seng*] cannot be said to be objectionable as usurping judicial power or being contrary to the rule of law. There is no abrogation of judicial power. It is erroneous to contend that the rule of law has been abolished by legislation and that Parliament has stated its absolute and conclusive judgment in applications for judicial review or other actions. Parliament has done no more than to enact the rule of law relating to the law applicable to judicial review' (at 515).

[64] Chua J in the High Court had clearly decided all these issues in favour of the government. So did Lai Kew Chai J in a High Court decision concerning another detainee: *Cheng Vincent* v. *Minister of Home Affairs* [1989] SLR 499.

[65] The effect of the amendments is not free from doubt. Section 8B decreed that the law 'shall be the same as was applicable and declared in Singapore on the 13th day of July 1971; and no part of the law before, on or after that date of any other country in the Commonwealth relating to judicial review shall apply'. While it is true that that was the day on which *Lee Mau Seng* (which stood for subjective review) was decided, it is not entirely clear that a High Court decision could declare the law of Singapore with finality. *Lee Mau Seng* could have been wrong the day it was decided. See *Ex Parte Rossminster* [1980] AC 952, at 1011: 'the time has come to acknowledge openly that the majority . . . in *Liversidge* v. *Anderson* . . . were expediently and, at that time, perhaps, excusably, wrong'. Moreover,

some fundamental feature of the constitution.[66] The economy of the judgment is surprising, coming so quickly after its seemingly gratuitous ruling on justiciability in the earlier decision. It did seem very much like a strategy of running away to live and fight again another day. The judges eventually ruled in favour of the government, but much thought appeared to have gone into 'damage control' – for the decision is of very limited precedential value in a future case.[67]

What lessons are to be learnt? For the judges, there is a price to pay for asserting themselves against a determined government, especially if the spectre of legislative and constitutional amendment is never very far off.[68] Some might justifiably think that it would have been better if the judges had not come out at that time so strongly in favour of judicial review – there would not then have been the 'indignity' of legislative and constitutional amendments explicitly meant to rein them in. But the dilemma was acute – if the courts do not intervene in a case as clear as this, the thinking public might begin to wonder if they ever will. So the judges played both ends, finding in favour of the detainees on the law, but in favour of the government on the facts. Only history will tell if this act of partial judicial resistance will come to mean anything to posterity. For the executive government, one hopes that those who are responsible for the powers of detention without trial will at least entertain the possibility that detention of the alleged 'Marxist Conspirators' was an over-reaction[69] – it is one thing to learn from history, it is quite another to be spooked by the ghost of Communist United Fronts past. The detainees had been released after televised 'confessions', and then re-detained when they alleged that the confessions were false and had been

the limitation of judicial review in section 8B(2) 'to compliance with any procedural requirement' relies on a substantive-procedural distinction that has never been clear. Taking into account an irrelevant consideration can easily be cast as a 'procedural' error in that the decision maker had adopted the wrong process in arriving at the decision.

[66] See *Kesavananda Bharati* v. *State of Kerala* AIR [1973] SC 1461. The idea of an implied limitation on the power to amend 'fundamental features' of the constitution was fashioned to deal with a situation where the government of the day can command the technical majority to effect any constitutional amendment it chooses (as is the case in Singapore and Malaysia today).

[67] The only conceivable value it has as a precedent is the way in which it applied the hypothetical objective test to the facts – this renders it very vulnerable to being distinguished on the facts.

[68] See also the much more dramatic Malaysian experience, note 40.

[69] The short history of the Internal Security Department on its website (http://www2.mha. gov.sg/mha/isd/newisd_earlyyears.html) makes no mention of the 'Marxist Conspirators'. It is odd that a recent major operation, in terms of the number of detainees (sixteen) receives no attention, in contrast with the operation against the members of the Jemaah Islamiyah, involving eighteen detentions: Government press release on the Jemaah Islamiyah members, 28 Nov. 2002, http://www2.mha.gov.sg/mha/detailed.jsp?artid= 631&type=4&root=0&parent=0&cat=0& mode=arc.

obtained by threats and inducements while in custody. They were ultimately released when they agreed to sign statutory declarations that their earlier confessions were true and that they were once again repentant. Were detainees such as these the stuff of threats to national security? Would a reasonable member of the thinking public have come away with the comforting assurance that the government had been vigilant, or with the niggling fear that the whole affair was tinged with official paranoia? For the legislature, it is expected of it that when it chooses to create and sustain such powers, it is mindful of the significant possibility that the powers, created as they were in the context of an armed insurrection and a polity on the verge of collapse, might be used in circumstances far less urgent. It should be especially circumspect when it contemplates measures to eliminate any form of meaningful judicial review – governments, as with individuals, have all sinned and fallen short, some time or other.

There was to be a Malaysian ripple to the exertions of the Singapore judges. Following the Singapore legislature's example, its Malaysian counterpart enacted similar exclusion clauses to prevent judicial review of detention without trial.[70] In the wake of the detention of a former Deputy Prime Minister, widely believed to be the result of a power struggle against the Prime Minister, several of his supporters were subsequently detained,[71] it appeared, for allegedly plotting violent protest demonstrations. The detainees filed for habeas corpus and the matter reached the Federal Court, which thought the matter serious enough to convene a bench of five judges.[72] It was the Malaysian judiciary's turn to be inspired by the developments in Singapore. They could or would do nothing about the exclusion clauses ousting review, but in a surprising turn, the court pointed out that the exclusion clauses applied only to ministerial detention.[73] They did not immunize police detention, a species of detention which normally precedes ministerial detention and is thought to facilitate 'investigations' in order to help the minister decide whether or not to impose ministerial

---

[70] Section 8B, inserted by the Internal Security (Amendment) Act 1989, Act A739, decreed that 'there shall be no judicial review in any court of . . . any act done or decision made by the Yang di-Pertuan Agong [i.e. King] or the Minister in the exercise of any discretionary power in accordance with this Act', except in regard to procedural requirements. The Singapore inspiration was evident.

[71] Former Deputy Prime Minister Anwar Ibrahim was himself detained. See generally, Therese Lee, 'Malaysia and the Internal Security Act – The Insecurity of Human Rights After September 11' [2002] *Sing JLS* 56; Nicole Fritz and Martin Flaherty, 'Unjust Order: Malaysia's Internal Security Act' (2003) 26 *Fordham International Law Journal* 1345.

[72] It has a quorum of three judges.

[73] *Mohamad Ezam bin Mohamad Noor v. Ketua Polis Negara* [2002] 4 MLJ 449. The decision was all the more remarkable because the court had to overrule several of its own precedents which had declared that police detention under section 73 was inextricably linked with ministerial detention under section 8.

detention.[74] Although the detainees had, by the time the applications were heard, been served with ministerial detention orders, the Federal Court was at pains to declare the prior police detention illegal. In a bold exercise of judicial review, the court explicitly adopted the objective test propounded by the Singapore court in *Chng Suan Tze*,[75] and seized upon evidence that interrogation following police detention was completely unconcerned with the alleged plans for violent demonstrations, but had instead attempted to probe the strength of support for the former Deputy Prime Minister. The police detention was, in administrative law terms, made mala fide and therefore illegal. However, the court held that it could not issue an order of habeas corpus because the detainees had, by then, been issued with ministerial detention orders. The brinkmanship was obvious, but to what end? Notwithstanding the rhetoric, the government had its way at the end of the day – the court was in no mood to force the issue and actually release the detainees.[76] It could not have escaped the court that the ministerial detentions were on exactly the same grounds as the prior and now infirm police detentions. Whilst of no apparent practical value, declaring the police detention illegal had at least a symbolic effect – a demonstration of judicial resistance against the wrongful use of executive powers to detain without trial. This must have been a big step indeed for a judiciary which had, not too long ago, been the victim of a direct attack by the government, resulting in the forcible removal of several of its most senior judges.[77]

IV. Law and emergency powers

It is a peculiarity of the constitutions of Malaysia and Singapore that there are formally two sets of exceptional powers which may be exercised in derogation of the usual constitutional norms. We have encountered the set of powers against 'subversion' – essentially the Emergency Regulations of the communist

---

[74] Section 73 of the ISA (Malaysia). Any police officer may arrest and detain if 'he has reason to believe' that there are grounds to justify ministerial detention, or that the person 'has acted or is about to act or is likely to act in any manner prejudicial to the security of Malaysia'. It is for a maximum period of sixty days. The 1989 amendments affecting ministerial detention left section 73 untouched.

[75] And again overruling its own precedents in the process.

[76] That the Federal Court was unwilling to go any further was confirmed by a later decision, *Kerajaan Malaysia v. Nasharuddin Nasir* [2004] 1 CLJ, where the Court again held that the objective review of *Chng Suan Tze* applied only to police, not ministerial, detentions. See also the account of (the former) Chief Justice Tun Mohamed Dzaiddin Abdullah, 'National Security Considerations Under the Internal Security Act 1960 – Recent Developments' (http://www.mlj.com.my/free/articles/dzaiddin.htm).

[77] See note 40.

insurgency enshrined.[78] Then there are the 'emergency powers' proper which follow on a declaration of emergency.[79] These are far more potent than the subversion laws – capable of overriding almost every other constitutional provision.[80] A declaration of emergency is a more overtly drastic measure, theoretically bearing much greater political, and perhaps economic cost,[81] to a government than the use of subversion laws. Independent Singapore has been very sparing with its use of emergency powers in its nearly forty years of existence.[82] Malaysia has used it on two major occasions – the Indonesian Confrontation in 1964, and the 13th May race riots of 1969.[83] While this record of sparing use is commendable, what is disturbing is the strange phenomenon of an unending emergency. Singapore was part of Malaysia when a national emergency was declared in 1964 – Indonesia had looked unkindly upon the creation of a federation of the former British possessions of Malaya, Sarawak, Sabah and Singapore, and in effect initiated limited military operations to destabilize the federation.[84] When Singapore parted ways with the federation in 1965, it appears to have taken along with it the 1964 declaration of emergency

---

[78] Article 149 in both Constitutions.

[79] Article 150 in both Constitutions. In 1965, when Singapore separated from the Federation of Malaysia, article 150 of the Malaysian document was adopted in its entirety into the Singapore Constitution: section 6, Republic of Singapore Independence Act 1985. Revised Edition. Both Constitutions have since been (independently) amended from time to time. Malaysia's original Constitution (in 1957) was much more parsimonious, allowing a state of emergency to last no longer than two months – that was quickly amended to give it an unlimited lifespan: Act 10 of 1960.

[80] The Singapore Constitution makes an exception for constitutional provisions 'relating to religion, citizenship or language' (article 150(5)). The Malaysian Constitution, in addition, states that emergency powers 'shall not extend the powers of Parliament with respect to any matter of Islamic law or the custom of the Malays, or with respect to any matter of native law or customs in the State of Sabah or Sarawak' (article 150(6A)).

[81] Although the technically continuing emergencies of both Singapore and Malaysia do not seem to have, in practice, exacted such a price.

[82] The reported decisions show examples of the use of emergency legislation in *Osman v. PP* [1965–68] SLR 19 (concerning events in the context of the Indonesian Confrontation, when Singapore was part of Malaysia), and *PP v. Goh Seow Poh* [1972–74] SLR 461(emergency offences concerning the verification of sources of publications).

[83] The race riots became a seminal event in Malaysian race relations. The fuse was a victory parade in Kuala Lumpur following a General Election in which the predominantly ethnic Chinese opposition made impressive electoral gains. This sufficiently inflamed Malay sentiments into sparking off a series of race riots. Speculations as to the deeper causes continue, ranging from mischief making to the growing economic inequality. In response, the government put in place several overt affirmative action institutions and policies.

[84] Indonesian President Sukarno had opposed the formation of Malaysia in 1963, on apparently 'anti-colonial' sentiments. The reasons were complex and alternative motivations might be found in Sukarno's sympathy for communist movements and the perceived need to create a diversion from domestic problems. The confrontation ended in 1966 when Sukarno himself was deposed.

together with its accompanying legislation.[85] The proclamation has never been explicitly revoked and the emergency legislation remains in the statute books,[86] evidence of an official view that would come as a shock to anyone who did not know it before – that Singapore in 2004 is still under a state of emergency and has been for forty years. Unlike the Internal Security Act and its provision for detention without trial, the proclamation and legislation based thereon have escaped scrutiny. The reason is simple – its powers have, to the credit of the government, very seldom been used.[87] Yet it remains, with the result that at any time, without a fresh proclamation, the legislature is at liberty to enact or promulgate laws in derogation of almost all other constitutional provisions. In addition, the existing emergency laws stand ready to be used at any time the government thinks fit.[88]

The problem of a government growing obsessively attached to emergency proclamations and powers is much more acute in Malaysia where emergency laws are, to this day, frequently resorted to. Neither the 1964 nor the 1969 proclamations have ever been revoked, and legislation thereunder seems to have gone from strength to strength, appearing in several updated incarnations.[89] The Malaysian courts have long grappled with such dubious use of emergency powers. Matters came to a head in the late 1970s when a criminal trial for possession of firearms, tried under emergency modifications, came before the Privy Council, then the highest court in Malaysia.[90] It was a charge which carried a mandatory death penalty and the accused was tried under emergency procedure, which deprived him of a preliminary inquiry and trial by jury. In a judgment which must have annoyed the government tremendously,[91] the Privy Council declared that the executive promulgation which contained the altered procedure was ultra vires – such powers having lapsed when Parliament sat.[92] This defect, though inconvenient, was easily

---

[85] Presumably by virtue of section 13 of the Republic of Singapore Independence Act, a continuation of 'existing laws' provision.

[86] The Emergency (Essential Powers) Act, Chapter 90, 1985 Revised Edition, and the subsidiary legislation made thereunder.

[87] See note 82.

[88] The Malaysian practice has been to proclaim a fresh emergency even though existing emergency powers could have been used.

[89] Now the Emergency (Essential Powers) Act 1979, 2001 Reprint.

[90] *Teh Cheng Poh* v. *PP* [1979] 1 MLJ 50. See Vincent Hoong, 'The Validity of Emergency Legislation and the Saga of Teh Cheng Poh's Case' [1981] *Malaya Law Review* 174; L. R. Penna, 'The Diceyan Perspective of Supremacy and the Constitution of Singapore' [1990] *Malaya Law Review* 207, 222–5. For a study pre-dating this decision, see S. Jayakumar, 'Emergency Powers in Malaysia: Development of the Law 1957–1977' [1978] 1 MLJ ix.

[91] Expressed in the constitutional amendments which followed quickly.

[92] The point was not crystal clear on a literal reading of the constitutional provision (article 150(2)) which seemed to say only that the power of the government to make *primary* law lapsed when Parliament sat – nothing explicit was said about *subsidiary* law.

remedied – Parliament could either itself make the procedural changes,[93] or it could pass a law delegating discretion to the executive to make subsidiary legislation.[94] The Privy Council expressly refused to deal with the much more significant argument that the 1969 proclamation itself cannot legally be in force because the cause of the emergency had by then clearly long lapsed into history.[95] But the court appeared to leave no doubt where it was leaning, and this could be seen in the way it treated another very similar power of proclamation under the Internal Security Act.[96] The accused had been charged for unlawful possession of firearms in a place proclaimed to be a 'security area' under the Internal Security Act. The relevance of this proclamation was that possession in a security area carried a mandatory death penalty. The whole of Malaysia was declared to be a security area shortly after race riots broke out in 1969 and this had never been revoked. Judicial manoeuvring was again the order of the day. The Privy Council declared that the power of proclamation of a security area under the Internal Security Act was governed by the normal principles of administrative law[97] – if the executive was no longer convinced that the proclamation was necessary, it would be an abuse of discretion for it not to revoke the proclamation. It then

[93] As parliamentary (as opposed to executive) emergency legislation.
[94] As it subsequently did. The Privy Council was unhappy with the executive continuing to make subsidiary legislation (after Parliament sat) on the authority of its own emergency ordinance, promulgated before Parliament sat.
[95] In these terms: 'it is unnecessary to decide whether or not they [the relevant regulations made under the proclamation of emergency] were invalid on the alternative and more far-reaching ground advanced by the appellant: namely, that by the time the Regulation was made the emergency proclaimed 15 May 1969 was over and the Emergency Proclamation of that date had ceased to be in force'.
[96] Section 47(1), ISA (Malaysia) confers discretion on the executive government to make a security area proclamation for any place 'seriously disturbed or threatened by reason of any action taken or threatened by any substantial body of persons, whether inside or outside Malaysia, to cause or to cause a substantial number of citizens to fear organized violence against persons or property'. The proclamation carried with it increased governmental powers, and in the context of the case, the imposition of a mandatory death penalty for illegal arms possession.
[97] Lord Diplock wrote: 'But, as with all discretions conferred upon the Executive by Act of Parliament, this does not exclude the jurisdiction of the court to inquire whether the purported exercise of the discretion was nevertheless *ultra vires* either because it was done in bad faith ... or because as a result of misconstruing the provision of the Act by which the discretion was conferred upon him the Yang di-Pertuan Agong has purported to exercise the discretion when the conditions precedent to its exercise were not fulfilled or, in exercising it, he has taken into consideration some matter which the Act forbids him to take into consideration or has failed to take into consideration some matter which the Act requires him to take into consideration' (at 55). Lord Diplock was well on the way to formulating his famous 'illegality, irrationality and procedural impropriety' summation in the famous 'GCHQ' case: *Council of Civil Service Unions* v. *Minister for the Civil Service* [1985] AC 374.

took a curious turn and held that even if there was an abuse of discretion, the proclamation cannot simply be declared invalid – the aggrieved had to apply for an order of mandamus against the executive to revoke the proclamation. No such application having been made, the court did not have to decide if mandamus ought to issue in this case.[98] It was the familiar theme of the judiciary striking out in favour of meaningful judicial review, but shrouding it in a result which went in favour of the government. The conceptual implications of the judgment were, however, far-reaching. There are many other discretions contained in both the emergency and subversion provisions, amongst them the discretion of the executive to proclaim and maintain an emergency and to promulgate emergency ordinances, and the discretion of the legislature to enact emergency legislation, and for that matter subversion laws like the Internal Security Act itself.[99] All of them would potentially be reviewable by the court.

All this was not lost on the government and legislative action was taken to plug all the 'loopholes'. The flawed emergency trial regulations were put on a legislative footing, and the accused retried thereunder – this time with success.[100] A last ditch attempt, this time by another person accused of a similar offence to argue that the trial modifications had breached fundamental features of the Malaysian constitution, failed.[101] In a strategy that was to foreshadow what the Singapore court was to do in the detention cases, the Federal Court, now the highest court of the land,[102] avoided making a final ruling on that mysterious Indian constitutional doctrine of implied limitations to the power of constitutional amendment[103] and held that, even if there were such a limitation on legislative power, no fundamental feature was

---

[98] Lord Diplock's treatment deserves quotation: 'This, however, does not mean . . . that the Security Area Proclamation can be treated by the court as having lapsed *ipso facto* as soon as there are no longer any grounds for considering it still to be necessary . . . if he [the government] fails to act the court has no power itself to revoke the proclamation in his stead. This, however, does not leave the courts powerless . . . Mandamus could, in their Lordships' view, be sought against the members of the Cabinet requiring them to advise the Yang di-Pertuan Agong to revoke the Proclamation . . . No such steps to obtain revocation of the Security Area Proclamation had been taken' (at 55).

[99] *Teh Cheng Poh* was invoked in Singapore more than ten years later in *Chng Suan Tze*, which declared the power of detention without trial to be reviewable on normal administrative law principles.

[100] See *Teh Cheng Poh v. PP* [1979] 2 MLJ 238 (Federal Court ordering a retrial); *PP v. Teh Cheng Poh* [1980] 1 MLJ 251 (trial court convicting the accused).

[101] *Phang Chin Hock v. PP* [1980] 1 MLJ 80. See note 70.

[102] Recourse to the Privy Council was terminated in Malaysia soon after *Teh Cheng Poh*. Singapore adopted a similar course following *Chng Suan Tze*; an appeal to the Privy Council was barred as part of the package of retrospective amendments (the now repealed section 8C of the ISA). The governments of Malaysia and Singapore were obviously unnerved by the flowering of judicial review in the UK.

[103] See note 66 above.

implicated. In addition, comprehensive ouster clauses in the form of consti-tutional amendments were clamped into place in an effort to forestall mean-ingful judicial review of any kind.[104] To this day emergency criminal law, substantive and procedural, is occasionally invoked by the Public Prosecutor in Malaysia. Famously (or infamously), the unhappy dismissed Deputy Prime Minister was charged for and convicted of an emergency offence in the late 1990s,[105] some twenty years after the decision of the Privy Council. The state of emergency, proclaimed in 1969, is, apparently, still of tremendous vitality in Malaysia, and the courts, it appears, rendered powerless to do anything about it.

V. Law and extraordinary times

One could be cynical about the whole enterprise of any legal analysis of anti-terrorism measures in Singapore and Malaysia.[106] Perhaps it is nothing more than an elaborate fiction – a theatrical apology for what governments and politicians will do in any event whatever the law or lawyers might say. Some expect the judiciary to temper and moderate governmental excesses, but there appears to be little the judges can do when governments almost invariably control a sufficient majority in the legislature to push through constitutional amendments to immunize anything they want to do.[107] Perhaps the answer is in democratic accountability at the ballot box, but experience has shown that this does not mean much when the electorate either has no real choice of an

---

[104] Act A514 of 1981 inserted article 150(8) to the Malaysian Constitution. Subparagraph (a), for instance, provides that the 'the satisfaction of the Yang di-Pertuan Agong ... shall be final and conclusive and shall not be challenged or called in question in any court on any ground'.

[105] *PP v. Dato Seri Anwar bin Ibrahim* (No. 3) [1999] 2 MLJ 1 (trial); *Dato Seri Anwar bin Ibrahim v. PP* [2000] 4 MLJ 286 (Court of Appeal), [2002] 3 MLJ 193 (Federal Court). See also note 71.

[106] Wu Min Aun, 'Sacrificing Personal Freedom in the Name of National Security', Fourth Professor Ahmad Ibrahim Memorial Lecture, 12 July 2003, International Islamic University of Malaysia, http://www.cdu.edu.au/lba/law/staff/wu/wu1.htm. Professor Wu said despairingly, but not without justification: 'In the past, governments around the world have sought new powers to deal with various threats in the name of national security only for those powers to be later used against their own citizens or their political opponents. They become laws that never seem to end, even long after their original purpose had ended.'

[107] Independent Singapore has had nothing but a government which controlled at least two-thirds (the requirement of most amendments – article 5, Singapore Constitution) of the seats in Parliament. Malaysian governments have enjoyed a similar domination in Parliament (the two-thirds majority requirement also pertains to Malaysia – article 159, Malaysian Constitution), save for a brief period following the 1969 elections which sparked off the race riots. Election campaigns in Malaysia are routinely fought on the basis that a two-thirds majority is necessary for any government to be effective.

alternative government, or if elections are seldom fought and won on the basis of legal issues such as these. But socio-political climates change and with it conceptions of the extent to which judges are allowed or even expected to intervene in extraordinary situations. Perhaps also public acceptance, tolerance or apathy towards the maintenance of a set of perpetual subversion or emergency laws will turn. Great revolutions in collective values do not often happen without a struggle with the old order. One can be hopeful that when the struggle begins,[108] if it ever does, these symbolic acts of judicial resistance to the wrongful use of extraordinary law designed to deal with insurgency, subversion and terrorism will be a source of inspiration.

---

[108] One also hopes that the struggle will be a peaceful and constitutional affair.

14

Indonesia's Anti-Terrorism Law

HIKMAHANTO JUWANA

Introduction

Soon after the Bali Bombing occurred on 12 October 2002 killing 202 people, mostly foreigners and holidaymakers, the government was quick to legislate an Anti-Terrorism Law. On 18 October 2002 the President issued Government Regulation in Lieu of Law[1] (hereinafter referred to as GRL) No. 1 of 2002 concerning the Eradication of Criminal Acts of Terrorism.[2] On the same day the Government issued GRL No. 2 of 2002 making GRL No. 1 retroactively applicable to the Bali bombings.[3] In 2003, both GRL 1 and 2 of 2002 were confirmed by the legislature and have become law (GRL 1 is referred to as the 'Anti-Terrorism Law').[4]

This chapter will describe Indonesia's Anti-Terrorism Law and the difficulties and public controversy the government has faced in trying to implement it. The chapter will show how the judiciary has attempted to curb some of the Law's perceived excesses and it will review recent legal developments. It will be argued that, for Indonesia, terrorism is a complex and multi-faceted issue that cannot be addressed simply by promulgating a new law.

I. The substance

The Anti-Terrorism Law provides four reasons for its promulgation. First, terrorism had 'claimed human lives intolerably and raised widespread fear among the community [and] caused loss of freedom and damage of

---

[1] GRL is a form of legislation enacted by the President in emergency circumstances. In the hierarchy of Indonesian law *Perpu* is one rank below a Law or Act (*Undang-undang*). Under the Constitution it is required for the Perpu to be brought to the parliament within one year after its promulgation to be confirmed or rejected as law.

[2] For an English translation, see: http://www.law.unimelb.edu.au/alc/indonesia/perpu_1.html.

[3] For an English translation, see: http://www.law.unimelb.edu.au/alc/indonesia/perpu_2.html.

[4] The GRL No. 1 of 2002 becomes Law No. 15 of 2003 and GRL No. 2 of 2002 becomes Law No. 16 of 2003. This chapter uses the unofficial translation of these laws into English as found in the sources cited above, notes 2 and 3.

property'.[5] Second, terrorism had maintained extensive networks, posing a threat to national and international peace and security.[6] Third, national legislation was required to implement international conventions relating to terrorism.[7] Lastly, the Anti-Terrorism Law was a matter of urgency because existing legislation in Indonesia was inadequate and failed to deal comprehensively with combating criminal acts of terrorism.[8]

The Anti-Terrorism Law applies to any person (including a corporation[9]) who commits or intends to commit a criminal act of terrorism in Indonesia and/or another nation that has jurisdiction and expresses an intention to prosecute that person.[10] It also applies to criminal acts of terrorism which are committed: '(a) against the citizens of Indonesia outside the territory of Indonesia; (b) against the state facilities of Indonesia overseas, including the premises of the diplomatic officials and consuls of the Republic of Indonesia; (c) with violence or threats of violence to force the Government of Indonesia to take or not to take an action; (d) to force any international organization in Indonesia to take or not take an action; (e) on board a vessel sailing under the flag of Indonesia or an aircraft registered under the laws of Indonesia at the time when the crime is committed; (f) by any stateless person who resides in Indonesia'.[11]

Terrorism is defined generally under the Anti-Terrorism Law as the intentional use of 'violence or the threat of violence to create a widespread atmosphere of terror or fear in public or to create mass casualties, by forcibly taking the freedom, life or property of others or causes damage or destruction to vital strategic installations or the environment or public facilities or international facilities'.[12] Those who *commit* this kind of act of terrorism can be sentenced to death, or life imprisonment, or a minimum sentence of four years and a maximum of twenty years.[13] Those who have the *intention to commit* an act of terrorism can be sentenced to a maximum of life imprisonment.[14]

Specific acts of terrorism defined under the Anti-Terrorism Law include a range of specific offences relating to various aspects of aviation security,[15] explosives, firearms, and ammunition,[16] and the use of chemical, biological, and other weapons to 'create an atmosphere of terror or fear in the general population, causing danger and destruction to vital strategic installations or the environment or public facilities or international facilities'.[17] Penalties for these offences range from life imprisonment or death to incarceration for a period of between three or four years and twenty years. It should be noted,

---

[5] See GRL No. 1 of 2002, considerations section (b). The full text in Bahasa Indonesia is available at http://www.ri.go.id/produk_uu/isi/perpu2002/perpu1'02.htm.
[6] Ibid., considerations section (c).   [7] Ibid., considerations section (d).
[8] Ibid., considerations section (e).   [9] Ibid., Article 17.   [10] Ibid., Article 3 (1).
[11] Ibid., Article 4.   [12] Ibid., Article 6.   [13] Ibid.   [14] Ibid., Article 7.   [15] Ibid., Article 8.
[16] Ibid., Article 9.   [17] Ibid., Article 10.

however, that the Anti-Terrorism Law provides that the various acts of terrorism will not be applicable to 'political criminal acts or criminal acts relating to criminal crimes nor criminal acts with political motives nor criminal acts with the political objective of obstructing an extradition process'.[18]

Those who intentionally provide or collect funds[19] or assets[20] with the 'objective that they be used or if there is a reasonable likelihood that the funds will be used partly or wholly' for criminal acts of terrorism will bear criminal responsibility under the Anti-Terrorism Law and can be sentenced to a minimum three years or a maximum of fifteen years imprisonment.[21]

A person also commits an act of terrorism if such person intentionally provides or collects assets with the objective or if there is a reasonable likelihood that the assets will be used partly or wholly for: (a) committing any unlawful act of receiving, possessing, using, delivering, modifying or discarding nuclear materials, chemical weapons, biological weapons, radiology, microorganisms, radioactivity or its components that causes death or serious injuries or causes damage to assets; (b) stealing or seizing nuclear materials, chemical weapons, biological weapons, radiology, micro-organisms, radioactivity or its components; (c) embezzling or acquiring illegally nuclear materials, chemical weapons, biological weapons, radiology, microorganisms, radioactivity or its components; (d) requesting nuclear materials, chemical weapons, biological weapons, radiology, micro-organisms, radioactivity or its components; (e) threatening to: (1) use such nuclear materials, chemical, biological weapons, radiology, microorganisms, radioactivity or its components to cause death or injuries or damage to property; or (2) commit criminal acts as stipulated in (b) with the intention to force another person, an international organization, or another country to take or not to take an action; (f) attempting to commit any criminal act as stipulated in (a), (b) or (c); and (g) participating in committing any criminal act as stipulated in (a) to (f). The sentence for those found guilty is imprisonment with a minimum sentence of three years and a maximum of fifteen years.[22] Any person found guilty of intentionally providing assistance to any perpetrator by: 'providing or lending money or goods or other assets to any perpetrator of criminal acts of terrorism; harbouring any perpetrator of any criminal act of terrorism; or hiding any information on any criminal act of terrorism' is liable to imprisonment for a minimum term of three years and a maximum of fifteen years.[23] Planning or inciting another person to commit any criminal act of terrorism can result in the death sentence or life imprisonment.[24]

---

[18] Ibid., Article 5.   [19] Ibid., Article 11.   [20] Ibid., Article 12.
[21] Ibid., Articles 11 and 12.   [22] Ibid., Article 12.   [23] Ibid., Article 13.
[24] Ibid., Article 14.

Moreover, any one who 'conducts any plot, attempt, or assistance to commit any criminal act of terrorism' will be sentenced the same as those who are committing such an act of terrorism.[25]

One interesting point to note is that the Anti-Terrorism Law can also be applied to those who provide any assistance, facilities, means or information for any criminal acts of terrorism committed extraterritorially. The sentence is the same as for committing the act of terrorism itself.[26] Indonesia is obliged to cooperate with other nations in the areas of 'intelligence, policing and other technical cooperation connected with anti-terrorism measures in accordance with the applicable legislative provisions'.[27]

The Anti-Terrorism Law introduces a novel procedure from that of ordinary criminal procedure, namely that an investigator may use any intelligence report as preliminary evidence.[28] However, the Anti-Terrorism Law provides that the adequacy of the preliminary evidence obtained must be determined through an inquiry process by the Head or Deputy Head of the District Court. The inquiry process is conducted in closed session within a maximum period of three working days.[29]

Various extraordinary powers are conferred on investigators, public prosecutors or judges. Investigators may detain any person strongly suspected of committing a criminal act of terrorism based on adequate preliminary evidence for a maximum period of seven times twenty-four hours.[30] Investigators, public prosecutors or judges are authorized to order banks and other financial institutions to freeze the assets of any individual whose assets are known or reasonably suspected to be the proceeds of any criminal act connected to terrorism.[31] In addition, for the purpose of investigation, the investigators, public prosecutors or judges are authorized 'to request information from banks and other financial institutions regarding the assets of any person who is known or strongly suspected of having committed a criminal act of terrorism'.[32]

Furthermore, investigators are authorized: 'to open, examine and confiscate mail and packages by post or other means of delivery' and 'to intercept any conversation by telephone or other means of communication suspected of being used to prepare, plan and commit a criminal act of terrorism'.[33] However, investigators may only intercept based on an order of the Head of the District Court for a maximum period of one year.[34]

The Anti-Terrorism Law stipulates other criminal offences related to acts of terrorism. For example, any person who uses violence or the threat of violence or who intimidates detectives, investigators, public prosecutors, solicitors and/or judges who are handling any criminal act of terrorism, so as to hamper the judicial process, is guilty of an offence subject to a minimum

---

[25] Ibid., Article 15.   [26] Ibid., Article 16.   [27] Ibid., Article 43.   [28] Ibid., Article 26 (1).
[29] Ibid., Article 26.   [30] Ibid., Article 28.   [31] Ibid., Article 29 (1).
[32] Ibid., Article 30 (1).   [33] Ibid., Article 30.   [34] Ibid., Article 31 (1) a and b.

sentence of three years and a maximum of fifteen years. And a person who provides false testimony, submits false material evidence, or unlawfully influences a witness during a court session or attacks a witness, including the officials in the trial of a criminal act of terrorism, is guilty of an offence subject to a minimum sentence of three years and a maximum of fifteen years. Witnesses, investigators, judges, and their families are entitled to protection by the state before, during, and after the investigation process.[35]

The Anti-Terrorism Law also imposes an obligation on the state to pay compensation and restitution to victims and families of victims of terrorist acts.[36] In addition, any individual shall be entitled to rehabilitation if he or she is discharged of all legal charges of terrorism by the court.[37]

Provisions of the Anti-Terrorism Law may be applied retroactively to acts of terrorism that occurred prior to the promulgation of this Anti-Terrorism Law.[38] The Anti-Terrorism Law has been used retroactively to arrest and try a number of terrorist suspects, such as Amrozi, Imam Samudera and Ali Imron in connection with the Bali bombing. They have all been sentenced either to death, life or a term of imprisonment.

II. The challenges in implementation

Indonesians greeted the Anti-Terrorism Law with ambivalence. Although they hoped terrorism would soon cease with the issuance of the Law, they were also suspicious that the Law would give rise to authoritarian government and the revival of the military. In addition, people were afraid that Indonesia had joined an American-led war against Islam, not terrorism. The public ambivalence should be understood in the Indonesian context. Indonesia has a majority Muslim population. Although most Indonesian Muslims are moderate, many believe that the war against terrorism is a war against Islam.

As a country Indonesia is not free from terrorism. Terrorism involves not only religious attacks but communal conflict and separatist movements. There are concerns that terrorism may destabilize the government. At the same time, there is a feeling in some quarters that terrorism is justified as a means to attack western arrogance and dominance. There is a feeling that Indonesia is the victim of bullying by foreign countries who are interested in making sure that Indonesia does not become a safe heaven for terrorist suspects. But at the same time, the public understand the image of Indonesia as a place where terror attacks have taken place. The image has hurt the economy and the trust of foreign investors.

---

[35] Ibid., Article 33.   [36] Ibid., Article 36.   [37] Ibid., Article 37.
[38] Ibid., Article 46. See also GRL No.2 of 2002.

The Anti-Terrorism Law has affected human rights in Indonesia. Promotion and protection of human rights are considered important because Indonesia fell under authoritarian regime for almost three decades. The public is very sensitive to any neglect and violation of human rights.

For the Indonesian public, the US and Australia have lost their persuasiveness and moral authority because their anti-terror efforts are perceived to be inconsistent with their prior human rights sermons to Indonesia. Such double standards have become a convenient means for the Indonesian public to attack the US and Australia who in the past had been perceived to be constantly bullying Indonesia to respect human rights. In addition, the Indonesian public believes that the war against terror should not be fought at the expense of human rights. For example, the Chairman of Indonesia's second largest Muslim organization, Muhammadiyah, has stated that the war against terror has confused the government, but that the government should not ignore human rights.[39]

For the public, the war against terror has had a negative impact on the promotion and protection of human rights in Indonesia for the following reasons.

First, the Indonesian government has been criticized for not protecting its nationals abroad where they may have suffered human rights violations. For example, Australian authorities went to the house of Indonesian Muslims residing in Australia with guns drawn and sledgehammers to break down doors.[40] The Indonesians were suspected of having connections with Abu Bakar Ba'asyir who is believed by the US and Australia to be the leader of Jemaah Islamiyah (JI). In Indonesia, the public believed this event not to be in accordance with human rights. The Indonesian parliament, DPR, urged the government to lodge a protest against what they called a human rights violation.[41] To appease the public, the Ministry of Foreign Affairs lodged a protest to the Australian government through its Embassy in Jakarta,[42] but shied away from DPR's demand to investigate the matter in Australia.[43] The public also demanded that the Indonesian government ask the Philippines government to explain the unnatural

---

[39] 'Religious leaders want police to respect human rights', *The Jakarta Post*, 13 November 2002, available at http://www.thejakartapost.com/Archives/ArchivesDet2.asp?FileID=20021113.A03.

[40] 'Australian police raid terror suspects', *BBC News*, 30 October 2002, available at http://news.bbc.co.uk/2/hi/asia-pacific/2374505.stm. Also: 'Eye-witness describes violent police raid in Australia', *World Socialist Web Site*, 2 November 2002, available at http://www.wsws.org/articles/2002/nov2002/raid-n02.shtml.

[41] 'Rights abuses occur in Australian raids: House', *The Jakarta Post*, 20 November 2002, http://www.thejakartapost.com/Archives/ArchivesDet2.asp?FileID=20021120.C01.

[42] 'Australian envoy summoned over antiterrorism raids', *The Jakarta Post*, 2 November 2002, http://www.thejakartapost.com/Archives/ArchivesDet2.asp?FileID=20021102.@03.

[43] 'Legislator wants probe into raids in Australia', *The Jakarta Post*, 18 November 2002, available at http://www.thejakartapost.com/Archives/ArchivesDet2.asp?FileID=20021118. A02.

death of terrorist suspect Al-Ghozi, who is believed to have been executed extra-judicially by the Philippines military on the eve of US President Bush's visit to the country.[44] There are also concerns about the exact whereabouts and treatment of Al-Faruq and Hambali who are currently in US custody. And there are calls that they should be extradited back to Indonesia for trial.[45] The Minister of Foreign Affairs has defended government inaction on the grounds that acts of terrorism are 'non-traditional criminal acts' that do not warrant protection.[46] Moreover, doubts have been raised whether some suspects are Indonesian nationals that the government should protect.[47]

Second, international pressure is mounting on the Indonesian government to arrest several Muslim leaders, including Abu Bakar Ba'asyir. The police and prosecutors have proceeded against him even when they had no solid ground for prosecution. The lower court found Abu Bakar Ba'asyir guilty of treason in a plot to overthrow Indonesia's secular government, but cleared him of charges of being the leader of the Jemaah Islamiyah.[48] Later on, the Appeal Court reduced his sentence from four to three years and found him guilty only of forging identity documents. On 9 March 2004 the High Court ruling was overturned by the Supreme Court, leaving only minor immigration offences outstanding. Ba'asyir's sentence was reduced to eighteen months.[49]

On the eve of his release on 30 April 2004, Indonesian police rearrested Abu Bakar Ba'asyir. The police said they had new evidence that he was a senior leader of JI.[50] Ba'asyir, who has served his sentence for immigration offences, denies being the group's spiritual leader and any involvement in the Bali bombing. As he was about to be taken into police custody from the jail, hundreds of his supporters clashed with police. Targeting Muslim leaders has offended the public and as a result, the public has been very critical of Anti-Terrorism Law enforcement.

---

[44] 'Philippine president denies JI bomb-maker was executed', *AFP*, 14 October 2003, http:// quickstart.clari.net/qs_se/webnews/wed/bl/Qphilippines-attacks.Rcn4_DOE.html.
[45] 'RI interested in interrogating Hambali', *The Jakarta Post*, 17 August 2003, available at http://www.thejakartapost.com/Archives/ArchivesDet2.asp?FileID=20030817.@01.
[46] 'Hassan seeks US permission to question Hambali', *The Jakarta Post*, 27 August 2003, available at http://www.thejakartapost.com/Archives/ArchivesDet2.asp?FileID=20030827.B02
[47] For example Hambali and al-Ghozi's nationality was doubted by Indonesian authorities as Indonesian as they were using several passports. See: 'Police say al-Ghozi is Canadian national', *The Jakarta Post*, 22 January 2002, available at http://www.thejakartapost.com/ Archives/ArchivesDet2.asp?FileID=20020122.G10.
[48] 'Indonesian appeals court reduces sentence of militant leader', *Associated Press*, 1 December 2003, available at http://www.startribune.com/stories/1576/4241535.html.
[49] 'Indonesian cleric "free in weeks"', *BBC News*, 9 March 2004, available at http://news. bbc.co.uk/1/hi/world/asia-pacific/3545209.stm.
[50] 'Indonesian cleric faces Bali charge', *BBC News*, 30 April 2004, available at http://news. bbc.co.uk/2/hi/asia-pacific/3668975.stm.

Third, a number of persons have reportedly disappeared or have been forcibly taken into custody by the police because of their alleged terrorist links.[51] The police have apprehended without due process of law persons thought to have received training in Afghanistan during the Afghan war. Human rights watchdogs and the Muslim community have criticized such police actions for violating basic human rights.[52] The police have denied accusations that they have kidnapped a Muslim activist by reference to their powers under the Anti-Terrorism Law.[53] Concerns have been expressed about the targeting of Muslims. Pesantren, an Islamic boarding school, has been suspected by the US government as a place to train Islamic militants who support terrorism.[54] The police have raided Pesantren as part of a terrorism investigation.[55]

The war on terror has relieved external pressure on the Indonesian government to respect human rights. Foreign countries are ready to overlook Indonesia's human rights abuses so long as the government is cooperative in the war against terror. The US, which had in the past expressed concerns about the condition of human rights in Indonesia, has not been exerting such pressure because the US needs Indonesia's support in its war on terror.

The public in Indonesia has resented the silence of international NGOs about human rights abuses of Indonesian nationals abroad who are suspected of terrorism. There is a perception of unfair double standards when NGOs fiercely criticize Indonesia for human rights abuse but are silent about the abuse of the human rights of Indonesians by other countries. The negative impact of the war against terror on human rights has caused the public in Indonesia to question whether human rights are only an instrument to weaken Indonesia as a country, including its government and military.

The war on terror has led to Western countries traditionally seen as 'defenders of human rights' to encourage and expect abuses of human rights

---

[51] 'Arrested or disappeared? Families, police at odds', *The Jakarta Post*, 16 September 2003, available at http://www.thejakartapost.com/Archives/ArchivesDet2.asp?FileID=20030916.C01.

[52] 'Police arrests human rights', *The Jakarta Post*, 17 September 2003, available at http://www.thejakartapost.com/Archives/ArchivesDet2.asp?FileID=20030917.G04.

[53] 'Police meet Muslim leaders over arrests of activists', *The Jakarta Post*, 20 September 2003 available at http://www.thejakartapost.com/Archives/ArchivesDet2.asp?FileID=20030920.@01.

[54] According to Virtual Information Center, there were many reports indicating that the children at Pesantren spend their entire childhood, in many cases, learning to hate the West and to blame it for all the ills of their society. Many of these graduates return home, committed to running *jihads* and to creating Islamic states governed by *sharia* (Islamic law), see http://www.vic-info.org/RegionsTop.nsf/0/43dd40e1787c7bfd0a256d98001231b5? OpenDocument. The US government for this purpose has been funding the Indonesian government to insert anti-terrorism in Pesantren's curriculum. See: 'Anti-terrorism now part of curriculum', *The Age*, 30 August 2003, available at http://www.theage.com.au/ articles/2003/08/29/1062050665721.html?from=storyrhs.

[55] 'Police negotiating with "pesantren" over suspects', *The Jakarta Post*, 20 November 2002, available at http://www.thejakartapost.com/Archives/ArchivesDet2.asp?FileID=20021120.@01.

to recur in Indonesia. For example, Australia announced in August 2003 a plan to resume ties with the Indonesian special force, Kopassus, which were broken off in 1999 when the latter was accused of orchestrating mass violence in East Timor.[56] Cooperation with Kopassus had been seen as necessary because Kopassus provides Indonesia's main counter-terrorism capability. The proposed cooperation received criticism within Australia,[57] causing the Australian Foreign Minister to argue that the ties would be qualified and limited.[58] The cooperation has been placed on hold after the Chief of Kopassus was refused entry into Australia and Kopassus became reluctant to engage in joint exercises.[59]

Human rights protection and promotion in Indonesia can be undermined if powerful states condone or encourage such a state of affairs. This leads to the conclusion that foreign governments do not have a sincere intention of upholding human rights in Indonesia. They rather have used human rights issues as a political instrument against Indonesia. Since the launch of the war against terror, Indonesia's human rights cause has become one of its casualties through the revival of legislation legitimizing human rights abuses from what was thought to be a bygone era.

There has been public criticism that the former Megawati government has erroneously bowed to the US and its allies in the fight against terrorism,[60] despite the fact that Indonesia has itself fallen victim to terrorism.[61]

III. Judicial review

In November 2003 the application of Anti-Terrorism Law in the Bali bombing was challenged in the Constitutional Court by Masjkur Abdul Kadir, who was sentenced to fifteen years' imprisonment for his involvement in the

---

[56] 'Canberra renews Kopassus ties,' *CNN.com*, 11 August 2003, available at http://edition.cnn.com/2003/WORLD/asiapcf/auspac/08/10/australia.kopassus/.
[57] 'Aust Defence-Kopassus ties questioned,' *ABC Online*, 1 August 2003, available at http://www.abc.net.au/worldtoday/content/2003/s915466.htm.
[58] 'Kopassus cooperation "limited": Downer', *ABC Newsonline*, 13 August 2003, available at http://www.abc.net.au/news/newsitems/200308/s922681.htm.
[59] 'Kopassus chief's trip to Perth vetoed', *The Age*, 13 October 2003, available at http://www.theage.com.au/articles/2003/10/12/1065917273113.html?from=storyrhs. Also: 'Kerjasama Kopassus-SAS Australia Dibatalkan Sampai Waktu Tidak Terbatas (Cooperation Kopassus-Australia's SAS Delayed for Unlimited Period)', *Republika Online*, 16 October 2003, available at http://www.republika.co.id/berita/online/2003/10/16/143277.shtm.
[60] 'Legal, human rights experts worried about dangerous trend', *The Jakarta Post*, 21 September 2001, available at http://www.thejakartapost.com/Archives/ArchivesDet2.asp?FileID=20020921. A04.
[61] Indonesia had been experiencing numerous bomb attacks. Notable attacks occurred in Bali in October 2002 and in Jakarta at the J.W. Marriot Hotel in August 2003.

deadly attack in Bali. The basis for the challenge was that the Anti-Terrorism Law cannot be applied retroactively.[62] It was argued that the retroactive application of the Anti-Terrorism Law contradicted the Constitution which states that a person has the right not to be tried under a law with retroactive effect.[63]

On 23 July 2004 the Constitutional Court gave its decision that the retroactive principle in the Anti-Terrorism Law violated the Constitution. Five out of nine judges agreed while the other four were against. The Constitutional Court argued that since acts of terrorism do not constitute international crimes, or 'gross violation of human rights', the retroactive principle may not be applied.

The decision raised controversy among Indonesians. Some were concerned that the ruling could lead to the acquittals of those convicted in the Bali bombing. But others felt that the Constitutional Court decided correctly. The government is of the opinion that, despite the Constitutional Court's ruling, those convicted of the Bali bombings will not be automatically released. It remains to be seen whether the Constitutional Court decision will be used by those convicted as new evidence prompting their release or, alternatively, whether the Supreme Court will annul its decision based on the Constitutional Court's ruling. As of October 2004, there has not been any legal action by lawyers for those convicted in the Bali bombings.

The Attorney General's Office has decided to follow the Constitutional Court ruling and charge those who have not been convicted of the Bali bombings with other crimes. For example, Abu Bakar Ba'asyir will not be charged in relation to the Bali bombings based on the Anti-Terrorism Law. Instead, the Attorney General's Office will use the Anti-Terrorism Law to charge him with masterminding the J. W. Marriot Hotel bombing which occurred after the Anti-Terrorism Law was promulgated.

IV. The Kuningan bombing

Despite the Anti-Terrorism Law and after two noted terrorist bombing incidents in Bali and Jakarta, on 9 September 2004 Indonesia experienced another huge bomb blast. The bomb was targeted at the Australian Embassy located in the Kuningan area, South Jakarta. Although no Australian Embassy personnel died, the blast killed 11 people and injured more than 150.

The government condemned the terrorist act and people deplored the attack. The police were quick to react. Within a few days they revealed that

---

[62] 'Court reviewing law on terror', *The Jakarta Post*, 21 January 2004, available at http://www.thejakartapost.com/yesterdaydetail.asp?fileid=20040121.C06.

[63] Constitution, art. 28 (I) (1) which provides as follows: 'The rights to life, freedom from torture, freedom of thought and conscience, freedom of religion, freedom from enslavement, recognition as a person before the law, and the right not to be tried under a law with retroactive effect are all human rights that cannot be limited under any circumstances.'

the bomb had been detonated by a suicide bomber. The police have arrested persons suspected of having involvement in the attack. The police, however, have not been successful in capturing the most wanted suspects, Dr Azahari bin Husin and Noordin Mohammed Top, both Malaysian nationals.

V. Further amendment

Currently there are preparations to amend the Anti-Terrorism Law.[64] The Ministry of Law and Human Rights which has responsibility for preparing the draft amendment has made some proposed revisions. Revisions include providing that the sale of bomb materials be considered an act of terrorism punishable by up to fifteen years' imprisonment. Persons who know about a terrorism act but who do not report it could also be jailed for up to fifteen years. Persons who become a member of an organization that has the intention to commit acts of terrorism could also receive jail terms of three to fifteen years. This proposed offence would include wearing clothes associating a person with the organization. Those who plan acts of terrorism, whether they occur or not, could also be punished by death or three to fifteen years of imprisonment under the proposed amendments. The amendments also propose that officers of an organization can be held responsible for terrorist acts committed by the organization.

The rules of procedure would also be revised. A person suspected of acts of terrorism could be detained longer that at present, up to 120 days. Investigators would be allowed to detain any person suspected of terrorism based on sufficient preliminary evidence for up to 30 days without notifying the detainee of his status as a suspect. Police would also have more power to arrest suspects. In addition, investigators may open, examine and seize letters and goods sent by post and eavesdrop based on sufficient preliminary evidence.

The proposed amendments have received fierce criticism from human rights proponents and some law professors, on the basis that they have the potential to violate human rights. To take one example: the criminal rule of procedure provides that a person can be arrested for a day, but the prevailing Anti-Terrorism Law has extended this period to seven days and the amendments would further extend it to thirty days. There are also concerns that fishermen may be suspected of acts of terrorism because they commonly use small detonators to fish.

VI. Conclusion

The enactment of the Anti-Terrorism Law has not prevented Indonesia from being a target of national and international terrorist attacks. Implementation

---

[64] 'Revisi UU Antiteroris Potensial Langgar HAM (Revision to Anti-Terrorism Law has Potential to Violate Human Rights)', *Kompas*, 31 October 2004.

and enforcement of Anti-Terrorism Law has not been an easy task. The fact that combating terrorism is led by Western countries has caused the Indonesian public to be suspicious. Debate has shifted from fighting terrorist acts to concerns that Western countries are undermining Indonesia's sovereignty.

The Anti-Terrorism Law gives legitimacy to law enforcement agencies that use legal measures different from those available for other criminal offences. Moreover, it imposes severe sanctions on those who commit acts of terrorism. Yet the Anti-Terrorism Law has not been effective in eradicating terrorist acts in Indonesia. The threat of severe sanctions including the death penalty will not deter those who believe they are fighting a *jihad* that will reward them a place in heaven. Those with such beliefs will go anywhere in Indonesia or elsewhere for the opportunity to die in a holy war.

The problem of terrorism in Indonesia runs deeper than promulgating a law to combat terrorism. Terrorism for Indonesia is a complex and multifaceted issue. The government has taken firm actions supported by the majority of the people. Nevertheless, these actions have yet to satisfy countries such as the US and Australia whose nationals are threatened. Facing the Indonesian condition and context it would be relatively difficult for any government in Indonesia to combat terrorism. It should be understood that Indonesia's challenge in combating terrorism is different from that faced by the US or Australia.

15

The Philippines: the weakest link in the fight against terrorism?

H. HARRY L. ROQUE, JR.

Terrorism has become a franchise. Its manufacturers had astutely recognized early on that the southern part of the Philippines is an ideal market. The Philippines is not a very large country but it has played a significant role in the spread of terrorism even beyond the boundaries of Asia. The country's location, history and geopolitics offered an ideal breeding ground for terrorism to spread. The same factors that made it attractive to terrorists, however, offer significant potentials that could be tapped by the Philippine authorities to make the country play an equally significant role in the fight against terrorism.[1] To make this happen, it is important that the government of the Philippines acknowledges the true extent of the problem within its boundaries, proclaims a commensurate policy and exhibits true political will.

While the rest of the countries in the region are busy apprehending and trying suspected terrorists, the Philippines achieved unprecedented embarrassment when one of the region's most wanted terrorists, Indonesian Fathur Roman Al Ghozi, escaped from the national headquarters of the Philippine National Police.[2] Al Ghozi was suspected of masterminding the 30 December 2001 bombing of a commuter train that resulted in the death of more than fifty individuals.[3]

Al Ghozi was subsequently killed following a massive manhunt[4] but his escape highlighted the Philippines' weakness when it comes to dealing with

---

[1] The Philippines was colonized by Spain despite the country's lack of economic promise as it was thought to be a valuable stepping stone to China and Japan. The Philippines was also intended to be Spain's base for conquest of neighbouring nations. It was also a transshipment base for regular trade between Mexico and China through the galleon trade. See Renato Constantino, *The Philippines: A Past Revisited* (Quezon City, Tala Publishing, 1975), 56–57.

[2] See 'Al-Ghozi had "walked out" to escape from police camp', *The Nation*, 14 October 2003 http://www.inq7.net/nat/2003/oct/14/text/nat_7-1-p.htm.

[3] Maria Ressa, *Seeds Of Terror: An Eyewitness Account Of Al -Qaeda's Newest Center Of Operations In Southeast Asia* (New York, Free Press, 2003), at 134–135.

[4] See 'Profile: Fathur Rohman al-Ghozi', 13 October 2003, *BBC News*, http://news.bbc.co.uk/2/hi/asia-pacific/3064345.stm.

terrorism: there is an official policy[5] but it is lacking when it comes to implementation and sustainability.

The escape of one of Asia's most wanted terrorists was not an isolated incident of negligence or complicity. During the two incidents when foreigners were kidnapped, repeated news reports cited the complicity of officials with terrorists.[6] Hostages themselves alluded to high-ranking military officials demanding their share of the ransom pie.[7] Certainly, Manila's failure to conduct an impartial investigation into these complaints created the perception that, in addition to failing to have a workable and credible national policy against terrorism, some of the country's policy-makers and high ranking officials may in fact be part of the problem.

I. The Philippines and terrorism

The Philippines is no stranger to terrorism. Even before 9/11, it figured in the global news for the abduction of no less than twenty European tourists from a high-end dive resort in Sipadan, Malaysia.[8] The kidnapping happened on a Malaysian island but the victims were brought to Mindanao in the Philippines. The culprit was the Abu Sayyaf, a group that exhorted Islamic fundamentalism at the same time that it was engaged in kidnapping for ransom, beheading, and bombing of public places.[9]

Prior to the Sipadan hostage taking, the Abu Sayyaf was involved in the bombing and pillage of Ipil town, in the Province of Zamboanga, in Mindanao.[10] Two years later, the Abu Sayyaf made the headlines again for the kidnapping of tourists from another high-end resort. This time the

---

[5] The Philippine policy on terrorism is contained in Memorandum Order No. 37 dated 12 October 2001 signed by President Gloria Macapagal-Arroyo. It is referred to as the 'Fourteen Pillars versus Terrorism'. These are: (1) Supervision and Implementation of Government Policies and Actions of the Government against Terrorism, (2) Intelligence, (3) Strengthen Internal Focus against Terrorism, (4) Accountability of Public and Private Corporations, (5) Synchronize Internal Efforts with Global Outlook, (6) Legal Measures, (7) Christian Muslim Solidarity, (8) Vigilance against Movement of Terrorism, (9) Contingency Planning, (10) Security Plan, (11) Support to Overseas Filipino Workers, (12) Modernization of the Armed Forces and the Police, (13) Seek Media Support, and (14) Political, Social and Economic Measures.

[6] See 'Negotiator says Aventajado wanted ransom cut', 12 December 2003, *Inquirer News Service*, http://www.inq7.net/nat/2003/dec/13/nat_3-1.htm.

[7] Gracia Burnham (with Dean Merrill), *In the Presence of My Enemies* (Wheaton, Tyndale House, 2003), at 223.

[8] See 'Libya and the Jolo Hostages', 20 August 2000, *ICT*, http://www.ict.org.il/articles/articledet.cfm?articleid=126.

[9] For a history of the Abu Sayyaf, see Marites Vitug and Glenda Gloria, *Under The Crescent Moon: Rebellion In Mindanao* (Quezon City, Ateneo Center for Social Policy and Public Affairs; Institute for Popular Democracy, 2000), 235–6.

[10] See http://www.mahk.com/sc1522.htm.

kidnapping happened on the Philippine island of Palawan. The equation had changed for a government that had been a long-time American ally. For the first time the Abu Sayaff kidnapped American nationals: Christian missionaries Martin and Gracia Burnham and Guillermo Sobero.[11]

The Philippine government was quick to publicly denounce the Abu Sayyaf and to announce a policy of no ransom and no negotiations with terrorist groups on both kidnappings.[12] This was lip service.

In the Sipadan incident, the German publication *Der Speigel* alleged that no less than the chief hostage negotiator, Roberto Aventajado, a member of then President Joseph Estrada's cabinet, was heard on a satellite telephone conversation intercepted by German authorities as 'haggling for a sizeable amount of the ransom' paid by the Libyan government to effect the release of the hostages.[13] Aventajado would later deny this vehemently in a book that would be published in 2003.[14] To date, however, Aventajado has not demanded a public apology or initiated a libel suit against the German publication.

In another hostage taking incident that occurred earlier, one victim narrated an incident when she overheard a conversation between the bandits and an official of the armed forces of the Philippines regarding the schedule of a future military initiative against the bandits.[15] The incident is only one of a number of reports that confirm the collusion between the Philippine military and the bandit group.

A more graphic first hand account would be provided later by Gracia Burnham, the only one of the three American hostages who survived the incident. She wrote a book about her experience. In one instance she recalled a conversation between her captors and, apparently, someone from the Philippine military talking about splitting the ransom paid by private groups to effect their release.[16] She also narrated how she and her captors would rendezvous with military appointed liaisons for the sale of arms to the bandit group coming from the armoury of the armed forces of the Philippines.[17] Philippine authorities later disputed Burnham's allegations. There was a

---

[11] Burnham, *My Enemies*, at 1–20.
[12] See '"My Conscience is Clear" Aventajado on the hostage negotiations', *Asiaweek*, 29 September 2000, http://www.asiaweek.com/asiaweek/magazine/2000/0929/nat.phil. aventajado.html.
[13] See 'Ransom for Jolo hostages went to politicians', *Der Spiegel*, 11 December 2000. http://babel.altavista.com/babelfish/urltrurl?lp=de_en&url=http%3a%2f%2fwww.spiegel. de%2 fspiegel%2fvorab%2f0,1518,107009,00.html.
[14] Roberto Aventajado, *140 Days of Terror in the Clutches of the Abu Sayyaf* (Pasig City, Philippines, Anvil Publishing, 2003), 104–10. It was also stated that $25 million was paid to release the Sipadan hostages (at 195).
[15] Jose Torres, Jr., *Into the Mountains: Hostaged by the Abu Sayaff* (Manila, Claretian Publications, 2001), at 33.
[16] Burnham, *My Enemies*, at 223. [17] Ibid. at 150.

public outcry in the Philippines following the publication of Burnham's book. No less than Acting Justice Secretary Merceditas Gutierrez flew to the US to see Burnham, only to be told that there had been in fact many other incidents that she had chosen to omit in the book.

Five days after the Burnham abduction there was an incident that best corroborated the reports about the collusion. On 1 June 2002, an irate President Gloria Macapagal-Arroyo, fresh from her assumption of the Presidency, ordered an all out military attack on the Abu Sayyaf whose members had been sighted in Lamitan. It was curious that despite the red alert status following the abduction, the bandits were able to transfer their hostages from Palawan to Basilan, 'dodging' military checkpoints in the process.[18] There was a heavy firefight between the military and the bandits. The bandits took their victims to a hospital at the centre of the Lamitan town. No less than 3000 military personnel were involved in the encounter. Helicopters were deployed to the town and all possible exits from it were sealed. The hardware was enough to convince any observer that the Palawan hostage taking would end swiftly afterwards. To the surprise and condemnation of many people, soldiers guarding the rear end of the hospital were ordered by their superiors to abandon their posts. This gave the bandits an opportunity to leave town with the Americans and the hostages, except for two Filipinos.[19] The police and the civilians refused to leave the area and were left to engage the bandits while the latter made their hurried escape.

An International Peace Mission, reporting on its investigation of the Lamitan siege, reported:

> A few hours before the Abu Sayyaf's escape, Brig. Gen. Romeo Dominguez allegedly met with the family of one of the hostages in a hotel in Zamboanga City. Several hours after the meeting, the general arrived at Lamitan carrying a black briefcase containing bundles of P1000 bills. Asked by a nurse as to when the fighting would end, the general smiled and said, it will end soon .... The General left still carrying the attaché case. When he went back to the hospital, the attaché case was no longer with him but two of the hostages were. Witnesses inside the hospital claimed to have heard conversations among the Abu Sayyaf members signifying the ransom had been paid for two of the hostages. Other witnesses narrated how they tried to warn the soldiers about the kidnappers escape but were ignored .... A captain of the military alleged that everything in the Lamitan siege was scripted. As early as two days before the incident, he was already instructed to handle hostage crisis in Lamitan, hinting that his superiors knew what was going to happen beforehand. When they reached Lamitan, most of them were not issued firearms. Upon reaching the scene of the fight, they were left defenseless and three of his men were

---

[18] Basilan: The Next Afghanistan?: The International Peace Mission Report, at 17. See also Burnham, *My Enemies*, at 79–92.

[19] Ibid.

killed .... What happened in Lamitan in June last year, based on collated testimonies of witnesses who have no motive to lie and who are endangering their own lives by speaking is credible: Ranking leaders of the military and the local government facilitated the payment of ransom to the Abu Sayyaf in exchange for the freedom of some of the hostages. A general received a brief-case full of cash from the family of a hostage, gave it to the Abu Sayyaf, and ordered his troops to let the kidnap group escape.[20]

Understandably, the Philippine Government was quick to criticize the fore-going findings of the International Peace Mission. Former National Security Adviser Roilo Golez, said the mission members were people of 'doubtful credentials' and 'imported military bashers'.[21] Despite such stinging criti-cism, the Administration was rebuffed by its own Senate. After conducting an investigation on the Lamitan incident, the Philippines Senate gave credence to the International Peace Mission report when it concluded that there was 'strong circumstantial evidence to support the allegation of collusion'.[22] Despite the Senate's call on the President and the Ombudsman to prosecute those behind the Lamitan collusion, none of them have been charged; the highest-ranking general involved in the incident was even promoted.[23]

II. The Abu Sayyaf and the Burnhams

Literally, Abu Sayyaf means 'bearer of the sword'.[24] It is a splinter group of the Moro National Liberation Front (MNLF), a group that seeks Muslim autonomy in the Philippines. The MNLF has signed a peace agreement with the government, but another secessionist group, the Moro Islamic Liberation Front (MILF), continues its campaign for an independent Mindanao. The story of the Abu Sayyaf mirrors the rise and fall from American favour of other extremist groups such as the Taliban regime in Afghanistan. Abduragak Abubakar Janjalani founded the Abu Sayaff. Janjalani is a Muslim who

---

[20] Ibid. at 18.
[21] Carlito Pablo, 'Golez hits Foreign Intervention', *Philippine Daily Inquirer*, 26 March 2002
[22] Senate Committee Report No.72 dated 19 August 2002, p. 44
[23] The Senate Committee on Defense, headed by Sen. Ramon Magsaysay, Jr. recommended that 'the Department of Justice and/or Ombudsman, continue the investigation on the charge of collusion between the Abu Sayyaf and high ranking military officials, including Maj. Gen. Romeo Dominguez, former chief of the 1st Infantry Division; Gen. Jovenal Narcise, former chief of the 103rd Infantry Brigade; and Maj. Eliseo Campued, executive officer of the 18th Infantry Battalion'. The same finding was arrived at by investigators from the Army Inspector Investigators Office. See 'AFP chief blamed for Basilan fiasco', *Philippine Headline News Online*, 10 September 2001, http://www.newsflash.org/2001/09/hl/hl014277.htm. Gen. Romeo Dominguez was later given a second star. See *Philippine Headline News Online*, 17 August 2002, http://www.newsflash.org/2002/08/hl/hl016296.htm.
[24] Tolin, 'The Response of the Philippines Government and the Role of AFP in Addressing Terrorism', National Defense College of the Philippines, p. 3 (unpublished manuscript).

trained in Afghanistan and fought against the Russians side by side with the then American supported Talibans.[25] Janjalani started as a staunch critic of the MNLF's decision to sign a peace treaty with the Manila government. To diffuse his criticisms, he was sent to study in Libya where he instead continued his criticisms of the MNLF. Upon his return to Mindanao he recruited from the ranks of dissatisfied members of the MNLF to form the Abu Sayaff which, he claimed, would wage the true '*jihad*'.[26]

Ideologically, it is unclear where the Abu Sayyaf stands. In fact it is difficult to classify the group for the purpose of applying international humanitarian law. Although it has made pronouncements that it is for an independent Islamic state of Mindanao, its very limited membership, its resort to prohibited means and methods of warfare,[27] and torture, would render it ineligible to become a combatant group either for purposes of the Geneva Convention or the latter's optional protocols.[28] At the same time, some believe that normative considerations dictate that international humanitarian law should be made applicable to the group in order to provide the legal basis for the exercise of universal jurisdiction against its members. Foreign courts have in fact exercised universal jurisdiction against members of the Abu Sayyaf for breaches of Common Article Three of the Geneva Conventions.[29]

The Philippine government initially treated the group as nothing more than common criminals. When the military repeatedly failed to rescue the American couple, the government revised its policy and labelled the Abu Sayyaf as part of an international network of terror groups to justify the operation of US troops in Philippine territory. This deployment of foreign troops to fight the Abu Sayyaf, partly owing to the Philippine military's collusion with the rogue group, has been the only effective means by which the Philippines has dealt with the problem of terrorism, albeit one which was beset with constitutional infirmities.

The Burnham abduction did get substantial media coverage in the mainstream American press. And expectedly, after 9/11, a connection was soon made between the 'war against terror' as the proper response to the bombing of the World Trade Center in New York, and the need to wage the same war in other parts of the world where American interests were imperilled. It was

---

[25] Vitug and Gloria, *Crescent Moon*, at 213.   [26] Ibid. at 205.
[27] Such as taking of hostage for ransom, wilful killing (even beheading) of civilians. See the prohibitions found in Common Article Three, Geneva Conventions. Additional protocol II provides that IHL shall be applicable if, *inter alia*, the combatant engaged in an armed conflict against a state is able to implement provisions of the protocol.
[28] 1977 Additional Protocol II Art. 1.1
[29] See 'COMM other Robot is before German court', *Der Spiegel*, 16 December 2003, http://babel.altavista.com/babelfish/urltrurl ?lp=de_en& url=http%3a%2f%2fwww.spiegel.de%2fpanorama% 2f0,1518,278589,00.html.

expected that the second leg of the so-called war against terror was going to be brought onto the shores of the Philippines.[30]

There was, however, a legal obstacle. The Philippines' new Constitution, crafted and ratified after the ouster of the Marcos dictatorship,[31] specifically banned the presence of foreign troops in Philippine territory, unless it is covered by a treaty duly concurred in by the Senate of the Philippines.[32] There was thus a need to find a legal basis for American involvement and the solution was found in the Mutual Defense Treaty and the Visiting Forces Agreement between the US and the Philippines. The Mutual Defense Treaty of 1951[33] between the Philippines and the United States, crafted at the height of the Cold War, provides that either party may seek the other party's help in the case of an 'external armed attack.' Article III of the Treaty provides:

> The Parties, through their Foreign Ministers or their deputies, will consult together from time to time regarding the implementation of this Treaty and whenever in the opinion of either of them the territorial integrity, political independence or security of either of the Parties is threatened by an external 'armed attack' in the Pacific ... [t]hey shall declare publicly their sense of unity and their common determination to defend themselves against external armed attack, so that no potential aggressor could be under the illusion that either of them stands alone in the Pacific area.

The Visiting Forces Agreement (VFA),[34] on the other hand, defines the status of Visiting American Forces in the country whenever they are on Philippines territory in connection with the conduct of joint military exercises.

President Arroyo invoked the Mutual Defense Treaty and the VFA to authorize a joint military exercise which became known as 'Balikatan 02-1'. Unlike other military exercises, this *Balikatan* was unique because it involved an alleged war exercise in an actual battlefield: the jungles of Basilan and Zamboanga, where the Americans were held by the Abu Sayyaf. In order to circumvent the constitutional ban on the presence of American troops which was obviously intended as a rescue mission, the Terms of Reference (TOR) of the military exercise described it as: 'a mutual counter terrorism advising,

---

[30] 'US Senator says RP Next Afghanistan', *Philippine Daily Inquirer*, 18 January 2000.
[31] Historians credit the survival of the Marcos regime to US support. In turn, this support was given because of the American desire to continue its military presence in the Philippines. The US then maintained its biggest military facilities outside of mainland United States in the Philippines, most noteworthy of which were Clark Airbase in Pampanga and Subic Naval base in Zambales. See Renato Constantino and and Letizia R. Constantino, *The Philippines: A Continuing Past* (Quezon City, Foundation for Nationalist Studies, 1978).
[32] Art. XVIII, Section 25, 1987 Constitution.
[33] See Mutual Defence Treaty, http://www.chanrobles.com/mutualdefensetreaty.htm #MUTUAL%20DEFENSE%20TREATY.
[34] See the Visiting Forces Agreement, http://www.dfa.gov.ph/vfa/frame/frmvfa.htm.

assenting and training exercise relative to Philippine efforts against the Abu Sayyaf Group'.[35] The TOR also provided that 'US exercise participants shall not engage in combat, without prejudice to their right of self defense'.[36] Consequently, the United States sent a total of 660 military personnel to the Philippines, a first since the United States closed its military bases in the country in 1991. Of these numbers, 167 special operatives were sent to the jungles of Basilan ostensibly to rescue the Burnham spouses.[37]

On 1 February 2002, two members of the Philippine Bar, Arthur D. Lim and Paulino P. Ersando filed a petition for certiorari and prohibition, attacking the constitutionality of the joint exercise, arguing that the exercises contravened the spirit and intent of the VFA. They were joined subsequently by Sanlakas and Partido Ng Manggagawa, both party-list organizations, which filed a petition-in-intervention on 11 February 2002.

The Supreme Court disposed of the issue of whether 'Balikatan 02-1' is covered by the VFA by citing Section 3 of the Vienna Convention on the Law of Treaties, which contained provisions on the interpretation of international agreements.[38] The Supreme Court noted that the VFA permitted United States personnel to engage, on an impermanent basis, in activities in the Philippines during war exercises, the exact meaning of which was left undefined. The High Court said the expression was ambiguous, permitting a wide scope of undertakings subject only to the approval of the Philippine government. But the Supreme Court said that, based on the Vienna Convention, the cardinal rule of interpretation must involve an examination of the text, which is presumed to verbalize the parties' intentions. Hence, a careful reading of the TOR would arrive at the conclusion that it rightly fell within the context of the VFA. It declared:

> After studied reflection, it appeared farfetched that the ambiguity surrounding the meaning of the word 'activities' arose from accident. In our view, it was deliberately made that way to give both parties a certain leeway in negotiation ... In this manner, visiting US forces may sojourn in Philippine territory for purposes other than military. As conceived, the joint exercises may include training on new techniques of patrol and surveillance to protect the nation's marine resources, sea search-and-rescue operations to assist vessels in distress, disaster relief operations, civic action projects such as the building of school houses, medical and humanitarian missions, and the like.[39]

---

[35] Cited in the dissenting opinion of Mr Justice Kapunan, in *Arthur D. Lim and Paulino R. Ersando v. Honorable Executive Secretary as alter ego of Her Excellency Gloria Macapagal-Arroyo, and Honorable Angelo Reyes in his capacity as Secretary of National Defense* (G.R. No. 151445. 11 April 2002), p. 2

[36] Ibid.

[37] See 'Row grows over U.S. troops in the Philippines', 24 January 2002, *CNN.com*, http://edition.cnn.com/2002/WORLD/asiapcf/southeast/01/24/philippines.us/.

[38] See Section 3 – Interpretation Of Treaties, Articles 31 and 32.

[39] Above note 35, majority opinion at 6.

It further held:

> Under these auspices, the VFA gives legitimacy to the current Balikatan exercises. It is only logical to assume that Balikatan 02-1, a mutual anti-terrorism advising, assisting and training exercise, falls under the umbrella of sanctioned or allowable activities in the context of the agreement. Both the history and intent of the Mutual Defense Treaty and the VFA support the conclusion that combat-related activities – as opposed to combat itself – such as the one subject of the instant petition, are indeed authorized.[40]

But on the second issue of the constitutionality of allowing US troops on Philippine soil under the new arrangement, the Supreme Court demurred. First, it asked itself, granting that 'Balikatan 02-1' is permitted under the terms of the VFA, what may US forces legitimately do in furtherance of their aim to provide advice, assistance and training in the global effort against terrorism? The Court said:

> Differently phrased, may American troops actually engage in combat in Philippine territory? In our considered opinion, neither the MDT nor the VFA allow foreign troops to engage in an offensive war on Philippine territory.[41]

The Supreme Court then said the Mutual Defense Treaty and the Visiting Forces Agreement, as with all other treaties and international agreements to which the Philippines is a party, must be read in the context of the 1987 Constitution. In particular, the Mutual Defense Treaty was concluded way before the present Charter, though it nevertheless remained in effect as a valid source of international obligation. It noted that the present Constitution contained key provisions useful in determining the extent to which foreign military troops are allowed in Philippine territory, in particular in the Declaration of Principles and State Policies,[42] and its provisions regulating the foreign relations powers of the Chief Executive when it provided that '[n]o treaty or international agreement shall be valid and effective unless concurred in by at least two-thirds of all the members of the Senate'.[43] Even more pointedly, the Supreme Court noted that the Transitory Provisions of the 1987 Charter also stated:

---

[40] Ibid. [41] Ibid.
[42] Citing the following provisions in the 1987 Charter: Sec. 2. – The Philippines renounces war as an instrument of national policy, adopts the generally accepted principles of international law as part of the law of the land and adheres to the policy of peace, equality, justice, freedom, cooperation, and amity with all nations. Sec. 7. – The State shall pursue an independent foreign policy. In its relations with other states the paramount considera-tion shall be national sovereignty, territorial integrity, national interest, and the right to self-determination. Sec. 8. – The Philippines, consistent with the national interest, adopts and pursues a policy of freedom from nuclear weapons in the country.
[43] Sec. 21, Art. VII.

Sec. 25. – After the expiration in 1991 of the Agreement between the Republic of the Philippines and the United States of America concerning Military Bases, foreign military bases, troops or facilities shall not be allowed in the Philippines except under a treaty duly concurred in by the Senate and, when the Congress so requires, ratified by a majority of the votes cast by the people in a national referendum held for that purpose, and recognized as a treaty by the other contracting state.[44]

The Philippine Constitution, said the Supreme Court:

> betrays a marked antipathy towards foreign military presence in the country, or of foreign influence in general. Hence, foreign troops are allowed entry into the Philippines only by way of direct exception. Conflict arises then between the fundamental law and our obligations arising from international agreements.[45]

It then discussed the relation of international law vis-à-vis municipal law in Philippine jurisprudence – that is, whether the High Court may invalidate a treaty on the ground of unconstitutionality – by citing the case of *Philip Morris, Inc.* v. *Court of Appeals*, where the court held that:

> Withal, the fact that international law has been made part of the law of the land does not by any means imply the primacy of international law over national law in the municipal sphere. Under the doctrine of incorporation as applied in most countries, rules of international law are given a standing equal, not superior, to national legislation.[46]

It also cited the case *Ichong* v. *Hernandez*,[47] where the High Court ruled that the provisions of a treaty are always subject to qualification or amendment by a subsequent law, or to the police power of the state, and the case of *Gonzales* v. *Hechanova*,[48] where it made the declaration that:

> As regards the question whether an international agreement may be invalidated by our courts, suffice it to say that the Constitution of the Philippines has clearly settled it in the affirmative, by providing, in Section 2 of Article VIII thereof, that the Supreme Court may not be deprived 'of its jurisdiction to review, revise, reverse, modify, or affirm on appeal, certiorari, or writ of error as the law or the rules of court may provide, final judgments and decrees of inferior courts in – (1) All cases in which the constitutionality or validity of any treaty, law, ordinance, or executive order or regulation is in question.' In other words, our Constitution authorizes the nullification of a treaty, not only when it conflicts with the fundamental law, but, also, when it runs counter to an act of Congress.[49]

---

[44] CONST. (1987) Art. XVIII.   [45] Above note 35 at 8.
[46] 224 SCRA 577 (1993).   [47] G.R. No. L-7995, 101 PHIL 1155 (1957).
[48] G.R. No. L-21897, 9 SCRA 230 (1963).   [49] Ibid.

The Supreme Court thus unequivocally declared that the Constitution prohibits the deployment of foreign combatants in the Philippine territory. However, it refused to declare the Balikatan as unconstitutional on the ground that a determination of whether or not the American troops were in Mindanao exclusively for war exercises or for the purpose of rescuing the Burnhams involved a decision on an issue of fact which it 'understandably loathed to do'.[50]

Gracia Burnham was later rescued but her husband died during the operation.[51] American operatives later allegedly killed Commander Abu Sabaya, a central figure in the Palawan hostage taking.[52] It was never mentioned in reports that the killing was done in 'self defence'.

Quite apart from its notoriety, what is even more disturbing is the persistent belief that the Abu Sayyaf was a creation of no less than the armed forces of the Philippines. MILF leaders insist that the Abu Sayyaf is the creation of the armed forces of the Philippines and/or the US Central Intelligence Agency in order to discredit the Muslim secessionist movement and to stop the peace talks between the government and the MILF. MILF leaders are always quick to point out that one of the group's founders, Edward Angeles, was a police agent.[53] This point was given credence by two of the Philippines' top investigative journalists:

> Exactly how the Abu Sayyaf was formed is a question for which neither the military nor Janjalani has a solid answer. The group remains as nebulous as its beginnings, and as shadowy as its charismatic founder. There is absolutely no doubt that it has been infiltrated by the military. What is uncertain is whether or not Janjalani, who was admired by many in the Muslim community, formed the Abu Sayyaf precisely to work for the military or if he had simply lost control over his own men.[54]

III. Lessons from Lamitan and the Burnhams

There are lessons to be learned from the Lamitan incident and the US military operations that led to the rescue of Gracia Burnham. First, some Philippine officials at the time of the kidnapping actively became part of the problem and even prolonged it to suit their own agenda. Secondly, the government was not able to deal with this kind of terrorism and was quick to run to its

---

[50] Above note 35 at 10. [51] Burnham, *My Enemies*, at 251–66.

[52] See 'Search for Abu Sayyaf leader's body', 22 June 2002, *Cnn.com*, http://www.cnn.com/2002/WORLD/asiapcf/southeast/06/21/philippines.rebel/.

[53] Eric Gutierrez, 'New Faces of Violence in Muslim Mindanao', in Kristina Gaerlan and Mara Stankovitch (eds.), *Rebels, Warlords, and Ulama: Reader on Muslim Separatism and the War in Southern Philippines* (Quezon City, Institute for Popular Democracy, 2000), at 234.

[54] Vitug and Gloria, *Crescent Moon*, at 210–11.

former colonizer and continuing ally, the United States, for assistance. The government may have been able to justify American military intervention in the Burnham incident, but there must be doubt as to what it could have done if American nationals had not been involved. The Mutual Defense Treaty and the Visiting Forces Agreement cannot be a satisfactory substitute for a genuine and comprehensive policy against terror groups.

It is also disturbing how Philippine policy-makers were quick to tap opportunities offered by the United States' global 'War Against Terror' to address its festering and decades-old problems with local communist groups, while ignoring threats from Muslim extremist groups. The Philippine government lobbied for the inclusion of the Communist Party of the Philippines (CPP) and its military arm, the New Peoples Army (NPA) as 'terror groups' within the meaning of the US Patriot Act.[55] The European Union followed suit.[56] As a result, the founder and head of the CPP-National Democratic Front (CPP-NDF), the political arm of the CPP, Jose Maria Sison, may soon be deported back into the Philippines from his exile in the Netherlands. Prior to his classification as a terrorist, the CPP-NPA founder was an asylum seeker in Utrecht under the 1951 Convention on Refugees.

The government has refused to seek this option against the Moro Islamic Liberation Front despite evidence linking the group with both the Jemaah Islamiah (JI) and the Al Qaeda network. The link is far from tenuous. In her book 'Seeds of Terror', CNN correspondent Maria Ressa cited intelligence reports and wrote that JI and al Qaeda have been training combatants in MILF military camps.[57] According to Ressa, the Philippine government has deliberately turned a blind eye to this evidence.[58] The involvement, in terms of al Qaeda in the Philippines, goes beyond maintaining training camps in MILF lairs. In 1995, Philippine policemen uncovered an al Qaeda cell intending to assassinate the Pope who was going to visit. Abdul Hakkim Murad, a Pakistani, was arrested. During his interrogation, Murad admitted to his participation in the 1993 bombing of the World Trade Center. His confession led to the arrest in Pakistan of the alleged mastermind, Ramzi Ahmed Yousef. Murad and Yousef have been tried and found of guilty of perpetrating the 1991 World Trade Center bombing. They are serving life sentences in New York.[59]

Familial ties link al Qaeda and the Abu Sayyaf. Muhammad Jamal Khalifa, a brother-in-law of Osama bin Laden, provided financial support to Abu Sayyaf's founder, Abdukurak Janjalani, to go on a pilgrimage to Mecca and on trips to Syria, Afghanistan, and Pakistan. It was in one of the trips financed

---

[55] See 'Powell declares CPP-NPA "foreign terrorists"', 10 August 2002, *Minda News*, http://www.mindanews.com/2002/08/3rd/nws10terror.html.
[56] See http://www.dfa.gov.ph/news/pr/pr2002/oct/pr240.htm.
[57] Ressa, *Seeds Of Terror*, at 7–8.   [58] Ibid. at 15.   [59] Ibid. at 32–40.

by Khalifa to Afghanistan that Janjalani met Abdul Rasul Sayyaf, the Muhajadeen leader of the resistance against Russians in Afghanistan. Janjalani named his group after this person.[60] Intelligence reports also indicated that it was Osama Bin Laden who introduced Janjalani to Ramzi Yousef.[61] No less than twenty members of the Abu Sayyaf allegedly graduated from al Qaeda training camps.[62]

Despite President Gloria Macapagal-Arroyo's continuing dismissal of evidence available as early as 2001,[63] the recent arrest of an Egyptian national who confessed to have trained al Qaeda operatives within MILF camps in Mindanao now confirms the link between al Qaeda and a 'faction' of the MILF.[64] Despite this validation, the Philippines still has not asked the United States and Europe to classify the MILF as a terrorist group. The avowed reason why President Arroyo has not asked for the inclusion of the MILF in the American list of terror groups is her stubborn insistence that the MILF is a purely domestic issue. According to her, by dealing with the MILF militarily and politically, despite its links with al Qaeda, 'we can get them to understand that they must break all links – if any – with terrorist groups, and that there is more life for their people, who are of course, our people, if they go on the road of peace talks'.[65] Ressa though believes there are more convincing reasons:

> In one Southeast Asian country after another, I witnessed a level of denial from political leaders who did not even admit that there was a threat. There were several reasons: acknowledging the threat required action; sometimes, leaders were afraid of its impact on terrorism; other times, officials had different priorities and terrorism didn't seem like an unmanageable problem.[66]

The lack of a genuine policy against terrorism explains why the Philippines does not have any special laws against terrorism.[67] The Philippines adopts the American form of government where powers are vested in three co-equal branches: the executive, the legislative, and the courts. This system allows the President to ask Congress to act with dispatch on bills duly certified by it as urgent. The President usually officially conveys her legislative agenda to

---

[60] Ibid. at 100. [61] Ibid. at 101. [62] Ibid. at 109. [63] Ibid. at 15
[64] See 'Arrested Al-Qaeda suspect links terror group to MILF', 3 June 2004, AFP, http://www.inq7.net/brk/2004/jun/03/text/brkpol_19-1-p.htm.
[65] Ressa, Seeds Of Terror, at 16. [66] Ibid.
[67] The failure to legislate an anti-terror law was described as 'a weak link in anti-terror law enforcement efforts', see Ma. Cristina E. Cruz, et al., 'The Need For A Responsive Terrorism Prevention Legislation', p. 2 A, Confidential National Security Advisory Paper, Office of the President, Policy and Strategy Office, National Security Council, a copy of which is deposited with the Institute of International Legal Studies (IILS), UP Law Center.

Congress in the annual State of the Nation Address held to open each session of Congress. President Arroyo has never asked Congress to prioritize any measure specifically against terrorism.[68] This omission indicates that as a matter of policy, the Arroyo government has not characterized the passage of a special law against terrorism as being urgent.

Nonetheless, there are pending bills in both Houses of the Philippine Congress addressing modern day terrorism.[69] The daughter of the late dictator Ferdinand Marcos, authored one of the bills.[70] This is ironic because Marcos' twenty-year reign in the Philippines was a classic example of state-sanctioned terrorism.[71] The legislative measures are not identical but they differ on minor points. Substantially, all of them seek to define terrorism by borrowing the definition of the American Patriot Act.[72] The bills also provide penalties for particular types and forms of terrorism. These bills also seek to amend the country's rules of criminal procedure to expand the scope of police power, often to the detriment of universally recognized human rights.

A starting point in an analysis of these pending legislative initiatives is an attempt to define terrorism. And just as the international community has failed to arrive at a universally accepted definition of terrorism,[73] this attempt to legislate a domestic definition of terrorism is likely to derail and prevent the passage of an anti-terrorism law. The Philippines has been dealing with two armed conflicts, both of which may be argued to be in exercise of the right to self-determination. The MILF seeks the secession of Muslim Mindanao from the Republic and the establishment of an independent

---

[68] For the President's State of the Nation remarks on terrorism, see http://www.gov.ph/sona/_04302004_5.asp.
[69] Senate Bill No. 2540 filed in substitution of Senate Bill Numbers 1458, 1980, 2263 and 2296 prepared by the Senate Committee on Public Order.
[70] House Bill 2057 authored by Rep. Imee R. Marcos.
[71] When President Ferdinand Marcos declared Martial Law in 1972 in the Philippines, he unleashed the full might of the state to combat what he claimed to be 'lawless elements' and employed 'state terrorism' to curtail the democratic rights and liberties of the Filipino people. See Sarmiento, 'Terrorism, the Terrors of Anti-Terrorism Bill and Human Rights' in Final Report, Conference on the Proposed Anti-Terrorism and Anti-Terrorist Financing Bill, Institute of Government and Law Reform, University of the Philippines Law Center, October 2002, at 35.
[72] H. R. 3162 'Uniting and Strengthening America Act by Providing Appropriate Tools Required to Intercept and Obstruct Terrorism (USA PATRIOT) Act of 2001'.
[73] See Roque, 'The Changing face of Terrorism: A New Crime Against Humanity?' (Jan-June, 2002), World Bulletin, vol. 18, nos. 1–3, at 30–46; Higgins, 'The General International Law of Terrorism' in Rosalyn Higgins and Maurice Flory (eds.), Terrorism and International Law (London, Routledge, 1997), at 1329; Proust, 'Nonprotected Persons or Things', in Alona E. Evans and John F. Murphy (eds.), Legal Aspects of Terrorism (Lexington Books, 1978), at 341, 367; M. Cherif Bassiouni, 'A Policy Oriented Inquiry of International Terrorism' in Bassiouni (ed.), Legal Responses To International Terrorism (Dordrecht, Nijhoff, 1988), at xviii.

Islamic state;[74] the CPP-NDF seeks the overthrow of the Philippine constitutional institutions in favour of a Maoist state.[75] From the standpoint of both international human rights and humanitarian law, it does not matter if the purposes of the groups are legitimate, or appropriate to the Philippines. International law recognizes the right to self-determination as being not only a fundamental human right, but as a right *ergo omnes* and recognizes no derogations therefrom.[76]

International humanitarian law (IHL), furthermore, does not inquire into the legitimacy of the use of force. Instead, it classifies armed conflicts into international and non-international armed conflicts and provides for non-derogable norms applicable to combatants.[77] There is now substantial authority that under both international and Philippines domestic laws, these norms of IHL are recognized as being *jus cogens*.[78] The Geneva Convention defines an international armed conflict as, among other things, one fought between a state and an armed group in the exercise of the right to self-determination.[79] International human rights law in turn defines the right to self-determination to be the right of a people to choose its form of government, including whether or not such a government shall be independent from any other state, or whether it should be appended to an existing state.[80] Under international law, both the MILF and the NPA are entitled to the status of national liberation movements in the exercise of self-determination. The first flaw of the bills before the Philippines Congress is thus in its definition of terrorism as the 'use or threatened use of serious violence, principally directed against civilians or noncombatants, or against properties with the intention of instilling a common danger, panic, or fear, or of coercing or intimidating the public or the government'.[81] The foregoing definition does not make any exception, even for those acts which are in the exercise of the *ergo omnes* right of self-determination. This would penalize as offences acts of the MILF and the NPA in pursuance of their armed struggle, in contravention of both international humanitarian and human rights law.

---

[74] Ressa, *Seeds Of Terror*, at 367–71.
[75] See http://www.au.af.mil/au/aul/bibs/tergps/tgnew.htm.
[76] *Portugal* v. *Australia*, ICJ Report 1995, p. 102.
[77] See Article 2 and Common Article Three, Geneva Conventions One of 1949. See also Art. 1(4) Optional Protocol 1, 1977.
[78] Barcelona Traction Case, ICJ Report 1970, p. 3; *Kuroda* v. *Jalandoni*, 83 Phil 171 (1948); *Yamashita* v. *Styler* G.R. No. L-129, 19 December 1945.
[79] 1977 Additional Protocol 1, Art. 1 (4).
[80] Article 1, International Covenant on Civil and Political Rights. See also Rosalyn Higgins, *International Law, Problems and Process: International Law and How We Use It* (Oxford, Clarendon Press, 1999), 125.
[81] Sec. 3, SB No. 2540.

Furthermore, the proposed bill, in so far as it purports to amend the existing rules of criminal procedure relating to search and seizure, appears to violate constitutional norms protecting the people from arbitrary search and seizures. Under the Constitution and existing rules, no search may be made unless pursuant to a judicial warrant.[82] The intent of such a seemingly tedious procedure is to safeguard the people's right to be secure against unreasonable searches on the part of agents of the state.[83] The proposed bill seeks to do away with the requirement of a search warrant. In fact, the proposed bill only requires a 'suspicion'[84] on the part of the police that the place to be searched contains terrorist persons or property. This is in spite of the fact that the right to be secure from arbitrary searches is a fundamental human right recognized by the Philippine Constitution and international human rights law.[85] It has even been argued that it is a *jus cogens* right.[86]

The bill also removes the requirement for a warrant of arrest in instances where the existing law would require one.[87] One version of the bill allows the police to detain any person on mere suspicion provided such person is in a ship, aircraft, vehicle or train.[88] Consequently, people may be legally detained on the strength of mere suspicions. As stated by the Supreme Court in the case of *Umil* v. *Ramos*:[89]

> Personal knowledge must have been designed to obviate the practice in the past of warrantless arrests being effected on the basis of or supposed reliance on an information obtained from third persons who merely profess such knowledge, or worse, concocted such reports for variant reasons not necessarily founded on truth.[90]

The proposed measures also allow wiretapping on the basis only of a court application.[91] The existing law requires an examination under oath or affirmation of any witness produced.[92]

No doubt, 9/11 has become a 'turning point of post-modern international law'.[93] The word that best describes the situation is 'backlash'. The reverberations of the American-launched war on terrorism are felt everywhere:

---

[82] CONST. (1987) Art. III.   [83] Stonehill versus Diokno 20 SCRA 383 (1967).
[84] Section 24 (2) Inter-Agency Draft Bill 'An Act Defining the Crime of Terrorism'.
[85] Art. 17, International Covenant on Civil and Political Rights 1966, 999 U.N.T.S. 171; Art. 12 Universal Declaration of Human Rights, G.A. Res. 271 A (III), G.A.O.R., 3rd Session, Part 1, Resn., p. 71.
[86] (1993) 14 H.R.L.J. 370.   [87] Sec. 6, Rule 116, Rules of Criminal Procedure.
[88] Above note 84, s. 24(1).   [89] 203 SCRA 251 (1991).   [90] Ibid. at 296.
[91] Above note 84, s. 23 (1).   [92] Sec. 3, RA 4200.
[93] Baxi, 'Operation Enduring Freedom: Towards a New International Law and Order?' Speech delivered at the Kalinaw-Asian People Speak Up for Peace Conference, University of the Philippines, Diliman, Quezon City, February 9, 2002.

international law scholars and civil libertarians have rung the alarm bells over what they say is the retreat of human rights and established principles of humanitarian law in the face of the new order that the Bush administration and its allies, including President Arroyo, are seeking to carve. Amnesty International charges that the anti-terror war has set back whatever gains the cause of human rights has made in fifty years as governments around the world pass legislation seeking to combat terrorism which curtail many fundamental liberties as well as guarantees for human rights, humanitarian law and international law.[94] The proposed legislation in the Philippines appears to be consistent with this worldwide trend.[95] Perhaps it is best to heed the urgent appeal of the Special Rapporteur to the UN High Commissioner for Human Rights:

> [The Special Rapporteur and Independent Experts] express alarm at the growing threats against human rights, threats that necessitate a renewed resolve to defend and promote these rights. They also note the impact of this environment on the effectiveness and independence of special procedures.
>
> Although they share in the unequivocal condemnation of terrorism, they voice profound concern at the multiplication of policies, legislation and practices increasingly being adopted by many countries in the name of the fight against terrorism which affect negatively the enjoyment of virtually all human rights – civil, cultural, economic, political and social.
>
> They draw attention to the dangers inherent in the indiscriminate use of the term 'terrorism', and the resulting new categories of discrimination. They recall that, in accordance with the International Covenant on Civil and Political Rights and pursuant to the Convention against Torture and Other Cruel, Inhuman or Degrading Treatment or Punishment, certain rights are non-derogable and that any measures of derogation from the other rights guaranteed by the Covenant must be made in strict conformity with the provisions of its article 4 . . .
>
> [The Special Rapporteurs and Independent Experts] deplore the fact that, under the pretext of combating terrorism, human rights defenders are threatened and vulnerable groups are targeted and discriminated against on the basis of origin and socio-economic status, in particular migrants, refugees and asylum-seekers, indigenous peoples and people fighting for their land rights or against the negative effects of economic globalization policies.

[94] See http://web.amnesty.org/library/Index/engACT300272001?OpenDocument&of= THEMES\DISCRIMINATION.

[95] It is certain that the legality of any special law on terrorism will be decided upon by the Philippine Supreme Court. In the recent case of Francisco et al., versus Speaker De Venecia, G. R. N. 160261, 10 November 2003, the court (at 44–5) ruled that judicial review in the Philippines is 'expressly provided for in the Constitution, is not just a power but also a duty, and it was given an expanded definition to include the power to correct any grave abuse of discretion on the part of any government branch or instrumentality'.

They strongly affirm that any measures taken by States to combat terrorism must be in accordance with States' obligations under the international human rights instruments.[96]

IV. Is a new law necessary?

Under existing laws, the Philippines can deal with terrorism through various provisions of the Revised Penal Codes,[97] and on the basis of special laws enacted as implementing legislation to international treaty obligations dealing with particular forms of terrorism. For example, when the Abu Sayyaf resorts to kidnapping for ransom and murder, they are liable for prosecution for the capital offences of kidnapping and murder penalized under articles 267 and 248 of the Revised Penal Code (RPC), respectively. When they commit rape and other gender-based violence against women, they may be held liable for rape under RA 8353, an act amending Art. 266 of the RPC, and Presidential Decree No. 532. Likewise, both air-jacking and piracy are penalized under RA 6235 and Art. 122 of the Revised Penal Code, respectively.

As to the issue of terrorist access to modern technology such as email and other audio-graphic technologies, RA 8792, otherwise known as the E-commerce law, and the Supreme Court-promulgated rules on electronic evidence[98] have since filled the lacunae for the criminal prosecution of those who may utilize technologies such as email and other modern day devices.

By way of adherence to international treaties that seek to address specific aspects of terrorism, the Philippines is the model of a state adhering to all existing treaties that deal with specific aspects of terrorism.[99] Where it probably needs to improve is in its compliance with treaty obligations to legislate domestic enabling legislation pursuant to treaties that it has voluntarily adhered to. For instance, with respect torture and genocide, which of

---

[96] See http://www.unhchr.ch/Huridocda/Huridoca.nsf/(Symbol)/E.CN.4.2004.4.En?Open document.

[97] Act No. 3815, as amended.   [98] Rules on Electronic Evidence effective August 1, 2001.

[99] The Philippines is a party to all existing conventions relating to particular aspects of terrorism. The author concedes that this could form part of a bigger and more responsive national policy against terrorism. The Philippines is a state party to: Convention on the High Seas , UN Doc A/Conf. 13/L 52–55 (1958); Convention on Offenses and Certain Other Acts Committed on Board Aircraft, 860 U.N.T.S. 219 (1963); Convention for the Suppression of Unlawful Seizure of Aircraft, 860 U.N.T.S. 105 (1970) Convention for the Suppression of Unlawful Acts Against the Safety of Civil Aviation, 974 U.N.T.S. 177 (1971); Convention on the Prevention and Punishment of Crimes Against Internationally Protected Persons including Diplomatic Agents, 1035 U.N.T.S. 167 (1973); International Convention Against the Taking of Hostages, UN Doc. A/Res/34/ 146 (1979); Convention on the Physical Protection of Nuclear Materials, IAEA Doc. IFCIR/225 (March 3, 1980); Convention on the Law of the Sea (UN Doc. A/Conf. 62/ 122 (1982); Protocol for the Suppression of Unlawful Acts of Violence at Airports Serving

late have been resorted to by terror groups, the Philippines has failed in its treaty obligation to criminalize these kinds of conduct under its domestic law.[100] Likewise, modern day acts of terrorism, when targeted on civilian populations and other protected persons and installations, such as schools, hospitals, power plants and water treatment facilities constitute war crimes or crimes against humanity prohibited by the Geneva Conventions.[101] Contrary again to its treaty obligation, the Philippines has failed to penalize under its domestic law grave breaches of the Geneva Convention, as well as serious breaches of the same in armed conflicts of a non-international character.[102]

Likewise, despite the fact the Philippines has contributed greatly to the principle of international criminal responsibility for those who commit international crimes, including war crimes and crimes against humanity, as well as the principle that customary international law is a legal basis for the prosecution of war crimes and crimes against humanity, it has failed to submit for ratification the Rome Statute of the International Criminal Court.[103]

Moreover, despite Philippine jurisprudence that Philippine courts may in fact exercise jurisdiction in criminal cases for the prosecution of war crimes and other recognized international crimes, its Supreme Court has not acted on proposals to amend the existing rules of court to provide for an appropriate conflict rule that a court which first exercises jurisdiction over an international crime covered by universal jurisdiction does so to the exclusion of others.[104] Such a rule will remove any doubt as to the competence of Philippine courts to exercise universal jurisdiction on matters involving international crimes.

International Civil Aviation, ICAO Doc. 9518 (February 24, 1998); Convention for the Suppression of Unlawful Acts against Safety of Fixed Platforms Located at the Continental Shelf, IMO Doc. A/Conf./16/Rev. 2 (1988); Convention on the Marking of Plastic Explosives for the Purpose of Detection, S/22393 & Corr. 1 (March 1, 1991); Convention on the Safety of United Nations and Associated Personnel, UN Doc. A/49/742 (1994); International Convention for the Suppression of Terrorist Bombing, UN Doc. A/Res/52/164 (1998); Convention for the Suppression of Financing of Terrorism, UN Doc. A/AC.252/L.7 (1999).

[100] Art. V of Convention on the Prevention and Punishment of the Crime of Genocide, 78 U.N.T.S 277 (1951); Article 4 of Convention against Torture and Other Cruel, Inhuman or Degrading Treatment or Punishment, 23 *I.L.M.* 1027 (1984).

[101] Art. 51.2, Protocol 1 and Art. 13.2, Protocol 2.

[102] Art. 45, Second Geneva Convention.

[103] Philippines is a signatory to the Rome Convention creating the International Criminal Court. It has, however, not become a member of the court since it has not ratified the treaty. For status of signatures and ratifications, see http://untreaty.un.org/ENGLISH/bible/englishinternetbible/partI/chapterXVIII/treaty17.asp.

[104] Proposal was made by the author in a letter addressed to the Committee on the Revision of the Rules of Court dated 20 May 2003.

As to the specific innovations in the proposed bill on terrorism, it would seem that while faster apprehension of suspected terrorists is a laudable goal, such a goal should not be to the extent of violating internationally recognized principles of human rights. It would seem that because of events like the Lamitan incident, the answer lies not in the enactment of the proposed bill, but in addressing a recognized malaise in Philippine society: that of corruption and enforcement of existing laws.

16

Japan's response to terrorism post-9/11

MARK FENWICK

I

Formulating an appropriate response to terrorism presents all governments with an acute political dilemma. On the one hand, by failing to act decisively a government runs the risk of providing terrorist groups with the opportunity to consolidate in order to launch further and even more devastating attacks. On the other hand, there is the opposite danger of over-reacting. After all, one of the key objectives of terrorism is to provoke states into adopting security policies that expose the commitment to constitutional rule as being shallow, hypocritical and contingent upon circumstances. By inviting a 'terror against terror', the terrorist hypothesis is that violent attacks can cause governments to derogate from key constitutional principles, and that such a suspension of norms exposes the limits of the rule of law and undermines the moral authority of the state. Striking an appropriate balance between the need for action and the danger of over-reaction has, post-9/11, become a pressing issue for all governments as they formulate counter-terrorism policy.

This chapter will examine some of the key issues raised by Japan's response to the 9/11 attacks and the global 'war on terrorism' that has followed. In responding to 9/11, many liberal democracies substantively expanded the coercive powers of the criminal law as well as the investigative powers of state agencies. In some cases, constitutional rights have been curtailed or even suspended. However, in Japan no significant changes to the Criminal Code or the Code of Criminal Procedure were enacted as a result of 9/11. Although legislative measures related to terrorist financing were introduced to ensure that Japan complied with its obligations in international law, no comprehensive anti-terrorism law of the kind passed in many jurisdictions was introduced. In fact, the principle legal instrument for countering terrorism, the Subversive

I would like to express my appreciation to all the participants in the Comparative Anti-Terrorism Law and Policy Symposium organized by National University Singapore, June 2004, and, in particular, to C. H. Powell and Simon N. M. Young for their insightful comments on an earlier draft.

Activities Prevention Law was not amended, in spite of well-documented deficiencies. At first glance, the Japanese response to 9/11 appears to be a controlled one.

And yet, 9/11 has instigated a significant shift in Japanese legal culture. Unlike many jurisdictions where discussion of counter-terrorism has focused on balancing the civil liberties of suspect populations with national security interests, the Japanese debate has involved an altogether different question, namely what is an appropriate *military* contribution for a sovereign nation to make in the global war on terrorism. More practically, this has meant delimiting the role for the Japanese Self-Defence Forces (SDF) in counter-terrorism operations overseas. The legal context for this discussion is, of course, Article 9 of the Japanese Constitution, which on an initial reading, at least, explicitly renounces war and prohibits the maintenance of any military forces. Rather than embrace the values of Article 9, however, successive Japanese governments have come to regard the provision as being incompatible with Japan's national interest and international obligations, and, in particular, the demands of the US–Japan security framework.

The chapter will examine this issue *via* a discussion of perhaps the most important piece of post-9/11 legislation, the Anti-Terrorism Special Measures Law. This law is significant in practical terms because it provides the legal basis for the overseas deployment of Japanese forces in the context of counter-terrorism operations. It will be suggested, however, that the military importance of the law is of less significance than its constitutional implications. The Anti-Terrorism Special Measures Law marks a clear break with the previous official view vis-à-vis Article 9. In order to justify the overseas deployment of the SDF in the context of counter-terrorism, the government has had to abandon the last vestiges of an earlier justification for the constitutionality of the SDF based around a narrowly defined concept of self-defence in favour of a more expansive and ambiguous standard inspired by international cooperation in eradicating terrorism. The principle contention of the chapter, therefore, will be that the attacks of 9/11 have weakened constitutional rule in Japan, not by provoking the state into adopting draconian domestic counter-terrorism measures, but by instigating a controversial re-interpretation of the Constitution that permits the overseas deployment of the SDF and exposes the lack of normative force of Article 9.

II

Immediately after the 9/11 attacks Prime Minister Junichiro Koizumi pledged his government's strong support for the United States. Within one week a Ministerial Meeting Concerning Measures against Terrorism had been convened and a package of counter-terrorism measures – Japan's Measures in Response to the Simultaneous Terrorist Attacks in the United States – was confirmed.[1] As 'Basic Policy' it provided that Japan would 'actively engage' in the fight against terrorism, which it regarded as 'Japan's own security issue', and that Japan would strongly support the US, its most important ally, in both a military and humanitarian capacity. Seven 'Immediate Measures' were outlined.[2] What is striking about these immediate measures and the government's response to 9/11 more generally is the focus on external measures and the absence of any significant reform of domestic security laws. This decision is even more surprising when one considers the current state of counter-terrorism laws in Japan. This section will therefore offer a brief overview of counter-terrorism law in Japan and examine some of the reasons for the decision not to significantly reform them post 9/11.

As a preliminary observation, it is important to note that in spite of having extremely low rates of 'street crime' politically motivated violence has been a recurring problem in modern Japan. The image of Japan as a harmonious, well ordered and 'crime free society' is somewhat undermined when one considers Japanese history.[3] After 1945, the Japanese Communist Party and the North Korean League engaged in radical protest against the pro-US policy and increased anti-communism of the new administration. Between 1948 and 1952 there were a series of violent clashes with the police resulting in thousands of arrests.[4] Such demonstrations flared up again in 1959–60 when 4.7 million demonstrators confronted a mobilized police force of around 900,000, and 1967–70 when 18.7 million demonstrators clashed with security forces numbering 6.7 million.[5] Since the late 1960s the activities of extreme left groups became increasingly violent. The most well-known of these groups, the Japanese Red Army Faction, carried out a series of attacks both domestically and abroad.[6] Between 1969 and 1989, over 200 bombing incidents occurred and 570 'guerilla attacks' were recorded between 1978 and

---

[1] An English language version of this document is available on-line at http://www.mofa.go.jp/region/n-america/us/terro0109/measure.html.

[2] The seven 'Immediate Measures' were: (1) SDF 'support' for US response to terrorist attacks'; (2) SDF assistance in 'securing US facilities inside Japan'; (3) dispatch of SDF ships for 'information' (i.e. surveillance) purposes; (4) greater 'information sharing' with other countries, particularly in the context of immigration; (5) humanitarian aid to regions affected by the war on terrorism; (6) assistance to displaced persons, including 'the possibility of humanitarian assistance by SDF'; and, (7) measures to 'avoid confusion in the international and domestic economic systems'.

[3] See P. J. Katzenstein, *Cultural Norms and National Security: Police and Military in Post-War Japan* (Ithaca, Cornell University Press, 1996).

[4] The following statistics derive from P. J. Katzenstein and Y. Tsujinaka, *Defending the Japanese State: Structures, Norms and the Political Responses to Terrorism in Post-war Japan* (Ithaca, Cornell University Press, 1991), Appendix.

[5] Ibid, 8–9.

[6] For a general account of the Red Army, see A. Gallagher, *The Japanese Red Army* (New York, Rosen, 2003).

1989. Right wing extremists have also engaged in violent campaigns, including a series of political assassinations and attempted *coup d'états* (including the incident in November 1970 when novelist Yukio Mishima committed ritual suicide after failing to persuade SDF recruits to join his attempted revolution). More recently, there has been a growth in religiously motivated violence, notably that associated with the cult Aum Shinrikyo.[7] Aum is well known for the sarin gas attack on the Tokyo subway in March 1995 that killed 17 and injured more than 5,000. However, prior to this incident Aum members had been implicated in as many as 80 individual murders and a string of attempted chemical and biological attacks.[8] In fact, Aum began developing weapons of mass destruction in 1990 and successfully manufactured anthrax and botulinus toxin, in addition to sarin.[9] None of this is to suggest that Japan has been plagued by civil unrest or political violence, but rather to highlight that such incidents have occurred periodically and that any limitations in security laws cannot be accounted for by the absence of a terrorism problem.

In response to specific incidents, successive governments enacted a number of special laws to supplement the provisions of the Criminal Code. For example, after a series of bomb attacks involving 'Molotov cocktails' the Law for the Punishment for the Use of Glass-Bottle Grenades was enacted in 1972, which criminalized the use, possession or manufacture of gasoline bombs. More recently, the Law Concerning the Prevention of Bodily Harm Caused by Sarin Gas was enacted in 1999 after the Tokyo subway attack. As might be apparent from these two examples, such legislation was usually narrow in scope and the content was framed in response to specific incidents. The result of this approach has been an ad hoc collection of laws whose utility is sometimes difficult to discern. These laws are rarely, if ever, enforced and seem designed as short-term measures to appease public anxieties during periods of uncertainty rather than as elements of a coherent counter-terrorism strategy. And yet, such laws are not usually repealed, even when the threat they were designed to counter has long since passed. They remain on the statute books for possible future use as and when it may be necessary or expedient.

The most important of the special laws relating to terrorism is the Subversive Activities Prevention Law of 1952 (SAPL). It is worth considering the SAPL because it illustrates many of the difficulties associated with enforcing security laws in Japan. Enacted during the Korean War and escalating US–Soviet tensions, the SAPL was initially intended to suppress the Japanese

---

[7] For general accounts of Aum, see D. A. Metraux, *Aum Shrinrikyo and Japanese Youth* (New York, University Press of America, 1999); and I. Reader, *Religious Violence in Contemporary Japan: The Case of Aum Shinrikyo* (New York, Curzon, 1999).

[8] R. J. Lifton, *Destroying the World to Save It: Aum Shinrikyo, Apocalyptic Violence and the New Global Terrorism* (New York, Metropolitan, 1999), at 37–9.

[9] Ibid., 39.

Communist Party and other left-wing groups. In principle, however, it can be utilized against any 'subversive' organization or individual belonging to such an organization. The purpose of the SAPL is 'to contribute to the preservation of public safety by establishing regulatory procedures for taking action against organizations which have carried out terrorist activities as organizational activities and supplementing the Criminal Code with additional penalties'.[10] Certain designated crimes (including riot, arson, the use of explosives, endangering the passage of public conveyances, murder, robbery, interference in the exercise of duties of public officials) normally prosecuted under the Criminal Code can be prosecuted under the SAPL if committed with a 'political purpose' by 'a person or persons affiliated with a subversive organization'.[11] Those prosecuted under the terms of the SAPL are liable for more severe punishments than if prosecuted under the Criminal Code. However, there have been very few such prosecutions and all related to minor offences carried out by members of radical left-wing groups in the period up to the early 1970s.[12] In each case the legal proceedings were extremely protracted. For example, several left-wing radicals arrested between 1969–71 only had their convictions confirmed by the Supreme Court twenty years later in 1990.

The SAPL also contains provision for an organization to be banned or restricted from engaging in certain activities.[13] An intelligence agency was established – the Public Security Investigation Agency (PSIA) – that may designate an organization as 'a danger and appropriate for surveillance and investigation', and may implement proceedings for the banning of such an organization.[14] The process is initiated when the Director-General of the PSIA makes an application to dissolve an organization. A government committee on security matters reviews the application. Details of the application, including the rationale for applying the law, are then printed in the government gazette and representatives of the targeted group are allowed to state their views at public hearings. Finally, the Public Security Commission (PSC) – a different and independent administrative body – decides whether to apply the law against the organization. The legal standard for the decision to ban a group involves three elements, namely that the targeted organization has (i) engaged in 'destructive activities' that (ii) they have 'a political purpose' and (iii) that the organization 'poses an ongoing threat'. Even then the law will only be applied 'within the minimum extent necessary to assure public safety'.[15]

---

[10] SAPL, Article 1.   [11] Ibid., Article 4.
[12] See Katzenstein and Tsujinaka, *Defending the Japanese State*, 70–5.
[13] SAPL, Articles 5–9.
[14] The PSIA is an external branch of the Ministry of Justice and is the government agency responsible for the investigation and surveillance of domestic subversive organizations.
[15] SAPL, Article 2. Moreover, Article 3(1) prohibits the 'unreasonable restriction to freedom of thought and freedom of association', and Article 3(2) prohibits the 'restriction of and interference with the legitimate activities of any organization through the abusive use of the SAPL'.

MARK FENWICK

Although a number of groups have been, and continue to be, placed under surveillance by the PSIA (including Korean Japanese groups, as well as radical left-wing and nationalist groups) no organization has ever been dissolved under the terms of the law. The most recent case of dissolution proceedings being initiated against an organization involved the Aum cult. After it carried out the sarin gas attack on the Tokyo subway proceedings were initiated to dissolve Aum. However, the PSC on 31 January 1997 rejected the PSIA's application for a dissolution order. Although the PSC acknowledged (somewhat controversially) that the cult had a political motive in carrying out the attacks, they concluded that Aum no longer posed an ongoing threat, i.e. as a result of the post-1995 police crackdown on the cult, there was no longer a danger that Aum would repeat its subversive activities in the future. Consequently, the request for a dissolution order was rejected. However, the PSC went on to note that the PSIA's future performance of its duties regarding Aum should be strictly separated from the decision not to ban the cult. The PSIA, therefore, continues to monitor Aum's activities. This kind of PSIA intelligence gathering work would appear to be the only aspect of the SAPL that is currently in operation, and this is largely because it (perhaps necessarily) occurs outside the glare of publicity.

Given the degree of public anger directed against the cult in the wake of the 1995 attack, one might imagine that the decision of the PSC not to ban Aum would have been criticized. However, the decision was met with almost unanimous approval. For example, the *Mainichi* newspaper labelled the ruling 'sound',[16] while the left-leaning *Asahi* newspaper, praised the commission for their 'calm appraisal of the facts'.[17] An editorial in the *Asahi* went so far as to call into question the very existence of the SAPL and the PSIA. It was suggested that the law was 'draconian' and 'likely to violate basic human rights'.[18] An analogy was made to the repressive conditions of pre-war Japan and the SAPL compared to the Peace Preservation Law of 1925, under which a number of religious and other groups were suppressed. Finally, the most conservative of the dailies, the *Yomiuri* newspaper, pointed out that 'the judgment shows that the SAPL is almost useless in stemming the rising tide of organized crime . . . Japan has no law that effectively prevents or checks organized crime or terrorism'.[19] Politically progressive groups, such as the Japanese Civil Liberties Union and the National Bar Association joined those critical of the SAPL. They argued that the SAPL violates the due process provisions of the Constitution because any decision made by the PSC regarding the dissolution of an organization is made by an administrative agency and not a court and it excludes the application of administrative law, notably those provisions that permit the appeal of the decision of an administrative agency. Moreover, the fact that the law allows for the dissolution of an organization

[16] *Mainichi Shimbun*, 1 February 1999, 2.
[17] *Asahi Shimbun*, 1 February 1999, 5. [18] Ibid. [19] *Yomiuri Shimbun* 1 February 1999, 4.

infringes upon the freedom of association, the freedom of expression and mental freedom provisions of the Constitution. Although the Supreme Court has confirmed the constitutionality of the SAPL, it is difficult, given the criticism of the law from all sides of the political spectrum, to regard it as an effective instrument of counter-terrorism.

It is against this background that one must consider the Japanese government's decision post-9/11 not to enact a comprehensive anti-terrorism law or to amend existing special laws relating to terrorism. In accounting for this decision, a number of factors should be mentioned. Firstly, unlike in many jurisdictions there was no public outcry in the immediate aftermath of 9/11 demanding stronger domestic counter-terrorism legislation. This may reflect a general perception that Islamic terrorism is not a Japanese problem or, at least, not a problem within Japan.[20] In addition, there has been little external political pressure placed on the Japanese government from the United States to enact more comprehensive domestic security laws. Such pressure – so-called *gaiatsu* – is often an important factor in Japanese lawmaking. As we shall see in the next section, the external pressure that has been placed on the government post-9/11 has involved the overseas deployment of the SDF rather than a call for tougher internal security laws. Given the sensitivity measures relating to the SDF, perhaps the government simply felt that it would be politically unwise to introduce another piece of controversial legislation at the same time as it was expanding the scope of SDF activities.

The government may also have felt that a more comprehensive anti-terror law is unnecessary because existing criminal law, criminal procedure law and immigration law provides the authorities with sufficient powers to deal with terrorism effectively. Most obviously, the Code of Criminal Procedure is widely regarded as favouring the interests of investigating authorities.[21] For example, the Code permits suspects to be detained for up to twenty-three days prior to indictment. During this time, investigators have constant access to suspects for the purpose of interrogation and legal representation is limited and subject to prosecutorial control. Although the Constitution provides for an extensive range of rights for suspects and defendants, the courts, and particularly the Supreme Court, have tended to favour the investigating authorities and rights, such as the right to silence, have been eroded. Moreover, immigration law has permitted the tightening of border

---

[20] More recently, however, public anxiety has been raised by the disclosure that a French citizen, Lionel Dumont, who is suspected of having links with Al Qaeda, had allegedly been attempting to form a terrorist cell inside Japan, see *Time*, 7 June 2004, 37.

[21] For more on Japanese criminal justice, see D. Foote, 'The benevolent paternalism of Japanese criminal justice' (1992) 80 *California Law Review*, 317; D. T. Johnson, *The Japanese Way of Justice: Prosecuting Crime in Japan* (Oxford University Press, 2002); S. Miyazawa, *Policing in Japan: A Study on Making Crime* (Albany, State University of New York Press, 1992).

controls and the more active pursuit of illegal immigrants.[22] Certainly measures of this kind have been prominent post-9/11 in Japan. With such extensive powers already at their disposal, the government may have felt it was unnecessary to enact further counter-terror laws.[23]

And yet, a noteworthy feature of the Aum saga was that state agencies were apparently unwilling to utilize their powers in spite of widespread evidence of criminal activity including evidence of the production of weapons of mass destruction.[24] This points to a final factor why there has been no overhaul of counter-terrorism law. An important legacy of the history of state abuse of power that occurred in pre-1945 Japan is an ongoing concern with possible infringements of civil liberties by state agencies, particularly in cases involving questions of political and religious freedom.[25] A painful history of state-sponsored terror has meant that it is politically difficult to enact and then enforce counter-terrorism laws. The narrow scope of earlier counter-terrorism law confirms this point. One reason for the failure to act against Aum was that the cult had been designated a religious corporation in 1989. Such a designation may well have shielded Aum from the gaze of the authorities who would have been criticized for violating religious freedoms if they had aggressively pursued the cult. In a society such as Japan where 'face' is important this kind of public criticism would be awkward for the investigating authorities, even if the allegations of criminal activity were subsequently proven. Legislation passed in the wake of the Aum attacks was controversial. In particular, the Wiretapping in Criminal Investigations Law, which for the first time in Japanese criminal procedure authorized the use of wiretapping, was subject to much public criticism.[26] In the absence of a specific attack

[22] See H. Mizukoshi, 'Terrorists, terrorism and Japan's counter-terrorism policy' (2003) 53 *Gaikko Forum*, 53.

[23] Aside from tightening immigration controls, perhaps the most significant government operational measure post-9/11 has been an organizational one, namely the creation of a Foreign Policy Bureau and an International Counter-Terrorism Cooperation Division within the Ministry of Foreign Affairs. Their principle task is to facilitate closer cooperation amongst government agencies concerned with terrorism, as well as with the international community. This measure seems designed to overcome a limitation of the SAPL, namely its exclusive focus on domestic terrorism.

[24] See R. J. Lifton, *Destroying the World to Save It*, ch. 1.

[25] For general accounts of pre-1945 repression, see R. Tipton, *The Japanese Police State: Tokko in Inter-war Japan* (Honolulu, University of Hawaii Press, 1991); R. M. Mitchell, *Janus Faced Justice: Political Criminals in Imperial Japan* (Honolulu, University of Hawaii Press, 1992); P. Steinhoff, *Tenko: Ideology and Social Integration in Pre-War Japan* (New York, Garland, 1999).

[26] On this and other reforms, see S. M. Lenhart, 'Hammering Down Nails: The Freedom of Religious Groups in Japan and the United States: Aum Shinrikyo and the Branch Davidians' (2001) 29 *Georgia Journal of International and Comparative Law* 491. It is also worth noting that more than ten leading figures within the cult – including the guru Shoko Asahara – have been sentenced to death as a result of their role in the 1995 attack.

within Japan, the public appears to lack the appetite for enacting or enforcing counter-terrorism laws. Moreover, as the Aum case illustrates, where such an attack does occur, public scepticism about security legislation means that it can be politically difficult for the government to introduce any measures that are perceived as infringing upon civil liberties.

In fact, the most significant legislative measures that the Japanese government introduced post-9/11 were concerned with terrorist financing. These measures are interesting because they highlight another feature of post-war Japanese policy towards terrorism, namely that the government is keen to be seen as a responsible and cooperative member of the international community. When an international instrument concerning terrorism is concluded and a consensus exists, the government will act to implement any necessary domestic measures. Japan is a signatory of all twelve UN Conventions relating to terrorism and as at September 11, 2001 had ratified eleven of them, the exception being the International Convention for the Suppression of the Financing of Terrorism. As a result of the events of 9/11, the ratification process was accelerated and the process of incorporating the Convention into domestic law was concluded on 11 June 2002. In order to implement the Convention, as well as various UN Security Council Resolutions, a series of reforms were introduced that considerably strengthened surveillance and control of money flows related to terrorism, together with the targeting of terrorist financing. Most significantly, a series of amendments were made to the Foreign Exchange and Foreign Trade Law in order to implement the more effective control of criminal assets. These powers were utilized to freeze assets of groups identified by the UN Security Council as associated with the Taliban and al Qaeda. By aggressively targeting terrorist financing, the Japanese authorities have followed the lead of the international community post-9/11.

One might be tempted to conclude from the above that Japan's response to 9/11 has been a controlled and relatively uncontroversial one. For those accustomed to the kind of aggressive counter-terrorism measures adopted in the US, Canada or UK post-9/11, the stance of the Japanese government appears to be something of an anomaly. Stated somewhat starkly, there has been an apparent unwillingness on the part of the Japanese government to mobilize the full force of state authority against terrorism preferring instead a more cautious, or at least less visible, approach. In this respect, the post-9/11 response is a continuation of earlier policy. The only significant legislative measures relate to the disruption of terrorist financing, an issue that is relatively uncontroversial domestically and sanctioned by the international community. In the absence of a specific incident within Japan it is difficult to envisage this situation changing. However, it would be a mistake to conclude that 9/11 has not had a significant impact upon Japanese law or politics. Quite the contrary, 9/11 has resulted in an important shift in government policy in so far as it relates to the SDF. However, this focus on delimiting an appropriate military role in the international 'war on terrorism' rather than on reforming domestic counter-terrorism law is the distinctive feature of events post-9/11 in Japan.

III

When PM Koizumi met personally with President Bush on 25 September 2001, he confirmed his government's decision to deploy the SDF abroad in support of US retaliation for the attacks. In fact, four of the seven 'immediate measures' adopted by the Ministerial Meeting Concerning Measures against Terrorism in the days following 9/11 directly related to the activities of the SDF.[27] Amongst these measures was the declaration that the government would enact legislation to allow for the SDF to provide support for US forces overseas. On 5 October the government agreed to the text of three bills that would facilitate such deployments and submitted them to the Diet. After legislative deliberation in both the House of Representatives and the House of Councilors the package of bills was passed on 29 October. The principle piece of legislation was the enactment of the Anti-Terrorism Special Measures Law (ATSML), which came into effect on 2 November 2001.

Three weeks was an extremely short period of legislative deliberation, particularly for legislation concerning the SDF. This was largely because the opposition parties – and in particular, traditional opponents of an expanded role for the SDF, namely the Communist Party and Social Democratic Party – felt unable, given the circumstances surrounding 9/11, to adopt the kind of stalling tactics that they customarily utilize.[28] The quick passage of the law invited the suggestion that the government had used the events of 9/11 in order to enact legislation that would have been extremely difficult, if not impossible, under ordinary circumstances. Critics pointed to the fact that the Diet had taken nine months to enact the Peacekeeping Law in 1992 and over a year to enact legislation to provide US forces with logistic support under the revised defence guidelines in 1999. This is not to mention earlier efforts to legislate in this area that had to be abandoned due to political and public opposition.[29]

---

[27] See above note 2.

[28] The politics of pacifism in Japan are complex and cut across party political lines. For example, former Cabinet Secretary Hiromu Nonaka, one of the most conservative members of the ruling Liberal Democrat Party (LDP) and key figure in the Hashimoto faction is well-known for his strong objection to Japan's assumption of a greater security role. One of the governing coalition parties, the New Komei Party – the political wing of Buddhist sect Sokka Gakkai – also has serious reservations about Koizumi's security policy. In contrast, two of the leading factions of the opposition Democratic Party (DPJ), those of former leader Yukio Hatayama and Ichiro Ozawa, took a rather strong stance in favour of a more active security role.

[29] A detailed review of failed attempts to enact legislation pertaining to the SDF is beyond the scope of this chapter; for an overview, see Katzenstein, *Cultural Norms*, ch. 5.

Unlike in other jurisdictions, however, the speed of the legislative process post-9/11 should not be regarded as a case of populist democracy. The ATSML was not enacted on a wave of public anger over the attacks, but as a result of PM Koizumi's ideological commitment to expand Japan's security role and, it seems, direct pressure from the United States. It has been suggested that the decision to involve the SDF in international counter-terror operations was prompted, at least in part, by comments made to the Japanese Ambassador in Washington by Deputy Secretary of State Richard Armitage, who apparently suggested that Japan should 'show the flag' in any future military action.[30] Given that PM Koizumi has constructed his foreign policy around strengthening ties with the United States often at the expense of relations with his regional neighbours, he may well have been keen to comply with this request. Nevertheless, the fact that this kind of story is given credence indicates the degree to which Japanese security policy is subject to US influence. The dilemma for Japanese governments – particularly post-9/11 – is in reconciling the reality of the US–Japan security relationship with the sometimes competing desire to be a responsible member of the international community.

And yet, read in isolation the ATSML appears to be an uncontroversial piece of legislation. The purpose of the law is defined as 'specifying certain "response measures" that enable Japan to contribute actively and effectively to the efforts of the international community to prevent and eradicate international terrorism, thereby ensuring the peace and security of the international community including Japan'.[31] This includes (a) 'measures Japan implements in support of the activities of the armed forces of the US and other countries which aim to eradicate the threat of the terrorists responsible for the 9/11 attacks and thereby contribute to the purpose of the Charter of the UN'; and, (b) 'measures Japan implements in a humanitarian spirit based on the relevant resolutions of the UN'.[32]

Response measures include three broad categories of activity, namely 'Cooperation and Support activities', 'Search and Rescue activities' and 'Assistance to Affected Peoples'.[33] Each of these three broad categories is then defined. Cooperation and Support activities include the provision of materials and services and other measures in support of foreign forces; Search and Rescue activities include measures implemented by Japan to search for and rescue combatants in distress due to combat in the case of the activities of foreign forces. Assistance to Affected Peoples is defined as the transportation of necessary provisions, including food, clothing and medicine, medical services and other humanitarian activities implemented by Japan with regard

---

[30] See G. MacCormack, 'Japan's Afghan Expedition', *Japan World*, 5 November 2001: http://www.iwanami.co.jp/jpworld/text/Afghanexpedition01.html.
[31] ATSML, Article 1.
[32] Ibid., Article 1.   [33] Ibid., Articles 2–3.

to terrorist attacks.[34] All the above measures can be carried out by various government agencies including the SDF,[35] but crucially they must not involve the 'threat or use of force'.[36] Members of the SDF responsible for any measures may proportionately use weapons only when an 'unavoidable and reasonable cause exists for their use in order to protect the lives of SDF members or those who have come under SDF control during the implementation of operations'.[37]

Response measures can be adopted in the following areas – '(a) the territory of Japan; (b) the high seas and airspace above; and, (c) the territory of foreign countries' (subject to the condition that the country consents to the presence of Japanese forces).[38] Significantly, in the case of (b) and (c), implementation is limited to cases where 'combat is not taking place or expected to take place, while Japanese activities are being implemented'.[39] The ATSML requires that the Prime Minister 'seek the approval of the Diet for all response measures within three weeks of their initiation'. In the event that the Diet does not approve, any response measure must be 'terminated immediately'.[40] Finally, the law is subject to periodic legislative review. On 10 October 2003, the Diet confirmed a government request to extend the law for a further two years.[41]

Thus far, measures adopted under the ATSML have, at least from a military point of view, been small-scale. On 9 November 2001 two destroyers and a supply ship were deployed in the Indian Ocean in support of US Navy operations. On 25 November, a destroyer, a supply ship and a minesweeper were also deployed. More controversially, on 16 December 2002 Japan sent a surveillance class destroyer to the Indian Ocean. Other operations have been of a similar scale, mostly involving resupply of US and UK vessels, as well as intelligence gathering. The modest nature of SDF deployments in the 'war on terrorism' highlights that what is at stake here is not necessarily a revival in Japanese militarism, but rather the status of the Japanese Constitution.[42]

Complicating discussion of the ATSML, however, is Article 9 of the Constitution and the history of Japanese aggression that preceded its promulgation. The renouncing of war and the concomitant prohibition of maintaining any war potential together constitute one of the fundamental principles that the occupying US forces imposed on the defeated Japanese

---

[34] Ibid., Article 3(1), 3(2), and 3(3).   [35] Ibid., Article 3(4).   [36] Ibid., Article 2(2).
[37] Ibid., Article 12.   [38] Ibid., Article 2(3).   [39] Ibid., Article 2(3).   [40] Ibid., Article 5.
[41] *Japan Times*, 11 October 2003, 2.
[42] There are two main arguments as to why Japanese remilitarization is unlikely, firstly, the extreme dependence of Japan on the US for security, and secondly, the genuine culture of anti-militarism that exists amongst a significant proportion of the population in Japan. On the latter issue, see I. Buruma, *The Wages of Guilt: Memories of War in Germany and Japan* (London, Phoenix, 1994); and N. Field, *In the Realm of a Dying Emperor: Japan at Century's End* (New York, Vintage, 1992).

government in August 1945.[43] This principle is given effect by Chapter III, Article 9 of the Constitution:

1. Aspiring sincerely to an international peace based on justice and order, the Japanese people forever renounce war as a sovereign right of the nation and the threat or use of force as means of settling international disputes.
2. In order to accomplish the aim of the preceding paragraph, land, sea, and air forces, as well as other war potential, will never be maintained. The right of belligerency of the state will not be recognized

There are other examples of how this principle more generally informs the Constitution and Japanese law. For example, Article 66(2) of the Constitution states that the PM and other Cabinet posts must be held by civilians. The prohibition on 'involuntary servitude' found in Article 18 is understood by constitutional scholars to include conscription to the military and no legal provision in the Constitution provides for martial law or for dealing with acts of war such as declaring war or concluding peace. The pre-war Criminal Code – which in contrast to the Code of Criminal Procedure was not completely revised during the US occupation – was subject to minor amendments; notably, those offences that were predicated on the existence of a war situation were deleted.

It is well known that Article 9 has been an ongoing source of controversy since the Constitution came into effect on 3 November 1947. A literal inter-pretation of Article 9 would seem to suggest that the existence of the SDF is unconstitutional because Article 9(2) contains a clear prohibition on the maintenance of any kind of military forces or 'other war potential'. Certainly, this is the view of most mainstream Japanese constitutional law scholars. They regard Japan's acceptance of the terms of the Potsdam Declaration on 2 September 1945 as crucial. Under the terms of the Potsdam Declaration, Japan was to be 'completely disarmed' and the author-ity of those who 'misled the people' would be eliminated 'for all time'.[44] As John Dower, the most prominent English language historian of post-war Japan, puts it, Potsdam 'made clear that disarmament and demilitarization were not merely to be "complete" but also "permanent"'.[45]

In the 1950s, however, and with the explicit support of a US government concerned about Soviet expansion in East Asia, Japan began a programme of

---

[43] The other principles were the sovereignty of the people (as opposed to the Emperor) and the guarantee of fundamental human rights (under the earlier Meiji Constitution all rights of 'subjects' were under reservation of law).
[44] Quoted in Dower, *Embracing Defeat*, 74.
[45] Ibid., p.75. See also, K. Inoue, *MacArthur's Japanese Constitution: A Linguistic and Cultural Study of its Making* (University of Chicago Press, 1991); and S. Koseki, *The Birth of Japan's Postwar Constitution*, (Boulder, Westview Press, 1998).

rearmament that has continued through to the present.[46] The procedural obstacles to constitutional reform as well as the political sensitivities surrounding Article 9 meant that an amendment to the Constitution was unlikely.[47] In fact, it is worth noting that no amendment of the Japanese Constitution has ever been enacted. Instead, the government adopted an interpretation of Article 9 in which they denied that the SDF constituted 'forces' or 'other war potential' prohibited by Article 9(2). The logic of this position derives from the argument that all sovereign nations – including Japan – enjoy an 'inherent right' of self-defence in international law.[48] This principle is expressly stated in Article 51 of the UN Charter although it also has a basis in customary international law.[49] Since the Constitution does not expressly prohibit the possession of a minimum level of armed strength necessary to exercise the right of self-defence, the maintenance of the SDF for the purpose of self-defence is constitutional.

In order to understand the Japanese government's position it is important to distinguish between an individual right of self-defence and a right of collective self-defence. An individual right of self-defence refers to the right of a country which is directly attacked (e.g. Japan) to repel such an attack, whereas the right of collective self-defence refers to the right of Japan, in a situation where Japan is not directly attacked, to deem an attack against another country that is in an alliance with Japan (e.g. US) as an attack on itself and then counter-attack. Over the course of the last five decades, the Japanese Government and Defence Agency have consistently taken the

---

[46] For details of this expansion, see Katzenstein, *Cultural Norms*, chs. 5–6. Fearful of Communist insurrection, the occupying US forces authorized the creation of a 75,000 National Police Reserve (NPR) to safeguard internal security in the late 1940s. Following the end of the US occupation in 1952 and the conclusion of the US – Japan Security Treaty, the NPR was transformed into the SDF. It seems the name SDF was adopted to indicate the defensive nature of the force. It is often suggested that Japan has the second largest military budget in the world: see, for example, D. Hayes, *Japan: The Toothless Tiger* (Tokyo, Tuttle, 2003), p. 131, although such claims are difficult to verify. The SDF currently consists of around 150,000 ground troops, a maritime force of 43,000 troops and 160 vessels, and an air force of 45,000 troops and 5,100 planes.

[47] The procedure for amending the Constitution is found in Article 96: 'Amendments to this Constitution shall be initiated by the Diet, through a concurring vote of two-thirds or more of all the members of each House and shall thereupon be submitted to the people for ratification, which shall require the affirmative vote of a majority of all votes cast thereon, at a special referendum or at such election as the Diet shall specify. (2) Amendments when so ratified shall immediately be promulgated by the Emperor in the name of the people, as an integral part of this Constitution.'

[48] See generally I. Brownlie, *International Law and the Use of Force by States* (Oxford University Press, 1963), 231–80, and 'The Nicaragua Case' 1986 *ICJ Reports* 14.

[49] 'Nothing in the present Charter shall impair the inherent right of individual or collective self-defence if an armed attack occurs against a Member of the United Nations' UN Charter, Article 51.

position that maintaining military force necessary for individual self-defence is constitutional, but that collective self-defence is not permissible under Article 9. The following is an indicative statement of the government view:

> The Constitution, upholding pacifism, sets forth in Article 9 the renunciation of war, non-possession of war potential and denial of the right to belligerency of the state. As long as Japan is a sovereign state, *it is recognized beyond doubt that the provision in the article does not deny the inherent right of self-defence that Japan is entitled to maintain as a sovereign nation.*
>
> Since the right is not denied, the government remains firm in the belief that *the Constitution does not inhibit the possession of the minimum level of armed strength necessary to exercise the right of self-defence.* On the basis of such understanding the government has adopted the *exclusively defence-oriented policy* as its basic policy of national defence and has maintained self-defence as an armed organization, and has taken steps to improve its capabilities and to ensure their efficient operation. These measures do not present any constitutional problem.[50]

Although official documents, such as this, do not explicitly refer to *individual* self-defence, the phrase 'exclusively defence-oriented policy' has always been understood in this way both by the government and its critics. The government interpretation of Article 9, therefore, derives the constitutionality of the maintenance of the minimum necessary level of armed strength for individual self-defence from the existence of Japan's right in international law to defend itself if directly attacked.

Further support for the government's view can be found in the legislative history of Article 9. Of crucial importance in this discussion is the fact that the original draft of Article 9 was amended – with, it should be noted, the consent of the occupying US authorities – during the final stages of its deliberation in the Diet.[51] The original English language version of Article 9 drafted by the occupying forces and presented to the Diet was as follows:

1. War as a sovereign right of a nation, and threat or use of force, is forever renounced as a means of settling disputes with other nations.
2. The maintenance of land, sea and air forces, as well as other war potential, will never be authorized. The right of belligerency of the state will never be recognized.

Discussion of the amendment process is complex and involves rather subtle questions of language, but the government position is that the effect of the

---

[50] Japanese Defence Agency, *Annual Report* (Tokyo, Japan Times, 1993), 63–7, 127–8 (emphasis added).
[51] The 1947 Constitution was formally enacted as an amendment to the 1889 Meiji Constitution, and so was subject to limited legislative review. For more on the history of legislative debate surrounding Article 9, see Dower, *Embracing Defeat*, 75–90.

so-called Ashida amendment was to clearly establish a right to individual self-defence in contrast to the original draft. According to this argument, the first clause of the revised version of Article 9 establishes international peace as the article's objective. The words added to the second clause as a result of the Ashida amendment – namely 'In order to accomplish the aim of the preceding paragraph', indicate that what was being renounced was, in contrast to the earlier draft, not the maintenance of military force *per se*, but the maintenance of a capacity for an aggressive war that would disturb international peace. This, according to the government view, left open the possibility that military force necessary for self-defence would be constitutional.

Although historians as well as constitutional lawyers have repeatedly criticized the government's position on Article 9, the courts have taken a more cautious view.[52] The leading cases on this question have generally accepted the government position that Article 9 does not proscribe the country's right of individual self-defence. On the question of whether a right to maintain military force can be derived from this right of self-defence there is something of a division between courts of first instance who have on a number of occasions rejected the government position, and appeal courts who have consistently refrained from ruling on this matter on the grounds that it is a political matter.

The 'exclusively defence-oriented' interpretation of Article 9 thus provided the justification with which Japanese governments conducted defence policy during the Cold War. This proved to be both an enabling and disabling interpretation of Article 9. On the one hand, the 'minimum level of armed strength necessary to exercise the right of individual self-defence' is an unclear standard that on a critical view has allowed the Defence Agency to construct a military capability free from any kind of restriction on the scale or composition of the SDF. And yet, although this justification for the existence of the SDF has imposed little in the way of quantitative restriction on Japanese rearmament, it has imposed limits of a different order, namely in restricting the areas and circumstances where the SDF may be deployed. By formulating the justification for the SDF's existence in terms of individual self-defence, the government has been limited in how the SDF may be utilized. Most significantly, this has meant that any overseas deployment of the SDF, including the use of the SDF in support of an ally who is under attack (i.e. collective self-defence) has been considered to be unconstitutional even by the government and their supporters.

---

[52] The leading Supreme Court judgments relating to Article 9 can all be found in translation in L. W. Beer and H. Itoh (eds.), *The Constitutional Case Law of Japan 1970 through 1990* (Seattle, University of Washington Press, 1996). On the topic of judicial independence in Japan more generally, see J. Haley, 'Judicial independence in Japan revisited' (1995) 25 *Law in Japan* 1, and M. J. Ramseyer and E. Rasmussen, *Measuring Judicial Independence: the Political Economy of Judging in Japan* (University of Chicago Press, 2003).

However, over the course of the 1990s the self-defence justification became increasingly strained in the face of the changing geopolitical situation. Of particular importance in this context was international criticism of the Japanese role in the first Gulf War of 1990–91. Although Japan made significant financial contributions, they did not contribute any military assistance to coalition forces on the grounds that it was incompatible with the 'exclusively defence-oriented policy'. Stung by US criticism of this so-called 'checkbook diplomacy', the government introduced a number of new measures. Foremost amongst these were the Law Concerning Cooperation with UN Peacekeeping Operations and Other Operations Law of 1992 (the PKO Law) and the Law Concerning Measures to Maintain the Peace and Security of Japan in Situations Surrounding Japan Law of 1999 (SASJL).

The purpose of the PKO Law was to provide appropriate and prompt cooperation for UN Peacekeeping Operations and humanitarian relief operations. Under the terms of the PKO Law the overseas deployment of the SDF became legally possible for the first time provided that five conditions were met, including the existence of a UN Security Council resolution authorizing the peacekeeping operation and the existence of a ceasefire agreement. Moreover, the use of weapons is limited to the minimum necessary in order to protect the lives of SDF personnel. Based on this law, the SDF have participated in PKOs in Cambodia (September 1992–September 1993), Mozambique (May 1993–January 1995), the Golan Heights (February 1996–present), and East Timor (March 2002–present).[53] SASJL was enacted in 1999 and made it possible for the SDF to provide so-called 'Rear Area Support', i.e. the provision of logistical support, in cooperation with US forces in areas 'surrounding Japan' that may lead to a direct military attack on Japan if they are not addressed.[54]

However, under the terms of the PKO Law and the SASJL it was not possible for the government to take measures in support of US forces outside of Japan or 'areas surrounding Japan'. Under the PKO Law there were clear limits to the overseas deployment of the SFD, notably the existence of a specific UN resolution and a ceasefire agreement. Under the terms of SASJL, SDF activities were limited to 'areas surrounding Japan'. Although these reforms facilitated the overseas deployment of Japanese forces – which in itself is clearly controversial from the point of view of the 'exclusively defence-oriented policy' – the situations authorized were still clearly

---

[53] It is worth noting the shift in public opinion that has occurred as a result of these activities. According to government surveys only 20.6% of the population 'approved' of Japan's participation in PKOs in 1991 compared with 40.5% in 2000. The number of those opposed decreased from 18.8% in 1991 to 2.7% in 2001. See *East Asian Strategic Review 2003* (Tokyo, Japan Times) 311.

[54] This law gave legal effect to the 1997 Guidelines negotiated between Japan and the US under the terms of the US–Japan Security Agreement.

restricted. The ATSML removed these limits and enables the government to deploy the SDF on completely new grounds, based neither on cooperation with the UN nor solely on the basis of US–Japan cooperation in defending Japan and surrounding areas. The key question then is whether the new law is inconsistent not only with the clear meaning of Article 9, but – perhaps more significantly – with the previously held government interpretation of Article 9.

In addressing how the ATSML marks a break with earlier policy, critics of the law pointed to a number of issues.[55] Most significantly, Article 2 of the ATSML adds the open-ended category of the 'territory of foreign countries' and 'the high seas and space above' to the areas where the SDF can lawfully operate. This goes beyond the PKO Law and the SASJL and makes it possible for the government to deploy the SDF overseas in the name of international cooperation against terrorism without any geographical restrictions or a clear UN mandate. Although SD deployment is limited to activities that aim to 'eradicate international terrorism' and thereby 'contribute to the purpose of the UN Charter', this is an open-ended and unclear standard. Particularly, when one considers that international terrorism is not clearly defined and the reference is to the UN Charter rather than specific Security Council Resolutions.

The ATSML would also appear to be incompatible with the previously held government interpretation of Article 9 as it would seem to permit 'response measures' in support of collective self-defence and perhaps even pre-emptive attacks if they are conducted with the goal of eradicating terrorism. This would involve stretching the earlier concept of self-defence – which is already a contentious one given the plain meaning of Article 9 – to breaking point. The law also provides that implementation shall be limited to cases where combat is not taking place. However, it can be difficult to distinguish between areas of combat and areas of non-combat, particularly in cases of terrorism.[56]

In addition, the ATSML emphasizes that 'response measures' do not constitute the use of force as prohibited by Article 9 by providing in Article 2(2) that these measures must not constitute a 'threat or use of force'. The issue here relates to the kind of activities that are specified as cooperation and support activities. As mentioned above, these include supply, transportation, repair and maintenance, medical services and communication. These would generally be thought of as logistical activities. However, since the use of force

---

[55] The following discussion draws upon the contents of an open letter of 9 October 2001 signed by over fifty Japanese constitutional law scholars written in protest over the ATSML. For the Japanese language version, see http://www.jca.apc.org/kenpoweb/appeal.html. It also uses arguments found in a special issue of the Japanese language law journal *Jurist* 2004 vol. 1260, which discusses Article 9 post-9/11.

[56] A similar restriction exists in the Special Law relating to Iraq. SDF forces can only be deployed if combat has ceased. In spite of the worsening security situation in Iraq, the Japanese government has argued that combat is not taking place in the *area* where the SDF forces are deployed, and that the deployment is therefore lawful.

is impossible without such logistical support – that is to say logistical support is a necessary pre-condition for the exercise of military force – the distinction that the law makes between 'response measures' and the 'use of force' has been questioned. A rather graphic illustration of this particular argument was posed by one newspaper editorial when it wondered whether a Japanese vessel would be permitted to provide fuel to US destroyers launching cruise missiles against terrorist training camps in NW Pakistan.[57]

Finally, under the ATSML the implementation of response measures by the SDF can be taken without advance parliamentary approval and an after-the-event validation of the Diet is permitted. This is to be contrasted with the PKO Law and the SASJL, which both provide for advance Diet approval for the overseas deployment of the SDF. The argument has been made that in this regard civilian control of the SDF has been diminished. Given the history of the Japanese military, this is an extremely sensitive question and it is not surprising that this was one aspect of the law that was strongly contested in the, albeit brief, parliamentary deliberations.

The government was clearly aware that in enacting the ATSML they were stretching the self-defence justification, and acknowledged that a different justification for the constitutionality of the SDF was required. The argument that the government proposed focused on the suggestion that there is a 'gap' between the Preamble of the Constitution and the earlier interpretation of Article 9. The government's recourse to the Preamble is interesting, not least because the Preamble has often been utilized in support of the argument that Article 9 amounts to an absolute prohibition and the conclusion that the SDF is unconstitutional. However, the new government position has been to suggest that a fundamental principle underlying the Preamble is the principle of international cooperation.[58] It is argued that when read in the context of the Preamble, Article 9 can legitimately justify the use of force not only in the case of individual self-defence but also in the broader case of international cooperation in pursuit of peace and security (i.e. collective self-defence). Overseas deployment of the SDF in support of operations aimed at eradicating terrorists is now considered constitutional by the Japanese government.

Constitutional scholars have met this suggestion with scepticism, arguing that the new government position means that Article 9 is meaningless as almost any joint deployment of the SDF could be justified on the grounds of international

---

[57] *Nihon Keizai Shimbun*, 11 November 2001.

[58] It has been suggested that this can be found most clearly, for example, in the following section of the Preamble, '*We desire to occupy an honored place in an international society striving for the preservation of peace, and the banishment of tyranny and slavery, oppression and intolerance* for all time from the earth . . . We recognize that all peoples of the world have the right to live in peace, free from fear and want. *We believe that no nation is responsible to itself alone*, but that laws of political morality are universal; and that obedience to such laws is incumbent upon all nations . . .' (emphasis added).

cooperation. Critics argue that there is no 'gap' between the Preamble and Article 9. Quite the contrary, the principles of the Preamble – namely pacifism and an absolute rejection of military force – are to be found in every Article of the Constitution, including Article 9. According to this view, it is a unique feature of the so-called 'Peace Constitution' that it adopts international cooperation based on the principle of pacifism. As such, critics have questioned both the legality of the government's position and the belief that military force, even if it is cooperative, can ever succeed in eradicating terrorism.

One further point of discussion concerns the relationship between international law, Article 9 and the ATSML. As was mentioned above, successive Japanese governments have relied upon the existence of an 'inherent right' of self-defence in international law in arguing that the SDF is constitutional in so far as it adopts an 'exclusively defence-oriented policy'. As such, the government view of Article 9 imposed a more severe standard than Article 51 of the UN Charter since only acts of individual self-defence are permitted. Given the fact that Article 51 explicitly mentions collective self-defence, is it possible for the government to rely upon international law as a legal basis for the ATSML?

Chapter X (Articles 97–99 of the Constitution) establishes the hierarchy of norms in Japanese law. Of crucial importance in this context is Article 98:

1. This Constitution shall be the supreme law of the nation and no law, ordinance, imperial rescript or other act of government, or part thereof, contrary to the provisions hereof, shall have legal force or validity.
2. The treaties concluded by Japan and established laws of nations shall be faithfully observed.

The 'prevailing view' is that the effect of this provision is that the Constitution has priority over international law.[59] The Cabinet's power to conclude treaties and the Diet's power to approve them derive from the Constitution, therefore it is logically not possible to justify the superiority of a treaty.[60] On this view, Article 51 of the UN Charter cannot provide a legal basis for the exercise of collective self-defence, if Article 9 is understood (as it has been even by the government) to exclude such acts.

The alternative (minority) view is to suggest that Article 98(2) constitutes a limitation on 98(1).[61] That is to say, treaties and the 'established laws of nations' (i.e. customary international law) have priority over the Constitution. This view leads to the conclusion that Article 51 of the UN Charter would have

---

[59] H. Oda, *Japanese Law* (Oxford University Press, 2001), 50.
[60] A further argument in support of this view is that the procedure for amending the Constitution is much more difficult than that for concluding treaties.
[61] See, for example, K. Sorimachi, 'Internationalization and globalization demand changes in judicial interpretation' (2003) *21st Century Shape of Japan, No.3* (http://www.lec-jp.com/speaks/info_003.htm).

superiority over the provisions of Article 9 and that collective self-defence is permitted as a result of Japan's ratification of the Charter. It is interesting to note that the Japanese government has not adopted this line of argument, preferring instead the reinterpretation of Article 9 discussed above.

Although international law may provide a legal basis for acts of *collective* self-defence, it is a much more controversial question whether it would be of assistance to the Japanese government if the response measures adopted under the ATSML were in support of *pre-emptive* action, e.g. if the SDF were to re-fuel a US aircraft involved in a pre-emptive strike against a terrorist group located in a third country. As has been well-documented, post-9/11 the US administration has actively sought to extend the scope of the right of self-defence to include action in anticipation of a terrorist attack against any state that willingly harbours such terrorists.[62] Such acts would appear to be problematic from the point of view of Article 51 of the UN Charter, as well as customary international law.[63] If the Japanese government were to rely upon international law as the basis for action under the ATSML they might, at some stage, be obliged to defend the view that such pre-emptive strikes are permissible in international law. Given the delicacy of this issue within the international community, this is a course of action the government would presumably be unwilling to take. Reinterpreting the Constitution to broaden the scope of Article 9 would seem to be a more expedient approach.

The ATSML has thus resulted in a reinterpretation of Article 9 that is hard to reconcile with the plain meaning of the text or, perhaps more importantly, the previous government position that limited the SDF's activities to defending Japan in the event of a direct attack. This more assertive approach reflects, in part, the ideological preferences of the Koizumi administration, as well as the demands of the US–Japan security relationship post-9/11. By presenting military force as a legitimate and effective means of responding to terrorism, the Koizumi administration seems to stand square with current US thinking that regards terrorists as hybrid paramilitaries who are engaged in a form of quasi-warfare rather than thinking of terrorist acts as crimes and terrorists as criminals. The message that is communicated to the Japanese public by the ATSML about the nature of the current terrorist threat and the most effective response to that threat seems designed to confirm anxieties that may lead many to question the values found in Article 9.

The policy of strong support for US military measures against suspected terrorists and their supporters continued with the enactment of The Law Concerning Special Measures on Humanitarian and Reconstruction

---

[62] See, for example, M Byers, 'Terrorism, the use of force and international law after 9/11' (2002) 51 *International and Comparative Law Quarterly* 401.
[63] Ibid., 413–4.

Assistance in Iraq in July 2003.[64] Under the terms of this law, the SDF are permitted to undertake humanitarian and reconstruction assistance in 'non-combat zones' in support of the US-led occupation.[65] The decision to actually deploy troops was repeatedly postponed largely as a result of public opposition to such a move. However, after the killing of two Japanese diplomats on 29 November 2003 in a terrorist attack inside Iraq, the government decided to push ahead with the deployment, citing the importance of maintaining Japan's alliance with the US and cooperating with the international community. In March 2004, 550 ground troops arrived in Samawah, South East Iraq where they engaged in 'reconstruction activities', principally involving the reconnection of water supplies.

A final illustration of the government's more aggressive stance on security issues occurred more recently in July 2003 when a Law to Respond to Armed Attacks (so-called emergency legislation) was enacted. As mentioned above, the Constitution contains no provision for the suspension of the rule of law in wartime or other national emergency. Since 1977 governments have unsuccessfully attempted to pass laws that would delimit the domestic powers of the PM and the role of the SDF in the event of an armed attack on Japan. The recent escalation of tensions with North Korea highlighted the need for some contingency plans. After failing once in the 2002 legislative session, the Koizumi administration succeeded in 2003 in passing a package of measures that delimited the powers of the state and the role of the SDF in the event of such an emergency situation.

IV

In conclusion, it would appear that the Japanese government is now confronted with a choice. On the one hand, it could choose to amend Article 9 in order to reflect the government's preferred interpretation. On the other, it could leave the provision unchanged and continue to interpret the text in a way that re-defines the scope of self-defence to include measures in

---

[64] Japan was quick to express its support for the US-led attack on Iraq. In February 2003, when many members of the UN Security Council were expressing reluctance to approve a new resolution that would have authorized an attack, Japan declared its backing for such a move. And in May 2003, when Koizumi met with President Bush, he promised Japanese help with the post-war reconstruction effort, implicitly suggesting that this would include dispatch of the SDF. The negative effects of this poicy were highlighted after the 11 March 2004 train bombings in Madrid when the group with alleged links to the al Qaeda terrorist network that claimed responsibility for the attack named Japan as a potential future target, *Japan Times*, 13 March 2004, 2.

[65] The Law Concerning Special Measures on Humanitarian and Reconstruction Assistance in Iraq, 2003, Article 2.

support of collective and possibly pre-emptive action. Current indications are that for the moment the government will pursue both options. Certainly, the enactment of the laws on Iraq and the emergency legislation indicates that this trend to enact laws that expand the scope of SDF activity is set to continue. And yet, the government are also preparing the groundwork for constitutional amendment. In January 2000, a Constitutional Review Panel was established to examine a wide range of proposals, including revision of Article 9. It is scheduled to conclude deliberations in 2005 and, if agreement is reached, to introduce proposals to the Diet in 2008. However, as was mentioned above, the Constitution has never been amended and the high procedural obstacles found in Article 96 (a two-thirds majority in both chambers of the Diet and a national referendum) make any change politically difficult. On a conceptual level, it is interesting to note that whereas many continental European constitutions have provisions explicitly prohibiting amendments that contradict fundamental principles, the Japanese Constitution has no such limitation. Despite the absence of an explicit provision, basic principles such as sovereignty of the people, respect for human rights and pacifism are understood by most constitutional scholars to be unchangeable even by formal amendment.[66] The results of current attempts at constitutional reform are, therefore, difficult to predict.[67] It goes without saying that the status of the SDF is an issue that arouses a great deal of controversy internationally, particularly in Asia. However, perhaps less well-documented, at least in the international news media, is reaction inside Japan where a significant section of the population – including members of the governing coalition – are troubled by PM Koizumi's decision to actively involve the SDF in international conflicts of this kind, and to align himself so closely with the US doctrine that regards military force as the principle means for responding to terrorism.

It is often suggested that terrorism can be successful when it provokes a state into a response that exposes the rule of law as hypocritical and contingent upon circumstances. The Japanese response to 9/11 is interesting because it has not involved the adoption of aggressive domestic counter-terrorism policies, in spite of widespread criticism of existing law. However, 9/11 has resulted in a controversial reinterpretation of Article 9 that has, in the view of critics, undermined the promise of the 'Peace Constitution'.

---

[66] See Oda, *Japanese Law*, 37–9.
[67] For the moment, the Japanese public appear to be comfortable with the government's approach. Public opinion polls indicate support for the government's policy towards terrorism, including the overseas deployment of the SDF in the context of counter-terrorism. For example, a survey conducted by the Mainichi newspaper found 63% for the ATSML. See Y. Tasumi 2002, 'Japan's homeland security: police or SDF?' Center for Strategic and International Studies, http://www.csis.org/japan/japanwatch/jw0204.htm.

The government has affirmed a position regarding Article 9 that is hard to reconcile with the plain meaning of the text, or even the earlier 'exclusively defence-oriented' interpretation. By exposing the lack of normative force behind Article 9, the attacks of 9/11 have, it could be argued, weakened constitutional rule in Japan. Not by provoking a 'terror against terror', but by instigating a controversial reinterpretation of a constitutional norm that apparently negates its intended effect.

17

Legal and institutional responses to terrorism in India

V. VIJAYAKUMAR

I. Introduction

Few countries have seen the ugly face of terrorism to the extent that India has since its independence in 1947. The situation in Jammu and Kashmir, the North-East states, the naxalite movement in Andhra Pradesh and Orissa, developments in the states of Punjab and West Bengal, recent violence in Gujarat and bomb blasts in Bombay have constantly challenged constitutional values and institutions. India has suffered terrorists' attacks on civilian, military and other governmental institutions (including the attack on the Indian Parliament) and on individuals, resulting in death and destruction. There has been hostage taking, and damage to property. Two examples will suffice. In Jammu and Kashmir alone, during the third week of May 2004, there were 29 civilian, 34 security personnel and 19 terrorist deaths, making a total of 82 deaths in only one week. The North-Eastern states have the dubious distinction of being home to Asia's longest running insurgency. With about 30 banned insurgency groups, the states of Assam, Manipur, Tripura and Nagaland have witnessed 11,000 casualties. During the first nine months of 2003, more than 300 people fell victim to the insurgency in the state of Assam alone. Religious and ideological differences, and demands for autonomy have been the major reasons for terrorism in India.

These developments have compelled policy-makers in India to respond appropriately, both domestically and through regional initiatives such as the South Asian Association for Regional Cooperation (SAARC) Regional Convention on Suppression of Terrorism. The need for additional governmental powers to deal with terrorism has proven irresistible. Greater powers create opportunities to abuse those powers. However, aspects of Indian democracy operate to ameliorate the worst excesses: a progressive and living Constitution, periodic elections, judicial independence, press freedom, and a strong opposition both at the centre and in the states. What follows is a brief account of India's legal response to terrorism, and in particular recent specific legislation dealing with terrorism. It advances the view that India has, in recent years, been able, more or less, to steer an acceptable course between giving too little power to the government so that it is unable to deal with terrorism, and too much power so that an intolerable violation of human rights is risked.

II. Legal response to terrorism

After India's independence in 1947, many of the colonial statutes were modified and adapted. Many are relevant to tackle and punish terrorists in India even today, such as the Explosive Substances Act 1908.[1] More specific laws include the Bengal Suppression of Terrorist Outrages (Supplementary) Act 1932,[2] and the Bombay Public Security Measures Act 1947.[3] Some of these remain on the statute book.

In 1950, the year of the commencement of the Constitution, the Preventive Detention Act was enacted.[4] Although the Minister promised that this Act would be in force for only one year, it existed till it was substituted by the Maintenance of Internal Security Act 1971.[5] The constitutional validity of the Preventive Detention Act 1950 was upheld by the Supreme Court in *A. K. Gopalan v. State of Madras*.[6] In between, the Armed Forces (Special Powers) Act 1958[7] and the Unlawful Activities (Prevention) Act 1967[8] were enacted and their validity upheld by the Supreme Court in *Naga People's Movement of Human Rights v. Union of India*[9] and *Jamat E-Islami Hind v. Union of India*[10] respectively. The Maintenance of Internal Security Act was enacted during the war with Pakistan and it continued in force till it was repealed in 1978.[11] This became a piece of legislation much abused by the then Congress government. It led to its downfall at the general elections in 1978. The next in the series was the National Security Act, enacted in 1980.[12] The validity of this law was upheld by a constitution bench of the Supreme Court in *A. K Roy v. Union of India*[13] despite the fact that the *détenu* did not have the right to be represented by a lawyer before the Advisory Board. As with many other laws, the state of Jammu and Kashmir was excluded from the application of this National Security Act. This law was the first serious attempt to tackle terrorism and its effectiveness was strengthened by an amendment in 1984, mainly to address insurgency in the state of Punjab.

With the escalation of terrorist activities in India, a more specific law, the Terrorist and Disruptive Activities (Prevention) Act 1985 (TADA) was enacted.[14] This law had a 'sunset' clause and ceased to be in force in 1987. As Parliament was not in session at that time, the President of India promulgated the Terrorist and Disruptive Activities (Prevention) Ordinance 1987 under article 123 of the Constitution. It came into force on 24 May 1987. Apart from including the provisions of TADA (1985), this Ordinance provided for a more deterrent punishment for terrorist acts, enabled the central

---

[1] Act No. 6 of 1908.   [2] Act No. 24 of 1932.   [3] Act No. 6 of 1947.
[4] Act No. 4 of 1950.   [5] Act No. 26 of 1971.   [6] AIR [1950] SC 27.
[7] Act No. 28 of 1958.   [8] Act No. 37 of 1967.   [9] (1998) 2 SCC 109.
[10] (1995) 1 SCC 428.
[11] Maintenance of Internal Security (Repeal) Act 1978 (Act No. 27 of 1978).
[12] Act No. 65 of 1980.   [13] AIR [1982] SC 710.   [14] Act No. 31 of 1985.

government to constitute Designated Courts, and vested rule-making power with the central government. TADA was re-enacted in 1987 with some changes. Unauthorised possession of arms and ammunition specified in the Arms Rules 1962 in a notified area (so notified by the state government) was made punishable with imprisonment for not less than five years, but which may extend to imprisonment for life and a fine. Confessions made by a person before a 'high ranking police officer' (not lower than a Superintendent of Police) and recorded by such police officer in writing or on any mechanical devise was made admissible in trial. The 'Designated Courts' could presume that an accused had committed an offence where arms or explosives or any other substance so specified were recovered from his possession. They were also empowered to try certain offences summarily[15] in accordance with the procedure prescribed in the Code of Criminal Procedure 1973.[16] The TADA of 1987,[17] unlike previous detention laws,[18] was made applicable to the state of Jammu and Kashmir as well.

The validity of TADA (1987) was challenged, but the Supreme Court in *Kartar Singh* v. *State of Punjab*[19] upheld its validity in spite of the sweeping powers given to the authorities. However, the Supreme Court also observed that this law was being used to circumvent the existing ordinary criminal law and criminal procedure even when the offence fell outside the scope of TADA. In spite of the growing acts of violence and terrorism in the state of Jammu and Kashmir, a much larger number of people were detained in the state of Gujarat,[20] where there was no such insurgency. Many innocent people, petty criminals and political opponents were charged under TADA because police and security personnel were acting under the dictation of their political bosses. Convictions under TADA could be secured in no more than 3 per cent of the cases. The courts instead convicted them under the Indian Penal Code, 1860[21] in a majority of cases. This led to a large number of people being detained, very few being charged (about 6 per cent) and even less being convicted under TADA.

TADA had a sunset clause, but it was extended three times, each time for a period of two years from 1989. A law that should have existed only for two years, continued for eight years and was not extended beyond that because of

---

[15] In *Sanjay Dutt* v. *State (Central Bureau of Investigation, Bombay)* (1994) 5 SCC 410, the Supreme Court held that the phrase 'arms and ammunition' must be read conjunctively and acquitted the petitioner who had only a country-made pistol and no ammunition.
[16] Act No. 2 of 1974.   [17] Act No. 28 of 1987.
[18] Preventive Detention Act 1950; Maintenance of Internal Security Act 1971; and National Security Act 1980.
[19] 1994 (2) J.T (SC) 423.
[20] About 20,000 people were detained in Gujarat under TADA while the number so detained was far less in the state of Jammu and Kashmir.
[21] Act No. 45 of 1860.

public pressure, the intervention of the National Human Rights Commission (NHRC), as well as the then forthcoming general elections. It is even more interesting to note the emergence of a more specific enactment in 1993 called the South Asian Association for Regional Cooperation (SAARC) (Suppression of Terrorism) Act[22] that sought to give effect to the SAARC Convention on Suppression of Terrorism 1987.[23] According to section 3 of the Act of 1993, the provisions of Articles I to VIII of the SAARC Convention were declared to have the force of law and given precedence over any other existing law in India.[24] Article I of the SAARC Convention provided a wider definition of a terrorist act and provided that such an act shall not be regarded as a political offence, or an offence connected with a political offence, or as an offence inspired by political motives. Two specific courses of action, extradition or prosecution, were prescribed to states to proceed against a person who had committed an offence as specified under Article I and found in any of the contracting states.[25] Accordingly, section 6 included offences committed outside India. There is no sunset clause in this Act. TADA was also extended for the third time in that year, 1993.

Probably the first legislation to define 'terrorism' was the Terrorist Affected Areas (Special Courts) Act 1984.[26] Section 3(1) of the Act gave the power to the central government to declare an area to be terrorist affected, if to do so was necessary to cope with terrorism. This Act also enabled the government to constitute Special Courts for the speedy trial of suspected terrorists (ss. 4–8), and the appointment of an Additional or Special Public Prosecutor (s. 9). A 'terrorist' was defined as:

> A person who indulges in wanton killing of persons or in violence or in the disruption of services or means of communications essential to the community or in damaging property with a view to:
>
>   i. putting the public or any section of the public in fear; or
>   ii. affecting adversely the harmony between different religions, racial, language or regional groups or castes or communities; or
>   iii. coercing or overawing the government established by law; or
>   iv. endangering the sovereignty and integrity of India.

---

[22] The SAARC Convention (Suppression of Terrorism) Act 1993 (Act No. 36 of 1993).
[23] The SAARC Convention on Suppression of Terrorism was ratified by all the states in the region (Bangladesh, Bhutan, India, Maldives, Nepal, Pakistan and Sri Lanka) and is the second regional Convention to emerge in the sphere of Public International law.
[24] Section 3 of the SAARC (Suppression of Terrorism) Act 1993 provides that 'Notwithstanding anything to the contrary contained in any other law, the provisions of Article I to VIII of the Convention shall have the force of law in India.'
[25] See Article IV of the SAARC Regional Convention on Suppression of Terrorism 1987.
[26] Act No. 61 of 1984.

Section 3(1) of the Terrorist and Disruptive Activities (Prevention) Act 1985[27] contained a more comprehensive definition of a terrorist:

> Whosoever with intent to overawe the Government as by law established or to strike terror in the people or any section of the people or to alienate any section of the people or to adversely affect the harmony amongst different sections of the people does any act or thing by using bombs, dynamite, or other explosive substances or inflammable substances or fire-arms or other lethal weapons or poisons or noxious gases or other chemicals or any other substances (whether biological or otherwise) of a hazardous nature in such a manner as to cause, or as is likely to cause, death of, or injuries to, any person or persons or damage to, or destruction of, property or disruption of any supplies or services essential to the life of the community.

There are also various state enactments in force to deal with particular situations like organized crimes, dangerous activities, anti-social activities and dacoity. They include legislation like the Disturbed Areas (Special Courts) Act 1976,[28] Armed Forces (Punjab and Chandigarh) Special Powers Act 1983,[29] and the Armed Forces (Jammu and Kashmir) Special Powers Act 1990.[30]

With an increasing number of terrorist attacks in the state of Jammu and Kashmir, the North Eastern states, Andhra Pradesh, Mumbai (Bombay), Coimbatore and other cities in India, the non-Congress government at the centre[31] initiated steps to introduce new legislation as TADA ceased to exist and the SAARC (Suppression of Terrorism) Act 1993 was considered inadequate.

III. Institutional responses to a new terrorism law

Two contradictory, yet well-considered, conclusions were arrived at by the Law Commission of India and the NHRC concerning the introduction of new legislation to counter terrorism. The new law is not a 'reactionary' one in India, but the result of a process of meaningful consultation.[32]

A. Responses of the National Human Rights Commission

The NHRC was set up by the Protection of Human Rights Act 1993.[33] It reiterated the core of the Vienna Declaration and Programme of Action 1993 that 'the acts, methods and practices of terrorism in all its forms and manifestations ... are activities aimed at the destruction of human rights ... The international community should take the necessary steps to enhance

---

[27] Act No. 31 of 1985. [28] Act No. 77 of 1976. [29] Act No. 34 of 1983.
[30] Act No. 21 of 1990.
[31] National Democratic Alliance led by the Bharatiya Janata Party.
[32] This seems to contradict the view that a high profile event, such as a terrorist attack will inevitably be followed by a spate of hastily enacted anti-terrorism laws.
[33] Act No. 10 of 1994.

cooperation to prevent and combat terrorism.' Referring to a series of UN Resolutions and Declarations, the NHRC stated that 'the nation, its police and armed forces have a duty to fight and triumph over terrorism. It must be done in a manner that respects the Constitution of our Republic, the laws of our land and the treaty commitments to which we have entered, which set out the provisions of international law and standards we must observe.'[34]

Referring to the violations of the rule of law by the state machinery, NHRC was opposed to the renewal of TADA and insisted on transparency and accountability in the handling of allegations of human rights violations, regardless of who is responsible for the violations.[35] NHRC also stated that 'any worthwhile strategy to combat insurgency and terrorism requires strong citizen support that can be achieved by dialogue with the respective societies affected by the acts of terrorism'.[36] The NHRC also welcomed the government's decision to find political solutions to the problems of insurgency and terrorism, thus emphasizing good governance through which the grievances of the past and the present may be addressed meaningfully. The NHRC had registered 259 cases against the members of Border Security Force up to 31 March 1997, including 12 officers. In 31 cases where investigation against army personnel was conducted, 81 including 29 officers, were eventually punished for human rights' violations.[37] The NHRC also welcomed the steps being taken to strengthen the international legal regime in this respect.[38]

The NHRC attempted to balance human rights with the concerns of terrorism and observed that this was 'essential, both to the cause of human rights and to the fight against terrorism'. It even recommended to the government of India that a suitable financing of terrorism law be enacted.[39] However, in expressing its opposition to the Prevention of Terrorism Bill 2000, the NHRC unanimously decided that

> There is no need to enact a law based on the Bill of 2000 and the needed solution can be found under the existing laws if properly enforced and implemented, and amended if necessary. The proposed Bill, if enacted, would have the ill-effect of providing unintentionally a strong weapon capable of gross misuse and violation of human rights which must be avoided particularly in view of the experience of the misuse in the recent past of TADA and earlier MISA in the emergency days.[40]

In the context of terrorism financing, it is not clear why the NHRC recommended new legislation. The Unlawful Activities (Prevention) Act 1967 (that has no sunset clause) deals with the funds of unlawful associations. If needed, the same law could be amended, instead of enacting a new law.

---

[34] Annual Report 1996–1997, National Human Rights Commission, New Delhi, at 8–10.
[35] Ibid.   [36] Ibid., at 11.   [37] Ibid., at 11–12.   [38] Ibid., at 10.   [39] Ibid., at 11.
[40] Ibid., at 12.

The NHRC has acted both on the basis of complaints as well as *suo moto* on reports of human rights violations by the police, security and armed forces in the state of Jammu and Kashmir. The Commission issued directives to state authorities, and the Ministry of Defence of the government of India. The Army eventually initiated investigations against 96 persons in Jammu and Kashmir and 26 in the North Eastern states during 2000–2001.[41] The Commission issued notice to the Ministry of Home Affairs of the Government of India and the government of the state of Manipur to show cause as to why immediate interim relief should not be accorded to the next-of-kin of the victims of military action. In some cases, the Commission directed that the compensation be paid to the next-of-kin of the victims killed by the Army, police and security forces.[42]

The NHRC also considered it essential to examine the Draft Prevention of Terrorism Bill 2000.[43] Accordingly, the Commission, chaired by J. S. Verma, former Chief Justice of India, formulated a unanimous opinion. The Commission thought that there was no need to enact a new law such as the Prevention of Terrorism Bill 2000. The concerns of the draft Bill were substantially taken care of under existing laws.[44] The Commission went on to say that the main problem facing the country related to proper investigation, adjudication and punishment, a problem which could not be solved by enacting a new law. The Commission also pointed out that the draft Bill would hinder, rather than enhance the effective implementation of international treaties and instruments on human rights, to which India is a party. Yet, the Commission supported new laws dealing with financing of terrorism, a matter on which the draft Bill was silent.[45]

Nevertheless, the Government of India decided in favour of a specific terrorism law. However, as the Parliament of India was not in session, the Government recommended immediate action to the President. Accordingly, the President promulgated the Prevention of Terrorism Ordinance[46] on 24 October 2001 under Article 123 of the Constitution. The NHRC opposed the Ordinance. It observed that:

> undoubtedly national security is of primary importance. Without protecting the safety and security of the nation, individual rights cannot be protected. However, the worth of the nation is the worth of the individuals

---

[41] Ibid., at 13–17.   [42] Ibid., at 18.
[43] Annual Report 2000–1, National Human Rights Commission, New Delhi, at 41.
[44] The Indian Penal Code 1860; Arms Act 1959; Explosives Act 1884: Explosive Substances Act 1908; Armed Forces (Special Powers) Act 1958; Unlawful Activities (Prevention) Act 1967; Suppression of Unlawful Activities against the Safety of Civil Aviation Act 1982; other Preventive Detention laws of the centre as well as of many states were referred to.
[45] Note 43 above at 43.
[46] Prevention of Terrorism Ordinance 2001 (Ordinance 9 of 2001).

constituting it. Article 21 of the Constitution which guarantees a life with dignity, is non-derogable. Both national integrity as well as individual dignity are core values of the Constitution, the relevant international instruments and treaties, and respect the *principles of necessity and proportionality (emphasis added).*[47]

The Commission went on to add that the purpose of anti-terrorism measures must therefore be to protect democracy and human rights, which are fundamental values of our society, not undermine them.[48] The NHRC had also intervened in preventing the TADA from being further extended beyond 1996.

B. Responses of the Law Commission of India

With the background of continued terrorist attacks, the Ministry of Home Affairs of the Government of India requested the Law Commission to undertake a fresh examination of the need for new legislation to combat terrorism and other anti-national activities in India. The Law Commission came to the conclusion that specific legislation to fight terrorism is a necessity in India. The Law Commission observed that it is not that the enactment of such legislation would by itself subdue terrorism. It may, however, arm the state to fight terrorism more effectively.[49] On the question that power is likely to be misused, the Law Commission was quick to refer to the decision of the Supreme Court of India in *State of Rajasthan* v. *Union of India*[50] which observed that:

> It must be remembered that merely because power may sometimes be abused, it is no ground for denying the existence of power. The wisdom of man has not yet been able to conceive of a government with power sufficient to answer all its legitimate needs and at the same time incapable of mischief.

However, the Law Commission felt that it should not be a permanent enactment and pointed out that the draft Bill had provided a specific period for its operation.

The Commission rejected the observation made by the Joint Secretary in the Ministry of External Affairs that 'the constitution of Special Courts and Special Laws are objected to by western governments as they give rise to complications in dealing with the extradition applications'. The Commission observed that it is a matter of policy for the government to decide whether to

---

[47] Annual Report 2001–2002, National Human Rights Commission, New Delhi, at 26.
[48] Ibid.
[49] 173rd Report of the Law Commission of India on Prevention of Terrorism Bill 2000, April 2000, Chapter –III.
[50] 1978 SCR 1; AIR [1977] SC 1361.

dispense with special courts or special procedures. The Commission agreed that the right of appeal should also be given to the prosecution to challenge the grant of bail.[51] The release of the working paper by the Law Commission was followed by the hijacking of an Indian Airlines plane and the release of three notorious terrorists in order to save the passengers and crew. 9/11 and terrorist attacks on the legislature of Jammu and Kashmir convinced the Government of India to persuade the President of India to promulgate the Prevention of Terrorism Ordinance on 24 October 2001. The Ordinance of 2001 was not of a reactionary nature, but the subject of detailed consideration.

IV. Prevention of Terrorism Act 2002

The Prevention of Terrorism Bill 2002 was introduced in the Lok Sabha by the National Democratic Alliance (NDA) led by the Bharatiya Janata Party (BJP). BJP had earlier criticised the TADA for its misuse but became a major partner of the NDA in introducing the Bill of 2002. More ironically, the Congress Party that was responsible for all the preventive detention laws, the Unlawful Activities (Prevention) Act 1967 and TADA, vehemently opposed the Bill of 2002.

After a prolonged debate in the Lok Sabha, the Bill was passed. However, it was defeated in the Rajya Sabha (Council of States), the Upper House of Parliament. The Constitution requires a Bill to be approved by both Houses of Parliament in identical terms.[52] To break this deadlock, the President convened a Joint Sitting of both the Houses of Parliament to discuss the Bill on 26 March 2002.[53] The Bill was finally passed at this joint sitting, convened only for the third time since the commencement of the Constitution in 1950, with 425 members voting in favour and 296 against the Bill. The Bill received the assent of the President on 28 March 2002 and became the Prevention of Terrorism Act (POTA).[54] Among the twenty-eight states in the Indian Union, POTA was opposed by sixteen states, fourteen led by Congress and two by Communist parties.

A. Salient features of POTA

POTA is organized under six chapters, consisting of sixty-four sections. The last chapter has been subject to an amending ordinance[55] followed by an

---

[51] For details see the 173rd Report of the Law Commission of India on Prevention of Terrorism Bill 2000.
[52] Article 107 (2) of the Constitution of India.   [53] Article 108 of the Constitution of India.
[54] Act No. 15 of 2002.
[55] Prevention of Terrorism (Amendment) Ordinance 2003 (Ordinance 4 of 2003).

amendment Act[56] to strengthen the role of the Review Committee. Some important features of POTA are these, and at many points it can be seen that an attempt has been made to strike a balance between empowering the government and checking abuse of power:

a. Section 1(6) provides that POTA shall remain in force for a period of three years from the date of its commencement. The same section also provides an explanation for the word 'commencement'. POTA is retroactive and deemed to have come into force on 24 October 2001, although it was enacted in 2002. In other words, the sunset clause under POTA begins retrospectively from the date of commencement of the first Prevention of Terrorism Ordinance dated 24 October 2001. The new Government that assumed power early this year promised to repeal POTA even before that date.[57] That promise was kept on 23 September 2004 when POTA was repealed by an executive ordinance, just a month before it was due to expire.

b. Holding the proceeds of terrorism is made illegal and the central as well as state governments are empowered to forfeit such proceeds whether or not there is any prosecution or conviction, subject to the procedure prescribed in POTA.[58] However, such power of forfeiture cannot be exercised arbitrarily as a number of checks, both procedural and substantial, are provided in the Act.[59] An appeal to the High Court against an order of forfeiture is also provided for as a check on arbitrary exercise of power.[60]

c. The central government has the power to amend the schedule to POTA[61] to exclude a Terrorist Organization included in the schedule, on the application of the organization concerned or any person affected by its inclusion.[62] On refusal, an appeal is provided to the Review Committee.

d. On the request of an investigating police officer, either the Court of a Chief Judicial Magistrate or the Court of a Chief Metropolitan Magistrate may direct the accused to give samples of handwriting, fingerprints, foot-prints, photographs, blood, saliva, semen, hair or voice to the police officer.[63] If the accused person refuses to give such samples as directed, the courts shall draw an adverse inference against the accused.[64]

---

[56] Prevention of Terrorism (Amendment) Act 2003 (Act No. 4 of 2004).

[57] The Information and Broadcasting Minister Mr S. Jaipal Reddy said that the decision to repeal POTA was in keeping with the promise made to that effect in the Common Minimum Programme of the UPA government led by the Congress Party. The government would rather strengthen the Provisions of the Prevention of Unlawful (Activities) Act 1967 through major amendments in the absence of POTA. 'Bill to Repeal POTA Soon', *Deccan Herald*, 11 August 2004. Also http://www.deccanherald.com/deccanherald/aug11, 2004/i2.asp.

[58] Section 6.   [59] Sections 6–17.   [60] Section 10.   [61] Section 18(2).   [62] Section 19.

[63] Section 27(1).   [64] Section 27(2).

e. A Special Court can, on application by a witness, or the Public Prosecutor, or on its own motion, keep the identity and address of a witness secret, if it is satisfied that the life of the witness is in danger.[65]

f. Certain confessions made to a police officer have been made admissible, notwithstanding prohibitions in existing laws. However, there are a series of checks to protect the rights of the accused. Confessions are to be made only to a high-ranking police officer not below the rank of a Superintendent of Police.[66] Before taking such confessions, the police officer should explain to the accused in writing that he is not bound to make a confession and that if he does so, it may be used against him. The police officer shall not compel or induce the person to make any confession if he decides to remain silent. The confession shall be recorded in the same language as it is given. Such confessions shall be produced before a Chief Metropolitan Magistrate or a Chief Judicial Magistrate, in the original form, within forty-eight hours. If there is a complaint of torture, then such person shall be directed to be produced for medical examination before a Medical Officer, not lower in rank than an Assistant Civil Surgeon and thereafter he shall be sent to 'judicial custody'.[67]

g. Appeals against a decision of a Special Court to the High Court shall be heard by a bench of two judges.[68] However, such appeals shall be preferred within a period of thirty days from the date of the decision unless the appellant has sufficient cause.[69]

h. Chapter V provides for an elaborate power to intercept communication, which section 36 defines to include electronic communication, oral and wire communication. All applications for authorization of interception must be approved by the 'Competent Authority' to be appointed by the central or state government.[70] A series of procedural safeguards have been built into POTA to prevent arbitrary exercise of power, including the submission of an order of interception to a Review Committee.[71] The central and state governments shall cause an annual report of interception to be laid before their respective legislatures. However, governments are permitted to exclude any matter in the annual report if its inclusion is prejudicial to the security of the state or to the prevention and detecting of any terrorist act.[72]

i. There is a specific provision for punishment as well as compensation for malicious action. The provision for 'personal officer liability' for malicious action is a welcome one that can to an extent prevent even high-ranking police officers from exercising their powers maliciously.[73]

---

[65] Section 30.   [66] Equal to the chief Police Officer of a district.   [67] Section 32.
[68] Section 34(1) and (2).   [69] Section 34(5).   [70] Section 37.   [71] Sections 38 to 47.
[72] Section 48.   [73] Section 58.

j. 'Review Committees' are provided for, consisting of a Chairman who is a sitting or retired judge of a High Court and not more than three members.[74] The Prevention of Terrorism (Amendment) Act 2003 inserted new subsections to section 60,[75] resolving several federal issues as well as questions concerning the consequences of directions issued by Review Committees. The constitutional validity of this amendment was upheld by a division bench of the Madras High Court in *State of Tamil Nadu* v. *Union of India*.[76]

POTA is a balanced piece of legislation that has taken national security seriously without diluting too much the rights and liberties of individuals. A number of checks have been incorporated to prevent abuse or misuse of power. The nationwide consultations have contributed to this balanced approach. Yet, POTA has not escaped judicial scrutiny in its brief period of existence.

B. Judicial response

Like the earlier preventive detention and anti-terrorism laws, the constitutional validity of POTA has been questioned. The constitutionality of POTA was questioned before the Division Bench of Punjab and Haryana High Court in *Simranjit Singh Mann* v. *Union of India*,[77] but without success. The High Court relied on a Supreme Court decision[78] which had approved of the Terrorist and Disruptive Activities (Prevention) Act 1987, a piece of legislation that POTA had borrowed heavily from.

A batch of petitions were also filed before the Supreme Court of India challenging the constitutional validity of POTA, including a public interest petition filed by the People's Union for Civil Liberties.[79] All these petitions were clubbed together by the Supreme Court in *People's Union for Civil Liberties* v. *Union of India*.[80] The Division Bench of the Supreme Court relied on the Constitution Bench decision in *Kartar Singh* v. *State of Punjab*.[81] It rejected the contention of the petitioners questioning the legislative competence of Parliament. Similarly, the court also rejected the contention that POTA is likely to be misused and pointed out that TADA's misuse had resulted in a large number of acquittals. The court observed that 'once the legislation is passed the government has an obligation to exercise all available options to prevent terrorism within the bounds of the Constitution'. Following earlier

---

[74] Section 60.   [75] Section 60(4), (5), (6), and (7).
[76] Writ Petition Nos. 1238, 1239 and 1240 of 2004 and W.P.M.P. Nos. 1297, 1298 and 1299 of 2004, as decided on 4 February 2004.
[77] 2002 Cri.L.J. 3368.   [78] *Kartar Singh* v. *State of Punjab* (1994) 3 SCC 569.
[79] Writ Petition (Crl) 89/2002, W.P. (Crl) 129/2002, W.P. (Crl.28/2003 and W.P. (Crl) 48/2003.
[80] (2004) 9 SCC 580.   [81] (1994) 3 SCC 569.

decisions,[82] the court held that mere possibility of abuse cannot be grounds for denying the vesting of powers or for declaring a statute unconstitutional. The petitioners argued that section 3(3) of POTA gave rise to the possibility of misuse as the term 'abet' had not been defined in POTA. The court held that the term 'abet' as defined in the Indian Penal Code would apply to POTA as well and rejected the argument of the petitioners. The petitioners also challenged the validity of section 4 which provides for punishment for 'unauthorised possession' of arms or other weapons, on the basis that the knowledge element is absent in that provision. The court rejected this argument by pointing to the decision in *Sanjay Dutt* v. *State (II)*[83] and held that the section presupposes the requirement of knowledge.

The petitioners challenged the validity of the sections concerning notification and denotification of terrorist organizations. They contended that inclusion in the schedule was without any legislative decision. They also argued that it excessively delegated power to the central government in the appointment of members to the Review Committee. The Supreme Court rejected these arguments and upheld the validity of these provisions on the ground that there is a post-decisional hearing, alternative constitutional remedies are available, and that the Review Committee is headed by a person who is or has been a judge of the High Court.

The petitioners assailed sections 20, 21, and 22 on the ground that no requirement of *mens rea* for offences is provided in these sections. Referring to similar provisions in the Terrorism Act 2000 of the United Kingdom[84] and the need for such laws all over the world, the Supreme Court held that these sections are limited only to those activities that have the intent of encouraging, furthering, promoting or facilitating the commission of terrorist activities. There cannot be any misuse if these sections are understood that way, the court said.[85]

The petitioners challenged the validity of section 27 under which a police officer can obtain a court direction for obtaining samples of handwriting, fingerprints, foot-prints, photographs and intimate body samples, and also the threat of adverse inferences if an accused refused to comply. The court rejected this challenge and pointed out that the courts have discretionary power and have to record the reasoning for allowing or rejecting a request made by an investigating officer. The Supreme Court also referred to an

---

[82] *State of Rajasthan* v. *Union of India*, AIR [1977] SC 1361; *Collector of Customs* v. *Nathella Sampathu Chetty*, AIR [1962] SC 316; *Keshavananda Bharathi* v. *State of Kerala*, AIR [1973] SC; and *Mafatlal Industries* v. *Union of India* (1997) 5 SCC 536.
[83] (1994) 5 SCC 410.   [84] Sections 11, 12 and 15 of Terrorism Act 2000.
[85] The court seems to have ignored the misuse of POTA by the Government of Tamil Nadu in detaining the leader of MDMK party for addressing a public meeting in support of LTTE.

earlier decision by a bench consisting of eleven judges in *State of Bombay* v. *Kathi Kalu Oghad*[86] in which the court had observed that requiring an accused person to provide such samples does not amount to compelling the accused person to testify as a witness in his own trial.

The petitioners challenged section 30 that provides for the protection of the identity of witnesses on the ground that the right to cross-examine, and thus the right to fair trial had been impaired. The court relied on *Kartar Singh* which upheld a similar provision (section 16) in the TADA. The court observed that the right to cross-examine as such is not taken away, but confers necessary discretion to keep the identity of witnesses secret, if their lives would otherwise be in danger. In the opinion of the court, a fair balance has been maintained among the competing interests of the accused, the witness and the public.

Thus the Supreme Court followed the tradition of upholding the constitutional validity of POTA, like the previous preventive detention and terrorism laws. One advantage is that the Supreme Court as well as the state High Courts retain their appellate as well as supervisory jurisdiction to correct any injustice caused to the individuals. Judicial review of administrative action has been a foundation of constitutional governance in India.

Mention should also be made of a few judicial decisions in the application of POTA. In spite of section 34 (2) that mandates the appeals to be heard by the High Court division bench consisting of two judges, many appeals have been disposed off by single judge benches of the High Courts. However, some of these decisions of a single judge bench of the High Courts have been set aside by the Supreme Court on second appeal in accordance with section 34 (2).[87] In a few cases, the High Courts have intervened to provide appropriate relief to appellants for non-compliance with the provisions of POTA by the authorities or by the Special Courts.[88] In an interpretation of

---

[86] 1962 (3) SCR 10; AIR [1961] SC 1808.

[87] *State (Central Bureau of Investigation, New Delhi)* v. *Navjot Sandhu & Afshan Guru and others*, (2003) 6 SCC 641; *State of Gujarat* v. *Salimbhai Abdulgaffar Shaik and others*, (2003) 8 SCC 50; and *State of Tamil Nadu* v. *Vaiko*, Writ Appeal No. 4065 of 2003 as decided by the Madras High Court on 15 December 2003.

[88] *Mohammad Gausuddin* v. *State of Maharastra*, Criminal Appeal Nos. 3 and 679 of 2002 as decided by the Nagpur division bench of the Bombay High Court on 5 March 2003; *Kamlakar & Others* v. *State of Maharastra*, Criminal Appeal Nos. 597 and 676 of 2002 as decided by the Nagpur division bench of the Bombay High Court on 30 April 2003; *R. R. Gopal* v. *State*, Criminal Appeal No. 1219 of 2003 as decided on 19 September 2003; *Shahul Hammeed* v. *State of Tamil Nadu*, Criminal Appeal No. 310 of 2004 as decided on 18 March 2004; *Paranthaman* v. *State of Tamil Nadu*, Criminal Appeal No. 363 of 2004 as decided on 5 April 2004; *Madurai Ganesan & Others* v. *State of Tamil Nadu*, Criminal Appeal No. 1397 of 2003 as decided on 12 January 2004; *P. Nedumaran & others* v. *State of Tamil Nadu*, Criminal Appeal No. 749, 750–2, 764–6 of 2003 as decided on 18 December 2003 by various division benches of the Madras High Court.

section 49 (7) of POTA, a division bench of the Madras High court held that there is no bar to move bail petitions within one year of detention, as decided by the Special Court.[89] The High Court of Madras has also directed the closure of a POTA case against a fifteen-year-old minor and directed that he may be proceeded against under the Juvenile Justice (Care and Protection of Children) Act 2000.[90]

V. POTA in practice

The short duration of POTA's existence has proved its effectiveness as well as its misuse. When compared with TADA, the previous terrorism law, the number of people detained has come down drastically.[91] There are about 440 persons detained under POTA, mainly from six states. About 93 are detained in the state of Maharastra, 90 in Jharkhand, 83 in Gujarat, 46 in Delhi, 42 in Tamil Nadu and 36 in Andhra Pradesh.[92] The number of persons arrested but not detained is, of course more. Some were released on bail and some discharged by the state governments. The reasons for release may be many, yet the safeguards provided under POTA are possibly among them.

However, the misuse of POTA could not be prevented altogether, primarily because of the lack of accountability and the inability to fix personal responsibility for such abuse of power. Nonetheless, the misuse has been, to a large extent, minimized during its short existence when compared to the previous legislation. The instances of misuse of POTA include cases from the state of Jharkhand. This state alone witnessed the arrest of about 218 people (as of February 2003) and included persons as young as twelve and as old as eighty-one. The state government directed the Crime Investigation Department (CID) to review the cases filed by the police. The CID reviewed 84 cases and found insufficient evidence in 41. Out of 277 persons arrested, 71 were granted bail (as of 1 January 2004). The Review Committee constituted by the state government of Jharkhand also discharged 114 persons.[93] These developments clearly indicate abuse of power as well as the effectiveness of safeguards provided under POTA. However, there is no information as to the compensation paid to those detained illegally.

---

[89] *Paza Nedumaran and others* v. *State of Tamil Nadu*, Criminal Appeal Nos. 1606, 1607, 1639, 1640, 1779 and 1780 of 2002 and Criminal Miscellaneous Petition No. 11999 of 2002 as decided on 3 March 2003.

[90] *Prabakaran* v. *State of Tamil Nadu*, Writ Petition No. 4511of 2003.

[91] In the State of Gujarat alone about 20,000 people were detained under TADA.

[92] See 'Interpretation of the Draconian: An Analysis of the POTA Judgement and POTA Amendment Review', Asian Centre for Human Rights, http://www.achrweb.org/Review/0104.htm.

[93] Ibid.

The Central Review Committee received about 180 complaints. Out of this, 40 were from Tamil Nadu, 39 from Maharastra, 28 from Delhi, 26 from Uttar Pradesh, 16 from Jammu and Kashmir and 15 from Jharkhand.[94] The Central Review Committee has been giving directions in favour of both the individuals detained as well as in favour of the state. Yet, some of the directions issued by the Review Committee have not been implemented by the states in spite of the clear terms of section 60 (7) of POTA.

VI. POTA repealed

The issue of repealing POTA was discussed by the present Home Minister of India and it was very clearly expressed to him that if POTA was repealed the security forces in the country would be unable to take action against terrorist and anti-national outfits. The concerns relating to money laundering and the inability of the security forces to act without a law like POTA as well as the limitations in banning terrorist organizations under the Unlawful Activities (Prevention) Act 1967 were also raised.[95]

In spite of these developments, the new government at the centre attempted to introduce a bill to repeal POTA as promised in the Common Minimum Programme of the United Progressive Alliance, led by the Congress party, despite the fact that POTA would automatically cease to exist on 23 October 2004. However, the government could not introduce a bill in the current budget session for want of time. Yet, the Union Cabinet recommended to the President its decision to repeal POTA, based on which two Ordinances were issued by the President under article 123 of the Constitution on 23 September 2004, just one month before POTA's expiry. The first Ordinance repealed POTA[96] and the second to amend the existing Unlawful Activities (Prevention) Act 1967[97] in an attempt to strengthen its provisions. This Act of 1967 has no sunset clause. However, the Central Review Committee would continue to function and dispose of all petitions before it within one year.[98]

Politics seems to have sidelined the importance and relevance given to prevention of terrorism on the Indian soil. Thus, POTA probably became the first law to be repealed even before the operation of the sunset clause built into it. The repeal is not by any law made by the Parliament, but by an

---

[94] Ibid.
[95] See 'Home Minister, Officials Mull POTA-Less Scenario', *Deccan Herald*, 16 July 2004, http://www.deccanherald.com/deccanherald/july162004/n11.asp.
[96] Prevention of Terrorism (Repeal) Ordinance 2004 (Ordinance 1 of 2004).
[97] The Unlawful Activities (Prevention) Amendment Ordinance 2004 (Ordinance 2 of 2004).
[98] Section 3 of the Prevention of Terrorism (Repeal) Ordinance 2004 (Ordinance 1 of 2004).

executive Ordinance under article 123 of the Constitution. POTA has been, as already mentioned, a balanced law to combat terrorism, providing some safeguards to protect the rights of the accused. Yet the present government that was responsible for all the previous enactments, brought a premature end to POTA. It remains to be seen whether the amended Unlawful Activities (Prevention) Act 1967 will be sufficient to tackle terrorism or whether the Indian government will be able to live without a piece of legislation like POTA, and if not, how terrorism legislation which might be enacted in the future will differ from POTA.

18

Enacting security laws in Hong Kong

SIMON N. M. YOUNG

I. Introduction

This chapter outlines the events surrounding the resisted and, at times, frustrated attempts to enact security laws in Hong Kong from 2001 to 2004. It will be argued that the resistance was attributable to a number of factors, the most important of which was the absence of a grassroots concept of security, conceived in Hong Kong as a result of a genuine and informed public consultation process. In respect of both the anti-terrorism and national security initiatives, the misguided strategy of the government was to impose a set of proposals at the outset, adopt a defensive attitude in the consultation process, and make significant concessions at the final hour as acts of appeasement. This chapter will conclude with a discussion of ideas for developing a new implementation strategy that will take the discourse on security in Hong Kong to a new level.

II. Initiatives to enact security laws 2001–2004

A. Security regime before September 11

While under British rule, seven of the major international treaties on terrorism were extended to Hong Kong after ratification by the United Kingdom.[1] The

I would like to thank Mark Fenwick, Michael Hor and Kent Roach for their comments on an earlier draft.

[1] See Convention on the Prevention and Punishment of Crimes Against Internationally Protected Persons, including Diplomatic Agents (1973), extended on 2 May 1979; International Convention Against the Taking of Hostages (1979), extended on 22 Dec. 1982; Convention on Offences and Certain Other Acts Committed on Board Aircraft (1963), extended on 4 Dec. 1969; Convention for the Suppression of Unlawful Seizure of Aircraft (1970), extended on 22 Dec. 1971, effective 21 Jan. 1972; Convention for the Suppression of Unlawful Acts against the Safety of Civil Aviation (1971), extended on 25 Oct. 1973; Protocol for the Suppression of Unlawful Acts of Violence at Airports Serving International Civil Aviation (1988), extended on 21 May 1997; Convention on the Marking of Plastic Explosives for the Purpose of Detection (1991), extended on 28 April 1997.

colonial government in turn implemented these treaties.[2] It was never considered necessary to apply the general anti-terrorism laws enacted in the United Kingdom to Hong Kong.

Following the resumption of sovereignty by China in 1997, Hong Kong's obligations under international instruments were to cease unless they continued in accordance with the new constitutional framework of The Basic Law of the Hong Kong Special Administrative Region of the People's Republic of China ('Basic Law').[3] This framework was similar to the previous one in that treaty obligations of China did not automatically apply to Hong Kong, but required a separate decision by the Central People's Government after seeking the views of the Hong Kong government.[4] Showing respect for Hong Kong's high degree of autonomy, the Basic Law made it possible for previous implemented international agreements to continue their implementation even if China was not a party to those agreements.[5] After 1997 the seven anti-terrorism instruments and their implementations were allowed to continue.[6]

Hong Kong also adhered to the anti-terrorism measures contained in United Nations Security Council decisions made under Chapter VII of the United Nations Charter. On 16 July 1997 Hong Kong's Provisional Legislative Council enacted the United Nations Sanctions Ordinance (Cap 537) (UNSO), which gave the Chief Executive a lawmaking power (using subsidiary legislation) for the purpose of implementing Chapter VII sanctions.[7] There were two main prerequisites to the exercise of this power. First, there had to be instructions from the Central People's Government to implement such a sanction.[8] This was consistent with the framework under the Basic Law, which reserved matters of foreign affairs to the central

---

[2] See Internationally Protected Persons and Taking of Hostages Ordinance (Cap 468), originally Ord. No. 20 of 1995; Fugitives Offenders (Internationally Protected Persons and Hostages) Order (Cap 503H), originally L.N. 205 of 1997; Aviation Security Ordinance (Cap. 494), originally 52 of 1996; Fugitive Offenders (Safety of Civil Aviation) Order (Cap 503G), originally L.N. 204 of 1997; Crimes Ordinance (Cap 200), Part VIIA, originally Crimes (Amendment) Ordinance 1994, Ord. No. 52 of 1994.

[3] Adopted by the 7th National People's Congress at its Third Session on 4 April 1990 ('Basic Law').

[4] Basic Law, Art. 153.   [5] Ibid.

[6] At the time, China was a party to all of the instruments except for the Convention on the Marking of Plastic Explosives for the Purpose of Detection (1991). The International Convention for the Suppression of Terrorist Bombings (1997) was applied to Hong Kong on 13 Nov. 2001.

[7] The Ordinance was originally Ord. No. 125 of 1997, coming into operation on 18 July 1997. Prior to 1 July 1997, Orders in Council made under English legislation (i.e. the United Nations Act 1946) were used to extend Chapter VII sanctions to British colonies. These Orders in Council were first made by Her Majesty in Council, then laid before the British Parliament, and once published in the Hong Kong Gazette, had legal force in Hong Kong.

[8] United Nations Sanctions Ordinance (Cap 537), s. 2(2) ('UNSO').

government.[9] Secondly, the sanctions had to be 'mandatory measures decided by the Security Council of the United Nations, *implemented against a place outside the People's Republic of China*' (emphasis added).[10] These two conditions were more than prerequisites since their satisfaction made it mandatory for the Chief Executive to exercise the power.[11] Strangely, regulations made under this power, unlike normal subsidiary legislation, were not subject to scrutiny by the Legislative Council of the Hong Kong Special Administrative Region ('LegCo').[12] As discussed below, it was the restrictiveness of this condition and also the second prerequisite that drew significant criticisms from legislators in late 2002 in the course of implementing legislation in response to September 11.

Using the power conferred by the UNSO, Hong Kong passed a regulation, the United Nations Sanctions (Afghanistan) Regulation (Cap 537K) (UNSAR), to implement the economic sanctions against the then Taliban regime in Afghanistan required by Security Council Resolution 1267 (R. 1267) adopted on 15 October 1999.[13] This regulation, for the first time, provided for the listing of individuals, groups, and property related to the Taliban, who were designated by the Committee established by R. 1267, in the Hong Kong Gazette for the purposes of enforcing the sanctions. When the Security Council extended these sanctions on 19 December 2000 by applying a general arms embargo to Taliban territory and against Osama bin Laden and the al Qaeda organization, Hong Kong made a further regulation to implement the extended sanctions.[14]

Overall, the Hong Kong measures against terrorism before September 11 were limited in terms of both the type of terrorist activity proscribed and the persons targeted. There were no general criminal offences proscribing terrorists or terrorist activities. Indeed, no definition of terrorist or terrorist activity was ever codified. There was no offence of financing terrorism. Terrorist acts that did not come within any of the implemented offences were left to be addressed by Hong Kong's ordinary criminal laws, e.g. murder, kidnapping, criminal damage to property, causing explosion likely to endanger, etc. The listing of persons in the Gazette was restricted to Osama bin Laden and members of the Taliban and the al Qaeda organization. Measures to cut off the flow of funds to terrorists were restricted to these persons.

---

[9] Basic Law, Art. 13.   [10] UNSO, s. 2(1).
[11] Ibid., s. 3(1) which provides that the 'Chief Executive shall make regulations to give effect to a relevant instruction'.
[12] Normally, subsidiary legislation is subject to either positive or negative vetting according to ss. 34 and 35, respectively, of the Interpretation and General Clauses Ordinance (Cap 1). Subs. 3(5) of the UNSO provides that these sections are not to apply.
[13] Originally L.N. 229 of 2000, which came into effect on or about 15 June 2000.
[14] See United Nations Sanctions (Afghanistan) (Arms Embargoes) Regulation, L.N. 211 of 2001, which came into effect on or about 11 October 2001 and expired on 18 January 2002.

B. Legal response to September 11 (Part I)

1. Two stage strategy to implementation

The Security Council's first Chapter VII response to the September 11 attacks was in Resolution 1373 (R. 1373), adopted on 28 September 2001. This resolution required all states to implement measures against the financing of terrorism generally and to cut off all forms of support to terrorists and terrorist groups. On 16 January 2002, the Security Council adopted further Chapter VII action in Resolution 1390 (R. 1390), which strengthened its existing measures aimed at Osama bin Laden, members of the al Qaeda organization and the Taliban, and all their controlled entities and associates.

Unlike other jurisdictions, Hong Kong did not respond urgently and rashly with new anti-terrorism legislation after September 11. Since the matter concerned 'foreign affairs', Hong Kong itself was not free to enact laws until it received the relevant instructions from the central government, which were reportedly given in October 2001.[15] In late November 2001, the Security Bureau presented a paper in a LegCo joint meeting between the Panel on Administration of Justice and Legal Services and the Panel on Security outlining measures to combat terrorism.[16] During the course of the meeting, it became apparent that the Administration had internally debated the possible legal responses to September 11.[17] As R. 1373 was a Chapter VII measure, one might naturally have thought that the implementation would be by executive regulations made under the UNSO. However, it was not possible to do this since R. 1373, being a resolution adopted against terrorists anywhere in the world, did not come within the second prerequisite condition of containing measures 'implemented against a place outside the People's Republic of China'.[18] It was decided that this would be the first Security Council sanction to be implemented by ordinary legislation. Whether the Administration intended it or not, this was a positive move since the use of the UNSO executive power would have bypassed public scrutiny and the checks and balances of the legislative process. However,

---

[15] Security Bureau, '[LegCo] Brief: [the Bill]', SBCR 2/16/1476/74, 10 April 2002, para 2 ('LegCo Brief'). This document and others from the Security Bureau or LegCo Secretariat can be found on the LegCo website: www.legco.gov.hk.

[16] See Security Bureau, 'Measures to combat terrorism', LC Paper No. CB(2)490/01–02(01) for Joint Meeting of the Panels on Administration of Justice and Legal Services, Financial Affairs and Security, 30 Nov. 2001.

[17] See LegCo Secretariat, 'Minutes of joint meeting held on Friday, 30 November 2001 at 10:45 am in the Chamber of the [LegCo] Building', LC Paper No. CB(2) 916/01–02 for LegCo Panels on Security and Administration of Justice and Legal Services, 8 January 2002 ('Minutes of Joint Meeting').

[18] UNSO, above n 8, s. 2(1). In the Minutes of Joint Meeting, ibid., para 28, the Solicitor General acknowledged this problem and made statements to the effect that the UNSO would have to be amended if it was to be used to implement R. 1373.

as will be seen below, the UNSO was not completely out of the picture since it was used to implement R. 1390.

In the November joint meeting, the Secretary for Security, Regina Yip, announced the two-stage strategy to implementation.[19] In the first stage, the 'essential elements' of R. 1373 were to be implemented in a new bill to be introduced in late February 2002.[20] The Administration later identified the 'essential elements' as paragraphs 1(a), (b), (c), (d) and 2(a) of R. 1373, which generally related to the financing and material support of terrorism and freezing of terrorist funds.[21] Added to the first stage was the implementation of Recommendations II, III and IV of the Special Recommendations of the Financial Action Task Force on Money Laundering (FATF).[22] While these recommendations overlapped somewhat with R. 1373, they widened the scope of implementation with new duties related to confiscating terrorist assets and reporting suspicious transactions related to terrorism.[23] In the second stage, the Administration was intending to implement the less urgent 'non-mandatory elements' of R. 1373 and other international conventions against terrorism, and to 'give full effect to the FATF's Special Recommendations'.[24]

While the Administration had planned to introduce legislation in late February 2002, it was not until 17 April 2002 that the United Nations (Anti-Terrorism Measures) Bill was first read in LegCo.[25] Apparently, the drafting of the Bill had 'taken more time than expected'.[26] Unfortunately, as it would turn out, this delay took away a critical amount of time for legislators and the public to scrutinize the Bill. The government was determined to pass the legislation by June 2002. There appeared to be three other reasons for this urgency. First, the FATF had imposed a deadline of June 2002 for countries to comply with its Special Recommendations on terrorist financing. Failure to comply could have resulted in countermeasures from FATF members. As Hong Kong held the Presidency of the FATF during this period, it would have been very embarrassing and a poor example for other countries if it did not comply with this deadline.[27]

---

[19] Minutes of Joint Meeting, ibid., para 3.   [20] Ibid., paras 3, 9.

[21] LegCo Brief, above note 15, para 4.   [22] Ibid.

[23] On 28–30 October 2001, the FATF held an extraordinary plenary meeting on the financing of terrorism, which led to eight Special Recommendations. See the FATF website: http://www1.oecd.org/fatf/. Hong Kong has been a member of the FATF since 1990. It held the Presidency in 2001–2002.

[24] LegCo Brief, above note 15, para 4.

[25] The Bill was gazetted on 12 April 2002. See the Government of the HKSAR Gazette website at http://www.gld.gov.hk/cgi-bin/gld/egazette/index.cgi?lang = e&agree = 0.

[26] See reply of Secretary for Security in LegCo Secretariat, 'Minutes of special meeting held on Tuesday, 5 February 2002 at 8:30 am in the Chamber of the [LegCo] Building', LC Paper No. CB(2) 1478/01–02 for LegCo Panel on Security, 25 March 2002, para 30.

[27] The Security Bureau described the consequence for Hong Kong as 'serious reputational risk as the FATF may publicly announce the jurisdictions which fail to comply with certain Special Recommendations'. It went on to say that this would 'reflect badly on HKSAR

Secondly, China had reported to the Counter-Terrorism Committee (CTC), established by R. 1373, on 22 December 2001 that Hong Kong would soon be enacting legislation to implement R. 1373.[28] The CTC replied with preliminary comments on the report and a request 'to provide a response in the form of a supplementary report by 24 June 2002'.[29] As it is unusual for China to accept United Nations reporting obligations, it would have been a loss of face if by June 2002 it could not report back to the CTC that concrete measures had been enacted in Hong Kong. China eventually provided its supplementary report in a letter dated 17 July 2002, five days after the Bill had passed through LegCo.[30]

Thirdly, China itself had implemented R. 1373 by enacting anti-terrorism laws for the mainland in late December 2001.[31] It would have greatly displeased China if the Hong Kong authorities had excessively delayed the implementation of R. 1373, especially since the instruction to Hong Kong was issued in October 2001.[32] As discussed below, these three reasons were the source of an immense amount of pressure to have the legislation passed before the 2002 summer recess.

2. United Nations (Anti-Terrorism Measures) Ordinance (UNATMO)[33]

a. The Process   There is no doubt that the pressure to pass the Bill in less than three months resulted in faulty legislation. Indeed, the second stage of implementing anti-terrorism laws, which began in May 2003, was partly devoted to correcting the flaws in the UNATMO. The Bills Committee for the Bill met for the first time on 17 May 2002. Although the Bills Committee managed to hold fifteen meetings before the Bill was passed by LegCo on 12 July 2002, the last twelve meetings were packed within a period of 24 days, leaving on average a day between each meeting. No wide public consultations

especially given our leading role as the President of the FATF'. See '[the Bill]', Paper No. CB(2)1930/01–02(03) for the Bills Committee on [the Bill], 17 May 2002.

[28] Jeremy Greenstock, 'Letter dated 27 December 2001 from the Chairman of the [CTC] addressed to the President of the Security Council', UN Doc. S/2001/1270, Annex.

[29] Jeremy Greenstock, 'Letter dated 10 April 2002 from the Chairman of the [CTC] addressed to the President of the Security Council', UN Doc. S/2002/399.

[30] Jeremy Greenstock, 'Letter dated 31 July 2002 from the Chairman of the [CTC] addressed to the President of the Security Council', UN Doc. S/2002/884, Annex.

[31] See the Government of China's supplementary report in the Annex to Jeremy Greenstock, 'Letter dated 4 January 2002 from the Chairman of the [CTC] addressed to the President of the Security Council', UN Doc. S/2001/1270/Add.1.

[32] As these instructions have never been revealed, it is not clear if the Chinese authorities imposed any deadline or timetable for implementation.

[33] Originally Ord. No. 27 of 2002. Partly in operation on 23 August 2002, see L.N. 137 of 2002.

were held on the Bill. While various public interest groups, media and business associations, legal academics and legal professional groups were invited to make written submissions, only two meetings were held to receive deputations from invited persons and groups.[34]

A common criticism amongst the commentators was the insufficient amount of time the government had allowed for review of the original Bill and the many proposed amendments that were being made. For example, in its written submission the Hong Kong Bar Association deplored 'the lack of proper time for full public consultation on the Bill when there is obviously no urgency to enact any anti-terrorist legislation in Hong Kong'.[35] From as early as the seventh meeting on 17 June 2002, the Administration began introducing a set of committee stage amendments (CSAs) that were constantly being updated and altered. The manner in which these amendments were being proposed, considered and modified was chaotic. Commentators were not properly informed of the latest changes to the proposed CSAs.[36] These sudden changes to rashly formulated proposals frustrated persons participating in the process.

The legislators who sat on the Bills Committee repeatedly criticized the government's moves to rush the Bill through LegCo. The following translated excerpt from legislator Audrey Eu's speech in the final debates captures the frustration felt by the Bills Committee members at the time:

> Actually, over the past one and a half months, Members have worked non-stop to scrutinize the Bill, convening 15 meetings in total. If my reckoning is correct, the Administration has submitted more than 10 revised drafts. Last Wednesday, when the last meeting of the Bills Committee was held, the Government could not submit a printed version of the finalized draft in time, and so, the draft had to be dictated to Members at the meeting, and Members were required to submit their amendments to the Government's finalized draft before midnight that day. This shows that the Bills Committee has never had any opportunity to discuss the Bill and submit appropriate amendments. It is extremely irresponsible, Madam President,

---

[34] See LegCo Secretariat, 'Minutes of the second meeting held on Monday, 3 June 2002 at 8:30 am in the Chamber of the [LegCo] Building', LC Paper No. CB(2)2323/01–02 for Bills Committee on the Bill, 17 June 2002, and LegCo Secretariat, 'Minutes of the 10th meeting held on Tuesday, 25 June 2002 at 8:30 am in Conference Room A of the [LegCo] Building', LC Paper No. CB(2)2880/01–02 for Bills Committee on the Bill, 7 Oct. 2002.

[35] See Hong Kong Bar Association, 'Submissions on [the Bill]', LC Paper No. CB(2)2548/01–02(01) for the Bills Committee on the Bill, 9 July 2002, para 5. To the same effect, see submissions of JUSTICE in '[The Bill]: Main Points and Suggested Draft Amendments', LC Paper No. CB(2)2390/01–02(01) for the Bills Committee on the Bill, June 2002, p 1.

[36] See generally Simon Young, 'Hong Kong's Anti-Terrorism Measures Under Fire', Occasional Paper No. 7 (Hong Kong: Centre for Comparative and Public Law, 2003) 8–10, which can be found at www.hku.hk/ccpl.

to handle a bill like the anti-terrorism Bill, which is so very complicated in nature and extensive in implications.[37]

On the day of the ninth meeting in the Bills Committee, i.e. 24 June 2002, the government, somewhat high-handedly, gave notice to resume the second reading of the Bill on 10 July 2002.[38] This was done even though it was clear that the work of the Bills Committee was incomplete and members of the Committee objected to such notice being given.[39] This move was like adding fuel to the already fired atmosphere of the Committee. Three days later, in a show of protest, the Bills Committee passed, without objection, the following motion proposed by legislator Cyd Ho:

> That this Bills Committee expresses deep regret that the Executive has given notice to resume the Second Reading debate on the United Nations (Anti-Terrorism Measures) Bill on 10 July 2002 before scrutiny of the Bill has been completed, which is at variance with the established practice of the Legislative Council.[40]

The so-called 'embarrassing hiccup' with the enactment of the terrorist recruitment offence was symbolic of the defects resulting from the rushed and unconsidered passage of the Bill.[41] The original proposal made it an offence for a person to 'become a member of, or begin to serve in any capacity with, a person specified in a notice'.[42] This offence was drawn so broadly that it could have included the family members of the specified person and anyone providing a service to that person, including his or her legal counsel or someone as innocuous as a laundry delivery person. It was also problematic because it lacked express *mens rea* requirements. The government acknowledged these problems and prepared committee stage amendments to address some of them.[43] The embarrassing moment occurred in the Council meeting when due to a dinner break there were an insufficient number of legislators who

---

[37] *Official Record of Proceedings of the Legislative Council of the Hong Kong Special Administrative Region* ('*HK Hansard*'), 11 July 2002, 8863–4 (translated from Cantonese).

[38] Legislators questioned whether there had been a breach of R. 54(5) of the LegCo Rules of Procedure, which required consultation with the chairman of the House Committee before effective notice could be given. See LegCo Secretariat, 'Minutes of the 29th meeting held in the [LegCo] Chamber at 2:30 pm on Friday, 28 June 2002', LC Paper No. CB(2) 2490/01–02 for House Committee of the [LegCo], 25 Sept. 2002, para 78–120.

[39] Ibid., para 99.

[40] See LegCo Secretariat, 'Minutes of the 11th meeting held on Thursday, 27 June 2002 at 8:30 am in Conference Room A of the [LegCo] Building', LC Paper No. CB(2)2881/01–02 for the Bills Committee on the Bill, 7 Oct 2002, para 2.

[41] See Ambrose Leung, Angela Li and Alyssa Lau, 'Embarrassing hiccup for terror bill', *South China Morning Post*, 12 July 2002.

[42] Bill, above note 25, clause 9(1)(b).

[43] LegCo Secretariat, 'Report of the Bills Committee on [the Bill]', LC Paper No. CB(2)2401/ 01–02 for House Committee meeting on 28 June 2002, para 44.

supported the government's amendment.[44] A competing amendment proposed by legislator Margaret Ng aimed at narrowing the provision even more
was also defeated. After the absent legislators had returned, there was little
choice for the government supporters but to accept the original proposal,
which even the government acknowledged was faulty. The enacted proposal
contained another obvious anomaly in that it referred only to persons
specified by the Chief Executive and not to those specified by court order,
which was a second form of specification added only in the CSAs.[45]
Subsequently, the Administration stated that the provision would not be
brought into operation until it was corrected in the second stage of
implementation.[46]

b. The Substance   In formulating its proposals, the Administration stated
that it was adopting a 'minimalist approach' to implementing R. 1373.[47] To
some extent, this was true. The Bill was relatively short, with only nineteen
clauses and three schedules, spanning only twenty-two pages in the Gazette.
Except in one respect, the proposals stayed within the aims and purposes of
R. 1373 and the FATF Special Recommendations. None of the controversial
detention powers or provisions affecting fair trial rights, as seen in other
countries such as the United States and Canada, were proposed.[48]
Nevertheless, the original proposals were often drawn in such broad terms
without sufficient safeguards or clear limits that their impact on human
rights seemed far from minimal.

One of the most pressing concerns with the proposals was the risk that the
new specification system might be used to marginalize groups, such as the Falon
Gong, that China had branded as 'terrorists' or counter-revolutionaries.[49]
Whether this was possible turned on how 'terrorist act' was defined in the Bill
since the definitions of 'terrorist', 'terrorist associate' and 'terrorist property'
were all based on the concept of 'terrorist act'. The definition in the original Bill

---

[44] See *HK Hansard*, 11 July 2002, above note 37, 8990–9004; 'Embarrassing hiccup for terror
     bill', above note 41.
[45] See UNATMO, above note 33, s. 10.
[46] Legal Services Division, 'Legal Service Division Report on Subsidiary Legislation Gazetted
     on 23 August 2002', which is Annex III to LegCo Secretariat, 'Paper for the House
     Committee Meeting on 4 October 2002', LC Paper No. LS 131/01–02 for House
     Committee, 2 Oct. 2002.
[47] Security Bureau, 'Legislative Proposals to Implement Anti-terrorism Measures under
     United Nations Security Council Resolution (UNSCR) 1373', LC Paper No. CB(2)1021/
     01–02(01) for LegCo Panel on Security, January 2002, para 5.
[48] See, in this volume, Roach, Chapter 23; Fenwick and Phillipson, Chapter 21; Banks,
     Chapter 22.
[49] Minutes of Joint Meeting, above note 17, para 6(b).

together with the superimposed changes in the final enacted definition is shown below:

'terrorist act' (恐怖主義行為) –

(a) subject to paragraph (b), means the use or threat of action where–
   (i) the action (including, in the case of a threat, the action if carried out) –
      (A) ~~involves~~ causes serious violence against a person;
      (B) ~~involves~~ causes serious damage to property;
      (C) endangers a person's life, other than that of the person committing the action;
      (D) creates a serious risk to the health or safety of the public or a section of the public;
      (E) is ~~designed~~ intended seriously to interfere with or seriously to disrupt an electronic system; or
      (F) is ~~designed~~ intended seriously to interfere with or seriously to disrupt an essential service, facility or system, whether public or private; and
   (ii) the use or threat is–
      (A) ~~designed~~ intended to ~~influence~~ compel the Government or to intimidate the public or a section of the public; and
      (B) made for the purpose of advancing a political, religious or ideological cause;
(b) in the case of paragraph (a)(i)(D), (E) or (F), does not include the use or threat of action in the course of any advocacy, protest, dissent or ~~stoppage of work~~ industrial action.[50]

As shown by the amendments, the original definition used imprecise language, such as 'involves' and 'designed', unfamiliar to the criminal law. Legislators also felt that the exception clause for legitimate protest and dissent had to be extended to other non-directly violent forms of terrorism.[51] Despite these improvements to the original definition, there was one issue that the administration and legislators could not agree on. Margaret Ng, one of the main critics of the Bill and legislative process, proposed that the definition of 'terrorist act' should not include threats of action.[52] It was argued that this made the definition unjustifiably broad as it could catch merely mischievous behaviour.[53] Threats and other inchoate harm were already caught by the definition of 'terrorist', i.e. a 'person who commits, or attempts to commit, a terrorist act or who participates in or facilitates the commission of a terrorist act'.[54] The Secretary for Security, however, insisted

---

[50] See Bill, above note 25, clause 2(1); UNATMO, above note 33, s. 2(1).
[51] LegCo Secretariat, 'Report of the Bills Committee on [the Bill]', LC Paper No. CB(2)2537/01–02 for House Committee, 9 July 2002, paras 12–17 ('UNATMO Report').
[52] HK Hansard, 11 July 2002, above note 37, 8916–18.   [53] Ibid.
[54] UNATMO, above note 33, s. 2(1).

on keeping the threat component mainly because other countries had it in their definition and threats of terrorist acts would inevitably cause public panic.[55]

The original proposed specification system contributed to concerns that it could be misused against certain groups. The original proposal gave the Chief Executive the exclusive power to specify persons and property as 'terrorists', 'terrorist associates' or 'terrorist property' on reasonable grounds to believe.[56] Once a person or property was specified and gazetted, the person or property was presumed to be a terrorist, terrorist associate, or terrorist property, as the case may be, until proven to the contrary. It was left to persons specified to bring proceedings in the Court of First Instance to contest the specification. Without a system of prior judicial authorization, there was a real concern that Beijing might try to influence the Chief Executive on what individuals and groups to specify.

To the government's credit, it accepted these criticisms and revamped the system by introducing a number of safeguards.[57] While specification by the Chief Executive was maintained, it was restricted to only persons and property already specified by a United Nations sanctions committee.[58] If other persons or property were to be specified, it had to be by the Chief Executive's application to the Court of First Instance.[59] There were further judicial checks on this second form of specification by way of review and appeal.[60] Another safeguard that was added was a compensation provision for persons wrongly specified.[61] But one of the threshold preconditions for obtaining compensation required the court to be satisfied that 'there has been serious default on the part of any person concerned in obtaining the relevant specification'.[62] To many legislators and commentators critical of the Bill, this threshold was so high that it essentially nullified the provision.[63] Until recently, the government has always held that the threshold is appropriate to cap government expenditure and also because it is the same standard as for the compensation provisions in Hong Kong's money laundering laws.[64]

Specification facilitates the freezing and forfeiture of terrorist property, which under the Bill (later accepted unchanged in the UNATMO) was defined as:

(a) the property of a terrorist or terrorist associate; or
(b) any other property consisting of funds that–
    (i) is intended to be used to finance or otherwise assist the commission of a terrorist act; or
    (ii) was used to finance or otherwise assist the commission of a terrorist act.[65]

---

[55] *HK Hansard*, 11 July 2002, above note 37, 8912–8914.   [56] Bill, above note 25, clause 4.
[57] See UNATMO Report, above note 51, paras 29–38.   [58] UNATMO, above note 33, s. 4.
[59] Ibid., s. 5.   [60] Ibid., ss. 2(7), 17.   [61] Ibid., s. 18.   [62] Ibid., s. 18(2)(c).
[63] See criticisms in UNATMO Report, above note 51, paras 83–91.
[64] *HK Hansard*, 11 July 2002, above note 37, 9045–6.
[65] See Bill, above note 25, clause 2(1); UNATMO, above note 33, s. 2(1).

By virtue of the first limb of the definition, 'terrorist property' was defined very broadly. The first limb presumptively tainted all property connected to the terrorist or terrorist associate; in other words, there was no need to show that the property was in fact crime tainted. In the Bill, it was proposed that the Secretary for Security would have the exclusive power to freeze funds that were terrorist property, subject to subsequent review by a court.[66] A scheme of executive freezing was controversial not only because of the absence of prior judicial scrutiny but also because it deviated from the general approach under Hong Kong's money laundering laws of obtaining court orders to restrain suspected proceeds of crime.[67] Ultimately, the government insisted upon maintaining the scheme on grounds that urgency and swift action required executive control.[68] It was moderately mitigated by added safeguards such as the power of the Secretary for Security and of the courts to grant a licence to release frozen funds to pay reasonable living and legal expenses, the reduction in the time limit of a freeze notice from three years to two years, and the need to show a 'material change in the grounds' if an application was made to re-freeze previously but no longer frozen funds.[69]

The scheme of forfeiting terrorist property was also somewhat unique to Hong Kong because it involved civil forfeiture, i.e. it was not predicated on a criminal conviction; the standard of proof was the civil standard, and hearsay evidence was admissible.[70] One important safeguard of this scheme was that not all terrorist property was forfeitable. It had to be shown to have some connection to crime, which was true for the second limb of the definition but not for the first. Merely being property of a terrorist or terrorist associate was insufficient for forfeiture; it also had to be property which:

i. in whole or in part directly or indirectly represents any proceeds arising from a terrorist act;

ii. is intended to be used to finance or otherwise assist the commission of a terrorist act; or

iii. was used to finance or otherwise assist the commission of a terrorist act.[71]

---

[66] Bill, ibid., clause 5.

[67] See Drug Trafficking (Recovery of Proceeds) Ordinance (Cap 405), s. 10 ('DTROPO'); Organized and Serious Crimes Ordinance (Cap 455), s. 15 ('OSCO'). An exception is seen in Part IVA of the DTROPO, which allows a limited warrantless power to seize money suspected to be proceeds of drug trafficking going across the border.

[68] See Security Bureau, 'Summary of Written Submissions and the Administration's Response', Paper No. CB(2)2424/01–02(04) for Bills Committee on the Bill, 26 June 2002.

[69] See HK Hansard, 11 July 2002, above note 37, 8945–8947.

[70] Civil forfeiture does exist on a limited basis in Part IVA of the DTROPO, above note 67. On the use of such powers in other countries, see Davis, Chapter 9, in this volume.

[71] UNATMO, above note 33, s. 13(1)(a).

One of the implications of this narrower forfeiture power is that the power to freeze is more extensive than the power to forfeit, since the former applies to all terrorist property in the form of funds. This raises the issue of the legitimacy of allowing the government to hold on to property that it cannot forfeit. Ultimately, this is an issue of whether the first limb of the 'terrorist property' definition is too broad.

Another area of great controversy in the Bills Committee was the enactment of new criminal prohibitions.[72] The fiasco concerning the terrorist recruitment offence has already been mentioned.[73] There were five other new criminal prohibitions. Two of the new provisions concerned the financing of terrorism and appeared to overlap each other substantially, leaving one to wonder if more time should have been given to their formulation. The first was concerned with providing or collecting funds to be supplied or otherwise used by a person known or reasonably believed to be a terrorist or terrorist associate.[74] The second was concerned with making funds or financial (or related) services available to or for the benefit of a person known or reasonably believed to be a terrorist or terrorist associate.[75] A third provision prohibiting the supply of weapons to terrorists was relatively uncontroversial.[76]

One debated issue that was common to all three offences was the repeated use of the *mens rea* standard of has or having 'reasonable grounds to believe', a standard that appears five times in these three provisions.[77] It is controversial since Hong Kong courts have interpreted it as an objective standard. Having actual belief is not required; it is enough if sufficient objective grounds for the belief exist and one is aware of those objective grounds.[78] Calls for a purely subjective standard were rebuffed by the Administration primarily on the basis that the standard was well established in Hong Kong's money laundering offences.[79] In stage two of the implementation, the Administration has softened its position on this point. Signs of this change were already seen in respect of the *mens rea* standard for the disclosure offence. In the Bill, it was proposed that any person who knew or had 'reasonable grounds to suspect' that any property was terrorist property had a duty to make a secret disclosure to the police.[80] This was an offence

---

[72] For a discussion on the limits of the criminal law in preventing terrorism, see Roach, Chapter 7, in this volume.
[73] See text accompanying above note 41.   [74] UNATMO, above note 33, s. 7.
[75] Ibid., s. 8.   [76] Ibid., s. 9.
[77] By comparison, see the discussion of *mens rea* standards in the Canadian and United States offences in Davis, Chapter 9, in this volume.
[78] See *HKSAR* v. *Shing Siu Ming & Others* [1999] 2 HKC 818 at 825 (CA), leave to appeal to CFA refused, [1999] 4 HKC 452 (CFA AC); *HKSAR* v. *Yam Ho Keung* [2002] 1230 HKCU 1 (CA).
[79] *HK Hansard*, 11 July 2002, above note 37, 8985–6.
[80] Bill, above note 25, clause 11(1).

that had the greatest potential impact on ordinary persons, particularly those in the financial and business sectors. After significant concerns were expressed by the business and professional community, the government yielded by replacing the objective element with the subjective standard of 'knows or suspects'.[81]

The most controversial new criminal offence introduced was the prohibition against false threats of terrorist acts.[82] Legislators and media groups objected to the proposal for various reasons, including the chilling effect on press freedoms, being outside R. 1373 or the FATF recommendations, and being already covered by offences in the Public Order Ordinance (Cap 245).[83] In the words of Margaret Ng, the 'Secretary [had] not kept her word' of applying a minimalist approach.[84] While the government acknowledged that it was outside the scope of R. 1373 and the FATF recommendations, it nevertheless said that the offence was necessary because of the incidences of false threats of anthrax after September 11.[85] Ultimately, without achieving any reconciliation of these divergent views, the offence provision was passed with only an amendment to confine the scope of the *mens rea* requirement.[86]

There were two other major amendments to the original Bill that were important from the perspective of human rights. The first amendment removed two lengthy schedules that would have conferred controversial new police powers to enforce the provisions in the Bill.[87] The other amendment, to the relief of various legal and media groups, provided for express preservation of legal professional privilege, the privilege against self-incrimination and the protective regime governing journalistic materials in the Interpretation and General Clauses Ordinance (Cap 1).[88]

After all the amendments were made, the enacted legislation had transformed significantly from the original Bill.[89] One ponders why the Bill in its original form was so short-sighted and over-broad to begin with. It was certainly not for lack of preparation time since the instructions from China had arrived in October 2001, six months before the Bill was gazetted. As argued below, it was due to insufficient consultation with the public and experts at the 'Bill formulation stage', and not only at the 'Bill amendment

---

[81] UNATMO Report, above note 51, paras 60–72.   [82] Bill, above note 25, clause 10.
[83] UNATMO Report, above note 51, paras 53–9.
[84] *HK Hansard*, 11 July 2002, above note 37, 8861.   [85] Ibid., 9004–16.
[86] The original proposal made it an offence to communicate information known or believed to be false to another person 'with the intention of inducing in him or any other person a false belief that a terrorist act has been, is being or will be carried out'. The enacted provision confines the added intent element to that of 'causing alarm to the public or a section of the public by a false belief that a terrorist act has been, is being or will be carried out'. See UNATMO, above note 33, s. 11.
[87] Bill, above note 25, Schedules 2 and 3.   [88] Ibid., paras 26–7.
[89] See Young, above note 36 for discussion of the legislative process.

stage'. This is a problem that reoccurs with the National Security Bill. The critical tasks of formulating policies and drafting the bill, carried out from October 2001 to April 2002, were largely completed by government lawyers and officials with no outside participation.

The willingness of the government to make concessions was more likely due to the June 2002 deadline than an earnest desire to safeguard fundamental rights and freedoms. Where the government was unwilling to change a proposal, there was a tendency to try to justify its position by reference to finding the same provision in other Hong Kong laws or in the laws of other countries. But this approach to justification is narrow-minded because, in respect of existing Hong Kong laws, it fails to question whether those laws are themselves illegitimate (particularly in the areas of police powers and *mens rea* standards) or otherwise inappropriate for the anti-terrorism context. In respect of the anti-terrorism laws of other countries, it cannot be assumed that what is appropriate for country A, B and C is necessarily appropriate for Hong Kong, particularly having regard to its relatively low risk of attracting terrorist-related activity.

3. United Nations Sanctions (Afghanistan) (Amendment) Regulation 2002

On the same date the UNATMO was passed through LegCo, the Chief Executive made the United Nations Sanctions (Afghanistan) (Amendment) Regulation 2002 (UNSAAR), which amended the UNSAR in light of R. 1390, adopted by the Security Council on 16 January 2002.[90] To the outsider, this new regulation came as a bit of a surprise since it suddenly emerged as law without any prior consultation with the public or even the elected members of the legislature. It would also have been surprising for the legislators who had just completed an intense one and a half month exercise of scrutinizing the UNATMO. The UNSAAR and UNATMO had much in common in terms of origin, purpose and provisions, yet the manner in which both were enacted could not have been more unique. It did not take long for legislators and the legal advisors in the LegCo Secretariat to start questioning the legal basis of the UNSAAR and the manner in which it came into being.

On 4 October 2002, legislators discussed three issues concerning the UNSAAR identified by LegCo's Legal Service Division.[91] First, legislators questioned whether R. 1390 was a sanction to be implemented 'against a

---

[90] Published in the *Hong Kong Gazette* on 19 July 2002, amending the United Nations Sanctions (Afghanistan) Regulation (Cap 537K).

[91] LegCo Secretariat, 'Minutes of the meeting held in the [LegCo] Chamber at 2:30 pm on Friday, 4 October 2002', LC Paper No. CB(2) 2886/01–02 for House Committee, Oct. 2002, paras 20–5.

place' as required by the UNSO.[92] If it was not, then there had to be a legal basis for the amendment regulation other than the UNSO, possibly the Basic Law itself. While the antecedents of R. 1390 certainly arose out of events in Afghanistan, by January 2002, it appeared the real focus of R. 1390 was on certain individuals and entities linked to Osama bin Laden and al Qaeda, persons who were probably no longer physically in Afghanistan. The Administration's position was that R. 1390 was a sanction implemented against a place and the use of the UNSO was appropriate.[93] In making this argument, it cited the number of references to 'Afghanistan' in R. 1390, and the antecedent resolutions, R. 1267 and R. 1333, which were more clearly applied against a place.[94]

The second issue identified by the Legal Service Division was the overlap of the supply of weapons offences in the UNATMO with three offences in the UNSAAR.[95] The difficulty was that the offences in the UNSAAR involved strict liability, subject to statutory defences for the accused to satisfy on balance. The equivalent offences in the UNATMO required proof of *mens rea*. In theory, if a relevant case arose, the prosecution could avoid this *mens rea* requirement by choosing to prosecute under the UNSAAR offences. In its response of 26 November 2002 the Administration acknowledged that there was overlap, but said that this was inevitable since there was overlap between R. 1373 and R. 1390.[96] Recognizing that the offence in the UNATMO was wider, it was prepared to repeal the strict liability offences in the UNSAAR.[97] The LegCo Legal Service Division later questioned whether the Hong Kong government could amend the sections in the UNSAR that overlapped with those in the UNATMO without fresh instructions from the Central People's Government.[98]

In respect of the third issue, the Legal Service Division noticed the 'wide powers of search and investigation' contained in six provisions of the

---

[92] LegCo Secretariat, 'Legal Service Division Report on Subsidiary Legislation gazetted from 19 July 2002 to 27 September 2002', LC Paper No. LS 131/01–02 for the House Committee Meeting on 4 October 2002, 2 Oct. 2002, Annex I, paras 5–7 ('Report on regulations').

[93] Commerce, Industry and Technology Bureau, '1: Whether the [UNSAAR] (Amendment Regulation) is within the regulation making powers of the UN Sanctions Ordinance? (Raised by the Hon James To)', Paper No. CB(2)164/02–03(01) for House Committee, October 2002.

[94] Ibid.   [95] Report on regulations, above note 92, para 9.

[96] Anita Chan for Secretary for Commerce, Industry and Technology, Letter to Clerk to Subcommittee on UNSAAR and United Nations Sanctions (Angola) (Suspension of Operation) Regulation 2002, Paper No. CB(2)477/02–03(01), 26 Nov. 2002.

[97] Ibid.

[98] LegCo Secretariat, 'Report of the Subcommittee on [UNSAAR] and United Nations Sanctions (Angola) (Suspension of Operation) Regulation 2002', LC Paper No. CB(2)3003/02–03 for the House Committee meeting on 3 October 2003, Appendix II, paras 6–10.

UNSAAR.[99] R. 1390 did not expressly require the inclusion of these new police powers. The Administration's response was that these powers were necessary to facilitate the enforcement of the new sanctions in the UNSAAR and that they also existed in a previous UNSO regulation relating to Liberia.[100]

Legislators in the House Committee were not satisfied with these responses.[101] Concerns about the UNSO and its regulations dragged on in two subcommittees of the House Committee.[102] Three further issues developed. The first was whether the implementing instructions from the Central People's Government should be disclosed to legislators. While the Administration was prepared to advise as to the contents of the instructions, it refused to make disclosure on grounds that they are intended for internal use only and disclosure would be unprecedented.[103] The second issue concerned the means by which to implement United Nations sanctions, and particularly when administrative measures, regulations or primary legislation should be used.[104] Finally, the third issue, and the more fundamental one, was whether the regulations made under the UNSO should be subject to legislative scrutiny. These issues remained unresolved at the conclusion of LegCo's 2000–2004 term.

C. The Article 23 episode[105]

With the first stage of the anti-terrorism initiative completed, the path was clear for the Security Bureau to commence its national security initiative in

---

[99] Report on regulations, above note 92, para 10.   [100] Ibid.

[101] See LegCo Secretariat, 'Minutes of meeting held on Monday, 31 March 2003 at 4:30 pm in Conference Room A of the [LegCo] Building', LC Paper No. CB(2)2064/02–03 for the Panel on Administration of Justice and Legal Services, 13 May 203, paras 45–51; LegCo Secretariat, Minutes of the meeting held in the LegCo Chamber at 2:30 pm on Friday, 3 October 2003, paras 53–6.

[102] The Subcommittee on UNSAAR and United Nations Sanctions (Angola) (Suspension of Operation) Regulation 2002 held four meetings from 30 Oct. 2002 to 25 Feb. 2003. The Subcommittee on the United Nations Sanctions (Liberia) Regulations 2003 held five meetings from 11 Dec. 2003 to 21 June 2004.

[103] Donald Tsang, Chief Secretary for Administration, Letter to Hon Miriam Lau, Chairman of the House Committee dated 13 Nov. 2003.

[104] The problem of having multiple listing mechanisms in domestic law has also been the subject of criticism in Canada. See E. A. Dosman, 'For the Record: Designating "Listed Entities" for the Purposes of Terrorist Financing Offences at Canadian Law' (2004) 62 University of Toronto Faculty of Law Review 1.

[105] The events surrounding the rise and fall of the National Security (Legislative Provisions) Bill together with a detailed examination of all the government proposals is the subject of a book, National Security and Fundamental Freedoms: Hong Kong's Article 23 Under Scrutiny, edited by Fu Hualing, Carole Petersen and Simon Young published by Hong Kong University Press in March 2005 ('Article 23 Book').

late 2002. Only two months after the enactment of the UNATMO, the Security Bureau released *Proposals to Implement Article 23 of the Basic Law: A Consultation Document ('Consultation Document')*.[106] Article 23 of the Basic Law required Hong Kong to enact laws on its own to prohibit acts of treason, secession, sedition, and subversion against the Central People's Government. It also required laws against the theft of state secrets and foreign political organizations or bodies conducting activities in Hong Kong or forming ties with Hong Kong political organizations or bodies. It is well known that Article 23 was inserted in the Basic Law by China following the mass demonstrations in Hong Kong against the 1989 Tiananmen incident in Beijing.[107] After several months of public consultation, the National Security (Legislative Provisions) Bill ('National Security Bill') was introduced in LegCo on 26 Feb 2003.[108]

The legislative exercise to implement Article 23 probably would have occurred even if September 11 did not happen. Nevertheless, following as it did after the first stage of implementing anti-terrorism laws, the two initiatives were closely related in many ways. It was very much the same group of officials responsible for implementing both initiatives. The Secretary for Security, Regina Yip, was the person-in-charge of both. This can probably explain why some of the same tactics and strategies to legal drafting, consultation and concession-making were employed. As well, the substance of the proposals shared many commonalities. Professor Kent Roach has argued that the National Security Bill 'combined an older vision of security based on betrayal of the state with a newer vision of security found in post-September 11 anti-terrorism laws'.[109] Two of the more noteworthy commonalities were found in the National Security Bill's definition of 'serious criminal means' and its use of the proscription mechanisms to ban local organizations.

As was true with the anti-terrorism Bill, though for different reasons, there was a significant amount of criticism of both the consultation and legislative processes. Two critical observations were generally made about the *Consultation Document*.[110] Although a significant amount of research from

---

[106] Security Bureau, *Proposals to Implement Article 23 of the Basic Law: A Consultation Document* (Hong Kong Government, 2002) was released on 24 September 2002.

[107] See Fu Hualing, 'The National Security Factor: Putting Article 23 of the Basic Law in Perspective' in Steve Tsang, ed., *Judicial Independence and the Rule of Law in Hong Kong* (Hong Kong University Press, 2001) 73–98.

[108] National Security (Legislative Provisions) Bill, gazetted on 14 February 2003 ('National Security Bill').

[109] Kent Roach, 'Old and New Visions of Security: Article 23 Compared to Post-September 11 Security Laws', in *Article 23 Book*, above note 105.

[110] See generally, Carole Petersen, 'Hong Kong's Spring of Discontent: The Rise and Fall of the National Security Bill in 2003' in *Article 23 Book*, ibid.; Carole Petersen, 'National Security Offences and Civil Liberties in Hong Kong: A Critique of the Government's "Consultation" on Article 23 of the Basic Law' (2002) 32 *Hong Kong Law Journal* 457–70.

international sources was reflected, the document presented what seemed to be *fait accompli* proposals rather than different options for reform. The second critical observation was that the 62-page document contained proposals often described in vague and ambiguous language. One of the most common sayings floated by commentators at the time was that the 'devil was in the details'; until the details were revealed, it was difficult to come to any final opinions on the proposals. It was not long after the publication of the *Consultation Document* that commentators began asking the government to publish a 'white bill' before presenting the 'blue bill' for first reading in LegCo.

The government ultimately declined to issue a white bill, saying that amendments would still be possible when the blue bill was scrutinized.[111] Legislators and public interest groups, aware of how difficult it was to amend a blue bill without support from the government, were greatly disappointed. Before the issuance of the Bill in February 2003, the government suffered another blow to its credibility with the *Compendium of Submissions* fiasco, which led some legislators to condemn the Administration for compiling a compendium 'in a slipshod, incomplete and inequitable manner, distorting the views expressed by the public and organizations'.[112]

There was much in the substance of the National Security Bill that was indeed positive from the viewpoint of modernization and rationalization of the law. Hong Kong's laws concerning treason and sedition have never been updated since they were introduced pre-World War II.[113] If some of these offences and related police powers were to be applied now, they would surely be challenged on constitutional human rights grounds, e.g. freedom of expression.

Unlike with the anti-terrorism initiative, the Administration never claimed to take a 'minimalist approach' to implementation. There were at least three main proposals that were not expressly required by Article 23.[114] The first related to the creation of a new offence of illegal access to protected information and a new category of protected information related to 'international relations or affairs concerning the Hong Kong Special Administrative Region which are, under the Basic Law, within the responsibility of the Central Authorities'.[115] This proposal was of great concern to

---

[111] Ravina Shamdasani and Jimmy Cheung, 'Officials stand firm against white bill', *South China Morning Post*, 24 December 2002, 2.

[112] Words taken from a condemnatory motion, introduced by legislator Sin Chung Kai, which did not pass. See debates in *HK Hansard*, 26 February 2003, above note 37, 4182–257. See also Press Release, 'Transcript of remarks by Secretary for Security', 6 February 2003.

[113] See generally Crimes Ordinance (Cap 200), Parts I and II.

[114] See generally Benny Y. T. Tai, 'The Principle of Minimum Legislation for Implementing Article 23 of the Basic Law' (2002) 32 *Hong Kong Law Journal* 579–614.

[115] See National Security Bill, above note 108, clauses 10 and 11.

journalists.[116] The second overreaching proposal was to give the Secretary for Security a new power to proscribe organizations endangering national security.[117] The power could be exercised if the organization was subordinate to an organization proscribed on the mainland. With this proposal, the earlier fears that the anti-terrorism laws might be used to marginalize religious groups undesired by the mainland were re-emerging in a new and real way.[118] The third proposal was to give the police a new warrantless entry and search power to gather evidence in urgent circumstances.[119] The difficulty with this proposal was that there was no empirical necessity for the power or anything to suggest that existing powers were inadequate.[120]

Although the Administration had always said that amendments to the blue bill were possible during the legislative process, it became clear as the work of the Bills Committee progressed that the Administration would only agree to minor changes and not budge on the main proposals.[121] Indeed, it was this very defensive attitude taken by the Secretary for Security and other staff and colleagues that angered legislators and commentators causing much resentment.

The boiling point of this anger and resentment was reached on 1 July 2003 (a public holiday celebrating Hong Kong's reunification with China) when approximately half a million people marched in protest primarily against the National Security Bill but also against the Administration generally.[122] At the time of the 1 July march, the Bills Committee for the National Security Bill had already completed its work, and Second Reading debate on the Bill was scheduled to continue on 9 July 2003.[123] Four days after the march, the Chief Executive announced three significant amendments to the Bill: (1) deletion of the 'subordinate to a mainland organization' triggering condition to the proscription power; (2) introduction of a 'public interest' defence for unlawful disclosure of certain protected information; and (3) deletion of the

---

[116] See Doreen Weisenhaus, 'Article 23 and Freedom of the Press: A Journalistic Perspective' in *Article 23 Book*, above note 105.

[117] National Security Bill, above note 108, clause 15.

[118] See Lison Harris, Lily Ma and C. B. Fung, 'A Connecting Door: The Proscription of Local Organizations' in *Article 23 Book*, above note 105.

[119] National Security Bill, above note 108, clause 18B.

[120] See Simon Young, '"Knock, knock. Who's there?" Entry and search powers for Article 23 Offences' in *Article 23 Book*, above note 105.

[121] LegCo Secretariat, 'Report of the Bills Committee on [National Security Bill]', LC Paper No. CB(2)2646/02–03 for House Committee on 27 June 2003, 27 June 2003 ('BC Art 23 Report').

[122] Ambrose Leung, Klaudia Lee and Ernest Kong, 'Hopes for freedom float upon a sea of political discontent', *South China Morning Post*, 2 July 2003, 3; Jimmy Cheung and Klaudia Lee, 'Turnout piles the pressure on Tung administration', *South China Morning Post*, 2 July 2003, 3.

[123] BC Art 23 Report, above note 121, para 156.

warrantless entry and search power.[124] Having made these major concessions
at the last minute, the Chief Executive still insisted on proceeding with the
second reading on 9 July.[125]

It soon became apparent that these concessions raised further issues,
particularly the scope and definition of the public interest defence.
Legislators and members of the public expressed concerns over the insufficient amount of time they had to consider the new amendments. These
concerns escalated until they climaxed when James Tien, legislator and leader
of the Liberal Party, resigned from the Executive Council, an unelected body
of special advisors to the Chief Executive.[126] This hurt the Administration
because the Liberal Party, representing mostly business and corporate interests, held a sizeable number of votes in LegCo.

On the day after Tien's resignation, 7 July 2003, the Chief Executive
announced that the second reading would be deferred and efforts would be
stepped up to explain the amendments to the public.[127] Nine days later, the
Secretary for Security and another principal official, who had been embroiled
in a car buying scandal, announced their decisions to resign.[128] Shortly
afterwards, the Chief Executive said that the government was going to 'put
forward the Bill to the whole community for consultation again'.[129] He
promised a 'more extensive [consultation exercise] than the previous one'
and 'to win the maximum understanding and support of the community as a
whole'.[130] The timeline was to 'depend very much on how the consultation
[went]'.[131] After the summer recess, however, the Chief Executive announced
on 5 September 2003 that the National Security Bill was being withdrawn to
allow the public sufficient time to 'study the enactment question' and for the
Security Bureau to establish a special working group to review the legislative
work afresh.[132] In September 2004, the Chief Executive announced that there
were no immediate plans to resume the legislative exercise.[133]

It has never been disclosed how much of a role the Chinese authorities
played in the making of the three amendments and the withdrawing of the
Bill. The general perception is that the Chief Executive consulted the central
authorities as these decisions were being made. It became rather clear that the
Hong Kong government was not fully in charge of the legislative exercise
when, shortly before his resignation, James Tien traveled to Beijing to determine from officials that there was no deadline to implementing Article 23.[134]

---

[124] Press Release, 'Chief Executive's transcript on Basic Law Article 23', 5 July 2003.
[125] Ibid.   [126] Press Release, 'Statement by CE', 7 July 2003.   [127] Ibid.
[128] Press Release, 'Statement by Secretary for Security', 16 July 2003.
[129] Press Release, 'CE's transcript', 17 July 2003.   [130] Ibid.   [131] Ibid.
[132] Press Release, 'CE's opening remarks on Basic Law Article 23', 5 September 2003.
[133] Press Release, 'Chief Executive Comments on Basic Law Article 23', 16 September 2004.
[134] See Albert Chen, 'Hong Kong's Political Crisis of July 2003' (2003) 33 *Hong Kong Law Journal* 265, 267; Petersen, above note 110.

D. Legal response to September 11 (Part II)

Even before the march on 1 July 2003, stage two of the implementation of anti-terrorism laws had commenced with the introduction of the United Nations (Anti-Terrorism Measures) (Amendment) Bill 2003 ('Amendment Bill') in LegCo on 21 May 2003.[135] The Amendment Bill contained proposals to expand the freezing power, to implement three additional anti-terrorism treaties,[136] to replace the recruitment offence provision with a new one, to add a new warrant-based power to search and seize terrorist property, to add three additional investigation powers involving prior judicial authorization, and to provide for limited international sharing of information obtained using the new powers.

In this second stage, there were a number of signs that the Administration, with its new Secretary for Security, had modified its approach after learning from the failings and problems of the two earlier legislative exercises. Indeed, the change was so apparent that it attracted the following complimentary comments from the staunchest critic of the original Bill, Margaret Ng:

> Thankfully, the Government changed its attitude in the end, and worked together with the Bills Committee with a more open mind. The many amendments to be introduced by the Government is a result of that process. Although it has caused us much effort, I am pleased that it has happened, and I do sincerely thank the Government for its co-operation.
> I took some time to revisit the Committee stage amendments I proposed last year. I am pleased to say that many of them are now being effected through the Government's amendments. I would like to mention the most significant improvements from the point of view of better legislation and better regard for human rights.[137]

This time there was no externally imposed deadline and more time was given to legislators and the public to study the Amendment Bill. A total of sixteen

---

[135] Gazetted on 9 May 2003. The Amendment Bill was passed on 3 July 2004, and signed and promulgated by the Chief Executive on 8 July 2004. The United Nations (Anti-Terrorism Measures) (Amendment) Ordinance, Ord. No. 21 of 2004 ('Amendment Ordinance') comes into operation on a day to be appointed by the Secretary for Security by notice published in the Gazette.

[136] The International Convention for the Suppression of Terrorist Bombings (1997), Convention for the Suppression of Unlawful Acts against the Safety of Maritime Navigation (1988), and Protocol for the Suppression of Unlawful Acts against the Safety of Fixed Platforms Located on the Continental Shelf (1988). When the Bill was introduced, the latter two instruments had neither been ratified by China nor applied to Hong Kong. However, the Administration indicated that they would be applied to Hong Kong in due course. See LegCo Secretariat, 'Legal Service Division Report on [Amendment Bill]', LC Paper No. LS 107/02–03 for House Committee Meeting on 23 May 2003, 21 May 2003, para 2.

[137] HK Hansard, 3 July 2004, above note 37, 470.

Bills Committee meetings were held over the course of eight months from 10 October 2003 to 18 June 2004. The rushed and confused atmosphere that marked the first stage of implementation was not repeated, and interested groups had ample opportunity to comment on both the original Amendment Bill and the draft CSAs to that Bill. A mutually acceptable deadline was naturally set by the 2004 summer recess, which concluded LegCo's first complete four-year term since the transfer of sovereignty.

This open public consultation process contributed to an informed, balanced and acceptable piece of legislation. The Administration showed a willingness to revisit the UNATMO to correct and improve defects resulting from the rushed enactment. The United Nations (Anti-Terrorism Measures) (Amendment) Ordinance narrowed the definition of 'terrorist act' with new *mens rea* qualifiers,[138] enacted a narrower recruitment offence with subjective *mens rea* requirements,[139] removed some of the objective *mens rea* standards in the existing criminal prohibitions,[140] and removed the 'serious' from the 'serious default' precondition to obtaining compensation.[141] Important amendments were also made to clarify and restrict some of the new police powers introduced in the original Amendment Bill.[142]

III. Ideas for a new implementation strategy

The defects with Hong Kong's security laws and policies have been more procedural than substantive. It is not so much the substance of the laws (in their final enacted or proposed form) that is problematic. And it is not so much the policy behind the law that is troubling because most Hong Kong people accept the reasons for having to implement anti-terrorism and national security laws. Instead, this chapter has shown that the problems lie more in how the laws and policies are formulated, debated, subjected to

---

[138] Under part (a)(i) of the definition, a terrorist act must now involve the use or threat of action where the action 'is carried out with the intention of, or the threat is made with the intention of using action that would have the effect of' realizing one of the harmful consequences enumerated in clauses (A) to (F). See s. 3 of the Amendment Ordinance, above note 135.

[139] Section 10 of the UNATMO now makes it an offence to: (a) recruit another person to become a member; or (b) become a member, of a specified terrorist body knowing that, or being reckless as to whether, it is a body so specified. See s. 9 of the Amendment Ordinance, ibid.

[140] The objective standard of 'having reasonable grounds to believe' in ss. 7 to 9 of the UNATMO has now been replaced with fault standards of recklessness, knowledge and intention. See ss. 6 to 8, and 14 of the Amendment Ordinance, ibid.

[141] See s. 17 of the Amendment Ordinance, ibid.

[142] See ss. 3, 5, and 12 of the Amendment Ordinance, ibid., the significance of which is explained in LegCo Secretariat, 'Report of the Bills Committee on [Amendment Bill]', LC Paper No. CB(2)2915/03–04, 25 June 2004.

public consultations, reformulated and finally enacted. In other words, it has been the implementation strategy that has been plagued by problems. If the Administration is to win the public's trust and confidence behind future legislative initiatives, it must first understand the reasons why the public resisted and frustrated its previous attempts at implementation. These reasons and possible ways of addressing them are discussed under the following three headings.

A. External imposition without internal need

With both the anti-terrorism and national security initiatives, there was no empirical necessity in Hong Kong for new laws. Instead, the public perception was that these new measures were being externally imposed on Hong Kong, in which case adopting a 'minimalist approach' seemed to follow logically. Closer examination revealed that the external imposition came from China in both cases. This form of imposition touches upon a particularly sensitive area for Hong Kong people. The Basic Law promised a 'high degree of autonomy' for Hong Kong which meant that China's socialist political system would not be applied in Hong Kong. Naturally any steps taken by China that appear to interfere with this high degree of autonomy are viewed with mistrust by Hong Kong people.[143]

Both the anti-terrorism and national security initiatives were matters under the Basic Law that required intervention from the central authorities. As a matter of political reality, both initiatives were of great interest and concern to China. The Hong Kong Administration had the responsibility of mediating between China and the Hong Kong people. This was a challenging task since it required, on the one hand, upholding Hong Kong's autonomy, while, on the other hand, carrying out the mainland instructions.[144] Judging from its performance and the public reaction, the Administration failed to strike the proper balance by insufficiently upholding Hong Kong's autonomy. Indeed, the manner in which the proposals were initiated, the inability to compromise on certain issues until the final hour and the imposition of artificial deadlines were strategies that clearly reinforced the external imposition perception.

Contributing to the distrust were two other factors: the internal policy not to disclose the instructions from China in respect of UN sanctions and the

---

[143] This mistrust was exacerbated in early 2004 when the Standing Committee of the National People's Congress adopted an Interpretation of the Basic Law and made a Decision that ruled out universal suffrage for 2007/2008, which was an aim that many in Hong Kong had hoped to realize.

[144] In respect of the national security initiative, it is unknown if China gave further instructions beyond Article 23.

proposal to make information concerning Hong Kong and China affairs protected information under the Official Secrets Ordinance (Cap 521). Without transparency about China's instructions to Hong Kong in respect of both initiatives, there would always be a lingering suspicion that the Administration's hard bargaining and imposed deadlines were a product of Chinese interference.

B. Faulty consultation processes

Where there is no apparent empirical need for new criminal laws and police powers, the need for genuine public consultation at the earliest possible moment is greatest. Even where there is an empirical need, subject matters such as anti-terrorism and national security can involve very technical legal proposals, which is another reason for ensuring early and full consultations. A third reason for having early consultations is that it helps to remove the perception of external imposition. When the public is involved as early as the proposal formulation stage then the public can take ownership in the final product. This is a strategy that engenders autonomy over the initiatives.

Unfortunately this has not been a strategy used by the Administration. Some have criticized the Administration for not using the Hong Kong Law Reform Commission (HKLRC) in developing the Article 23 proposals.[145] Using the HKLRC would have involved the public in a wide consultation during the proposal formulation stage. However, the HKLRC may not be the best vehicle for implementing laws on security in Hong Kong. It is not unknown for governments to ignore completely the recommendations of an independent law reform agency. When this is the case, the initiative goes back to the drawing board, although with the benefit of the work done by the law reform body. To avoid this potential roadblock, it may be necessary to include some of the responsible government officials in the law reform process. By having the officials actively involved in the formulation process (but not in any leading role), there is a greater chance that the formulated proposals will later be accepted. More importantly, the officials will have the opportunity to gain broader perspectives by interacting directly with the independent experts forming part of the body. The present system of consultation, in the formal and politically charged atmosphere of a bills committee, leaves very little room for focused and rational discussion and exchange. A plurality of expert views in the drafting process is very important in order to avoid the formulation of short-sighted and overreaching proposals, as was seen in the initial drafts of the anti-terrorism and national security bills.

---

[145] See Petersen in *Article 23 Book*, above note 110, 21–3.

Another limitation of the HKLRC is that its subcommittees are generally non-permanent made up of the volunteer services of members of the community. Typically the subcommittee is disbanded once the specific law reform reports are complete. There are no standing committees in the HKLRC devoted to the study of specific areas of law. In the area of security laws, it is probably a good idea to have a standing committee of experts that not only proposes new laws when needed but also reviews existing ones. This standing committee will also be able to formulate policies and principles governing security issues in Hong Kong. The aim is to develop a new discourse on security that arises from the grass roots rather than from outside of Hong Kong.[146]

C. Defects in policy and practice

The anti-terrorism initiative revealed some serious defects in the Administration's present policies and practices in implementing Security Council sanctions. The UNSO is in dire need of a complete overhaul.[147] The triggering condition of implementing sanctions 'against a place' needs to be reconsidered for at least two reasons. First, it falsely assumes that Chapter VII decisions are always against a particular place. R. 1373 proved this assumption was false, and increasingly, there is a greater tendency to employ 'smart sanctions' that target specific persons or subject matters without territorial boundaries.[148]

The other difficulty with the condition and the general scheme is that Chapter VII sanctions against a place must necessarily require implementation using the UNSO (assuming instructions from the central authorities have been received). In other words, regardless of the urgency of the matter, the Chief Executive has no choice but to implement the measure by making regulations that are not subject to scrutiny by the legislature. This raises important issues concerning the accountability of the executive and the

---

[146] Although it has not been a problem in Hong Kong, this informed standing committee can also help to avoid the problem, which Victor V. Ramraj discusses, of having an overreacting populist democracy motivated by misperceptions of risk and public fear. See Ramraj, Chapter 6, in this volume.

[147] The UNSO was originally enacted in a matter of days without question or dissent in the first few weeks after the resumption of sovereignty. The expediency was a product of the need to ensure that the existing UN sanctions continued to apply in Hong Kong after 1 July 1997. Unfortunately, it was enacted by the Provisional Legislative Council, an unelected body put in place by China to facilitate the resumption of sovereignty. The body was notoriously known to be uncritical of legislation put forward by the government.

[148] See Security Council Resolution 1540 (2004) (Non-proliferation of Weapons of Mass Destruction) and Peter L. Fitzgerald, 'Managing "Smart Sanctions" Against Terrorism Wisely' (2002) 36 New England Law Review 957.

separation of powers. It has been seen that these implementing regulations can contain wide police powers and strict liability offences. There has yet to be any reasonable justification on policy grounds for R. 1390 being implemented with UNSO regulations while R. 1373 was implemented with primary legislation. Having these two overlapping laws has also given rise to confusion due to their separate terrorist listing mechanisms.[149] Currently there are two lists published in the Gazette on a regular basis as required by both the UNATMO and UNSAR. While the names on the two lists have been the same, this will not always be the case since the power to specify under the UNATMO is broader than the power under the UNSAR.

The urgency in having the sanction implemented may be one explanation for why executive regulations should be used over primary legislation, but presently this is not a triggering condition in the UNSO. Even if regulations are the desired method of implementation in urgent circumstances, it still does not explain why there cannot be tabling of the subsidiary legislation before LegCo for negative vetting. Ironically, even with the present scheme of executive regulations under the UNSO, there has still been considerable delay in implementing UN sanctions. Some of this delay may be explained by the existing practice of the Chief Executive seeking views from the Executive Council. Conferring this task on the proposed standing committee may very well lead to a more expeditious process of implementation.

In reforming the UNSO Hong Kong can learn from the enabling legislation used in Canada and Singapore, both of which share the same name and are very similar in nature.[150] Both laws give the executive a discretionary power to implement Chapter VII sanctions by regulations 'as appear to him to be necessary or expedient for enabling the measure to be effectively applied'.[151] Neither have the anomaly of restricting the lawmaking power to Chapter VII resolutions implemented 'against a place'. Both laws also preserve legislative scrutiny by requiring the regulations to be tabled before their respective parliaments within a short time after they are made.[152]

---

[149] See similar problems in Canada, E. A. Dosman, above note 104.

[150] See the United Nations Act, R.S.C. 1985, c. U-2 (CAN) originally enacted in 1945 ('Canada UNA'), and the United Nations Act, Chapt. 339, originally No. 44 of 2001, Republic of Singapore Government Gazette, enacted on 17 October 2001 ('Singapore UNA').

[151] See s. 2 of the Canada UNA, ibid., and s. 2(1) of the Singapore UNA, ibid. However, this formulation is not without its difficulties; see criticisms of the Singapore UNA in C. L. Lim, 'Executive Lawmaking in Compliance of International Treaty' [2002] *Singapore Journal of Legal Studies* 73–103.

[152] See s. 4 of the Canada UNA, ibid., and s. 2(4) of the Singapore UNA, ibid.

IV. Conclusion

There are signs from stage two of the anti-terrorism initiative that the Administration is changing its strategy to implementation. Indeed, the decision to withdraw the National Security Bill, even though its passage through LegCo was imminent, reflected the Administration's willingness to heed public sentiment despite the absence of genuine democratic accountability in Hong Kong. In the next four year term of LegCo, starting in October 2004, the issue of Article 23 is bound to return together with ever-increasing new global anti-terrorism initiatives. No time should be wasted in implementing the procedural and consultative mechanisms that will lead to the development of grass roots security laws and policies for Hong Kong.

PART FOUR

Regional Cooperation

19

Southeast Asian cooperation on anti-terrorism: the dynamics and limits of regional responses

SIMON S. C. TAY AND TAN HSIEN LI

I. Introduction

Some have seen Southeast Asia as a potential 'second front' in the US-led war on terrorism. The sharpest evidence of this was the 2002 Bali bombings. Problems in Aceh (Indonesia), Mindanao (the Philippines) and in southern Thailand have been linked with Muslim groups that have differences with their respective capitals. They have resorted to action that has been described as 'terrorist'. Member states in the Association of Southeast Asian Nations (ASEAN) have responded differently to issues within their own borders, as well as to US-led action in other arenas. Public opinion in much of the region has grown in opposition to the US-led war on terrorism, especially the decision to intervene in Iraq.

Generally, however, ASEAN states have sought to cooperate with the US or at least to limit their disagreement. The US has largely acted on a bilateral basis with the different governments. This draws from and reinforces the dominant security architecture in the region that existed pre-9/11 and since the end of World War II. The US has been anchored to Asia by a number of bilateral alliances and agreements, as the centre of a hub-and-spoke arrangement. Each Southeast Asian state has often more to do with the US than with each other. The points on the hub do not coalesce.[1] While this has been the dominant structure of security arrangements in Southeast Asia, it is not the only one. There have also been declarations, treaties and examples of cooperation among the states in the region that do not have a direct or explicit American involvement.

Beyond terrorism, ASEAN has sought to bring the region together to cooperate on many issues. While ASEAN is not explicitly a security alliance, it has developed its own modes for increasing cooperation and conflict avoidance among its member states. ASEAN hosts the ASEAN Regional Forum (ARF) as a multilateral dialogue on security. The ARF covers a 'footprint' that extends beyond the immediate domain of Southeast Asia into Northeast Asia and includes many non-regional powers with interests in the area, including the US, Russia and even the European Union (EU), India and Australia. Its 'road

---

[1] See Simon S. C. Tay, 'Asia, U.S. Primacy, and Global Governance', (2004) 10 *Global Governance* 139.

map' expresses the ambition that the ARF will move from confidence-building to preventive diplomacy and then to conflict resolution. It is an effort in norm-building and institutionalization, intended to supplement but not displace, the more realistic and military efforts of the bilateral US-centric security arrangements. The differences between the latter and regional cooperation in Southeast Asia hold the key to real understanding of the dynamics and limits of regional anti-terror responses. While declarations of intention, plans of action and treaties can be agreed between governments, the viability of concerted efforts depends on at least two other elements. First is the strength (or weakness) of regional institutions. Second, terrorism, unlike more traditional kinds of inter-state conflict, has strong domestic factors.

This chapter will first survey the efforts against terrorism in Southeast Asia that involve ASEAN as a whole, or one of its member states. Secondly, it will contextualize these efforts by considering the prevailing security architecture in the region, and the role that the US plays in these arrangements. It will also consider attempts to shift the focus from the violent outcomes of terrorism to its 'root causes'. The chapter then examines the context of prevailing ideals. Third, the chapter will analyze the need for interstate cooperation to deal with terrorism and the longstanding concepts of sovereignty and security. Fourth, there will be consideration of the interplay of interstate cooperation with international law norms of cooperation, justice and power.

In sum, the argument is that, while ASEAN member states have offered declarations, treaties and a considerable measure of response to American concerns on terrorism, their commitment (and thus the effectiveness of the response) depends on the absolute sovereignty practice in the region which limits cooperation where domestic issues may be involved. In this chapter we suggest that while cooperation in the region is limited, there is a need for 'root causes' to be addressed to better provide justice in the world order. The challenge is therefore for the US and her allies in the war on terrorism not merely to press for cooperation, but to fashion policies that better recognize regional attitudes and practices and which will have the support of governments and peoples of the region.

II. What has been promised: ASEAN, security and terrorism

ASEAN was established in 1967 for the member states to attain economic, social and cultural aims through 'joint endeavours' and 'active collaboration and mutual assistance'.[2] Membership of ASEAN has always accommodated

---

[2] See the ASEAN founding document, the Bangkok Declaration 1967, at http://www.asean sec.org/1212.htm. For an overview of ASEAN, see http://www.aseansec.org/64.htm. See also the ASEAN 1976 Treaty of Amity and Cooperation at http://www.aseansec.org/1217.htm.

the varied political and economic policies of its member states. Different political structure or type of government is not a barrier to membership. The present make-up of ASEAN ranges from the Philippine democracy to the Myanmese military dictatorship.

ASEAN has been explicitly premised on shared convictions about national priority objectives, such as economic development and political stability. Moreover, ASEAN was an anti-communist grouping during the Cold War and relied upon the US as a guarantor of stability. The contrast between an explicit and an implicit rationale for ASEAN and its relationship with the US can be seen in the individual foreign policy stances of its constituent member states. Two ASEAN member states – Thailand and the Philippines – are formal US allies, while Singapore is a close trading partner and affords port and other facilities for American military use. Conversely, two founding member states – Indonesia and Malaysia – have cultivated a more neutral public stance, and shown themselves to be closer to Third World and non-aligned movements, while maintaining vital relations with the USA.

While ASEAN has become an important regional grouping in political and economic affairs, there is no imperative for ASEAN member states to be unanimous in security and political policies. Member states maintain independent laws and legal systems, and the sovereign right to determine internal and external affairs, except for mutually agreed cooperation programmes which must be established by a consensus among ASEAN member states. This tradition of seeking uniform approval on all important policy decisions and of non-intervention in each other's affairs has resulted in a certain degree of 'bureaucratic inertia'. This is especially so in the field of counter-terrorism as countries in the region 'differ very much in their susceptibility to and experience of terrorism and hence it is extremely difficult to obtain an effective ASEAN-wide response to it'.[3] Security processes have remained limited to political dialogue and confidence-building, rather than actual military measures. Indeed – while ASEAN has fostered dialogue in almost all areas from foreign affairs to health – military and defence matters have not been emphasized.

There are current considerations of forming an ASEAN Security Community, a goal accepted by ASEAN leaders at their 2003 Bali summit.[4] There are, however, those who argue that ASEAN is already a security community because, through more than thirty years of dialogue and cooperation,

---

[3] *Per* Professor Robert O'Neill, former director and chairman of the International Institute for Strategic Studies, at the Shangri-La Dialogue 2003 (May 30 to June 1, 2003), at http://www.iiss.org/confPress-more.php?confID = 306.

[4] Among the steps proposed is for the formation of an ASEAN peace-keeping force, which remains controversial.

major interstate armed conflict has been avoided, notwithstanding some territorial and other disputes.

While some may argue that the 'ASEAN way' is excuse for the lack of political will to commit resources to solve problems,[5] others defend ASEAN by focusing on the need to understand the organization in its local context. ASEAN is only a norm-setting body which defines principles to guide actions. This does not mean that ASEAN is not doing enough, for actual operational cooperation is better done on a bilateral or trilateral basis. Full ASEAN multilateral cooperation against terrorists is unlikely to occur in the near future as 'many wish to maximize the freedom to act according to their own lights'.[6] This is exemplified by how Malaysia constantly asserts that while there must be maritime cooperation with the US, there is no question of the US Navy patrolling the waters of the Malacca Straits.

This basic ASEAN characteristic remains, even with the ARF's purpose of dealing with the new security environment. Rather than promising a revolution, the ARF has taken an evolutionary approach in regional affairs. It plans to extend its use over three broad stages: promoting confidence-building among participants, developing preventive diplomacy, and elaborating approaches to conflict prevention. This enables ARF participants to deal constructively with political and security issues that bear on regional peace and stability. Initially, ARF participants included ASEAN members, other Southeast Asian states that were not yet ASEAN members, ASEAN's then seven dialogue partners, Papua New Guinea (an ASEAN observer), China and Russia (then still 'consultative partners' of ASEAN). India became a participant in 1996. Mongolia and the Democratic People's Republic of Korea were admitted in 1999 and 2000.[7]

While the ARF has emerged as the leading process for multilateral dialogue in the region, it has faced criticism for its inability to respond to different crises such as the situation in East Timor (when violence erupted after the vote for independence). Additionally, Myanmar, an ASEAN member, has been under international pressure to proceed with its 'roadmap to democracy' by restoring elections and a civilian government.

---

[5] *Per* Jusuf Wanandi, Indonesia Centre for Strategic and International Studies, at the Shangri-La Dialogue 2003, at http://www.iiss.org/confPress-more.php?confID = 306.

[6] *Per* Amitav Acharya, Singapore Institute of Defence and Strategic Studies, at the Shangri-La Dialogue 2003, at http://www.iiss.org/confPress-more.php?confID = 306.

[7] The current participants in the ARF are as follows: Australia, Brunei Darussalam, Cambodia, Canada, China, European Union, India, Indonesia, Japan, Democratic Peoples' Republic of Korea, Republic of Korea, Laos, Malaysia, Myanmar, Mongolia, New Zealand, Papua New Guinea, Philippines, Russian Federation, Singapore, Thailand, United States, Vietnam. At http://www.aseansec.org/3536.htm.

Southeast Asian counter-terrorism initiatives

With the resurgence of Islamic fundamentalism within many Southeast Asian states, ASEAN counter-terrorism efforts have been discussed at the highest intra-regional level – the seventh, eighth and ninth ASEAN Summits.[8] Counter-terrorism is of such critical importance to safeguarding regional political stability and prosperity that new measures are constantly debated, not only within ASEAN or with its cooperative partners, but also among individual ASEAN member states. For example, the most recent point of contention is the security of shipping lanes in the Straits of Malacca and other waters flanked by Indonesia, Malaysia and Singapore, and whether foreign powers such as the US should be allowed to help these countries patrol their territorial waters.[9] These trading lanes are susceptible to piracy, and the potential for traditional armed aggression and biochemical attacks from terrorist groups is believed to be very high.

Every ASEAN Summit after 9/11 has produced a declaration for joint effort to eliminate terrorist activities.[10] These Summits advance ASEAN's efforts to fight terrorism by undertaking practical measures such as the review and strengthening of national mechanisms to combat terrorism, and the early signing and ratification of or accession to all relevant anti-terrorist conventions including the International Convention for the Suppression of the Financing of Terrorism.

Enhanced cooperation among front-line law enforcement agencies in combating terrorism and sharing 'best practices' among ASEAN states has been also exhorted. This includes intelligence exchange to facilitate the flow of information on terrorists and terrorist organizations. Other measures include the study of relevant international conventions on terrorism with the view to integrating them with ASEAN mechanisms for combating international terrorism, strengthened cooperation and coordination between the ASEAN Ministerial Meeting on Transnational Crime (AMMTC)[11] and other relevant ASEAN bodies, and the development of regional capacity-building programmes to enhance existing capabilities of ASEAN member countries to investigate terrorist acts.

The ASEAN Ministers have tried to realize the Summits' decisions, culminating in joint communiqués such as the *Joint Communiqué of the Fourth ASEAN Ministerial Meeting on Transnational Crime (2004)* and the *Joint*

---

[8] The 7th, 8th and 9th ASEAN Summits were held in Brunei Darussalam, November 2001; Cambodia, November 2002; and Indonesia, October 2003 respectively.

[9] 'Malaysia rejects US sea-patrols', 4 April 2004, BBC News, at http://news.bbc.co.uk/2/hi/asia-pacific/3598977.stm.

[10] The declarations can be found at www.aseansec.org/5318.htm, www.aseansec.org/13154, www.aseansec.org/15159 respectively.

[11] For more on AMM counter-terrorist activities, see their joint communiqués at http://www.aseansec.org/89_3644.htm.

Communiqué of the Third AMMTC (2001) that detail ASEAN efforts to eradicate regional problems such as terrorism.[12] There was even a Special ASEAN Ministerial Meeting on Terrorism convened in Kuala Lumpur in May 2002 that further communicated ASEAN's counter-terrorism activities and sought to establish the *Work Programme to Implement the ASEAN Plan of Action to Combat Transnational Crime, Kuala Lumpur, 17 May 2002*,[13] a document that detailed a six-pronged strategy, including the establishment of legal facilities and institutional capacities within the ASEAN member states.

ASEAN also carried out counter-terrorism training programmes in 2003. Courses on bomb and explosive detection, post-blast investigation, airport security and passport and document security and inspection have also been planned. After the 2002 Bali bombings, a Regional Conference on Combating Money-Laundering and Terrorist Financing was held in December 2002. The implementation of these counter-terrorism measures have since been reviewed in the third annual Senior Officials Meeting on Transnational Crime (SOMTC) in June 2003 in Hanoi.

Recognizing international cooperation as vital to Southeast Asian anti-terror efforts, ASEAN has also included counter-terrorism in discussions with its three partners, Japan, China and South Korea, at ASEAN + 3 (APT) summits.[14] This resulted in a *Joint Declaration on the Promotion of Tripartite Cooperation among the People's Republic of China, Japan and the Republic of Korea* at the Bali Summit of October 2003.[15] The APT framework was extended to the AMMTC during the Bangkok meeting in January 2004. The *Joint Communiqué of the First ASEAN Plus Three Ministerial Meeting on Transnational Crime* noted that though substantive measures had not yet been drafted, APT leaders reemphasized their determination to strengthen cooperation in the field of non-traditional security issues, especially in intensifying joint efforts to combat international terrorism in the region, and to support the *Bali Concord II*, which includes close cooperation in developing the ASEAN Security Community.[16] ASEAN has also intensified talks on transnational crime with its three partners in the first SOMTC + 3 meeting in June 2003 in Hanoi.

---

[12] At http://www.aseansec.org/15649.htm and http://www.aseansec.org/5621.htm respectively.

[13] For greater detail of the action plans at the intra- and extra-regional levels, including the work of ASEANAPOL, see *Joint Communiqué of the Special ASEAN Ministerial Meeting on Terrorism, Kuala Lumpur, 20–21 May 2002*, at www.aseansec.org/13075.htm and the *Work Programme* at www.aseansec.org/5616.htm.

[14] The 5th, 6th and 7th APT Summits were held simultaneously with the 7th, 8th and 9th ASEAN Summits in Brunei, 2001; Cambodia, 2002; and Indonesia, 2003.

[15] See http://www.aseansec.org/15284.htm.   [16] See http://www.aseansec.org/15159.htm.

ASEAN has also held individual talks with each partner state, termed ASEAN + 1 Summits, on issues pertinent to the bilateral relations between itself and its three partners. Beyond trade issues, there is discussion on terrorism, nuclear proliferation and security matters on a deeper level than at the APT meetings. ASEAN and China issued a *Joint Declaration of ASEAN and China on Cooperation in the Field of Non-Traditional Security Issues* in November 2002 where counter-terrorism was included as one of the priorities for ASEAN-China cooperation.[17] This cooperation was reinforced in the *Joint Declaration of the Heads of State/Government of the Association of Southeast Asian Nations and the People's Republic of China on Strategic Partnership for Peace and Prosperity* in October 2003.[18]

There has been increasing desire to engage the other (potential) Asian power, India, which has been ASEAN's partner in the Asia-Pacific security framework set up by the ASEAN Regional Forum since 1996. Expanding on this relationship, the 1st and 2nd ASEAN-India Summits of 2002 and 2003 saw the two parties agree to jointly contribute to the promotion of peace, stability and development in the Asia-Pacific region and the world, including cooperation in the area of security and counter-terrorism.[19] This led to the eventual institution of the *ASEAN-India Joint Declaration for Cooperation to Combat International Terrorism* at the Bali Summit 2003.[20]

On the periphery of Asia, Russia has also been invited. On 19 June 2003 in Phnom Penh, ASEAN and Russia signed the *Joint Declaration of the Foreign Ministers of the Russian Federation and ASEAN on Partnership for Peace and Security, and Prosperity and Development in the Asia-Pacific Region*, signalling closer cooperation and greater effort to counter terrorism. At the 14th ASEAN-EU Ministerial Meeting in Brussels on 27 January 2003, the European Union (EU) signed an *ASEAN-EU Joint Declaration on Co-operation to Combat Terrorism*. Similarly, the US and ASEAN signed the *ASEAN-United States of America Joint Declaration for Cooperation to Combat International Terrorism* on 1 August 2002 at the 35th ASEAN Ministerial Meeting in Brunei. Again, these political agreements aim to prevent and combat international terrorism through the exchange of information, intelligence and capacity-building assistance.

Counter-terrorism has also come under the ARF's ambit in managing Asia-Pacific security. However, the ARF has focused on general issues of security like preventive diplomacy, military and maritime security challenges.[21] Much effort has been channelled to questions of financing and linkages to transnational

---

[17] See http://www.aseansec.org/13185.htm.   [18] See http://www.aseansec.org/15265.htm.
[19] The 1st and 2nd ASEAN-India Summits were held simultaneously with the 8th and 9th ASEAN Summits in Cambodia, 2002 and Indonesia, 2003.
[20] See http://www.aseansec.org/15276.htm.
[21] These activities were part of the 10th and 11th ASEAN Regional Forum during the Inter-Sessional years of 2002–2003 and 2003–2004 respectively.

crime. For instance, at the 9th Ministerial Meeting of the (ARF) in Brunei in July 2002, the *ARF Statement on Measures against Terrorist Financing* was adopted. The participating states and the EU agreed on concrete steps that included the freezing of terrorist assets, implementation of international standards, and cooperation on exchange of information and outreach, and technical assistance.[22] However with the resurgence of violence in Southeast Asia, most notably southern Thailand, traditional counter-terrorism measures need supplementation. Border security and maritime security are increasingly areas of urgency for the region. Thus, the ARF Statements on *Cooperation Against Piracy and Other Threats to Maritime Security*[23] and *Cooperative Counter-Terrorist Action on Border Security*[24] at the 36th AMM in July 2003 in Phnom Penh, are indispensable to setting a seamless security architecture.

On a smaller scale, similar efforts have been undertaken by smaller groupings of ARF member states outside the ASEAN framework. These collaborations appear to be more effective, involving actual police work, information exchange and the establishment of anti-terror operatives. For instance, the signing of the *Agreement on Information Exchange and the Establishment of Communication Procedures* between Indonesia, Malaysia and the Philippines in May 2002 – Thailand and Cambodia have since acceded – is significant in the international campaign against terrorism.[25] Indonesian and Malaysian police will soon launch joint operations to tackle international crimes occurring at mutual border areas and a terrorism crisis centre is to be established in Indonesia. The head of the Indonesian National Police Operations has said that the operation, called *Aman Malino* (Safe Malaysia–Indonesia), was also targeted at securing the Straits of Malacca, which the US believes to be a prime terrorist target.[26] Other intra-regional bilateral efforts include the Thai-Malaysian border crackdowns on Islamic fundamentalist groups that have increasingly caused much civil disturbance.[27]

---

[22] 10th ASEAN Regional Forum (2002–2003 Inter-Sessional Year) Workshop on Counter-Terrorism Measures Japan, Republic of Korea and Singapore, September/October 2002. 11th ASEAN Regional Forum (2003–2004 Inter-Sessional Year). Inter-Sessional Meeting on Counter-Terrorism and Transnational Crime of the ASEAN Regional Forum in Karambunai in March 2003. Inter-Sessional Meeting on Counter-Terrorism and Transnational Crime Manila, 30–31 March 2004. On terrorist financing, see ARF Statement on Measures Against Terrorist Financing, 30 July 2002, at www.aseansec.org/12001.htm.

[23] See http://www.dfat.gov.au/arf/statements/index.html.

[24] See http://www.dfat.gov.au/arf/statements/10_borders.html.

[25] See www.aseansec.org/14825.htm.

[26] 'Malaysia, Indonesia To Launch Joint Action On Terrorism', 24 April 2004, Bernama – Malaysian National News Agency (http://www.bernama.com/bernama/v3/news.php?id = 63104).

[27] 'Malaysia supports Thai crackdown', 12 April 2004, CNN.com, http://www.cnn.com/2004/WORLD/asiapcf/04/12/thailand.malaysia/.

Other more long-standing bilateral agreements have been made between non-Asian and Asian ARF members to counter terrorist operations. In 2002, Australia signed individual agreements with Indonesia, Malaysia and Thailand. Such Memoranda of Understanding provide frameworks for Australia and these states to improve border controls, combat identity fraud and eliminate the illegal traffic in arms and explosives. In addition, it strengthens counter-terrorist capabilities through training, seminars and exchange visits by officials and specialists. This has reaped results particularly for Australia and Indonesia in the capture and prosecution of terrorist suspects related to the Bali bombings.

The US remains a bulwark in Southeast Asian security. Unsurprisingly, its presence in Southeast Asian counter-terror efforts has been the strongest. Apart from the sole anti-terror agreement signed with ASEAN, the US has largely preferred to enact bilateral agreements, practical plans of action and information-sharing with many ASEAN states like Singapore and Thailand.[28] This effectively affords the US a greater say and direction over counter-terrorism efforts.

Traditional supporters of the US, the Philippines and Singapore, have cooperated closely with the US in the global war on terrorism in the immediate aftermath of 9/11. In the Philippines, President Arroyo has allowed US troops to conduct joint counter-terrorism military exercises in the south of the country. While on a brief visit to the Philippines in October 2003, President Bush promised to 'help the country weed out terrorism'.[29] By sending troops to aid Filipino forces in defeating the Abu Sayyaf, the Philippines has become the only country besides Afghanistan to receive direct involvement of US troops in the fight against terrorism. Though their precise role remains unspecified, to avoid further controversy and perceived intrusion by the Philippine domestic population, US troops will (officially) only provide technical support, advice and training and take part in joint military exercises, but will not participate in combat.[30] In January 2004, Manila announced its readiness to deploy air marshals on Philippine Airline flights to the US if it reciprocates on US flights to the Philippines.

Singapore too supports the US as best as it can. As its Defence Minister put it, 'We will continue to support the anti-terrorism effort within our capabilities to make a useful contribution.'[31] Domestic measures were undertaken

---

[28] See *ASEAN-United States of America Joint Declaration for Cooperation to Combat International Terrorism*, 1 August 2002.

[29] 'Bush promises to help Philippines weed out terrorism', 8 October 2003, *USA Today*, http://www.usatoday.com/news/world/2003-10-18-bush-philippines_x.htm.

[30] 'Al-Qaeda in Southeast Asia: Evidence and Response', 8 February 2002, Reyko Huang, Center for Defense Information, at http://www.cdi.org/terrorism/sea-pr.cfm.

[31] The comment was notably made at a news conference after awarding the commander in chief of the US Pacific Command, Admiral Dennis Blair, the Meritorious Service Medal.

with laws to allow the country to implement UN Security Council resolutions readily.[32] Singapore authorities have also arrested over thirty alleged Jemaah Islamiyah operatives in 2002, two-thirds of whom were arrested after the Bali bombing, and a Southeast Asian-wide network of alleged terrorist groups said to be linked to al Qaeda has since been uncovered. The Singapore government subsequently published a Parliamentary White Paper on terrorism on 10 January 2003, detailing the aims and activities of the Jemaah Islamiyah terrorist group.[33] The US has also aided Malaysia and Indonesia extensively. Although Malaysia had suppressed Islamic radicals even before 9/11 with its Internal Security Act (ISA) that empowers the government to actively pursue counter-terrorism measures domestically, it has also granted the US access to intelligence and over-flight clearance.[34] Not only did the US consequently help Malaysia establish the first Southeast Asian anti-terror centre, it has extended a non-military assistance to Indonesia, including US$10 million to train Indonesian police, customs officers and the banking sector, and an offer to enhance intelligence sharing. In January 2004, Indonesia and the US signed an agreement on the peaceful exploitation of nuclear energy designed to protect Indonesian facilities from terrorist attacks.

In this plethora of different statements, a number of key promises of action can be identified. They are, in summary, undertakings for:

1. *Non-discrimination.* A particular point stressed in the ASEAN meetings was that the region must ensure that efforts to eliminate terrorism must avoid the identification of terrorism with any particular religion or ethnic group, and that counter-terrorism cooperation respects and has regard to regional sensitivities.

2. *Examination of root causes.* In addition to the current social and development projects undertaken by ASEAN, 'root causes' of terrorism such as poverty, economic development, education and other human security issues should should be addressed.

See 'Singapore pledges continued support for US-led anti-terror war', 29 January 2002, Agence France Presse, at http://www.singapore-window.org/sw02/020129a2.htm.

[32] As early as September 2001 the government established an inter-ministerial anti-terrorism task force, and in October 2001 issued regulations to facilitate implementation of UN Security Council Resolutions on counter-terrorism; for example, UNSC Resolution 1373 on the suppression of terrorist financing. The Monetary Authority of Singapore (MAS) instructed all banks and financial institutions to identify customers suspected of financing terrorist operations or involved in money-laundering activities, while the police stringently reviewed all financial transactions in Singapore.

[33] See Singapore *White Paper – The Jemaah Islamiyah Arrests and The Threat of Terrorism*, http://www2.mha.gov.sg/mha.

[34] For more information on counter-terrorism action in South-East Asia, see 'The Shape of Anti-Terrorist Coalitions in Southeast Asia' by Dana R. Dillon, Heritage Lecture #773, 17 January 2003, at http://www.heritage.org/Research/AsiaandthePacific/hl773.cfm.

3. *Transnational crime and connection to terrorism.* It has been recognized that there is a close connection between international terrorism and transnational organized crime As such, further initiatives like the Regional Conference on Combating Money Laundering and Terrorist Financing, held in Bali in December 2002, and the ongoing work of the Bali Process on People Smuggling, Trafficking in Persons and Related Transnational Crime should be encouraged to complement regional counter-terrorism efforts as well as to consider adopting confiscation of the proceeds of crime provisions to prevent funds obtained through illicit activities being used for terrorist activities.

4. *Safeguarding economic progress and APEC.* Sustained economic development has undoubtedly been a priority in the region. Thus ASEAN ministers and its collaborators acknowledge the need for effective counter-terrorism measures to provide a conducive climate for business activities. Consequently, ASEAN Ministers welcomed the Asia-Pacific Economic Forum's (APEC) newly-created Counter-Terrorism Task Force and the development of the APEC Counter-Terrorism Action Plans as a practical means to assist APEC members in fighting terrorism and promoting economic growth. Other APEC measures lauded were the Secure Trade in the APEC Region (STAR), the Energy Security, Countering the Financing of Terrorism and the Cyber Security Strategy initiatives. APEC's decision to establish a regional trade and financial security initiative within the Asian Development Bank to support projects that enhance port security, combat terrorist finance and achieve other counter-terrorism objectives was also encouraged.

5. *Maritime and aviation security.* Related to economic prosperity is the need for enhanced maritime security, especially in combating sea piracy and armed robbery at sea, to prevent and suppress maritime terrorism so that the trade routes remain safe. In addition, there are renewed calls for further steps to ensure aviation security to prevent aviation terrorism.

6. *Training and capacity-building programmes.* There has been constant emphasis on the importance of capacity building in law enforcement and mutual legal assistance in dealing with terrorism.

III. Asian security architecture: who will act and for whose benefit?

The declarations, treaties and plans summarized above are part and parcel of public diplomacy. It is a more difficult question to ask if they have borne results. It has often been said that collective regional efforts are mere political documents while practical substantive action is taken at the national level, especially in conjunction with the US. At the very least, they can be said to evidence a norm in the region, both unilaterally and collectively, against terrorism and non-state actors who perpetuate terrorist acts. Furthermore, the central importance of the USA to the security and politics of the region is explicitly demonstrated.

It is acknowledged that Southeast Asian relations are premised upon absolute state sovereignty and non-interference in neighbouring states' internal affairs. A stronger regional grouping that possesses the potential to diminish sovereign integrity and personality especially in the area of security may be too radical for current political sentiment. If the declarations are merely non-binding political expressions, how does Southeast Asia actually combat terrorism?

The coordination of legal initiatives for joint investigation, information-exchange, and the setting up of legal mechanisms for extradition and prosecution require more cooperation and unity of purpose than what has been evidenced thus far. Despite the many political documents signed, ASEAN member states still refrain from actively pursuing the activation of such plans, preferring anti-terror operations in smaller bilateral or multilateral initiatives, especially where the US is involved. It may even be said that there is implicit agreement that while declarations are signed, the actualization of plans will occur at the level of smaller groupings. This has been the long-standing mode of operation and it is unlikely that things will change, notwithstanding strong criticism.

It is implicitly understood that US presence in the region is necessary to maintain peace and security. While some dissent, the thinking that it is better to ally with the US prevails. Its policies of 'benign selfishness' offer the closest match to world interest – the desire for free trade, rule of law, free movement of capital and people, as well as security for persons and property.[35] Stability in Southeast Asia, in this view, is provided by a hegemonic power, provided it is relatively benign. To many security analysts, such realist bilateral relationships are vital to the region. They see multilateral institutions and processes like the UN, APEC, ARF and ASEAN as epiphenomenal – nice to have, but not essential. The leverage the US holds is therefore substantial.

However, the American agenda is not always deferred to. Due to the large Muslim population in Southeast Asia, governments have had to balance domestic public opinion and tread very carefully in identifying too closely with the US. This is especially true when there does not seem to be a radical difference in opinion among the ASEAN member states as to actual or perceived terror threats. There are no asymmetries in threat perception but rather varying degrees of how urgent the terror threat is according to whether fundamentalist ideology is rife, the presence of dissatisfied Muslim

---

[35] See 'The acceptability of American power', *The Economist*, 29 June 2002, at 10, for more on countries jumping onto the American 'bandwagon'.

populations and other human security factors. Indeed, at the Shangri-La Dialogue 2004 Singapore and Malaysia agreed that the United States needs to adopt a more 'balanced approach' towards the Palestinian-Israeli issue so that the rage which fuels terrorist acts is quelled. Singapore's Deputy Prime Minister, Tony Tan, said that the Israeli-Palestinian conflict and fighting in Iraq remain 'catalysts for rage, resentment and suicide bombers' while Malaysian Deputy Prime Minister Najib Tun Razak declared that injustices committed against the Palestinian people 'appear crystal clear to over one billion Muslims around the world, and yet there are countries that continue to promote an imbalanced view of this long-running conflict'.[36]

These statements echo what then Singapore Prime Minister, Goh Chok Tong, frankly expressed at the Council on Foreign Relations in Washington in May 2004. He said that

> While most Muslims do not approve of suicide bombings, they all do empathise with the plight of Palestinian Muslims. They are angered and disappointed by what they perceive as America's acquiescence in Israel's disproportionate use of force against the Palestinians and, most recently, its policy of 'targeted assassinations'. They are critical of what they regard as America's double standards, citing, for example, the US' determination in taking action against Iraq but not Israel for non-compliance of UN Security Council resolutions. These are views expressed consistently by leaders of Muslim nations ... including those most strongly supportive of America ... I can think of no Muslim society anywhere in the world where the Palestinian issue does not provoke a basic, common emotional response no matter how it may be expressed or intellectually articulated.[37]

Southeast Asian states do object to over-intrusion on the part of the US into their sovereign realms, most notably the recurring Malaysian rejection of the US offer of naval patrols in the Straits of Malacca in April 2004. Moreover, the Thai government reacted bluntly to suggestions from the US National Republican Congressional Committee that the US expands its anti-terrorism activities to Thailand, saying that Thailand would exercise its full right to make its own foreign policy decisions. Government spokesman, Jakrapob Penkair, said that while Thailand was happy to listen to suggestions from all of its allies, US suggestions that it could extend its foreign policy ideals into Thailand was unacceptable.[38]

---

[36] See speeches of the Shangri-La Dialogue 2004, International Institute of Strategic Studies, at http://www.iiss.org/shangri-la.php.

[37] 'Madrid: Winning against Terrorism', speech by PM Goh to the Council of Foreign Relations, Washington DC, 7 May 2004, at http://app.mfa.gov.sg/pr/read_content.asp?View,3900,_.

[38] 'We can deal with terrorists ourselves', 29 March 2004, MCOT News, at http://etna.m cot.net/query.php?nid=26714.

With the upsurge in radical Islamic terrorism in the Middle East and Southeast Asia, and the intense sporadic revolts by Iraqi guerillas, fears of heightened terrorism by transnational terrorist cells have also increased in Asia, especially in states with major US interests. Moreover, as a result of the increasing anti-American sentiment around the world with regard to the controversy over the Iraq occupation, the US itself is also circumspect about over-zealousness in its foreign policy, not wanting to incur greater opposition and more losses by being where it is not welcome.

Perhaps this could be the opportunity for greater progress in Asian regionalism in counter-terrorism and security, especially in the light of the proposed ASEAN Security Community (ASC) described in the Bali Concord II. This is envisaged to bring ASEAN's political and security cooperation to a higher plane. In this regard, the ARF remains the main forum for regional security dialogue. The ASC is to fully utilize the existing institutions and mechanisms within ASEAN with a view to strengthening national and regional capacities to counter terrorism and other transnational crimes, and will work to ensure that the Southeast Asian region remains free of all weapons of mass destruction. It may enable ASEAN to demonstrate a greater capacity and responsibility of being the *primary driving force* of the ARF and Southeast Asian regional security in general.[39]

Impetus for a Southeast Asian-led security mechanism could come from the importance of a peaceful and stable region for continued economic growth and prosperity. Southeast Asian nations give utmost precedence to economic development and financial security. This emphasis can propel an array of counter-terror initiatives.

However, such action needs a leader. Who would be the best choice to lead such a security community? It is debatable whether this question poses a debilitating obstacle to Southeast Asian anti-terror efforts. As has been sometimes argued, the leadership of ASEAN is not an issue as equality is greatly stressed in ASEAN, especially by the less prosperous new members like Cambodia, Laos, Myanmar and Vietnam (CLMV). Furthermore, the ASEAN agenda progresses by having different states champion different issues and proposing them at regional meetings. For example, the Philippines is traditionally the leader on issues of civil rights, while Malaysia and Singapore have always propounded economics. Indonesia is now spearheading the ASEAN Security Community discussed during the 9th ASEAN Summit in October 2003.

On the other hand, it has also been said that Southeast Asian states are too small to have much impact and tend to be tied down by domestic concerns. Moreover, the mutual rivalry between ASEAN states makes it difficult for any

---

[39] For more on the ASEAN Security Community, see http://www.aseansec.org/15159.htm.

one of them to assume a leadership role. If anything, ASEAN as a whole unit *may* be a possible contender to influence regional security. It was declared at the first East Asia Congress in Kuala Lumpur in June 2003 that ASEAN as a whole has better standing than its individual states.

Resources and infrastructure are an equally pressing concern. Faced with the need for domestic development and limited budgets, it is unlikely that many, if any, can contribute extensively to a collective security or anti-terror mechanism. There is the need for manpower, basic education and training, and the establishment of civil institutions before any form of effective cooperation and coordination can occur. Even if Indonesia has been the erstwhile leader of ASEAN security affairs, it is questionable whether it is in a position to lead when the level of its own domestic unrest is high and resources are stretched. Moreover, with the upcoming Indonesian Presidential elections, it is uncertain that this project initiated by former President Megawati Soekarnoputri will be continued if there is a change in leadership in the upcoming elections. In addition, other ASEAN states may chafe at an equal's leadership. It would perhaps be better if an external player continues to exercise leverage in regional security.

It is possible then that the region would be looking at a 'multiplex' of players, one of which is the US. The UN is not inconsequential to Southeast Asians. Indeed, Asia has been an arena for prominent and successful UN operations. The Cambodian and East Timorese efforts were, in their time, the largest in UN history. They also signalled a first by establishing protectorates to help reconstruction efforts in fragile states. For Asians with longer-memories, UN approval ushered in US-led forces during the Korean War.

However, in the aftermath of the 1997–98 Asian financial crisis, states in the region have realized their own vulnerabilities. Continued American primacy and the importance of its markets have been the central hope for countries seeking to increase their exports as a means to stimulate recovery. The Asia–Pacific regional self-image of parity, equity and community has given way to a realistic assessment of what and who matters. The increasing fear was not of a unilateralist and overbearing America but of a self-satisfied one that would retreat into itself, uninterested in Asia. Against this background, the post-9/11 agenda has again turned US attention outwards.

The agenda of the UN and the Bretton Woods institutions are framed, and their operations determined, by American power. This is not news. During the Korean War American soldiers stood behind the UN flag. China's accession into both the UN and the WTO resulted not from consensus on the part of existing members but from improved relations with Washington. In the post-Cold War period, Asians witnessed the ascendance within the UN of such issues as democracy and human rights in response to changing American moods. In the wake of the financial crisis, many Asians expressed concerns that the International Monetary Fund wrongly prescribed policies that deepened the crisis but were unable to sway the organization from the prescription of the so-called Washington consensus. A regional idea for an Asian Monetary Fund was also set aside after protests from the US.

In these, as in so many other instances, global institutions have not responded so much to the majority of member states or even to the Security Council, but to the US. Asians, for the most part, perceive that American policy and power is embedded in the UN and Bretton Woods institutions, serving as multilateral façades for American imperatives. Others recognize, however, the importance of such power in upholding norms in global institutions. In this regard the UN is at most a second-best to the US. Most Asians are content to be involved in such institutions as a 'hedging' strategy, to go along when there is convergence between American hegemony and their own interests.

What can be used to eliminate or deter terrorist groups like Jemaah Islamiyah, the Moro Liberation National Force and al Qaeda? As evidenced by the US offensive in Afghanistan, it is impossible to use traditional military means to counter terrorists. Other means of combating terrorism must be examined, especially the prevention of terrorism at the foundational stage.

IV. Radical Islam and the 'root causes'

Many in Asia believe that thorough eradication of terrorism requires 'root causes' to be addressed. Poverty, the isolation of Muslim groups because of terrorism misconceptions, ethnicity, and an underlying sense of injustice are among the main causes Asian commentators commonly cite. Without such concomitant efforts, it is hard to convince Muslims in Southeast Asia, and elsewhere, that the US is not anti-Islam.

It may be asked how something as far removed as the actual and ideological conflict in the Middle East can affect Southeast Asian security so gravely. Radical Islam in Southeast Asia is widely acknowledged as an import from the Arab world with little influence in the mainstream of Southeast Asian societies. Thus many Asian governments' anti-terror operations work on the premise that 'as long as the terrorists have not acquired a critical mass and deep roots in local societies they can be isolated and hunted down if countries of the region can marshal the will and capacity to take effective action'.[40] Therefore, even if human security issues are not the real causes of terrorism, they do provide terrorist groups with something to exploit. Hence, the

---

[40] '9/11: Two Years On, ASEAN Breaks Terrorism's Deadly Lock'. Daljit Singh, senior research fellow at the Institute of Southeast Asian Studies, Singapore, contributed the article to the *Straits Times* on 11 September 2003. See http://www.iseas.edu.sg/viewpoint/dssep03.pdf.

rectification of the root causes of terrorism within Southeast Asia itself has not been overlooked, but instead has rightly been given an increasing focus. This is especially true of Southeast Asia where there are constantly growing links with international militant Islamic terrorist groups. The Abu Sayyaf and Moro Islamic Liberation Front (MILF) in the Philippines have received funding from al Qaeda, while other Islamic fundamentalists allegedly linked to Osama bin Laden have infiltrated Muslim non-government organizations and are preachers in mosques, teaching that it is the duty of all good Muslims to fight for all oppressed Muslims worldwide and to become *syahids* (martyrs) by dying for the cause.[41] With the transfer of Arab Islamic ideology, larger numbers of Southeast Asian Muslims are identifying with the cause of the Arab Muslims and the Islamic 'brotherhood' call to *jihad*. Anger is directed at the Israel–Palestine conflict, the occupation of Iraq and the recent Abu Ghraib mistreatment of Iraqi prisoners, especially in the context of the apparent hypocrisy of the US in its continued exhortation to spread its democratic and capitalist ideals worldwide.

Southeast Asia therefore cannot avoid the security implications of the worldwide radicalization of Islam and the emergence of post-modern terrorism. The long-term solution to the problem of Islamic extremist militancy in Southeast Asia lies with dealing with its fundamental causes, which has at its root socio-economic issues and grievances.

Even if some terrorists are from the educated middle class, it is undeniable that the bulk of fundamentalist support comes from those who are poor and dispossessed. Eradication of poverty is a near-impossible task with regional resources constricted by competing concerns of national development like housing, civil institutions and government and education. Constructing a hierarchy to which resources may be allocated is fraught with disagreement. Even if the international community were to offer aid, developmental issues are primarily the duty of the state. States wishing to develop must agree to abide by the international financial institutions' terms in the restructuring and development of their economies and industries as the concomitant duty in return for the money.

In addition to direct counter-terrorist operations like intelligence gathering, infiltration of terrorist cells and the use of preventive detention, an ideological strategy to minimize the impact of fundamentalist teaching must be formulated, for example, through the promotion of moderate theology and encouraging debate within Islam.[42]

---

[41] See Senior Minister Lee Kuan Yew's interview with the Far Eastern Economic Review on the Jemaah Islamiyah militant attacks, reproduced at the Singapore Ministry of Home Affairs press releases, at http://www2.mha.gov.sg/mha/.

[42] 'The emergence of post-modern terrorism and its implications for Southeast Asia', Andrew Tan, Asst. Professor at the Institute of Defence and Strategic Studies (IDSS), Perspectives-IDSS, at http://www.ntu.edu.sg/idss/Perspective/research_050107.htm.

This could be the right time to promote moderate Islamic ideologies. The Muslim populations of Malaysia and Indonesia appear to be strongly supportive of moderate Islam. The results of Malaysia's eleventh General Election have shown that moderate Islam is the people's democratic choice. Strong support was given to Prime Minister Abdullah Badawi's vision of a modern, moderate and progressive Islam. He defeated the main Islamist political party, the Parti Islam Se-Malaysia (PAS), which promised Islamic law to the states in which it won control of local government. PAS garnered less than 16 per cent of the vote nationwide and only retained six of the twenty-seven seats it held in the previous Parliament.[43]

It is significant that amid the increasing Islamic fundamentalism globally, the Malaysian PAS is perhaps the first Islamic political party to be so badly defeated. Such democratic victories within Muslim communities are all the more legitimate when Islamic parties are part of the political process, as they are in Malaysia.

In Indonesia, much the same is expected to occur in the country's first direct presidential election in the third quarter of 2004. Already the big established nationalist-secular parties have won the most seats, but newer parties have made gains on an anti-corruption agenda. Indonesia's once long-ruling Golkar Party captured the most votes in the April election with 22 per cent. President Megawati Sukarnoputri's Indonesian Democratic Party of Struggle came in second with slightly less than 19 per cent.[44] A recent survey by political scientists Saiful Mujani and R. William Liddle found that while more than 70 per cent of Indonesians supported the concept of *Sharia* 'in the abstract', when asked about specific aspects of Islamic law, such as requiring women to wear the veil or banning women from politics, this support dropped off dramatically.[45]

It has been propounded widely that education and the closer scrutiny of *madrasahs* and their curricula help in combating terrorism at the foundational levels. Measures such as these have been implemented in Singapore, where the government is strongly promoting moderate Islam and seeking the help of the Islamic Council in doing so. For most Singaporean Muslims, 'moderate' beliefs are held and such measures have been quite uncontroversial. For the rest of the Southeast Asian region, the converse would probably be true.

---

[43] 'A template for moderate Islam in Southeast Asia?', 31 March 2004; Lawrence Pintak, Howard R. Marsh visiting professor of journalism at the University of Michigan contributed this commentary to the *Daily Star*, at http://www.lebanonwire.com/0403/04033115DS.asp.

[44] 'Golkar Wins Indonesian Parliamentary Elections', 5 May 2004, *Epoch Times*, at http://english.epochtimes.com/news/4-5-5/21270.html.

[45] Above note 43.

When Indonesian President Megawati Sukarnoputri ordered a review of the teaching of religion in Indonesian schools on 18 May 2004, stating that the current modes of education encouraged fundamentalism, her initiatives were met with a lot of opposition by many Muslim scholars and leaders, who dismiss views that *pesantrens* (Islamic boarding schools) are breeding grounds for Islamic militancy, arguing that these *pesantrens* have been stalwarts of Islamic education in Indonesia for decades and generally produce students with tolerant religious views.[46] Given that such schemes are highly sensitive and could even be perceived as contrived and perhaps even 'un-Islamic' by supporters of moderate Islam who prefer taking a less constructed route based on the traditional Southeast Asian type of moderate interpretation and practice of Islam, it is uncertain how the ideological arm of counter-terrorism is to be carried out and what degree of success it will be able to achieve.

It is also questionable what role, if any, foreign states, most notably the US, can play in this process. It is to be surmised that the US would be more than willing to contribute to this cause. However, such altruism could easily be perceived as indoctrination and imperialism. What should the US then do? Perhaps in such matters, the US should recognize that it *cannot* lead the ideological battle and as such refrain from any overt action. The US seem to have exercised self-restraint, correctly in our view, when it congratulated Malaysia's PM Abdullah Badawi on his election victory on 23 March 2004. It prudently did not play up the implicit message of support for moderate Islam in Malaysia's election and the forthcoming elections in Indonesia. Paradoxically, in this area, inaction on the part of the US could be a more successful form of 'action' for the US agenda, advancing the forces of democratic change in these countries. In Indonesia but also increasingly in other Southeast Asian nations, being too closely identified with the US in its war on terrorism (with all the attendant perceptions of that war) can be detrimental to their standing in political domestic opinion.

Nevertheless, other ASEAN countries must also realize their own limitations. If the state conducts intensive 'moderate Islamicization', the risk of the ideological campaign appearing contrived and even 'un-Islamic' runs very high and there could be a backlash. This has already been pointed out by then Singapore PM Goh, stating simply that the 'ideological struggle is far more complex ... because it engages not just reason but religious faith ... non-Muslims have no *locus standi* to engage in this struggle for the soul of Islam. It is a matter for Muslims to settle among themselves'. He also said that it was

fortunate that the Singapore Muslim community and Islamic leaders trusted the Government sufficiently to be willing to offer their help; they understood

---

[46] 'Religious education review ordered', 18 May 2004, *Jakarta Post*, at http://www.the jakartapost.com/yesterdaydetail.asp?fileid=20040518.A04.

that unless *they* acted, all Muslims could have been tarred by a few. Hence, a number of Islamic religious teachers have already volunteered their services to our security authorities to undertake religious counseling and rehabilitation of the *Jemaah Islamiyah* (JI) detainees. While the government welcomed their help, it acknowledged that as a secular Government, it could not direct religious teachers as to what they must preach. Religious leaders regarded as too pro-government would not be credible.[47]

While the US should not spearhead the ideological campaign, it must, in its interaction with the international Muslim community, recognize the differences among separate Muslim populations. As PM Goh pointed out,

> even though the RAND report released in March 2004 tried to understand Muslims better, its categorization of Muslims into fundamentalists, traditionalists, modernists and secularists, fails to recognise what all Muslims share in common. There is the real presence of a vibrant Islamic *ummah* (global Islamic community) but this *ummah* is not monolithic. The identification that all Muslims feel for events affecting other Muslims has become real and visibly stronger and more widespread since global communications have facilitated the missionary activities of the Arab states, especially Saudi Arabia preaching and spreading *Wahhabism* with its oil wealth.[48]

Perhaps even more importantly the international community as well as the media should expressly recognize that much of the Muslim world rejects extremism. Instead of constantly exhorting the global Muslim community to embrace moderate Islam, steps taken by the community should be duly acknowledged. When Pakistani President Pervez Musharraf told students to reject extremism at a national student convention in May 2004, and when Dr Muhammad Sayyid Tantawi, an *ulama* of Islam and professor of Egypt's Al-Azhar University, spoke out against Islamic extremists at the Conference of the Supreme Council for Islamic Affairs during April 2004 in Cairo, both incidents were overlooked by the international community and media. Hence, it is important that the US and the international community recognize these efforts and avoid over-generalizing the Muslim world.[49]

V. Cooperation and sovereignty: the needs and limits in Southeast Asia

From the many declarations, it would seem that ASEAN member states are intent on cooperating with each other, with the USA and even indeed with other states outside the region on anti-terrorism efforts. Yet from this chapter's analysis of the American actions and regional reactions to date, it is also

---

[47] Speech by PM Goh to the Council of Foreign Relations, Washington DC, above note 37.
[48] Ibid.   [49] 'When voices of moderation go unheard', 8 June 2004, *Straits Times*.

clear that there are many impediments to cooperation or even a contestation about what really needs to be done. There is a divide between the official policies made by the ASEAN member states that have largely supported the USA or limited their differences, and public opinion, which has increasingly turned against America. This creates what may be called a democratic deficit in the region between governments and their citizens. It also reveals something of a paradox in that American policies to date have been accepted by ASEAN member states at one level and yet are also quizzed or even opposed at another level.

One way of understanding this paradox is to examine the type of cooperation that is needed for anti-terrorism efforts and compare that to the ideas of sovereignty that prevail, both internationally and within the region. Interstate cooperation in Southeast Asia is not new. ASEAN was formed in 1967 and has, in its thirty plus years of existence, undertaken cooperation in diverse fields including issues of geopolitics in challenging the Vietnamese intervention in Cambodia, trade and economic cooperation with the ASEAN Free Trade Area (AFTA) and ASEAN Economic Community, and environmental protection, including efforts to address the recurring Indonesian fires and haze. The different areas of cooperation however intrude – in different ways and to different degrees – upon what would otherwise have been considered the domestic jurisdiction of the sovereign states.

In trade issues, for example, AFTA was largely an exercise in getting states to cut and limit the tariffs imposed on different items. This is a minimal intrusion on state sovereignty, as tariffs may be viewed as an external gate that can be altered with little impact on domestic policy. In the case of Cambodia, the cooperation among ASEAN member states (which did not include either Cambodia or Vietnam at the time) largely involved their foreign policies and efforts at the United Nations. There was no cooperation in terms of military efforts, or in dealing with refugees or other aspects of the situation. In contrast, the ASEAN Economic Community seeks to integrate the markets of the ASEAN member states across eleven product sectors. This involves not just tariffs, but internal policies and practices such as non-tariff barriers, competition policy and market access. If ASEAN is to successfully cooperate in addressing the issue of the Indonesian fires and resulting regional haze, this must necessarily impact on Indonesian law and policy internally; and indeed it is for this reason that the regional treaty negotiated by ASEAN may be necessary but insufficient in itself.

Terrorism is an issue that deeply challenges cooperation between states, especially those in Southeast Asia. While the USA has led military interventions in Afghanistan and Iraq akin to conventional warfare, much more of the effective cooperation against terrorism involves non- military measures, such as the sharing of intelligence, border control measures, effective monitoring of illicit bank and financial transactions – measures that the ASEAN member states have agreed upon. While tariffs and military interventions deal with different actions between states, these types of anti-terrorism measures have much more bite *within* states. Many more different and diverse units of the state are involved too, ranging from immigration and customs to financial authorities, police and intelligence agencies. The nature of anti-terrorist measures and of the agencies involved grows even more diverse and complex if 'root causes' of poverty, exclusion and injustice are addressed, as many Asians feel ought to be the case.

Seeing anti-terrorist measures in this way warns us that declarations and treaties such as those undertaken by ASEAN and surveyed in the first part of this chapter are only the beginning, even if they are sincerely intended and pursued. Cooperation on anti-terrorism is, in many cases, deeply intrusive on what states would otherwise consider matters within their domestic jurisdiction. This characteristic of cooperation is additionally challenged in the ASEAN practice of sovereignty. As noted by many observers, the ASEAN member states and ASEAN as a whole propound and practice a principle of 'non-intervention' that goes beyond the usual international standard. In the international community, non-intervention is largely a shield against the illegitimate use of force or threat of force. Within ASEAN, there are often cases in which no more than a public comment is made, against which the protest of 'interference' or 'intervention' is raised.

The reasons chiefly relate to the nature of these states. These are largely recent, post-colonial creations and have multiple and diverse characteristics of race, language, religion and ethnicity. The result is an ASEAN that is avowedly an association, and not a union like the European Union. The institutional capacity and purposes of ASEAN are measured out accordingly, with a declared distrust for a larger regional bureaucracy and against 'legalistic', binding approaches to cooperation. Changes have been made to enable and enhance cooperation within ASEAN in a number of fields, especially in economic affairs. But there has been little change in terms of the ASEAN approach to political and security issues. Suggestions for 'flexible engagement', while appealing to those of liberal persuasion, have not been adopted by ASEAN as a whole.

Thus, while Indonesia suffers from a long-standing and often violent secessionist movement in Aceh, Thailand from a similar problem in its southern provinces and the Philippines from separatists in Mindanao, there is no concerted and open cooperation on these issues among ASEAN as a whole. Bilateral understandings with the US have been reached in the case of the Philippines and perhaps Aceh. Quieter but no less help has been given in some cases by an ASEAN neighbour. But these have not been issues for ASEAN. The shield of sovereignty is instead held up against 'interference'. The most recent example of this is that of Thailand's response to the problems in its southern provinces, where it first decried Malaysia's (alleged) failure to control their shared border, and then seemed to refuse to seek deeper cooperation with Malaysia.

With this norm and practice of 'non intervention', the prospects of effective cooperation against terrorism in Southeast Asia are pressured not only by capacity and political will; they are running up against strongly held norms of state practice. Even when there may be some recognition of the needs of cooperation, there are still quite narrow limits to that cooperation because of concerns over sovereignty.

VI. The context of principles and concepts: human rights and world order

The promises and limits of cooperation in Southeast Asia may also be seen in the context of principles of international law or of conceptions of the international community. Two principles or concepts that may be especially of interest are, first, the protection and promotion of human rights; and, second, principles about power, justice and world order.

Human rights has assumed considerable prominence in world politics and international law. While many limitations remain, there has been considerable progress by the modern human rights movement since the end of World War II. There has been the growth of a body of treaties accepted by very many of the states in the world. Even states which are not legally bound by ratification often face the political need to respond. There has been the growth of institutions that can also bring these treaties and norms to life, such as the ad hoc tribunals on crimes in the former Yugoslavia and the fledgling International Criminal Court. Most controversially perhaps there has been the first modern war waged in the ostensible defence of human rights: the bombing of Belgrade by NATO forces, in response to human rights violations in Kosovo. In many ways, in the post-Cold War world, democracy and human rights have emerged as the most important legitimating factors for governments.

However, the post-9/11 American-led war against terrorism has had an ambivalent impact on the role of human rights. Very often, the Bush administration has made the protection of human rights and the promotion of democracy part of its legitimacy in taking action. This is strongly evident in the US justifications for intervention in Iraq. This emphasis moves beyond the more legalistic approaches of the UK and others who have instead emphasized the UN Security Resolution 1441 and the recommencement of the long dormant authorization for the use of force in the first Gulf War, a decade before. There has been notable rhetoric and even academic opinion in favour of using the might of the US in the service of rights, and of bringing democracy to the Middle East.

On the other hand, however, human rights have suffered in the post-9/11 war on terrorism in a number of ways. First and perhaps foremost has been the action of the US administration in refusing to give full recognition and protection to Iraqi captives as prisoners of war. This has exposed them to legal uncertainties in their captivity, whether in Guantanamo Bay or in various prisons across Iraq. The recent exposure of gross human rights violations against Iraqi prisoners by their American captors must be seen in the context of this systemic evasion of existing international norms and a slippage of legitimacy. A second post-9/11 weakening of human rights protections has been felt domestically in the USA, with the Patriot Act and other measures that erode (to many people) the extent of civil liberties and protections that US citizens, residents and even visitors to the USA have usually enjoyed. A third weakening of the legitimating role of human rights in the post-9/11 efforts is highly relevant to the states of Southeast Asia. This is that, when compared to its fervour in the post-Cold War flush, the US appears to be less strongly interested and committed to human rights in other countries where their governments can be of help and support to its war on terrorism. A trade-off has been struck between human rights beliefs and post-9/11 exigencies. This has impacted on US relations with Indonesia and the Philippines.

The post-9/11 efforts against terrorism also may be seen in the context of the international principles and concepts concerning justice, power and world order. For while the fact of American primacy as the only superpower left in the world preceded 9/11, there has been a much stronger purpose and drive to the American use of that primacy, post-9/11, and much more suspicion and resistance to it as well.

VII. Conclusion: cooperation as *realpolitik* or as principle?

'The United States possesses unprecedented and unequalled strength and influence in the world. Sustained by faith in the principles of liberty, and the value of a free society . . . the great strength of this nation must be used to promote a balance of power that favors freedom.'

US President George W. Bush, the National Security Strategy, September 2002

Southeast Asian states have offered their cooperation to the US-led war on terrorism. They have done so bilaterally with the US as well as amongst themselves, sometimes acting as ASEAN and sometimes in ad hoc arrangements. They have done some of this with a sense of American expectation and pressure. Relations between the US and Southeast Asia cannot be seen as an equation of growing equality or even a partnership. Southeast Asia is instead another region that must deal with the US on its terms and in response to the agenda that Americans set, post-9/11. There is a growing sentiment in Asia and elsewhere of resistance and even anger against America. There may be no immediate penalty for the US, given its primacy. Yet it is striking that the declared values of the country, and the goodwill and sympathy that many in the world felt immediately after 9/11, have not led to a greater and sustained support for the US in Asia or indeed the wider world. This has considerable implications for US-Southeast Asian relations.

ASEAN and other Asian countries are right to seek to engage the US on the 9/11 agenda. American inattention or resentment can otherwise have a negative impact. However, they can and should make stronger efforts to increase the terms of this engagement. America can and should be more multilateral in both process and substance. Univalent attention to narrow security and military concerns should be broadened with an agenda that considers the needs for peace-building, sustainable development and prosperity.

The efforts in ASEAN and ASEAN + 3 regionalism serve best to help the states in Asia address what issues they can, among themselves. They may also serve as an occasional platform for dialogue and consultation with America. In the short to medium term, there is little prospect that they will displace the primary importance of bilateral relations with America. The hub-and-spoke arrangement of relations will continue between the different, disunited Asian states at the rim. For the longer term, however, there is a growing need for the dialogue to grow to include wider issues such as world order and values like human rights.

The Bush administration has referred to many traditions and values in America's thinking about the world. These include the need to 'champion aspirations of human dignity', 'ignite a new era of global economic growth through free markets', and 'expand the circle of development by opening societies and building the infrastructure of democracy'.[50] If these values are pursued alongside the global war against terrorism, American leadership in the world would be much more acceptable to many more people. It remains to be seen if the Bush administration, in its second term, will live up to these declared aims. If it does, it will find states in Asia who are willing to cooperate. It is not an end to the American presence that most in Asia desire. Indeed, American presence is what they have known, lived with and largely prospered from. The overarching wish of Asian states is instead that American primacy continues to provide stability and be generally benevolent for all, even in the face of post-9/11 American exigencies and imperatives.

Cooperation must therefore move from being based on a sense of *realpolitik* and obeisance to American power. If it does not, there will always be

---

[50] 'The National Security Strategy of the United States of America', Titles of sections II, VI and VII respectively, at http://www.whitehouse.gov/nsc/nss.html.

limits to the extent of that cooperation in meeting the complex challenges of terrorism, and growing resistance to American dictates. Efforts to help grow trust and common perspectives must instead be increased. These may help assure the region that American might is indeed used for what, collectively, is thought to be right. A reciprocal result would be that the US might be better able to find states that would more genuinely and fully support their efforts. Principles of international law and the community of nations must guide and direct cooperation in directions that many more can accept and support.

20

Anti-terrorism law and policy: the case of the European Union

JÖRG MONAR

Introduction

Since the 9/11 terrorist attacks the European Union (EU) has increasingly emerged as an actor in its own right in the fight against international terrorism, providing a framework for collective action both inside the EU and on the international level. Based on the Treaty of Amsterdam in 1999, the scope of EU anti-terrorism law and policy has expanded significantly since 2001, and the Madrid terrorist attacks of 11 March 2004 have given a new impetus to this process.

This chapter analyses the role of the EU in the fight against international terrorism by first looking at the legal, structural and political bases of the EU, and then by analyzing the Union's response to 9/11 and the 11 March 2004 attacks. It will provide an overall evaluation of the Union's potential and limits as a political and legal actor in this field, taking into account reform proposals of the European Convention's Draft Constitution for the EU.

I. The bases for EU action

A. Legal bases

At the time of 9/11 EU Member States could already look back to a quarter of a century of cooperation against terrorism. The TREVI cooperation, which had come into operation in 1976 and can be regarded as the ancestor of the 'third pillar' of the 1990s, had originally focused entirely on the cross-border fight against the terrorist groups which were trying to destabilize several of the EC Member States at that time, especially Germany, Italy and the UK. Yet TREVI had remained a loose inter-governmental structure without legal bases, competences, permanent institutions and financial means, largely limited to information exchange. It was only with the introduction of Title VI TEU through the Treaty of Maastricht (1993) that EU action was for the first time provided with a legal basis, a basis which was then strengthened and expanded by the Treaty of Amsterdam which entered into force in May 1999.

At the level of fundamental treaty objectives, the most important provision is Article 2 TEU which provides for the maintenance and the development of the Union as an 'area of freedom, security and justice'. That internal security lies at the core of this objective is made clear by the major emphasis placed in Article 29 TEU on providing 'citizens with a high level of safety' within the Union. This objective is repeated in almost identical terms in Article 61(e) TEC. The Union has therefore been given an explicit mandate as a provider of internal security – which in itself is a major innovation. Article 29, second paragraph, specifically mentions terrorism as a form of crime which should be targeted 'in particular'. Although there is no explicit mention of terrorism in the provisions on the 'common foreign and security policy' (CFSP) in Title V TEU, Article 11(1), second sub-paragraph, defines the strengthening of 'the security of the Union in all ways' as one of the central objectives of the CFSP. This is broad enough to include international action against security threats posed by global terrorism.

At the level of the specific competences to act, the most extensive set of provisions is to be found under Title VI TEU, the 'third pillar' as reformed by the Treaty of Amsterdam. Of primary importance are the following:

- police cooperation between the Member States in the prevention, detection and investigation of criminal offences, data collection, joint training and the common evaluation of investigative techniques (Article 30(1) TEU),
- the further development of Europol, including the support of specific investigative actions, the initiation and coordination of investigations, and the promotion of liaison arrangements between prosecuting/investigating officials (Article 30(2) TEU),
- the facilitation and acceleration of cooperation between judicial authorities and competent ministries, including the facilitation of extradition, ensuring the compatibility of applicable rules and the prevention of conflicts of jurisdiction (Article 31(a)–(d) TEU),
- the progressive adoption of measures establishing minimum rules relating to the constituent elements of criminal acts (including terrorism) and penalties, (Article 31(e) TEU),
- the possibility of concluding agreements with third countries or international organizations over matters falling under Title VI TEU (Article 38 TEU in conjunction with Article 24 TEU).[1]

Although all these competences to act are of a non-exclusive nature and remain in the inter-governmental sphere of Title VI TEU, they nevertheless offer substantial possibilities for increased cooperation between national police and judicial authorities, a stronger role for Europol and a harmonization of national penal laws.

---

[1] Article 24 TEU governs the negotiation and conclusion of international agreements in the CFSP context.

Two of the communitarized areas of Title IV TEC are of relevance to terrorism:

- standards and procedures to be followed by Member States in carrying out checks on persons at external borders (Article 62(2)(a) TEC), and
- rules on visas for intended stays of no more than three months, including the list of third countries whose nationals must be in possession of visas when crossing external borders (Article 62(2)(b) TEC).

The legal instruments to be used depend on the legal basis. In the communitarized areas of Title IV TEC, well-established EC instruments, primarily regulations and directives, apply. The primary instruments in the intergovernmental domain of Title VI TEU are 'decisions' and 'framework decisions'. The latter are comparable in their legal effects to EC regulations and directives, the only major difference being that they do not have direct effect.[2] The availability of decisions and framework decisions as legal instruments represents a significant improvement to the situation before the Treaty of Amsterdam when 'soft law' instruments were an often used option for the Member States.[3] The Council can also agree on 'conventions'.[4] These, however, are subject to ratification by the Member States, a procedure which can take years and makes 'conventions' a very cumbersome instrument to use. All these instruments are open to judicial review by the European Court of Justice (ECJ), but in the Title VI TEU domain only national courts of last instance can seek a preliminary ruling from the Court. The Court has no jurisdiction over the validity or proportionality of law enforcement measures by national authorities and where there is a dispute regarding the interpretation of an EU measure, the Court can only come in after the Council has failed to resolve the issue within six months.[5]

Because of the 'cross-pillar' dimension of the threats posed by global terrorism, two further legal bases for EU action need to be mentioned. One is the residual power of Article 308 TEC which can be used for attaining an objective of the Treaty even if the Treaty does not provide for explicit powers. As a high level of internal security is now clearly an objective also of the EC, Treaty Article 308 TEC can also be used as a basis for common action. The other legal basis to be mentioned concerns the CFSP. The broadness of the CFSP aim 'to strengthen the security of the Union in all ways' (Article 11 TEU) provides sufficient justification not only for the use of specific CFSP instruments listed in Article 12 TEU (e.g., common strategies, joint actions) and Article 17(2) TEU (rescue, peace-keeping and crisis management tasks),

---

[2] See Article 34(2)(b) and (c) TEU.
[3] On the legal instruments, see Steve Peers, *EU Justice and Home Affairs Law* (Harlow, Longman 2000), 49–50.
[4] Article 34(2)d) TEU.   [5] Article 35 TEU.

but also for the use of external economic sanctions via Articles 301 TEC and Article 60 TEC.

However, the instruments mentioned here, with few and rather marginal exceptions,[6] are subject to a major constraint – the need for a unanimous decision in the Council.

B. Structural bases

As a result of the rapid development of EU justice and home affairs in the 1990s the structural bases for the fight against terrorism at EU level have improved considerably. The loose inter-governmental structures of TREVI have been fully integrated into the Council structure, with the Justice and Home Affairs Council (of Ministers) (JHA Council) at its top. This Council brings together representatives of the national ministries of the interior and of justice and the responsible Member of the European Commission. The Council deals with all anti-terrorism measures of a justice and home affairs nature. CFSP related aspects are left to the General Affairs Council which regroups the Foreign Ministers. General coordination of the decision-making process below the ministerial level is formally the task of the Committee of Permanent representatives (COREPER). Yet in the justice and home affairs domain COREPER normally plays an active role only when there are difficulties in reaching an agreement in the specialized senior Council committees, or if there are cross-cutting issues such as inter-pillar coordination, or the use of the EC budget. In practice, therefore, a substantial role in preparing ministerial decisions on anti-terrorism measures is played by the Article 36 Committee (CATS) which regroups senior national and Commission officials dealing with judicial and police cooperation. CATS also gives instructions to the Council Working Party on Terrorism (WPT) which regroups national and European Commission desk officers dealing with anti-terrorism measures in the 'third pillar' context. While WPT is in charge of working out details of anti-terrorism measures, issues more specifically relating to judicial cooperation and police cooperation are discussed and negotiated in other specialized Council working parties.

In the CFSP context, there is a different set of decision-making bodies which ranges from the General Affairs Council at the? to the Counter-Terrorism Working Party (COTER) which deals with the details of anti-terrorism measures in foreign and security policy. This separation of decision-making may not appear optimal, but it mirrors a similar separation between the justice and home affairs, and the foreign and security policy domains, in the national administrations.

---

[6] Such as visa policy measures (see Article 67(3) TEC).

Since 1999, when its non-exclusive right of initiative was extended to all justice and home affairs areas, the European Commission has set up a Directorate-General of 'Justice and Home Affairs'. Initially the Commission's role was hampered both by a lack of personnel and a relatively cautious political strategy in this domain. The Prodi Commission, however, has also adopted a much more proactive role in justice and home affairs than its predecessor, with Commissioner Antonio Vitorino opting for an ambitious agenda and an extensive use of the Commission's right of initiative, although its non-exclusive nature and the unanimity requirement continue to limit the Commission's political weight in the decision-making process.

The European Parliament only needs to be consulted on legally binding acts in justice and home affairs, and has no blocking or amending powers. Europol is clearly the most significant EU institution. In 1999 – as a result of a strong Spanish insistence – its remit was extended to the fight against international terrorism. Yet its current role is limited to the collection, transmission and analysis of data provided by national police forces through national contact units. Europol does not enjoy any operational powers, and even the supply of data from the national sources has tended to vary considerably from one Member State to another. Nevertheless, it is the only permanent central police structure of the EU with a substantial infrastructure. Europol must clearly be regarded as a major EU resource in the fight against terrorism. The 'Police Chiefs Task Force' (PCTF) was established in 2000 and is intended to facilitate – in cooperation with Europol – the exchange of experiences, common evaluations and the planning of common operations in the fight against cross-border crime.[7] Unlike Europol, however, PCTF is not an institution with legal competences and a permanent infrastructure, but a high level coordination group which meets at least once per presidency with changing priorities.

The European Police College was established by a Council Decision of December 2000. It has the task of providing training courses for senior law enforcement officers in dealing with cross-border crime, including terrorism, with a focus on the different national police systems and structures of other Member States and Europol, and international policing instruments and methods. The College currently functions only as a network of national training institutions, with a small and under-resourced Secretariat.[8]

In the area of judicial cooperation, the most important structure is the newly established cross-border prosecution agency Eurojust which was fully established in April 2003 following the adoption of the final Council Decision of 28 February 2002.[9] Eurojust is in many respects the judicial counterpart to Europol. It facilitates cooperation between national prosecution authorities,

---

[7] See Leo Schuster, 'Europäisierung der Polizeiarbeit', *Kriminalistik* 2000, 74–6.
[8] Council document No. 5136/04.   [9] OJL 63/1 of 6.3.2002.

including the speeding up of legal assistance and extradition, support for the coordination of parallel prosecution operations in several Member States and information exchange. It does not enjoy any operational powers. Yet Eurojust has been given a broad mandate covering cross-border crimes, including terrorism, and can ask competent authorities of the Member States concerned to consider the launching of investigations or prosecution of specific acts, or to set up joint investigation teams.

C. Political bases

Even before 9/11, there was a consensus among the Member States that international terrorism had to be regarded as a major challenge to the democratic societies of the European Union. In the 1970s, cooperation among the Member States had actually started with cooperation against terrorism in the TREVI context. In the 1990s, at the informal Council meeting in La Gomera on 14 October 1995, the ministers agreed on the 'Declaration of La Gomera', which was subsequently adopted by the Madrid European Council of December 1995. It identified terrorism as a fundamental threat to democracy, human rights and economic and social development which could not be countered by national measures alone. It emphasized the need for common action.[10] Since the mid-1990s, there has also been a growing awareness in the EU of new forms of Islamic terrorism marked by increased ideological radicalism, more extensive international networks and unprecedented logistical capabilities. France, the object of a series of bloody terrorist attacks in 1995, has been at the forefront, monitoring the activities of radical Islamic groups and warning about terrorist threats posed by them.[11]

Yet there are at least four factors which make the political consensus amongst the Member States slightly less homogeneous than the official declarations suggest:

1. Differences in national experiences with terrorism: threat perceptions vary widely between Member States which have been engaged in a protracted fight against terrorism – such as France, Spain and the United Kingdom – and others which have experienced only a temporary, or even hardly any, terrorist threat. This makes it more difficult for the Council to arrive at common priorities and programmes of action.
2. Variation in national capabilities: specialized forces, organisational structures, training and equipment vary considerably between the Member

---

[10] Council document No. Press 00400/95, Annex III.
[11] See Thérèse Delpech, 'Le terrorisme international et l'Europe', *Cahiers de Chaillot* no. 56 (Paris, Institut d'Études de Sécurité, 2002), 8–10.

States. Whereas some Member States, such as the UK, have well-established integrated anti-terror structures which cut across the boundaries between ministries (interior and defence) and involve effectively the police, the armed forces and intelligence services, others have not gone beyond small investigation and operational units. This is often a cause of frustration for those involved in cooperative efforts.

3. The emergence of informal, bilateral and multilateral cooperation relationships: these often involve non-EU countries such as the US. Law enforcement authorities in the Member States still tend to prefer such 'proven' working relationships to the often cumbersome 'new' cooperation structures involving all of the twenty-five Member States. This also applies to the sharing of sensitive information.

4. Diverging political and legal positions: there was conflict, for instance, between Spain and Belgium in the 1990s over the treatment of suspected ETA terrorists as asylum seekers on Belgian territory. Major differences have also appeared as regards acts of violence committed by Palestinians, and in relation to initial attempts by the Italian Berlusconi government – in the context of the riots on the occasion of the G-8 summit in Genoa – to classify certain violent demonstrators as terrorists.

Overall, one can assume a high degree of consensus amongst the Member States as to the need for a common front against international terrorism, but when it comes to deciding on common action, these differences remain.

II. EU responses to the 11 September 2001 attacks[12]

The unprecedented terrorist attacks of 9/11 presented the EU with both an internal and external challenge. It had to provide an effective response in terms of internal security, which meant primarily action in the context of the Union's 'third pillar', backed up by some measures in the 'first pillar' context. But the attacks also required a parallel response on the external security side, which meant primarily action in the context of the 'second' (CFSP) pillar.

Taking into account the inevitable difficulties of consensus building among the (then) fifteen governments, the initial reaction by the EU was both quick and substantial: a forceful text was agreed upon on September 12 by the General Affairs Council, and was followed two days later by a common declaration of the heads of state or government, the Presidents of the European Parliament and of the Commission and the CFSP High

---

[12] This section is largely based on information obtained through interviews with Commission and Council officials and the successive versions of the Council 'road map' for the implementation of the September 2001 European Union action plan to combat terrorism (latest version available: Council document no. 13909/1/02 REV 2).

Representative.[13] Both texts emphasized full solidarity with the US and the need for both internal and external action, indicating certain priorities which were further developed in the 'European Union Action Plan to Combat Terrorism' adopted on 21 September by the European Council.[14] This Action Plan, agreed upon in record speed, was subsequently revised several times, and in the end contained over 200 measures across all three pillars.[15]

A. Internal measures

1. Legislative measures

9/11 revealed one of the most glaring deficits of EU action against terrorism. Although there had been more than a quarter of a century of cooperation against terrorism, and in spite of the increased potential for action created by the treaty reforms of the 1990s, the EU had never created a common legal basis for the cross-border prosecution of terrorists. There was no common legal definition of terrorist acts, no harmonized system of penalties and – with the extradition agreements of 10 March 1995 and 27 September 1996 still not being ratified by all Member States – no basis for accelerated extradition. Removing these deficits became a priority for EU action after 9/11. The European Council itself set the extremely tight deadline of December 2001 for reaching agreement on several legal acts. Most prominent amongst these was the adoption of framework decisions on the introduction of a European Arrest Warrant, on the definition of terrorist offences in combination with a minimum harmonization of penalties for those offences, and on the freezing of assets of terrorist groups.

The EU decision-making process was greatly helped by the fact that the Commission had already been working on proposals for a European arrest warrant and a common definition of terrorist acts for many months – so that it was in position to submit legislative proposals to the Council on 20 September 2001. Yet in spite of the common emphasis on the need for rapid action, negotiations on the framework decisions – which were largely carried out by the Article 36 Committee – ran into serious difficulties and made only slow progress during the first few weeks. In the case of the European Arrest Warrant there were major differences over the list of offences to which the Warrant should apply and over the full abolition of the principle of double criminality. In the case of the framework decision on terrorist offences, the main points of contention were the scope of the definition, and the level of minimum penalties. Yet intense pressure by the European Council and continuous efforts by the Belgian Presidency made it

[13] Council document no. 11795/01 and Press release 140/01.
[14] Council document no. SN 140/01.
[15] See Council documents nos. SN 14925/01 and 10773/2/02.

possible for the JHA Council at its meeting of 6/7 December 2001 to come to an agreement on both the Framework Decision on combating terrorism and on EC Regulation 2580/2001 authorizing the freezing of assets of terrorists and terrorist organisations.

The Framework Decision on combating terrorism, whose final adoption was delayed because of parliamentary scrutiny until 13 June 2002,[16] defines terrorism in relation to one or all of the following list of intentions (Article 1):

- serious intimidation of a population,
- undue compelling of a Government or international organization to perform or abstain from performing any act,
- serious destabilization or destruction of the fundamental political, constitutional, economic or social structures of a country or an international organization.

Political intention is the basic criterion for distinguishing a terrorist offence from other offences. Yet the Framework Decision does not classify all acts pursuing one of these intentions as a terrorist offence but limits it to a series of explicitly listed acts (Article 1(a)–(i)). Some are more 'traditional' offences, such as kidnapping, hostage taking, hijacking airplanes or the use of firearms or explosives. Others such as research into and development of biological and chemical weapons and interfering with or disrupting the supply of water, power or any other fundamental natural resource the effect of which is to endanger human life, take into account the EU's widened threat perception regarding international terrorism. Yet according to Article 1, it is left to the Member States to define terrorist acts under national law.

The Framework Decision also comprises a further element of minimum harmonization. Each Member State is to take necessary measures for terrorism offences to be punishable by effective, proportionate and deterrent criminal sanctions, possibly entailing extradition (Article 5). Member States are obliged to make individuals responsible for a violation liable to a prison term of a minimum term of not less than fifteen years for leading a terrorist group and eight years for participating in terrorist activities. Participation in a terrorist group receives a wide definition which includes supplying information or material resources and the funding of terrorist activities in any way, with knowledge of the fact that such participation will contribute to the criminal activities of the terrorist group (Article 2(2)(b)). Special provision is to be made for 'terrorist-linked offences' such as aggravated theft, extortion and the drawing up of false administrative documents (Article 3), as well as inciting or aiding or abetting a terrorist offence (Article 4(1)), but no minimum penalty levels are set for those. There is also a special provision on

---

[16] OJL 164 of 22.06.2002.

possible penalty reduction for terrorist offenders who cooperate with the judicial authorities (Article 6).

The Framework Decision is a significant step ahead for EU action in the fight against terrorism. It should be recalled that several Member States did not have substantive anti-terrorism legislation in force at the time of 9/11. The Framework Decision ensures that some basic provisions will be common to all. Yet it does not go beyond a minimum harmonization of the Member States' penal laws, leaving them a wide margin of discretion. There were also serious concerns expressed by the European Parliament and several NGOs about a clear enough distinction between terrorist acts and demonstrators. Responding to them, the Council inserted into the Preamble the statement that nothing in the Framework Decision should be 'interpreted as being intended to reduce or restrict fundamental rights or freedoms such as the right to strike, freedom of assembly, of association or of expression, including the right of everyone to form and to join trade unions with others for the protection of his or her interests and the related right to demonstrate'.

Regulation 2580/2001 on 'specific restrictive measures ... with a view to combating terrorism'[17] was based on definitions from relevant existing international agreements, especially the International Convention for the Suppression of the Financing of Terrorism, and was intended to allow the freezing of assets and other financial measures against terrorist individuals and organizations. The Regulation was based on a combination of Articles 60, 301 and 308 TEC and a CFSP 'Common Position' adopted on the same day, which made it in formal terms a CFSP- motivated economic sanction. This interesting case of cross-pillarization happened as a result of the need for implementation of UN Security Council Resolution 1373(2001). The Regulation uses a broad definition of both financial assets, which include assets of every kind, whether tangible or intangible, movable or immovable, however acquired (Article 1), and of financial services, which include insurance and insurance-related services, and banking and other financial services (Article 3). Estimates of assets frozen throughout the EU during the first year of application (2002) vary from Euro 40 million to 100 million.[18]

Regulation 2580/2001 was complemented by an agreed list, adopted by written procedure as a Council 'Decision' of 27 December 2001.[19] It comprised a total of twelve organizations and thirty individuals, including the Basque terrorist organisation ETA, and several armed Irish Protestant and

---

[17] OJL 344 of 28.12.2001. The Regulation was followed by further implementing legislation such as Decision Implementing Article 2(3) of the Regulation adopted on 17 June 2002 (OJL 160 of 18.06.2002).
[18] Europol: 2002 Organised Crime Report (File number: 2530–108 REV. 1), The Hague 2002, p. 17.
[19] OJL 344 of 28.12.2001.

Catholic groups. The list, which has been amended several times,[20] should be regarded as an important piece of harmonization in its own right. It should be mentioned that on 6 March 2001 the Council had adopted another EC Regulation (467/2001)[21] on the freezing of funds belonging to members of the Taliban and entities connected to Osama bin Laden. This was later modified to take into account the end of the Taliban regime and to extend the sanctions to all 'economic resources'.

The most controversial legislative measure turned out to be the Framework Decision introducing a European Arrest Warrant. Agreement was only reached in December 2001 after the Belgian Presidency brokered a compromise with the Italian Government which had wanted to exclude corruption and a number of other offences from the list covered by the warrant.[22] Italy in the end accepted the original list but insisted successfully on the amendment of certain constitutional provisions in Italy as a prior condition for implementation. Parliamentary scrutiny reserves then delayed the formal adoption of the Framework Decision until 13 June 2002.[23] The European Arrest Warrant, which entered into force on 1 January 2004 for initially only eight Member States[24] (as the others had not yet adopted all necessary legislative measures at the national level), makes it possible to arrest and transfer suspects between Member States without formal extradition procedures, eliminating in particular all possible political intervention by national governments. In contrast with existing extradition practices, which could take years, the final decision on executing a European arrest warrant must be taken within sixty days from the arrest of the wanted person (Article 17). The Framework Decision sharply restricts the grounds for a refusal to execute the European Warrant (Articles 3 and 4). Although the European Commission had fought hard for the abolition of the double criminality principle, the Framework Decision confirmed that principle as a condition of execution of the warrant, making however a substantial exemption from it for a total of thirty-two offences. These are enumerated in a 'positive list' (Article 2), which includes acts of terrorism. The Framework Decision on the

---

[20] Council Decisions of 2 May, 17 June, 28 October and 12 December 2002 implementing Article 2(3) of Regulation (EC) No 2580/2001, OJL 116 of 03.05.2002, OJL 160 of 18.06.2002, OJL 295 of 30.10.2002, OJL 337 of 13.12.2002 and OJL 229 of 12.12.2003. After its last amendment in September 2003 the list comprised fifty-two persons and thirty-four groups and entities.

[21] This Regulation was later replaced by Council Regulation 881/2002 (OJL 139 of 29.5.2002) which has to date (April 2004) been amended thirty-one times by Commission Regulations.

[22] On the negotiations on the Arrest Warrant, see Wenceslas de Lobkowicz, *L'Europe et la sécurité intérieure* (La documentation française, Paris 2002), 183–5.

[23] OJL 190 of 17.06.2002.

[24] Belgium, Denmark, Finland, Ireland, Portugal, Spain, Sweden and the United Kingdom.

Arrest Warrant constitutes a major breakthrough for cross-border judicial cooperation in the EU.[25] The impetus given by 9/11 also contributed to the agreement reached by the JHA Council of 6/7 December 2001 on the Council Decision setting up the cross-border prosecution unit Eurojust.[26] The Decision enabled the replacement of the 'Provisional Judicial Co-operation Unit' by the permanent Eurojust. The Member States were able to agree on a broad mandate for Eurojust as to the types of cross-border crime (which includes terrorism) in the prosecution of which Eurojust can support competent authorities of the Member States. Agreement was also reached in that Eurojust – if acting as a College – would be able to ask competent authorities of the Member States to consider launching investigations or prosecutions.

Other legal instruments were less forthcoming. The adoption of the Framework Decision on joint investigation teams between the competent authorities of two or more Member States for the purpose of carrying out cross-border criminal investigations, which was already under negotiation well before 9/11, was delayed by several months by a Danish reserve and finally adopted only in June 2002.[27] It took the Member States until July 2003 to agree to a Framework Decision providing for the simplified and accelerated cross-border execution of orders to freeze property, and even then the deadline for implementation was only set for August 2005.[28] To the considerable frustration of the European Commission, the Member States were extremely slow in ratifying the 2000 EU Convention on Mutual Assistance in Criminal Matters[29] and its 2001 Protocol, which includes cross-border requests for interception of communications and monitoring of bank accounts. By the end of 2002, only Portugal had ratified this important instrument. This demonstrated again the drawbacks of the traditional 'third pillar' instrument with its need for ratification by all national parliaments. Some of the Member States also failed to fully implement by the end of 2002 the Framework Decision of 26 June 2001[30] on money laundering. Finally, negotiations also proceeded rather slowly in the Council on proposed Framework Decisions on attacks against information systems, on the application of the principle of mutual recognition to confiscation orders, on a European Evidence Warrant for obtaining cross-border evidence in criminal proceedings and on the confiscation of crime-related proceeds. All these had

---

[25] See on this point Emmanuel Barbe, 'Le mandat d'arrêt européen: en tirera-t-on toutes les conséquences?' in Gilles de Kerchove and Anne Weyembergh (eds.), *L'espace pénal européen: enjeux et perspectives* (Brussels, Editions de l'Université de Bruxelles, 2002), 113–17.

[26] OJL 63 of 06.03.2002.   [27] OJL 162 of 20.6.2002.

[28] Council Framework Decision of 22 July 2003 on the execution in the European Union of orders freezing property or evidence, OJL 196 of 2.8.2003.

[29] OJC 197 of 12.7.2000.   [30] OJL 182 of 5.7.2001.

not yet been formally adopted by the time of the 11 March 2004 terrorist attacks in Madrid.

2. Structural and operational measures

a. The enhanced use of existing EU structures.   During the first weeks after 9/11 it became apparent that there were problems of coordination between the two principal Council working parties dealing with terrorism: the third pillar Working Party on Terrorism (WPT) and the second pillar CFSP Working Party on Counter-Terrorism (COTER). The two key working parties were instructed to cooperate more closely. This led in October 2003 to an agreement that the two working parties would produce under each of the EU's half-yearly Presidencies a threat assessment report on threats posed by terrorism within Europe (under the responsibility of the WPT), and in third countries (under the responsibility of COTER). The Presidency could ask for special consideration to be given to particular types of threats, or to particular countries.[31]

Europol is an obvious asset in the EU's operational response. Immediately after 9/11 it was asked to give a situation report on terrorist activities within the EU to the Council. The Member States committed themselves in the context of the September 2001 Action Plan to the systematic transmission of data relevant to terrorism to Europol, which had previously received rather fragmentary information. The Director of Europol has since been giving situation reports to the Council on a regular basis. As a result of a decision adopted by the Brussels European Council on 21 September 2001, a team of anti-terrorist specialists has been set up within Europol comprising of intelligence or police specialists of the Member States. Some problems persist, however. Europol's task force seems to have experienced problems with handling real-time data, and some national authorities have continued to be reluctant to share information about terrorism. Europol has no power to force them to do so.[32]

Under a mandate by the Council the PCTF has held several meetings to discuss cross-border operational cooperation. The PCTF was able to agree on recommendations for the strengthening of cooperation between the heads of anti-terrorist units. These were implemented in April 2002. In April 2002 the PCTF agreed to set up a new structure involving the current, previous and forthcoming EU presidencies, Europol and the Commission which should meet between PCTF meetings to improve coordination.[33] Eurojust has been asked to strengthen cooperation between anti-terrorist magistrates and has

---

[31] Council document no. 11994/3/03 of 28 October 2003.
[32] Nora Bensahel, *Counterterror Coalitions. Co-operation with Europe, NATO, and the European Union* (Santa Monica, Rand 2003), 40.
[33] Council document no. 13909/1/02 REV 1, Annex p. 28.

started to act as an intermediary between them. In order to increase the information flow to both Europol and Eurojust, the Council decided on 19 December 2002 that Member States should designate specialized services as contact points within their police services, and a Eurojust national correspondent for collecting and forwarding all relevant information.[34]

It should be added that providing high-level joint training on cross-border cooperation against terrorism has also become an important element in the EU's operational strategy. In its work programmes for 2002, 2003 and 2004, the European Police College (CEPOL) has included special training for senior police officers on investigation techniques. In November 2003, special anti-terrorism training needs were identified for the ten new Member States joining in May 2004, some of which will be provided by CEPOL.[35]

b. New structures and mechanisms.   One of the most innovative responses to 9/11 in operational terms was the introduction of regular meetings of the heads of intelligence services which had until then remained entirely outside of EU justice and home affairs cooperation. The first of these meetings already took place on 11 November 2001 and was followed by one on 20 February 2002 which agreed on further common work on terrorist profiles. Europol has been associated with these meetings. In April 2002 the Council also agreed on the creation of multinational ad hoc teams consisting of national experts for the gathering and exchanging of information on terrorists in the pre-judicial phase of investigation.[36]

Most noteworthy amongst the new mechanisms is the introduction of a system of peer evaluation of national arrangements for combating terrorism. A common mechanism for evaluating national legal systems was formally agreed on by the Council on 28/29 November 2002.[37] It provides for an elaborate process which starts with the forwarding of a detailed questionnaire drawn up by a team of independent experts to the evaluated Member State. The team then visits the respective Member State to seek clarification on the answers given to the questionnaire, following an itinerary agreed with that Member State, which involves meetings with relevant political, administrative, police, customs or judicial authorities there. The evaluation team prepares a confidential draft report to be sent to the Council. The Council discusses the report and adopts any conclusions and recommendations by consensus. The Council may invite the evaluated Member State to report on progress made on recommendations made. The implementation of the Decision on the evaluation mechanism runs parallel to the production of

---

[34] Council Decision of 19 December on the implementation of specific measures for police and judicial cooperation to combat terrorism, OJL 16 of 22.1.2003.
[35] Council document no. 14307/1/03 REV 1 of 26 November 2003.
[36] Council document no. 13788/03 of 21 October 2003.   [37] OJL 349 of 24.12.2002.

an inventory of national measures and early warning plans, for which the Council Working Party on Terrorism and the PCTF are responsible.

c. Specific security measures. Specific security measures taken in response to 9/11 included a temporary strengthening of checks at external Schengen borders, an agreement reached by the Article 36 Committee on 23 November 2001 on a definition of a terrorist threat of exceptional gravity which would justify the re-establishment of internal border controls,[38] the inclusion of improved terrorist alert input possibilities into the list of desirable new functionalities of the new Schengen Information System ('SIS II') and the setting up of a Community mechanism for the coordination of civil protection measures which was adopted by the Council on 23 October 2001. Regulations were also adopted on civil aviation security (2320/2002 and 1486/2003).

B. External measures

The Union's CFSP has not acquired the best reputation in dealing with international crisis situations. Yet after the events of 9/11, it not only came up quickly with several strong statements in support of the US and international action against terrorism, but also provided the framework for intense diplomatic activity aimed at building up a broad international coalition. It started with ministerial Troika visits to several Middle East countries, Saudi Arabia, Pakistan, Iran, Uzbekistan, Turkmenistan and Tajikistan. A second high level round of visits by Guy Verhofstadt and Romano Prodi followed. Efforts in Central Asia continued with a tour of the Regional Directors Troika from 10 to 14 June 2002. The EU convened on 20 October 2001 a meeting of the European Conference dedicated to combat terrorism. This brought together not only the candidate and EFTA countries, but also the Balkan countries of the Stabilization and Association Process, the Russian Federation, Moldavia and Ukraine. Both the ministerial level meeting of the Euro-Mediterranean partnership on 5/6 November 2001 and the ministerial week of the UN 56th General Assembly in mid-November were used, not only for intense bilateral and multilateral efforts on maintaining the fragile international coalition, but also to achieve progress on tougher measures against the financing of terrorist activities. Another example of the EU's multilateral efforts was the 'Copenhagen Declaration on Cooperation against International Terrorism' adopted on the occasion of the 4th Asia-Europe Meeting in Copenhagen on 23–24 September 2002 by the EU and its ASEM partners. Bilateral cooperation was also stepped up with Russia through the decision to

---

[38] Council document no. 14181/1/01.

set up a network of contact points, negotiations on an agreement with Europol, and discussion of further common action at an EU-Russian ministerial meeting in Moscow on 5 November 2002.

This was backed up by economic and financial instruments such as the signing of a cooperation agreement with Pakistan – a crucial partner in the coalition against the Taliban – on 24 November 2001, the adoption of the negotiating directives for trade and a cooperation agreement with Iran on 12 July 2002, and the provision of (until May 2002) of Euro 559 million of emergency aid for Afghanistan. On 7 October 2001 all Member States signed the UN Convention for the Suppression of the Financing of Terrorism, and by the end of December 2001, an EC Regulation was in place implementing UN Security Council Resolution 1373 (2001) on the freezing of terrorist financial assets.

The Council also agreed on a systematic evaluation of the EU's relations with third countries in the light of their possible support for terrorism, with the possibility not only of incorporating terrorism clauses into trade and cooperation agreements with third countries,[39] but also taking measures on technical assistance and other trade instruments ('carrot and stick' approach). In 2002, special clauses on anti-terrorism were inserted into agreements with Algeria, Chile and Egypt, and a special exchange of letters on this issue was attached to a new cooperation agreement with Lebanon,[40] constituting a major move towards the 'mainstreaming' of the fight against terrorism in conventional relations with third countries.

For obvious reasons, bilateral cooperation with the US ranked particularly high on the EU's agenda after 9/11: the Union had to demonstrate solidarity with the US, its most important international partner, which in this situation clearly expected more than just words. As both the military support offered by individual Member States – primarily by the United Kingdom – for the operations in Afghanistan and the invocation of the collective defence clause of Article 5 of the North Atlantic Treaty took place outside of the EU framework, it might appear as if the US did not get much in terms of solidarity from the Union. Yet outside the military field the EU's support was far from negligible. Deploying the full range of its diplomatic instruments in the CFSP context (see above) it made a substantial contribution to the build-up of the international coalition. Its diplomatic efforts were particularly useful in countries with whom the US had a rather strained relationship, such as Iran.

The Union went out of its way to upgrade cooperation with the US in the areas of justice and home affairs, not one of the easiest domains of trans-atlantic cooperation because of some fundamental differences over the death

---

[39] Council document no. 7750/02, agreement reached on 17 April 2002.
[40] See Council document no. 13909/1/02 REV 1, Annex p. 22.

penalty, powers of law enforcement authorities and protection of personal data. On 20 September 2001 the Council gave the green light to a joint assessment with the US of terrorist threats and to the participation of US representatives in meetings of the heads of EU counter-terrorism units meeting at the instigation of the PCTF. To this was added the possibility of representatives of US authorities participating in EU joint investigation teams. All this amounted to an unprecedented opening of EU structures towards a third country.[41]

On 19 November 2001, an official mission of the provisional Eurojust went to Washington. This resulted in the appointment of a US contact point for Eurojust and an agreement on regular bilateral meetings. At the margins of the Justice and Home Affairs Council of 6 December 2001, an agreement was signed between the Director of Europol, Jürgen Storbeck, and US Ambassador Rockwell Schnabel, on the exchange of strategic and technical information and of liaison officers.[42] Although this agreement does not yet provide for the exchange of data on persons it was presented as a first step to be followed by a more comprehensive agreement. Its significance was underlined by the presence of US Secretary of State Colin Powell at the signing. In December 2001 the Council agreed on a mandate for Europol to negotiate a second agreement with the US, including the exchange of personal data. On 1 February 2002 an FBI agent was appointed on secondment to Europol, and in April 2002 two Europol liaison officers were designated for Washington. The negotiations on the second Europol–US agreement were not without difficulties. A range of NGOs expressed major concerns about a potential undermining of EU data protection rules, and several Member States were not satisfied with the initial guarantees offered by the US which were significantly lower than in the EU. A further problem was the question of Europol's immunity in case of US citizens seeking compensation for injury suffered as a result of transfers of data by Europol. After the US Government had given additional reassurances in a letter clarifying the content of relevant US legislation on data protection, the agreement was signed in Copenhagen on 20 December 2002.[43]

Yet data protection issues continue to be a problem. In 2003/4, the European Parliament adopted three highly critical Resolutions on an agreement negotiated in February by the European Commission with the US Administration obliging trans-Atlantic carriers (air and sea) to provide electronic reservation system passenger details ('Passenger Name Records', PNR) to US Customs.[44] While the US made a number of minor concessions, a new agreement reached by the Commission with the US on 16 December 2003 still left the European Parliament and numerous civil liberties groups highly dissatisfied. The Commission found itself in an extremely

---

[41] Council document no. 13788/03 of 21 October 2003, p. 5.
[42] Council document no. 14586/01.   [43] Council document no.15231/02.
[44] See EP documents no. P5 TA(2003)0097, P5 TA(2003)0429 and P5 TA(2004)0245.

uncomfortable position, between severe pressure by the US, civil liberties concerns and different attitudes adopted by Member States. The Commission's Article 29 Data Protection Working Party declined to adopt or approve the text on the ground that the transfer of PNR to the US was 'in any case illegal' and that 'nothing should be done to blur that fact'.[45] The approval of the European Parliament not being necessary under current EU procedures, the EU–US agreement on PNR was eventually signed on 28 May 2004.[46] Yet on 25 June 2004, the Parliament requested the ECJ to annul the controversial agreement because of a violation of fundamental EU data protection rights and procedural requirements. This case is still pending.

In response to strong US interest in a bilateral extradition treaty, the JHA Council adopted on 26 April 2002 a negotiating mandate for an extradition and mutual legal assistance agreement with the US. The negotiations started in June 2002 but proved difficult because of the obvious problem of the death penalty in the US, US demands to be treated in a similar way as EU Member States, and the seizure of property. A positive impetus was provided by a meeting of the US Attorney General with EU JHA ministers in Copenhagen on 13/14 September 2002 at which it was agreed to arrange for regular meetings of EU and US law enforcement experts on threat assessments and profiling of terrorism, for the sharing of information on action plan implementation and for cooperating on the setting up of joint investigative teams.[47]

On the issue of extradition and death penalty, a compromise was finally reached in February 2003 according to which EU Member States may extradite to the US on the condition that the death penalty shall not be imposed on the person sought, or if imposed, shall not be carried out. Should the US not be in a position, in a given case, to accept these conditions, EU Member States can refuse the extradition request. The EU, concerned about US practices and military justice in the Guantanamo Bay camp, insisted on an explicit reference to the right to a fair trial before an independent tribunal. Agreement was also reached on the possibility of the EU and the US setting up 'joint investigative teams'. This will enable US officials to participate in investigations in the EU Member States (and vice versa), although the exercise of law enforcement powers will be reserved to authorities of the country in which the investigation takes place. The compromises reached were codified in two agreements – one on extradition and one on mutual legal assistance – both of which were signed in Washington on 25 June 2003.[48]

There can also be little doubt that the extraordinarily rapid progress made by the Union on key aspects of its internal anti-terrorism agenda, such as the

---

[45] Quoted from Commission Communication, 'Communication on Transfer of Air Passenger Name Record (PNR) Data', COM(2003) 826, 16.12.2003, 7.
[46] OJL 183 of 20.05.2004, 84–5.   [47] Council document no. 13909/1/02 REV 1.
[48] Text of the agreements: Council document no. 9153/03.

European Arrest Warrant, was in part motivated by an intention to prove to the US that the EU could be a credible partner. Justice and home affairs issues have clearly acquired a new salience in EU–US relations, widening the scope of trans-Atlantic security partnership, but also creating friction over data protection and extradition.

III. EU responses to the Madrid attacks of 11 March 2004

While the terrorist attacks in Madrid on 11 March 2004 sent shock waves across Europe, they were not totally unexpected. Especially after the participation of the United Kingdom, Spain and several other European countries in the US-led intervention in Iraq, there had been repeated warnings about a heightened risk of large-scale attacks in Europe. Europe had come more than ever before into the potential firing line of Muslim extremists.

The attacks highlighted the persistent deficiencies in of the implementation of the September 2001 EU Action Plan to Combat Terrorism. The much vaunted European Arrest Warrant, for instance, had by mid-March only been fully implemented by ten of the (then) fifteen Member States. Similarly, at the time of the attacks three Member States had still not reported on implementation of the crucial Framework Decision on combating terrorism of June 2002, which provides for crucial criminal law definitions and penalty levels. Europol, which had been vested with an enhanced analysis function and a special terrorism task force following the 2001 Action Plan, had been experiencing considerable difficulties because several Member States, fearing potential leaks of sensitive information, had only provided it with limited and highly-filtered intelligence. Six Member States had by the time of the attacks not yet notified transposition of the June 2002 Framework Decision on joint investigation teams, two had not yet established the national contacts points provided for by the December 2002 Decision on specific judicial and police cooperation measures to combat terrorism, and no less than eleven had still not formally ratified the 2000 Convention on Mutual Assistance in Criminal Matters. These and a range of other deficiencies were clearly brought out in a European Commission memorandum to the Council on 18 March 2004[49] which was followed by another memorandum[50] proposing action on implementation and several new measures. These were discussed at a special meeting of the EU's Justice and Home Affairs Council on 19 March. The ministers agreed on the need to tackle, in particular, the deficiencies of cooperation between the relevant security services, and the existing implementation problems, with a range of concrete action points to be formally adopted by the European Council meeting scheduled for the week after.

---

[49] European Commission Memo/04/63, 18 March 2004.
[50] European Commission Memo/04/66, 18 March 2004.

The meeting on 19 March 2004 was not without tension. Some governments felt misled by the Spanish Aznar government who, in order not to lose
the Spanish general elections, had tried, almost to the last minute, to link the
Madrid attacks to ETA in spite of mounting evidence of al Qaeda involvement. German Minister, Otto Schily, was particularly outspoken in his criticisms. Several Member States felt that the involvement of Spain and other
partners in the war in Iraq had weakened international action against terrorism and increased rather than decreased terrorist risks. There were also
disagreements over the preference expressed by Austria and the Benelux
countries for the establishment of a new anti-terrorism agency, France and
Germany preferring instead a more informal information network.

On 22 March the General Affairs Council put the finishing touches to a
draft 'Declaration on Combating Terrorism', largely based on JHA Council
deliberations on 19 March. This was then, with very few changes, formally
adopted by the Heads of State and Government at the end of a two-hour
session during the European Council meeting in Brussels on 25 March 2004.
The Declaration[51] is explicitly linked to the previous (September 2001) Action
Plan. It provided for a substantial package of measures which were laid out in
detail in an updated version of the EU Action Plan on Combating Terrorism
which was adopted by the Council on 15 June 2004.[52] Four new elements
emerge from these texts and their implementation.

A. Solidarity

The European Council not only expressed its full solidarity with the Spanish
people but also, in a 'Declaration on Solidarity', took the unusual step of
committing itself to the application of the 'solidarity clause' of Article I-42 of
the not yet ratified draft EU Treaty establishing a Constitution for Europe,
whose final text was only approved in June 2004.[53] This clause provides for
the full mobilization of Member States' resources, including the military, to
prevent terrorist threats to any of them, and to assist affected Member States
upon their request. While this clearly marked a higher degree of commitment
to solidarity than before, it has to be noted that the Declaration left it to each
Member State to decide how to comply with this commitment and does not
mention, for instance, the use of the EU budget.

B. Improved implementation

The European Council Declaration had set June 2004 as the deadline for full
implementation of six key legislative acts of relevance to the fight against

---

[51] European Council: Declaration on Combating Terrorism, 25 March 2004.
[52] Council document no. 10586/04.   [53] See below section IV. C.

terrorism, including the Framework Decisions on the European Arrest Warrant. The same deadline was set for completing negotiations on a number of other instruments, such as the Framework Decisions on attacks against information systems, on the confiscation of crime-related proceeds, and on the mutual recognition of confiscation orders. The German government, struggling with difficulties of German Länder competencies in the internal security domain, would have preferred an 'as soon as possible' formula to these binding deadlines, but failed to convince its partners.

It was decided to speed up the designation of national correspondents for Eurojust, and the putting into place of the new Europol Information System, to ensure that Member States pass on all criminal intelligence on terrorism to Europol and to reactivate Europol's Counter-Terrorist Task force which had been increasingly marginalized as a result of limited input by the national authorities. Europol and Eurojust representatives should also be associated with the work of Joint Investigation Teams as soon as possible; and a Eurojust/Europol cooperation agreement was signed on 9 June 2004.

C. New anti-terrorism measures

The Declaration instructed Ministers to start work on a number of new legislative measures. These include rules on the retention of communications traffic data by service providers (such as mobile phone companies), the creation of European databases on convictions (European Criminal Record) and disqualifications as well as forensic materials, and rules on the facilitation of cross-border hot pursuit – a difficult issue because of the territoriality of law enforcement powers. The Commission was invited to come up with proposals on the protection of witnesses in terrorist cases, the exchange of personal information (DNA, fingerprints and visa), the use of passenger data for border and aviation security, and for an integrated system for the exchange of information on stolen and lost passports (to be in place by the end of 2005). The Council was also instructed to adopt Commission proposals on the incorporation of biometric features into passports and visas by the end of 2004. On 29 March the Commission came up with a first set of concrete proposals. These included the creation of a system of national bank account registries allowing for the identification of the true owners of accounts, and streamlining of national information collection on terrorist offences through specialized services, and wide-ranging obligations for Member States to ensure the passing on of this information to Europol and Eurojust.[54]

---

[54] COM(2004) 221.

In order to arrive at a new quality for the sharing of intelligence, Secretary-General/High Representative Solana was asked to integrate within the Council Secretariat an intelligence capacity on all aspects of terrorist threats in Europe. This came as a compromise between Member States who had advocated the creation of a new permanent intelligence agency on terrorism, and those who had instead favoured the enhanced use of existing informal networks. The centralization of intelligence tasks poses the problem of a potential overlap with Europol's task, and to some extent penalizes Europol for shortcomings in analysis capabilities which were largely due to the unwillingness of some Member States to provide it with relevant information. The Declaration made it clear, however, that increased use should also be made of information provided by intelligence services – which had so far been made available only to a limited extent – and that cooperation between Europol and intelligence services should be enhanced to that effect.

The Declaration promised more support to vulnerable third-countries on building up their counter-terrorism capabilities. It also announced that the Union 'will analyse and evaluate the commitment of countries on an ongoing basis', which is declared to be an 'influencing factor' in EU relations with them. This is a rather strong hint at an enhanced 'carrot and stick' approach to countries seen as being not fully cooperative in the fight against terrorism.

D. Appointment of a Counter-terrorism Co-ordinator

The most 'visible' innovation brought by the new anti-terrorism package was the appointment of a 'Counter-terrorism Co-ordinator'. The appointment of the former Dutch President of the Liberal Group in the European Parliament (1994–1998), Junior Minister in the Dutch Interior Ministry (1998–2002) and Dutch representative in the European Convention, Gijs de Vries, came as a surprise to some observers as he had no specific credentials in the anti-terrorism field. Yet de Vries brought with him considerable experience within the EU system and a reputation as a highly skilled negotiator who is considered unlikely to pose difficulties to Secretary-General Solana under whose authority he will have to work. To what extent the new Co-ordinator will be able to make a difference remains to be seen. The March 2004 Declaration did not confer any specific powers on Mr de Vries, and national law enforcement and intelligence agencies have so far proved extremely reluctant to subject themselves to common guidelines and systematic cooperation. The mandate given to the new Coordinator only rather vaguely provides for him 'to maintain an overview of all the instruments at the Union's disposal', and to regularly report back to the Council on the effective follow-up of Council decisions, which is an implicit admission that implementation is seen as a key problem.

E. Assessment

Overall, the March 2004 anti-terrorism package clearly addressed some of the most urgent problems in the implementation of the 2001 Action Plan. The new deadlines for legislative action and enhanced information sharing can increase the Union's role in the fight against terrorism. At the same time, the Member States have not transferred any new real powers to the EU institutions and the role of Europol could actually have been weakened as a result of the stronger coordinating role of the Council Secretariat. The new Counter-terrorism Co-ordinator will have to struggle to develop and define his role.

The proposed creation of a range of new data-collection and analysis instruments almost immediately caused considerable concern, not only amongst civil liberties groups, but also in some parliaments. The Select Committee on European Scrutiny of the British House of Commons, for instance, questioned the proportionality of the compulsory registration of bank accounts envisaged in the Commission proposals and expressed doubts about the compatibility of the proposed Council Decision on the exchange of information with the European Convention on Human Rights.[55] The House of Lords Select Committee on the European Union made it clear that it was unconvinced of the need for a European Criminal Record, expressing concerns about its impact on privacy and the protection of personal data and stating that it could violate the principle of the presumption of innocence if the data stored extended beyond convictions.[56]

Effective implementation also remains a crucial problem. A Commission report on the implementation of the Framework Decision on combating terrorism of 8 June 2004 indicated that only eight of the fifteen 'old' Member States had by then specifically criminalized terrorist offences as a separate category of crimes, which is one of the crucial requirements of the Framework Decision.[57] By mid-June 2004, only ten Member States had reported completion of implementation measures of the Framework Decisions on joint investigation teams and on money laundering.[58]

---

[55] House of Commons, European Scrutiny Committee, 21st Report Session 2003–2004, 'Exchange of Information and Cooperation Regarding Terrorist Offences', 7 HO (25536), 17 June 2004.

[56] House of Lords, European Union Committee: 23rd Report Session 2003–2004, Judicial Cooperation in the EU: the role of Eurojust, HL Paper 138, 21 July 2004, para. 102.

[57] European Commission: Report based on Article 11 of the Council Framework Decision of 13 June 2002 on combating terrorism, COM(2004) 409, 08.08.2004, 6.

[58] Council document no. 10586/04, 26–27.

IV. Conclusions

A. *The emergence of the EU as actor in its own right*

According to a 2003 Eurobarometer opinion poll, 80 per cent of EU citizens count terrorism amongst their primary fears and 90 per cent of them think that the fight against terrorism should be one of the priorities of the Union.[59] Substantial expectations exist, and the question is whether the EU is capable of meeting them. The EU has taken important steps towards a 'comprehensive' actor capability in the security domain, which also enables it to play a substantial role in the fight against international terrorism. This corresponds fully with the treaty objective of Article 29 TEU, according to which the Union should provide citizens with a 'high level of safety'. While most of the expertise and operational means remain obviously with the Member States, the EU has the legal instruments, structures and political will to play, at least, a significant complementary role. The EU responses to 9/11 – and more recently the decisions of March 2004 and the revised Action Plan of June 2004 in response to the Madrid attacks – amply demonstrates this capacity.

Taken together the legislative and the operational measures are quite substantial. The EU has not only used all available instruments and structures, but did so in some cases with extraordinary speed. Before 9/11 most observers had expected the Union to need several more years to agree on a common definition of terrorism and the introduction of a European Arrest Warrant. In the event it proved possible within three months. The new Amsterdam Treaty legal instruments – especially the Framework Decisions – clearly demonstrated that they were far more suitable for effective legislative action than the former Maastricht legal instruments, although national parliamentary scrutiny reserves took their toll in the delays for formal adoption. The Commission was able to play a substantial role in the process, partly because of having some of the necessary legislative proposals ready 'in the drawer'. Both Europol and Eurojust were, within a few months, given enhanced functions, and a lot of effort was put into ensuring adequate cooperation and synergy between the different EU structures and national authorities. The introduction of intelligence services into EU cooperation and the creation of the anti-terrorist team within Europol also indicated flexibility in response to the terrorist threat. These and several other changes have substantially increased common analysis and planning capacity.

Externally, both CFSP and economic instruments have been effectively used to shore up the international coalition against terrorism in an unprecedented and sustained effort of 'cross-pillar' action. The US were not only offered international support through these instruments but also a new

---

[59] Standard Eurobarometer 59, July 2003, 9 and 58–9.

quality of cooperation in the justice and home affairs domain which went as far as opening EU structures to the participation of US representatives and the negotiation of formal agreements.

Through the adoption of the September 2001 Action Plan which has been reaffirmed and revised after the Madrid attacks, the EU has arrived at something which it did not have before: a common strategy based on a common approach on key issues.

B. Capability and legitimacy problems

The EU's reaction to 9/11 has brought out a number of persistent capability weaknesses. The most obvious is that all operational capabilities remain exclusively with the Member States. So far no EU institution is vested with any coercive or judicial powers. In essence the EU's role remains limited to information, coordination and framework legislation.

Then there is the unanimity requirement in the Council. The speed of the agreement on the European Arrest Warrant should not make one overlook the fact that the whole process very nearly failed because of Italian objections which had nothing to do with the fight against terrorism. Yet even without the Italian 'intermezzo', the negotiations in the Council bodies often enough came to a complete standstill over objections by individual delegations staunchly defending what they regarded as unchangeable elements of their legal systems. The unanimity requirement encourages inflexibility of national positions. The unanimity principle also prevented the complete abolition of the double criminality principle under the European Arrest Warrant and, significantly, delayed the adoption of other legal instruments such as the Framework Decisions on attacks against information systems, on the confiscation of crime-related proceeds, and on the mutual recognition of confiscation orders.

The EU's 'pillar' division and the absence of a cross-cutting legal base for action against terrorism is an additional 'systemic' weakness. It necessitated complex combinations of different legal bases and the involvement of different strings of decision-making.

While decision-making may have been relatively fast by EU standards, the same cannot be said about implementation. The fact that key instruments such as the Framework Decisions on combating terrorism and on the European Arrest Warrant had not been fully transposed by several Member States at the time of the 11 March 2004 terrorist attacks highlights a significant discrepancy between decision-making and implementation. This endangers both the effectiveness and the credibility of EU action in this domain.

Europol had to struggle to get all necessary data from the Member States for a comprehensive assessment of the terrorist threat within the EU, highlighting the problem of a central European police office without real powers, which in many respects continues to be dependent on the goodwill of national police forces, although its remit has been increasingly expanded. The PCTF has had difficulties in finding its own role in the process, ending up with making recommendations but without producing any major results in the operational sphere. The Union has been creating more and more structures, the most recent addition being the EU Counter-Terrorism Co-ordinator, without ensuring an effective division of tasks and coordination between them.

The very limited role of the European Parliament in the adoption of the vast array of EU anti-terrorism measures, which is mainly due to its merely consultative powers in this domain under current EC/EU treaty provisions, is clearly one of the negative points on the EU's post-September 11 balance sheet. This is all the more true as national parliaments are more often than not faced with the fait accompli of negotiated EU Council compromises on anti-terrorism measures which national ministers are extremely reluctant to get back to because of concerns of their own parliaments. Adequate parliamentary control should be regarded as all the more important as some of the EU measures have given rise to serious concerns about negative effects on civil liberties in the EU.[60]

The EU cooperation framework has clearly contributed to the strengthening of the role of the executive branches in the fight against terrorism. National governments can actually use the European level for reducing not only parliamentary scrutiny, but also – as there is no such thing as a 'European public opinion' or a 'European press' – for escaping potentially difficult debates in the media on some of the measures adopted in the name of the fight against terrorism. Once a measure has been agreed on at EU level, they can use the claimed legitimacy and importance of a common EU approach to push through certain measures at the national level, which would have been more difficult to pass if they had been national measures only. A good example is the Draft EU Framework Decision on the retention of data processed and stored in relation with publicly available electronic communication services, proposed on 28 April 2004 by France, Ireland, Sweden and the UK in line with the Anti-terrorism Action Plan.[61] It extends the period of storage of telecommunication data from a minimum of twelve to a maximum of thirty-six months, to location as well as traffic data and for the purpose not only of investigation and prosecution but also of prevention of criminal acts. This goes partially beyond existing legislation in the proposing countries, and definitely beyond legislation in other EU countries, showing

---

[60] For particularly sharp criticisms of EU action, see Tony Bunyan, 'The War on Freedom and Democracy', *Statewatch Analysis* no. 13, London, September 2002 (http://www.state watch.org/).
[61] Council document no. 8958/04.

clearly the risk of the EU level being used by national governments to push through more invasive legislation at the national level.

C. Future prospects

Over the next few years, the EU will not only have to implement the revised Action Plan of June 2004 but also – at least potentially – the provisions of a new Treaty establishing a 'Constitution' for Europe. The draft of this Treaty was adopted by an EU Inter-governmental Conference in June 2004 and now needs to be ratified by the twenty-five Member States.[62] It introduces a number of reforms which are likely to enhance the Union's capabilities in the fight against terrorism. The cumbersome pillar structure will be abolished, qualified majority voting will become possible on a range of criminal justice cooperation issues, including minimum rules regarding the definition of criminal offences and sanctions for terrorism and other serious crimes, and new EU action possibilities are provided for as regards the adoption of common minimum rules in the domain of criminal law procedures and crime prevention as well as the conditions and limitations under which national police authorities may operate in the territory of another Member State.[63] Article III-274 even provides for the possibility of establishing a European Public Prosecutor's Office, emanating from Eurojust, which shall be responsible for investigating, prosecuting and bringing to judgment the perpetrators of serious crimes, although the establishment of such an Office remains subject to unanimity, and not a few political controversies. Democratic accountability will be strengthened by the introduction of co-decision powers of the European Parliament for all legislative measures. The protection of fundamental rights in the EU will benefit from the full incorporation of the EU Charter of Fundamental Rights, which includes wide-ranging provisions on judicial rights and the protection of personal data, and the removal of most of the remaining restrictions on the role of the ECJ. Also new is the introduction of the 'solidarity clause' for terrorist threats, which includes the mobilization of all instruments at the Union's disposal to prevent terrorist threats, to protect democratic institutions and the civilian population and to assist a Member State in the event of an attack.[64]

The new Treaty has its flaws. The formally abolished 'pillars' continue to exist in a sort of shadowy existence because decision-making procedures still vary between former first and third pillar areas. Despite the obvious difficulties, Europol has neither been redefined nor strengthened. Another example on the negative side is the so-called 'emergency brake' introduced by Articles III-270(3) and III-271(3) which allows a Member State to ask for a

---

[62] Text: EU Council document no. CIG 86/04.
[63] Articles III-271 to III-272 and III-277 s. 3 and III-329.   [64] Article I-42.

suspension of the legislative process in substantive or procedural criminal law if it considers that the proposed legislative measure affects fundamental aspects of its criminal justice system, thereby reintroducing a national veto through the backdoor. While these and other weaknesses should not be underestimated, a successful ratification of the new 'Constitution' would certainly enhance the Union's capability to respond to the challenges of international terrorism. This is something which, having regard to the Eurobarometer opinion polls, European citizens clearly seem to expect, although effective EU action in the fight against terrorism will ultimately always depend on the common political will of the Member States to fully realize its potential.

PART FIVE

Anti-Terrorism Law and Policy in the West

21

Legislative over-breadth, democratic failure and the judicial response: fundamental rights and the UK's anti-terrorist legal policy

HELEN FENWICK AND GAVIN PHILLIPSON

I. Introduction: policy options and loci of opposition

Three standard governmental policy responses to terrorism have been identified:[1] a military one, treating the fight against terrorism as a form of warfare; a police-based one, treating it simply as a form of criminal activity, to be detected and then defeated using (perhaps some modified version of) the criminal justice system; and a political one, viewing it as a form of armed rebellion to be resolved through negotiation and the political process. The UK Government's response to political violence in Northern Ireland, for example, was to use a mixture of police-based and political strategies. In this light, the UK Government's response to the al Qaeda threat (leaving aside its military aspect, such as the war in Afghanistan) is police-based: it has involved a very significant ratcheting up of the state's coercive powers in terms of surveillance, data-sharing and detention. The main change in UK anti-terrorist policy in recent years has been described as being 'the shift to intelligence-based and proactive methods [with] the primary aim of preventing terrorist attacks, rather than responding to events and attempting to solve crimes after they occur'.[2] The use of preventive detention, rather than

We are grateful to Kent Roach, George Williams and William C. Banks for their very useful comments on earlier drafts of this chapter. [Editorial note: this chapter was written before the ruling of the House of Lords in A. v. *Secretary of State for the Home Department* [2004] UKHL 56, and should be read in light of that ruling. See 'Postscript', Chapter 28, in this volume]
[1] Noel Whitty, Therese Murphy and Stephen Livingstone, *Civil Liberties Law – The Human Rights Act Era* (London, Butterworths, 2001), at 128–9.
[2] Ibid., at 143. As Clive Walker, a leading commentator on UK anti-terrorist law and policy, puts it, 'The trend [of UK anti-terrorist policy] ... represents a part of a fundamental switch away from reactive policing of incidents to proactive policing and management of risk', in 'Terrorism and Criminal Justice: Past, Present and Future' [2004] *Crim L. R.* May, 311 at 314. Walker further cites R. V. Ericson and K. D. Haggerty, *Policing the Risk Society* (Clarendon Press, Oxford, 1997). Clearly, preventive measures are the only possible strategy in relation to the threat of suicide bombers: those who *plan* to die in carrying out attacks self-evidently cannot be 'punished' after the event and are unlikely to be deterred by the threat of conviction and imprisonment; however, imprisonment of those

charging suspects with offences actually committed, is the logical conclusion of this approach: persons may be imprisoned, not because of what they have actually done, but for fear of what they might do, based upon suspicion of their involvement with al Qaeda generally.

It should be pointed out that the experience of the use of such 'special powers' in relation to Northern Ireland is not a happy one: there is substantial evidence of the use of powers in an oppressive manner, of their use against persons later turning out to be innocent,[3] and of more oppressive practices being carried on in secret.[4] A further lesson from Northern Ireland is that the use of draconian security methods of fighting terrorism diminished when they were seen as counter-productive, because they were obstructing movement towards a *political solution* to the terrorist problem – the Northern Ireland peace-process. For example, it appears that governmental policy towards the use of lethal force against IRA members preparing to carry out violent acts changed, *not* because of a finding in *McCann* v. *UK*[5] that such use had violated the suspects' right to life under Article 2 of the European Convention on Human Rights (ECHR), but because a political calculation was made that the creation of 'republican martyrs' would hinder the British Government's attempts to reach a political settlement with the IRA.[6] Given that there appears to be absolutely no possibility of political negotiation with al Qaeda and its associates,[7] this obvious 'political route' towards less repressive security measures against terrorist suspects seems to be unequivocally closed off. Nevertheless, there are good reasons for reconsidering the current measure of executive detention discussed below: there is now substantial evidence that the use of this measure exclusively against Muslim men has created substantial resentment and alienation in the Muslim community and a loss of faith in the British justice system and Western democratic values generally.[8] This in turn may both increase support for extremist Islamic groups within the wider Muslim community and hamper intelligence gathering by the security services within that community. Unfortunately, however, the Government at present shows little or no appreciation of these counter-productive effects. Thus there

engaged in planning and preparation for such attacks (e.g. on conviction for proscription offences or for conspiracy (below text to notes 23, 24) would assist in preventing them.

[3] 80% of those arrested under the PTA were released without charge.

[4] E.g. the use of the so-called 'five techniques' of intensive interrogation used in Northern Ireland against terrorist suspects in the 1970s, eventually found to breach Art. 3 European Convention of Human Rights in *Ireland* v. *UK* (1978) 2 EHRR.

[5] (1995) 21 EHRR 97.

[6] T. Harnden, *Bandit country: the IRA and South Armagh* (1999), 303.

[7] Note however, that M. Ignatieff in a new book, *Lesser Evils* (Toronto, Penguin, 2004) suggests the possibility of negotiating with groups broadly sympathetic to al Qaeda but with less extreme agendas and methods.

[8] See the Liberty paper on the ATCSA: *Reconciling Security and Liberty in an Open Society: Liberty Response* (2004), Ch. 2, esp. pp. 9–10.

appear to be only two means by which amelioration, in human rights terms, of the current statutory powers could at present come about: political pressure from other sources and the use of legal challenge.

Political pressure from civil libertarians in Parliament and the media has not to date had any significant effect, mainly because of strong support in much of the press for 'tough action' against terrorism, and cross-party backing for it. Indeed, Parliament's role in relation to the Anti-terrorism, Crime and Security Act 2001 (ATCSA) – the main legislative response of the UK Government to September 11 – reveals not only an absence of any effective *democratic* opposition to the draconian powers it granted, in particular those in Part 4 giving powers to detain non-British nationals without trial, but also a lack of willingness to subject them to the kind of sustained, careful scrutiny that might be expected of a country with (purportedly) a strong allegiance to the rule of law and basic human rights values. The ATCSA was passed with strong support from the main opposition party in the House of Commons[9] and the overwhelming backing of MPs generally. Indeed, the 124-page long ATCS Bill, which partially abrogated habeas corpus and made the UK the only country in Europe to derogate from Article 5 of the European Convention on Human Rights,[10] was passed with just sixteen hours of debate; of the 135 clauses of the Bill, precisely 86 were debated in the Commons.[11]

---

[9] The Conservative Party; there was opposition from the much smaller Liberal Democrat party.

[10] Article 5 ECHR, as relevant, provides:

1. Everyone has the right to liberty and security of a person. No one shall be deprived of his liberty save in the following cases and in accordance with a procedure prescribed by law:
   a. the lawful detention of a person after conviction by a competent court;
   b. the lawful arrest or detention of a person for non-compliance with the lawful order of a court or in order to secure the fulfilment of any obligation prescribed by law;
   c. the lawful arrest or detention of a person effected for the purpose of bringing him before the competent legal authority on reasonable suspicion of having committed an offence or when it is reasonably considered necessary to prevent his committing an offence or fleeing after having done so . . .
   d. the lawful arrest or detention of a person to prevent his effecting an unauthorised entry into the country or of a person against whom action is being taken with a view to deportation or extradition . . .
2. Everyone arrested or detained in accordance with the provisions of paragraph 1(c) of this Article shall be brought promptly before a judge or other officer authorised by law to exercise judicial power and shall be entitled to trial within a reasonable time or to release pending trial . . .
3. Everyone who is deprived of his liberty by arrest or detention shall be entitled to take proceedings by which the lawfulness of his detention shall be decided speedily by a court and his release ordered if the detention is not lawful.

[11] See H. L. Deb. Vol. 629 col. 1533, 13 Dec. 2001 (Baroness Williams).

Despite powerful reports from the Joint Committee on Human Rights,[12] warning that the Bill as drafted almost certainly violated the ECHR, the Commons imposed not a single amendment against the Government,[13] and then, as and when instructed to by Government Whips, obediently and repeatedly overturned amendments passed in the House of Lords[14] intended to safeguard human rights and keep the proposed new powers within reasonable, internationally endorsed limits.

Thus the route of legal challenge has always appeared to be the only one likely to result in *significant* amelioration of the authoritarian aspects of the anti-terrorist legislation.[15] However, it should be noted that under the UK's Human Rights Act 1998 (HRA), due to the doctrine of parliamentary sovereignty, the courts have no power to strike down statutory provisions that violate fundamental rights guaranteed under the ECHR. The courts are limited instead to seeking to *interpret* legislation compatibly with such rights 'if possible',[16] and if they cannot do so, making a formal declaration of incompatibility between the provision in question and the ECHR right[17] that has no effect upon the legal validity or enforceability of the incompatible provision.[18]

This chapter focuses on a number of central characteristics of the UK's current counter-terrorist response[19] and on the future discernible trends. The

---

[12] Second Report, H. C. 37, H. L. 372 (2001–02); Fifth Report, H. C. 51, H. L. 420 (2001–02).

[13] The Government did bring forward some amendments in the Commons, in response to reports by various Select Committees, in particular the Joint Committee: see its Fifth Report (ibid.), at 8.

[14] The second, unelected, chamber of the UK Parliament did impose some improvements on the Bill: the deletion of the proposed creation of an offence of incitement to religious hatred; the insertion of 'sunset' clauses against Government resistance, whereby the more draconian aspects of the legislation would automatically lapse after a specified period (crucially re ss. 21–23, the powers to detain without trial); and the restriction of the provisions re retention of communications data to crime that '*may relate directly or indirectly to national security*' (s. 102(3)(b)), not *any* criminal offences.

[15] See further on this, Ramraj, Chapter 6, in this volume.

[16] Section 3(1) HRA: 'So far as it is possible to do so, primary legislation and subordinate legislation must be read and given effect in a way which is compatible with the Convention rights.'

[17] Section 4(2) HRA states: 'If the court is satisfied that [a provision of primary legislation] is incompatible with a Convention right, it may make a declaration of that incompatibility'.

[18] Sections 3(2) and 4(6) HRA.

[19] We do not consider the European Council Framework Decision on Combating Terrorism, (COM (2001) 521; Framework Decision [2002] O JL 164/3). The UK Government considers that, 'the proposal does not go further than existing UK legislation, which is considered to be adequate and not to require change' (House of Lords Committee on the European Union, (1999–00 HL 34, App.3). For discussion of EU anti-terrorist policy, see Monar, Chapter 20, in this volume, and Walker, 'Terrorism and Criminal Justice', at 323–5.

current Labour Government introduced a new counter-terrorism scheme with the introduction of the Terrorism Act 2000 (TA) and the ATCSA of 2001. This scheme offers a strong contrast to the previous one of the 70s, 80s and 90s. This chapter demonstrates that the new scheme represents a new model of counter-terrorist legislation that is more open to the criticism that it fails the test of proportionality – 'a recurring theme in the interpretation of the Convention'[20] – discussed below. The test derives from the principle encapsulated in Article 15 of the ECHR, which allows for derogation from certain fundamental rights protected by the Convention in states of emergency, but only to the extent 'strictly required by the exigencies of the situation'. This chapter will argue that the current Government shows little recognition of the need to tailor provisions more precisely to the particular emergency in order to avoid unnecessary impairments of human rights.

II. UK counter-terrorism legislation – the criminal justice model

The previous UK counter-terrorist scheme – essentially the Prevention of Terrorism (Temporary Provisions) Act 1989 (PTA) and the Northern Ireland (Emergency Provisions) Act 1996 (EPA) as amended – revealed some acceptance of the principle that emergency measures should be adopted only in the face of immediate and severe need. The old model for the counter-terrorist legislation – temporary, graduated to levels of threat, incrementally developed in the face of particular emergencies, with localized effect – was viewed in many quarters as deeply flawed, not least in that the legislation became more far-reaching as the terrorist activity diminished. It was at its most extensive, as a temporary measure, in 1998, although the Irish peace process was in being. Nevertheless, it had not entirely lost touch with the principles often put forward by government Ministers and by civil libertarians: that in a democracy, steps taken in abandonment of a commitment to human rights should be subject to the most rigorous tests for proportionality derived from Article 15 ECHR: an immediate and serious threat should be evident; the measures adopted should be effective in combating it and should go no further than strictly necessary to meet it. The additions to the original legislation were relatively minor and usually had at least an apparent justification as a response to an actual terrorist act. In contrast, the counter-terrorist scheme post-2000, aimed mainly at extreme Islamic groups and at 'international terrorists' generally, is more extensive than in the worst years of Irish terrorist violence. Its cornerstone is formed by the Terrorism Act 2000.

---

[20] D. J. Harris, M. O'Boyle, C. Warbrick, *Law of the European Convention on Human Rights* (London, Butterworths, 1995), at 11.

A. The definition of terrorism in the 2000 Act

The TA, s. 1(1) provides that 'terrorism' means the use or threat, 'for the purpose of advancing a political, religious or ideological cause', of action 'designed to influence a government or to intimidate the public or a section of the public', which involves serious violence against any person or serious damage to property, endangers the life of any person, or 'creates a serious risk to the health or safety of the public or a section of the public, or is designed seriously to interfere with or seriously to disrupt an electronic system'. This extraordinarily wide definition covers such action occurring anywhere in the world (under s. 1(4)). It is not an offence to 'be a terrorist' under this definition unless, as indicated below, the group to which the 'terrorist' has links is proscribed since membership of such a group is an offence in itself. The definition covers the actions of the most extreme and dangerous terrorist groups, such as al Qaeda, but it also covers on its face forms of direct action adopted by protest groups. In Australia and South Africa, such groups were expressly exempted from those countries' equivalent terrorist legislation when the definition of terrorism was borrowed from the UK's TA, s. 1.[21] Significantly, the s. 1(1) definition creates a potential effect that is far wider in practice than the effect of the previous definition (under s. 20 PTA) since the new legislation, unlike the PTA, allows the *definition itself* to determine the application of the special powers.[22]

B. Proscription-related offences

Under the TA, the power of proscription and all the proscription-related offences (formerly under the PTA) are retained, and their impact is greatly extended. The power to add to or delete groups from the relevant TA Schedule is exercised under s. 3(3) by the Secretary of State, by order. Thus the initial exercise of the proscription power is retained within the executive domain. Under s. 3(4) the power may be exercised 'only if he believes that [the organization] is concerned in terrorism'. The proscription power is wider therefore than the application of the s. 1(1) definition itself would warrant, since groups which do not themselves fall within the s. 1 definition can be proscribed. Parliament's approval is required for additions to, or deletions from, the list, as it was under

---

[21] See Chapters 24 and 25, respectively, in this volume.
[22] 'Terrorism' was defined in section 20(1) of the PTA 1989 as: 'the use of violence for political ends and includes any use of violence for the purpose of putting the public, or any section of the public in fear'. But the special powers conferred applied only to 'terrorism connected with the affairs of Northern Ireland' or (in certain narrow instances) to international terrorism.

the PTA provisions.[23] Under s. 11(1) TA a person commits an offence if s/he belongs or professes to belong to a proscribed organization. It is notable that there is no *mens rea* requirement.[24]

C. Special 'terrorism' offences

The TA applies all the special 'terrorism' offences that were developed in the context of the PTA or EPA to an extremely wide range of organizations. Unless and until the Home Secretary proscribes a range of international political groups advocating terrorist tactics in their own countries to bring down oppressive regimes,[25] or domestic extremist groups covered by the s. 1 definition, the proscription-related offences will not apply to them. But all the special terrorist offences, which have no equivalents in ordinary criminal law, apply, as does the special criminal justice regime under the TA for suspected terrorists, affording them lesser rights within the criminal justice system (in relation to stop and search, arrest and detention) than 'ordinary' criminals.[26] In so far as the offences discussed below curb expression or association rights protected under the HRA (Articles 10 and 11 ECHR), it was assumed that no derogation from those Articles was required, on the basis that the offences, even coupled with the very broad definition of terrorism, set permissible limits on those rights.

A range of very broad offences are available. Section 56 TA makes it an offence, carrying a maximum sentence of life imprisonment, to direct 'at any level' a terrorist organisation. Under Section 19 TA it is an offence to fail to report information to the police that comes to one's attention in the course of a trade, profession, business or employment and which might be of material assistance in preventing an act of terrorism or in arresting someone carrying

---

[23] s. 123(4). Al Qaeda itself and its associated groups are of course proscribed, along with other groups not linked to it, including the PKK and various groups associated with Northern Ireland.

[24] A maximum penalty of ten years' imprisonment is imposed. Under s. 11(2) it is a defence to prove that the organization was not proscribed when the person became a member or that he has not taken part in the activities of the organization since it was proscribed. S. 12(1) provides that it is also an offence to solicit support, other than money or other property, for a proscribed organization. See also the offences under s. 12(2) and 12(3) of arranging, managing or speaking at meetings designed to support or further the activities of a proscribed organization and s. 13, relating to the wearing of badges or uniforms signalling support for such organizations.

[25] Some of these groups, such as the PKK, are already proscribed; see note 23 above.

[26] See H. Fenwick, *Civil Liberties and Human Rights* (3rd ed, London, Cavendish Publishing, 2002), Ch. 11.

out such an act.[27] Section 38B ATCSA broadens this provision immensely: it makes it an offence, subject to an unexplicated defence of reasonable excuse, for a person to fail to disclose to a police officer any information which he knows or believes *might* be of material assistance in preventing an act of terrorism or securing the apprehension or conviction of a person involved in such an act. Family members are not exempted from the duty. A further wide range of people are potentially subject to criminal penalties under s. 58(1) TA, the provision relating to the collection of information, which is based on s. 16B PTA.[28] S. 57(1) TA is particularly draconian in imposing a reverse burden of proof: it provides that a person is guilty of an offence if he has an article in his possession in circumstances giving rise to a reasonable suspicion that the article is in his possession for a purpose linked to terrorism. Under s. 57(2) the accused can rebut this presumption of guilt by proving that the article was not in his possession for the purpose mentioned in s. 57(1).[29]

These offences could probably originally only have been introduced in the context of the threat from Irish terrorism, in some instances at a time when the number of deaths from bomb attacks had been very high in the preceding years. But the TA does not act only as the 'trigger' applying the old PTA or EPA offences to a wider range of groups; it also creates new offences of inciting terrorism abroad, which apply under ss. 59–61.[30] Reviewing the existing powers available to the executive in fighting terrorism, the Joint Committee on Human Rights commented, 'the UK's armoury of anti-terrorism legislation is widely regarded as the most rigorous in Europe'.[31] The very broad scope of the offences described above must be borne in mind when considering the *necessity* of introducing the further power of detention without trial.

---

[27] Subs. (5) preserves an exemption in respect of legal advisers' privileged material.

[28] S. 58(1) provides: 'A person commits an offence if (a) he collects or makes a record of information of a kind likely to be useful to a person committing or preparing an act of terrorism, or (b) he possesses a document or record containing information of that kind.' The offence lacks any requirement of *knowledge* regarding the nature of the information or any requirement that the person *intended* to use it in order to further the aims of terrorism, though a defence of 'reasonable excuse' is provided.

[29] Under s. 57(4), if it is proved that the article and the accused were both present on the premises or that the article is present on premises which he occupies or habitually uses, this may be sufficient evidence of possession, unless he proves that he did not know of its presence or had no control over it.

[30] Under s. 59(1) the offence is made out if the act of terrorism incited would, if committed in England and Wales, constitute one of the offences listed in subs. (2), which include the more serious offences against the person, including murder.

[31] Second Report (note 12) above, at 35.

III. UK counter-terrorism legislation – the detention without trial scheme[32]

A. The introduction of Part 4 of the Anti-Terrorism, Crime and Security Act, and the Derogation Order

The problem faced by the Government after September 11 was presented to Parliament and a number of parliamentary committees[33] in the following terms: a dilemma arises in respect of persons suspected of being international terrorists but who cannot be placed on trial due to the sensitivity of the evidence and the high standard of proof, and cannot be extradited, or deported to their country of origin, because there are grounds to think that they would there be subject to torture or inhuman and degrading treatment, in breach of Article 3 ECHR.[34] The dilemma arose due to the decision of the European Court of Human Rights in *Chahal* v. *UK*,[35] in which it found that a breach of Article 3 will arise where a country deports a person to another country, knowing that he or she will face a substantial risk of Article 3 treatment in that other country.[36] Article 3 imposes an absolute obligation on signatory states. Further, the UK has ratified Protocol 6 of the Convention and therefore cannot deport persons to countries where there is a real risk that the death penalty will be imposed.[37] As a matter of domestic law, it is clear that the power to detain persons prior to deportation under Schedule 3, paragraph 1 of the Immigration Act 1971 is limited to such time as is reasonable to allow the process of deportation to be carried out, and that deportation should follow promptly after the making of the order: *R* v. *Governor of Durham prison ex parte Singh*.[38] Thus current powers of detention prior to deportation did not provide the Government with a solution since the suspected terrorists in question could not be deported within a reasonable time, or, in some instances, at all.

The Government's preferred solution to the dilemma was to introduce detention without trial for foreign nationals suspected of involvement with

---

[32] The ATCSA had a large number of provisions many of which were not counter-terrorist measures: see H. Fenwick 'The Anti-Terrorism, Crime and Security Act 2001: A proportionate response to September 11?' [2002] 65 *MLR* 724–762. This section draws to an extent upon that article.

[33] Home Affairs Select Committee, *The Anti-Terrorism, Crime and Security Bill* (HC (2001–02) 351, 10 Nov. 2001).

[34] Article 3 provides: 'No one shall be subjected to torture or to inhuman or degrading treatment or punishment'.

[35] (1996) 23 EHRR 413.   [36] Ibid. at 74.

[37] *X* v. *Spain* DR 37 (1984) 93; *Aylor-Davis* v. *France* (1994) 76-A DR 164; *Raidl* v. *Austria* (1995) 82-A DR 134. Protocol 6 prohibits the death penalty in time of peace: it was ratified by the UK on 27 Jan. 1999.

[38] [1984] 1 WLR 704.

terrorism, even where they could not be deported. But it considered that the new provisions would be incompatible with Article 5(1) ECHR, which protects the right to liberty and security of the person, afforded further effect in domestic law under the Human Rights Act (HRA). Although there is an exception under Article 5(1)(f) allowing for detention of 'a person against whom action is being taken with a view to deportation or extradition', it was clear, following *Chahal*, that it would not cover the lengthy detentions envisaged during which deportation proceedings would not be in being.[39]

Therefore, in order to introduce the new provisions it was necessary to derogate from Article 5(1). The derogation was made by giving notice to the Secretary-General of the Council of Europe under Article 15(3) ECHR. Article 15 provides that 'in time of war or other public emergency threatening the life of the nation' any of the contracting parties may take measures derogating from its obligations under the Convention, 'to the extent strictly required by the exigencies of the situation, provided that such measures are not inconsistent with its other obligations under international law'. No derogation from Articles 3, 4(1), 7 or 2 ('except in respect of deaths resulting from lawful acts of war') can be made under Article 15. Before giving notice to the Secretary-General the Government made an order under s. 14 HRA, the Human Rights Act (Designated Derogation) Order 2001,[40] setting out the derogation from Article 5(1). The derogation itself is expressed to subsist until it is withdrawn, but for HRA purposes it will cease to have effect after five years unless its extension is approved by the positive resolution procedure in both Houses of Parliament.[41] The schedule to the Derogation Order, which takes the form of a draft letter to the Secretary-General, points out that the UN Security Council recognized the 11 September attacks as a threat to international security and required states in Resolution 1373 to take measures to prevent terrorist attacks, which include denying a safe haven to those who plan, support or commit such acts. The schedule argues that on this basis there is a domestic public emergency, which is especially present since there are foreign nationals in the UK who threaten its national security. Therefore, it argues, the measures in Part 4 ATCSA are clearly and strictly required by the very grave nature of the situation. The Government also derogated from Article 9 of the International Covenant on Civil and Political Rights as a further method of safeguarding the new measures from challenge.[42]

---

[39] See *Chahal* v. *UK* (1996) 23 EHRR 413, [113]. In order to detain, deportation proceedings should be in being and it should be clear that they are being prosecuted with due diligence.
[40] SI 2001 No. 3644. It was laid before Parliament on 12 November 2001, coming into effect on the following day. It designates the proposed derogation as one that is to have immediate effect.
[41] S. 16 HRA.
[42] Under Article 4(1) of the Covenant: see *UK Derogation under the ICCPR*, 18 Dec 2001.

The Part 4 provisions are sometimes spoken of as amounting to 'indefinite detention'. This is not strictly so: the detention powers in Part 4 will expire on 10 November 2006.[43] Detention is therefore limited to a little less than five years for those arrested immediately after the Act was passed in December 2001. Moreover, Part 4 must be renewed by order, subject to Parliamentary approval, every fifteen months.[44] However, it appears that the Government's intention is to introduce legislation to Parliament in order to retain these powers, once they lapse, assuming that the current 'emergency' is considered to be ongoing at that point.[45] Therefore in practice the detention may be termed indefinite.

B. The Part 4 detention provisions

Detention under Part 4 ATCSA depends on certification by the Home Secretary as – in a sense – a substitute for a trial. Under s. 21(1) the Home Secretary can issue a certificate in respect of a person on the basis of (a) a reasonable belief that the person's presence in the UK is a 'risk to national security' and (b) reasonable suspicion that he or she is a terrorist. Under s. 21(2) a 'terrorist' is a person who 'is or has been concerned in the commission, preparation or instigation of acts of international terrorism' or (b) is a member of or belongs to an international terrorist group or (c) has 'links' with such a group. Under s. 21(4) such links will exist only if the person 'supports or assists' the international terrorist group. 'Terrorism' has the meaning given to it in s. 1(1) of the Terrorism Act 2000 (TA).[46] Thus the TA and ATCSA must be read together. But the detention provisions in Part 4 of ATCSA do not apply to all those within the definition in s. 1(1) TA; the power to detain only applies to 'suspected international terrorists' who are non-British citizens. Under s. 21(5) ATCSA a 'suspected international terrorist' is a person who falls within the definition of terrorism in s. 1 TA and who has been certified under s. 21(1).

It is crucial that the definition of a 'suspected international terrorist' should be precise since such a person can be subject to lengthy – perhaps indefinite – detention without trial. But, as indicated, the definition of 'terrorism' under s. 1 TA, on which it is centrally based, is itself immensely broad and imprecise. No full definition of an 'international' terrorist is contained in the Act, but s. 21(3) provides that an international terrorist group is a group subject to the control or influence of persons outside the UK and the Home Secretary suspects (not qualified by 'reasonably') that it is concerned in the commission, preparation and instigation of acts of terrorism. Further, a person can be termed a 'suspected international terrorist' on the basis that he or she has 'links' with an international terrorist group.

---

[43] S. 29(7).   [44] S. 29(1)–(6).
[45] As appears from the Government's discussion paper (note 119 below).   [46] S. 21(5).

The power of certification can only be exercised in respect of persons who, under s. 22 ATCSA, can be subject to various immigration controls.[47] Under s. 23(1) persons falling within s. 21 'may be detained under a provision specified in subs. (2) despite the fact that his removal or departure from the UK is prevented (whether temporarily or indefinitely) by (a) a point of law which wholly or partly relates to an international agreement or (b) a practical consideration'. S. 23(2) refers to Schedule 2 paragraph 16 of the 1971 Act (detention of persons liable to examination or removal) and Schedule 3 paragraph 2 of that Act (detention pending deportation). No definition or explanation of the terms used in s. 23(1) is offered. Provision under (a) must be taken to relate to Article 3 and Protocol 6 of ECHR, while the 'practical consideration' covers *inter alia* a failure to identify a country which will take the person. The detention powers were used immediately to detain eleven persons in Belmarsh Prison in London. Two of them stated that they were prepared to leave the country and did so.[48] Since that time a further five persons have been detained.

As the Joint Committee on Human Rights pointed out, the provisions go beyond answering the dilemma the Government claimed to be addressing.[49] The scheme covers on its face a range of persons unconnected with al Qaeda – the terrorist group which was almost certainly responsible for the September 11 attacks. On its face, it would cover those who pose a threat only to other countries, such as Tamil Tigers, and also those who merely have 'links' with such groups; it could, for example, cover a Kurd who supports the PKK.[50]

A number of qualifying provisions that would have improved this scheme in human rights terms are notable by their absence. For example, it is not necessary prior to certification for the Home Secretary to receive an assessment from legal advisors regarding the feasibility of bringing any of the potential detainees to trial rather than relying on this scheme. Nor must an interim assessment be made on the basis that fresh evidence has been obtained while the detainee is in detention, rendering a prosecution feasible. The significance of this omission was high-lighted in the case of *Abu Qatada v. Secretary of State for the Home Dept.*[51] The Special Immigration Appeals Commission (SIAC) found that the evidence against Qatada was very strong and the extensive evidence against him was reviewed. Clearly, the question why Qatada could not be prosecuted under one of the TA offences arises. The

[47] Defined widely to include powers concerning asylum seekers: see ss. 3, 3B, 3(6), 5(1), 8–10 and 12–14 Immigration Act 1971 and s. 10 Immigration and Asylum Act 1999.
[48] See the *Guardian* 15.4.02.   [49] Fifth Report (note 12 above), at 6.
[50] Such an individual could alternatively be arrested and charged with one of the proscription-linked offences under the TA: s. 12(1) would provide the obvious one.
[51] File No. SC15/2002.

offence under s. 59(1) TA, for example, might well have been applicable. Obviously some of the evidence might be difficult to present in court, but SIAC's judgment gives the impression that sufficient evidence exists that could be presented in a trial, probably with safeguards such as anonymity for certain witnesses.

No particular conditions of detention are prescribed for the detainees, and bearing in mind that it is de facto indefinite, they are under particular mental stress. On 22 April 2004, the Special Immigration Appeals Tribunal ordered the release of one of those detained under Part 4 ATCSA, known as 'G', on the grounds that his prolonged detention without trial had affected his mental health so badly that he had become psychotic. SIAC ordered that G be placed under a form of house arrest in which his movements would be closely monitored, he would be denied access to means of electronic communication and electronically tagged. Another detainee who has recently been released[52] has told the press that a number of the detainees have become mentally ill as a result of their detention. The detainees are subject to the same conditions as remand prisoners in general – albeit in high security detention applicable to category A prisoners – although their status differs greatly from that of a remand prisoner who can expect to be detained for a relatively short period of time.

There is no express provision allowing for the release of the detainee if, for example, the group to which he allegedly belongs, or has links to, renounces terrorist activity. No obligation is placed on the Home Secretary to receive independent and continuing assessments of the degree to which a particular detainee is at risk of Article 3 treatment if deported. There is no *express* provision allowing persons at risk of Article 3 treatment abroad to leave if they are prepared to take the risk of that treatment. There is no requirement that detainees must be deported or removed, if they wish to be, when and if a safe third country can be found, or indeed imposing any duty at all to find a safe third country. However, it was argued before SIAC and the Court of Appeal that such a duty should be *implied*: if safe deportation by arrangement with the receiving country appears a possibility as an alternative to detention without trial, then such detention surely cannot be said to be 'strictly required' under Article 15. Article 15 could therefore be said to impose a positive duty upon the Secretary of State to seek to deport those detained. However, this argument was summarily rejected by the Court of Appeal in its 'generic judgment'.[53]

---

[52] See *M* v. *Secretary of State for the Home Department* (2004) EWCA Civ 324.

[53] Laws LJ said that he rejected this suggestion 'out of hand': *A, B, C, D, E, F, G, H, Mahmoud Abu Rideh, Jamal Ajouaou* v. *Secretary of State for the Home Department* [2004] EWCA 1123.

C. Legal challenges to the derogation and the Part 4 scheme

The Special Immigration Appeals Commission (SIAC), established under s. 1 of the Special Immigration Appeals Commission Act 1997 (SIACA), plays a crucial role in this scheme since in most instances it will represent the only means of challenging the decision to detain. Under s. 6(1) HRA, SIAC, as a public authority, is bound to act compatibly with the ECHR.[54] Under s. 21(8) ATCSA, the Secretary of State's decision in connection with certification can only be questioned under ss. 25 or 26, which deal with challenges to the certificate or reviews of it in SIAC. There are two methods of judicial control enshrined in Part 4. Under s. 25 a detainee may appeal to SIAC which has the power to cancel the certificate of the Home Secretary, if it finds that there were no reasonable grounds for a belief or suspicion of the kind referred to in s. 21(1)(a) or (b), or that for 'some other reason' the certificate should not have been issued. The Commission can allow the appeal and cancel the certificate, but the Home Secretary can then issue a further certificate under s. 27(9).

There is also a distinct power of review of the certificate under s. 26, which is not instigated by the applicant and which must occur in SIAC.[55] However, it is of crucial significance to note that the grounds upon which SIAC may quash a certificate under the review power are very significantly narrower than they are on the original appeal under s. 25. On review, s. 26(5) states that the Commission:

a. '*must* cancel the certificate if it considers that there are no reasonable grounds for a belief or suspicion of the kind referred to in s. 21(1) [i.e. that the person is a risk to national security or that he or she is a terrorist] and

b. otherwise *may not make* any order . . .'[56]

Therefore a finding at some future point by a court that the derogation order is unlawful,[57] would *not* provide grounds for SIAC to cancel the certificate of those who had already unsuccessfully appealed, under s. 25, against their detention, precisely because the catch-all ground for cancelling the certificate

---

[54] There is an exception in subs. (2) of section 6: a public authority is relieved from acting compatibly with the Convention if primary legislation either requires it to (subs. (2)(a)) or otherwise if it is acting to give effect to primary legislation that cannot be interpreted compatibly with the Convention rights: subs. (2)(b). Neither exception has been found to be relevant to SIAC's role under ATCSA.

[55] The first review must occur as soon as is reasonably practicable after six months from the issue of the certificate under s. 26(1). However, if there is an appeal this will delay the point of the first review, under s. 26(2), which will occur six months from the point at which the appeal is finally determined.

[56] Emphasis added.

[57] At the time of going to press the House of Lords is expected to give its judgment very shortly (in November or December 2004) on whether the derogation is lawful. [Editorial note: In

in s. 25(1)(b) – 'some other reason' – applies only on initial appeal, not on subsequent reviews. Therefore any attempt to detain further suspects could be frustrated by successful appeals to SIAC, which could cancel the certificates,[58] relying on this ground. This could create an extraordinary situation in human rights terms in which those *already* detained could continue to be held, despite the fact that the derogation underpinning the detention power had been found to be unlawful.[59]

SIAC represents an example of what Dyzenhaus refers to in this book as 'imaginative institutional design', intended to provide for the continuing operation of the rule of law, even in emergency situations, without threatening the integrity of the regular legal system.[60] Clearly, Dyzenhaus accepts that the standard of due process in SIAC will inevitably be lower than in a criminal trial, although he views this as a necessary compromise in preserving that integrity. However, following the generic judgments in SIAC and the Court of Appeal,[61] it is now clear that the SIAC procedure has three very significant weaknesses, the first two of which were at least partly avoidable through robust judicial interpretation of the relevant Part 4 rules. The first relates to the standard of proof for certification. It was argued before the Court of Appeal that, 'having regard to the fundamental importance of the right to liberty and security of a person and to the prospect of indefinite detention inherent in Part IV of the 2001 Act, a very high standard is required ... when scrutinising the issue of a certificate under Section 21'.[62] (Any notion that the detentions might in practice be short-lived has now been dispersed: most of the detainees have been in detention for three years.) However, in its generic judgment, the Court rejected this contention, and confirmed that, given the use of the terms 'reasonable belief' and 'reasonable suspicion' in section 21 ATCSA, SIAC could not apply a rigorous

---

December 2004 the House of Lords issued its ruling in *A. v. Secretary of State for the Home Department* [2004] UKHL 56. See 'Postscript', Chapter 28, in this volume]
[58] It is of course impossible to say in advance whether SIAC *would* cancel certificates on appeal on this basis, although the language of s. 25(b) is clearly broad enough to allow them to do so.
[59] Under the HRA, it is also the case that primary legislation incompatible with Convention rights remains valid and of full effect (ss. 3(2) and 4(2)) and moreover, may still be enforced by public authorities (s. 6(2)). There is of course the further possibility that specific appeals against SIAC's refusal under s. 25 to cancel certificates authorizing detention could reach the House of Lords *after* it had found the derogation unlawful (*if* it makes such a finding in its forthcoming judgment): in such a case, presumably, the Lords could direct SIAC to release the detainees under s. 25(1)(b) on the basis that there is *now* 'some other reason' for cancelling the certificates. SIAC's determinations under s. 25 are presumably not exhausted until all appeals against its findings are concluded.
[60] See further Chapter 4 at 67.
[61] See SIAC's generic judgment of 29 October 2003 on appeals SC/1,6,7,9,10/2002 at 117 and note 53 above – the CA judgment.
[62] Ibid., at 28 per Pill LJ.

standard in testing the Secretary of State's evidence. As Laws LJ succinctly put it:

> In order to be persuaded that 'reasonable grounds' exist, SIAC does not have to be satisfied on the balance of probabilities either that the appellant is a threat to national security, or that he is a terrorist.[63]

In other words, there is no 'burden of proof' as that concept is commonly understood. Instead, SIAC is 'merely concerned with deciding whether there are reasonable grounds for [the Secretary of State's] belief or suspicion.[64] Thus the Secretary of State's belief is tested to a standard *below* that of the civil standard of proof.

The second key due process concern is that the normal rules of evidence do not apply to SIAC – it may admit evidence inadmissible in a court of law.[65] The concern was raised in hearings before SIAC that at least some of the evidence relied upon by the Secretary of State might have been obtained by torture or ill-treatment,[66] given revelations about the treatment of prisoners in Guantanemo Bay and elsewhere. It was argued that it would be unlawful for SIAC to admit such evidence, since it would create an abuse of process at common law or a breach of Article 6 ECHR, or both. This argument did not succeed before SIAC and was recently rejected, by a two to one majority in the Court of Appeal's generic judgment.[67] It was also pointed out that admission of evidence obtained by torture would breach Article 15 of the UN Convention on Torture (UNCAT), which specifically prohibits the admission of such evidence 'in any proceedings'.[68] The Court of Appeal, however, found that the provisions of UNCAT, as an unincorporated treaty, could not be directly enforced by domestic courts. Further, neither SIAC's rules of procedure nor the common law could, it was found, be reinterpreted to impose this prohibition indirectly:

> It would be contrary to the exercise of the statutory power as intended by Parliament, and also unrealistic, to expect the Secretary of State to investigate each statement [relied upon as evidence] with a view to deciding whether the circumstances in which it was obtained involved a breach of Article 3.[69]

It must be stressed that both the Court of Appeal and SIAC thought that no such evidence had in face been relied upon.[70] However, it is extraordinarily

---

[63] Ibid., at 364.   [64] Ibid., at 369.   [65] Rule 44(3), SIAC Procedure Rules.
[66] See SIAC's generic judgment (note 61 above) and the Court of Appeal judgment (note 53 above) for discussion of the relevant hearings.
[67] Neuberger LJ alone accepted that admission of torture evidence by SIAC would create a breach of Article 6(1): note 53 above, at 467).
[68] The wording is clearly not confined to criminal proceedings.
[69] Note 53 above, at 129. See also 133.   [70] Ibid., at 239.

disturbing to find that the UK courts are prepared, even in principle, to countenance the use of evidence that may have been obtained in breach of a norm of international law. Such use is specifically outlawed by international treaty (UNCAT) and fundamentally undermines the rule of law. The concern is all the more pressing when such evidence is used as the basis for a practice that amounts to a further fundamental violation of human rights norms: executive detention.

The third due process concern relates to natural justice within SIAC. Its Rules of Procedure[71] are intended to amount to a compromise between due process values and the Government's need to protect sensitive evidence and intelligence gathering methods from those it believes to be terrorists. The Rules allow for hearings in the absence of the person bringing the proceedings and his or her legal representative. In such instances a Special Advocate (SA) will be appointed who has had security clearance. The procedure is divided between closed and open sessions. Under SIACA s. 5(3)(b) and Rules of Procedure, rule 19, the appellant and his or her advocate are excluded from the closed sessions in which the sensitive intelligence-based evidence against the applicant is disclosed to SIAC. The advantage of the closed sessions is that SIAC can hear all the evidence, including the sensitive evidence, before making its determination. The SA *is* permitted to attend these sessions, and hear such evidence, and obviously can seek to challenge it. However, the crucial problem in due process terms is that the SA cannot discuss this evidence with his or her client. Therefore the applicant cannot be informed as to what may in many cases be the crucial evidence against him and cannot therefore challenge it. He is also disadvantaged when under cross-examination since he is unable to appreciate the significance of a number of the questions – a matter that SIAC itself has recognized.[72]

Clearly, therefore, the position of the applicant is weak before SIAC: the extent to which the evidence can genuinely be tested is questionable. As White puts it in relation to this type of Tribunal: '[it] attempts to create an adversarial forum where one of the parties is severely hampered in presenting his or her case'.[73] As a matter of law the procedure in SIAC could be challenged as incompatible with Article 6, the fair trial guarantee. This argument was raised in both SIAC and the Court of Appeal;[74] it was accepted in the latter that challenges to detention under SIAC do fall within the remit of Article 6 since they were viewed as a determination of civil

---

[71] SI 1998 No. 1881, amended by SI 2000 No. 1849.
[72] SIAC's generic judgment of 29 October 2003 on appeals SC/1,6,7,9,10/2002 at 117.
[73] For discussion see C. White 'Security Vetting, discrimination and the right to a fair trial' [1999] *PL* 406–18, at 413. See also C. Walker *The Prevention of Terrorism* (Manchester University Press, 1986), at 82; he advocates an inquisitorial system for such Tribunals.
[74] *A, X, Y and Others* v. *Secretary of State for the Home Dept* [2003] 1 All ER 816.

rights.[75] However, Lord Woolf found that within the national security context, which demanded some flexibility in applying due process values, the procedure satisfied the requirements of Article 6(1). This is clearly questionable: Lord Woolf's assertion once again failed to take account of the factor of indefinite detention, which clearly calls for strong due process protection within the Article 6 civil rights context, even if it is to fall short of that demanded by a criminal trial. However, his approach was echoed by Laws LJ in the generic judgment, who repudiated the suggestion that 'the Article 6 right should in some way be marginalised in the name of national security', but insisted 'that the right's application, and its scope in practice, is highly dependent upon the practical context in which it is asserted'.[76]

So far, in the eleven cases determined by SIAC following appeal against certification, the Home Secretary's decision to certify has been upheld in all but one of them. The Court of Appeal has agreed with SIAC's decision in all instances,[77] with the result therefore that one detainee has been released. However, in *M v. Secretary of State for the Home Department*[78] the Special Advocates were able to mount an effective challenge in the closed sessions to the evidence that M had links to al Qaeda. As a result SIAC decided that reasonable suspicion under the tests of ss. 21 and 23 was not established, and the Court of Appeal upheld this ruling. This instance indicates that the SIAC procedure has some efficacy as a means of testing the basis of the certification. However, as the Joint Committee on Human Rights recently pointed out, it is deeply concerning 'that an individual can be wrongly detained without charge for some fifteen months before the error in authorising such detention is established'.[79]

The Court of Appeal in *M* deferred to SIAC's assessment of the demands of national security, even though its view was opposed to that of the Home Secretary. This was the exact converse of the approach of the House of Lords in *Secretary of State for the Home Dept ex parte Rehman*,[80] in which the House of Lords refused to uphold SIAC's assessment of the risk to national security, deferring instead to the Home Secretary's view. This was despite the fact that SIAC was empowered to review the Home Secretary's decision on the widest

---

[75] Ibid., at 57: the Court of Appeal and SIAC determined that the proceedings therefore fell within Article 6(1) which guarantees 'a fair and public hearing within a reasonable time by an independent and impartial tribunal established by law'. However, it was also found that SIAC proceedings do *not* concern a 'criminal charge': therefore Art. 6(2), which sets out a series of minimum rights in relation to criminal trials, including the presumption of innocence, legal assistance and knowledge of the case against, was held not to apply. For further discussion, see H. Fenwick note 26 above at 750–4.

[76] Note 53 above, at 260.

[77] See *M v. Secretary of State for the Home Department* SIAC – SC/15/2002; CA 2004 EWCA Civ 324.

[78] Ibid.   [79] Eighteenth Report (2003–4), at 32.   [80] [2002] 1 All ER 123.

possible grounds, including his findings of fact, or if it considered that his discretion should have been exercised differently.[81] The difference in approach between the two decisions can presumably only be justified (if at all) by the argument that the more draconian provisions at issue in *M*, allowing for detention without trial, required a greater degree of judicial oversight.[82] However the Court of Appeal, in its later generic judgment, appeared to reject the argument that the context of indefinite detention justified a stricter standard of review than that applied in *Rehman*: there are explicit dicta to this effect,[83] and *Rehman* was cited approvingly in its judgment at several points.

All eleven detainees challenged the designated derogation itself in SIAC, under s. 30 ATCSA.[84] They also challenged the detention scheme in relation to the Convention rights scheduled in the Human Rights Act 1998. SIAC's decisions were then appealed to the Court of Appeal.[85] SIAC had to consider first whether there had been compliance with the requirements for derogation, meaning that it had to examine the demands of Article 15. The Government had not claimed that this is a time of war and therefore the first question which the court had to consider was whether there was a public emergency threatening the life of the nation, within the meaning of Article 15.

The European Court of Human Rights itself has never found that a claim for a derogation is unjustified on the basis that such a state of emergency does not exist. However, the Commission was prepared to make such a finding in the *Greek* case[86] since it considered that the threat was largely imminent rather than actual. In *Lawless v. Ireland*[87] the Court found that any terrorist threat must affect the whole population, must be in being or be imminent, and must have produced a situation in which the usual law enforcement mechanisms are unable to function.[88] The introduction of special powers in Ireland, including internment, in 1971 was found to be justified by an upsurge in terrorist activity, together with serious and prolonged rioting.[89]

[81] S. 4 SIACA 1997.

[82] Dyzenhaus is heavily critical of *Rehman*, arguing that it wholly undermined the special position and powers of SIAC: see Chapter 4, at 82–3.

[83] 'I have not been able to understand the submission that less deference should be paid to the Secretary of State in [relation to there being a state of emergency] than in the [national security situation at issue in *Rehman*]' – note 53 above, at 237, per Laws LJ.

[84] *A and others* v. *Secretary of State for the Home Dept*, determination: 30 July 02, unrep.

[85] *A, X and Y and Others* v. *Secretary of State for the Home Dept* – note 74 above.

[86] 12 YB 1 (1969).   [87] A 3, (1961) at 28.

[88] Ibid. It found that these conditions were satisfied in 1957 due to the existence of a 'secret army' operating in Ireland and in the UK and because of the alarming rise in terrorist activities in the previous year.

[89] *Ireland* v. *UK* A 25 (1978) at 23.

In introducing the ATCSA the Home Secretary said that the Government held secret information suggesting that members of some international terrorist groups are currently in Britain.[90] The Government took the view, taking into account the September 11 atrocities and Britain's support for America, that a state of public emergency affecting the life of the nation could be said to exist. The Joint Committee on Human Rights, however, expressed concern in its Second Report about the lack of specificity in the reasons given for taking this view.[91] It examined the Home Secretary in oral evidence on the reasons for thinking that a state of emergency existed differing from that facing the country when the TA 2000 was enacted; he replied that the current threat is greater than that posed by the IRA since the 1970s because the terrorists in question are thought to have access to weapons of mass destruction.[92] The Committee found that there might be evidence of a state of public emergency but that no evidence of it had been disclosed by the Home Secretary. In its more recent report the Committee reiterated its concern that it was unable to advise Parliament on the necessity and proportionality of the UK's derogation, on the evidence that had been made available to it. It suggested that the consequent democratic deficit in terms of scrutiny of the executive assertion of a public emergency could be cured by empowering the parliamentary Intelligence Services Committee to investigate and report on the matter itself.[93] Given the wide margin of discretion granted by the *courts* to the executive in assessing this matter, discussed below, it is submitted that this suggestion of the development of an independent, *democratic* forum within which this assessment could be made in a more rigorous manner, is a compelling one.

SIAC took the view that it had to decide 'whether the decision that there was such an emergency as justified derogation was one which was reasonable on all the material or . . . one that he was entitled to reach'.[94] This standard of scrutiny appears to resemble the *Wednesbury* approach and therefore, it is argued, was too low.[95] Having adopted this approach, SIAC accepted the existence of an emergency within the terms of Article 15 due to the fact that 'the UK is a prime target, second only to the US[96] . . . an emergency can exist

[90] See HC Debs 15 Oct. 2001, col. 924; evidence of the Home Secretary given to the Joint Committee on Human Rights, Second Report (note 12 above), Questions 3–7 and 9.
[91] Ibid., at 29.
[92] Second Report (note 12 above) and Oral Evidence appended to the report, Questions 3–7 and 9, at 29.
[93] Note 79 at 23.   [94] Note 84 above at 21.
[95] This point was raised on behalf of the applicants in the Court of Appeal; the Court considered that these words merely meant that SIAC recognized that it must afford a reasonably wide margin of discretion (*A, X and Y and Others* v. *Secretary of State for the Home Dept* [2003] 1 All ER 816 at 59.
[96] Note 84 above, at 35.

and can . . . be imminent if there is an intention and a capacity to carry out serious terrorist violence even if nothing has yet been done'.[97] The Court of Appeal[98] also accepted the existence of an emergency in Article 15 terms. Taking into account the breadth of the definition of an emergency under Article 15 and the fact that the domestic courts considered that they had to assess, on the basis of very sensitive intelligence, not an overt but a covert, implicit and speculatively imminent state of emergency, it was unsurprising that they concluded that one is currently in existence in the UK, although such an assessment would clearly be open to future revision if al Qaeda's operational effectiveness appears to diminish. In this respect it should be noted that in its notification of derogation from Article 15, the UK Government pledged that the derogation would be withdrawn as soon as it was no longer necessary.[99] The House of Lords is about to consider the question whether a state of emergency can be said to exist, and is likely to take account of the fact that other European countries, including Spain – which has suffered a severe terrorist attack – have continued over the past three years to find it unnecessary to derogate from Article 5.[100]

The second question to be asked under Article 15 is whether the derogation applies 'only to the extent strictly required by the exigencies of the situation'. This is a much more problematic issue. The Joint Committee on Human Rights concluded that even if the requisite state of emergency exists, it was doubtful whether the measures in the Bill could be said to be strictly required, bearing in mind the array of measures already available to be used against terrorism.[101] Other legal opinion on this issue was quite firmly to the effect that the detention scheme is unjustified on the basis that it goes further than is required by the exigencies of the situation.[102]

In determining the question of proportionality SIAC relied on the relevant Strasbourg jurisprudence in considering the need to introduce the Part 4 detention scheme, bearing in mind the other available measures which have not themselves necessitated derogation.[103] SIAC found that so long as the

---

[97] Ibid., at 24. [98] [2003] 1 All ER 816.

[99] As the Opinion prepared for JUSTICE's evidence to the Joint Committee pointed out, the fact that a state of emergency could be viewed as currently in being may not *continue* to justify the existence of the derogation since the assessment is based on the continued operational effectiveness of al Qaeda (Second Report, note 12 above at 10–11).

[100] Spain suffered the bombing of Madrid, apparently perpetrated by al Qaeda, on 11 March 2004. See the Second Report of the Joint Committee on Human Rights (note 12 above) at [30] on the position of other countries.

[101] Second Report (note 12 above) at 30.

[102] Both David Pannick QC in his Opinion for *Liberty* and the Opinion prepared for JUSTICE (note 12 above) came to the conclusion, on different grounds, that the derogation was unjustified.

[103] See: *Lawless v. Ireland* A 3, (1961) at 36; *Ireland v. UK* A 35, (1978) at 212.

detention scheme fell within the range of reasonable legislative responses it should not be viewed as over-broad merely because other alternatives were available. It went on to consider the key issue of over-inclusiveness and found that account should be taken of the potential effect of s. 3(1) HRA (providing that legislation should be rendered compatible with the Convention rights if at all possible) and the power of SIAC to set aside the certificate under s. 25(2)(b) ATCSA. Section 3(1) could be used, it was found, to narrow down the provisions of ss. 21–23 so that they only applied to members of al Qaeda and those linked to it. Moreover, if the powers were exercised against a person unconnected with al Qaeda that would provide a basis for setting aside the certificate under ss. 25(2)(b). Thus the detention scheme was found to satisfy the test of proportionality. The Court of Appeal agreed with SIAC in accepting that the measures taken were strictly required in the circumstances, taking into account the limited class of foreign nationals at which they were aimed. The judges found that it was well established that in some circumstances, particularly in times of emergency, states may distinguish between nationals and non-nationals.

Lord Woolf considered that s. 3(1) HRA need not be used to narrow down the detention provisions: he said that they would have to be read narrowly in any event so as to ensure that they were covered by the derogation Order, since otherwise they would conflict with Article 5. However, this point appears to ignore the fact that primary legislation incompatible with a Convention right remains valid: s. 3(2) HRA, and that s. 3(1) is the mechanism to be used to seek to ensure that incompatibility does not arise. On the basis that the provisions would in any event have to be read narrowly, Lord Woolf accepted the Government's undertaking that the detention power would only be used in relation to the emergency which was the subject of the derogation.[104] This was a very significant reading down of the statute and imposes a proportionality on the scheme which was not originally present since only members of al Qaeda or those with links to al Qaeda can now legitimately be detained.

D.   Tension between Part 4 and the rights to liberty, to freedom from discrimination, torture or inhuman or degrading treatment

The Court of Appeal agreed with SIAC that all other Convention Articles protected under the HRA were applicable[105] and could be claimed in relation

---

[104]   Note 74 above, at 42.
[105]   Ibid. This was on the basis that, regardless of the reference in Article 15 to 'other obligations in international law' which might include other Convention rights, such rights can in any event be invoked by the applicants, presumably under the HRA, although Woolf CJ was not explicit on this point: ibid. at 36.

to the detention scheme. The possibility that the application of the scheme itself amounts to Article 3 treatment was raised before both SIAC and the Court of Appeal. It was argued before SIAC that Article 3 treatment arises where the only means of escape from indefinite detention without trial is to accept the risk of such treatment abroad. If the deportation or extradition of a person to a country where she will face Article 3 treatment is in breach of Article 3, it is arguable that one could say the same, in principle, of forcing a person to choose between indefinite detention without trial and accepting the risk of Article 3 treatment abroad, since the 'choice' is so circumscribed. The application of Part 4 can place – and is intended to place – some detainees in the position of being forced to 'choose' between the exercise of two fundamental rights. It is therefore arguable that ss. 21 and 23 combined are incompatible with Article 3 since they are so deeply opposed to the values it enshrines.[106] This argument was summarily rejected by both SIAC and the Court of Appeal on the basis that the scheme was set up to *protect* the appellants' rights under Article 3, not to undermine them.[107]

The key argument put before SIAC was that the scheme is discriminatory on the ground of nationality and therefore breaches Article 14 which provides: 'The enjoyment of the rights and freedoms set forth in this Convention shall be secured without discrimination on any ground such as sex, race ... national or social origin, association with a national minority'. In general, a breach of Article 14 can be established where other persons in an analogous position enjoy differential treatment (in relation to another Convention guarantee) and there is no objective and reasonable justification for the distinction.[108] In the domestic courts it has been found under Article 14 that there will be an objective justification for different treatment where it pursues a legitimate aim and the treatment bears a reasonable relationship or proportionality with the aim sought to be realized.[109] SIAC found that since a number of British nationals would fall within the definition of a 'suspected international terrorist' under s. 21 ATCSA but could not be subject to detention under Part 4, the detention scheme creates discrimination on grounds of nationality. A breach of Article 14 read with Article 5(1) was therefore established. SIAC proceeded to quash the Derogation Order and made a declaration of incompatibility (under s. 4 HRA) between s. 23 ATCSA and Article 14 read with Article 5. This was clearly a highly significant finding. It meant that a key

---

[106] In particular, where detention is very prolonged; the detainee is a torture victim who is subject to severe psychological disturbance; he has already suffered prolonged detention without trial abroad; death or torture abroad as the alternative is a near certainty.
[107] SIAC judgment note 84 above, at 68, CA judgment note 74 above, at 58.
[108] *Stubbings v. UK* (1996) 23 EHRR 213.
[109] *Michalak v. London Borough of Wandsworth* [2002] EWCA Civ 271 at 20.

aspect of the UK's response to September 11 was deeply flawed since it had failed to comply with the fundamental principle of non-discrimination.

However, the Court of Appeal disagreed. The Court, unanimously, 'reached a different conclusion on the basis that British nationals are not in an analogous situation to foreign nationals who currently cannot be deported because of fears for their safety'.[110] Lord Woolf CJ said that he reached this conclusion partly on the basis of the tension between Articles 14 and 15.[111] Article 15, as indicated above, debars the taking of action to meet the emergency that is more than is strictly necessary. The Home Secretary had come to the conclusion that it was only necessary to take action in respect of non-national suspected terrorists and that was a conclusion that should be treated deferentially by the courts. Action taken also against *national* suspected terrorists might have been more effective but could not be viewed as strictly necessary in Article 15 terms, bearing in mind the Home Secretary's decision. The basis for singling out non-national suspected terrorists – that they, unlike nationals, are liable to be deported, even if, perforce, there is a delay before deportation can occur – was, in Lord Woolf's view, rational. Thus, the different treatment could be justified since it had a reasonable relationship or proportionality with the aim – of meeting the emergency – sought to be realized. In any event, Lord Woolf found, and the other members of the Court of Appeal agreed, that the comparators – nationals who are suspected terrorists – are not in an analogous position to non-national suspected terrorists since they have a right of abode, whereas the non-nationals merely have a contingent right not to be removed (due to the risk of Article 3 treatment abroad or where no country can be identified that is prepared to accept them). The use of nationality as the determinant of the reach of the scheme was found to be non-discriminatory and thus the appeal from SIAC's decision was allowed.

This decision was founded on the idea that targeting all 'suspected international terrorists' would have created a greater invasion of human rights than the current scheme creates since the rights of nationals would also have been invaded. This misses the point that a much more narrowly targeted scheme – aimed *on its face* only at al Qaeda members or supporters – national and non-national – would have created a much more confined invasion. The choice to target instead the much wider group, based on the necessarily unconnected factor of nationality – since al Qaeda is a group defined by ideology, not nationality – is very difficult to defend in terms of rationality. (It may also be noted that the choice of nationality as the key determinant of the reach of the scheme means that it also creates indirect discrimination on grounds of race.) The Court of Appeal succeeded in accepting the

---

[110] Note 74 above, at 56.   [111] Ibid. at 45.

Government defence only by adopting a strikingly deferential stance towards the Home Secretary's contention that an emergency created by al Qaeda would be most effectively addressed by targeting persons on the ground of nationality rather than on that of involvement in al Qaeda.[112] Clearly, a scheme that had included British citizens would have been viewed as more draconian since they cannot be deported and so would not be able to leave detention. However, almost all the suspects who were detained cannot in any event leave detention, and therefore that distinction is not of great significance in practice. Moreover, in accepting the argument that the detention of non-nationals is non-discriminatory, it may be argued that the Court of Appeal failed to uphold the role of courts in protecting minorities – minorities who have no other means of seeking protection since, as they are debarred from voting, they cannot employ the democratic process to do so. Deference is context-dependent[113] and the courts clearly have expertise in determining questions of discrimination.

IV. Prospects for the future: reviews of the ATCSA and the Government's response

In this part, we consider the future – the probable course of the UK government's anti-terrorist security strategy. This is revealed primarily in its responses to statutory reviews of the ATCSA carried out both by Lord Carlile, an independent reviewer, and also by a group of Privy Counsellors under Lord Newton[114] ('the Newton Report'); of particular significance is the strongly argued view of the latter that the detention without trial provisions in Part 4 ATCSA should be repealed and replaced as a matter of urgency. The Joint Committee on Human Rights has also recently produced a report on Part 4 and the Government's discussion paper;[115] it too urges the immediate repeal of Part 4, whilst Lord Carlile has suggested prosecution under a new, broader terrorist offence as an alternative to the detention scheme.[116] It is worthy of note therefore that the three independent reviews of Part 4 that have been carried out all recommend its repeal.

---

[112] Ibid. at 40 of the judgment.   [113] But see text to notes 75 and 76.

[114] That is, senior parliamentarians, and other holders of high office, whose technical role is to advise the Queen. Their report, *Anti-Terrorism, Crime and Security Act 2001 Review: Report* HC 100 (2003–04), is available at www.homeoffice.gov.uk/docs3/newton_committee_report_2003.pdf.

[115] Eighteenth Report (2003–04).

[116] 'If the criminal law was amended to include a broadly drawn offence of acts preparatory to terrorism, all could be prosecuted for criminal offences and none would suffer executive detention': 2003 Review (note 117 below), at 101.

A. The Government's response to the Newton Report's rejection of the retention of the powers of detention without trial[117]

It is a matter of concern, in the light of the above remarks, to find that the Government, having included in the ATCSA provision for a review of the Part 4 detention scheme by Privy Councillors,[118] then unequivocally rejected its central recommendation – that Part 4 should be repealed. The manner in which this was done is also revealing.[119] The Home Secretary dismissed this recommendation on the same day that the report came out:[120] a report of such length and over which so much time had been spent surely deserved more deliberate consideration than the few hours that the Home Secretary, David Blunkett, took to put together a press release dismissing the proposals. Further, in his more detailed response, considered below, the Home Secretary failed to engage seriously with the arguments put to him. The poor quality of argument in this 'discussion paper' discloses, we will argue, a dismissive attitude on the part of Government to the human rights concerns of those independent bodies who would take issue with its policy.

The Newton Report identified a number of particular points of concern with Part 4, in particular the low standard of proof and the fact that the suspects 'are not presented with and given the opportunity to refute, all the evidence against them', leading to a risk of a miscarriage of justice.[121] The Report concluded, in its most important finding of principle: 'we strongly recommend that the Part 4 powers which allow foreign nationals to be detained potentially indefinitely should be replaced as a matter of urgency'. In their place, the Report found that new legislation should be introduced that would:

> a. deal with all terrorism, whatever its origin or the nationality of its suspected perpetrators; and
> b. not require a derogation from the European Convention on Human Rights.[122]

Point (a) refers to matters of both human rights principle and security: the Report attacked the discrimination involved in applying such draconian

---

[117] Note that further statutory reviews of the *operation* of Part 4 have been carried out by Lord Carlile. These largely vindicated the *operation* of the scheme, the certifications made under it, and the fairness of the hearings before SIAC; (his first report is, *Anti-Terrorism, Crime and Security Act 2001: Part IV Section 28 Review 2002* (2003), his second is the 2003 review, dated (2004). Both are available at www.homeoffice.gov.uk/docs.

[118] Pursuant to s. 122(5) ATCSA 2001.

[119] The Government's response appeared as *Counter-Terrorism Powers: Reconciling Security and Liberty in an Open Society, A Discussion Paper* Cm 6147 and is available at www.homeoffice.gov.uk/docs3/CT_discussion-paper.pdf (hereafter, 'Discussion Paper').

[120] See www.homeoffice.gov.uk/n_story.asp?item_id=743.

[121] Note 114 above, at 188–9.   [122] Ibid., at 135.

sanctions on grounds of nationality, but also the irrationality of introducing a scheme, intended to respond protectively to the threat posed by al Qaeda, that affords no powers to use against dangerous members of that group who happen to be British nationals.[123] The Joint Committee has since said that it 'strongly agrees' with this key finding.[124] Newton therefore urges the Government to consider an alternative that could be effective in combating terrorism but that would be nationality-neutral. The Home Secretary's response is, in effect, as follows: the UK had to derogate in response to September 11, and that derogation had to be as narrow as possible.[125] Therefore the Government decided to act against foreign nationals only, as that amounts to the least draconian action, in accordance with Article 15 ECHR. The problem, clearly, is that the whole argument rests upon the assumed necessity for derogation, which *itself* assumes the need for detention without trial. In other words, using strikingly circular reasoning, the Home Secretary responds to an argument against using detention without trial, by saying that *since* it had to introduce such a measure, it could only be used against foreign nationals to keep its use as limited as possible. It thus gives the appearance of engaging in reasoned argument whilst, in reality, wholly avoiding the central issue.

The Home Secretary's attempt to refute Newton's argument that non-discriminatory alternative counter-terrorist measures should be introduced, is equally worthy of note:

> Immigration powers and the possibility of deportation could not apply to British citizens. While it would be possible to seek other powers to detain British citizens who may be involved in international terrorism it would be a very grave step. The Government believes that such draconian powers would be difficult to justify.[126]

This response again avoids reasoned engagement with Newton. The Home Secretary characterizes the argument that anti-terrorist legislation should treat all nationalities equally as a suggestion that the powers to detain or deport foreign nationals should be extended to include British citizens. He

---

[123] The Government itself admits that the threat faced by the UK comes at least partly from UK nationals: see note 119 above, Pt I, [24]; the Newton Report (note 114 at [193]) found that 'almost 30%' of Terrorism Act 2000 arrestees in the past year have been British and 'nearly half' of those suspected by the authorities of involvement in international terrorism are British nationals.

[124] Note 115 above, at 4.

[125] 'It was the unprecedented threat posed by al Qaeda and its associated networks which led to the derogation. The Government, in seeking a proportionate response, therefore undertook to limit its use, and the application of Part 4, to the international terrorist threat posed by al Qaeda and its associated networks. The Government's action was designed to meet the requirement in Article 15 that the measures leading to the derogation "were strictly required by the exigencies of the situation".' (Discussion Paper, Pt I, at 35).

[126] Discussion Paper, Pt I, at 35–6.

then replies (a) that deportation of British nationals is impossible; and
(b) that detention without trial of British nationals would be too draconian
a step. The argument deliberately misstates Newton's position and thus
provides no argument at all against proposals to introduce a non-discriminatory scheme. It argues only against extending the current scheme to British
nationals – an irrelevance, since Newton does not propose this.

Newton further makes a powerful objection to the use of deportation as an
alternative to indefinite detention:

> Seeking to deport terrorist suspects does not seem to us to be a satisfactory
> response, given the risk of exporting terrorism ... While deporting such
> people might free up British police, intelligence, security and prison service
> resources, it would not necessarily reduce the threat to British interests
> abroad, or make the world a safer place more generally.[127]

The Home Secretary's response to this objection is as follows:

> It can be argued that as suspected international terrorists their departure
> for another country could amount to exporting terrorism ... But that is a
> natural consequence of the fact that Part IV powers are immigration
> powers: detention is permissible only pending deportation and there is
> no other power available to detain (other than for the purpose of police
> enquiries) if a foreign national chooses voluntarily to leave the UK.[128]

Here, the Home Secretary again reverts to circularity: he simply accepts the
problem of potentially exporting terrorism as a corollary of the course it has
chosen; he does not seem to be prepared to engage with it *as a reason for
changing the Government's course of action* – an extraordinarily closed form of
reasoning, especially for what is supposed to be a discussion paper. His only
substantive response to this argument is to point out that, 'deportation has
the advantage moreover of disrupting the activities of the suspected terrorist'.[129] This may be a valid point, but with use of the internet and mobile
phones, it is possible that such a person could regain contact with his cell
quite easily.

In short, the Government's response to the fundamental arguments of
principle and efficacy against the detention scheme reveal an obduracy and
unwillingness to engage in serious discussion that bode ill for the possibility
that reasoned pressure, such as that represented by the Newton Report, might
bear any fruit in the future. The Government seems wholly unmoved by the
fact that no other European country has derogated from the Convention:
Spain suffered a serious terrorist attack upon its soil very shortly after the
Government's Discussion Paper was published, but has made no move to
derogate from the Convention in response.

---

[127] Newton Report, at 195.   [128] Discussion Paper, Pt I, at 32.   [129] Ibid.

B. Alternatives to detention without trial: the Newton and Carlile proposals and the Government's response

The Newton Report made a series of wide-ranging and imaginative proposals that could act as alternatives to the detention scheme in Part 4 ATCSA, whilst Lord Carlile[130] suggested that those detained could instead be charged under a new substantive offence of 'being or having been concerned in the commission, preparation or instigation of acts of terrorism'. This was not, however, a proposal that found favour with the Joint Committee in its 2004 review of Part 4.[131] It appears that the Government is minded to take up this suggestion,[132] but only as an *addition* to the Part 4 powers, not, as Carlile intended, as a substitute for them. So the result may merely be that a further, very broadly drafted, special offence may be added to the existing ones considered above.

Despite the fact that the Government's response was characterized as opening a period of consultation on the operation and necessity for Part 4, it dismisses Newton's proposals on *alternatives* to Part 4 at the very outset: 'the Government does not believe any of [the proposals] provide a workable solution to the challenges [Newton] poses'.[133] The proposals would have allowed the Government to avoid a derogation that at the present time looks increasingly like being a long-term departure from its human rights obligations. They are also precisely representative of the methods that other democracies are using in fighting global terrorism. But these factors failed to carry any weight. As the Joint Committee pointed out, in reviewing comparative research on anti-terrorism law and policy prepared by the House of Commons,[134] only the USA has also resorted to administrative detention. Other democracies have adopted instead a common cluster of methods that do not require derogation from basic human rights norms and, importantly, are nationality-neutral: that is, they do not suffer from the discrimination inherent in the UK scheme and can therefore be used against *all* those threatening the state, not just foreign nationals. These methods include:

> the creation of new terrorism or terrorism-related offences, the adoption of new investigative techniques, new protections for sensitive information, changes to criminal procedure including longer pre-charge detention, and the imposition of higher sentences for terrorism-related offences.[135]

Newton's most important proposals are on similar lines since they relate to methods of seeking to *prosecute* terrorist suspects, rather than detaining them

---

[130] First report, note 117 above, at 6.5.   [131] Eighteenth Report (2003–04) at 67.
[132] Discussion Paper, at 48.   [133] Ibid., at 34.
[134] Note 131 at 83. The countries surveyed include: Australia, Belgium, Canada, Denmark, Finland, Sweden, USA, France, Germany, Italy and Spain.
[135] Ibid., at 83.

without trial, thereby allowing for withdrawal of the UK's derogation from Article 5 ECHR. Much evidence against such persons consists of telephone intercept material obtained by the security services, but there is a statutory prohibition, contained in the Regulation of Investigatory Powers Act 2000 (s. 17) against the admissibility of such material as evidence in court. Newton therefore suggests removing this 'self-imposed blanket ban'.[136] As LIBERTY comments, 'Lifting the bar [on the admissibility of such material] would ... remove the primary obstacle to bringing trials in criminal cases',[137] while the Joint Committee finds that there is 'overwhelming support for this proposal'.[138] Lord Carlile, in oral evidence to the Committee, described the absolute ban as 'a nonsense', indicating that both the police and MI5 are in favour of lifting it.[139] Carlile's stance is unsurprising, in view of the fact that only Ireland also maintains a blanket ban on the use of such material.[140] As the Joint Committee puts it: 'More tailored and precise ways of protecting sources and methods should be developed which do not depend on blanket prohibitions.'[141] Newton suggests on this point:

> We can also see the case for modifying the normal rules governing the disclosure of evidence so that, for example, the prosecution would not be obliged to disclose intercept evidence, or even its existence, unless they chose to rely on it. This would need to be done with care to minimise the risk of miscarriages of justice, but those risks should not be greater than under the present system where the prosecution is forbidden from disclosing intercepted communications, even if they are exculpatory.[142]

Newton also puts forward the more radical alternative of making 'a security-cleared judge responsible for assembling a fair, answerable case, based on a full range of both sensitive and non-sensitive material [including intercept material]. This would then be tried in a conventional way by a different judge.'[143] Newton points out that a similar system is used in France. The key difference between this and a conventional trial would be that only the investigating judge, not the accused or his legal advisers, would see sensitive evidence that was not then used. As Newton points out, in a normal trial, 'the defence normally has the right to see all potentially relevant material, even if the prosecution is not relying on it (because it may undermine the prosecution's case)'.[144]

It is not, however, immediately clear that such an approach would answer fully to the problem identified.[145] Assuming that some sensitive evidence was

[136] Newton Report, at 208.   [137] Note 8 above, at 44.   [138] Note 131 above, at 55.
[139] Ibid., Q 22.   [140] Newton Report, at 211.   [141] Note 131 above, at 56.
[142] Newton Report, at 213.   [143] Ibid., at 224.   [144] Ibid., at 228.
[145] LIBERTY make a similar point in their response to the Discussion Paper, see note 8 above at 31); see also the negative conclusion of the Joint Committee on this point: note 131 above, at 58.

used at trial,[146] it would still become known to the accused, so that the original governmental objection (compromising sources or revealing the capabilities of the security services) would still apply. Alternatively, if the prosecution applied for a PII (Public Interest Immunity) certificate to exclude the evidence on the ground of its sensitivity, and the judge accepted it, the trial could not proceed if that evidence was central to the case. In any event, the Government deals with this, one of the more complex and interesting proposals of Newton, albeit one that requires further working out, with a flat rejection: 'It does not offer a solution to the need to protect sensitive information whilst enabling the defendant to know the full case that has been put against him.'[147]

Newton's other recommendations rely upon the possibility of prosecution, and seek only to maximize the potential impact of such prosecution. They do not therefore in themselves address the fundamental problem of the use of intercept material in court, and therefore would not, without further reform, operate as substitutes for the Part 4 scheme. They advocate the use of a greater and more structured use of plea-bargaining so that an individual would know with greater certainty that he could obtain a reduction in sentence in return for providing information about others or his own activities.[148] The Government merely stated briefly and dismissively in response that it is already considering making the current informal system of plea-bargaining more transparent in criminal cases generally.[149] It was equally unreceptive to the suggestion of using terrorist involvement as an aggravating factor in sentencing[150] – a practice used both in the USA and France.[151]

The other main strand of proposals made by Newton were those intended to remove the need for detention without trial by suggesting less draconian alternatives that would apply even in cases in which it was not thought possible to obtain a criminal conviction. The first of these focused upon the immigration route and picked up on the concern expressed by Lord Carlile that the Government does not always appear to be actively seeking to deport those it is detaining where that is a possibility:

---

[146] If the investigating judge decided not to use certain sensitive evidence this would presumably be because it was non-probative. But in such an instance, whilst some evidence that would otherwise have been seen by the defence would be excluded before trial, it would by its nature be non-crucial evidence (otherwise it would have been deemed probative).

[147] Discussion Paper, Pt II, at 37.

[148] Newton Report, at 240 ff. Newton cites the Council Framework Decision of 13 June 2002 on combating terrorism: it provides for the reduction of offences if the offender provides assistance to the authorities in the anti-terrorism struggle or renounces terrorist activity.

[149] Discussion Paper, Pt II, at 39.   [150] Discussion Paper, Pt II, at 33–4.

[151] Newton Report, at 216 ff.

> ... we have seen no evidence that it would be illegal for the Government to detain the deportee while taking active steps in good faith to reach an understanding with the destination government to ensure that the deportee's human rights were not violated on his return. This is what some other countries seem to have been able to do, at least in some cases ... [this conclusion] is reinforced by the observation that two of those certified under Part 4 as un-deportable suspected international terrorists have been able to leave the country without apparently putting themselves at risk.[152]

The Government's response to this points out:

> Case law is quite clear. For immigration detention to be lawful, there has to be a reasonable prospect of removal within a reasonable period. Without derogation, and section 23 of the ATCS Act, we would have no option but to release if an acceptable undertaking could not be obtained within a reasonable period.[153]

While this is correct as a matter of law, there is a further possibility put forward by Newton: of 'seek[ing] to establish framework agreements in advance with some of the main countries involved, in order to minimise the delay in dealing with individual cases'.[154] The Government asserts in response that 'work is underway' to establish such agreements, but doubt is cast on this by the 2003 report of Lord Carlile on the operation of Part 4. As this generally uncritical reviewer comments:

> ... Whereas France appears to enter into bilateral discussions with third countries as to what would happen to at least some detained persons following transfer, as I understand it the practice of the Foreign and Commonwealth Office has been to take only a generic approach as to the receiving country. Some of the detainees left their countries of origin as youths, and a more particular and individualised approach to the potential receiving country might in some cases reveal a very low risk to them on return provided that they are law-abiding thereafter.[155]

It may therefore be that the Government, whilst protesting that it uses detention genuinely as a last resort, is simply failing to put in the diplomatic leg-work in order to allow it to avoid detention. It will be interesting to note whether the Government does in fact announce the establishment of such agreements with possible receiving countries in the near future.

The other main *alternative* to detention offered by Newton is the use of surveillance and restrictions upon the movement of suspects. Such lesser restrictions on liberty would have 'the aim of monitoring potentially dangerous

---

[152] Newton Report, at 154–5.   [153] Discussion Paper, Pt II, at 46–7.
[154] Newton Report, at 28c.
[155] *Anti-Terrorism, Crime and Security Act 2001: Part IV Section 28 Review 2003* (2004), at 96.

individuals to prevent them from engaging in terrorist or terrorist-facilitating activity'. The Report suggested imposing restrictions on

a. the suspect's freedom of movement (e.g., curfews, tagging, daily reporting to a police station);
b. the suspect's ability to use financial services, communicate or associate freely (e.g., requiring them to use only certain specified phones or bank or internet accounts, which might be monitored);
   subject to the proviso that if the terms of the order were broken, custodial detention would follow ... [156]

As LIBERTY points out, intensive surveillance, coupled with the threat of custodial sentences, is the method used by the French and Swedish governments against those targeted by Part 4 in the UK.[157] The Joint Committee considers that the use of civil restriction orders, as outlined above, 'is worthy of further exploration', although clearly such orders are also problematic in human rights terms.[158] In contrast, the Government peremptorily rejects this suggestion, except in relation to those persons that present a low level of threat:[159]

> Modern technology, such as pay as you go mobiles, easy access to computers and other communications technology mean that tagging by itself would not prevent these individuals from involvement in terrorism and the Government cannot guarantee the success of such an approach.[160]

It is suggested that where a distinguished group of Privy Councillors recommends alternatives to a scheme that has necessitated derogation from a fundamental provision of the European Convention on Human Rights, it requires more serious consideration than a one-line dismissal that makes no attempt to explain its lack of efficacy in considered terms.

It has been argued that the Government would be likely to use the provisions for review in ss. 28 and 122 ATCSA[161] in any legal challenge to Part 4 as evidence that the Government accepts their extraordinary nature and is for that reason keeping them under careful, independent review.[162] The generic Court of Appeal judgment indicates that judges are indeed minded to accept this Government argument; in particular, Laws LJ attached 'no little importance'[163] to the requirement for review of the operation of Part 4 in section 28.[164] But the summary dismissal by the Government of the Privy

---

[156] Newton Report, at 28a.   [157] Note 8 above, at 36–7.   [158] Note 131 above, at 80.
[159] Discussion Paper, Pt II, at 44.   [160] Ibid., at 45.
[161] By a Government appointee (Lord Carlile), and by the Privy Councillors.
[162] C. Warbrick, 'Emergency Powers and Human Rights: the UK Experience' in C. Fijnaut, J. Wouters, and F. Naert (eds.), *Legal Instruments in the Fight against Terrorism* (Leiden, Nijoff, 2004), at 399.
[163] Note 53 above at 235.
[164] See also Pill LJ, ibid., at 129 re parliamentary monitoring of the situation.

Councillors' key findings and recommendations discussed above gives the strong impression that the statutory provision for review amounts only to a fig-leaf – intended to lend respectability to the scheme, but not to be taken seriously as a means of generating alternatives to the need for detention without trial. In the result, the review provisions arguably have a doubly negative effect: they appear to have helped protect the scheme from successful *legal* challenge whilst doing nothing in practice to help bring it to an end or ameliorate its worst aspects through politico-legislative means.

V. Conclusion

Democratic governments are clearly entitled to take extraordinary measures if faced with a threat of atrocities on anything like the scale of those that occurred on September 11. But as a matter of international law democracies are expected to place especial value on the fundamental right of non-discrimination, and in general would be expected to seek to impair human rights as little as possible in the course of adopting such measures. The under- and over-inclusivity of the current scheme means that it fails to satisfy both the minimum impairment and the efficacy test. The over-breadth of the definition of terrorism in the TA set the scene for the introduction of further over-inclusive provisions in Part 4 ATCSA. Part 4 is not a 'response' to September 11; on its face it is a response to certain previous decisions that stood in the way of the deportation of suspected international terrorists generally. The response of the Court of Appeal to Part 4 indicates that the Human Rights Act has enhanced the protection of fundamental rights in the UK in the context of national security, but the acceptance of the derogation demonstrates that the protection remains limited. Thus, it may still be necessary to seek that protection at Strasbourg.

At present, as this chapter has shown, two parallel schemes are operating in Britain in respect of the counter-terrorist response: indefinite detention without trial based on certification for a tiny group of suspected terrorists, defined by nationality, and a nationality-neutral scheme[165] based on a range of broad special terrorism offences, but dependent on trial and conviction, for all suspected terrorists. The creation of the two schemes reveals a clear disjunction of aim between the creation of ever-broader substantive offences and the due process demands of criminal trials. Ironically, the special terrorist offences are viewed by the Government as ineffective in relation to those that pose the greatest security threat. The creation of Part 4 of ATCSA amounts to an admission of the failure of the criminal law to deal with this threat. So far the Government has not sought to introduce modifications to the criminal trial

---

[165] At least on its face, unlike Part 4.

itself[166] – such as allowing the use of intercept material in evidence – with a view to bringing members of the relevant groups to trial. The key proposals from the Newton Committee had that objective in mind: they were intended to allow for the use of the special terrorism and proscription offences in prosecutions against members or supporters of al Qaeda, in order to remove the need for indefinite detention without trial. Their apparent rejection by the Government, coupled with its view that the UK 'now faces a near-permanent emergency'[167] – there being no prospect of a *political* solution – leaves the UK with the prospect of a long-term derogation from the European Convention.[168] As the Joint Committee has recently commented, such derogations:

> have a corrosive effect on the culture of respect for human rights on which the effective protection of all rights depends. They undermine the State's commitment to human rights and the rule of law, and diminish the State's standing in the international community.[169]

Unfortunately, the failure of democratic controls, the Government's resistance to reasoned pressure from the Newton Committee and others, and the wide margin of discretion granted by the courts to the executive in this area, give little grounds for optimism that this bleak scenario can or will be avoided.

---

[166] Save for the introduction, in places, of reverse burdens of proof, as in s. 57 TA – above text to note 29.

[167] Note 131 above.

[168] Unless the House of Lords declares it unlawful in its judgment expected in late 2004.

[169] Note 131 above at 4–5.

United States responses to September 11

WILLIAM C. BANKS

The violent destruction of life and property incident to war, the continual effort and alarm attendant on a state of continual danger, will compel nations the most attached to liberty to resort for repose and security to institutions which have a tendency to destroy their civil and political rights. To be more safe, they at length become willing to run the risk of being less free.[1]

The September 11 attacks profoundly affected the United States. Apart from the destruction of so many lives and the damage done to two of our most symbolically important buildings, the visual images of the attacks inflicted a level of trauma unknown to many Americans. The collective sense of fear and dread created by September 11, along with an understandable and palpable collective determination to rise up and 'do something' about terrorism, precipitated changes in laws and policies designed to counter the terrorist threat.

Acknowledging the risks of making judgments about the longer term from a perspective of three years from the event, the law and policy changes that are still being made by the United States may be part of what many inside and outside government now refer to as the 'new normal'. In short, a longer term permanent realignment of the relative importance of security among our government's objectives may be taking place, perhaps at the expense of a thoughtful examination of terrorism and its antidotes. The new measures have emerged from virtually all quarters of government in the United States, and many of the reforms have significant if not profound implications for our nation's law and governance. A range of civil liberties protections have been called into question, compromised or, some would say, undermined by new investigative and criminal authorities, along with programmes to detain and interrogate those captured in the 'war on terrorism'. The largest overhaul of government structure since World War II resulted in the creation of a new executive branch department to oversee the nation's homeland security.

I thank Helen Fenwick, Kent Roach, and George Williams for helpful comments on an earlier draft.
[1] Clinton Rossiter (ed.), *The Federalist No. 8* (Alexander Hamilton, New York, 1961), at 50.

The traditional distaste for a military role in domestic affairs is being replaced with a domestic command structure and an invigorated role for the military in homeland defence. In the international sphere the war against terrorism spilled over when President Bush launched a war against Iraq, justified at the time on the grounds that Saddam Hussein had weapons of mass destruction poised to strike the United States, and that Saddam had ties to the al Qaeda terrorist network and thus actively supported the terrorists' war against America. The Congress was an active partner with the executive in these initiatives early on, and has been largely quiet since authorizing the use of force against Iraq in October 2002. The courts are being tested, and the record so far is mixed. In critically important matters recently decided by the US Supreme Court, decisions were made that may limit principles of the new normal in the name of due process. It is equally possible, however, that the rebuke to our government delivered by the Supreme Court in June 2004 will only provide legal cover for the unlimited detention and coercive interrogation techniques already practised by the Administration. Only time will tell.

It may well be that the war on terrorism is not our gravest crisis. Our nation was born through the cauldron of violent revolution, and the Civil War was the contemporary equivalent of an all-out nuclear attack on the nation. In their time, the war with France soon after the founding and the two World Wars were potentially more calamitous for us. In each of these wars, the judicial branch was an active participant, sometimes generously deferent to the government's expansive interpretation of its wartime constitutional prerogatives, other times especially attentive to what have been viewed as unchanging constitutional values. Despite these historical parallels, there is evidence that our government has begun to realign our institutions, laws, and policies toward security in a way that is unprecedented.

Part I of this chapter will assess selected important law changes, beginning with statutory and executive rule-based reforms, some designed to enhance authorities to prevent terrorist attacks and others crafted to facilitate detention and trial of accused terrorists. The critical role of the courts in monitoring the legal developments will also be considered. Part II will examine policy shifts by our government, in national and homeland security strategy and in civilian/military relations, which upset long-standing models for governance by the United States. A brief conclusion will critique both sets of reforms.

I. The post-September 11 legal landscape

Within a few days of the World Trade Center and Pentagon attacks, Congress passed a joint resolution authorizing the President to 'use all necessary and appropriate force' against those responsible for September 11 'in order to prevent any future acts of international terrorism against the United States by such ... persons'.[2] No geographic or time limit was placed on the authority granted by the Authorization for the Use of Force, and the authorization to 'prevent any future acts' raises the possibility that military activities and other actions short of the use of force could take place against an unidentified enemy inside and outside the United States for the foreseeable future. In short, the scope of the discretion given to the Commander-in-Chief is unprecedented in United States history. In addition, for the first time since the Civil War, our Government recognized that the battlefield in the war on terrorism could include our cities. The breadth of the Resolution was underscored when the Supreme Court found in June 2004 that it empowered the President to detain as an enemy combatant an American citizen allegedly captured on the battlefield in Afghanistan.[3]

The USA PATRIOT Act

A few weeks after September 11, after minimal hearings and scant debate, Congress enacted the USA PATRIOT Act.[4] Perhaps more than any other legal development, the Patriot Act has become a magnet for galvanizing supporters and defenders of the Bush Administration response to September 11. Anyone who has taken the time to read the 352-page Act must wonder just where to find the magnetism. The Patriot Act is hardly a code for fighting the war on terrorism, nor one for saving the United States homeland from another attack. Instead, it is an amalgam of often unrelated pieces of authority, most of which simply amend existing laws, and the larger share of which are unremarkable complements to existing authority.

That is not to say that the Patriot Act lacks importance. The few really significant changes in investigative authorities and criminal law were made subject to a three-year sunset provision, and controversy really surrounds only several pages of the 352. An entire subtitle of the Act that would have authorized lengthy detention of any alien immigrant on the say-so of the Attorney General[5] has not been utilized, because existing immigration statutes and regulations conferred equally expansive authority.

One change wrought by the Patriot Act permits the FBI secretly to gain access to the personal information of Americans – including library, medical, education, internet, telephone and financial records – without having to show that the target of the investigation has any involvement in espionage or terrorism. Prior to the Patriot Act, the FBI could seek an order for

---

[2] Authorization for the Use of Force, Pub. L. No. 107–40, 115 Stat. 224 (2001).
[3] See discussion of *Hamdi* v. *Rumsfeld*, below.
[4] Uniting and Strengthening America by Providing Appropriate Tools Required to Intercept and Obstruct Terrorism (USA PATRIOT) Act, Pub. L. No. 107–56, 115 Stat. 272 (2001).
[5] Ibid. §§ 411–18, 8 U.S.C. § 1226a ff.

production of certain transactional records from third-party custodians, such as banks and telephone companies, if the government certified that it had 'reason to believe that the person to whom the records pertain is a foreign power or agent of a foreign power'.[6] As the authority was broadened by the Patriot Act, commercial vendors may be compelled to produce the requested records following a statement from the FBI that the information is for an investigation 'to protect against international terrorism or clandestine intelligence activities'. No showing is required that the target has anything to do with terrorism. The same provision then makes it a crime for the vendor to reveal that the FBI has obtained the requested information.[7] Provisions requiring a limited judicial approval before exercising this expanded authority to examine business records were later eliminated, when Congress in 2003 amended the law again to permit the Attorney General to issue administrative subpoenas (with no judicial role) in these investigations, and expanded the categories of those subject to the subpoenas to include securities dealers, currency exchanges, car dealers, travel agencies, post offices, casinos and pawnbrokers, among others.[8]

Since the Patriot Act, the volume of administrative subpoenas, known as national security letters, has increased dramatically, although the government has resisted Freedom of Information Act requests for the relevant data.[9] The American Civil Liberties Union (ACLU) sued the Justice Department in April 2004, challenging the constitutionality of the expansion of this authority to obtain personal records as it applies to electronic service providers. The ACLU claims that the FBI can obtain information from traditional Internet service providers, as well as universities, businesses, public interest organizations and libraries. The principal arguments by the ACLU are that the expanded authority chills protected expression, that it invades personal privacy, and that it constitutes a search that should be attended by a probable cause determination and warrant procedure to meet constitutional Fourth Amendment requirements.[10]

A second controversial Patriot Act provision amended the Foreign Intelligence Surveillance Act,[11] the authority that has, since 1978, allowed intelligence investigators to bypass the regular law enforcement warrant process by obtaining authorization for electronic surveillance or (since 1994) a physical search from a special secret court. Instead of having to

---

[6] 50 U.S.C. § 1862.   [7] Ibid. § 215, 115 Stat. 287.
[8] Intelligence Authorization Act for FY 2004, Pub. L. No. 108–77, § 374, 117 Stat. 2599, 2628 (2003).
[9] Dan Eggen and Robert O'Harrow, Jr., 'US Steps Up Secret Surveillance', *Washington Post*, 24 March 2003, A1.
[10] *American Civil Liberties Union* v. *Ashcroft*, No. 04 Civ. 2614 (S. D. N. Y. filed April 2004).
[11] 50 U.S.C. §§ 1801 ff.

demonstrate to a magistrate probable cause to believe that a crime is being or has been committed before being given permission to conduct electronic surveillance or a physical search, the judge of the secret court has merely to find probable cause that the requested surveillance is to obtain 'foreign intelligence' from an 'agent of a foreign power'. In other words, there should be a reasonable belief that the target is connected to an international terrorist organization.

Of course, intelligence and law enforcement investigations often overlap, utilize the same methods, and may concern the same targets. Because of the importance attached to personal privacy as enshrined in our Fourth Amendment requirements for probable cause of a criminal act and a warrant issued by a neutral magistrate, law enforcement and intelligence officials have historically walked a fine line. To gather foreign intelligence, agents could forego the traditional Fourth Amendment processes, but if they were intending to build a criminal case against the target, the probable cause and warrant requirements had to be followed. Until amended by the Patriot Act, to avoid tainting a criminal prosecution, investigators who found criminal activity in the course of a FISA investigation effectively had to show that the primary purpose of the surveillance approved by the secret FISA court was to obtain foreign intelligence. Once that showing was made, the fact that evidence turned up that could be used in building a criminal case would not undermine the rights of the accused.

This 'wall' between law enforcement and intelligence investigations permitted parallel law enforcement and intelligence investigations to coexist and protected the constitutional rights of the potential accused, but the government argued that the various procedures designed to insure the integrity of the wall stood in the way of effective cooperation and information sharing between the law enforcement and intelligence investigators. The Patriot Act thus changed FISA to permit an investigation to proceed by means of the secretive and less burdensome FISA procedure so long as a 'significant purpose' of the investigation is to gather foreign intelligence.[12] Thus, a terrorism investigation that is seeking to build a criminal case from the beginning may bypass the traditional law enforcement warrant process and attendant Fourth Amendment protections for individuals[13] through use of the FISA procedures, so long as some foreign intelligence is also sought.[14]

---

[12] Patriot Act, § 218, 115 Stat. 291.
[13] The Fourth Amendment provides: 'The right of the people to be secure in their persons, houses, papers, and effects, against unreasonable searches and seizures, shall not be violated, and no Warrants shall issue, but upon probable cause, supported by Oath or affirmation, and particularly describing the place to be searched, and the persons or things to be seized'. US Const., Am. IV.
[14] See *In re: Sealed Case*, 310 F. 3d 717 (Foreign Intelligence Surveillance Court of Review 2002).

This 'significant purpose' amendment, along with provisions in the Act to authorize broader sharing of law enforcement and intelligence information, are regularly touted as cornerstones of the investigative portion of the paradigm of prevention in the war on terrorism proclaimed by Attorney General John Ashcroft.

Detention and trial by military commission

In those same sombre weeks after September 11, the Bush Administration crafted a legal scheme for detaining and then trying suspected al Qaeda and Taliban operatives captured in the war on terrorism. Perceiving that it would have far more latitude to detain, interrogate, and decide the fate of suspected terrorists or their sympathizers or financiers if it fashioned a military-type regime for holding and trying those it then characterized as 'enemy combatants', the Bush Administration promulgated a Military Order and there claimed the authority to detain without time limit any non-citizen whom the President has 'reason to believe' is a member of al Qaeda, is involved in international terrorism, or has knowingly harboured such members or terrorists.[15] The same Order authorized trials of suspected non-citizens accused of committing 'violations of the laws of war and other applicable laws' by military commissions, outside the traditional civilian and military justice systems. By early 2002 the United States military removed several hundred persons from Afghanistan to the United States Naval Base at Guantanamo Bay, Cuba. In July 2003, the Defense Department announced that six current detainees at Guantanamo had become eligible for trial by military commission. In February 2004, the Department of Defense announced that two Guantanamo Bay detainees, one from Yemen and one from Sudan, had been charged with conspiracy to commit war crimes and that each would be tried by military commission.[16]

Several of the detainees at Guantanamo Bay and their representatives sought to petition courts in the United States for habeas corpus, on grounds that the detentions violated a range of protections in the Bill of Rights of the United States Constitution. They asked for release from custody, access to legal counsel, and freedom from interrogation. The federal statute providing for habeas corpus relief states that federal district courts may entertain habeas petitions 'within their respective jurisdictions'.[17] The government argued that detainees at Guantanamo could not sue in any federal court because

---

[15] Military Order of 13 November 2001, Detention, Treatment, and Trial of Certain Non-Citizens in the War Against Terrorism, 66 Fed. Reg. 57,833 (2001).

[16] 'First Charges Filed Against Guantanamo Detainees', http://www.defenselink.mil/releases/2004/nr20040224-0363.html.

[17] 28 U.S.C. § 2241.

no federal court can have jurisdiction where the United States is not sovereign. Lower courts reached inconsistent results on the petitions,[18] prompting the Supreme Court to grant review. Arguments were heard in April 2004, and in late June the Supreme Court held that the habeas corpus petitions could be brought in a federal court in the United States.[19] According to the Court, 'respective jurisdiction' refers to the place where the responsible detaining officials may be found. When the government holds detainees in foreign territory over which it exercises effective and permanent control but not otherwise within the jurisdiction of any federal court, a petition for habeas corpus may be brought in any federal court that has jurisdiction over the President. United States control over Guantanamo was based on an effectively permanent lease granted by Cuba in 1915. Writing in dissent for three members of the Court, Justice Scalia warned that the decision would have disastrous consequences because prisoners held by the Americans anywhere in the world under the effective 'jurisdiction and control' of the United States, including those in Iraq and Afghanistan, could take advantage of domestic laws and sue the United States in its courts.

The Administration also acted in 2002 to detain indefinitely two American citizens it labelled as enemy combatants, without charges and without access to counsel. Unable to rely for authority on the Military Order, the Administration justified the citizen detentions on the basis of the September 2001 Use of Force Resolution and on the President's authority as Commander-in-Chief. Yaser Hamdi was allegedly captured on the battlefield in Afghanistan, transferred to Guantanamo Bay, and then to a military brig in South Carolina once his United States citizenship was determined. Jose Padilla was detained as he stepped off a commercial flight in Chicago. At first Padilla was held in civilian confinement in New York City as a material witness to the September 11 attacks, but then he was declared an enemy combatant and was transferred to the same military facility as Hamdi.

On the same day it announced the ruling permitting the Guantanamo Bay detainees to sue in federal court, the Supreme Court ruled on the appeals of Yaser Hamdi and Jose Padilla. Hamdi's father brought a habeas corpus petition on his son's behalf and alleged that Hamdi was not fighting with the Taliban against the United States, but had travelled to Afghanistan as a relief worker. The government answered with an affidavit signed by a Department of Defense official that Hamdi was with a Taliban unit and had a Kalashnikov rifle in his possession when his unit surrendered to the

---

[18] See *Odah v. United States*, 321 F. 3d 1134 (D.C. Cir. 2003) (non-resident aliens cannot appeal to the protection of the Constitution or laws of the United States); *Gherebi v. Bush*, 352 F. 3d 1278 (9th Cir. 2003) (habeas corpus may be available because the detention facility at Guantanamo Bay is effectively subject to US jurisdiction and control).

[19] *Rasul v. Bush*, 124 S. Ct 2686 (2004).

Northern Alliance. Hamdi's father then asked either that his son be released or that the government substantiate its claims in support of the affidavit. Although the lower federal court agreed with Hamdi, the court of appeals ruled that the Constitution empowers the President to detain any person captured in a theatre of military operations and that no court could review the President's designation of such an enemy combatant.

The Supreme Court reversed the decision of the court of appeals and ordered new proceedings in the district court.[20] According to the controlling plurality opinion of Justice O'Connor, Congress had authorized the detention of enemy forces captured in battle in its September 2001 Use of Force Resolution. The question was not one of the President's authority then, but whether the detention of American citizens without judicial review violates the Fifth Amendment command that no 'life, liberty, or property' be taken without 'due process of law'. After balancing the competing interests of Hamdi and the government, Justice O'Connor found that the detainee 'must receive notice of the factual basis for his classification, and a fair opportunity to rebut the Government's factual assertions before a neutral decisionmaker'.[21] Hamdi has the right of access to counsel for his further proceedings and because the only legitimate purpose of detention without trial is to prevent an enemy from fighting again, the citizen may not be detained when hostilities have ended in the place he allegedly fought.

The case of Jose Padilla was more difficult for the government to defend and for the Court to decide because Padilla was not captured on a battlefield and, once detained, never presented a security danger to the United States. After he was transferred from civilian detention as a material witness in New York to the same military detention facility as Hamdi in South Carolina, his lawyer filed a habeas corpus petition in the federal court in New York, naming Secretary of Defense Rumsfeld as defendant. In contrast to the Hamdi proceedings, the district court ruled that the President has unreviewable discretion to detain enemy combatants, while the court of appeals reversed and held that the government could not detain Padilla without charging him with a crime.

The Supreme Court reversed in a 5–4 decision and held that Padilla's lawyer sued the wrong person in the wrong court.[22] Based on the majority's reading of the habeas corpus statute, Padilla had to sue his immediate custodian, the commander of the naval brig in South Carolina, in the federal court in South Carolina. Although the four dissenters accused the Court of using an unnecessarily rigid reading of the statute to effectively decide 'questions of profound importance to the nation', the Court was able to decide

---

[20] *Hamdi* v. *Rumsfeld*, 124 S. Ct 2633 (2004).   [21] Ibid.
[22] *Rumsfeld* v. *Padilla*, 124 S. Ct 2711 (2004).

Hamdi, the case with facts more favourable to the government, by mildly rebuking the government, and then duck the harder case on a technicality.

II. Changes in policy

Organizing for Homeland Security

September 11 also produced an almost immediate policy response, in the form of creating a White House Office of Homeland Security, charged 'to develop and coordinate the implementation of a comprehensive national strategy to secure the United States from terrorists' threats or attacks'.[23] Within a few months, the difficulties associated with a subordinate White House official attempting to influence the activities and spending in a range of federal agencies led the President to agree to propose that the Congress approve a new cabinet-level department with a Secretary subject to approval by the Senate. In November 2002 the Department of Homeland Security (DHS) was created,[24] in the largest restructuring of government functions and agencies since the creation of the Department of Defense in 1947. The Act merges all or part of 22 agencies and 170,000 employees into the DHS, and it charges the Department with analyzing terrorist threats, guarding borders and airports, protecting critical infrastructure, and coordinating the response to future emergencies.

After nearly two years, DHS has little to show for its efforts beyond a maddening colour-coded threat advisory scheme,[25] an ill-advised mention by DHS officials that Americans should stock up on duct tape,[26] and a massive agenda. More than $6 billion has been spent on airline security since September 11, although it is commonplace to criticize policies like those of the Transportation Safety Administration as 'fighting the last war'. The technological centrepiece of the plans for enhanced airline security – the Computer Assisted Passenger Pre-Screening or CAPPS II programme – suffered a serious setback when privacy concerns and technical problems persuaded the agency not to implement the programme and to consider other security options. The CAPPS II programme would utilize data mining

---

[23] Office of the Press Secretary, The White House, President Establishes Office of Homeland Security, 8 Oct. 2001, summarizing Exec. Order 13,228, 66 Fed. Reg. 51,812.
[24] Homeland Security Act of 2002, Pub. L. No. 107–296, 116 Stat. 2135 (2002).
[25] *See* Edward N. Luttwak, 'Damage from the Alert System is Alarming', *Los Angeles Times*, 19 Jan. 2004, B.13; Dan Eggen, 'GOP Lawmaker Urges Reform of Terror Alert System; Rep. Cox Backs Legislation That Would Mandate a More Regional Approach', *Washington Post*, 29 December 2003, A07.
[26] John Mintz, 'Terror Attack Steps Urged; Officials Suggest Water, Other Supplies,' *Washington Post*, 11 February 2003, A01; Kenneth Chang and Judith Miller, 'Threats and Responses: Protective Devices; Duct Tape and Plastic Sheeting Can Offer Solace, if not Real Security', *New York Times*, 13 February 2003, A21.

technology to scan passenger lists against a wide array of threat information and, through the high-speed screening, identify passengers who should undergo additional scrutiny before they are allowed to fly.[27] The Fourth Amendment may not protect passengers against inappropriate government mining of personal information from private databases because individuals have no reasonable expectation of privacy in information voluntarily submitted to third parties. Nonetheless, the spectre of sweeping up millions of innocent airline passengers in a data mining exercise designed to identify a few security risks caused officials to revisit the programme in search of more finely tuned measures.[28]

The Department's efforts to centralize the coordination of homeland security intelligence information have faltered due to the continuing presence of independent intelligence missions in the FBI and CIA, which are not tasked with reporting to DHS. The DHS Directorate for Information Analysis and Infrastructure Protection (IAIP) collects intelligence from agencies throughout the government, analyses it, and disseminates it for use in counterterrorism.[29] Its objective is to 'connect the dots' in ways that avoid the intelligence failures that preceded September 11. However, the Terrorist Threat Integration Center (TTIC), managed by the Director of Central Intelligence, was created by the Bush Administration in 2003 to perform largely the same tasks, although the TTIC mission extends to threats to the United States abroad.[30] Later in 2003, the President ordered the creation of a third counter-terrorism intelligence entity – the Terrorist Screening Center, administered by the FBI.[31] There is considerable overlap in function among the three agencies, and confusion within federal and state government about their roles.

One of the principal roles for DHS is to provide a systematic and unified federal response to a terrorist attack. The Department absorbed the Federal Emergency Management Agency (FEMA), along with other agencies that have specialized roles in crises. With the creation of DHS, the Department supplies centralized communications and guidance toward coordinating the work of other federal, state and local agencies. A series of Presidential

[27] Ricardo Alonso-Zaldivar, 'US Rethinks Air Travel Screening', *Los Angeles Times*, 16 July 2004.

[28] Jeremy Torobin, 'TSA Grounds Controversial Passenger-Screening System Due to Privacy Concerns', *Cong. Qtly. Daily*, 15 July 2004.

[29] Homeland Security Act of 2002, Pub. L. No. 107–296, 116 Stat. 2135 (2002), §§ 201(d); 202(b)(2).

[30] White House News Release, Fact Sheet: Strengthening Intelligence to Better Protect America, 28 January 2003.

[31] Homeland Security Presidential Directive/HSPD-6, Integration and Use of Screening Information, 16 September 2003.

directives have begun to spell out roles and missions for the important players in responding to a terrorist incident. However, to date no clear guidance has been given to make clear the specific lines of responsibility of federal, state, and local agencies and officials.[32] In addition, the effort to interdict or minimize the effects of a domestic terrorist attack with weapons of mass destruction has been complicated by the assignment of a domestic combatant command for the military, without further elaboration of its roles and missions, and by the structural difficulties posed by our federal system, where authority to respond to domestic emergencies resides primarily with the states and cities.

Pre-emption and the Iraq war

During the consideration of the new Department in Congress, the National Security Strategy of the United States and National Strategy for Homeland Security[33] were announced by President Bush, both of which emphasized the increasingly important role for the military in protecting the United States from terrorism. The National Security Strategy proclaims for the first time in the history of the United States the doctrine of pre-emption – striking terrorists before they strike.

> The United States can no longer solely rely on a reactive posture as we have in the past. The inability to deter a potential attacker, the immediacy of today's threats, and the magnitude of potential harm that could be caused by our adversaries' choice of weapons, do not permit that option. We cannot let our enemies strike first ... Traditional concepts of deterrence will not work against a terrorist enemy whose avowed tactics are wanton destruction and the targeting of innocents; whose so-called soldiers seek martyrdom in death and whose most potent protection is statelessness ... The greater the threat, the greater is the risk of inaction – and the more compelling the case for taking anticipatory action to defend ourselves, even if uncertainty remains as to the time and place of the enemy's attack. To forestall or prevent such hostile acts by our adversaries, the United States will, if necessary, act preemptively.[34]

Arguably, pre-emption is only the next step in the gradual metamorphosis of the customary doctrine of self-defence. Classically, self-defence by nations was permitted only when the need was immediate, when there was

---

[32] In February 2003, the White House published Homeland Security Presidential Directive/ HSPD-5, *Management of Local Incidents.* HSPD-5 announces the development of a *National Response Plan* (NRP). A draft plan, 30 September 2003, is available at http://www.dhs.gov/interweb/assetlibrary/Initial_NRP_100903.pdf.
[33] Both available at http://www.whitehouse.gov/homeland.   [34] Ibid., at 9–10.

no moment for deliberation.[35] Yet the speed and lethality of modern weaponry and the lack of warning associated with a covert attack render the traditional doctrine unworkable in a world of terrorists with weapons of mass destruction.[36] However, if not anchored by some standard of proof, to link the pre-emptive strike to a reasonably likely provocation, and some indication of the imminence of an attack, or the repetition of an attack that has already occurred, pre-emption as a defensive strategy against terrorism is too blunt an instrument and risks merely escalating cycles of violence.[37]

The 2003 war with Iraq is illustrative. Unlike the 1991 Gulf war, the 2003 war was not conducted with the approval of the United Nations Security Council. Although the Security Council 'deplored' Iraq's failure to disclose fully or grant United Nations inspectors unconditional access to its programmes and sites for weapons of mass destruction, and found Iraq to be in 'material breach' of its various earlier resolutions, Iraq was given one 'final opportunity to comply' in November 2002.[38] However, on 16 October 2002, Congress approved a joint resolution that authorized the President to use military force against Iraq 'as he determines to be necessary and appropriate in order ... to defend the national security interests of the United States against the continuing threat posed by Iraq'.[39] Thus, when the President launched the war in March 2003, he likely had all the domestic law authority he needed.

It was generally agreed, however, that the war was initiated by the United States in violation of international law. There was no imminent threat to the United States from Iraq in March 2003. The factual predicates for a defensive use of force – a serious, imminent, and continuing threat of a lethal attack – were simply not present. Although the congressional resolution cited such a threat and the President described Iraq in such terms in his 2003 State of the Union message, the threat was neither serious nor imminent. No weapons of mass destruction have been found in Iraq, and the Senate Select Committee on Intelligence has found that most of the information available in the October 2002 National Intelligence Estimate concerning Iraq's weapons programme was 'overstated' or 'not supported by' the underlying

---

[35] See, VI *The Works of Daniel Webster* 261 (1851), quoted in Stephen Dycus, Arthur L. Berney, William C. Banks, and Peter Raven-Hansen, *National Security Law* (New York, Aspen Publishers, 2002), at 355.

[36] Ruth Wedgwood, 'Responding to Terrorism: The Strikes Against bin Laden' (1999) *24 Yale J. Int'l L.* 559.

[37] Jules Lobel, 'The Use of Force to Respond to Terrorist Attacks: The Bombing of Sudan and Afghanistan' (1999) *24 Yale J. Int'l L.* 537.

[38] S.C. Res. 1441, U.N. Doc. S/RES/1441 (2002).

[39] Authorization for Use of Military Force Against Iraq Resolution of 2002, Pub. L. No. 107–243, 116 Stat. 1498 (2002).

intelligence.[40] In a similar vein, before the war the President also asserted ties between the government of Iraq and al Qaeda, and some members of his Administration claimed links between Saddam and September 11. After an exhaustive study, the 9/11 Commission found 'no evidence [of] a collaborative operational relationship' between Iraq and al Qaeda.[41] Still, President Bush continued to maintain that the war was justified: 'We removed a declared enemy of America who had the capability of producing weapons of mass murder and could have passed that capability to terrorists bent on acquiring them. In the world after September the 11th, that was a risk we could not afford to take.'[42] Whether the Iraq war foreshadows a longer term policy change toward pre-emptive uses of force by the United States remains to be seen.

An enhanced domestic role for the military

Fundamental changes have also been made in the organization of the military in relation to domestic security. After September 11, the military presence in the homeland increased literally overnight. The President approved orders for the Air Force to shoot down civilian airliners in the event of a hijacking, National Guard troops were deployed at the nation's airports, and more United States forces were deployed for security at the Salt Lake City Olympic Games in February 2002 than were then deployed fighting the Taliban in Afghanistan.[43]

The 30 September 2001 Qaudrennial Defense Review Report 'restores the defence of the United States as the Department's primary mission',[44] and the National Strategy for Homeland Security in July 2002 called for 'a concerted national effort to prevent terrorist attacks within the United States, reduce America's vulnerability to terrorism, and minimize the damage and recover from attacks that do occur'.[45] On 1 October 2002 a new combatant command, the United States Northern Command (NORTHCOM) became the first military entity with responsibility for military activities inside the United States since the Civil War.[46] NORTHCOM will provide support to civilian

---

[40] Report on the US Intelligence Community's Prewar Intelligence Assessments on Iraq, 9 July 2004, at 14, available at: http://intelligence.senate.gov/iraqreport2/pdf.

[41] National Commission on Terrorist Attacks Upon the United States, The 9/11 Commission Report, 335 (22 July 2004).

[42] Richard W. Stevenson and Jodi Wilgorin, 'Bush Forcefully Defends War, Citing Safety of US and World', New York Times, 11 July 2004.

[43] Gene Healy,'Deployed in the USA – The Creeping Militarization of the Home Front Policy' No. 503, The Cato Institute, 17 Dec. 2003, 1 at 5.

[44] Quoted in Operational Law Handbook (Charlottesville, VA, International and Operational Law Department, The Judge Advocate General's Legal Center and School, 2004), 355.

[45] Available at http://www.whitehouse.gov/homeland.   [46] See www.northcom.mil.

authorities for managing the consequences of natural and terrorism-related disasters, but it will also 'deter, prevent and defeat external threats against the American homeland'.[47] It remains unclear what forces will be assigned to NORTHCOM, and what roles NORTHCOM will play in homeland security. Still, a recent Judge Advocate's Corps Operations Law Handbook states that the 'role of the military in domestic operations has changed drastically'[48] since September 11. But just what *is* that military role? Will uniformed military be patrolling our streets, conducting surveillance and detaining citizens?

Among the nations of the world, the United States has been proudly unique in entrusting law enforcement to civilian forces, managed and controlled by civilians. Our federal system has helped cement control over and, thus, accountability for law enforcement activities and decisions at the lowest levels of government, closest to the operations being conducted. At the same time, our revolutionary and constitutional heritage, fed by experiences in England and with English military in the colonies, led to the creation of a sharp separation of civilian and military spheres in government, and to the unequivocal subordination of the military to civilian authority.

For more than 200 years, our laws and traditions have made military presence in the homeland exceptional. Still, the domestic use of troops has been a feature of government in this country since President Washington called out the militia to put down the Whiskey Rebellion in 1794. Since then, federal troops have been activated a number of times to help keep the peace, to aid local governments in natural disasters, and to enforce federal and state laws. State militia has been deployed even more often, especially in the first three decades of the twentieth century. Yet current concerns about the ongoing threat of terrorist attacks in the homeland, worsened by the spectre of weapons of mass destruction (WMD) threats, cause civilian authorities to consider what once would have been unthinkable – uniformed military enforcing the laws and undertaking military operations on our streets and in our neighbourhoods. To be sure, no other government entity has the training, equipment, and resources to bring force to bear when an attack occurs. Likewise, if the National Guard is counted, no other part of government is so widely dispersed to be available throughout the nation if its services are needed. But are military personnel capable of refining their role to be engaged in law enforcement at home, among the people they are charged to protect?

Express constitutional authority for such use is found in Article I, § 8, which provides, 'The Congress shall have the power ... to provide for calling forth the Militia to execute the Laws of the Union, suppress Insurrections and

---

[47] Ibid.   [48] *Operational Law Handbook*, at 355.

repel Invasions'.[49] Additional authority may be drawn from Article IV, § 4, which imposes on the federal government the obligation to protect each of the states 'against Invasion; and on Application of the Legislature, or of the Executive (when the Legislature cannot be convened) against domestic Violence'.[50] The President may also have authority to deploy troops in defence of the homeland from his Article II powers to faithfully execute the laws[51] and to act as Commander-in-Chief of the armed forces.[52] However, the Framers intended that part-time state-based militias would principally perform the homeland defence tasks. Experience with the militias has been uneven, but these small professional and state-governed forces largely sufficed except for wartime build-ups until the Cold War led to the development of a sizeable peacetime military establishment.

The most concrete manifestation of the American tradition of keeping the military out of domestic civilian affairs lies in the Posse Comitatus Act of 1878, which in its current form states:

> Whoever, except in cases and under circumstances expressly authorized by the Constitution or Act of Congress, willfully uses any part of the Army or the Air Force as a posse comitatus or otherwise to execute the laws shall be fined not more than $10,000 or imprisoned not more than two years, or both.[53]

Although the Posse Comitatus Act (PCA) supplies a general statutory prohibition against domestic use of troops to enforce the laws, the constitutional authorities of the President and a number of statutory exceptions undercut or at least counterbalance the rule. Some of the exceptions specifically apply to various forms of WMD attacks by terrorists, and, following appropriate inter-agency coordination, permit Defense Department personnel and equipment to be engaged in containing, disabling, or disposing of the weapons involved in an attack. In certain emergency circumstances, military personnel are permitted to perform law enforcement functions, where civilian authorities are not capable of taking appropriate action. Other statutes anticipate civil disorder or other emergencies and permit deployment of military units in various circumstances, certainly including in response to a terrorist attack. In addition, the President arguably may deploy military personnel to perform civilian law enforcement pursuant to his constitutional authorities.

The PCA remains as much a symbol of our nation's subordination of military to civilian control, and to the distaste for military involvement in domestic law enforcement, as it is a set of legal strictures. As conditions and threats have changed, however, so has the principle of posse comitatus. Construed literally, the PCA could compromise homeland defence or hinder a response to widespread disorder in society. Interpreted too generously, the

---

[49] US Const., Art. I, § 8, cl. 15.   [50] Ibid., Art. IV, § 4.   [51] Ibid., Art. II, § 3.
[52] Ibid., Art. II, § 2, cl. 1.   [53] 18 U.S.C. § 1385 (2000).

exceptions can give rise to regrettable excesses, such as those documented at Kent State University in 1970.[54]

III. Conclusions

> They that can give up essential liberty to obtain a little temporary safety deserve neither liberty nor safety.[55]

The rule of law in general and the United States Constitution in particular have served as societal anchors during national security crises. Our independent and life-tenured judiciary has been asked before, as it is being asked now, to uphold rule of law principles and core constitutional protections in challenges to central pieces of the post-September 11 legal regime. The Military Order and the military commissions, the Guantanamo Bay detention camp, and the detention as enemy combatants of United States citizens taken together constitute an argument for a separate track, outside the rule of law and constitutional protections, for those adjudged by the administration not to be worthy of the protections our system otherwise provides. The extent to which the Supreme Court decisions in late June 2004 are interpreted as a partial acquiescence in the separate track will establish an important cornerstone of the new normal.

Did the Court affirm or at least acquiesce in the separate track? In an apparent response to the warning voiced by Justice Scalia in the *Rasul* Guantanamo Bay cases that the ruling will open the floodgates to enemies captured in battles around the world, the Pentagon announced that it was creating a Combatant Status Review Tribunal, staffed by military officers, where detainees could challenge their combatant status. Although detainees could have the assistance of a 'personal representative' assigned by the government, they would not be entitled to a lawyer and they would have to overcome a 'rebuttable presumption in favor of the government's evidence'.[56] At least in the Pentagon's view, these proceedings comply with the

---

[54] Following President Nixon's announcement on 30 April 1970, that US combat forces had been deployed in Cambodia, student anti-war protests erupted on a number of college campuses. The Governor of Ohio called out Ohio National Guard troops equipped with loaded weapons to keep order at Kent State University. When a large group of students gathered for a rally there on 4 May, the Guard troops tried to disperse them, at one point firing into the crowd, killing four students and wounding nine others. See *Gilligan* v. *Morgan*, 413 US 1 (1973) (dismissing a suit, on political question grounds, that sought to restrain a state governor and National Guard leaders from future violations of students' rights of free speech, assembly and due process).

[55] Benjamin Franklin, Letter to Josiah Quincy, 11 Sept. 1773, John Bartlett, *Familiar Quotations* No. 3929 (10th ed., Boston, Little, Brown, 1919).

[56] Memorandum from the Deputy Secretary of Defense to the Secretary of the Navy, *Order Establishing Combatant Status Review Tribunal*, available at http://www.defenselink.mil/news/July2004/d20040707review/pdf.

rules the Supreme Court said are required for detaining citizens in the United States, and thus also satisfy any obligations to foreign detainees. According to the Supreme Court's *Rasul* decision, however, the Guantanamo detainees met the requirement of the habeas corpus statute of being in 'custody in violation of the Constitution or laws or treaties of the United States' because they are detained in territory subject to the long-term, exclusive jurisdiction and control of the United States, without access to counsel, and without being charged with any wrongdoing.[57] The Defense Department has thus sought to sustain the separate track, even in the face of apparently inconsistent commands from the Supreme Court. Additional litigation will be required to ascertain the scope of the right to counsel prescribed by the Court in *Rasul*.

Similarly, the apparent victory for Yaser Hamdi may be more symbolic than real. The neutral decision-maker prescribed by Justice O'Connor's plurality opinion in *Hamdi* could be a military commission rather than a civilian court. In addition, hearsay evidence and other evidentiary rules favourable to the government might be permitted, including the affidavit initially relied on to justify holding Hamdi, and the reversal of the normal presumption requiring Hamdi to prove that he is not an enemy combatant. Thus, Hamdi is allowed to see the evidence against him, but that may consist only of the sketchy and uncorroborated affidavit originally filed. And Hamdi has to prove that those allegations are false, even though finding witnesses to support his story under current circumstances in Afghanistan may be next to impossible. Although he must be released when the fighting there is over, the government may claim that the 'war on terrorism' is fought on many fronts simultaneously, including Afghanistan, for the foreseeable future.

Even the procedural ruling in the *Padilla* case portends an easing of the government's practical burdens in dealing with detainees in the war on terrorism. The effect of the Court's decision is to permit the government to 'forum shop' – to choose its forum by detaining persons where it can expect favourable conditions for litigation. Jose Padilla should expect less favourable outcomes from the court of appeals that includes South Carolina than the one in New York. Similarly, the government will likely either stop sending detainees to Cuba or will have such success with its Combatant Review tribunals that forum shopping will not be necessary. If the panels do not work out favourably for the government, the *Rasul* decision will afford those detainees the right to sue in any district court in the United States.

Since the November 2001 Military Order creating the military commissions for non-citizens, the Department of Defense has issued more detailed rules prescribing commission procedures. To a large extent the procedures improve the prospects for justice for those subject to trial by military

---

[57] *Rasul* v. *Bush*, 2693.

commission, although the commissions still provide considerably lesser protections for the accused than either United States civilian or regular military courts. Proceedings may be closed to outside scrutiny in the interest of 'national security', defence counsel will have their client consultations subject to government monitoring, and defence counsel may be denied access to potentially exculpatory evidence if the government asserts that it is 'necessary to protect the interests of the United States'.[58]

It remains to be seen whether the Supreme Court's decisions in June 2004 will limit significantly the government's detention and treatment of prisoners in the war on terrorism. It is as likely as not that the limited judicial role required by the *Rasul* and *Hamdi* decision will be played out as outlined here with little if any inconvenience to the government. The alternative possibility is that the due process balancing that Justice O'Connor invoked to limit the government's detention of Yaser Hamdi will be extended to other detainees, including non-citizens, and to conditions of confinement as well as the detention decision itself. The Iraqi prisoner abuse scandal first reported early in 2004 and the graphic images of torture and humiliation of prisoners by United States military and civilian personnel at Abu Ghraib prison near Baghdad has become the proverbial tip of an iceberg of detainee abuse in a range of locations around the world, including Guantanamo. In the face of shockingly candid efforts by government lawyers to construe narrowly legal proscriptions against torture (to constitute torture, 'physical pain must be equivalent in intensity to ... organ failure';[59] interrogation activities 'may be cruel, inhuman, or degrading, but still not produce pain and suffering of the requisite intensity'[60] to violate the law), ongoing investigations concerning the responsibility for abusive treatment may produce criminal charges and civil cases against those responsible. It is also possible that the due process protections applied for Yaser Hamdi could be extended to others, including non-citizens, detained and subject to coercive interrogation by United States officials.

Surely one aspect of the balancing employed by the Court in *Hamdi* – the harm to the detainee who is not in fact an enemy combatant – remains constant across citizens and non-citizens. The government's interests in *Hamdi*, preventing captured detainees from returning to the battlefield, is the same interest that produced the rules set out in the Geneva Conventions that permit tribunals to sort facts to determine which persons may be treated

---

[58] Department of Defense, *Military Commission Order No. 1* (21 March 2002).
[59] Department of Justice, Office of Legal Counsel, Memorandum for Alberto R. Gonzeles, Counsel to the President, Re: Standards of Conduct for Interrogation Under 18 U.S.C. §§ 2340–2340A, 1 Aug. 2002, at 1, available at: http://www.gwu.edu/~nsarchiv/NSAEBB127/ 02.08.01.pdf.
[60] Ibid.

as prisoners of war. In other settings, then, including those of Jose Padilla and non-citizens similarly detained, due process may require some meaningful and impartial assessment of each detainee's guilt or innocence as a combatant. The standard by which a tribunal will assess the evidence for and against the classification of a detainee as a combatant may well be the most important determinant of the outcomes of individual cases. If the 'some evidence' standard urged by the government in the *Hamdi* case is not acceptable, but the more protective 'beyond a reasonable doubt' standard of the United States criminal law is not required, fashioning the substitute standard will be of critical importance for future challenges brought by detainees.

The fifth and final annual report of the Advisory Panel to Assess Domestic Response Capabilities for Terrorism Involving Weapons of Mass Destruction (the Gilmore Commission)[61] recognized alternative visions of America's future relative to the threat of terrorism. Ranging from a version of do-nothing complacence at one extreme, to a 'fortress America' at the other extreme, the Gilmore Commission rejected the extremes and a reactive strategy in favour of what it calls 'the New Normalcy'.[62] The essence of this strategy is to plan so effectively for terrorism that the fear is dispelled. Terrorism is treated primarily as a criminal action.[63] However, while the panel opines that 'America's New Normalcy in January of 2009 should reflect . . . empowerment of individual freedoms',[64] the New Normalcy also includes sharing information and intelligence 'to the broadest possible audience rapidly' and it calls for strengthened roles for military domestically. According to the Commission, this win/win outcome may be achievable by overcoming the traditional assumption that security and civil liberties are in tension.[65] Assuming the classically conservative view that security is the most fundamental civil liberty, the Commission reminds us that our constitutional Framers chose to devolve governmental power and protect civil liberties, based on their experience that 'civil liberties and security are mutually reinforcing'.[66]

Explaining away the threat to liberty simply by defining security as the first liberty fails to confront a looming crisis in constitutional values. The Gilmore Commission views our common security as serving the inalienable rights of life, liberty, and the pursuit of happiness. While those are well and good, that list comes from the Declaration of Independence, an unenforceable prelude to the rights protections of the Constitution. The First Amendment expressive freedoms, Fourth Amendment privacy, and Fifth and Fourteenth Amendment due process and equal protection are enforceable rights, and steps taken by government to enhance our security must not violate those protections. To be sure, terrorism can threaten the most fundamental

---

[61] Available at http://www.rand.org.   [62] Ibid., at 13.   [63] Ibid.   [64] Ibid., at iv.
[65] Ibid., at 22.   [66] Ibid.

liberty – the right to life, and government must be afforded considerable discretion to take measures reasonably determined to protect our lives. At the same time, measures taken in furtherance of security must be assessed, like other laws, in light of their effects on other fundamental protected liberties.

To its credit, the Gilmore Commission acknowledges that broadening investigative and law enforcement powers in the service of security have the potential to chill freedom of speech and to invade personal privacy. The Commission also recognizes the dangers to liberty implicit in expanding a military presence domestically, and it recommends creation of an independent civil liberties oversight board to advise Congress and the President concerning changes to legal rules for fighting terrorism that are likely to have civil liberties implications, whether or not intended.[67]

Against the backdrop of the war on terrorism and the war against Iraq, President Bush has made reauthorization of the Patriot Act and removal or extension of its sunset provisions a regular theme in his campaign. President Bush made his Patriot Act appeal in Buffalo, New York, where the so-called Lackawanna Six were arrested and convicted last year for providing 'material support' to terrorism.[68] The President claimed that successes in the war on terrorism like that represented by the Lackawanna Six could not have occurred without the Patriot Act and its expanded investigative authorities. Although it is true that the above described amendments to FISA in the Patriot Act made it easier for investigators to obtain secret orders to listen in on the suspects' phone and email conversations, the break that made local investigators aware of these Yemeni-Americans came in the old fashioned way – from an anonymous letter left at a local FBI office. The 'material support' crime that carries such lengthy prison sentences that the six indicted suspects each took guilty pleas in return for slightly lesser prison sentences was not part of the Patriot Act, and was enacted in 1996, after the first World Trade Center and Oklahoma City bombings. Ironically, the Patriot Act amendment to 'material support', adding a crime for 'expert advice or assistance', was struck down as unconstitutional by a California federal court in January 2004, based on the court's conclusion that the prohibition was unconstitutionally vague.[69] Similarly, a material support prosecution of a Saudi student in Idaho for maintaining a website that urges '*jihad*' against the

---

[67] Ibid., at 23.

[68] Matthew Purdy and Lowell Bergman, 'Where the Trail Led: Between Evidence and Suspicion; Unclear Danger: Inside the Lackawanna Terror Case', *New York Times*, 12 October 2003, sec. 1, 1.

[69] *Humanitarian Law Project* v. *Ashcroft*, 2004 WL 112760 (C.D. Cal. 22 Jan. 2004); see also Timothy Egan, 'Computer Student on Trial Over Muslim Web Site Work: Case Hinges on Use of Antiterrorism Law', *New York Times*, 27 April 2004, A16.

United States failed when a jury acquitted the student, finding insufficient evidence that the student intended to aid al Qaeda.[70]

Just as measures to enhance investigative authorities may have compromised civil liberties, the doctrine of pre-emption is potentially a recipe for disaster. If every nation practised military pre-emption of its enemies, war would become the norm across much of the globe. The United States war on Iraq is merely an example of how misguided the application of the doctrine of pre-emption can be. The continuing insurgency in Iraq and the resurgence of the Taliban in Afghanistan suggest that the military response may inspire more terrorists while it disrupts others. Continuing rumblings about the threat to the United States posed by nuclear weapons programmes in Iran and North Korea render the possibility of further pre-emptive military action more than merely hypothetical. The fact that Congress asked so few questions about the evidence to back up the Administration's claims and then voted such a sweeping authorization for war against Iraq in October 2002 does not reflect positively on the Congress. The fact that the pre-emption approach permits a sort of shoot first, talk later approach is all the more reason to consider alternative schemes for responding to the threats of terrorism.

Similarly, the merging of national security and law enforcement spheres of governance in the United States is serving to inculcate in the citizenry the idea that emergency conditions that arose on September 11 have become routine, and that adding the national security emblem to terrorism-related law enforcement renders extraordinary measures legitimate. Unlike emergencies with a known duration, the unknowable boundaries of the war on terrorism supply licence to institutionalize these changes in governance. We all should pause before making that commitment.

---

[70] Patrick Orr, 'Sami Al-Hussayen Not Guilty of Aiding Terrorist Groups', *Idaho Statesman*, 11 June 2004.

23

Canada's response to terrorism

KENT ROACH

Canada's response to terrorism has been dramatically affected by 9/11. Canadians died in the horrific attacks on the World Trade Center, but so did the citizens of many other countries. What was unique about Canada's response to 9/11 was the border it shares with the United States. The border meant that Canada felt the repercussions of the swift American response to the attacks in an immediate and profound manner. For example, when the United States closed its air space that terrible day, it was Canada that accepted over 200 airplanes destined for the United States, including one plane that was erroneously believed to have been hijacked. Canada also was affected by erroneous claims that some of the terrorists had entered the United States through Canada, as indeed had occurred before and may likely occur again given the millions who cross the border each day.[1] Canada was also singled out in the USA Patriot Act[2] which contained a whole section entitled 'Defending the Northern Border' providing for increased border guards and scrutiny of those entering the United States. Important components of Canada's anti-terrorism and immigration policies have been established in border agreements with the United States. Canada has drafted broad new anti-terrorism laws and developed a new public safety department of government with an eye to American perceptions that Canada might provide a safe haven for terrorists.

Canada was not immune from terrorism before 9/11. In response to kidnappings by two cells of the Front de Liberation du Québec in 1970 (known as the 1970 October crisis), it invoked extraordinary emergency

---

[1] See my *September 11: Consequences for Canada* (Montreal, McGill-Queens University Press, 2003), ch. 1 for a fuller account of the dramatic consequences of the September 11 terrorist attacks for Canada.

[2] Uniting and Strengthening America by Providing Appropriate Tools to Intercept and Obstruct Terrorism (USA Patriot Act) Act of 2001 H. R. 3162 Title 4 Subsection A 'Protecting the Northern Border'. Even while recognizing that 500 million people cross its borders every year, the 9/11 Commission has more recently recommended increased border controls that would require Canadians and Americans alike to be subject to biometric identification at the border: The National Commission on Terrorist Attacks Upon the United States, *The 9/11 Commission Report* (New York, St Martins, 2004), at 12.4.

powers to declare that organization to be illegal and to detain suspected supporters and associates of that organization without ordinary legal safeguards. It is also prosecuting under the regular criminal law two men accused of participating in the 1985 bombing of an Air India aircraft, an event that killed 329 people in one of the world's most deadly acts of terrorism before 9/11. In the first part of this chapter I examine Canada's new Anti-Terrorism Act (ATA) that was quickly enacted in the months after September 11 and compare it to Canada's previous response to terrorism. I focus on the breadth of the definition of terrorism in the new law, its reliance on executive proscription of groups, its authorization of novel investigative powers and its status as permanent legislation. I also note that with a few exceptions, the new law has not been used.

One of the reasons why Canada's new anti-terrorism law has largely sat on the shelf is that Canadian authorities have focused on using immigration law as a means to detain suspected international terrorists. Although the ATA departs from some traditional criminal law principles, it still has requirements such as proof beyond a reasonable doubt of a prohibited act with fault, a three-day limit on preventive arrest and the ability of trial judges to stay proceedings if secret evidence will result in an unfair trial. In contrast, the administrative law apparatus of the Immigration and Refugee Protection Act[3] (IRPA) allows preventive detention and the removal of non-citizens on the basis of secret evidence not disclosed to the deportee. In the second part of this chapter, I examine how Canada's immigration law has been used to detain and deport suspected terrorists in a manner that challenges due process and equality values. I also examine how Canada's immigration policy with respect to refugees has been influenced by anti-terrorism concerns and relations with the United States.

In the last part of the chapter, I examine the likely effectiveness of Canadian anti-terrorism law and policy and a new and promising direction in Canada's approach to security. In late 2003–2004 Canada created a new Department for Public Safety and Emergency Preparedness and articulated a national security policy that has the potential to facilitate a more rational and effective approach not only to the risks of terrorism, but other harms relating to disease, nuclear and chemical accidents and the safety of food and water. It also finally enacted the Public Safety Act[4] which features administrative regulations designed to secure sites and substances vulnerable to terrorism. These new elements of Canada's security policy have the potential to be more effective than reliance on the criminal law and immigration law and may present less of a threat to due process and equality values.

---

[3] S. C. 2001 c.27.   [4] S. C. 2004 c.15.

I. The criminal law response: Canada's new Anti-Terrorism Act

Barely a month after 9/11, the federal government introduced a massive anti-terrorism bill that for the first time created and defined crimes of terrorism under Canada's Criminal Code. The bill's definition of terrorism was clearly inspired by the United Kingdom's Terrorism Act 2000 in requiring proof of religious, ideological or political motive and the commission of a broad range of harms that went well beyond violence against civilians. In some respects the Canadian bill was even broader. As first introduced, it would have defined as acts of terrorism politically motivated acts that intentionally caused a serious disruption of any public or private essential service. Such acts had to be designed to intimidate a segment of the public with regard to its security, but this could include its 'economic security'. Alternatively they had to be designed to compel a government, an international organization or any person to act. The only exemption from this sweeping prohibition was for '*lawful* advocacy, protest, dissent or stoppage of work'. This broad definition of terrorism inspired wide-spread concerns among many civil society groups that the Act would brand many illegal protests and strikes as terrorism.[5] This concern led to amendments before the bill became law that dropped the requirement that exempted protests must be lawful and provided that the expression of religious, political or ideological thought or opinions would not normally be considered terrorism.[6]

Although the amendments narrowed the definition of terrorism, the remaining definition of terrorism is still much broader than the functional definition of terrorism that was used during the 1970 October crisis. In 1970, groups that advocated 'the use of force or the commission of crime as a means of or as an aid in accomplishing governmental change within Canada' were declared to be unlawful associations under emergency regulations.[7] Another important difference was that the ATA was enacted as permanent legislation as opposed to the emergency orders of the October crisis. In response to criticisms, the bill was amended to require a Parliamentary review of its

---

[5] For essays largely critical of the proposed bill and this aspect of the definition of terrorism in particular, see R. Daniels, P. Macklem and K. Roach, *The Security of Freedom: Essays on Canada's Anti-Terrorism Bill* (University of Toronto Press, 2001). See also 'Special Issue' (2003) 14 *National Journal of Constitutional Law* 1ff. For an account of how various groups including unions, churches, charities, Muslim groups and Aboriginal people criticized the bill and the impact these criticisms made on the legislative process see Roach, *Consequences for Canada*, ch. 3.

[6] Section 83.01(1.1) of the Criminal Code provides: 'For greater certainty, the expression of a political, religious or ideological thought, belief or opinion does not come within paragraph (b) of the definition "terrorist activity" in subsection 1 unless it constitutes an act or omission that satisfies the criteria of that paragraph.'

[7] Public Order Regulations 1970 SOR/70–444 s. 3.

provisions and operations to commence late in 2004. Two of its most controversial provisions relating to preventive arrest and investigative hearings
were also subject to a renewable sunset after five years. Nevertheless the
permanent nature of the Act increases the risks that investigative and trial
powers introduced to combat terrorism will eventually spread to other parts
of the criminal law. The distinction between the broad definition of terrorism
and phenomena such as organized crime can be an illusive one.[8] The fact that
the legislation was designed as permanent legislation to be consistent with
the Canadian Charter of Rights and Freedoms and did not require any
emergency derogation from protected rights may also make it more likely
that new powers in the ATA may eventually be extended to apply to other
serious crimes.

The ATA was built on the premise that the ordinary criminal law was
inadequate to deal with the threat of terrorism after 11 September 2001. Both
with respect to the murder of a cabinet minister during the 1970 October
crisis and the bombing of Air India, Canada relied on the ordinary criminal
law which prohibited participation in crimes such as murders and bombings,
as well as conspiracies and attempts to commit such crimes. The ordinary
criminal law functioned under the traditional principle that motive was not
relevant and that a political or religious motive could not excuse the crime. In
contrast, the ATA requires proof that terrorist crimes were committed for
religious or political motives. Although this was defended as a means to
restrict the ambit of crimes of terrorism, it also requires the religion and
politics of terrorist suspects to be investigated by the police and to become a
central issue in any terrorist trials.

The ATA was defended as a necessary means to prevent terrorism. It
criminalized a broad array of activities in advance of the actual commission
of a terrorist act, including the provision of finances, property and other
forms of assistance to terrorist groups, participation in the activities of a
terrorist group, and instructing the carrying out of activities for terrorist
groups. There is not always a requirement of a proximate nexus to any
planned act of terrorism. In addition, offences under the former Official
Secrets Act were extended to apply to giving information to terrorist groups
and foreign governments.[9] The financing provisions of the ATA were
required to implement Canada's obligations under the 1999 Convention for
the Suppression of the Financing of Terrorism, but in my view the non-
financing offences relating to participation, preparation and harbouring
terrorists were not required to apprehend and punish those such as the
September 11 terrorists. The problem on September 11 was intelligence

---

[8] Andrew Ashworth, *Human Rights, Serious Crime and Criminal Procedure* (London, Sweet
and Maxwell, 2002), at 30, 95.
[9] Security of Information Act R. S. 1985 c.0–5 as amended by S. C. 2001 c.41 s. 25

gathering and coordination and the enforcement of the criminal law and not the ambit of the criminal law.[10] This raises the dilemma that much of the uncertain contours of the new criminal law against terrorism may be either cosmetic or overbroad. On one reading, the new terrorism offences may only duplicate existing provisions concerning inchoate crimes and participation in crime. If they go beyond the existing provisions, however, concerns about the extent of the criminal law and in particular guilt by association and status based crimes can be raised.

Another important feature of the ATA is that it applies to a broad range of acts committed inside or outside of Canada. This was done to make clear that Canada was implementing various international conventions concerning specific forms of terrorism. The extra-territorial application of the new terrorism laws also builds on precedents relating to war crimes and aircraft hijackings. People can be prosecuted in Canada for sending financial and other support to struggles fought in foreign lands. In noting the difficulty of defining terrorism, the Supreme Court of Canada has noted that 'Nelson Mandela's African National Congress was, during the apartheid era, routinely labeled as a terrorist organization, not only by the South African government but by much of the international community'.[11] The only exemptions from the scope of international terrorism targeted by the law are for armed conflict conducted according to customary or conventional international law or the official activities of a state military force 'to the extent that those activities are governed by other rules of international law'.[12] This would not necessarily apply to all resistance efforts against repressive regimes. Difficult issues may emerge should people in Canada be charged with sending financial or other forms of support to liberation struggles in foreign lands.

The first and so far only charges under the ATA were laid by the Royal Canadian Mounted Police (RCMP) on 31 March 2004. Charges of knowingly participating in the activities of a terrorist group and facilitating a terrorist activity were laid against Mohammad Momin Khawaja.[13] The Canadian-born

---

[10] Kent Roach, 'The Dangers of a Charter-Proof and Crime-Based Response to Terrorism' and 'The New Terrorism Offences and Criminal Law' in Daniels et al. (eds.), *Security of Freedom*. See also Michael Ignatieff, *The Lesser Evil: Political Ethics in an Age of Terror* (Toronto, Penguin, 2004), at 51. For arguments that the new offences were required, see Richard Mosley, 'Preventing Terrorism: Bill C-36, The Anti-terrorism Act' in D. Daubney et al. (eds.), *Terrorism, Law and Democracy: How is Canada Changing After September 11* (Montreal, Les Editions Themis, 2002).

[11] *Suresh v. Canada* [2002] 1 S.C.R. 3 at para 95.   [12] ATA s. 83.01(1)(b).

[13] The participation offence provides: 'Everyone who knowingly facilitates in or contributes to, directly or indirectly, any activity of a terrorist group for the purpose of enhancing the ability of any terrorist group to facilitate or carry out a terrorist activity is guilty of an indictable offence and liable to imprisonment for a term not exceeding ten years' (Criminal Code, s. 83.18). The facilitation offence provides: 'Everyone who knowingly

citizen is alleged to have participated in the activities of a terrorist group and facilitated terrorist activity in and around Ottawa, Canada and London, England in late 2003 and early 2004. Officials have linked his arrest with nine men in the London area and the seizure of a large amount of ammonium nitrate stored near Heathrow Airport. Some subsequent reports have suggested that charges against Mr Khawaja might not have been possible without the ATA. If true, this suggests that something short of a conspiracy to bomb may be the basis for the charge.[14] The fact that Mr Khawaja is a Canadian citizen precluded the use of the IRPA against him.

Like the emergency regulations enacted during the October crisis, as well as the use of terrorist lists by the United Nations, a central feature of the ATA is the ability of the cabinet of elected ministers to designate groups and even persons as terrorists.[15] So far 38 groups have been listed. Executive designation of a group as terrorist is designed to be conclusive proof in a criminal trial that the group is in fact a terrorist group.[16] Over 450 groups and individuals have been listed as terrorists under regulations enacted under the United Nations Act.[17] These lists are distributed to financial institutions and within government. Executive designation of terrorist groups and individuals is a common feature of many international and national anti-terrorism schemes. Nevertheless, it can be criticized as a challenge to judicial powers to decide in a particular case who is a terrorist. A person or group listed as terrorist receives no prior notice of the listing decision and a limited right of judicial review after the decision has been made. In Canada, at least one person, Liban Hussein, was wrongfully listed as a terrorist, an error that was corrected by the government after more than six months.[18]

There is a limited form of *ex post* judicial review of whether the Cabinet's listing decision was reasonable, but it is unlikely that such reviews would be

facilitates a terrorist activity is guilty of an indictable offence and liable to imprisonment for a term not exceeding fourteen years' (s. 83.19). The definition of a terrorist activity includes attempts, conspiracies, counselling and threats to commit a terrorist activity. The RCMP stresses that their focus is on individuals, not Canada's large Muslim community. 'RCMP lay terrorist charges' *Globe and Mail*, 31 March 2004; 'Ottawa man's arrest tied to terror raids in Britain' *Globe and Mail*, 3 April 2004.

[14] Five people in the United Kingdom have been charged with conspiracy to cause an explosion likely to endanger life or cause serious injury to property, an offence punishable by up to life imprisonment. 'British court hears of potential bomb targets' *Globe and Mail*, 17 April 2004.

[15] Criminal Code s. 83.05.

[16] But for an argument that this would violate the presumption of innocence, see David Paciocco 'Constitutional Casualties of September 11' (2002) 16 *Supreme Court Law Rev.* (2d) 199.

[17] United Nations Suppression of Terrorism Regs. SOR 2001–360 2 Oct 2001.

[18] E. Alexandra Dosman, 'For the Record: Designating "Listed Entities" For the Purposes of Terrorist Financing Offences at Canadian Law' (2004) 62 *University of Toronto Faculty Law Review* 1 at 15–19.

successful or remove the stigma of being officially listed as a terrorist. The procedure for judicial review is also open to criticism. Hearings can be closed and the group challenging the listing can be denied access to evidence before the judge because of national security concerns. In cases of intelligence received from other governments or international organizations, the applicant can be denied access to even a summary of evidence.[19] In a case decided after September 11 in a non-terrorist context, the Supreme Court of Canada emphasized the importance for Canada of assuring foreign governments that their intelligence will be kept secret because Canada relies heavily on such intelligence.[20]

The listing decision is in part designed to encourage financial institutions and individuals to refuse to associate with the listed person or group. The state effectively encourages third parties such as banks and landlords to impose their own sanctions on those listed as terrorists. Section 83.08(2) of the ATA encourages such actions by exempting from civil liability those who refuse to deal with property provided that they took 'all reasonable steps to satisfy themselves that the relevant property was owned or controlled by or on behalf of a terrorist group'. Section 83.1 requires all Canadians to report information about a transaction with terrorist property and provides that no 'criminal or civil proceedings lie against a person for [such] disclosure[s] made in good faith'. The Proceeds of Crime (Money Laundering) and Terrorist Financing Act[21] also requires reporting about money or property if there are suspicions of a terrorist connection. All of these financing provisions depart from the traditional criminal law model by conscripting non-state third parties in the state's anti-terrorism efforts. About two million reports about financial transactions are made each year and in the last nine months in 2003, twenty-nine cases involving $35 million were identified for investigation into terrorist financing.[22]

Another important feature of the ATA was its expansion of police powers. One provision provides for preventive arrest when there are reasonable grounds to believe that a terrorist activity will be carried out and reasonable suspicion to believe that detention or the imposition of conditions is necessary to prevent the carrying out of the terrorist activity. The period of preventive arrest under the Canadian law is limited to seventy-two hours. At the same time, the effects of a preventive arrest can last much longer. The suspect can be required by a judge to enter into a recognizance or peace bond for up to a year with breach of the bond being punishable by up to two years' imprisonment and a refusal to agree to a peace bond punishable by a year's imprisonment.[23] Governments are required to prepare reports on the use of the measure and in the first three years of the act, no preventive arrests were made. This may represent restraint on the part of

---

[19] ATA s. 83.05(6)(a), 83.06.   [20] *Ruby* v. *Canada* [2002] 4 S.C.R. 3 at para 44.
[21] S. C. 2000 c.17 as amended by S. C. 2001 c.41.
[22] '$35M funnelled to terror groups' *Toronto Star*, 29 March 2004.   [23] ATA s. 83.3.

Canadian police, a preference for keeping terrorist suspects under surveillance or difficulties identifying terrorist suspects.

A second new investigative power is a power to compel a person to answer questions relating to terrorist activities. The subject cannot refuse to answer on the grounds of self-incrimination, but the compelled statements and evidence derived from them cannot be used in subsequent proceedings against the person compelled. There is also judicial supervision of the questions and a right to counsel. An attempt was made to use the investigative hearing provision during the Air India trial. They were held to be procedural provisions that, as opposed to the new offences, can be applied to crimes committed before the enactment of the ATA. An initial hearing was held in secret without notice to the media or to the accused in the Air India trial. The person compelled to testify challenged the constitutionality of the procedure. In *Application under s. 83.28*[24] the Supreme Court upheld the constitutionality of this novel procedure in a 6:3 decision. Iacobucci and Arbour JJ held for the majority that the procedure did not violate Section 7 of the Charter given protections that compelled evidence or evidence derived from that evidence could not be used against the person in subsequent criminal prosecutions with the exception of those for perjury. They added that the Charter would prevent the use of an investigative hearing if the predominant purpose was to determine penal liability and would prevent the use of compelled testimony and evidence in subsequent extradition and deportation proceedings even though this was not specifically provided for in the impugned statute.[25] The Court's extension of immunity to deportation and extradition hearings add protections that are especially important in the context of international terrorism.

Two judges dissented on the basis that investigative hearings violated the institutional independence of the judiciary by requiring judges to preside over police investigations[26] and they, along with a third judge, dissented on the basis that the use of an investigative hearing in the middle of the Air India trial constituted an abuse of process because it was an attempt by the prosecution to gain an unfair advantage. The Court held that the presumption in favour of open courts applied to the conduct of investigative hearings as opposed to the application for an investigative hearing which would be held in private. Two judges dissented on the basis that such a presumption 'would normally defeat the purpose of the proceedings by rendering them ineffective as an investigative tool' and would harm the rights of third parties and the administration of justice.[27]

---

[24] [2004] 2 S.C.R. 248.   [25] Ibid. at para 78–9.   [26] Ibid. at para 180.

[27] The Court added the caveat that it may very well be that by necessity 'large parts of judicial investigative hearings' and 'the very existence of these hearings' might at times have to be kept secret and it was too early to tell how many hearings there would be and what form they would take' (*Re Vancouver Sun* [2004] 2 S.C.R. 332, at paras 41, 60).

Even though upheld as constitutional and subject to a rebuttable presumption of openness and active participation by judges and counsel representing the individual, investigative hearings represent an undesirable incursion on the adversarial traditions of criminal justice and one that could spread in an attempt to combat other serious crimes. It is also questionable whether investigative hearings are necessary or will be effective. Authorities already have the power to offer people associated with terrorists incentives to cooperate such as reductions of possible charges and witness protection.[28] The law assumes that an uncooperative person will suddenly cooperate and tell the truth simply because they are threatened with contempt of court or a prosecution for refusing to cooperate at an investigative hearing. This questionable assumption poses a dilemma that runs throughout anti-terrorism law. On the one hand, the law may be too tough should it be applied against those who are not determined terrorists but who may innocently associate with terrorist suspects, and against those who belong or associate with radical religious or political organizations. On the other hand, the law may not be tough enough to deter or stop committed terrorists prepared to die for their cause. In the third part of this chapter, I suggest that a necessary strategy with respect to determined terrorists is to attempt to deny them access to the substances and sites that are particularly vulnerable to terrorism.

The prior consent of a provincial or federal Attorney General is required before prosecutions for terrorism offences are commenced or the new powers of preventive arrest or investigative hearings are used.[29] Although this requirement may prevent some unjustified uses of the ATA, it is nevertheless significant that the Act will be administered by police officers throughout Canada. The McDonald Commission concluded that the Royal Canadian Mounted Police (RCMP) had engaged in illegalities and had trouble distinguishing radical dissent from terrorism in the wake of the 1970 October crisis.[30] In 1984, Canada created a new civilian security intelligence agency that was subject to a special watchdog with broad powers not only to respond to complaints, but to audit the activities of the agency to ensure that it did not stray beyond its legitimate mandate or engage in unlawful activities.[31] The commissioner to hear complaints against the RCMP has expressed concerns

---

[28] Two people based in Canada with reported links to al Qaeda, Ahmed Ressam and Mohammed Jabarah, are now in American custody and said to be cooperating with American authorities. See Stewart Bell, *Cold Terror* (Toronto, Wiley, 2004).

[29] ATA s. 83.24, 83.28(3), 83.3(1). The Security Offences Act RSC 1985 c.S-7 allows the federal Attorney General and the federal police to pre-empt provincial authorities with respect to offences involving threats to national security.

[30] Commission of Inquiry Concerning Certain Activities of the Royal Canadian Mounted Police, *Second and Third Reports* (Ottawa, Queens Printer, 1981).

[31] Canadian Security Intelligence Service Act R. S. 1985 c. C-23. A different review body oversees the legality of the actions of the Communications Security Establishment which

that she has not been given additional resources and powers to deal with the new mandate of the RCMP to administer the ATA.[32] Another complicating factor is that police were given expanded powers in 2001 to commit acts that would otherwise be crimes provided that they are authorized by senior police officers.[33] The Canadian government has announced its intention to create 'an independent arms' length review mechanism for the RCMP's activities with respect to national security' and has given a public inquiry a mandate to recommend such a scheme. These are welcome commitments, but at present the RCMP remains subject to less extensive review than Canada's civilian security intelligence agency.

The ATA included a new offence of hate motivated mischief against religious property and expanded powers to remove hate literature from the Internet. These provisions were defended on the basis of the connection between racial and religious hatred and terrorism. Although the government was prepared to proclaim its commitment to the anti-discrimination principle when it extended the criminal law, it was not prepared to introduce an anti-discrimination clause in the ATA that would bind state officials.[34] Such a clause might provide symbolic reassurance to those in Canada's multicultural community who have expressed concerns that they will be subject to heightened scrutiny because they may have the same origins and religion as some terrorists. Concerns have been raised about over-inclusive targeting of people by officials or financial institutions because of factors such as an Arabic name. The remedies available for discriminatory profiling of an innocent person are very limited.[35] It will be interesting to see if such a clause is added as part of a comprehensive review of the provisions and operation of the ATA by a Parliamentary committee, a process that must be completed by the end of 2005.[36] At the same time, however, an anti-discrimination clause by itself will not be self-executing and concerns about how the new law is

---

can intercept private communications from foreign sources without judicial authorization. National Defence Act Part VI as amended by S. C. 2001 c.41.

[32] Shirley Heafey 'Civilian Oversight in a Changed World' and A. Borovoy 'Watching the Watchers: Democratic Oversight' in Daubney et al. (eds.), *Terrorism, Law and Democracy.*

[33] Criminal Code s. 25.1.

[34] Those who advocated such a clause included Irwin Cotler, a noted human rights lawyer subsequently appointed as Canada's Minister of Justice. See his 'Thinking Outside the Box: Foundational Principles for a Counter-Terrorism Law and Policy' in Daniels et al. (eds.), *Security of Freedom.*

[35] Sujit Choudhry and Kent Roach, 'Racial and Ethnic Profiling: Statutory Discretion, Constitutional Remedies and Democratic Accountability' (2003) 41 *Osgoode Hall L. J.* 1; Reem Bahdi, 'No Exit: Racial Profiling and Canada's War Against Terrorism' (2003) 41 *Osgoode Hall L. J.* 293.

[36] ATA s. 145.

administered remain high, especially in Canada's Arab and Muslim communities.[37]

II. Immigration as the focus of Canada's anti-terrorism efforts

Although most of the post-9/11 debate has focused on the ATA, it is Canada's immigration laws under the Immigration and Refugee Protection Act (IRPA) that have been used most frequently against suspected terrorists. In some respects this follows patterns of reliance on immigration laws in both the United States[38] and the United Kingdom. Immigration law has been attractive to the authorities because it allows procedural shortcuts and a degree of secrecy that would not be tolerated under even an expanded criminal law.

A. Grounds of exclusion

Under the IRPA 'engaging in terrorism' or 'being a member of an organization that there are reasonable grounds to believe engages, has engaged or will engage' in acts of terrorism are grounds to make a non-citizen inadmissible to Canada for security reasons.[39] Terrorism is not, however, defined under IRPA. In the 2002 case of *Suresh v. Canada*, the Supreme Court implicitly rejected the broad definition of terrorism found in the ATA and used by lower courts. The Court defined terrorism for the purpose of immigration law as any 'act intended to cause death or serious injury to a civilian, or to any person not taking an active part in the hostilities in a situation of armed conflict, when the purpose of such act by its nature or context is to intimidate a population or to compel a government or an international organization to do or abstain from doing any act'. The Court described this definition of terrorism, taken in part from the 1999 International Convention on the Suppression of the Financing of Terrorism, as 'the essence of what the world understands by "terrorism"'.[40] The Court adopted this definition of

---

[37] As part of a new national security policy, the government has established an advisory cross-cultural round-table on security. Canada, *Securing an Open Society: Canada's National Security Policy*, April 2004, at 2.

[38] The United States' extraordinary rendition of Canadian citizen Maher Arar to Syria via Jordan is the focus of a major public inquiry in Canada headed by a respected judge. Arar, who was returning to Canada via New York, was detained in the United States, transported to Syria where he was detained for almost a year before being released. The inquiry will examine the role of Canadian officials in this matter. Neither Syria nor the United States will participate. The inquiry also has a mandate to make recommendations about an arm's-length review mechanism for the national security activities of the RCMP. See www.ararcommission.ca.

[39] Immigration and Refugee Protection Act S. C. 2001 c.27 s. 34.

[40] *Suresh v. Canada*, [2002] 1 S.C.R. 3 at para 98.

terrorism in the course of rejecting challenges that the law was unconstitutionally vague and unjustifiably restricted freedom of expression and freedom
of association. It also left open the possibility that Parliament might chose to
alter its definition of terrorism, perhaps by bringing the broader ATA definition into immigration law.

The fact that at present terrorism is defined more narrowly in IRPA than
in the ATA has not, however, limited the utility of immigration law as
anti-terrorism law. One reason may be that an alternative ground for the
declaration of inadmissibility is that of 'a danger to the security of Canada'.
The Supreme Court has indicated that after September 11 this term must be
interpreted broadly and is not limited to direct threats to Canada.[41]Another
reason is that detention or removal under IRPA can be achieved without the
need to prove beyond a reasonable doubt that a person has committed a
crime. Although the ATA stops short of making membership in a terrorist
group a crime, Section 34 of the IRPA allows a non-citizen to be declared
inadmissible on security grounds for being a member of an organization that
there are reasonable grounds to believe either engages, has engaged or will
engage in terrorism.[42] In addition, membership in a terrorist organization
can be proven under Canadian immigration law on the basis of a bona fide
belief in a serious possibility based on credible evidence.[43] This standard is
less onerous for the government than even the civil standard of proof on a
balance of probabilities, let alone the criminal law standard of proof beyond a
reasonable doubt.

B. Investigative detention

Procedures used under Canadian immigration law for preventive or investigative detention are more draconian than those available under the ATA. As
discussed above, the ATA provides for preventive arrest for a seventy-two

---

[41] The Court stated that 'it may once have made sense to suggest that terrorism in one
country did not necessarily implicate other countries. But after the year 2001, that
approach is no longer valid' (*Suresh*, at para 87). The Court went on to stress the global
nature of terrorism and Canada's interest in international cooperation. It also stated that
'preventive or precautionary state action may be justified; not only an immediate threat
but also possible future risks must be considered' (at para 88).

[42] IRPA s. 34(1)(f) provides that: 'A permanent resident or a foreign national is inadmissible
on security grounds for ... being a member of an organization that there are reasonable
grounds to believe engages, has engaged or will engage in acts ... [of] terrorism'. The
Supreme Court of Canada has read down this provision to allow a refugee applicant
'to establish that his or her continued residence in Canada will not be detrimental to
Canada, notwithstanding proof that the person is associated with or a member of a
terrorist organization. This permits a refugee to establish that the alleged association
with the terrorist group was innocent' (*Suresh* at para 110).

[43] *Chiau* v. *Canada* [2001] 2 F. C. 207 (C. A.). See also IRPA s. 33.

hour period, but with the possibility of peace bonds being imposed for a longer period. In contrast, the IRPA authorizes a much broader form of preventive detention on reasonable grounds that a non-citizen, including a permanent resident, is inadmissible and a danger to the public. As under the ATA, there would be review within forty-eight hours, but not by a judge but an official within the Immigration Division. Continued detention can be authorized on the basis that 'the Minister is taking necessary steps to inquire into a reasonable suspicion that they are inadmissible on grounds of security or for violating human or international rights'.[44] This is a form of investigative detention not contemplated under the ATA. There is no limit on this period of detention, but the reasons for the detention must be reviewed every thirty days.[45]

The above powers of investigative detention were used in August 2003 in Canada with respect to twenty-one non-citizens from Pakistan who were arrested for typical Immigration Act violations relating to misleading statements and a fraudulent school being used as a means to obtain student visas. Nevertheless, the arrests were headline news in Canada largely because of a sensational 'backgrounder' prepared by a Public Service and Anti-Terrorism Unit, composed of Mounties and immigration officials. The news release stated that the young men were: 'from, or have connections to, the Punjab province in Pakistan that is noted for Sunni extremism ... They appear to reside in clusters of 4 or 5 young males and appear to change residences in clusters and/or interchange addresses with other clusters ... All targets were in Canada prior to 5 September 2001 .... A confirmed associate of the group ... provided an offer of employment from Global Relief Foundation ... [which] has been identified by the United Nations as a fundraising group that provides financial support to terrorist groups, including Al Qaeda ... One of the targeted apartments is reported to have aeroplane schematics posted on the wall, as well as pictures of guns'. And then the allegation that was the lead in the newspapers: 'One of the subjects is currently enrolled in flight school to qualify as a multi-engine commercial pilot. His flight path for training purposes flies over the Pickering Nuclear Plant.'[46]

Not surprisingly given the dramatic nature of this extraordinary press release, the initial detention of nineteen men (the same number involved in the September 11 attacks) was highly publicized and initially raised many security concerns. The men were entitled to prompt administrative hearings, but most of them were detained under Section 58(1)(c) of IRPA on the grounds that 'the Minister is taking necessary steps to inquire into a reasonable suspicion that they are inadmissible on grounds of security or for violating human or international rights'.[47] The aftermath of these

---

[44] IRPA s. 58 (1) (c).   [45] IRPA s. 57(2).
[46] *Project Thread Backgrounder: Reasons for Detention Pursuant to 58(1)(c)*, undated.
[47] IRPA s. 58(1) (c).

detentions suggest that the front page news about a suspected al Qaeda cell with designs on a nuclear plant was grossly unfair. Many of the men have been released after adjudicators determined that they were not a security threat. Those who have been deported or detained have also been found not to be security threats. Ten of the men are making refugee applications on the basis that the publicity surrounding the case has made them liable to detention under Pakistan's harsh anti-terrorism laws.[48] The whole incident has caused widespread resentment among Canada's Muslim and Arab communities with some criticizing the apprehension of the men as the actions of a police state and others suggesting that it is an example of profiling that victimizes the innocent.

C. Security certificates and secret proceedings

Security certificates were introduced in Canadian immigration law in the early 1990's and about twenty-seven security certificates have been signed by the Ministers of Immigration and the Solicitor General declaring that a permanent resident or foreign national is inadmissible on security grounds. The security certificate is subject to judicial review in the Federal Court to determine its reasonableness, but it pre-empts other proceedings, including applications for refugee status. The procedure for reviewing security certificates is extraordinary because it involves the judge being required to hear the evidence in the absence of the person named in the certificate and their counsel if, in the judge's opinion, the disclosure of information would be injurious to national security or the safety of any person. Such information can be used by the judge in determining the reasonableness of the certificate, but it cannot even be included in a summary of other evidence that can be provided to the person named.[49] The Supreme Court of Canada upheld a somewhat similar procedure in an earlier Act, but stressed the importance of providing at least a summary of the evidence to the person named in the certificate.[50] Somewhat similar procedures are available under the ATA with

---

[48] 'Detained students seek refugee status' *Toronto Star*, 11 October 2003.
[49] Section 78 (e) of IRPA provides that at the government's request 'the judge shall hear all or part of the information or evidence in the absence of the permanent resident or the foreign national named in the certificate and their counsel if, in the opinion of the judge, its disclosure would be injurious to national security or to the safety of any person'. Section 78(h) provides that 'the judge shall provide the permanent resident or the foreign national with a summary of the information or evidence that enables them to be reasonably informed of the circumstances giving rise to the certificate, but that does not include anything that in the opinion of the judge would be injurious to national security or to the safety of any person if disclosed'.
[50] *Chiarelli* v. *Canada* [1992] 1 S. C. R. 711.

respect to preserving the confidentiality of information obtained in confidence from a foreign entity or for protecting national defence or national security. An important exception under the ATA, however, is that the criminal trial judge has the right to make any order, including a stay of the entire criminal proceedings, that he or she 'considers appropriate in the circumstances to protect the right of the accused to a fair trial'.[51] Such orders are not contemplated under Canadian immigration law. Indeed if the judge upholds the security certificate as reasonable, the person named is subject to removal without appeal and without being eligible to make a claim for refugee protection.[52]

The incursions that are made on standards of due process or adjudicative fairness in the name of keeping information affecting national security confidential but usable in security certificate proceedings are well-demonstrated by a 2002 speech given by a judge of the Federal Court, a specialized court in Canada that has jurisdiction over many security matters. He commented:

> We do not like this process of having to sit alone hearing only one party and looking at the materials produced by only one party and having to try to figure out for ourselves what is wrong with the case that is being presented before us and having to try for ourselves to see how witnesses that appear before us ought to be cross-examined.[53]

The judge ended his speech with an extraordinary confession: 'I sometimes feel a little bit like a fig leaf.'[54] He also suggested a more proportionate alternative to the present system, one based on the British system of allowing lawyers with security clearances to have access to confidential information and play the role of the adversary in the national security context.[55] Unfortunately, this suggestion has yet to be taken up.

Those subject to a security certificate may be subject to indefinite detention until the certificate has been reviewed by the judge and if upheld, they have been removed from Canada on the basis that they are 'a danger to national security or the safety of any person or are unlikely to appear at a

---

[51] CEA s. 38.14. [52] IRPA s. 81.

[53] James Hugessen 'Watching the Watchers: Democratic Oversight' in D. Daubney et al (eds.), *Terrorism, Law and Democracy*, at 384.

[54] Ibid., at 386.

[55] Under a previous Act, a review of security certificates issued against permanent residents was conducted by the independent review body for Canada's security intelligence agency and security cleared counsel for that agency played an adversarial role in challenging the security certificate. See Murray Rankin, 'The Security Intelligence Review Committee: Reconciling National Security with Procedural Fairness' (1990) 3 *Canadian Journal of Administrative Law and Practice* 173. The European Court of Human Rights wrongly assumed in *Chahal* v. *UK.* (1996) 23 E. H. H. R. 413 that such a special advocate procedure was also used in Canada's Federal Court.

proceeding or for removal'.[56] One refugee, Mahmoud Jaballah, alleged to have terrorist ties with the Egyptian al Jihad, has been detained since August 2001 on a security certificate ordering his deportation to Egypt.[57] Judges have rejected the idea that those detained under immigration law for national security reasons should have the same rights as those detained pending criminal trials.[58]

In terms of the eventual removal of a person on the basis that he or she is a threat to national security or a member of a terrorist organization, the Supreme Court has held that the right not to be deprived of life, liberty or security of the person except in accordance with the principles of funda-mental justice in Section 7 of the Canadian Charter will in most cases prohibit the deportation of a person to a country where there is a substantial risk of torture.[59] Interestingly, however, the Court did not articulate an absolute rule or indicate what exceptional circumstances might justify deportation to face torture or address the situation of those who may be subject to continued detention because their removal would not be constitutional. The Canadian courts have also refused to stay deportations to allow United Nations Committees such as the Human Rights Committee and the Committee Against Torture to hear complaints that they will be tortured if deported from Canada.[60]

Unlike the United Kingdom, Canada has not enacted legislation specifi-cally derogating from fair trial rights to allow the indefinite detention of

---

[56] The complex detention provisions, which also make it easier to detain a foreign national as opposed to a permanent resident, are found in ss. 82–4 of IRPA.

[57] A judge who found an abuse of process because of the Minister's delay in deciding whether a person subject to a security certificate was at risk if deported made an analogy to detention at Guantanamo Bay. 'Judge sorry for delay in terrorist suspect's case' *National Post*, 12 April 2003; *Re Jaballah* 2003 F. C. T. 640. The judge eventually upheld the security certificate without the Minister's decision but this was overturned by an appeal court. 'Detainee granted new hearing' *Toronto Star*, 14 July 2004. Mr Jaballah had previously been detained under a security certificate from March to November 1999 before that certificate was quashed.

[58] *Jaballah*, 2004 F. C. 299 at para 47.

[59] Although a refugee applicant facing the risk of torture is entitled to heightened due process in terms of written reasons from the Minister for the deportation, the Minister's decisions as to whether a person faces a substantial risk of torture or is a threat to the security of Canada will only be overturned by the courts if they are patently unreasonable.

[60] *Ahani* v. *Canada* (2002) 58 O. R.(3d) 107. The United Nations Human Rights Committee subsequently indicated that the deportation of Ahani before it had decided the complaint violated Canada's obligations under the International Covenant on Civil and Political Rights and reaffirmed the absolute prohibition on torture under international law. *Ahani* v. *Canada* Communication No.1051/2002: Canada 15/06/2004 CCPR/C/80/D/1051/2002. See generally Kent Roach, 'Constitutional, Remedial and International Dialogues About Rights: The Canadian Experience' (2005) 40 *Texas International Law Journal* (forthcoming).

suspected terrorists who cannot be deported because of concerns that they might face torture.[61] At the same time, the existing Canadian legislation places no limits on the time that a person subject to a security certificate may be detained. The government is arguing in at least one case that a person should be deported to Egypt even if that results in torture or, alternatively, that 'the threat to national security is so great that this man can never be released'.[62]

D. Changes in refugee policy

In December 2001 Canada and the United States agreed to implement a 'safe third country agreement' as part of a smart border agreement to increase security and ease the flow of goods and people at the border. When implemented the agreement will preclude most refugees who reach the United States from making a refugee application to Canada. Unless other measures are taken to increase refugee applications, this may significantly reduce the number of refugees Canada considers in any year. The agreement responds to perceptions that Canada's refugee policy is too liberal and generous. A recent report by the research division of the United States Library of Congress has concluded that 'Canada's immigration laws are arguably the foremost factor in making Canada hospitable to terrorists'. Although the report noted that the IRPA had decreased appeal rights and facilitated the use of detention, it also criticized it in part because its reference to the protection of refugees was 'an indication of the prevailing concern for or priority placed upon civil liberties in Canada'.[63]

E. Summary

The above sketch cannot do justice to the complexities of Canadian immigration law, but it does provide some basis for understanding why the Canadian government has been attracted to using the IRPA as opposed to the ATA as the main means to deal with suspected international terrorists. It is regrettable that most academic and civil society concerns focused on the ATA while provisions of IRPA that present an even greater threat to the values of due process and equality have largely escaped criticism. As my colleague Audrey Macklin has suggested 'laws that arouse deep concerns about civil

---

[61] Anti-terrorism Act, 2001 Part 4.
[62] 'Must deport Jaballah, court told' *Toronto Star*, 17 August 2004.
[63] Library of Congress Research Division, *Nations Hospitable to Organized Crime and Terrorism*, October 2003 at 152, 153 and 147. Note that the methodology and orientation of the report has been criticized by many in Canada. 'US terror study "crude" "inexpert"', *Toronto Star*, 17 February 2004.

liberties when applied to citizens are standard fare in the immigration context'.[64]

At the same time, there is little demand in Canada for more liberal immigration laws. Although the Supreme Court of Canada has held in a landmark equality rights case that non-citizens are a 'discrete and insular minority' vulnerable to discrimination by the majority,[65] it has also accepted that non-citizens do not have a right to remain in Canada and can be treated more harshly under immigration law than under the criminal law.[66] The IRPA indeed subjects non-citizens to considerably lower standards of adjudicative fairness than under even the enhanced criminal law of the ATA. It is in this context that the Canadian government has chosen to rely more on immigration law than the new criminal law to deal with suspected international terrorists.

III. Canada's evolving anti-terrorism policy: a new emphasis on public safety and security

There are reasons to doubt the effectiveness of ATA as an instrument to deter acts of terrorism. Even before its enactment, most acts of terrorism were already punished as serious crimes such as murder, hijacking and the use of explosives. The ATA may marginally increase the severity and certainty of punishment, but determined terrorists are not rational actors amenable to deterrence. The ATA will probably be most useful when it is directed at third parties, such as financial institutions, that could provide services to terrorists. These entities may well be encouraged to cease dealing with suspected terrorists. At the same time, there may be problems of overdeterrence and inflicting harms on the innocent if errors are made in determining who is a terrorist.

Reliance on immigration law in an attempt to decrease the risk of terrorism can also be both overinclusive and underinclusive. Policies such as the safe third country agreement will turn away many more legitimate refugees than deflect terrorists. The type of long-term and preventive detention that is allowed under Canadian immigration law may be successful in incapacitating suspected terrorists, albeit without a clear finding of guilt. Nevertheless, many of those detained will eventually be deported from Canada. Given the international nature of terrorism, it is not clear that deflection or deportation of suspected terrorists to other countries will actually increase security. It may simply displace the problem of global terrorism. In addition, the immigration

---

[64] Audrey Macklin, 'Borderline Security' in Daniels et al. (eds.), *Security of Freedom*, at 393.
[65] *Andrews* v. *Law Society of British Columbia*, [1989] 1 S. C. R. 143.
[66] *Canada* v. *Chiarelli*, [1992] 1 S. C. R. 711.

law approach that Canada has relied upon cannot be used against terrorist suspects who are Canadian citizens.

Reliance on military force such as Canada's participation in the war against the Taliban regime in Afghanistan may play some role in disrupting terrorist cells and state sponsors for terrorism. Nevertheless, the war has not incapacitated al Qaeda with its decentralized cell structure. Reliance on war will also result in loss of innocent lives and may have costs in terms of human rights. Canadian troops in Afghanistan participated in the transfer of some prisoners to Guantanamo Bay where they have been kept in what Lord Steyn has criticized as a 'legal black hole'.[67] A Canadian citizen, Omar Khadr is detained at Guantanamo Bay and alleged to have killed an American medic in combat on the Afghanistan/Pakistan border. As a result of the United States Supreme Court's decision in *Rasul* v. *Bush*, Khadr is seeking habeas corpus review before the American courts. He is also suing the Canadian government alleging a failure to provide consular access.[68] Should Khadr be charged, it is possible that he may be tried and face the death penalty before an American military tribunal even though he was sixteen years of age at the time of the alleged offence. Canada did not join the United States, the United Kingdom, Australia and other countries in the invasion of Iraq, a use of war that seems to have increased rather than decreased terrorism.

What then ought Canada and other countries do to respond to the very real risk of terrorism? Clearly doing nothing is not an option because of the dire consequences of even one successful act of biological, chemical or nuclear terrorism or the poisoning of food or water supplies. In my view, Canada ought to have placed greater emphasis on administrative and environmental controls that would help secure sites and substances that can be used to commit acts of terrorism. Some of these controls, including increased protection and surveillance of critical infrastructure such as pipelines, electricity lines, and seaports and airports, as well as increased control over dangerous materials such as explosives and toxins, are included in the Public Safety Act[69] which, after being introduced four times in Parliament, was finally enacted into law in May 2004. It is unfortunate that defining as crimes of terrorism much that was already illegal before 9/11 was a priority for the Canadian government while administrative measures to reduce the damage that could be caused by terrorists were not. At the same time, the criminal law approach taken in ATA, as well as the immigration law approach, was partially encouraged by the terms of United Nations Security Council

---

[67] Johan Steyn, 'Guantanamo Bay: The Legal Black Hole' (2004) 53 *International and Comparative Law Quarterly* 1.

[68] *Khadr* v. *Canada*, [2004] F. C. J. no. 1391. The family of the deceased American serviceman are suing Khadr and his family in American civil courts.

[69] S. C. 2004 c.15.

Resolution 1373 which called for criminalization of financing and participation in terrorism and better border controls.

An administrative and environmental approach designed to prevent terrorists from gaining access to substances such as explosives, chemical or nuclear materials or sites vulnerable to terrorism such as airplanes and nuclear plants might have a number of benefits. These are softer strategies that do not rely upon punishment and detention to the same extent as criminal and immigration law. They also work as a fail safe should it prove impossible to deter, incapacitate or identify all the terrorists. Measures such as more effective screening of all passengers and baggage on aircraft through technology may also limit the damage to values such as liberty, privacy and equality. Technology can be used to screen all passengers and not just those who fit into a profile of a terrorist. To be sure, technology such as the use of biometrics could have a negative impact on privacy. When applied to large-scale populations, it will also produce a considerable number of false positives and false negatives. It will not be possible to screen all passengers of mass transit, but it should be possible to provide better controls on explosives and other materials that can be used for bombs.

Some environmental measures such as better monitoring of public health and the safety of food and water have the important additional benefit of providing protections against diseases and accidental contamination of food and water, as well as terrorism. Better security for computer systems would protect them not only from a cyber-terrorism attack, but also from random attacks by hackers. Better emergency preparedness also serves a similar all risks function as it better prepares society to deal with a wide range of natural and man-made disasters such as earthquakes and black outs. The Public Safety Act[70] contains provisions that allow Ministers of Transport, the Environment, Health and Defence to take temporary measures in a wide range of emergencies, not just with respect to terrorism. The American National Research Council has concluded in a post-9/11 report, that we should invest in strategies that will make us safer not only from terrorist attacks, but from disaster, disease and accidents.[71] Such strategies also present less of a risk, both for the targets and for society, of targeting the wrong people.

The Canadian government has recently taken steps towards such a comprehensive all risks approach to national security. In response not only to

---

[70] The Act allows for emergency directions when necessary to deal with immediate risks to safety, security, health and the environment in relation to: aeronautics (part 1), environmental protection (part 3), health (part 6), food and drugs (part 9), hazardous products (part 10), navigable waters (part 15), pest control products (part 18), quarantines (part 20), radiation emitting devices (part 21), and shipping (part 22).

[71] National Research Council, *Making the Nation Safer: The Role of Science and Technology in Countering Terrorism* (Washington, National Academy Press, 2002).

September 11, but also the SARS crisis, black outs, and contamination of food and water, a new Ministry of Public Safety and Emergency Preparedness was created in late 2003. The Minister of this department chairs a new Cabinet committee on Security, Public Health and Emergencies. She also has responsibilities for a new Canada Border Services Agency and the Office of Critical Infrastructure and Emergency Preparedness. The new Ministry has over 55,000 employees and a $7 billion budget. It was designed in part to allow for better integration with the new American Department of Homeland Security.

The new Public Safety ministry has the potential to develop a more comprehensive and rational approach to the various risks that Canadians face to their well-being. It could allow for cost effective distribution of limited resources with a premium placed on strategies that protect Canadians not only from terrorism but other harms. This all risks approach was adopted in a national security policy released in April 2004 that includes commitments to better emergency preparedness, better public health, better transport security and better peace-keeping, as well as the more traditional terrorism specific proposals relating to better intelligence and better border security.[72] This national security policy can be contrasted with the new American policy with its emphasis on the pre-emptive use of military force.[73] At the same time, a recent report by a Senate Committee suggests that Canada, and in particular the federal Office of Critical Infrastructure and Emergency Preparedness, is not adequately prepared for emergencies including those caused by terrorism.[74]

The creation of the new Ministry of Public Safety is not a guarantee of a more comprehensive and creative all risks security policy. The new ministry has traditional responsibilities for policing and security intelligence and new responsibilities for the border and for security aspects of immigration. There has been increased spending on security intelligence, but problems remain with the coordination of multiple intelligence agencies in Canada and the degree to which they produce useable information. A report by the Auditor General of Canada found deficiencies in the communication and coordination of intelligence information within government.[75] A proposed new Parliamentarian committee on security may assist in coordination.

---

[72] 'This system is capable of responding to both intentional and unintentional threats. It is as relevant in securing Canadians against the next SARS-like outbreak as it is in addressing the risk of a terrorist attack.' Canada, *Securing an Open Society: Canada's National Security Policy*, April 2004 at 10.

[73] Banks, Chapter 22, in this volume.

[74] Standing Senate Committee on National Security and Defence *National Emergencies: Canada's Fragile Front Lines*, March 2004.

[75] *Report of the Auditor General of Canada to the House of Commons*, March 2004 ch. 3.

The ATA, as well as a new emphasis on intelligence based policing, puts pressure on the traditional distinction between policing and intelligence by criminalizing a wide variety of associations and support for terrorism. Although the government is committed to it in principle, a new independent review mechanism for the new role of the RCMP in national security remains to be developed and implemented.

A comprehensive all risks policy for human and national security must still be carefully monitored to ensure that it does not produce unwarranted threats to liberty, due process, equality and privacy. Many provisions in the Public Safety Act[76] facilitate the collection and sharing of information within governments and between governments. Although this may respond to some concerns that security information is not appropriately communicated within government, the information sharing provisions also raise concerns about privacy and transparency, as well as practical concerns about decision-makers being swamped by too much information. Vast databases can undermine privacy while producing information about potential terrorists that may not be accurate or helpful. At the same time, delays such as the average forty-eight days delay from publication of Interpol alerts to entry into police systems and Canadian watchlists are not acceptable either from a security perspective or from a fairness perspective to those who should be removed from watchlists.[77] The challenge for the new Ministry will be to make optimal uses of its resources to protect the security of Canadians while also minimizing intrusions on important democratic values such as equality, fairness and the right to engage in religious or political dissent.

IV. Conclusion

It remains to be seen the extent to which Canada's new Ministry of Public Safety and Emergency Preparedness will follow the pattern established after September 11 of relying on immigration law and to a lesser extent criminal law to respond to the risks of terrorism and of responding to American perceptions about Canada's vulnerabilities to terrorism. Canada has enacted broad new criminal laws against terrorism and given police enhanced powers, but so far has relied on the even broader powers available under immigration law as a means to deal with terrorist suspects. There are concerns in Canada about the fairness of immigration law when used to detain suspected

---

[76] S. C. 2004 c.15. For example, Part 5 permits the sharing of information with other governments and foreign organizations, Part 11 allows the collection and disclosure of information for national security purposes under immigration law. Part 17 extends the government databases and agencies that can be consulted in relation to terrorist financing.

[77] *Report of the Auditor General of Canada to the House of Commons*, March 2004 at 3.122.

terrorists and about the targeting of people on the basis of their race, religion or political beliefs and associations.

The enactment of the Public Safety Act, although not without controversy, may facilitate administrative measures to protect sites and substances that are vulnerable to terrorism. There is also a potential that Canada's new national security policy and its Ministry of Public Safety and Emergency Preparedness may result in a more creative and comprehensive approach to the broad range of risks to the security of Canadians.

24

The rule of law and the regulation of terrorism in Australia and New Zealand

GEORGE WILLIAMS

I. Introduction

Australia and New Zealand might seem unlikely targets for a terrorist attack.[1] They are geographically isolated and are only minor players in the 'War on Terror'. Nevertheless, Australia is an active military partner in the 'Coalition of the Willing' that went to war in Iraq in 2003 and both nations supplied troops for the conflict in Afghanistan. Australia has also come to the attention of terrorist organizations, with a recent statement purporting to be from al Qaeda declaring Australian Prime Minister John Howard to be 'wicked'. Howard responded: 'I've been insulted by everybody, so I suppose Al Qaeda can have a go as well.'[2]

Although there has not been a terrorist attack for more than a decade on Australian or New Zealand soil, both have been affected by terrorism. Many New Zealanders regard the 1985 sinking in Auckland Harbour of the Rainbow Warrior by French agents, with loss of one life, as an example of state sponsored terrorism. More recently, Australians and New Zealanders died in the September 11 attack. A year later, on 12 October 2002, 202 people were killed when two bombs exploded in the Sari Club and Paddy's Bar in Bali, Indonesia. Of the dead, 88 were Australian and 3 were from New Zealand. Like the effect of September 11 on the United States, the Bali bombing has had an enormous impact upon the culture and politics of these nations. My own memories of the attack resurface whenever I walk down to Coogee Beach, close to my home in Sydney, which features a

---

Thanks to Ben Golder for his research assistance and to Alex Conte for his comments.

[1] Compare the statement of the Director-General of the Australian Security Intelligence Organisation in 'ASIO Today', *AIAL Forum*, April 2004, No. 41, 25 at 25–6: 'we now know that al-Qaida had an active interest in carrying out a terrorist attack in Australia well before 11 September and that we remain a target'. See also *Transnational Terrorism: The Threat to Australia* (Australian Government White Paper, 2004) at 65–74 < http://www.dfat.gov.au/publications/terrorism/index.html >.

[2] '"Wicked" Howard shrugs off Al Qaeda slur', www.abc.net.au/news/newsitems/s1095558.htm. For other such references to Australia, see also *Transnational Terrorism*, note 1 above, at 66–7.

sculpture and memorial to those who died in the attack. Twenty of the Bali victims were from my local area and the point at Coogee Beach has been renamed Dolphin Point in remembrance of the six Coogee Dolphin rugby league players who died in the blast.

Australians and New Zealanders remember these terrorist attacks in their own way. However, an important point of similarity between them and other nations is how the law has formed a central part of their response. In this chapter I examine the range of new laws enacted after September 11 by the parliaments of Australia and New Zealand. My primary focus is upon the laws introduced into Australia and their effect upon the rule of law and basic principles of human rights. In the case of Australia, I also explore an historical parallel with the anti-communist legislation of more than half a century ago. In the next section I begin with the legal context in which Australia has enacted new terrorism laws.

II. The rule of law and human rights in Australia

Terrorism is an attack on our most basic human rights. It can infringe our rights to life and personal security and our ability to live our lives free of fear. Our response to terrorism also raises important human rights issues. Indeed, it poses some of the most important questions of law and policy of our time. Should we protest that the Bali bombers received the death penalty in Indonesia or should the death penalty be reintroduced into Australia and New Zealand for terrorism offences? Should, as Alan Dershowitz has argued,[3] the law provide for a 'torture warrant' whereby a terrorist suspect might be tortured to gain information about a large-scale, imminent danger to the community? Should the police be able to detain terrorist suspects without charge for one or more days? Should governments be able to access our emails without our knowledge to search for information? The list goes on.

Unfortunately, unlike New Zealand and every other western nation, Australia must search for answers to these questions without the benefit of a Bill of Rights.[4] This is made even more difficult when, after September 11, new laws have been made and old laws amended, often with great haste. These changes demonstrate how legal systems, and the basic principles that underlie them, such as the rule of law and the liberty of the individual, can come under considerable strain in the aftermath of a terrorist attack. Bills of Rights can play an important role at such a time. They remind governments and communities of a society's basic values and of the principles that might otherwise

---

[3] Alan Dershowitz, *Why Terrorism Works: Understanding the Threat, Responding to the Challenge* (Yale University Press, 2002).
[4] See generally George Williams, *Human Rights under the Australian Constitution* (Oxford University Press, 1999).

be compromised at a time of grief and fear. After new laws have been made, a Bill of Rights can also allow courts to assess the changes against human rights principles. This can provide a final check on laws that, with the benefit of hindsight, ought not to have been passed. The absence of such a check is one reason why Australian law after September 11 is stringent in its impact upon individual rights. The situation differs in New Zealand, in part because the New Zealand Bill of Rights Act 1990 shapes legislative, executive and judicial decision-making in this and other fields.

In Australia, there can occasionally be a role for judges in assessing new terrorism laws, but this is usually at the margins of the debate, such as where constitutional provisions are relevant to human rights enforcement or in the interpretation of legislation. In the latter context, the courts have developed the common law so that the infringement of rights is minimized. According to Chief Justice Mason and Justices Brennan, Gaudron and McHugh of the High Court of Australia in Coco v. The Queen:[5] 'The courts should not impute to the legislature an intention to interfere with fundamental rights. Such an intention must be clearly manifested by unmistakable and unambiguous language.' Hence, 'a statute or statutory instrument which purports to impair a right to personal liberty is interpreted, if possible, so as to respect that right'.[6]

Of course, this means that parliaments can still depart from fundamental rights by passing a new law if it operates within constitutional limits and is clear in its intent. There is no mechanism through which to analyse whether such abrogation is appropriate. Unlike in every other western nation, the issue in Australia is purely political. Moreover, without a Bill of Rights, political and legal debate is usually unconstrained by fundamental human rights principles and the rule of law. Instead, as was demonstrated by the legislation introduced into the federal Parliament after September 11 (discussed below), the contours of debate may match the majoritarian pressures of Australian political life rather than the principles and values upon which the democratic system depends. This means that any check upon the power of parliament or governments to abrogate human rights derives from political debate and the goodwill of political leaders. This is not a check that is regarded as acceptable or sufficient in some other nations.

The lack of a domestic reference point for basic rights in Australia means that it is difficult to determine the extent to which, if at all, rights and the rule of law should be sacrificed in the name of national security and in the fight against terrorism.[7] As in many other debates, the absence of a domestic Bill of Rights means that Australians turn to international law. The United Nations

---

[5] (1994) 179 CLR 427 at 437.
[6] Re Bolton; Ex parte Beane (1987) 162 CLR 514 at 523 per Justice Brennan.
[7] For the view of the current Australian Attorney-General on this issue, see P. Ruddock, A New Framework: Counter Terrorism and the Rule of Law (Speech delivered to the Sydney

has been a focus of debate and activity in responding to terrorism, and a number of international instruments are important, such as Resolution 1373 of the United Nations Security Council, made on 28 September 2001, which determines that States shall 'prevent and suppress the financing of terrorist acts' and 'take the necessary steps to prevent the commission of terrorist acts'. Other instruments ratified by Australia such as the International Covenant on Civil and Political Rights affirm that governments have an obligation to take action to protect their citizens from terrorism, but that any such action must be in accordance with accepted human rights principles.

Further guidance on the balance between national security and domestic freedoms has been provided by the Council of Europe, which has forty-four member States, including all members of the European Union. On 11 July 2002 the Council adopted *Guidelines of the Committee of Ministers of the Council of Europe on Human Rights and the Fight Against Terrorism*.[8] According to the Secretary General of the Council of Europe, Walter Schwimmer, the Guidelines 'enable our member States, and other countries, to combat terrorism whilst also observing the Council's fundamental values of human rights, democracy and the rule of law'.[9] In a resolution made on 16 December 2002, the United Nations General Assembly commended the Council of Europe 'for its contribution to the implementation of Security Council resolution 1373', taking note in this context of the Council of Europe *Guidelines*.

Although these instruments could provide useful assistance on human rights issues and national security, they do not form part of Australian law and lack political and legal legitimacy in Australia. For example, when there was criticism in 2000 from the United Nations Human Rights Committee of the mandatory sentencing regime for minor property offences then in operation in the Northern Territory, its Chief Minister Denis Burke stated: 'This is designed to cause embarrassment. This is designed to shame Australians. And to my mind an opportunity for Australians to tell them to bugger off.'[10] The response of the federal government was less direct, but the message was the same.[11] Prime Minister Howard rejected any international pressure, stating on Perth radio that 'we are mature enough to make decisions on these matters ourselves full stop'.[12]

Institute on 20 April 2004) http://www.ag.gov.au/www/ministerruddockhome.nsf/Web + Pages/B046617DB08691D9CA256E7D000ED953?OpenDocument.

[8] See http://portal.coe.ge/downloads/terrorism.en.pdf.

[9] 'Council of Europe Adopts the First International Guidelines on Human Rights and Anti-Terrorism Measures' (Media Release, 15 July 2002), at http://press.coe.int/cp/2002/369a(2002).htm.

[10] 'NT under fire again for mandatory sentencing', http://www.abc.net.au/pm/stories/s154694.htm.

[11] See generally D. Hovell, 'The Sovereignty Stratagem: Australia's Response to UN Human Rights Treaty Bodies' (2003) 28 *Alternative Law Journal* 6.

[12] http://www.pm.gov.au/news/interviews/2000/6PR2502.htm.

III. Australia's new anti-terrorism laws

Australia has little history of enacting laws aimed at terrorism.[13] In fact, before September 2001, only the Northern Territory had such a law.[14] Australia has now passed many anti-terrorism laws, although their impact has yet to be felt as the occasion to use many of them has thankfully not arisen. A consequence of this is that these laws have not yet been subject to judicial interpretation or to constitutional challenge. I examine the laws below, beginning with the form in which they were introduced into the federal Parliament.

The federal Government's legal response to September 11 was introduced into Parliament in March 2002 as two packages of legislation. The first contained several new Bills, the most important of which was the Security Legislation Amendment (Terrorism) Bill 2002 (the 'Terrorism Bill').[15] This Bill sought to introduce a definition of 'terrorist act' into the Criminal Code Act 1995 (Cth). Under section 100.1, a 'terrorist act' was an act or threat done 'with the intention of advancing a political, religious or ideological cause' that:

(a) involves serious harm to a person;
(b) involves serious damage to property;
(c) endangers a person's life, other than the life of the person taking the action;
(d) creates a serious risk to the health or safety of the public or a section of the public; or
(e) seriously interferes with, seriously disrupts, or destroys, an electronic system.

The section provided an exception only for industrial action and *lawful* advocacy, protest or dissent.

This definition lacked a focus on the intent associated with a terrorist act that distinguishes such violence from other non-terrorist acts. The reference to 'with the intention of advancing a political, religious or ideological cause' was so wide that it would have criminalized many forms of unlawful civil protest (unlawful perhaps only due to a trespass onto land) in which people, property or electronic systems were harmed or damaged. The section could have extended to protest by farmers, unionists, students, environmentalists

---

[13] For a history of terrorism laws in Australia, see J. Hocking, *Terror Laws: ASIO, Counter-Terrorism and the Threat to Democracy* (Sydney, UNSW Press, 2003).

[14] Criminal Code Act (NT), Pt. III Div. 2. The provisions were modelled on the Prevention of Terrorism (Temporary Provisions) Act 1974 (UK).

[15] The others were the Suppression of the Financing of Terrorism Bill 2002; Criminal Code Amendment (Suppression of Terrorist Bombings) Bill 2002; Border Security Legislation Amendment Bill 2002; Telecommunications Interception Legislation Amendment Bill 2002.

and online protestors. Moreover, a penalty of up to 'imprisonment for life' applied where a person engaged in a terrorist act.

The Terrorism Bill failed to pass in this form. It was substantially amended after being strongly criticized by legal and community groups and after a highly critical, unanimous report by the Senate Legal and Constitutional Committee,[16] an upper house committee composed of members of each of the major parties. The Bill as amended contains the following additional element as part of the definition of terrorism:

> the action is done or the threat is made with the intention of:
>
> (i) coercing, or influencing by intimidation, the government of the Commonwealth or a State, Territory or foreign country, or of part of a State, Territory or foreign country; or
> (ii) intimidating the public or a section of the public.

In addition, advocacy, protest, dissent or industrial action (whether lawful or not) is excluded so long as it is not intended to, among other things, cause serious physical harm to a person or create a serious risk to the health or safety of the public. This definition provides the basis for a number of new criminal offences. These include committing a 'terrorist act' or even possessing a 'thing' connected with terrorism.

In provisions seemingly modelled on the anti-communist legislation of the early 1950s (discussed below), the Terrorism Bill in its original form also empowered the federal Attorney-General to proscribe (or ban) organizations,[17] accompanied by a penalty of up to twenty-five years' imprisonment for their members and supporters and people who have provided training for, or have been trained by, it.[18] Section 102.2 would have enabled the Attorney-General to ban an organization for reasons including that the organization 'has endangered, or is likely to endanger, the security or integrity of the Commonwealth or another country'. 'Integrity' could have included the geographical, or territorial, integrity of a nation, and hence this power could have been applied to proscribe an organization that supported non-violent independence movements within other nations. Over recent years, this would have included bodies supporting independence for East Timor from Indonesia.

---

[16] Senate Legal and Constitutional Legislation Committee, Parliament of Australia, *Consideration of Legislation Referred to the Committee: Security Legislation Amendment (Terrorism) Bill 2002* [No. 2] (2002).

[17] See for an extended summary of the legislative history of this proscription power, Parliamentary Joint Committee on ASIO, ASIS and DSD, *Review of the listing of the Palestinian Islamic Jihad (PIJ)* (June 2004), at http://www.aph.gov.au/house/committee/ pjcaad/pij/report.htm, Chapter 1.

[18] The Anti-terrorism Bill (No. 2) 2004 would also introduce a new offence in s. 102.8 of associating with terrorist organizations.

The power to ban organizations could have been exercised unilaterally by
the Attorney-General and not as part of a fair and accountable process. The
Attorney-General's decision to ban would not have been subject to meaningful independent review (although judicial review upon limited, essentially
procedural, administrative law grounds would have been possible under the
Administrative Decisions (Judicial Review) Act 1977).[19] By contrast, the
separation of powers in Australia, including the notion that power should
not be concentrated in any one arm of government, suggests instead that the
decision to ban organizations should be made by an independent judge, or at
least should be subject to strict scrutiny by a court. The dangers of not doing
so were expressed by Justice Dixon of the High Court of Australia in 1951 in
the *Communist Party Case*:[20]

> History and not only ancient history, shows that in countries where
> democratic institutions have been unconstitutionally superseded, it has
> been done not seldom by those holding the executive power. Forms of
> government may need protection from dangers likely to arise from within
> the institutions to be protected.

The Terrorism Bill was also amended to remove the Attorney-General's proscription power. As enacted, it did not grant the Attorney-General a unilateral
power of proscription but allowed for the banning of terrorist organizations
identified by the United Nations Security Council. However, the Government
continued to press for a broader power. After Parliament passed specific legislation to enable the banning of the Hizballah, Hamas and Lashkar-e-Tayyiba
organizations, it agreed to the Criminal Code Amendment (Terrorist
Organizations) Act 2004. This Act gives the Attorney-General the power to
determine that a body is a terrorist organization if 'satisfied on reasonable
grounds that the organisation is directly or indirectly engaged in preparing,
planning, assisting in or fostering the doing of a terrorist act (whether or not
the terrorist act has occurred or will occur)'. While it would be difficult, if
not impossible, to challenge the decision to make such a regulation in court,
s. 102.1A of the Criminal Code Act as amended provides that the decision can be
reviewed by a parliamentary committee and can be disallowed by Parliament.
The first review undertaken by the Parliamentary Joint Committee on ASIO
Australian Security and Intelligence Organization, ASIS Australian Secret
Intelligence Service and DSD Defence Signals Directorate into the proscription
of Palestinian Islamic Jihad was encouraging. The Committee decided its role

---

[19] Even if a judge were to proceed to review a decision made under s. 102.2, the grounds of
review under the Act are narrow and procedural. There would be no scope for review on
broader proportionality grounds. In other words, it could not be argued that a decision
was wrongly made because it was not 'reasonably appropriate and adapted' to the relevant
purpose or object.
[20] *Australian Communist Party* v. *Commonwealth* (1951) 83 CLR 1 at 187.

was to examine the decision not only according to procedural criteria but also as to its merits (in part because of the lack of merits review by a judicial body.)[21] However, the capacity of the Committee to be effective in this role is limited by it only being given a non-extendable period of fifteen days to report.

Australia's second major package of anti-terrorism legislation contained only the Australian Security Intelligence Organisation Legislation Amendment (Terrorism) Bill 2002, which sought to confer unprecedented new intelligence gathering powers on ASIO. In its original form, the Bill allowed adults and even children who were *not* terrorist suspects, but who may have useful information about terrorism, to be strip searched and detained by ASIO for rolling two-day periods that could be extended indefinitely. The detainees could have been denied the opportunity to inform family members, their employer, or even a lawyer of their detention. There was no right to silence and a failure to answer any question put by ASIO would have been punishable by five years in prison. The regime applied to all Australians, including journalists who could not have protected the confidentiality of their sources. While the Bill stated that detainees 'must be treated with humanity and with respect for human dignity', there was no penalty for ASIO officers who subjected detainees to cruel, inhuman or degrading treatment. In fact, s. 92 of the Australian Security Intelligence Organisation Act 1979 still provides that it is an offence (punishable by imprisonment for up to one year) to even publish the identity of an ASIO officer.

The original ASIO Bill is consistent with the Howard Government's continuing acquiescence in the indefinite detention without charge of Australian David Hicks by the United States military at Camp X-Ray at Guantanamo Bay, Cuba. The ASIO Bill went further, however, in that Australians could have been held not because it was suspected that they had engaged in terrorism or were likely to do so, but because they may 'substantially assist the collection of intelligence that is important in relation to a terrorism offence'.[22]

I described the original ASIO Bill as being 'rotten to the core' and as one of the worst Bills ever introduced into the federal Parliament.[23] It would have conferred unprecedented new powers upon a secret intelligence organization that could have been used in ten, twenty or even fifty years' time against the Australian people by an unscrupulous government. In its original form, the ASIO Bill would not have been out of place in former dictatorships such as

---

[21] Parliamentary Joint Committee on ASIO, ASIS and DSD, *Review of the listing of the Palestinian Islamic Jihad (PIJ)* (June 2004), at para 2.8, http://www.aph.gov.au/house/committee/pjcaad/pij/report.htm.

[22] Australian Security Intelligence Organisation Legislation Amendment (Terrorism) Bill 2002 (Cth), cl 34G(3).

[23] For example, George Williams, 'Why the ASIO Bill is Rotten to the Core', *The Age* (Melbourne), 27 August 2002, 15.

General Pinochet's Chile. The Parliamentary Joint Committee on ASIO, Australian Secret Intelligence Service and Defence Signals Directorate unanimously found that the ASIO Bill 'would undermine key legal rights and erode the civil liberties that make Australia a leading democracy'.[24]

The ASIO Bill was finally passed fifteen months after it was introduced after one of the longest and most bitter debates in Australian parliamentary history. At one point in a continuous 27-hour debate in December 2000, the Government and Labour Opposition accused each other of bearing the blame for any Australian blood that might be spilt by terrorists because of the deadlock on the Bill. The original Bill is different in important respects from the final Act. As amended, the detention regime in the Australian Security Intelligence Organisation Act 1979 only applies to people aged sixteen years and over. Detainees have access to a lawyer of their choice, although ASIO may request that access be denied to a particular lawyer where the lawyer poses a security risk. Australians may be questioned by ASIO for 24 hours over a one week period. They must then be released, but can be questioned again if a new warrant can be justified by fresh information. A person can only be held and questioned under the Act when ordered by a judge, and the questioning itself will be before a retired judge. The questioning must be videotaped and the whole process will be subject to the ongoing scrutiny of the Inspector-General of Intelligence and Security (who is effectively the Ombudsman for ASIO).

These additional protections in the hands of independent people blunt some of the worst excesses of the original Bill. However, even in this form, the Act can be justified only as a temporary response to the threat to national security posed by terrorism. This is reflected in the sunset clause added to the law, which means that it will lapse after three years unless it is re-enacted. In this form, the law will hopefully not create a long-term precedent for law enforcement and intelligence gathering in Australia. Apart from other considerations, the Act conferred greater powers of detention over *non-suspect* Australians than the then federal Crimes Act 1914, which allowed only for the detention without charge of terrorist and other criminal *suspects* for a maximum of 12 hours.[25]

The passage of the Terrorism and ASIO Bills has not seen the end of new Australian anti-terrorism laws. Indeed, there has been a steady stream of new proposals and laws. In 2003, the ASIO Legislation Amendment Act was passed to increase the time allowed for the questioning of non-suspects by ASIO from 24 to 48 hours when an interpreter is involved. Another change

---

[24] Parliamentary Joint Committee on ASIO, ASIS and DSD, Parliament of Australia, *An Advisory Report on the Australian Security Intelligence Organisation Legislation Amendment (Terrorism) Bill 2002* (2002), vii.
[25] Crimes Act 1914 (Cth), ss. 23C and 23D.

brought about by that Act made it an offence, for two years after someone has been detained, to disclose 'operational information'[26] about detention under the Act. The penalty for doing so, even if the information is provided as part of a media story on the detention regime, is imprisonment for up to five years. The impact of this provision upon freedom of the press is of great concern. It means that two years must pass before abuses involving the operational activities of ASIO under the regime can be exposed through media reporting.

In all of the new federal law in Australia, there has until recently been a surprising omission. No attempt was made until 2004 to increase the time that police can question a terrorist suspect before the person must be charged or released. As the law stood, any criminal suspect could be questioned for up to 12 hours. By contrast, in the United Kingdom, the police may detain suspected terrorists for 48 hours extendable for a further 5 days,[27] and in Canada police may detain suspected terrorists for 24 hours extendable for a further 48 hours.[28] The United States legislation provides for the detention of 'inadmissible aliens' and any person who is engaged in any activity 'that endangers the national security of the United States' (detention is for renewable six month periods).[29] The Anti-Terrorism Act 2004[30] has now doubled the questioning time for terrorist suspects to 24 hours. In light of the time limits in other nations, this is surprisingly modest.

Other terrorism laws have been passed in Australia at the State level. These include laws[31] that refer legislative power to the Commonwealth to enable the federal Parliament to pass national terrorism laws that might otherwise be outside of federal constitutional competence.[32] Other State laws are the Terrorism (Police Powers) Act 2002 in New South Wales and the Terrorism

---

[26] This is defined by s. 34VAA as 'information indicating one or more of the following:

   (a) information that the Organisation [ASIO] has or had;
   (b) a source of information (other than the person specified in the warrant mentioned in subsection (1) or (2)) that the Organisation has or had;
   (c) an operational capability, method or plan of the Organisation'.

[27] Terrorism Act 2000 (UK), s. 41.

[28] Anti-Terrorism Act, SC 2001, c. 41 s. 4, inserting ss. 83.3(6) and (7) into Criminal Code, RS 1985, c C-46.

[29] USA Patriot Act 2001, Pub. L. No. 107–56, § 41, 115 Stat 272 (2001).

[30] Further changes to federal terrorism law are also contained in the Anti-Terrorism Bill (No. 2) 2004 and Anti-Terrorism Bill (No. 3) 2004.

[31] For example, South Australia's Terrorism (Commonwealth Powers) Act 2002.

[32] This is possible under s. 51(xxxvii) of the Australian Constitution, which enables the federal Parliament to pass laws with respect to 'Matters referred to the Parliament of the Commonwealth by the Parliament or Parliaments of any State or States, but so that the law shall extend only to States by whose Parliaments the matter is referred, or which afterwards adopt the law'. As the authors of *Terrorism and the Law in Australia: Legislation, Commentary and Constraints* (Department of the Parliamentary Library (Cth), Research Paper No. 12, 2001–2002) at 5 note, federal 'legislative power to deal with terrorism may

(Community Protection) Act 2003 in Victoria. Queensland is the most recent reformer, with the Terrorism (Community Safety) Amendment Act 2004 designed, according to Premier Peter Beattie, to deal with 'the ugly realities of the post-September 11 world'.[33] These new State laws reflect the fact that separate police forces exist in Australia at both the State and federal level and that in the event of a terrorist attack it would likely be the larger, locally based State police forces that would provide the first law enforcement response.

The State laws challenge accepted understandings of the rule of law because they confer greater powers upon law enforcement authorities than would normally be found in dealing with criminal activity and can deny courts any role in reviewing decisions made under the Act. For example, the New South Wales Act, in the event of an imminent terrorist attack or to prevent such an attack, empowers the police to use extraordinary powers that bypass existing warrant and other procedures in regard to, for example, conducting searches and entering property. The Act states as to the authorization to use such powers (which may be granted by a senior police officer):

> 13 Authorisation not open to challenge
> (1) An authorisation (and any decision of the Police Minister under this Part with respect to the authorisation) may not be challenged, reviewed, quashed or called into question on any grounds whatsoever before any court, tribunal, body or person in any legal proceedings, or restrained, removed or otherwise affected by proceedings in the nature of prohibition or mandamus.

An even more recent New South Wales Act, the Bail Amendment (Terrorism) Act 2004 (NSW) was enacted within 48 hours of terrorism suspect Bilal Khazal being granted bail. It amended the Bail Act 1978 (NSW) to provide a presumption against bail in regard to terrorism offences listed in the federal Criminal Code Act. The federal Parliament has also now changed federal law in response to this granting of bail to provide that 'despite any other law of the Commonwealth, a bail authority must not grant bail to a person' charged with, or convicted of, offences including terrorism offences 'unless the bail authority is satisfied that exceptional circumstances exist to justify bail'.[34]

---

be derived from a mosaic of various direct and indirect sources'. These sources include, among other things, the defence power, the external affairs power, the aliens power, the corporations power, the banking power, and the power over interstate and overseas trade and commerce.

[33] 'Premier Announces New Laws to Target Terrorism, Sabotage' (Ministerial Media Statement, 18 April 2004), http://statements.cabinet.qld.gov.au/cgi-bin/display-statement.pl?id=777&db=media.

[34] Crimes Act 1914, s. 15AA as amended by the Anti-Terrorism Act 2004.

IV. The historical parallel in Australia

The most direct historical parallel with events in Australia since September 11 can be found in the late 1940s and early 1950s when Australia grappled with the external and internal threats posed by communism. Community fear was fed by political and media hysteria. The 1946 federal election policy statement made by the Country Party asserted that it 'regards the Australian communist in the same category as a venomous snake – to be killed before it kills'.[35] Similarly, the editorial in the *Sydney Morning Herald* on 7 November 1947 stated, in words resembling President George W. Bush's rhetoric of 'either you are with us, or you are with the terrorists':[36]

> Communism is cold, harsh and ruthless, and it is building slowly and inexorably to the day when our democratic Government will be superseded by a Godless, tyrannical Communistic dictatorship in Australia ... Any Australian born in this country who embraces Communism is a traitor. There is no half way. There has to be a choice between good and evil, and people must be either loyal or disloyal.[37]

When Sir Robert Menzies became Prime Minister for the second time in 1949, one of his first actions was to introduce the Communist Party Dissolution Bill 1950. In the second reading speech to the Bill on 27 April 1950, Menzies listed fifty-three leading Australians as 'communists'. Unfortunately, he later had to admit that five of those persons were not actually communists. A similar mistake was made by the *Sydney Morning Herald* the day after Menzies' speech when it published as a 'named' communist the photograph of J. W. R. Hughes, the Deputy Commissioner of Taxation, instead of J. R. Hughes, an officer of the Federated Clerks' Union (the newspaper corrected its mistake the next day).

The Communist Party Dissolution Bill was introduced into Parliament on the day the first Australian forces landed in Korea, and the Labor-controlled Senate passed the Bill despite misgivings. It did so in part because the policy of banning communism received overwhelming public support, with one poll taken in May 1950 showing 80 per cent of electors in favour.[38] The new law provided for a term of imprisonment of five years for any person who knowingly carried or displayed anything indicating that he or she was in any way associated with the Party, such as a badge with the words

---

[35] B. McKinlay, *A Documentary History of the Australian Labor Movement 1850–1975* (1979), at 691.

[36] 'Address to a Joint Session of Congress and the American People' (20 September 2001), http://www.whitehouse.gov/news/releases/2001/09/20010920-8.html.

[37] P. Deery (ed.), *Labour in Conflict: The 1949 Coal Strike* (Sydney, Hale and Iremonger, 1978), at 21.

[38] L. F. Crisp, *Ben Chifley: A Political Biography* (London, Angus & Robertson, 1977), at 390.

'Communist Party Conference 1948'. It also empowered the Governor-General, acting on the advice of the government to ban organizations and to declare a person to be a 'communist', which the Act defined as 'a person who supports or advocates the objectives, policies, teachings, principles or practices of communism, as expounded by Marx and Lenin'. Under the law, a sanction could be applied not according to a person's acts but according to his or her beliefs. Once declared to be a communist, a person could not hold office in the Commonwealth public service or in industries declared by the Governor-General to be vital to the security and defence of Australia. Should a person wish to contest a declaration by the Governor-General, he or she could do so, but 'the burden shall be upon him to prove that he is not a person to whom this section applies'.

Fortunately, the law was struck down by the High Court,[39] although due to fundamental rule of law and separation of powers principles rather than on the grounds of human rights. As Justice Dixon remarked, the Australian Constitution:

> is an instrument framed in accordance with many traditional conceptions, to some of which it gives effect, as, for example, in separating the judicial power from other functions of government, others of which are simply assumed. Among these I think that it may fairly be said that the rule of law forms an assumption.[40]

The real significance of the decision was that the Court, in striking down the Communist Party Dissolution Act, entrenched its own position as the ultimate arbiter of the Constitution, and thus as an independent check upon the power of the legislature and the executive.

In the half-century since its enactment, the Communist Party Dissolution Act has been regarded as one of the most draconian and unfortunate pieces of legislation ever to be introduced into the federal Parliament. It threatened to herald an era of McCarthyism in Australia and to undermine accepted and revered Australian values such as the presumption of innocence, freedom of belief and speech, and the rule of law. In the focus upon Australia's present security situation after September 11, the Bali attack and the Madrid train bombing, it is easy to forget such history and its lessons. But, despite the many fundamental differences between the threats, other parallels are too striking to be denied. Today, the ideological enemy is not communism, but terrorism and Australia is at war not in Korea and Vietnam but in Afghanistan and Iraq. If Australia's new anti-terrorism laws are challenged in the High Court, it is likely that use of the decision in the *Communist Party Case* will form an important part of the attack.

---

[39] *Australian Communist Party* v. *Commonwealth* (1951) 83 CLR 1.   [40] Ibid. at 193.

V. The New Zealand response

Unlike Australia, New Zealand already had significant anti-terrorism laws[41] in place prior to September 11.[42] These included the International Terrorism (Emergency Powers) Act 1987 (enacted in part as a response to the 1985 bombing of the Rainbow Warrior), which confers 'emergency powers' upon the police and the armed forces after an 'international terrorist emergency' has been declared. Section 2 provides that such an emergency can only arise in regard to terrorist acts undertaken 'for the purpose of furthering, outside New Zealand, any political aim'. A controversial aspect of the Act is that, under s. 14, the Prime Minister may prohibit publication or broadcasting of matters relating to the international terrorist emergency. This power has never been used because a declaration of an international terrorist emergency has not been made under the Act.

Prior to September 11, New Zealand had passed legislation implementing eight of the dozen major international conventions on terrorism.[43] A further Bill that sought to implement two more of the conventions, the Terrorism (Bombings and Financing) Bill 2001, was before the New Zealand Parliament on September 11. After the attack, it became a 'convenient vehicle'[44] to respond to the requirement imposed on nations to combat terrorism by United Nations Security Council Resolution 1373. Indeed, a focal point of the debate became how the Bill could be redrafted to comply with the Resolution, and the Resolution was added as a Schedule to the Bill. The Bill was renamed and was ultimately enacted in October 2002[45] with overwhelming cross-party support[46] as the Terrorism Suppression Act 2002.[47] Before its

---

[41] Indeed, a recent study has found that 'a comprehensive legislative and substantive counter-terrorist framework had been established by the New Zealand state prior to New Zealand having any "real" contact with terrorism'. This was attributed to factors including 'a degree of caution' and 'a desire to be part of a broader anti-terrorist effort to strengthen ties with other "like-minded" states': B. K. Greener-Barcham, 'Before September 11: A History of Counter-terrorism in New Zealand' (2002) 37 *Australian Journal of Political Science* 509 at 514.

[42] See ibid., for accounts of the evolution of New Zealand's anti-terrorism laws. For an overview of New Zealand law on terrorism before and after September 11, see J. E. Smith, *New Zealand's Anti-Terrorism Campaign: Balancing Civil Liberties, National Security, and International Responsibilities* (December 2003), http://www.fulbright.org.nz/voices/axford/docs/smithj.pdf.

[43] A. Conte, 'A Clash of Wills: Counter-Terrorism and Human Rights' (2003) 20 *New Zealand Universities Law Review* 338 at 340 n. 7.

[44] M. Palmer, 'Counter-Terrorism Law' [2002] *New Zealand Law Journal* 456 at 456.

[45] Concerns raised prior to enactment included the definition of terrorism, the scope for designating terrorist organizations and the effects of such a designation: T. Dunworth, 'Public International Law' [2002] *New Zealand Law Review* 255 at 270.

[46] The Bill was passed with a margin of 106 to 9 votes, with only the Greens voting against it: J. E. Smith, *New Zealand's Anti-Terrorism Campaign*, note 42 above, at 30.

[47] As amended by the *Terrorism Suppression Amendment Act 2003* (NZ).

enactment, the Bill was vetted by the government's Crown Lawyer for compliance with the New Zealand Bill of Rights Act. Under s. 70, the Act must also be the subject of a parliamentary inquiry that must report by 1 December 2005 on whether the Act should be amended or repealed.

'Terrorist act' is defined by s. 5 of the Terrorism Suppression Act in three alternative ways.[48] First, under s. 5(1)(a) an act is a 'terrorist act' if it 'falls within subsection (2)'. S. 5(2) then provides:

> An act falls within this subsection if it is intended to cause, in any 1 or more countries, 1 or more of the outcomes specified in subsection (3), and is carried out for the purpose of advancing an ideological, political, or religious cause, and with the following intention:
>
> (a) to induce terror in a civilian population; or
> (b) to unduly compel or to force a government or an international organisation to do or abstain from doing any act.

Subsection (3) further states:

> The outcomes referred to in subsection (2) are –
>
> (a) the death of, or other serious bodily injury to, 1 or more persons (other than a person carrying out the act):
> (b) a serious risk to the health or safety of a population:
> (c) destruction of, or serious damage to, property of great value or importance, or major economic loss, or major environmental damage, if likely to result in 1 or more outcomes specified in paragraphs (a), (b) and (d):
> (d) serious interference with, or serious disruption to, an infrastructure facility, if likely to endanger human life:
> (e) introduction or release of a disease-bearing organism, if likely to devastate the national economy of a country.

Subs. (4) exempts acts of war made during situations of armed conflict and made in accordance with applicable international law from subs. (2), while subs. (5) states:

> To avoid doubt, the fact that a person engages in any protest, advocacy, or dissent, or engages in any strike, lockout, or other industrial action, is not, by itself, a sufficient basis for inferring that the person –
>
> (a) is carrying out an act for a purpose, or with an intention, specified in subsection (2); or
> (b) intends to cause an outcome specified in subsection (3).

---

[48] Under s. 25(1), 'planning or other preparations to carry out the act, whether it is actually carried out or not', a 'credible threat to carry out the act' or an 'attempt to carry out the act' also constitute a terrorist act.

Second, under s. 5(1)(b) an act qualifies as a 'terrorist act' if it is an act 'against a specified terrorism convention' (the use of 'against' in this context is certainly awkward).[49] S. 4(1) defines a 'specified terrorism convention' as any of the nine treaties listed in Schedule 3, such as the Convention for the Suppression of Unlawful Seizure of Aircraft or the Convention for the Suppression of Unlawful Acts against the Safety of Maritime Navigation.

Third, under s. 5(1)(c) an act is a 'terrorist act' if it is a 'terrorist act in armed conflict (as defined in section 4(1)'. S. 4(1) defines 'terrorist act in armed conflict' to mean an act:

(a) that occurs in a situation of armed conflict; and
(b) the purpose of which, by its nature or context is to intimidate a population, or to compel a government or an international organization to do or abstain from doing any act; and
(c) that is intended to cause death or serious bodily injury to a civilian or other person not taking an active part in the hostilities in that situation; and
(d) that is not excluded from the application of the Financing Convention by article 3 of that Convention.

Surprisingly, committing a 'terrorist act' is not itself made an offence under statute. However, the concept is central to other offences, such as the financing of terrorism (s. 8) or harbouring or concealing terrorists (s. 13A). Other offences such as participating in terrorist groups (s. 13) relate to terrorist organizations, which can be 'designated' under the Act.

Under s. 22, the Prime Minister 'may designate an entity as a terrorist entity under this section if the Prime Minister believes on reasonable grounds that the entity has knowingly carried out, or has knowingly participated in the carrying out of, 1 or more terrorist acts'. In making this decision, he or she 'may take into account any relevant information, including classified security information' (s. 30) as well as information that suggests that the United Nations Security Council considers that a body is a terrorist organization (s. 31). In fact, 'in the absence of evidence to the contrary', the listing of a body by the United Nations Security Council or one of its Committees is deemed to be 'sufficient evidence of the matters to which it relates' (s. 31(1)) and hence no further evidence is required. A decision to designate is subject to judicial review and expires after three years, but can be extended by the High Court. Once designated, an organization is subject to a number of consequences, such as having its property seized and being unable to gain financial or related services.

A second major piece of terrorism legislation, the Counter-Terrorism Bill 2002, was introduced into the New Zealand Parliament two months after the

---

[49] M. Palmer, 'Counter-Terrorism Law', note 44 above, at 457.

enactment of the Terrorism Suppression Act. The Bill covered a wide range of matters in seeking to close gaps in the legislative framework. It sought to amend a range of New Zealand statutes and contained important changes relating to, for example, search warrants and tracking devices.[50] It also sought to implement the requirements of the last two international treaties on terrorism that had yet to be legislated for in New Zealand. After nearly a year of debate and committee inquiry, the Bill was split into six separate Bills[51] and then passed in October 2003 with the overwhelming support of Parliament.

Since the enactment of the Terrorism Suppression Act, the New Zealand Government has designated a number of organizations. However, it has only designated organizations that have also been listed by the United Nations. This illustrates a key difference from Australia. A primary aim of the New Zealand legislative response has been to bring its law into compliance with United Nations Conventions and determinations about terrorism. By contrast, this has only been of secondary importance in Australia, which has tended to look to the United States for leadership and was willing to take part in pre-emptive military action in Iraq that arguably breached international law.[52]

This difference explains in part why New Zealand has not sought to replicate some of the more draconian proposals put forward in Australia, such as the indefinite detention of non-suspects by a secret intelligence service. Indeed, amendments to the New Zealand Security Intelligence Service Act 2003 have been relatively minor[53] and the focus has instead been on designation of United Nations listed organizations combined with more traditional law enforcement processes. However, like Australia, law reform and debate about terrorism has not had a significant focus on immigration law. The one major exception in New Zealand relates to Algerian asylum seeker Ahmed Zaoui who, despite being granted refugee status by the independent Refugee Status Appeals Authority, has been held in detention since December 2002 on the basis of a 'security risk certificate' issued by the New Zealand Director of Security under the Immigration Act 1987.[54]

---

[50] See A. Conte, 'Tracking Devices, Search Warrants and Self-Incrimination' (July 2003) *New Zealand Law Journal* 235.

[51] Namely, the Crimes Amendment Act 2003 (NZ), Misuse of Drugs Amendment Act (No 2) 2003 (NZ), New Zealand Security Intelligence Service Amendment Act 2003 (NZ), Sentencing Amendment Act 2003 (NZ), Summary Proceedings Amendment Act 2003 (NZ) and Terrorism Suppression Amendment Act 2003 (NZ).

[52] See D. Hovell and G. Williams, 'Advice on the Use of Force Against Iraq' (2003) 4 *Melbourne Journal of International Law* 183.

[53] See New Zealand Security Intelligence Service Amendment Act 2003 (NZ).

[54] The issues are set out in J. E. Smith, *New Zealand's Anti-Terrorism Campaign*, note 42 above, at 62–7. See also, for example, http://www.freezaoui.org.nz/, and http://www.amnesty.org.nz/zaoui for a civil libertarian perspective.

Although New Zealand has enacted laws that impact less severely upon basic rights, their response has had other problems. The notion of being a 'good international citizen' has had a pervasive influence in New Zealand. Indeed, this has been of such importance that its response can be seen as too deferential to United Nations' determinations and too passive in not being more critical in adapting these to its own situation. For example, an act qualifies as a 'terrorist act' in New Zealand whenever it is an act 'against a specified terrorism convention'. A body can also be designated as a terrorist organization if the United Nations Security Council considers the body to be so, without any requirement for a further determination or assessment in New Zealand. While the Australian proscription regime lacks a sufficient judicial check, it does at least require the Attorney-General to satisfy him or herself that a body is a terrorist organization and also provides for scrutiny of this decision by Parliament.

VI. Conclusion

Australia and New Zealand have passed important new laws in response to September 11. However, while New Zealand Minister of Justice and Minister of Foreign Affairs and Trade Phil Goff has suggested that 'At this point, legislatively, I think we've pretty much got it covered',[55] Australia continues to see a succession of new proposals. The reasons for this lie as much in the political importance of national security and terrorism to the forthcoming federal election in Australia as in the fact that prior to September 11 Australia had no national legislation on the topic.

It is not surprising that political leaders in both nations, as members of parliament and law-makers, have turned to new laws after September 11 and the Bali attack. New legislation is at least within their control and is a symbolic and potentially practical response. However, it is important to acknowledge that new laws will not provide long-term solutions. Legislation is unlikely to tackle the causes of terrorism and will not deter a terrorist from a premeditated course of action. Further, law-making may also redirect attention away from debate over other responses to terrorism. Worse still, enacting draconian laws may lead to a sense of complacency on the part of the public and may also compromise the same democratic freedoms that are meant to be the subject of protection. This is of particular concern in Australia which, without a statement of rights that has political acceptance and legal force, lacks the tools needed to navigate through the current war on terror whilst still maintaining basic freedoms.

I do not mean to suggest that a nation's response to terrorism should be timid. Indeed, all nations have an obligation to protect their people from

---

[55] J. E. Smith, *New Zealand's Anti-Terrorism Campaign*, note 42 above, at 35.

terrorism. However, when the law is used as a primary tool in the war on terror, it can also pose a threat to the rule of law. In succession, such laws can undermine the basic values and assumptions that have been developed over the course of centuries. Unfortunately, this can occur without any real appreciation of the extent to which such laws are actually effective in combating terrorism.

PART SIX

Anti-Terrorism Measures in Africa, the Middle East and Argentina

25

Terrorism and governance in South Africa and Eastern Africa

Introduction

It has become axiomatic that terrorists, who have no respect for international borders, can be countered only through an internationally coordinated programme. For this reason, the Security Council of the United Nations has invoked its powers under Chapter VII of the UN Charter to insist that states cooperate in regional and international anti-terrorism efforts in addition to setting up domestic anti-terrorism regimes. This chapter examines the main features of the anti-terrorism regimes of four African states, namely, South Africa, Uganda, Tanzania and Kenya, all of which have had some experience of terrorism. It sets their anti-terrorism legislation in the international and regional context to establish how each state has integrated itself into the wider anti-terrorist framework. What emerges from this study is that the anti-terrorism regime in the four states has come to be dominated not only by the executive branches of government, but also by the powerful executive branches of other governments and the executive-like powers of the UN Security Council.

I. The international and regional anti-terrorism regime

UN Security Council Resolution 1373 of 2001, issued under Chapter VII of the UN Charter, requires all states to refrain from providing support of any kind to terrorist groups and to prevent terrorist acts through early warning systems and mutual assistance in investigation and prosecution.[1] States must establish and

Thank you to a wonderful team of students, colleagues and friends who helped with this chapter: to Jeremy Wilkin, Simon van Dugteren, Grant Tungay and Janse Rabie for their research support; to Jean Redpath, Adele Erasmus and P. J. Schwikkard for lessons on South African criminal procedure; to Ken Nyaundi, Alexandra Nkonge and Judge Anthony Bahati for information on the legal systems of Kenya, Uganda and Tanzania respectively; and to Tom Bennett, Christina Murray, Ken Nyaundi, Isabel Goodman, Michael Osborne, P. J. Schwikkard, Adele Erasmus, Francois Du Bois, Victor V. Ramraj, Jörg Monar and Lynn Welchman for comments on earlier drafts. The errors are my own.

[1] Articles 1(a), 2(a), and 2(b) of Security Council Resolution 1373 of 2001 (hereafter SCR 1373).

prosecute a range of terrorist offences within their domestic criminal justice system and must suppress recruitment to terrorist groups.[2] These measures must combat both terrorism *stricto sensu* and organized crime, which is seen to have an intimate connection to terrorism.[3]

SCR 1373 was followed and confirmed by a range of later resolutions[4] directed specifically at groups of individuals and organizations identified as terrorist by the Security Council.[5] They require that states freeze the financial assets of these entities, deny them entry into and transit through their territories and prevent them from selling and supplying military equipment, whether such sales and supplies are carried out from their territories or even by their nationals outside their territories.[6]

SCR 1373 calls on states to sign all international conventions and protocols which relate to terrorism,[7] including, specifically, the International Convention for the Suppression of the Financing of Terrorism of 1999.[8] All four states have ratified this Convention[9] as well as the International Convention for the Suppression of Terrorist Bombings of 1998.[10] Kenya, South Africa and Tanzania have also ratified the Organization of African Unity's Convention for the Prevention and Combating of Terrorism of 1999,[11] and Kenya and South Africa are parties to the Convention against Transnational Organized Crime of 2000.[12] Together, these treaties reflect the Security Council requirements, setting out a fairly detailed system arranged around two main phases of a counter-terrorism programme.

In the first phase, a wide range of measures attempt to prevent terrorism.[13] These measures include the surveillance of suspects and the monitoring, and occasionally freezing, of their assets. In addition, assets connected to terrorism may be permanently seized. Asset seizure often follows on conviction for one of the treaty crimes, but criminal conviction does not appear to be a

---

[2] Article 2.   [3] Article 4.
[4] See Security Council Resolutions 1390 of 2002, 1455 and 1456 of 2003 and 1526 of 2004.
[5] See note 162 below.
[6] Paragraphs 2(a) to (c) of Security Council Resolution 1390 of 2002 (hereafter SCR 1390), reaffirmed by Security Council Resolutions 1455 and 1456 of 2003 (hereafter SCR 1455 and SCR 1456 respectively) and Security Council Resolution 1526 of 2004.
[7] Article 3(d). See also article 2(a) of SCR 1456.
[8] Hereafter the Financing Convention. See http://untreaty.un.org/English/Terrorism.asp.
[9] See http://untreaty.un.org/ENGLISH/Status/Chapter_xviii/treaty11.asp.
[10] Hereafter the Bombing Convention. See http://untreaty.un.org/English/Terrorism.asp.
[11] Hereafter the Algiers Convention. Uganda has signed but not ratified this Convention. Information supplied by the African Union.
[12] Hereafter the Organized Crime Convention. Tanzania and Uganda have signed but not ratified this Convention.
[13] See articles 8, 12, and 18, Financing Convention; articles 12 and 20–1, Organized Crime Convention; article 4(2) Algiers Convention; and article 15 Bombing Convention.

prerequisite to seizure in all cases. In the monitoring of assets, neither states nor individuals may refuse to provide information on the basis of bank secrecy.[14]

The second phase concerns the prosecution and extradition of terrorists.[15] Both terrorism and transnational organized crime are considered to be particularly grave offences, for which punishment must be correspondingly harsh. Each Convention requires signatories to create a range of specific crimes and provide expressly for wide accomplice and attempt liability. Over and above the wide accomplice liability, two Conventions suggest that states proceed against criminal or terrorist groups. States must either prosecute or extradite persons accused of terrorism or organized crime. They may not grant reprieve from criminal proceedings on the basis that the offence is politically motivated or fiscal in nature.[16]

Close cooperation between states underpins the anti-terrorism programme as a whole: the conventions require an early warning system against terrorist threats[17] and oblige states to guard against the abuse of refugee status and asylum seeking.[18] States are expected to cooperate with one another to facilitate investigation, prosecution and extradition of offenders[19] and the confiscation and disposal of assets connected to the treaty crimes.[20]

Together, the treaties and the Security Council Resolutions attempt to create a worldwide, uniform system in which terrorist threats can be recognized and prevented, information shared among states and terrorists extradited and prosecuted. The entire regime rests, of course, on an internationally recognized, determinate definition of terrorism. The lack of one is a serious obstacle. The Security Council Resolutions do not attempt a definition, and almost all of the treaties prohibit a range of activities rather than defining the crime of terrorism itself.[21] The most recent attempt, which was made in the

---

[14] Article 12(2) Financing Convention; article 12(6) Organized Crime Convention.
[15] The key provisions referred to in this paragraph are found in articles 2, 4(b), 6, 10, 11, 13, 14 of the Financing Convention; articles 5, 6, 8, 11, 18, and 23 of the Organized Crime Convention; articles 2(a), 3(2), and 8 of the Algiers Convention; and articles 2, 4, 5, 8, 11 and 15(a) of the Bombing Convention.
[16] Note, however, the 'persecution' exemption, note 156 below.
[17] See generally: article 18 Financing Convention; article 2(b), (c), (f) and (i) Algiers Convention.
[18] Article 4(2)(g) Algiers Convention.
[19] Article 12 Financing Convention; articles 17–19, 21 and 27 Organized Crime Convention; and article 10 of the Bombing Convention. The OAU Convention on the Prevention and Combating of Terrorism even provides for a semi-judicial organ, a *commission rogatoire*, which is meant to have jurisdiction over states in its investigation of suspected terrorism. It is not clear who is expected to staff these commissions. See articles 14, 16 and 17 of the Algiers Convention.
[20] Article 8(3) Financing Convention; and articles 13 and 14 Organized Crime Convention.
[21] Only two international instruments attempt a normative definition. The 1937 attempt by the League of Nations, in its Geneva Convention for the Prevention and Punishment of

International Convention on the Suppression of the Financing of Terrorism, does provide a normative definition of terrorism, but only in the context of armed conflict. The armed conflict section of the Convention refers to acts 'intended to cause death or serious bodily injury to a civilian, or to any other person not taking part in the hostilities ... when the purpose of such act ... is to intimidate a population, or to compel a government or an international organisation to do or to abstain from doing any act'. However, the Convention describes 'peacetime' terrorism only by reference to the specific acts outlawed in the earlier Conventions.[22]

The main obstacle to formulating a definition, particularly relevant to Africa, is the right to self-determination.[23] Whether terrorism is seen as a list of proscribed activities or more generally as violence aimed at influencing the government, it renders methods typically used in armed liberation struggles unlawful. The fear that acknowledgement of the crime of terrorism will negate the right of self-determination finds expression in the definition of the offence by the OAU, which expressly excludes the struggle of a people for self-determination.[24]

Because the lack of a common definition of a crime hinders extradition, the UN Office on Drugs and Crime has provided a selection of the major models of definition in use in domestic jurisdictions. The most detailed model requires three elements before a criminal act becomes a terrorist act: that the act is of a particular level of violence, that there is an intention to intimidate, and that there is an underlying motivation of a particular sort – usually political, ideological or religious.[25]

Terrorism, defined 'acts of terrorism' as: 'criminal acts directed against a State and intended or calculated to create a state of terror in the minds of particular persons, or a group of persons or the general public' (LN Doc C.546(1) M 383(1) 1937 V, Art. 1 (2)). In 1994, the General Assembly Declaration on Measures to Eliminate International Terrorism defined terrorist acts as 'criminal acts intended or calculated to provoke a state of terror in the general public, a group of persons or particular persons for political purposes' (UN GA Res. 49/60, Annex, 9 December 1994, para. 3). Regional instruments which provide normative definitions include the Convention of the Organization of the Islamic Conference on Combating International Terrorism, adopted on 1 July 1999, the Algiers Convention and the Treaty on Cooperation among States Members of the Commonwealth of Independent States in Combating Terrorism of 4 June 1999.

[22] See generally C. L. Lim, Chapter 3, in this volume.
[23] The right to self-determination was accepted as an obligation *ergo omnes* by the *East Timor Case* (1995) *ICJ Reports* 90.
[24] Article 3(1) Algiers Convention. The Convention does not make clear how this article is to be reconciled with article 3(2), which states that 'political, philosophical, racial, ethnic, religious or other motives shall not be a justifiable defence against a terrorist act'.
[25] UN Office on Drugs and Crime *Legislative Guide to the Universal Anti-Terrorism Conventions and Protocols* (2003) at http://www.unodc.org/odccp/terrorism.html?id=11702 para 20. It suggests omitting the element of motivation for two main reasons: its inclusion could frustrate extradition requests and it would be impossible to prove without a confession from the accused.

The above model could cover acts of violence in both peace and war. In this discussion, however, terrorism will be viewed as a 'peacetime' phenomenon, ideologically motivated, aimed primarily at civilians and intended to cause terror in the targeted community. It is not immediately evident that this narrower view of terrorism is supported in the developed world, as anti-terrorist rhetoric creates contradictions within state practice. States frequently adopt a military discourse in responding to terrorism and claim that its threat confers on them the right to use force. In any discussion of the legal regime which should govern terrorism, however, states vigorously reject the framework of armed conflict. They insist that a terrorist attack is not military activity – even if such activity would also be prohibited by the laws of war. Under this view, terrorists are seen as serious but ordinary criminals. They are not considered war criminals, and states are not subject to international humanitarian law when they deal with them.[26] The ideological motivation behind terrorism therefore does not elevate terrorist attacks to the status of (possibly legitimate) acts of armed conflict.

II. Domestic politics

Despite Africa's long and painful history of violence and civil war, the continent as a whole has experienced relatively little terrorism in the narrower, 'peacetime' sense outlined above. Instead, terrorist attacks are encountered in two main forms – as a tactic of organized groups engaged in criminal activities such as the drug trade or trafficking of persons, and as a breach of humanitarian law when rebel groups terrorize, rob and coerce civilians to assist their military campaigns.[27] By contrast, South and Eastern Africa have had experiences of terror attacks carried out on civilian targets in a peacetime setting. The worst of these were possibly the bombing of the American embassies in Nairobi and Dar-es-Salaam in 1998, but there have

---

[26] This rejection of any connection between terrorism and war for definitional purposes is perhaps seen most clearly in the vehement response to a proposal by an ILA Committee to define terrorism with reference to International Humanitarian Law in 1982. The minority report insisted that terrorism 'is committed during a time of peace' by non-state groups which are not recognised as belligerents. See the Fourth Interim Report of the ILA Committee on Terrorism, 1982 in (1984) 7 *Terrorism: An International Journal* 131; Y. Dinstein, 'Comments on the Fourth Interim Report of the ILA Committee on International Terrorism (1982)' 7 *Terrorism* 163–5; and R. A. Friedlander, 'Comment: Unmuzzling the Dogs of War' 7 *Terrorism* 169.

[27] See generally J.-F. Bayart, S. Ellis and B. Hibou, *The Criminalization of the State in Africa* (Bloomingdale, Indiana University Press, 1999), 49–68 and C. Powell and I. Goodman, 'Reconciling the Fight against Terrorism and Organised Crime with Banjul' (2002) in *Africa and Terrorism* Monograph no. 74, Institute for Security Studies, Pretoria, 35–49.

also been other incidents. Examples include bombings and attempted bombings in Kampala, Uganda in 1997 and an attack on an Israeli hotel in Kikambala Beach, Mombasa, Kenya in 2002. South Africa experienced a series of bombings between 1994 and 2000,[28] although many of these may have had criminal,[29] rather than ideological, motivations.

Uganda is a special case in this study, as it also has extensive experience of armed conflict. Two rebel forces, the Lord's Resistance Army (LRA) and the Allied Democratic Forces (ADF), run military campaigns in the country and have been declared 'terrorist organizations' by the government.[30]

The presence of a terrorist threat within these four states might suggest that there would be a strong internal need and support for their anti-terrorism legislation. However, in all four states, there has been opposition to the new regime. In East Africa, commentators on the anti-terrorism regime accuse the government of introducing the measures in response to foreign pressure, particularly that of the United States. The perception that the anti-terrorism regime is externally driven is strengthened by the fact that the targets of the attacks in these countries have been foreign embassies and businesses, not local interests. In Kenya, the Bill is perceived to have been promulgated after the United States and Britain put pressure on the Kenyan government.[31] The Kenyan *Daily Nation* reports that Kenyans believe that the US authored the legislation, due to similarities to the US Patriot Act.[32] The Ugandan legislation had US support and the Ugandan rebel group, the LRA, was put onto the US list of terrorist organizations once the Ugandan Act had been passed into law.[33]

---

[28] H. Boshoff and M. Schönteich, 'South Africa's Operational and Legislative Responses to Terrorism' in (2002) *Africa and Terrorism* Monograph no. 74, Institute for Security Studies, Pretoria, 63; and Powell and Goodman, 'Reconciling the Fight', at 43–5. The South African Law Commission Report no. 92 of 2000 lists 338 bombings between 1994 and 1998.

[29] Chiefly the drug trade, the smuggling of weapons, gold, ivory and other valuable substances and the theft and export of cars and other valuables. See generally S. Ellis 'The New Frontiers of Crime in South Africa' in Bayart, Ellis, and Hibou, *Criminalization of the State*, at 49–68.

[30] The LRA receive support from Sudan, while the Ugandan government supports the Sudanese People's Liberation Army (SPLA), the principal Sudanese rebel group. Uganda was also a major player in the DRC conflict. It withdrew its forces in September 2003.

[31] See 'Anti-terror steps irk Kenyans' http://www.news24.com/News24/Africa/News/0,,2-11-1447_1393459,00.html.

[32] Kagari 'Anti-terror Bill an affront to human rights' *Daily Nation on the Web*, 18 November 2003 at http://www.nationaudio.com/News/DailyNation/18112003/Coment/Comment18112003.html.

[33] See Human Rights Watch World Report 2003 at http://www.hrw.org/wr2k3/africa13.html. See also H. Strydom, 'South Africa's Response to International Terrorism' (2002) 27 *South African Yearbook of International Law* 82, at 95–6.

To the extent that the anti-terrorism measures relate to the internal political landscape, commentators fear that anti-terrorism laws will be used not to protect the citizens of the country, but to suppress particular groups. In Uganda, Kenya and Tanzania, Muslim residents feel targeted by the legislation.[34] The Tanzanian government has been accused of torturing members of opposition groups, and critics believe the new legislation will allow the government to suppress and repress opposition with impunity.[35] In Uganda, civil organizations also assert that the legislation was not motivated by the war on terrorism but rather by Uganda's internal politics. The government in Uganda is accused of intolerance to opposition and large-scale mistreatment of opponents, including arbitrary arrests, detentions and assaults.[36]

III. Background to the anti-terrorism legislation of South and Eastern Africa

As indicated above, both Uganda and Tanzania already have legislation in force against terrorism, while the Kenyan executive produced a draft Suppression of Terrorism Act in 2003.[37]

South Africa's draft anti-terrorism legislation has had a difficult gestation period of over eight years. The term 'terrorism' has a particularly unfortunate history in South Africa, having been misused by the apartheid government in its suppression of political opposition. Ironically, South Africa's anti-terrorism Bill[38] can therefore be traced back to a project to repeal one of apartheid South Africa's most notorious pieces of security legislation, which included the infamous provision for indefinite detention.[39] Over time, the perceived need to reformulate rather than remove security legislation led to a draft of anti-terrorism legislation first by the South African Police in 1999, and then by the South African Law Reform Commission (SALRC) and two parliamentary portfolio committees. This draft, although accepted by the National Assembly, was further amended by the second house of Parliament, the

---

[34] Above note 31. Hitherto, persons arrested under the Ugandan Act have come largely from the *Tabliq* sect of Islam.

[35] See Amnesty International report at http://web.amnesty.org/library/Index/ENGAFR 560042001?open&of=ENG-TZA.

[36] Above note 33.

[37] Uganda's Anti-Terrorism Act ('Ugandan Act') came into force on 7 June 2002. Tanzania's Prevention of Terrorism Act ('Tanzanian Act') came into force on 15 June 2003. Kenya's legislation is still in draft form: the Suppression of Terrorism Bill 2003 ('Kenyan Bill').

[38] In its final version, the anti-terrorism Bill is called the 'Protection of Constitutional Democracy against Terrorist and Related Activities Bill'. It is referred to as 'the South African Bill' in this chapter.

[39] See SALRC Report *Project 105 Review of Security Legislation, Terrorism: Section 54 of the Internal Security Act 1982 (Act no. 74 of 1982)* August 2002 at 1.

National Council of Provinces (the NCOP). It was then referred back to the portfolio committees for discussion and reintroduced to Parliament after the elections of April 2004. It was finally passed on 12 November 2004.[40]

There seem to be two main themes running through the criticism of the South African Bill. The first, recalling South Africa's apartheid history, objects to the legislation on the basis of liberal principles of constitutionalism, the doctrine of separation of powers and human rights. The second theme is grounded more concretely in socio-political considerations: certain groups fear victimization under the legislation. Thus the various drafts have been heavily criticised by the Muslim community[41] and the trade union movement.[42]

In Eastern Africa, there was little consultation about the anti-terrorism legislation. The draft bills were not referred to the Law Reform Commissions in any of the three states. Despite criticism, the legislation was passed extremely quickly in both Uganda and Tanzania. Uganda's Human Rights Commission suggested extensive amendments to its draft Bill,[43] most of which were not adopted.[44] Kenya, which has not yet passed its Bill, may still adapt the Bill in response to some of the objections against it.

IV. The anti-terrorism regimes of South and Eastern Africa

The following description of the legislation in South and Eastern Africa is arranged around two main phases of the internal anti-terrorism regime of each state: the pre-trial phase, which revolves mainly around the prevention

---

[40] This Bill will become an Act of Parliament when it is signed by the President (see s. 74 (1) (d) of the Constitution).

[41] South African Law Reform Commission *Compendium of Recent Publications* 31 March 2004 at 22 and the submissions to the SALRC, available at http://www.law.wits.ac.za/salc/report/report.html.

[42] One of the final changes made to the Bill by the NCOP was meant to address concerns of the Congress of South African Trade Unions (COSATU). It aimed to ensure that workers who take part in unprotected strikes do not fall within the ambit of the definition of terrorism.

[43] In particular, it objected to the complete removal of the political offence exception, the vagueness of the definition, the duplication of offences, the reverse onus of proof, the disproportionately high sentences, the discretion enjoyed by the executive to declare organizations terrorist and the offence of wearing clothing which creates the reasonable apprehension that the wearer supports a terrorist organization.

[44] The final Act has reworded the definition of terrorism, adding significant detail but retaining much of the breadth of the previous definition (section 7). Offences are still duplicated and the executive retains its discretion to declare organizations terrorist (compare section 7 with sections 12–14 and sections 23–9, and see section 10). However, the previous blanket immunity of executive officials has been reduced to civil immunity only (section 32) and the offence of wearing clothing which creates the reasonable apprehension that the wearer supports a terrorist organization has been dropped (see clause 16 of the Ugandan Suppression of Terrorism Bill of 2001).

of terrorism, and the trial phase, which describes the range of possible offences, the rules of evidence which go to prove them, and the consequences of conviction. The description of the South African draft legislation includes an extra section on the constitutionality of the legislation. South Africa forms the focal point of the analysis and its draft Bill is situated in the context of both the constitution and other South African legislation. The Kenyan, Tanzanian and Ugandan regimes are set out more briefly.

The aim in this section is to demonstrate the similarities between the states in this region and to identify their points of agreement and disagreement with South Africa. In particular, this section will examine the role of the executive and identify how its powers have grown through the anti-terrorism regime. The extension of executive power is problematic, not just because it runs counter to human rights law, but also because it often leads to other dangerous results as well. By weakening the governmental institutions which are meant to keep a check on executive action, an imbalance of power threatens the rule of law. In extreme cases, where democracy is fragile or the government has doubtful legitimacy, the imbalance fails to achieve its underlying aim, the prevention of terrorism.

A. South Africa's draft anti-terrorism legislation

1. Prevention

Previous drafts of South Africa's anti-terrorism Bill introduced controversial changes to criminal procedure in the case of suspected terrorism and allowed the executive considerable freedom to act against suspected terrorists without judicial oversight.[45] Most of the objections to these changes have been met and detention without trial has been dropped completely.[46]

The regime of investigation into and prevention of terrorism has largely been integrated with the regime against organized crime. The Bill proposes extensive amendments to the Prevention of Organized Crime Act (POCA), expanding its ambit to include terrorism. Chapter 6 of POCA, which provides for civil forfeiture of property connected to a crime, would, once amended, also apply to 'property associated with terrorist and related

---

[45] For criticism of the various drafts see E. Steyn, 'The draft Anti-Terrorism Bill of 2000: the lobster pot of the South African criminal justice system?' (2001) 14 *South African Journal of Criminal Justice* 178–94; M. Cowling, 'The Return of Detention without Trial? Some Thoughts and Comments on the Draft Anti-Terrorism Bill and the Law Commission Report' (2000) 13 *South African Journal of Criminal Justice* 344–59; Powell and Goodman, 'Reconciling the Fight'; C. Powell, 'South Africa's Legislation against Terrorism and Organised Crime' 2002 *Singapore Journal of Legal Studies* 104–21; and I. Goodman, 'The Draft Anti-Terrorism Bill' 2002 *Responsa Meridiana* 1–21.

[46] See Strydom, 'South Africa's Response', at 96–7 for the history of the detention clause up to 2002.

activities'. By this process, the National Director of Public Prosecutions can get an order of forfeiture of property which was 'acquired, collected, used, possessed, owned or provided for the benefit of, or on behalf of, or at the direction of, or under the control of an entity which commits or attempts to commit or facilitates the commission' of the crimes in the anti-terrorism Bill. A criminal prosecution of any person involved in this 'entity' will not be necessary.[47]

In addition, clause 22 brings Chapter 5 of the National Prosecuting Authority Act (the NPA) into operation.[48] The powers of investigating officers in cases of suspected terrorism will, by this mechanism, be the same as those of officers investigating organized crime. Under Chapter 5 of the Act, the Investigating Director of the Directorate of Special Operations (the DSO)[49] may choose to conduct a particular investigation and assign particular officers to deal with it.[50] The officers assigned to such an investigation then enjoy expanded powers of search and seizure. In particular, although designated officers need to apply for a court order to search a suspect's property, they do not need to specify the particular articles they hope to find.[51]

Two additional procedures in the Bill complement the powers in the NPA. A judge can authorize the stopping and searching of vehicles, which order would be valid for ten days.[52] A more important addition to the normal South African criminal procedure, however, is contained in clause 23, which allows for an *ex parte* application by the National Director of Public Prosecutions to freeze the property of a terror suspect.[53] This last provision is worth emphasizing, because it provides an example of executive discretion without judicial oversight: under clause 23, to obtain a freezing order, the National Director of Public Prosecutions need prove merely that the assets in question are controlled by an entity identified by the UN Security Council as terrorist.[54] It is not necessary to show that the assets will in fact be used for a terrorist purpose, or that the entity identified by the UN Security Council is in fact a terrorist organization. As a corollary, the Bill does not provide that

---

[47] The schedule to the Bill amends s. 38 of POCA, which provides for civil forfeiture of property.
[48] Act no. 32 of 1998.
[49] Colloquially known as 'the Scorpions', the DSO has special powers to investigate organized crime.
[50] Section 28 of the NPA. See generally J. Redpath, *The DSO: Analysing the Scorpions* (2004) Monograph no. 93, Institute for Security Studies, Pretoria.
[51] Section 29 of the NPA.   [52] Clause 24 of the South African Bill.
[53] Persons who may be prohibited from dealing with property include persons with previous convictions for terrorism and associated offences, as well as entities identified as terrorist by the Security Council of the United Nations (see clause 25).
[54] Clause 23(1)(b) of the South African Bill, referring to clause 25.

persons affected by the freezing order may challenge the UN Security Council's categorization.

2. Trial

Once the terrorist suspects are brought to court, they face a substantial problem: the crimes of which they are accused are the most broadly and vaguely defined in all of South African law. The new Bill codifies a range of treaty crimes and introduces two main new offences: terrorism itself and a so-called 'offence connected with terrorist activities', which provides for extensive accomplice liability.[55] Faced with the problem presented by the right to self-determination and the criticism that previous definitions outlawed political opposition as well as terrorism, the drafters chose not to narrow the definition but to add two exceptions exempting acts committed in pursuance of advocacy, protest, dissent or industrial action as well as acts committed during armed struggles in the exercise of a legitimate right of self-determination.[56]

The offence of terrorism[57] consists of three elements: an act, an intention and a motivation. Each element is broadly defined. Part (a), which sets out the act, appears extremely detailed, but is nonetheless unclear and broad. For example, the 'systematic, repeated or arbitrary use of violence' constitutes 'terrorist activity'. It is difficult to imagine which form of violence could not be qualified by one of those three adjectives, which means that only the requirements of intention and motivation – themselves very broad – distinguish between *any* act of violence and the very serious crime of terrorism itself. The rest of part (a) lists activities which, for the most part, cause severe harm. Examples are the release of dangerous chemicals into the environment, seriously endangering life, causing serious risk to public health, causing destruction or substantial damage to property, a natural resource or an environmental or cultural heritage, causing major economic loss or extensive destabilization of an economic system and creating a serious public emergency or general insurrection. Within part (a), two extra *mens rea* requirements are inserted into the description of interfering with or disrupting an essential service, facility or system. In these cases, the interference or disruption must be 'intended or calculated'.[58] The Bill provides a non-exhaustive list of possible services, facilities or systems, including information,

---

[55] Clauses 2 and 3.   [56] Clause 1(3) and (4).

[57] This offence is set out, rather incongruously, in the definition section. 'Terrorist activity' is defined in clause 1(1)(xxv).

[58] See Steyn, 'The draft Anti-Terrorism Bill', at 186–7, for an argument, based on general rules of statutory interpretation, that this phrasing reduces the fault component of the offence to negligence.

telecommunication, banking and financial systems, emergency services, infra-structural facilities and public services generally.[59]

The three terrorist intentions listed in (b) are the intention to threaten the unity and territorial integrity of a state, to intimidate or cause feelings of insecurity in the public, and unduly to compel or induce a person, government or general public to do or abstain from any act. The already broad phrasing of these intentions is underscored by the lowering of the standard of proof. Under (b), the state can establish either that the accused had the intention or that such intention can, by its nature and context, reasonably be inferred. In inferring this intention, the court may rely on the accused's 'constructive knowledge' of a fact.[60] Part (c) of the definition sets out the requisite terrorist motivation. An act which satisfies one of the criteria in parts (a) and (b) of the definition becomes a terrorist activity if it is carried out for an individual or collective political, religious, ideological or philosophical cause.

Redundancy is a common feature of anti-terrorism legislation, because definitions of terrorism often duplicate crimes already found in the munici-pal legal system. But the South African legislation is remarkable in the extent to which the draft Bill duplicates itself. Clauses 4 to 10 of the Bill create a wide range of offences to implement separately the thirteen international conven-tions mentioned in the preamble.[61] The treaty offences prohibit bombing, financing, hijacking, hostage-taking and harming a range of particular per-sons or objects, namely, foreign representatives, fixed platforms and ships. The offences in clauses 4 to 10 fit comfortably into the main crime of terrorism, and the definition of terrorism incorporates the already existing South African crimes of murder, culpable homicide, assault, arson and mali-cious damage to property. However, it is in the area of accomplice liability that the duplication reaches ludicrous levels.

Accomplice liability is provided for more than four times. To the extent that the offences are consequence and not circumstance crimes,[62] the various forms of terrorism cover principal and accomplice liability already. Secondly, facilitation, participation, assistance, contribution and planning are expressly included within the crime of terrorism itself.[63] Thirdly, clause 3 separately criminalizes enhancing the ability of another to engage in terrorist activity,

---

[59] For almost all of these acts, the Bill includes acts which cause harm outside of the republic. The only exception, curiously, is creating a public emergency or general insurrection.

[60] Under clause 1(6), a person is deemed to have knowledge of a fact if he or she had actual knowledge, failed to obtain information to confirm the existence of a fact, or merely believed that there was a reasonable possibility that the fact existed.

[61] The conventions include the Financing Convention, the Bombing Convention and the Algiers Convention. The Organized Crime Convention is not included.

[62] See J. Burchell and J. Milton, *Principles of Criminal Law* (2nd ed., Cape Town, Juta, 1997), 107 for a discussion of the distinction between 'consequence' and 'circumstance' crimes.

[63] Clause 1(1)(iv).

providing or offering a skill and providing weapons or other logistical support. The distinction between this form of accomplice liability and that contained within terrorism itself is that clause 3 creates liability for assistance negligently given.[64] Fourthly, clause 14 creates the separate offence of conspiracy and inducing another to commit an offence. Fifthly, the offence of failing to report a suspected terrorist crime or person[65] may be seen as another form of accomplice liability.[66] Finally, the convention crimes of financing and harbouring also codify forms of accomplice liability.[67] It is worth noting that accomplice liability is incurred whether or not the terrorist activity takes place.[68]

On conviction of terrorism or a related offence, the maximum sentences are extremely high. Life imprisonment can be imposed for some of the offences in the Bill[69] and the maximum fine is R100 million – the highest in the statute books. In allowing the lower courts to impose some of these sentences, the draft Bill follows POCA's approach of raising the normal sentencing limits of these courts.[70] The Bill allows the district magistrates' courts sentencing limits of R250 000[71] and five years, and the regional magistrates' courts a maximum sentence of R100 million and eighteen years.[72] The rationale for the elevation of sentencing limits is unclear, and the wisdom of the change is questionable. The

[64] Liability arises when the person providing assistance 'knows or ought reasonably to have known or suspected' the existence of the main offence.

[65] Clause 12.

[66] This provision was introduced in earlier versions of the anti-terrorism Bill. It carried a severe sentence (the maximum penalty was five years' imprisonment with no option for a fine) and was problematic constitutionally. Failure to volunteer information could lead to imprisonment but persons who provided information were protected only by conditional indemnity (clause 21(2)). People caught under this provision also faced detention for interrogation if the NDPP was not satisfied that they had revealed *all* their information (clause 16). In its latest version, this provision forces people to reveal their information on terrorist crimes or persons, but no longer threatens them with detention should their information appear incomplete. However, the Bill does not grant indemnity to people who incriminate themselves while providing the information.

[67] See clauses 4 and 11. These forms of accomplice liability are also already offences under the common law.

[68] With regard to clauses 2, 3, 4, 11, 12(2) and 14; see also clause 17.

[69] Terrorism itself (clause 2) and all the convention offences.

[70] For example, POCA allows the regional magistrates' courts to impose fines of R100 million and imprisonment of thirty years, whereas the normal sentencing limit for the regional magistrates court is R300 000 and fifteen years' imprisonment. See s. 92 of the Magistrates Court Act 32 of 1944 and Government Gazette 19435, GN R1410 of 30 October 1998.

[71] See clause 18 of the South African Bill. The maximum sentence which the District Magistrates Court may impose in cases other than POCA cases is R60 000 or three years' imprisonment. See s. 92 of the Magistrates Court Act 32 of 1944 and Government Gazette 19435, GN R1410 of 30 October 1998.

[72] Clause 18.

magistrates' courts do not produce published judgments and are loath to engage with constitutional issues.[73]

On conviction, forfeiture of assets connected to the crime is mandatory.[74] Third parties have three years – the normal prescription period – to claim restitution or compensation for their interests in the property.[75] They face a reverse onus of proof, as they need to establish that they acquired the property in good faith and for consideration.[76] In addition, they must show either that the surrounding circumstances were not such as to arouse a reasonable suspicion of terrorist use of the property, or that they could not prevent such use.[77]

3. Constitutionality

Despite attempts to render the latest draft more human-rights friendly, its constitutionality is still in doubt. To the extent that the procedural rights of terrorist suspects have been restored, not to the usual position in South African criminal procedure, but to the regime applicable to organized crime, the Bill and POCA face similar constitutional challenges.[78] On its own, POCA can be challenged for infringing various constitutional rights, particularly the right to silence, the presumption of innocence, the right not to be deprived of one's property, the right to privacy, and the right to dignity.[79]

Most challenges to POCA have, however, been unsuccessful, and have focused on the merits of the particular case rather than on the constitutionality of the provisions of the Act. In addition, judgments which reject the occasional challenges to the constitutionality of POCA[80] do not provide detailed reasoning to

[73] The only limitation on magistrates courts' constitutional jurisdiction is that they may not pronounce on the constitutionality of legislation or the conduct of government ministers (s. 170 Constitution of the Republic of South Africa Act 108 of 1996). In practice, magistrates' courts tend to assume they have no constitutional jurisdiction at all. See S. Jagwanth, 'The Constitutional Roles and Responsibilities of the Lower Courts' (2002) 18 *SAJHR* 201 and Powell, 'South Africa's Legislation', at 110.

[74] Clause 19. A curious feature of this provision is the phrasing – the Court must order the forfeiture of property 'reasonably believed' to have been used in the commission of an offence. This formulation leaves unclear what standard of proof is to be applied.

[75] Clause 20.

[76] Compare clause 17(6) (those accused of financing terrorism under clause four of the Bill can defend themselves by showing that they dealt with the property concerned purely to preserve that property's value).

[77] Clause 20(1). The reverse onus of proof in cases of asset forfeiture is often justified on the basis that the proceedings are *in rem* and are civil and not criminal in nature. This construction is criticised by J. Pretorius and H. Strydom in 'The Constitutionality of Civil Forfeiture' (1998) 13 *South African Public Law* 385.

[78] See Powell, 'South Africa's Legislation', at 106–12.

[79] Sections 35(1), 35(3)(h), 25, 14, and 10 of the South African Constitution, Act 108 of 1996.

[80] *Director of Public Prosecutions: Cape of Good Hope* v. *Bathgate* 2000 (2) SA 560 (C), 2000 (2) BCLR 151 (C); *NDPP* v. *Phillips* 2002 (4) SA 260 (W); *NDPP* v. *Rebuzzi* 2002 (1) SACR 128 (SCA); *NDPP* v. *Mohamed* 2003 (2) SACR 258 (T).

explain why the limitations which POCA places on various constitutional rights are justified.[81] It is therefore difficult to forecast the fate of the terrorism provisions before the Constitutional Court. In general, courts might respond more sympathetically to legislation against organized crime than they would to legislation against terrorism,[82] as the former is a particular problem within South African society.[83] And indeed, the courts do refer to the menace which organized crime poses to South Africa when they approve the provisions in POCA.[84] However, a strong theme in the POCA case law is also the threat which organized crime presents to the international community.[85] If South African courts mould their judgments to the perceived needs of the international community, they might well accept that terrorism is even more of a threat than organized crime. Given the already sympathetic response to POCA, this suggests that the anti-terrorism Bill could for the most part survive constitutional review.

The courts are, however, fairly certain to interpret the anti-terrorism legislation restrictively – a mechanism whereby some provisions in POCA have been preserved as constitutional.[86] In this vein, the duty to report in clause 12 of the Bill might be saved by reading in a 'use indemnity',[87] whereby the information provided may not be used against the person who reported it. Similarly, a court may read into clause 23 a right to challenge the Security Council's view that a particular organization is terrorist.[88]

As for the substantive aspects of the Bill, the vagueness of the main definition of terrorism could possibly be cured by a very restrictive reading

---

[81] For suggested analyses of possible 'limitations' enquiries in the context of various drafts of the anti-terrorism legislation, see Cowling, 'Return of Detention', at 349–54 and Powell, 'South Africa's Legislation', at 118.

[82] See Powell, 'South Africa's Legislation', at 118.

[83] See Bayart, Ellis and Hibou, *Criminalization of the State*, at 49–68; Powell and Goodman, 'Reconciling the Fight' at 43.

[84] *Bathgate*, at para 86.

[85] See, for example, *NDPP* v. *Mohamed* 2002 (4) SA 843 (CC), in which Ackermann J commented that 'the rapid growth of organised crime, money laundering, criminal gang activities and racketeering has become a serious international problem and security threat, from which South Africa has not been immune'. See further paras 14–16 of the judgment.

[86] For example, in *Mohamed*, the court read a rule nisi procedure into an asset forfeiture provision, allowing persons affected to make representations after the initial order had been given. See also *National Director of Public Prosecutions* v. *Carolus and others* 1999 (2) SACR 27 (C); 2000 (1) SA 1127 (SCA) and *NDPP* v. *Seevnarayan* 2003 (2) SA 178 (C) at para 38.

[87] See *Phillips* and *Mohamed*. A use indemnity should not, however, be considered sufficient protection of the individual's rights under South African constitutional and international human rights law. See Powell and Goodman, 'Reconciling the Fight', at 47.

[88] This could raise serious problems, particularly if the Security Council's view is communicated through a chapter VII declaration. If the Security Council's decision is valid under international law (see below p. 578), South Africa's constitutional rights would be forcing the country to contravene international law.

of the text. Without creative interpretation, the phrasing of these clauses could easily be wide enough to infringe the *ius certum* principle.[89] The wide use of negligence as the required form of fault is extremely problematic and has yet to be tested in court. The Constitutional Court has interpreted s. 12 of the South African Constitution – the right not to be deprived of freedom arbitrarily or without just cause – to include a *substantive* component.[90] A penalty of imprisonment which is imposed for negligence could therefore be argued to violate s. 12 if the *reason* for which the state is depriving an individual of his or her liberty is insufficient.[91]

Finally, clause 23 of the Bill, which adopts the Security Council's list of terrorist organizations for the purposes of asset forfeiture, could be seen as an unconstitutional delegation of legislative power. Because the Constitution bestows legislative power on the legislature,[92] the Constitutional Court has already struck down a delegation of plenary legislative powers by the legislature to the executive.[93] It can be argued that a delegation of these powers to an international body, which has no democratic mandate from South Africa's citizens, is even less acceptable.

B. Anti-terrorism legislation and draft legislation in East Africa

1. Prevention

In comparison to South Africa, the executive in Kenya, Tanzania and Uganda enjoys a much wider discretion to decide who is suspected of terrorism and how to act on that suspicion. All three countries allow the relevant Cabinet Ministers to declare groups to be terrorist organizations. The Ugandan Act allows the Minister of Internal Affairs, together with cabinet, to amend the list of terrorist organizations created by the Act itself.[94] Although Parliament may

---

[89] See *State President* v. *Hugo* 1997 (6) BCLR 708 (CC) at para 99, citing *The Sunday Times* v. *The United Kingdom* 17 (1979) 2 EHRR 245: 'A norm cannot be regarded as a 'law' unless it is formulated with sufficient precision to enable the citizen to regulate his conduct: he must be able – if need be with appropriate advice – to foresee, to a degree that is reasonable in the circumstances, the consequences which a given action may entail.' See Steyn, 'The draft Anti-Terrorism Bill'.

[90] *Bernstein* v. *Bester* 1996 (2) SA 751 (CC) and 1996 (4) BCLR 449 (CC); *De Lange* v. *Smuts NO* 1998 (3) SA 785 (CC); *S* v. *Coetzee* 1997 (1) SACR 379 (CC); *Lawyers for Human Rights and Another* v. *Minister of Home Affairs* 2004 (4) SA 125 (CC) para 36.

[91] See V. Ramraj, 'Freedom of the Person and Principles of Criminal Fault' (2002) 18 *South African Journal on Human Rights* 225 on the substantive element of due process in Canadian and South African constitutional law and its impact on criminal fault.

[92] Section 44 of the Republic of South Africa Constitution Act no. 108 of 1996.

[93] *Executive Council of the Western Cape Legislature* v. *President of the Republic of South Africa* 1995 (10) BCLR 1289 (CC); 1995 (4) SA 877 (CC).

[94] Schedule 2 of the Act declares the Lord's Resistance Army, the Lord's Resistance Movement and the Allied Democratic Forces to be terrorist organizations.

subsequently annul changes to the list of declared terrorist organizations, it may not do so retrospectively.[95] The executive therefore has a period of up to two weeks of untrammelled power to take any measures it wishes against any organization it chooses. In Tanzania, the Minister of Home Affairs may declare a person or a group to be a terrorist or a terrorist organization.[96] The Minister's guidelines indicate that there must be a 'reasonable suspicion' of terrorism. This term suggests judicial oversight, but the guidelines, which refer to the view of the UN Security Council, may add support to the approach of the executive.[97] In Kenya, the draft legislation would allow the Minister of National Security to declare an organization terrorist if, in his or her *belief*, it meets the guideline criteria of terrorism provided in the section.[98]

Once an organization has been declared to be a terrorist organization, Uganda allows its Minister of Internal Affairs to dissolve and wind up terrorist assets and to declare them forfeit to the state[99] and Tanzania empowers the Minister to freeze the funds of a declared terrorist organization or person.[100] Kenya grants less special discretion to the executive to act against terrorist organizations. Pre-trial asset forfeiture is permitted as a general measure against terrorist suspects on an *ex parte* application to a court.[101]

Apart from organizations and persons declared to be terrorists, there will, of course, be a wide range of persons and organizations suspected of committing the crime. The question is then what extra help the executive, particularly the police, is given in investigating these persons and organizations. The legislation in Uganda and Kenya does not provide any special police powers in this respect and, in Tanzania, the Act states merely that police may arrest without warrant on reasonable suspicion.[102] They may also carry out search and seizure without warrant (notwithstanding the Tanzanian Criminal Procedure Act) if an application for a warrant would cause prejudicial delay.[103]

---

[95] Section 10 of the Ugandan Act.   [96] Section 12 of the Tanzanian Act.
[97] As discussed in the conclusion, reference to international bodies, and to the Security Council in particular, is likely to exacerbate executive domination in the domestic sphere.
[98] Clauses 9(4) and (5) of the Kenyan Bill. The Minister's declaration is nonetheless reviewable by a court as an administrative act, and would also be subject to constitutional review under s. 84(1) of the Constitution.
[99] Section 10(5) of the Ugandan Act.   [100] Section 12(5) of the Tanzanian Act.
[101] Clause 20 of the Kenyan Bill. It does not appear that a trial need ever be held to confirm that the owner of the property is in fact a terrorist. There is also no special provision for the rule nisi to allow those affected by the order a chance to be heard, although this might be read into the provision.
[102] By police officers of the rank of Station Commander or Assistant Superintendent. Section 28 of the Tanzanian Act. However, in itself, this power presents no unusual departure from the Criminal Procedure of most countries, and the 'reasonable suspicion' requirement admits of judicial oversight.
[103] Section 29 of the Tanzanian Act.

572   C. H. POWELL

All three states allow for seizure of property on suspicion of terrorist connections, but place different controls on executive discretion. In Uganda, Schedule 3 provides for court orders to search for and seize property if there are reasonable grounds to believe that the property will be of substantial value to an investigation.[104] In Tanzania, the Inspector-General of Police may issue a detention order against vessels and aircraft,[105] which order the Minister may vary. The police may seize property on suspicion of a terrorist connection, after which they must apply for a court order allowing for further detention of the property. The Court order, valid for sixty days, is renewable.[106] In Kenya, the procedure of search and seizure is permissible in three circumstances: if the person or institution fails to heed a court order compelling a bank or financial institution to reveal the account details of their clients, if search and seizure have been separately authorized by the court, or if such application would cause delay prejudicial to public safety and public order.[107] The phrasing of the latter provision[108] suggests that the lawfulness of the initial search is subject to judicial review. Two contradictory clauses in the Kenyan Bill each provide for a different regime of retention of seized articles. The most likely view is, however, that articles may be retained indefinitely, subject to periodic judicial review.[109]

All three states provide for surveillance of suspects. The Ugandan Minister may authorize surveillance operations, under which letters, electronic data and bank accounts of a suspect may be monitored.[110] In granting the authority to monitor, he or she is required to protect, inter alia, the public interest and national economy. The Tanzanian surveillance procedures may be authorized by both the Minister and the Court, both of whom may co-opt private bodies in the interception of information.[111] In Kenya, it is only on a court order that terrorist suspects or financial institutions must grant access to information and documents in their possession.[112]

Outside the arena of criminal investigation, the executive in Uganda, Tanzania, and Kenya is granted other powers to ward off possible terrorist attacks. The Tanzanian Minister may pass regulations to prohibit the entry of persons to Tanzania and to prohibit arms sales. The Tanzanian Director

---

[104] Certain items are excluded from the search warrant, including personal and journalistic material. See Schedule 3 to the Ugandan Act.
[105] Section 32 of the Tanzanian Act.   [106] See sections 33 (1) and (5).
[107] Clauses 19, 25, and 26 of the Kenyan Bill.
[108] Clause 26(4) may not be 'construed as a derogation from the lawful right of any person in the defence of person or property'.
[109] Under clause 40(4) of the Bill, property seized on suspicion of terrorist connections may be retained for as long as necessary; clause 21 provides for ninety-day renewable court orders to allow the executive to retain property until trial.
[110] Sections 18 and 19 of the Ugandan Act.   [111] Sections 30–1 of the Tanzanian Act.
[112] Clause 19 of the Kenyan Bill.

of Immigration may also refuse entry to suspected terrorists and the Minister may deport suspected terrorists already in Tanzania.[113] He or she may also refuse refugee status to applicants on the basis of suspected terrorist involvement.[114] Similarly, the Kenyan Minister may issue exclusion orders against non-nationals suspected of terrorist involvement, and even against Kenyan nationals if they have dual nationality.[115] Such an order both prevents the entry of persons and allows for the removal of persons already in Kenya.[116]

Finally, all three East African states grant immunity to members of the executive who act against suspected terrorists. The immunity covers damage to property and the causing of injury or even death.[117]

2. Trial

In all three states, the legislation creates the offences both of terrorism and of a range of ancillary and convention crimes.[118] The definition of terrorism is generally arranged around the three constituent elements of act, purpose and motivation, although these elements are not always set out schematically and it is not always clear whether all three elements are required.

The clearest outline is found in Kenya's legislation. Its first requirement is an action of particular severity, such as serious violence to a person, damage to property, endangering life, seriously risking health or public safety and seriously disrupting an electronic system.[119] The action must be intended to influence the government or intimidate the public and the motivation behind it must be political, religious or ideological.[120] Where weapons are used, the purpose of the action is irrelevant.[121] The Kenyan Bill also provides for specific offences, based on the two recent UN Conventions against terrorist bombings and against the financing of terrorism.[122] These specific offences criminalize weapons training, directing a terrorist organization, possessing articles for terrorist purposes, collecting information for terrorist purposes

---

[113] Section 46 of the Tanzanian Act.   [114] Section 47 of the Tanzanian Act.
[115] Clause 31 of the Kenyan Bill.   [116] Schedule Four, clause 4 of the Kenyan Bill.
[117] The Ugandan Act grants civil immunity to all public officers or persons assisting them for anything done by them in good faith in the exercise of functions conferred by the Act (s. 32). Under the Tanzanian Act, all police officers who seize property or cause injury, death or damage under the Act enjoy civil and criminal immunity (ss. 29, 33). Kenya grants immunity for injury, damage to property and death under clause 40(3) of its Bill.
[118] In an apparent oversight, the Kenyan draft Bill *defines* terrorism but does not expressly render it an offence. I am assuming that this will be corrected before the Bill is enacted.
[119] See clause 3(a) of the Kenyan Bill. The last-mentioned element has an additional *mens rea* requirement: the action must be 'designed' seriously to disrupt the electronic system.
[120] Clause 3(b) and (c) of the Kenyan Bill.   [121] Clause 3.
[122] K. Nyaundi 'Synopsis of the Suppression of Terrorism Bill, 2003 vis a vis International Conventions' (unpublished paper, 17 December 2003).

and inciting offences outside of Kenya.[123] A range of accomplice offences focus strongly on the financial support of terrorism[124] but are broad enough to include all forms of accomplice liability.[125] Finally, the Bill empowers the Minister to declare organizations to be terrorist after which membership in them becomes a criminal offence.[126]

Uganda's definition sets out a list of activities which constitute terrorism if they are carried out with the aim of influencing the government or intimidating the public, for a political, religious, social or economic aim, indiscriminately and without due regard for the safety of others.[127] The activities reflect both treaty offences and common-law crimes and include acts of violence (murder, bombing, hijacking and kidnapping), collecting funds for 'terrorist activities under this Act', interference with electrical systems and the manufacture of explosives and biological weapons. The Act provides for wide accomplice, attempt, conspiracy, and accessory liability and creates the separate offence of running or supporting a terrorist institution.[128] A separate list of financing crimes partly duplicates the main crime of terrorism.[129] A list of organizations is declared terrorist by the Act itself and membership therein is made an offence.[130]

Tanzania's definition is particularly unclear. Under s. 4(2), an act or omission which may seriously damage the country or an international organization, *or* is intended to influence the government, intimidate the population or destroy the fundamental social structure of the state, *or* involves attacks upon life, physical integrity and the freedom of a person are all terrorist acts. In addition, s. 4(3) sets out a list of accomplice terrorist activities, some of which overlap with s. 4(2). These activities occasionally have special *mens rea* requirements and generally deal with damage to life and limb, use of firearms or explosives, the release of dangerous substances into the environment and the disruption of essential services. Lawful protest activities are excluded from the definition.[131] Sections 5 to 10 then create wider sets of accomplice offences, all of which also count as terrorism under s. 4(5). Sections 13 to 27 set out more specific offences, covering financial support for terrorism, weapons training, membership of a terrorist organization and yet more accomplice liability in various forms.

In attempting to prove these charges, all three East African countries grant the state additional assistance by relaxing the rules of evidence. The most

---

[123] Clauses 4 to 8.   [124] Clauses 14 to 17.
[125] Clause 17(e) refers to the provision of 'any service, skill or expertise' either intentionally or negligently for the purposes of terrorism.
[126] Clauses 9–10.   [127] Section 7(2) of the Ugandan Act.
[128] Sections 8, 23, 25–28, and 9.
[129] Sections 12 to 14, duplicating in part s. 7(2)(d).
[130] Sections 10 and 11 and Schedule 2. The list can be varied by the Minister.
[131] Section 4(4) of the Tanzanian Act.

important example of this change to the normal rules is found in the introduction of a reverse onus of proof for many of the offences. In Uganda, for example, a person charged with helping to finance a terrorist organization bears the onus of proving that he or she did not know of the organization's terrorist nature and a person charged with hindering an investigation (either by making a prejudicial disclosure or by destroying evidence) must prove that he or she neither knew nor could reasonably have suspected that his or her actions would hinder the investigation.[132] In Tanzania, a person accused of membership of a terrorist organization must establish the organization was not a terrorist organization at the time of his or her membership.[133] The Kenyan Bill creates a reverse onus in the cases of weapons training,[134] the use of money and property for terrorist purposes, and membership of a terrorist organization. In prosecuting the crime of possession for terrorist purposes under clause 6, the state is relieved of two evidentiary burdens. It need prove only that the article was found on the premises which the accused habitually used, and that the surrounding circumstances 'give rise to a reasonable suspicion that his possession is for a purpose connected with the commission, preparation or instigation of an act of terrorism'. The accused must then either disprove the *mens rea* of possession or prove that the possession was *not* for a terrorist purpose. If charged with making available a document which is 'likely to be useful to a person committing or preparing an act of terrorism',[135] the accused must similarly establish that the document was *not* to be put to terrorist use. Collecting or transmitting information has a reverse onus in that the accused may establish a 'reasonable excuse'.[136] Finally, the Bill provides a reverse onus in the offence of membership of a terrorist organization. It is particularly interesting, as it allows the accused to prove that he or she was not a member of the organization at the time it was a declared a terrorist organisation,[137] but does not suggest that the accused can challenge the categorization of the organization as terrorist.[138]

In Uganda and Tanzania, penalties on conviction for terrorist offences are harsh. In Uganda, the death sentence is mandatory for acts of terrorism which result in death and may be imposed for all lesser forms of terrorism.[139] If convicted of financing terrorism under sections 12–14,[140] an accused faces a maximum sentence of ten years.[141] In Tanzania, the only offence with a

[132] Sections 13, 14, and 17 of the Ugandan Act.
[133] Or professed membership. See section 25(2) of the Tanzanian Act, which allows the Minister to declare organizations terrorist on a 'reasonable suspicion' of terrorism (s. 12).
[134] Clause 4(6). [135] Clause 7(1). [136] Clause 7(3). [137] Clause 10(2).
[138] Compare s. 25 of the Tanzanian Act. [139] Sections 7(1)(a) and (b) of the Ugandan Act.
[140] As opposed to under the 'terrorism' section itself, which also covers the financing of terrorism in section 7(d).
[141] Section 16(1) of the Ugandan Act.

minimum sentence below fifteen years is that of arranging a terrorist meet-ing,[142] for which crime the sentence ranges between ten and fifteen years. Funding terrorism, using and retaining terrorist property and recruiting for terrorism carry sentences of between fifteen and twenty years, while provid-ing property for terrorist use and dealing with terrorist property carry sentences of between twenty and twenty-five years.[143]

Kenya's draft legislation currently appears mild by comparison, but its clemency may be accidental. It provides a maximum sentence of ten years imprisonment for ancillary offences such as weapons training, possessing articles for terrorist purposes, collecting and transmitting information and membership of a terrorist organization.[144] By a curious anomaly, however, no penalty is attached to terrorism as such because terrorism is not expressly rendered an offence by the Bill.[145]

In both Kenya and Uganda, the courts have a discretion to order the forfeiture of property on conviction for a terrorist or terrorist-related offence. Kenya's draft Bill does not provide any guidelines for how a court should exercise this discretion, whereas Uganda allows the forfeiture order to be made if the court believes the property will be used for further terrorist offences. However, the onus rests on the person who attempts to preserve the property to prove that it will not be used in this way.[146] Both Kenya and Uganda allow third parties to establish their rights in the property.[147]

V. Conclusion

The international anti-terrorism regime threatens a range of human rights, including the right to property, the right to be presumed innocent until proven guilty, the right to a fair trial and various freedoms, such as freedom and security of the person and freedom of association.[148] However, as pro-ducts of negotiation, the anti-terrorism treaties are broad enough to allow for a range of interpretations, and they also defer expressly to the international

---

[142] Section 26 of the Tanzanian Act.

[143] Sections 13 to 17 and 21 of the Tanzanian Act.

[144] Clauses 4, 6, and 10 of the Kenyan Bill.

[145] See above note 118.

[146] Section 16(5) of the Ugandan Act.

[147] The Ugandan Act appears to expect interested parties to make an application immedi-ately after the conviction of the person who used the property for terrorist purposes as it does not set aside a period in which third parties can make their claims (s. 16(6)). The Kenyan Bill allows third parties six months to bring an application (clause 22 and the third schedule).

[148] S. Jagwanth and F. Soltau, 'Terrorism and Human Rights in Africa' in (2002) *Africa and Terrorism* Monograph no. 74, Institute for Security Studies, Pretoria, 27–8; Powell and Goodman, 'Reconciling the Fight', at 39–41.

human rights regime.[149] Where a norm of the international anti-terrorism regime threatens human rights, therefore, the domestic regime could be expected to implement the norm at only a minimal level.

Within the four states in this study, the approach to human rights varies widely. On the whole, legislation which passed through Parliament quickly, and avoided prolonged consultation, is the most draconian, while legislation which has run the gauntlet of a protracted and controversial consultative process has become considerably more rights-friendly. Nonetheless, a comparison between the domestic regimes and the treaties reveals that all of the domestic anti-terrorism regimes have to some extent adopted and even exceeded the treaties' repressive provisions. Thus, for example, the Financing and Organized Crime Conventions, the only conventions to provide for asset seizure,[150] do not mandate seizure before a criminal conviction is obtained. Yet all four states provide for seizure of property prior to criminal conviction[151] and both Uganda and South Africa provide expressly for permanent forfeiture of 'terrorist' property. While such forfeiture requires a court order in South Africa,[152] it can be achieved by executive fiat in Uganda.[153] Similarly, although only the Organized Crime Convention suggests that states might lower the standard of proof in criminal trials, all the states introduce a reverse onus into their criminal offences.[154]

Finally, there is no obligation in the treaties to deprive the judiciary of ultimate control over the process of counter-terrorism. However, our case studies demonstrate that the focus of power has shifted significantly to the executive. Many examples of unchecked executive power are obvious. They include the power to determine terrorist status and to act against persons and property, coupled with wide immunity protecting officials from the legal consequences of their actions. But other examples of executive discretion are more subtle. An almost invisible, but powerful, factor is the role of the executive in the foreign sphere. As the organ responsible for foreign affairs, the executive forms the interface between states and between international and domestic legal regimes. To the extent that a domestic anti-terrorism regime is being driven, not by internal necessities but by international law or

---

[149] Articles 15 and 17 Financing Convention; articles 3(1) and 22(1) Algiers Convention; and articles 12 and 14 Bombing Convention. See also article 3(f) of SCR 1373.

[150] Article 8 Financing Convention; article 12(1)(b) Organised Crime Convention.

[151] Tanzania and Kenya allow seized assets to be held indefinitely, but not necessarily disposed of. See s. 33 of the Tanzanian Act and Clauses 21 and 40(4) of the Kenyan Bill.

[152] On a lowered standard of proof. See above notes 47 and 77.

[153] Section 10(5) of the Ugandan Act.

[154] Clause 17(6) of the South African Bill; sections 13, 14(2) and 17 of the Ugandan Act; section 25(2) of the Tanzanian Act; clauses 4(6), 6(1) and (2), 7(1) and (3) and 10(2) of the Kenyan Bill.

the political pressure of other states, this regime can have a strong executive bias from its inception.

In the modern state, the executive usually initiates legislation, which may give it the power to import the international regime into its domestic system with little regard for internal needs. The legislature is meant to provide a democratic check on executive proposals, but it may not always be up to the task. This is evident not only in the repressive measures in the legislation but also in the outward-looking perspective which permeates it. Sometimes this perspective emerges clearly, as when the view of the UN determines which organizations are prohibited and which property may be forfeited. But it is also an underlying theme of the system as a whole, in that it moulds the domestic system towards the needs of other states and implicitly assumes the legitimacy of the international anti-terrorism regime.[155]

Uganda's removal of the political offence exception in its extradition regime[156] is a clear example of such an assumption. The measure demonstrates that Uganda assumes that violent opposition to the government of a foreign state is *illegitimate*. In a similar vein, Uganda must assume that the action of the foreign executive is *legitimate*, that is, that the executive speaks both for the rest of the government and for the state as a whole. These assumptions, which conform to classical international law, have been challenged by international human rights law. The human rights regime recognizes the potential disjunction between a government and the people of a state, and it vests statehood in the latter by insisting on democratic rule. Similarly, the doctrine of separation of powers reminds us that the executive should not be conflated with the government as a whole; it is but one power structure, which must be kept in check by the other two.

Conflicts between two international law regimes warn us against a blind adherence to international law as a system. From observation of the anti-terrorism regime, it is clear that international law is not a monolith but a patchwork of norms and values. Conflict between the norms results not only from differing goals within a single system (in this case, the promotion of human rights and the prevention of terrorism) but also from the fact that, as a legal system without a central legislature, international law reflects competing sources of authority.

---

[155] A view also reflected in South Africa's case law, as *Bathgate* and *Mohammed* demonstrate.
[156] By allowing states to recognize some forms of violence against another state as legitimate, the political offence exception mirrors the right to self-determination, although it is broader. The recent blossoming of the anti-terrorism discourse has avoided the seemingly impossible task of determining which politically inspired violence is acceptable by simply rejecting the political offence exception altogether. While all four states in this study exclude the political offence exception to differing extents, s. 5 of the Uganda Act excludes it for the entire range of offences.

In the international sphere, the Security Council has claimed the power to create a long-term, binding regime against terrorism, a shift by which it extends its role from a primarily executive organ[157] to a source of law. The precursor to this development was its creation of International Criminal Courts in the 1990s, but these judicial structures were at least independent of the Security Council.[158] SCR 1373 of 2001 now attempts to fast-track the usual process whereby states create treaty and customary international law. Although it does not *oblige* signature of the Financing Convention,[159] its *recommendation* that states become parties, coupled with article 25 of the UN Charter,[160] puts states under strong pressure to set up the long-term, legal regime proposed by this treaty.

As discussed above, the treaty regime may, with some effort, be capable of a fairly benign implementation. However, domestic implementation of the treaties seems to accord more closely with the approach of the Security Council, a role model which is showing scant regard for international human rights constraints in its counter-terrorism programme. The Council has itself gone well beyond the requirements of the treaty regime by declaring a list of persons and organizations to be terrorists and by obliging states to carry out a wide range of measures against them, including freezing of assets.[161] The Security Council acts without any judicial oversight, and with little consideration for the rules of natural justice. The party who is designated a terrorist does not receive a hearing and cannot apply directly to the Security Council to have its name removed from the list.[162]

---

[157] Although the UN cannot be divided neatly into the domestic categories of legislature, judiciary and executive, the Security Council most closely resembles an executive and is the most powerful body in the UN. Designed to take speedy action to deal with threats to world peace in the short-term, it was the only organ empowered to bind states to carry out particular courses of action (see article 25 and Chapter VII of the UN Charter).

[158] See *Prosecutor* v. *Tadić* , Case No. IT–94–1–AR72, Decision on the Defence Motion for Interlocutory Appeal on Jurisdiction, 2 Oct 1995 reprinted in (1996) 35 *I.L.M.* 32. Here the Court guarded its independence as a judicial organ from the Security Council (paras 5–22) and implied that the Security Council was bound to respect certain trial rights in the creation of the Court (para 42).

[159] Article 3(d) of SCR 1373 of 2001.

[160] By which states agree to abide by Security Council decisions.

[161] The list predates SCR 1373, but many of the measures are new. See note 162 below.

[162] The list of terrorist organizations and individuals is updated by the Security Council Committee established pursuant to resolution 1267 (1999) concerning al Qaeda and the Taliban and Associated Individuals and Entities. Names are added to the list via the 'no objection' procedure: a government circulates the names of organizations and individuals whom it wants designated terrorist. If no objections are received within 48 hours, the names are accepted. The delisting procedure is more onerous. Persons affected by the listing have no direct access to the Committee, and can appeal their listing only with the assistance of their own governments.

Terrorism is best countered if its incidents are prevented and not merely prosecuted. As a result, swift executive action, untempered by judicial or legislative oversight, may be needed to respond effectively to terrorist threats. But this does not dispense with the need for a legal framework for the executive action. The blurring of the line between the executive and judicial spheres is accompanied by a blurring of the distinction between law and power. Without a determinate definition at its foundation, the international anti-terrorism regime itself has doubtful status as a legal regime. At the same time, the indiscriminate application of anti-terrorism legislation at the domestic level leads to a conception of terrorism as any criminal behaviour. This is alarming, and not just because an overbroad concept of terrorism enables the government to use extra and repressive powers. An overbroad concept ceases to be a legal one. It suggests that the entire counter-terrorism programme is neither based on, nor subject to, law.

While domestic courts consider the proper limitations on executive power within the anti-terrorism regime, international courts and writers have begun to grapple with the charge that the Security Council is transcending its boundaries as an executive organ of the UN. This constitutional question accompanies criticism that the executive-led anti-terrorism regime ignores international law and particularly international human rights. It would appear that we cannot fight terrorism globally while restricting the doctrine of separation of powers to the domestic sphere.

26

Rocks, hard places and human rights: anti-terrorism law and policy in Arab states

LYNN WELCHMAN

Introduction

This chapter provides an overview of legislative developments in Arab states following the passage of Security Council resolution 1373 (2001), focusing on definitions of 'terrorism' and 'terrorist' offences. It considers the Arab Convention for the Suppression of Terrorism before proceeding to review the responses of a number of individual states. Moves towards political reform and the opening of public space for dissent and criticism are challenged by the exigencies of the 'war on terror'. Certain practices in violation of human rights in Arab states have apparently been endorsed by the US alongside a newly stated policy focus on 'democratization' in the region. Dissonance between law-related word and deed of the states leading the 'war on terrorism' – particularly the US, but also the UK – sustains the arguments of those who seek to undermine the discourse of rights and rule of law, complicates the considerable challenges posed to local and regional human rights groups, and seriously undermines the credibility of international law in the region; the efficacy of all of which in the 'global war on terrorism' must surely be open to question.

I. Regional context

The US overview of *Patterns of Global Terrorism* for 2003 confirmed that 'the Middle East continued to be the region of greatest concern in the global war on terrorism'.[1] At the same time, it is the lives and freedoms of the populations of Arab states in the region that have probably been the most directly affected by the anti-terrorism laws and policies being implemented and promoted by the US since 9/11. Uncounted thousands of non-combatants have been killed by the US-led forces in Afghanistan and Iraq. Hundreds of Arabs of different nationalities are held in Guantanamo Bay, and Arab men

---

[1] Office of the Coordinator of Counter-terrorism, *Patterns of Global Terrorism – 2003*, Washington, 29 April 2004, 58; available at http://www.state.gov/s/ct/rls/pgtrpt/2003/c12153.htm.

have been major targets of various domestic 'counter-terrorism' arrest and detention procedures which have been roundly criticized.[2] In the region, thousands have been arrested in Arab states, many held for prolonged periods without trial and others sentenced after trials that failed to meet international standards of due process.[3]

Nationals from different states in the region have been implicated in attacks attributed to or claimed by al Qaeda and various groups associated with it, both before and after 9/11. Since 2001, the Arab region has seen major bombings and other armed attacks in states such as Tunisia, Saudi Arabia and Morocco, with scores of dead and injured. Recent decades also saw considerable 'domestic' political violence, with thousands of lives lost. Arab states have underlined their prolonged exposure to terrorism and promoted the ways in which they have sought to deal with it as potential models which others in the international community might do well to follow. The Egyptian Prime Minister said that 'maybe Western countries should begin to think of Egypt's own fight against terror as their new model', and Syria's President Bashar al-Asad pressed the USA to 'take advantage of Syria's successful experiences'.[4] As a regional grouping, 'Arab states were among the first to reach an anti-terrorism agreement' and were 'the first to warn against the danger of terrorism and the importance of taking collective measures to combat it'.[5] All twenty-two state members of the Arab League have signed up to the 1998 Arab Convention on the Suppression of Terrorism.

Implicit in these statements are rebukes to states now seen to be leading the 'global war on terrorism' for their past criticisms of the Arab states; both Syria and Egypt have been heavily criticized for human rights abuses involved in precisely the approaches that they now present as potential models of efficacy. There is also reproach for a less than vigorous engagement with the 'terrorist threat' until the attacks of 9/11. In its first report to the Counter-Terrorism Committee (CTC), Algeria opened with these words:

---

[2] See, for example, Human Rights Watch, *United States: Abuses Plague September 11 Prosecutions*, 15 August 2002; and 'United States: Ensure Protection for Foreign Detainees' 1 December 2001; Neil Hicks, 'The Impact of the September 11 Attacks on Civil Rights in the United States' in Ashild Kjok (ed.), *Terrorism and Human Rights after September 11* (Cairo Institute for Human Rights Studies, 2002), 55–64.

[3] Two Amnesty International reports are pertinent: 'The Gulf and the Arabian Peninsula: Human rights fall victim to the "War on Terror"' AI Index: MDE 04/002/2004 22 June 2004; and 'Morocco/Western Sahara: Torture in the "anti-terrorism" campaign' AI Index MDE: 29/004/2004 24 June 2004.

[4] Joe Stork, 'The Human Rights Crisis in the Middle East in the Aftermath of September 11' in Kjok, *Terrorism and Human Rights*, 41–54, at 43 and 45.

[5] Respectively, the Secretary-General of the League of Arab States'Amr Mousa, in Kjok (*Terrorism and Human Rights*, 21–23 at 21) and the Saudi Arabian Interior Minister quoted after the May 2003 Riyadh bombings in the *Kingdom of Saudi Arabia* (newsletter, London Embassy) July 2003.

Having long suffered the ravages of terrorism often in the face of indifference and occasional complaisance on the part of certain sectors of the international community, Algeria welcomes the adoption of the resolution [1373] insofar as it reflects a welcome acknowledgement by the international community of the potential threats both to national stability and to international peace and security represented by the scourge of terrorism. On September 11, the world paid the price of underestimating the dangers posed by the terrorist threat and its potential for destruction. ... As a victim of terrorism, Algeria urges the international community to firmly commit itself to definitively abandoning erroneous and selective perceptions surrounding the phenomenon of terrorism.[6]

A particular concern voiced by Algeria, shared by other states in the region, concerns a feature of most new anti-terrorism legislation which criminalizes 'supporting actions abroad which satisfy the definition of terrorism'.[7] As the Algerian government put it, 'the need for rigorous counter-terrorism efforts concerns first and foremost the countries whose territories are known to harbour support networks and to be used by terrorist groups as staging areas'.[8] States such as Algeria and Egypt had long been objecting to the activities of dissident Algerians and Egyptians in the UK, urging the introduction of measures finally realized in the UK's Terrorism Act 2000 – according to Kent Roach, 'something of a gold standard after September 11' in Commonwealth countries.[9] Considerable scepticism has been voiced as to whether the critical distinction between 'dissident/opposition/resistance' and 'terrorism' is adequately preserved in new anti-terrorism legislation; practice (not only judicial but executive and security practice) rather than textual analysis alone is likely to be the key. Algeria went on to propose a 'series of concrete proposals' for a global counter-terrorism strategy.[10]

US officials have on various occasions indicated that they are listening. In 2004, the deputy commander of the US European command noted that 'we think we have a lot to learn from the Algerians'.[11] US Secretary of State Colin

---

[6] UN Doc S/2001/1280 27 December 2001, (first report of Algeria to the Counter-Terrorism Committee pursuant to paragraph 6 of Security Resolution 1373 (2001)), 4.

[7] Kent Roach, 'The World Wide Expansion of Anti-Terrorism Laws After 11 September 2001', (2004) 116 *Studi Senesi* 481 at 492. I am grateful to Professor Roach for providing me with this text.

[8] Note 6 above.   [9] Roach, 'World Wide Expansion', 3.

[10] UN Doc. S/2001/1280 Appendix 1: Aide-mémoire.

[11] Giles Tremlett, 'US sends special forces into north Africa', *Guardian*, 15 March 2004. Tremlett observes that 'states previously shunned by the international community, such as Algeria, are being provided with arms and military training and may become a cornerstone of US military interests in the region'. On plans by US Defence Secretary Donald Rumsfeld to 'thrust special forces into the lead role in the war on terrorism, by using them for covert operations around the world', see Jennifer D. Kibbe, 'The Rise of the Shadow Warriors' 83/2 *Foreign Affairs* March/April 2004, 102–15.

Powell agreed that Egypt was 'really ahead of us on this issue' and that the US had 'much to learn' from Egypt's anti-terrorist tactics, although Joe Stork of Human Rights Watch points out that such tactics 'have been used against non-violent critics as well'.[12] At the end of 2002, it was reported that CIA agents in Bagram and Diego Garcia were 'contracting out their interrogation to foreign intelligence agencies known to routinely use torture'; specifically, it was reported that 'low-level suspects have been handed over to Jordanian, Egyptian and Moroccan agencies ... with a list of questions from the CIA'.[13]

This indicates particular challenges for the Arab human rights movement. Implicit in Arab states' reports to the CTC is a vindication of existing draconian legislation and practice, in defiance of sustained criticism by domestic and regional human rights groups as well as by international human rights organizations and the dedicated United Nations mechanisms. The threat perceived to human rights in the 'global war on terrorism' is of course not limited to the Middle East. Irene Khan, Secretary General of Amnesty International, has said that 'in a world engaged in the so-called "war on terrorism", human rights were seen as an obstacle to ensuring victory and human rights defenders as defenders of "terrorists"'.[14] As mass arrests began after the Casablanca bombings in May 2003, the official Moroccan discourse accused human rights activists of being 'soft on terrorism' by indulging in 'knee-jerk criticism of the security services'.[15] In Egypt just after 9/11, the Prime Minister took the human rights movement to task for its long-standing campaigns against torture and unfair trials, criticizing groups for 'calling on us to give these terrorists their "human rights"'.[16] And in Yemen, Amnesty International reported a climate of fear in the period directly following 9/11 that stifled internal dissent to an unprecedented degree – fear of a possible US military attack or economic sanctions.[17] This last example, albeit lifting by late 2003, illustrates one of the specificities of the Arab world: a fear of being 'next on the list'. Another is the long-standing and profound grievance in the region at the treatment of the Israel/Palestine

---

[12] Stork, 'Human Rights Crisis', 45.

[13] Suzanne Goldenberg, 'CIA accused of torture at Bagram base: some captives handed to brutal foreign agencies', *Guardian*, 27 December 2002. Original *Washington Post* report 'US Denies Abuse but Defends Interrogations', 26 December 2002; see Human Rights Watch press release and intervention, 'United States: Reports of Torture of al Qaeda Suspects', 27 December 2002.

[14] Irene Khan, 'Human Rights Challenges following the events of September 11 and their impact on universality and the human rights movement' in Kjok, *Terrorism and Human Rights*, at 35.

[15] Eileen Byrne, 'Escaping from the Chains of History', *Financial Times*, 16 April 2004.

[16] Stork, 'Human Rights Crisis', 44.

[17] Amnesty International, 'Yemen: The Rule of Law sidelined in the name of security,' AI Index: MDE 31/006/2003 24 September 2003.

dispute by the major Western powers: specifically, the failure to hold Israel, as the occupying power, to its established duties under international law over the decades, exemplified most recently at George Bush's apparent endorsement of Israel's intention to keep control of major settlement blocks in the West Bank, and to deny Palestinian refugees the right to return inside the 1948 borders. The Director of the Cairo Institute for Human Rights Studies, Bahey el-Din Hassan, outlines the impact of such actions in producing an 'accumulated feeling of injustice':

> This undermines the credibility of international human rights law and international humanitarian law and increases the reservation of many people in the Arab and Islamic worlds as to the universality of human rights principles and values.[18]

The Iraq war has increased these reservations, fuelled most recently by the attack on Falluja and the release of photo documentation of the torture and inhuman treatment of Iraqi detainees. The situation of detainees in Guantanamo Bay is a further exacerbating factor. Governments of Arab states are likely to feel less pressure in regard to their own abusive practices. Domestic actors seeking socio-political reform are considerably constrained by the resulting dynamics.

II. Legislative themes

A regional overview of the Arab states presents a varied picture. It will clearly be important to have detailed country studies on a number of states in the region in order to meaningfully inform a 'global' comparative process and to integrate the Arab experience into the development of mainstream paradigms in this emerging area of study.

With this caveat, certain legislative themes can be identified across the region. All Arab states are party to the Arab Convention on the Suppression of Terrorism and to a growing number of related international conventions. All are party to two or more of the United Nations human rights treaties, although some are not yet party to the ICCPR or the ICESCR[19] and others have not yet signed up to the Convention Against Torture.[20] A number of Arab states are party to the African Charter on Human and Peoples' Rights. A regional human rights instrument, the Arab Charter on Human Rights, was criticized by international human rights groups for serious flaws and gaps upon its adoption in 1994 by members of the League of Arab States. The

---

[18] Bahey el-Din Hassan, 13–16 in Kjok, *Terrorism and Human Rights*, 15.
[19] These include Bahrain, Comoros, Mauritania, Oman, Qatar, Saudi Arabia and the United Arab Emirates.
[20] Iraq, Mauritania, Oman, Syria and the United Arab Emirates.

Charter failed to secure any ratifications in the years following.[21] Most recently (in 2003) a process of review for the 'modernization' of its contents was initiated in the Arab League, matching a number of governmental initiatives on human rights 'institutionalization'. Most Arab states have yet to ratify the statute of the International Criminal Court.[22]

Domestically, individuals are rarely able to realize human rights protections by directly invoking international human rights instruments in national courts. Weak and unempowered national judiciaries are usually unable to assert their independence against the executive to secure judicial protection of human rights, even though the rights enshrined in international instruments are also guaranteed in most of the constitutions of the region. The prospect of a 'dialogue' between courts and legislatures on the limits being set to rights and freedoms, particularly on 'security' issues, is minimal. Moreover, state security courts or other 'special tribunals' – including military courts – are often assigned jurisdiction over perpetrators accused of offences against state security. Such courts have fewer procedural protections than the ordinary court system. Unfair trials that fail to meet the standards set by international law or required in domestic law have been documented across the region well before 9/11.[23] Political opponents and non-violent critics have been the targets of such procedures, including alleged or suspected Islamists and communists, human rights defenders, journalists and newspaper editors. There are widespread reports of torture by police and security services, and all Arab states retain the death penalty, although it is used more commonly in certain states.[24] Some states have semi-permanent 'states of emergency' in force, and several face the threat of serious political violence from groups included in the 'proscribed' or 'terrorist' organizations listed by the US or the EU.[25] Tempering this picture are a set of developments indicating moves towards political and social reform with greater space for debate and dissent.

Legislatures in the region have generally acceded to the executives' determination of the exigencies of security in matters of new or amended

---

[21] See Mona Rishmawi, 'The Arab Charter on Human Rights: A Comment' 10 *INTERIGHTS* Bulletin 1996.

[22] Those that have are currently Jordan and Djibouti.

[23] See Amnesty International, 'State Injustice: Unfair Trials in the Middle East and North Africa' 16 April 1998 AI Index: MDE 01/002/1998.

[24] Robert Postawko, in 'Towards an Islamic Critique of Capital Punishment' [2002] UCLA *Journal of Islamic and Near Eastern Law* 269–320 at 270, notes (albeit based on an AI reference from the 1980s) that Bahrain and Djibouti can be considered 'abolitionist in practice'.

[25] Including the Abu Nidal organization, the Armed Islamic Group (GIA), al-Gama`a al-Islamiyya, Egyptian Islamic Jihad, and the Salafist Group for Call and Combat, as well as al Qaeda. See *Patterns of Global Terrorism*, Appendix B, 113 ff.

legislation; civil society groups have been more critical. Some states already had extensive and explicit anti-terrorism legislation, such as Egypt and Algeria; others have introduced amendments to their Penal Codes addressing the issue of terrorism, such as Jordan and Morocco. Tunisia, which already exercises particularly tight political control through its criminal legislation and press law, has promulgated a new Law Against Terrorism and Money Laundering. Syria at first gave the impression of not standing in need of amending its laws or regulations, satisfied that its existing penal code already met the requirements of Security Council resolution 1373, but its second report mentions a draft law on money-laundering.

This examination focuses on the definition of terrorism in legislative instruments, as well as measures taken that would not appear critical to the anti-terrorism mandate, but have the potential to considerably restrict the scope for non-violent political dissent. It is unlikely that the Arab states present an exception; as Christopher Harding has observed, it is 'in the interest of governments to take advantage of any opportunities for extending the scope of their measures of legal control when political circumstances are conducive to such developments'.[26]

Legislative responses of Arab states match those of the Anglo-American systems examined by Kent Roach:[27] the expansion of the definition of terrorism; the introduction of new offences, particularly regarding funding and financing activities, that apply 'long before an act of terror is committed'; the expansion of crimes of 'association'; and the expansion of police powers, in particular the extension of pre-arraignment detention (*garde à vue*) with counsel excluded. There are detailed listings of potential offences, frequently with 'catch-all' phrases, and an increase in penalties where 'ordinary crimes' are classified as 'terrorist offences'. Terrorism is not defined by identification of the act or threat with advancing a 'political, religious or ideological cause'; indeed, the phrase 'whatever the motives' may be added, to emphasize that the accused's possible political or ideological motive is not an element in the offence. In certain cases, the definition of 'terrorism' appears to be dissociated also from the 'much less controversial'[28] purpose of intimidation or causing fear to the public as well as from seeking to influence the actions of government or public bodies. The acts through which terrorism is established do not, in some cases, appear to have to be of particular severity or danger. There is a fairly standard exemption or reduction in penalty for those who inform the appropriate authorities of the preparation of an act of terrorism. In none of the legislation reviewed in this chapter is there an exemption such as Roach notes to be contained in Canadian and Australian laws for certain acts

---

[26] 'International Terrorism: The British Response' [2002] *Singapore Journal of Legal Studies* 16–29, 18.
[27] Roach, 'World Wide Expansion', 489.   [28] Ibid. 491–2.

of 'advocacy, protest, dissent or stoppage of work'.[29] Victor V. Ramraj observes that 'in jurisdictions where political opposition is otherwise minimally restricted, a broadly worded definition of terrorism may well have a chilling effect'.[30] In the Arab states, where political opposition is considerably restricted, such definitions may be more than chilling. On the other hand, they may be met with resilience by non-violent opponents and critics as 'more of the same', stronger tools in harder times, which may or may not be offset by the discourse of democratization running parallel. Their 'effectiveness' in relation to actual or would-be violent groups or individuals is open to question.[31]

III. The Arab Convention for the Suppression of Terrorism

The Arab Convention for the Suppression of Terrorism, adopted by member states of the Arab League in 1998, came into force in 1999. It is pointed to by Arab states in their reports to the CTC as evidence of forward-thinking and responsible action by governments in the region. The Convention defines 'terrorism' in Article 1(2) as:

> Any act of violence or threat thereof, whatever its motives or purposes, that occurs in execution of an individual or collective criminal undertaking, and is aimed at sowing fear among people, or causing fear by harming them or exposing their lives, liberty or security to danger, or causing damage to the environment or to a public or private installation or property, or occupying or taking over the later, or exposing a national resource to danger.

This definition requires the element of violence or threat thereof, together with an undertaking that is criminal under national legislation and aimed at one of the list of purposes or actions. The phrasing in Arabic does not seem to require that the element of 'sowing fear among people' or 'causing fear' condition the remainder of the purposes, which potentially renders many ordinary criminal activities acts of terrorism. However, if the intention is in fact that the clauses following the word 'danger' are to be read as conditioned by a necessary element of causing fear, the definition is still extremely broad. At the time of the Convention's promulgation, an Amnesty International report held that the definition was so broad that it 'does not satisfy the definition of legality in international human rights law' and that it could be read as posing a threat to the freedoms of association and of expression.[32] The

---

[29] Ibid. 496–7.
[30] 'Terrorism, Security and Rights: A New Dialogue' [2002] *Singapore Journal of Legal Studies* 1–15, at 4.
[31] Ibid.
[32] Amnesty International, 'The Arab Convention for the Suppression of Terrorism; a serious threat to human rights' 21 January 2002 AI Index: MDE 01/002/2002, 8.

definition could be applied to certain forms of attack not prohibited by international humanitarian law regulating non-international armed conflict, and that if it were indeed to render such conduct 'terrorism', 'armed political groups will lose an important incentive to comply with international humanitarian law'.[33] Three elements have been identified by the UN's Office of the High Commissioner for Human Rights that could be included in a definition of terrorism: 'criminal acts intended or calculated to provoke a state of terror in the general public, a group of persons or particular persons for political purposes'.[34] In the Arab Convention's definition, the only definite overlap is with the first element of 'criminal acts', although it adds the element of violence or threat thereof.

A 'terrorist offence' is defined in Article 1(3) as:

> Any offence or attempted offence committed for a terrorist purpose in any of the Contracting States, or against their nationals, property or interests, that is punishable by their domestic law. The offences stipulated in the following conventions shall be considered terrorist offences unless such offences have been excepted by the legislation of the Contracting State or the State has not ratified the said convention.

The 'terrorist purpose' here presumably relates to the definition of 'terrorism' in the preceding clause, and there follows a list of international terrorism-related conventions. In Article 2(a) come a clarification and a caveat:

> Cases of struggle by whatever means, including armed struggle, against foreign occupation and aggression for the sake of liberation and self-determination, in accordance with the principles of international law, shall not be considered an offence. Such cases shall not include any act prejudicing the territorial integrity of any Arab state.

This clause reflects the concern to exclude from the definition acts done in the Palestinian struggle for self-determination, while at the same time not to exclude acts committed in any self-determination struggle against any existing Arab state – implicitly even if such claims were recognized 'in accordance with the principles of international law'. This caveat clearly sits uneasily with the prior invocation of the general principle of self-determination. The insistence on the distinction between 'resistance to foreign occupation and aggression' and terrorism, inspired by the position of Palestine, is a cornerstone of the Arab states' promotion of a definition of international terrorism. The CTC asked Saudi Arabia a follow-up question:

> The CTC would welcome an indication of how Saudi Arabia would deal with a request by a state that is not party to that [Arab] Convention for

---

[33] Ibid.
[34] OHCHR, *Digest of Jurisprudence of the UN and regional organizations on the protection of human rights while countering terrorism*, Geneva n.d., 3, citing the Declaration on Measures to Eliminate International Terrorism annexed to UNGA resolution 49/60.

the extradition of a person accused of an offence against, say, the
International Convention for the Suppression of Terrorist Bombings committed in circumstances of the kind attracting the above-mentioned special
exception.[35]

Saudi Arabia's response was to deny that there was such a thing as an
exception, since struggles against foreign occupation and aggression are in
accordance with the principles of international law as reaffirmed by the
United Nations, and 'inasmuch as what is involved is the right of peoples to
engage in armed struggle for self-determination'.[36] Joe Stork critically
observes in this regard that without any conditioning language on the framework of international humanitarian law, the affirmation of 'any means of
armed struggle . . . politically represents merely a mirror image of the Israeli
contention that all forms of militant struggle, and certainly armed struggle,
are indistinguishable from terrorism'.[37]

The Convention then proceeds to the concept of political offences, which
would clearly be excluded from the provisions on extradition and rogatory
procedures with which much of the remainder of the text deals. Anything
already defined as a 'terrorist offence' is not to be considered a political
offence, along with a list of other specific offences which are also not to be
so considered 'even if they are politically motivated' (Article 2(b)). Offences
excluded from the 'political offence exception' for purposes of extradition
include 'attacks' on the kings and heads of Contracting States, their rulers,
wives (sic), ascendants or descendants, crown princes, deputy heads of state
or government ministers, and persons enjoying 'international protection'
including ambassadors and diplomats (Article 2(b) i, ii, iii). Also excluded
are 'intentional murder and theft accompanied by force against individuals,
or the authorities, or means of transport and communications'; 'acts of
sabotage and destruction of public property assigned to a public service,
even if owned by another Contracting State', and offences related to weapons,
munitions or explosives or other items 'that may be used to commit terrorist
offences'. In the first three clauses, the word used for 'attack' (ta'adda'ala) is
unqualified; that is, it is not necessarily restricted to physical attacks, or
attacks on the lives or liberty of such persons. Some Contracting States
have legislation criminalizing the 'defamation' or lampooning or otherwise
'undermining' of their leaders.

There is much to comment on in the remainder of the text, including
particular concerns over the lack of guarantees of fair trial or rights of
detainees, extended surveillance authorities threatening the right to privacy,
and an absence of reference to international law standards on any of these or

---

[35] UN Doc S/2003/583 (Third report of Saudi Arabia to the CTC) 13.   [36] Ibid.
[37] Stork, 'Human Rights Crisis', 49.

other issues.[38] Despite the urging by Arab states that an international definition of torture include a definition of state terrorism, the Arab Convention includes no such text, and fails to clarify that state officials or other agents of the state are capable of committing the crimes defined therein as 'terrorist offences'.[39] Some state parties however provide in their domestic legislation for increased penalties if terrorist offences are committed by agents of the state, notably members of the police or armed forces. The focus of such provisions appears to be hostile activities against the state by such individuals or groups, rather than state accountability for actions of its agents as 'state terrorism'.

IV. State responses

A. Egypt

The definition of terrorism in the Arab Convention is taken almost word for word from pre-existing (1992) Egyptian legislation.[40] Egypt tends to play a leading role in matters legislative in the region, and politically is one of the 'big three' (along with Saudi Arabia and Syria) in the Arab League. Egypt has officially been in a state of emergency since 1981, when President Anwar Sadat was assassinated, and has since suffered other attacks by domestic armed groups. Concern at 'the effects on the human rights situation' caused by this prolonged state of emergency and various 'security' measures associated therewith has been voiced by the UN Human Rights Committee.[41] The Committee had similar concerns when the Egyptian government legislated Law no. 97 of 1992 in direct response to 'the emergence of the phenomenon of terrorism'.[42] It declared:

> The definition of terrorism contained in that law is so broad that it encompasses a wide range of acts of differing gravity. The Committee is of the opinion that the definition in question should be reviewed by the Egyptian authorities and stated more precisely especially in view of the fact that it enlarges the number of offences which are punishable with the death penalty.[43]

---

[38] See above note 32.
[39] Amr Mousa, Secretary-General of the League of Arab States, told the Cairo meeting on terrorism and human rights that the UN should draft a convention 'including a definite definition of terrorism that discerns between terrorism and peoples' legitimate right to combat occupation and aggression and a definition of state terrorism' (in Kjok, *Terrorism and Human Rights*, 23). See also Amnesty International, above note 32, 16.
[40] UN Doc S/2001/1237 of 29 May 2002 (Egypt's first report to the CTC) 13.
[41] CCPR/10/76/EGY 2002, para 16. See also UN Doc CCPR/C/79/Add.23 of 9 August 1993 paras. 7, 9.
[42] UN Doc S/2001/1237 of 29 May 2002, 3.
[43] UN Doc. CCPR/C/79/Add.23 9 August 1992, para. 8.

Law no. 97 of 1992 introduced amendments to a number of laws.[44] It introduced the following definition of 'terrorism' as Article 86 of the Egyptian Penal Code:

> In application of the provisions of this law, terrorism shall mean any use of force or violence or threat or intimidation resorted to by the perpetrator in implementation of an individual or collective criminal undertaking aimed at disturbing[45] public order or jeopardizing the safety and security of society, which is of such nature as to harm persons or sow fear among them or imperil their lives, liberty or security; or [of such a nature as] to damage the environment, or to damage, occupy or take over communications, transport, property, buildings or public or private realty (amlak); or to prevent or impede the exercise of their functions by public authorities or places of worship or institutions of learning; or to thwart the application of the Constitution or the laws or regulations.

The similarities with the definition adopted by the Arab Convention are evident, but certain revisions were made. In the Arab Convention, causing fear or terror to persons is not an element of the definition, but in Egypt, the aim of violating public order or endangering public safety and security is. The first of these, violation of public order, is extremely wide. In contrast to the Convention, in the Egyptian text, a 'threat' is not necessarily of use of force or violence. The list of possible prohibited acts is similar but rather longer and considerably wider, in particular the final two clauses which are absent from the Arab Convention. The definition of terrorism cited in Egypt's first report to the CTC is a summary of the relevant article rather than the full text.[46]

Law no. 97 of 1992 sets out a series of offences as ordinary crimes, with increased penalties (including the death penalty and hard labour for life) if 'terrorism' is among the means used. For example:

> The penalty shall be prison for whosoever establishes, founds, organizes or directs, in violation of the law, an association or body or organization or group or gang the purpose of which is to call (da`wa) by any means for thwarting the provisions of the Constitution or the laws or preventing one of the government institutions or public authorities from exercising its functions, or attacking the personal freedom of the citizen or other public rights and freedoms guaranteed by the Constitution and the law, or injuring national unity or social safety. The penalty shall be temporary hard labour for whosoever, with knowledge of the purpose for which it calls,

---

[44] Law no. 97 of 1992, *Official Gazette* No. 29 bis of 18 July 1992. The legislation amended by the provisions of law no. 97 of 1992 included Penal Code and Code of Criminal Procedure, Law no. 105 of 1980 Regarding the Establishment of State Security Courts, Law no. 205 of 1990 Regarding the Confidentiality of Bank Accounts, and Law no. 394 of 1954 Regarding Weapons and Explosives.
[45] Or 'violating': *ikhlal bi*.   [46] UN Doc. S/2001/1237 3–4.

holds any kind of leadership within it, or supplies it with material or financial provisions.

The penalty shall be prison for a period of not more than five years for whosoever, with knowledge of its purpose, joins one of the associations, bodies, organizations, groups or gangs set out in the previous paragraph, or participates in it in any manner.[47]

This article already renders illegal mere membership in associations that have no necessary link with violence, let alone with terrorism, and may pose a considerable risk to freedom of expression and association. The following article (Article 86 *bis* (a)) stipulates that for offenders covered by the first paragraph of the previous article, the penalty shall be death or hard labour for life 'if terrorism is one of the means used in the realization or implementation of the purposes called for' by the association. For offenders under the second paragraph of Article 86 *bis*, the penalty in such circumstances becomes a sentence of hard labour if terrorism is among the means used.[48] There is further a prison sentence of up to ten years for anyone disseminating the purposes of such associations in any way or possessing materials for such dissemination, if terrorism is one of the means used by the association.[49] The accusation of terrorism may be made on the basis of the extremely broad terms of its definition.

Egypt has not amended these provisions following the promulgation of SCR 1373 (2001), although it has introduced new legislation on money laundering.[50] Human rights concerns have included the violent suppression of anti-war demonstrations in Cairo in the spring of 2002 and the arrest of alleged 'ringleaders'. In addition, Egypt's past criticisms of other states for refusing to hand over or curtail the activities of those it accuses of offences against Egyptian security appear to be bearing fruit, giving rise in some cases to fears for the safety of those extradited or returned to Cairo. In December 2001 two Egyptian asylum-seekers were forcibly repatriated by Sweden after secret evidence was relied on to dismiss their asylum claims; they then 'disappeared' into the system for more than three weeks with no access to family or counsel. Human Rights Watch reports other forcible repatriations from Jordan, Canada, Bosnia and Uruguay.[51]

---

[47] Article 86 *bis* of the Penal Code as amended by Article 2 of Law no. 97 of 1992.

[48] Article 86 *bis* (a) as amended by Article 2 of Law no. 97 of 1992. Offenders under Article 86 *bis* are also liable to hard labour for membership in such an association if they are members of the police or armed forces.

[49] Article 86 *bis* para. 3 and Article 86 *bis* (a) para. 3 as amended by Article 2 of Law no. 97 of 1992.

[50] Law to Combat Money Laundering, Law no. 80 of 2002 (*Official Gazette* no. 20 of 22 May 2002) and Law Amending Certain Provisions of the Law to Combat Money Laundering, Law no. 78 of 2003. See Sherif Sayyid Kamil, *Mukafihat jara'im ghasal al-amwal fi al-tashri' al-misri*, Cairo: Dar al-nahda al-`arabiyya, 2002.

[51] Stork, 'Human Rights Crisis', 46.

Egyptian human rights groups point out that they were among the first to focus the attention of the international NGO community on political violence by non-state actors.[52] The country has a diverse and active non-governmental human rights community, whose many activities, such as an energetic campaign against torture, rarely receive coverage in the domestic press. On the governmental side, and in line with recent 'reform-minded' moves in the region, the National Council for Human Rights has recently been established, functioning since the beginning of 2004 under the leadership of former UN Secretary-General Boutros Boutros Ghali. In what was considered its first real challenge, at the beginning of May, some observers saw a setback for the Council's potential in the apparently last-minute refusal by a majority of its members to endorse a memorandum prepared by its Legal Committee requesting the government to end the long-standing state of emergency.[53]

B. Syria

Syria is another state that has not found a need to amend its criminal legislation in the wake of SCR 1373 (2001). For the US, Syria remains one of 'the seven designated state sponsors of terrorism' because of its 'political and material support to Palestinian rejectionist groups'. Concerns that Syria might be the next target of the 'neo-cons' for invasion and 'regime change' reduced somewhat by 2004, and Syria for its part made positive moves to ensure it was not aligned with the 'enemy' in the 'global war on terror.' In its 2003 report, the US formally recognized Syrian cooperation 'against al-Qaida, the Taliban, and other terrorist organizations and individuals'[54] before announcing the imposition of sanctions against the country a fortnight later. Syria remains among the most tightly controlled of the Arab states despite recent moves towards the opening of the public space to civil society actors. Reports of discontent by Syrian Kurds in the north in March 2004, followed in April by 'mysterious gun battles' in Damascus, made uncommon

---

[52] Bahey el-din Hassan in Kjok, *Terrorism and Human Rights*, 13.

[53] *Al-Wafd*, 6 May 2004, 'Al-majlis al-qawmi li-huquq al-insan yataraji taht al-dughut al-hukumiyya.' See further Arab Program for Human Rights Activists, Press Release of 25 May 2004, 'Egypt: the National Council for Human Rights'.

[54] *Patterns of Global Terrorism 2003*, 85. Other Arab states on the list are Libya (although poised to be removed during 2004), Sudan, and Iraq. The list also includes Iran. The only non-Middle Eastern states on the list are Cuba and North Korea. The reports notes (at 93) that 'Syrian officials have publicly condemned international terrorism but continue to make a distinction between terrorism and what they consider to be the legitimate armed resistance of Palestinians in the Occupied Territories and of Lebanese Hizballah. The Syrian Government has not been implicated directly in an act of terrorism since 1986.'

news in the region.[55] Like Jordan and Morocco, Syria has recently come under new, comparatively young leadership with the accession of the former President's son, Bashar al-As`ad, to power, and his four-year-old programme of economic and financial reform is emphasized by increasingly dynamic Syrian inputs into international media.[56] Human rights groups have recently been allowed to form and operate, although still under considerable constraint.[57] In 2001, the UN Human Rights Committee reiterated its concern that a 1963 decree declaring a state of emergency remained in force.[58]

The Syrian Penal Code of 1949[59] was modelled on the Lebanese Penal Code, which was in turn inspired by French criminal law. The Syrian code contains three articles on 'terrorism' within the chapter on 'crimes against internal state security'. The following definition of terrorism in Article 304 is almost unchanged since the original promulgation of the law:

> Terrorist acts shall mean all deeds that aim at creating a state of panic (dhu`r) and which are committed by means such as explosives, weapons of war,[60] inflammable materials, poisonous or incendiary products or epidemic or microbe agents of a nature to cause public danger.

---

[55] Trouble between Kurdish and Arab supporters at a football match in Qamlish, and the reported killing of some twenty persons by the security forces, were followed by clashes between Kurds and the security forces in March 2004; Amnesty International cited reports of hundreds of Syrian Kurds arrested.

[56] For example in a glossy 14-page pull-out in the Lebanese *Daily Star*, which comes with the *International Herald Tribune* in the region, entitled *The Syrian Arab Republic: Commemorative Feature Supplement Celebrating the 58th Anniversary of Independence* (3 May 2004) the front page led with 'Facing a long list of international and regional pressures, Syria's reform efforts continue to take hold.'

[57] Several Syrian human rights activists were arrested in the opening months of 2004, including Aktham Nu`aisa, director of the Committee to Defend Democratic Freedom and Human Rights in Syria. Nu`aisa was brought before the State Security Court charged, apparently, with 'carrying out activities that contradict with the socialist regime of the state, opposing the goals of the revolution, and circulating false information damaging the reputation of the state'. See also the Law on Opposition to the Goals of the Revolution, Legislative Decree no. 6 1965.

[58] UN Doc. CCPR/CO/71/SYR para. 6; see OHCHR Digest, 18–19. The Committee referred to Legislative Decree no. 51 of 9 March 1963 declaring a state of emergency. In the article from the *Daily Star* supplement of 3 May 2004 (above note 56), reference was made to 'domestic political problems, including protests to lift the Emergency Law' as well as the 'Kurdish riots of March'. The article described the response to these problems as 'restrained'.

[59] Promulgated by legislative decree no. 148 on 22 June 1949 (*Official Gazette* no. 37 of 18 July 1949 p. 2025); with 15 laws amending it, the latest in 1979. Text annotated by Mamduh `Atari, *Qanun al-`uqubat: mùaddalan wa madbutan; `ala'l-asl*, Damascus: Mu'assasat an-nuri 2003.

[60] The phrase 'weapons of war' was added by Law no. 36 of 26 March 1978; `Atari 118.

The Syrian definition makes the creation of fear an element in the definition of the offence, although it does not specify among whom. It does not specify any further purpose, and although the means listed tend to a high degree of potential danger and damage, they are not presented as exhaustive ('means such as'). Article 305 imposes a penalty of hard labour of between fifteen and twenty years for 'every terrorist act' (not further defined) and of between ten to twenty years of hard labour for conspiracy. The death penalty is mandated if such an act 'results in the destruction – even partial – of a public building, industrial establishment, vessel or other installation or disruption of means of information, communication or transport, or if it leads to the death of a person'. The third of the three articles in the section on terrorism deals with associations that are established 'with the intention of changing the social or economic character of the state or the basic mores of society by one of the means set out in Article 304'. Such an association is to be dissolved and its members sentenced to hard labour, with a minimum seven year sentence for founders and directors. This description includes a political purpose missing from the definition of terrorism. Membership in such an association is here, as in Egypt, a punishable offence even if no specific terrorist act has been planned, attempted or carried out.

In its second report to the CTC, Syria sets out legislation imposing 'severe penalties for all acts relating to terrorism'.[61] The first provision it sets out is Article 278, which comes in a section entitled 'crimes affecting international law' and criminalizes the violation of arrangements made to maintain neutrality in a war, and punishes 'the author of acts, writings, or speeches for which the Government has not granted permission and which expose Syria to the risk of acts of hostility or disturb its relations with a foreign state or exposes Syrians to acts of revenge against their person or property'.[62] In a recent annotated copy of the Penal Code, this article is cross-referenced to Article 65 of the General Publications Law 1949,[63] which concerns the communication or publication of false news or falsified documents and imposes a criminal sentence of up to a year and/or a fine 'if such act was ill-intentioned or disquieted the public or disturbed international relations or undermined the standing or dignity of the state'. This provision may be used to serious effect in the constraint of political dissent and criticism of the government.

C. Jordan

In Jordan, an opportunistic expansion of government control was passed at the same time as legislation responding to Security Council resolution 1373 (2001), only to be changed back again after negotiations between the

---

[61] UN Doc. S/2002/1046 of 19 September 2002 3 (second report of Syria to the CTC).
[62] The penalty is a prison sentence.   [63] Law no. 53 of 8 October 1949; 'Atari 2003 111.

executive and key civil society actors. Many provisions of Jordan's Penal Code 1960[64] reproduce the Syrian text. This was the case in the three provisions in the Jordanian code on terrorism until their amendment in 2001; the only differences were that in its definition, Jordan had not followed Syria's amendment of its listed means of committing terrorism to include 'weapons of war', while in the second article stipulating penalties the Jordanian text substituted life hard labour for the death penalty in one case and a slightly lighter prison sentence in another.[65]

In October 2001 Jordan's government rushed out amendments to the Penal Code by way of a royal decree issued in accordance with a decision of cabinet, during an extended delay in convening Parliament that saw over a hundred such 'temporary laws' issued.[66] Temporary Law no. 54 of 2001[67] introduces a new definition of terrorism based on a combination of the Arab Convention and its Egyptian model. The element of 'causing panic' is no longer a necessary part of the definition of terrorism, and the 'means' listed in the above-cited Syrian Article 304 as part of the definition are transformed in the new Jordanian provision into aggravating factors at sentencing, giving rise to the death penalty when an act of terrorism under the new definition is committed.[68] The new definition of terrorism in Article 147 is as follows:

> Terrorism shall mean the use of violence or threat of use thereof, whatever its motivations or purposes, occurring in implementation of an individual or collective act aimed at disturbing public order or jeopardizing the safety or security of society, where such is of a nature to spread fear among the people and frighten them or to expose their lives and security to danger, or to cause damage to the environment, or to cause damage to, occupy or take over public facilities and realty or private realty, international facilities and diplomatic missions, endangering national resources or thwarting the provisions of the Constitution and laws.

---

[64] Law no. 16 of 1960 as amended 1988, 1991, 2001, 2003; *Official Gazette* no. 1487 of 11 May 1960. This Code replaced an earlier Temporary Penal Code of 1951 (Temporary Law no. 85 of 1951, *Official Gazette* no. 1077 of 17 July 1951). On the choice made by the newly independent and sovereign state of Jordan to follow French-based models from neighbouring states rather than adopting the 1936 Criminal Code issued by the British in Palestine (and which had therefore been in force in the Palestinian West Bank, incorporated into the territory of Jordan after the war), see E. T. Mogannam, 'Developments in the Legal System of Jordan' 6 *Middle East Journal* (1952) 194–204, at 196.

[65] Articles 147, 148, 149 of the Jordanian Penal Code 1960 before its amendment in 2001; paralleling Articles 304, 305 and 306 of the Syrian Code.

[66] Legislation issued in this manner is classified as 'temporary' and is supposed to be submitted for parliamentary scrutiny and decision when parliament is reconvened.

[67] Temporary Law no. 54 of 2001 amending the Penal Code, of 2 October 2001, *Official Gazette* no. 4510 of 8 October 2001.

[68] Article 148 (4)(c) of the Jordanian Penal Code as amended by article 3 of Temporary Law no. 54 of 2001.

This definition adopts the broader Egyptian text in some respects (including 'disturbing public order'), while staying closer to the Arab Convention definition in others (including the threat being of the use of force). Curiously, it omits the qualification of such acts as 'criminal'.

Article 148 adds to the original text penalties of hard labour for life for terrorist offences resulting, *inter alia*, in 'damage, even partial, to a public or private building'[69] or 'disabling means of communication and computer systems, or disrupting their networks, or the total or partial disabling or damaging of means of transport'. The death penalty is mandated where the act leads to death or is committed using means (such as explosives) that were previously included in the definition of terrorism.

The third of the three articles in the section on terrorism, Article 149, is also amended to show key differences from the Syrian text:

> A penalty of temporary hard labour shall be imposed on whosoever embarks upon any act of a nature to destroy the system of political rule in the Kingdom, or to incite to oppose it (*munahida*), and whosoever embarks on any individual or collective act with the intention of changing the economic or social character of the state or the basic mores of society.

The original wording of this provision was a word for word reproduction of the Syrian text. The new Jordanian text no longer refers to associations but to individual or collective acts, does not require that such acts be carried out by means elsewhere identified with the definition of terrorism, and adds as new the first half of the provision regarding the destruction of the system of political rule or incitement to opposition thereto.[70]

In the same temporary law, Jordan changed a text punishing 'every writing, speech and act intended to or resulting in the provocation of sectarian or racial chauvinism or urging discord between the sects and different elements of the nation' by a prison sentence of six months to three years plus a fine, to the following:

> Regardless of any other law, a prison sentence shall be imposed for any writing, speech or any act broadcast by whatever means, or publication of news in press or any publication, where such is of a nature to injure national unity or to incite commission of crimes or spread rancour and hatred and discord between individuals of the society or provoke racial or sectarian chauvinism, or injure the dignity, personal freedoms and reputation of individuals, or shake the basic foundations of society by promoting deviant behaviour or immorality or by publishing false information or

---

[69] Thus adding 'private' buildings to the Syrian text which stipulated 'public' buildings in Article 305 cited above.

[70] Subsequent clauses deal with hostage taking and with infiltration to and from the territory of the Kingdom. Article 147 (2) and (3) of the Penal Code 1960 as amended by article 4 of Temporary Law no. 54 of 2001.

rumours or incitement to agitation or vigils or the holding of public meetings in a manner contravening the applicable law, or by any other act liable to undermine the prestige, reputation or dignity of the state.

(Article 150).[71]

The second paragraph of this article as amended provided for the punishment of the editor-in-chief and owner of any publication used in such an act, plus the temporary or permanent closure of the newspaper or press 'in accordance with a decision of the court'. International human rights groups voiced concern at the attack on the right to freedom of expression and of the press represented by the extremely sweeping terms of this amended provision. In January 2002 the editor-in-chief of a political weekly was described by Amnesty International as 'the first known victim of the amendment of Article 150' when he was charged with 'writing and publishing false information and rumours that may harm the prestige and reputation of the state and slander the integrity and reputation of its members' after publishing a piece critical of the government.[72] The Jordanian Press Association and a number of newspaper editors and owners challenged the constitutionality of the amended article but the High Court of Justice rejected the suit for lack of interest of the petitioners;[73] interventions and negotiations about the role of the media and its regulation continued, with the Press Association drafting its own 'code of honour assuring objectivity and freedom of expression' and the Prime Minister promising that the article would be repealed.[74] In another temporary law issued in June 2003, the text of Article 150 was changed back to its original reading apart from an increase in the fine that could be imposed.[75]

In its first report to the CTC, Jordan set out in some detail examples of sentences passed by its State Security Court on persons convicted of

---

[71] Article 150 of the Penal Code 1960 as amended by Article 5 of Temporary Law no. 54 of 2001.

[72] The case of Fahd al-Rimawi, editor-in-chief of al-Majd weekly. See Amnesty International, 'Security measures violate human rights' AI Index MDE 16/001/2002 of 5 February 2002. See also Stork, 'Human Rights Crisis', 43.

[73] Jordan Times, 'High Court rejects JPA lawsuit contesting Penal Code provisions', 17 July 2002. See further AMAN News Center (the Arab Regional Resource Center on Violence Against Women) http://www.amanjordan.org.

[74] Jordan Times, 'Government announces procedures to repeal Article 150', 9 April 2003.

[75] Temporary Law no. 45 of 2003 amending the Penal Code, Official Gazette no. 4600 of 1 June 2003. The potential prison sentence of between six months to three years remains the same, while the fine rises from a maximum of 50 dinars in the original 1960 text to 500 in the new version. Another change made by Temporary Law no. 54 of 2001 however remains: this is an amendment to article 195 of the Penal Code, which deals with insults to the King; a new clause added to the list of offences that provoke a prison sentence of from one to three years for 'whosoever gossips about His Majesty the King or commits calumny by attributing to him words or deed which the King did not say or do, or acting to broadcast such or spread it among the people'.

terrorism-related offences, including the death penalty and life sentences with frequent *in absentia* judgments.[76] The State Security Court has been the focus of criticisms from human rights groups since it was reintroduced in 1991.[77] Already in August 2001 there had been an amendment (through a temporary law) to the Law establishing the State Security Court expanding its jurisdiction (for example to include 'any other crime related to economic security that the prime minister decides to transfer to the Court').[78] The amendment also permits the police to detain a suspect for up to seven days before bringing him or her before the Prosecutor, as compared to the twenty-four hours permitted under the regular Code of Criminal Procedure.[79] The Jordanian Bar Association voiced particular objections to the removal of the right to appeal for those convicted of 'misdemeanours' in the State Security Court.[80]

Jordan, rather like Morocco, emphasizes its positioning as a 'moderate middle course'.[81] Along with the introduction of these amendments to the Penal Code that potentially tighten the controls on political dissent, the institutionalization of human rights mechanisms is underway. The discourse of rights and reforms is prominent, and a well-known figure from the NGO human rights movement, advocate Asma Khadr, has been appointed spokesperson for the government. Significant changes to family law were also passed in the absence of Parliament, as were amendments to the controversial penal code provisions on 'crimes of honour', which had been the focus of advocacy for many years by women's groups and of attention by the international media. Not all of these changes have survived reviews undertaken subsequently by the newly elected parliament.

D. Morocco

A few years into his reign, the new Moroccan king had dismissed certain key elements of the 'old guard' and is considered to have been moving steadily if somewhat slowly along the path of socio-economic and political reform.

---

[76] UN Doc S/2002/127 of 29 January 2002 (first report of Jordan to the CTC) at 9–12.

[77] The State Security Court was first established in 1952, replaced by military martial courts from 1967–1990, and reintroduced (replacing the military martial court system) in 1991.

[78] Article 3 (a) iii) of Temporary Law no. 44 of 2001 amending the Law establishing the State Security Court, *Official Gazette* no. 4503 of 28 August 2001. An examination is made in a 'Working Paper on Law no. 16 of 2001 amending the Code of Criminal Procedure no. 9 of 1961' (Arabic text) by Advocate Abdel Ghaffar Freihat to a workshop of the Jordanian Banks Association in Amman, 15 October 2001.

[79] Article 7 of the Law establishing State Security Courts as amended by article 3 of Law no. 44 of 2001; Freihat, 'Working Paper', 10.

[80] The Bar Association took an 'unprecedented decision' to call on all its members to refrain from appearing before the Court for a week in June 2002, to protest the 2001 amendments. Saad Hattar, *Jordan Times*, 12 June 2002.

[81] UN Doc S/2002/127 29 January 2002 (Jordan's first report to the CTC) 3.

The 'public space' had enlarged and at the end of 2003 a new personal status code, heralded as broadly egalitarian, was issued with significant amendments to more traditional positions maintained in its predecessor. An Equity and Reconciliation Commission has been established to deal with past 'disappearances' and other abuses, which although still limited goes further than previous mechanisms. Nevertheless, human rights activists working on Sahrawi issues remain vulnerable to arrest, and the editor of the country's only satirical news journal was sentenced after the Casablanca bombings, although released by royal amnesty along with a number of Sahrawi activists in January 2004.[82] Observers comment that the 'security-minded administration' still holds that 'too much political liberalization is dangerous' and that their arguments were bolstered by the suicide bombings in Casablanca in May 2003 and the alleged involvement of Moroccan nationals in the Madrid bombings of 2004.[83] These events have exacerbated differences between the reform-minded and the 'old guard'. The 'security crackdown' began in 2002, and by November 2003 Amnesty International was reporting a sharp rise in the number of reported cases of torture or ill-treatment, with a rise in the number of political arrests being a 'significant factor' in this development.[84] Hundreds were arrested after the Casablanca bombings, with associated reports of torture and ill-treatment and concerns at unfair trials in which many were sentenced.

In its first report to the CTC Morocco noted that terrorist acts were already criminalized by the Moroccon Penal Code, but that 'the criminalization of terrorism as such' was being prepared. In May 2003 the Law on the Fight Against Terrorism was published amending certain sections of the Criminal Code 1962 and the Code of Criminal Procedure.[85] It introduces a section on 'Terrorism' into the Criminal Code[86] which provides a list of offences under criminal law that:

> shall be considered terrorist acts where they are intentionally related to an individual or collective undertaking aimed at seriously prejudicing public order by means of intimidation, terrorization (*tarhib*) or violence.[87]

---

[82] Eileen Byrne, 'Turning the page,' 717 *Middle East International* 23 January 2004, 24–5.

[83] Mark Huband, 'Reforms offer a means of reducing high jobless rate,' and Eileen Byrne, 'Escaping from the Chains of History', *Financial Times*, 16 April 2004.

[84] Amnesty International, 'Morocco/Western Sahara: Briefing to the Committee Against Torture', November 2003, AI Index MDE: 29/001/2003 of 11 November 2003.

[85] Dhahir no. 1.03.140 issued on 28 May 2003 promulgating Law no. 03.03 concerning the Fight against Terrorism (Mukafahat al-irhab), *Official Gazette* no. 5112 of 29 May 2003 Amending the Criminal Code 1962 (promulgated by Dahir no. 1.59.413 on 26 November 1962); and the Code of Criminal Procedure promulgated by Dhahir no. 1.02.255 on 3 October 2002, *Official Gazette* no. 5078 of 30 January 2003, 315.

[86] Inserted into the Criminal Code as Article 218 (1)–(9).

[87] Criminal Code article 218 *bis* (1) as amended by Law no. 03.03.

This definition includes purpose (prejudicing public order) and act (including a level of severity in 'seriously'), but not motivation. Thus, 'terrorism as such' is defined through the commission of certain offences for certain purposes. The list of offences attached to this definition includes *inter alia* intentional attacks on the lives or security or freedoms of persons, counterfeiting, sabotage, diverting or destroying planes, ships or other means of transport, forming a gang or making an agreement in order to prepare for or to carry out a terrorist act, and knowingly concealing gains made through a terrorist act. For such acts, where the penalty under ordinary criminal law is life imprisonment, the death penalty is imposed; life imprisonment is imposed where it would have been a maximum penalty of thirty years in prison, and otherwise the maximum penalties under ordinary criminal law are doubled so long as the final penalty does not exceed thirty years. Prison of two to six years plus a fine is imposed for 'anyone who commends acts constituting terrorist crimes by means of speech, shouts or threats in public places or meetings, or by means of writing, publications that are sold or distributed or offered for sale or exposed in public places or meetings or by means of placards exposed to public gaze by the various means of audio visual and electronic media'.[88] A prison sentence of ten to twenty years is provided for:

> Whosoever intentionally provides someone committing a terrorist offence or contributing or participating in such with arms or explosives or instruments to implement the offence, or monetary assistance or means of subsistence or communication or transport, or a place to meet or lodging or concealment; and whosoever helps to dispose of the results of the criminal act or knowingly gives any [other] kind of assistance.[89]

This provision clearly seeks to be all-inclusive of various possible acts of complicity or concealment, and there is a clear emphasis on intention and knowledge of purpose. If all that was provided was lodging or personal subsistence, Law no.03.03 allows the court to pardon from the set penalty 'relatives and in-laws of a person who committed or participated in or contributed to a terrorist offence, up to the fourth degree', and a similar dispensation is permitted to such relatives for the offence of not revealing to the relevant authorities knowledge that a person has of terrorist crimes.[90] This specific allowance for exemption from an otherwise mandatory penalty is also found in Tunisia, although there it applies only to the offence of failing to inform the authorities.

Law 03.03 provides for searches and other investigative procedures to take place outside the normal hours 'in cases of necessity' as well as the ordering of phone intercepts, taping and other forms of surveillance where certain

---

[88] Article 218 *bis* (2) of the Criminal Code as amended by Law no. 03.03.
[89] Article 218 *bis* (6) of the Criminal Code as amended by Law no. 03.03.
[90] Article 218 *bis* (8), providing for a penalty of five to ten years in prison.

offences are suspected. *Garde à vue* (pre-arraignment) detention is allowed for ninety-six hours, renewable twice for a similar period, with access to a lawyer being delayed 'where necessary' for up to forty-eight hours from the first renewal of the *garde à vue*.[91] Since most allegations of torture and ill-treatment relate to the period of *garde à vue*, this extension from the ordinary maximum of eight days in cases affecting state security has given rise to concern among human rights organizations. Even before the operation of the new rules, there were in addition concerns over the alleged falsification of the dates of arrest, a practice which illegally extends the period of *garde à vue* during which the detainee is isolated from anyone but the detaining agents. After the Casablanca bombings, among the hundreds arrested was a man accused of being the coordinator of the attacks. Abdelhak Bentasir died in custody, according to the authorities, of 'pre-existing illnesses of the heart and liver' two days after being arrested and 'before his questioning had been completed'. Amnesty International reported his family as stating he had been arrested five days earlier than acknowledged by the authorities and had been in good health; the autopsy was not made public, nor was his family enabled to appoint their own doctor to attend.[92] Praising Morocco's effective cooperation in the 'global war on terrorism', the USA's official update for 2003 reported that:

> Days after the [Casablanca] attacks, the Moroccan legislature passed a law that broadened the definition of terrorism ... and facilitated prosecution of terrorist suspects. Throughout the summer and fall, authorities arrested hundreds of terrorist suspects and sentenced dozens to lengthy prison terms and, in some cases, execution.[93]

Amnesty International's June 2004 report casts further light on the treatment of such 'terrorist suspects' in custody. Compared with the decrease in reports of torture and ill-treatment prior to 2002, this is clearly a set-back for the rights of Moroccan citizens, challenging internal actors working for socio-economic and political reform in different constituencies across the country.

E. Tunisia

Tunisia's Law no. 2003–75 regarding Support for International Effort to Combat Terrorism and the Repression of Money Laundering[94] shows some similiarities with the Moroccan amendments. The draft had already been prepared when in

---

[91] Article 5 of Law no. 03.03 amending articles 66 and 80 of the Code of Criminal Procedure.
[92] Amnesty International, 'Briefing to the Committee Against Torture', 6.
[93] *Patterns of Global Terrorism*, 65.
[94] Law no. 2003–75 of 10 December 2003, *Journal Officiel de la République Tunisienne* no. 99 of 12 December 2003 at 3592–601. French translation by the Tunisian government for purposes of information. French text also available at http://www.jurisitetunisie.com/

April 2002 a truck exploded outside a Djerba synagogue, killing twenty-one people. The Tunisian authorities have observed that they had 'long warned of the terrorist threat', but at the same time human rights groups have voiced concern at Tunisia's use of the security discourse for over a decade 'as a pretext for repression of political dissent and critical discourse across the political spectrum'.[95] Thus, while the official narrative of modernity, stability and rights (including substantial emphasis on women's rights) is fiercely promoted at home and abroad, Tunisia's public space remains extremely restricted in relation to criticism of the president or the government. Tunisia's new law reflects its official image in an aspirational opening statement:

> The current law guarantees society's right to live in security and peace, far from all that is of a nature to undermine its stability, to reject all forms of deviance, violence, fanaticism, racial segregation and terrorism which menace peace and the stability of societies. It contributes, moreover, to supporting the international effort to combat all forms of terrorism, to confront sources of finance that support it and to the repression of money laundering, within the framework of international, regional and bilateral conventions ratified by the Tunisian Republic and respect for constitutional guarantees.
>
> (Article 1)

This is the longest of the post-SCR 1373 (2001) legislative instruments under consideration here. The law's first major contribution is to amend the pre-existing definition of 'terrorist offence' under the Tunisian Penal Code.[96] The new Law 2003–75 contained the following definition of terrorist offences:[97]

> Shall be categorized as terrorist, every offence, regardless of its motives,[98] related to an individual or collective undertaking liable to intimidate a person or group of persons or spread alarm among the population with the intention of influencing the policy of the state and prompting it to do or abstain from doing any action, disturbing public order or international peace and security, causing harm to persons or property, damaging the headquarters of diplomatic and consular missions and international organizations, inflicting serious harm on the environment so as to endanger the life or health of inhabitants, or damaging vital resources, the infrastructure, transport, communications, information systems or public amenities.
>
> (Article 4)

---

tunisie/codes/terror/menu.html. (under the title *Lutte contre le Terrorisme et le Blanchiment d'Argent*). I do not yet have the Arabic text.

[95] Amnesty International, 'Tunisia: New draft "anti-terrorism" law will further undermine human rights', briefing note to the European Union, AI Index MDE 30/021/2003.

[96] In this case I am using the translation provided by the English text of Tunisia's second report to the CTC (S/2002/1024 of 13 September 2002).

[97] Article 103 Amending.

[98] *Quels qu'en soient les mobiles*. This phrase is not included in the translation in Tunisia's third report, which is otherwise used here from the phrase 'to intimidate' onwards.

In this wording, prospective intimidation of a person or group of persons or spreading fear among the population is a necessary element;[99] also necessary is intention, but while this includes influencing state policy, it may also include 'disturbing public order', or 'causing harm to property' or 'damaging public amenities'. There is no requirement of use of violence nor, in some phrases, of the level of damage that has to be done.

Amnesty International has voiced particular concern over what it considers a further broadening of the definition of 'terrorist offence' in Law 2003–75 in the light of the past use of the pre-existing Article 52 *bis* of the Penal Code against non-violent opponents of the Tunisian authorities. The organization notes that 'the Tunisian authorities have been casting the net of "terrorism" charges so wide as to include prisoners of conscience. Article 52 *bis* has been used to criminalize peaceful opposition activities'. The reinstatement since 1999 of the trial of civilians by military court has resulted in 'scores of civilians ... sentenced on charges of "terrorism" to heavy prison sentences after unfair trials'.[100]

A large number of accomplice offences are provided for, some of them requiring intention and some not. Membership of whatever form in any sort of group or organization which 'even coincidentally or incidentally'[101] has adopted terrorism as a means of achieving its goals is criminalized, as is putting any 'capabilities or expertise' at the disposal of such a group or supplying or disseminating information 'with the intention of assisting in the commission of a terrorist offence'.[102]

A prison sentence of five to twelve years can be imposed on whosoever:

> procures a meeting place for members of an organization, group or persons connected with terrorist offences, helps to lodge them or hide them or helps them to escape or ensures they are not discovered or punished, or benefits from the outcome of their misdeeds.[103]

---

[99] In the French text this is not necessarily the case, but I assume the Arabic original will confirm the meaning rendered in the English text of the UN report.

[100] See further Amnesty International, 'Tunisia: the cycle of injustice', AI Index MDE 30/ 001/2003. A particularly notorious attempt to apply article 52 *bis* – although ultimately the conviction was not made under the 'terrorist offences' terms of this article – came in the 1999 prosecution of Radhia Nasraoui, a prominent human rights lawyer, along with twenty-one co-defendants. For details of the charges against Nasraoui and her co-defendants, and of the trial proceedings, see Amnesty International, Human Rights Watch, and the Observatory for the Protection of Human Rights Defenders, *The Administration of Justice in Tunisia: Torture, Trumped-up Charges and a Tainted Trial*, March 2000, AID Index 30/04/00.

[101] Wording from S/2003/1038 11.

[102] Articles 13 and 17. The penalty is 5–12 years in prison for the first offences and 5–20 for the second set, plus a fine of 5,000 to 50,000 dinars in both cases.

[103] Article 18 of Law no. 2003–75.

There is apparently no requirement here of knowledge or intention. In the parallel provision of the pre-existing Penal Code broadly the same list of actions is criminalized with a maximum penalty of six years in prison for whosoever 'knowingly and voluntarily' commits them in relation to members of a criminal gang.[104] The comparable provision in the new Moroccan law also emphasizes that such acts incur liability where done 'knowingly' or 'intentionally'.[105] It is an offence under the Tunisian law not to give immediate notification to the relevant authorities of information regarding a terrorist offence, even where the person is bound by professional confidentiality; here, an exception is made for ascendants, descendants, brothers, sisters and spouse.[106] Article 12 of Law no. 2003–75 provides for a penalty of five to twelve years in prison for:

> whosoever, by any means, calls for the commission of terrorist offences or for joining an organization or group connected with terrorist offences, or uses a name, a term, a symbol or any other sign with the goal of condoning[107] a terrorist organization, one of its members or its activities.[108]

In Canada, Roach notes a new offence regarding 'knowingly participating in or contributing to any activity of a terrorist group', and the evidential use of frequent association with members of a terrorist group and of the use of terrorist-related symbols and representations.[109] In Tunisia, such use itself constitutes an offence.

V. Conclusion

Reform and 'democratization' in the Arab states were emphasized as a policy focus in developing US engagement with states in the region in a series of 'initiatives' developed in 2003 and 2004.[110] Considerable attention is paid to the findings of the set of Arab Human Development Reports by those seeking

---

[104] Article 133 of the Penal Code as amended by law no. 89–23 of 27 February 1989. Article 28 of Law no. 2003–75 provides for the minimum penalty for the initial offence in the event that the perpetrators of a terrorist offence establish they were drawn into the act by *inter alia* abuse of their situation.

[105] See above p. 602.   [106] Article 22 of Law no. 2003–75.

[107] The French text is *faire l'apologie de*; the Moroccan provision similarly translated (Article 218.2 above) uses an Arabic word (*ashad bi*) meaning praise or condone.

[108] The last part of this provision, from 'or uses a name', is not included in Tunisia's third report to the CTC.

[109] Roach, 'World Wide Expansion', 513.

[110] The Greater Middle East Initiative was not, as originally planned, announced at the G8 Summit of June 2004, although some Arab states did attend to discuss an apparently less ambitious 'Broader Middle East Initiative'. For a critique of the first for failing to establish 'a basis for genuine partnership', see Marina Ottaway and Thomas Carothers, 'The Greater Middle East Initiative: Off to a False start', Carnegie Endowment for International Peace, Policy Brief 29, March 2004.

to formulate policies in the 'global war on terrorism,' and in particular to extremely high levels of joblessness as well as lack of participation in social and political development. Different bodies in the United Nations have considered the role of the Organization beyond the CTC in combating terrorism, including through 'norm setting, human rights and communication'.[111] In a number of states new, albeit limited, human rights mechanisms have been instituted by governments, and certain other moves towards social, economic and political 'opening' (or 'reform') have been noted. Nevertheless, there is clearly a tension between these developments and the threats to core 'democratic' rights posed by legislation introduced or legitimated by the 'war on terror'. Helen Fenwick observes that 'democratic governments are perfectly entitled to take extra-ordinary measures if faced with a threat of atrocities' and explores the tension that necessarily arises between such measures and 'democratic values', with a view to proposing that such measures 'be subjected to the most rigorous tests for proportionality'.[112] The lack of space for public dissent and criticism, even given the opening up that has been going on in certain states over recent years, is a particular obstacle facing those in the Arab states who would agree with this statement, and who would seek to constrain within a similar principle of proportionality the reaction of their governments to serious domestic and international threats. A further obstacle is the apparent endorsement of legal and extra-legal practice by the US in particular. In the Yemen, a visiting delegation from Amnesty International, bringing up the mass arbitrary arrests and detentions that had taken place there since 11 September 2001, allegedly with FBI involvement, reported as follows:

> The authorities, while recognizing that they were in breach of their international human rights obligations and their own laws, argued that this was because they had to 'fight terrorism' and avert the risks of a military action against Yemen by the US in the wake of the 11 September events. The authorities said that they had 'no option' but to continue the practice of detention without charge or trial of those held contrary to their laws and international obligations, and that they had no plans to offer them an opportunity of access to lawyers or the judiciary to challenge the legality of their detention.[113]

Such deftly frank admissions of responding to pressure cannot excuse the state actor in such cases. Nevertheless, support – or pressure – for such

---

[111] UN Doc A/57/273 S/2002/875 Report of the Policy Working Group on the United Nations and Terrorism.

[112] Helen Fenwick, 'Responding to 11 September: Detention without Trial under the Anti-Terrorism, Crime and Security Act 2001' in Lawrence Freedman, *Superterrorism: Policy Responses* (Oxford, Blackwell Publishing 2002), 80–101, at 100–1.

[113] Amnesty International, 'Yemen: United Against Rights', AI Index 31/011/2003 24 September 2003. See also '200 held in Yemen to placate US', *Guardian*, 24 September 2003.

measures from the US sits uneasily with its public promotion of reform in the Middle East as critical in its future engagement with the region. It was also in Yemen that a CIA-controlled drone aircraft is reported to have launched a missile killing six men in a car in a suspected extra-judicial execution. Although Amnesty International reported receiving no response to its letters raising its concerns, Yemeni ministers have since confirmed that the government cooperated with the US in this operation within the 'global war on terrorism'.[114]

Alongside the current focus on 'democratization', human rights activists in the region report an increasing perception of the 'hypocrisy' of the international discourse of human rights and international law, in a region where it is already complicated by long-standing perceptions of selectivity, and where indeed the term 'international' is being increasingly read as meaning either US or US-driven. This is a concern not only for those who wish to see domestic reform initiatives take shape and continue rather than be interrupted or undermined. It needs no particular insight to suggest that such a development is of dubious efficacy in the effort to build international peace and security and to combat the phenomenon of terrorism.

---

[114] Amnesty International, 'Yemen: The Rule of Law Sidelined in the name of security', AI Index MDE 31/006/2003 24 September 2003. Amnesty reported the US as arguing that such actions did not constitute extra-judicial killings but rather 'military operations against enemy combatants' and therefore were governed not by Yemeni police procedures but by 'the international law of armed conflict'.

27

Terrorism in Argentina: government as its own worst enemy

WILLIAM C. BANKS AND ALEJANDRO D. CARRIÓ

Argentine society has experienced terrorism from domestic and external sources since the late 1960s. Domestic terrorism appeared mainly in the 1970s, first as leftist guerrilla movements that sought to attract attention when they failed to field an organized political movement. This small band of terrorists effectively paved the way for the appearance of brutal forms of state terrorism. The repressive state practices were first justified as a necessary antidote to the guerrilla activities, but quickly expanded into a blunt and massive campaign to eliminate any dissent to military rule. Unfortunately, the extra-legal methods employed by the Argentine government for fighting terrorist violence were mostly condoned or acquiesced in by the judiciary, and the legacy of the 'Dirty War' waged by the military *junta* continues to haunt the Argentine courts.

In more recent times international terrorism appeared. A massive attack destroyed the Embassy of Israel in Buenos Aires in 1992. In 1994, the building that harboured the two most prominent Jewish organizations in Argentina was targeted with another deadly bomb. In the combined attacks, conventional explosives caused in the aggregate about one hundred deaths and hundreds of injuries. In both cases criminal investigations have been ongoing for more than ten years, although there has been little success in bringing those responsible to justice. After one president was accused of interfering with the investigations of the bombings, a new president has promised to invigorate the investigation and to make its findings public.

After discussing the historical context for terrorism in Argentina and some legal aspects of the two types of terrorism in parts I and II of this chapter, we assess common elements of the domestic and international terrorism that have bedevilled Argentina for more than thirty years. Our conclusion, that the Argentine government is complicit in the terrorism experience in Argentina, derives from an examination of the common ground. Unabashed state terrorism was the government's tool for responding to the small band of guerrillas in the 1970s, and some state involvement, from knowing acquiescence to quiet support, accompanied brutal international terrorism in the 1990s. A new government has brought new candour and openness to addressing the wrongs of the

Argentine experience with terrorism in the past. Whether the frank admission of past wrongdoing will pave the way to more lawful and effective responses to terrorism in the future remains to be seen.

I. State terrorism in the 1970s

A. Historical background

Until 1930, Argentina had a relatively successful constitutional system and a growing experience with participatory democracy. When a military coup toppled the elected government in 1930, the retired General Jose F. Uriburu declared himself president. Although Uriburu promised his 'respect for the Constitution and basic laws in force',[1] subsequent history shows anything but respect, as is evidenced by five military coups between 1930 and 1976, a replacement constitution that lasted only from 1949 to 1955, a practice of sacking individual justices or the Supreme Court *en masse* for political purposes, and an enduringly strong influence of the military in civilian affairs.[2]

Terrorism first appeared in Argentina in the late 1960s and early 1970s. Violent guerrilla organizations were formed, during a period when Argentina was governed by a military regime. The ideologies of these groups varied. One of them, called *Ejército Revolucionario del Pueblo* (ERP), was mainly identified with Marxism. Another powerful group, *Monteneros*, had a nationalistic origin and clear links with the Peronist party, which had dominated Argentine politics since 1946. However, the *Monteneros'* support for Peronism was merely pragmatic; they wanted power and influence and believed that Peronist politics could provide their opportunity. The *Monteneros* were no more than twenty in number, and they came together in 1968 to launch a violent struggle against government authority. They assassinated General Pedro Aramburu, the president who sought to overturn Peronist influences. They carried out kidnappings, robberies, bombings and other attacks on military installations and other government properties and persons throughout 1971 and 1972.[3]

The party leader, Juan Perón, had been responsible for encouraging these groups through messages sent from Madrid, Spain, where he had been living in exile under the protection of General Franco.[4] By mid-1972, the ruling

---

[1] Quoted in Robert A. Potash, *The Army and Politics in Argentina, 1928–1945* (Palo Alto, Stanford University Press, 1969), at 58.

[2] Daniel Poneman, *Argentina: Democracy on Trial* (St Paul, Paragon House, 1987), 3–8.

[3] Gary W. Wynia, *Argentina: Illusions and Realities* (New York, Holmes & Meier, 1986), 77–80.

[4] 'Violence already exists and only violence will destroy it' and 'what other means, except violence is available for a humiliated people', are phrases attributed to Perón during those years. For a thorough description of the appearance of these extremist groups and the illegal response given by the Argentine state, see Jaime Malamud Goti, 'Terror y Justicia en la Argentina,' Ed. La Flor, 2000.

junta announced that elections would be held the following year, leading to a campaign to bring Perón back from Spain for another term as president. A democratic government was elected in 1973 and Héctor Cámpora, known to be the delegate of Perón, was sworn in as President. Cámpora resigned almost immediately, making room for Perón, who had conveniently returned from Spain earlier on. After another general election was held, Perón became President of Argentina for a third time. His wife, Isabel Martínez de Perón, who had no experience in holding public office, was elected Vice-President.[5]

Perón died in July 1974 after less than a year in office, and Isabel Perón became the new head of state. The *Monteneros* recognized that, while they were heard by the new Peronist government, they had not gained considerable influence. ERP, already rejected by Perón, attacked the Peronist left, leading the old guard Peronists to begin violent confrontations with the youthful ERP and *Monteneros*. By then, violence emanating from all groups became an everyday reality, each faction claiming to be the real heir of the Peronist doctrine. Bombings, kidnappings, and attacks directed at military bases, were part of the strategy followed by the guerrilla groups, especially ERP and the *Monteneros*. The *Monteneros* kidnapped wealthy businessmen, collected ransom, and used the $70 million to buy weapons which they used to assassinate labour and Peronist leaders. In 1975 and 1976 they expanded their attacks to military and police installations. In 1976 the *Monteneros* killed or seriously injured 300 persons.[6]

In early 1974, the government began to fight back. A former secretary of Perón and Minister of Social Affairs, José López Rega, became the strong man of an already ineffectual government.[7] López Rega was responsible for the creation of the Anti-Communist Argentine Alliance, or Triple A, a paramilitary group made up in part of retired police officers and gunmen from the ministry of social welfare. Triple A began to combat the guerrilla groups using their very same methods. In 1975, with violence dominating the political scene, the executive issued a decree giving the armed forces the task of carrying out the 'military and security operations they deem necessary to annihilate the subversive elements throughout the country'.[8] According to this decree and some complementary orders issued by the military, the whole

---

[5] Interestingly, Perón's wife was able to achieve what Eva Perón could not. When in 1952 Perón was running for a second period as President, the powerful military blocked the candidacy of Eva Perón for the Vice-Presidency. Only then 'Evita' delivered her famous speech of renouncement of that post.

[6] Wynia, *Argentina*, at 81–2.   [7] Goti, 'Terror y Justicia', at 23.

[8] Decree 2772 of October 6, 1975, published in the Boletín Oficial of Argentina, 4 November 1975. See generally Alejandro Garro and Henry Dahl, 'Legal Accountability for Human Rights Violation in Argentina: One Step Forward and Two Steps Backward' (1987) 8 *Human Rights Law Journal* 283.

of Argentina was divided into four defence zones, with a military commander in charge of each. The Army, under the command of Lieutenant General Jorge Rafael Videla, had overall control of all zones.

In 1976 the military seized power from an already exhausted government in another coup. General Videla was appointed President of the military *junta* that took control. The parliament was dissolved and heavy purges in the judiciary followed. Under these circumstances, the military *junta* took advantage of the state of siege[9] that had been declared in 1974 by the previous government, in order to escalate what became known as the 'Dirty War' against any individual suspected of left-wing ideologies. Instead of merely re-establishing order in society, the military government determined to root out what it viewed as the core sickness of Argentine society.

B. Fighting terrorism with more terrorism: states of siege

Although the United States Constitution influenced the Argentine Constitution of 1853, the Argentine Constitution retained a Spanish-style centralization of powers. In addition to designating the president as 'supreme head of the Nation',[10] the Argentine Constitution borrowed from the French revolutionary law of 1791 and the Chilean Constitution of 1833 to confer on the president the authority to declare a 'state of siege' and suspend constitutional freedoms when internal unrest threatened the Constitution or the government.[11] Although only the Congress may declare a state of siege during a period of 'internal disorder', the President may issue the declaration if the Congress is in recess, and Congress may approve or disapprove the declaration when it reconvenes.[12] This limitation on the executive has proven ineffectual in Argentine history. During the extended periods when Argentina has been ruled by the military, the president has unilaterally declared every state of siege; Congress has been dissolved during military rule.[13] States of siege have been imposed more than thirty times, for periods as short as six weeks and as long as nine years.[14]

---

[9] For an analysis of the prerogatives of the executive in Argentina under a state of siege and its comparison to emergency powers in the United States, see William C. Banks and Alejandro Carrió, 'Presidential Systems in Stress: Emergency Powers in Argentina and the United States' (1993) 15 *Michigan Journal of International Law* 1.

[10] Arg. Const. art. 99 (1).

[11] Ibid. art. 23. See Alejandro M. Garro, 'The Role of the Argentine Judiciary in Controlling Governmental Action Under a State of Siege' (1983) 4 *Human Rights Law Journal* 311, 316–317 (1983).

[12] Arg. Const. arts. 75 (29); 99 (16).   [13] See Banks and Carrió, 'Presidential Systems', at 11.

[14] Poneman, *Argentina*, at 131.

The government of Isabel Perón declared the entire nation to be in a state of siege in 1974. After seizing the government from Perón in 1976, and with augmented powers coming from laws enacted by the military leaders, the armed forces resorted to repressive activities. The Statute for the Process of National Reorganization, for example, declared that the Constitution would remain in force only 'to the extent that it does not oppose the main objectives set forth by the military *junta* or the provisions' of its law.[15] The 'Dirty War' was conducted by the military government between 1976 and 1983, relying for its legal legitimacy on the state of siege declared by the deposed constitutional government. The three service branches planned an orchestrated campaign of state terror and then carried it out throughout Argentina. The campaign of violence was carried out under the supervision of the highest levels of the military leadership, with orders in chain-of-command fashion filtering down to the Task Groups of young officers, civilians and off-duty policemen who executed the orders.[16]

Violent abductions of suspected 'subversive elements' became an everyday reality, followed by detention in 280 secret prison camps created near military bases, interrogation with the use of torture, and execution.[17] Systematic and prolonged torture of those abducted included the electric prod, sexual abuse, and a variety of forms of psychological torture. Many people became the famous 'disappeared ones', while courts summarily rejected most habeas corpus petitions brought by the families of those deprived of their freedom, simply relying on the information advanced by the Minister of the Interior that denied any knowledge of the whereabouts of the missing persons.[18] The commission that eventually investigated the 'disappeared' persons documented 9,000 cases, although human rights organizations claimed that 30,000 were executed by the government. All the while, as the state monopolized terror and repression, fear turned citizens into spies on their neighbours, who became informants to the state.[19]

[15] Estatuto para el Proceso de Reorganizacion Nacional of Mar. 24, 1976, XXXVI-B A.D.L.A. 1021, 1032 (1976).
[16] Luis Alberto Romero, *A History of Argentina in the Twentieth Century* (University Park, Pennsylvania State University Press, 2002), 212–220.
[17] The horrendous practices used by the Armed Forces were documented in a report prepared by a National Commission set up by President Alfonsin in 1983, when Argentina returned to democratic rule. The report was known as 'Nunca Más: Informe sobre la desaparición de personas,' published by Editorial Universitaria de Buenos Aires.
[18] See Banks and Carrió, 'Presidential Systems', at 32.
[19] Romero, *History of Argentina*, at 218–20.

C. The aftermath: open wounds

The disastrous adventure of the Argentine armed forces that resulted in the war with Great Britain over the Malvinas/Falkland Islands in 1982 precipitated the fall of the military government. General elections were held in 1983 and a new democratic President, Raúl Alfonsín, took office in December of the same year. Almost immediately the government implemented a policy of bringing to trial the heads of the military *junta* that ruled the country between 1976 and 1983 for their role during the 'Dirty War' against terrorism. The initial idea of the government had been to leave the trials to military tribunals, according to the existing legislation that gave them jurisdiction.[20] The procrastination of these tribunals paved the way for a decision of the Federal Court of Appeals of Buenos Aires to take jurisdiction over the case.[21] The Federal Court of Appeals convicted most members of the *junta*, handing out heavy sentences ranging from life imprisonment to extended periods of incarceration. The convictions were mainly for the crimes of murder, torture and illegal deprivation of freedom.[22]

In this section we examine some of the still festering wounds caused by the state terrorism employed by the armed forces in Argentina. To be sure, the guerrilla movements of the 1970s were a threat to Argentine society. However, these horrific injuries done to innocent civilians vividly illustrate the risks of using illegal means against terrorism, no matter how serious this threat might be.

1. Missing children, crimes against humanity and the extent of *res judicata*

One consequence of the policies implemented by the Argentine Armed Forces to deal aggressively with those who became the 'disappeared ones' was that many children were born while their mothers were held under secret detention. It is now known that many of those infants were appropriated by

---

[20] The existing Code of Military Justice, Act 14029, would give the military courts jurisdiction to try all offences committed by any member of the armed forces, even such serious offences as murder and torture. The policy implemented by the government was to amend the Code, adding to the processes held in military courts a mandatory appeal in front of the Federal Court of Appeals located in Buenos Aires. The amendment also made sure that if the military councils showed no progress in trying their own personnel, the Federal Court of Appeals could take jurisdiction to try the cases itself. See these amendments in Act 23049 passed by Congress on 14 February 1984, XLIV-A A.D.L.A. 8 (1984). For further analysis of the extent of this Act, see Garro and Dahl, 'Legal Accountability', at 306.

[21] Ibid.

[22] The case in which these convictions were imposed was identified as '13/84.' The full decision is published in 309 Fallos CSJN, Vol. 1 and 2 (1986). On appeal, the Argentine Supreme Court affirmed most of the convictions, while reducing some of the sentences imposed. See 309 Fallos CSJN 1657 (1986).

persons with connections to the military, who either tried to pass these children as their own, or initiated adoption proceedings. In both situations, false birth certificates issued in most cases by physicians belonging to the police or the armed forces were created.

Former President and Army General Videla was one of those convicted of murder, deprivation of freedom and torture, in the 1984 trial held in the Federal Court of Appeals. Although charged with six counts of abduction of minors, Videla was acquitted of all six counts. Some years later, Videla was charged again with the crime of abduction of four different minors, born while their mothers were held captive. In the interim and after the conviction of the heads of the military *junta*, Congress passed an Act that sought to put an end to the trials of members of the armed forces that were being brought to Justice.[23] In essence, what became known as the 'Due Obedience Law'[24] created an irrefutable presumption that all military, police officers and servicemen below a certain rank had acted following orders that they were in no position to question. However, this 'Due Obedience Law' made clear that the presumption did not apply to the crimes of abduction of minors and suppression of their real identity.[25] Because of this exception to the general rule, Videla could be charged in spite of the existence of the Act.

In the course of the process Videla made a motion claiming that in the main trial in which the heads of the *junta* had been partially convicted, his acquittal had encompassed all possible cases of illegal deprivation of freedom of minors. In his motion he relied on a passage of the decision by the Federal Court of Appeals, in which the court stated that the defendants had been indicted for all the events that occurred while in charge of their respective forces. Therefore, the Federal Court of Appeals added, no new criminal prosecution could be brought against these defendants, since the lack of specific charges for other counts amounted to an implied acquiescence in other conduct of the accused.[26] With express reliance on this passage of the decision that had acquitted Videla for the abduction of certain minors, his

---

[23] By March 1987 the situation had become very tense. Some fifty military and police officers had been arrested in connection with human rights violations during the 'Dirty War,' and members of the armed forces had begun to show their unrest. Especially lieutenants, colonels and other officers in active duty menaced with revolts against the government, claiming that they were those who had really risked their lives in the fight against 'subversion', while merely following orders from their superiors. A strong revolt took place during the Easter of 1987 when a military barrack was the scenario of many troops demanding an end to the trials held against all members of the armed forces. See Garro and Dahl, 'Legal Accountability', at 337.

[24] Act 23521 published in XLVII-B A.D.L.A. 1548 (1987). See especially art. 1.

[25] See ibid. art. 2.

[26] See decision of the Federal Court of Appeals, Vol. 309 Fallos CSN, at 306/307.

defence then sought to thwart the new charges brought against him for the abduction of different minors by relying on the principle of *res judicata*.[27]

The *res judicata* argument was finally rejected by the Argentine Supreme Court.[28] In a part of the opinion in which all members concurred, the Supreme Court held that Videla had been previously charged with specific acts of abduction of certain minors, that were individualized in the case that resulted in his partial acquittal. He had not been charged, the Supreme Court added, with unspecific crimes committed at some period of his life, or 'unspecific abductions', but rather with certain and concrete acts of murder, torture and abductions. As Justice Maqueda stated in his concurring opinion, 'the defense of *res judicata* could only encompass the historic event that the court (below) was legally in a situation to judge'.[29] Therefore, the Court concluded, there were no obstacles to trying Videla for the abduction of minors not included in the previous case.

2. Pardons

The tension created in the 1980s when the Argentine courts arrested many active duty military officers for their role in the 'Dirty War' was partially appeased by the approval by Congress of President Alfonsin's so called 'Due Obedience Law'. The courts routinely dismissed the charges brought against these lower ranking defendants, entering decisions of exoneration that, according to Argentine law, have the full effect of an acquittal, preventing new charges for the same crime.[30]

However, the solution embedded in the 'Due Obedience Law' of only blaming those responsible for handing down the illegal orders, while freeing those merely carrying them out, was not enough for the military. Under the presidency of Carlos Menem, who had assumed the office after the general elections held in

---

[27] Act 48 that regulates the access of cases to the Supreme Court mandates that only 'final decisions' can be appealed to the Argentine highest tribunal. See A.D.L.A, 1852–1880, 364, art. 14. However, this Court has consistently held that decisions of lower courts that reject the application of the double jeopardy clause actually qualify as 'final', because of the irreparable harm that can be caused by such a rejection. See, among many others, 'Ganra de Naumow,' 299 Fallos 221 (1977).

[28] Decided on 21 August 2003; 2003-F La Ley 84. The decision in full was published by the 'Asociación Argentina de Derecho Constitucional,' No 191 issue, XIII, July/October 2003, p. 105, with note by Alejandro Carrió.

[29] See Justice Maqueda's opinion, ibid. at 126.

[30] In the Argentine system of criminal justice, notions of double jeopardy attach at very early stages of the process, since the investigation of crimes is essentially a judicial function. Investigative magistrates are actually those in charge of deciding whether there are enough grounds to bring defendants to trial, and decisions of those magistrates to end an investigation have the full effect of an acquittal, barring a new investigation for the same event. See, generally, Alejandro D. Carrió and Alejandro M. Garro, 'Chapter 1, Argentina' in Craig M. Bradley (ed.), *Criminal Procedure: A Worldwide Study* (Durham, Carolina Academic Press, 1999).

1989, many superior officers not covered by the benefits of the 'Due Obedience Law' continued to press for the termination of the cases remaining open against them. President Menem eventually acceded to their demands and ordered the full pardon of more than 200 military officers and other members of the armed forces. Those pardons, unprecedented in size and scope, resulted in the termination of all legal proceedings still under way.[31] In another move that was highly criticized by the legal community, Menem also pardoned the heads of the military *junta* that had been convicted during the historic trial held by the Federal Court of Appeals, during the presidency of Alfonsin. As a result of these pardons, no member of the Armed Forces remained in jail or subject to criminal charges for the remainder of Menem's presidency.

In 2003, the election of a new President in Argentina, Nestor Kirchner, brought a new willingness to confront past abuses and to provide openness in government. Unresolved allegations of human rights abuses were subject to re-examination, as was the role of the armed forces while fighting terrorist groups during the 1970s. First, Congress passed a law that repealed and declared 'null and void' the 1987 'Due Obedience Law'.[32] New charges, even for the old crimes, were brought against those previously pardoned or benefited by the 'Due Obedience Law'. This time, courts justified the new indictments claiming that the policy employed by the armed forces of subjecting individuals to secret detention, forcing them to 'disappear', or imposing torture during questioning, amounted to 'crimes against humanity', not subject to the defences available for normal crimes governed by domestic law.

3. The incorporation of international humanitarian law in the courts of Argentina

Even though not necessary to solve the question under dispute in the Videla case, two concurring Justices of the Argentine Supreme Court invoked language of the Barrios Altos case decided in March 2001 by the Interamerican Court of Human Rights. In Barrios Altos the Interamerican Court dealt with the validity of a Peruvian amnesty law that exempted from criminal responsibility those members of the armed forces, the police, and civilians for human rights violations committed between 1980 and 1995. Declaring that Peruvian law inconsistent with several provisions of the American Convention of Human Rights,[33] the

---

[31] Banks and Carrió, 'Presidential Systems', at 34.

[32] See Act 25779, A.D.L.A. LXIII-D, 3843, passed on 21 August 2003, which declared null and void the previous Act 23521.

[33] Signed in San José, Costa Rica, on 22 November 1969. Argentina approved this Convention by Act 23054 on 19 March 1984. In an Amendment to the Argentine Constitution that took place in 1994, the text of this Convention was incorporated in the Constitution. See art. 75, subdivision 22.

Interamerican Court of Human Rights held:

> that amnesty provisions, those that declare the application of the statute of limitations and the acceptance of exemptions of responsibility intended to prevent the investigation and punishment of those responsible for serious violations of human rights such as torture, extralegal or arbitrary summary executions and forced disappearances of persons, all acts prohibited as a violation of inalienable rights acknowledged by International Law, are inadmissible.

In deciding the Videla case, Chief Justice Petracchi stated that any extensive interpretation of the principles of *res judicata* which prevents the prosecution of the defendant should be rejected.[34]

The decision to treat the crimes committed by the Argentine armed forces during the 1970s and early 1980s as 'crimes against humanity', proscribed by principles of international law, is having a significant effect on previously settled doctrines of Argentine law. In the Rivero case, decided by the Federal Court of Appeals of Buenos Aires on 7 August 2003,[35] the defendant had challenged his prosecution for the crime of abduction of minors and suppression of their identity, because the statute of limitations had run. The acting Court of Appeals rejected this claim, invoking principles of international law that make this type of crime subject to continuous prosecution, in spite of any limitations coming from the internal legislation of the country in which the trial is taking place. The decision also relied on two International Conventions: the Convention approved by the United Nations in 1968 declaring that 'crimes against humanity' are not subject to the statute of limitations, and the Interamerican Convention of Forced Disappearances of Persons, signed in Brazil, on 9 June 1994, that includes similar provisions.[36] The Federal Court of Appeals relied on these international instruments even though none of them had been ratified by Argentina at the time of the events judged in this case.[37]

In another case recently decided by the same Federal Court of Appeals, *Crespi*,[38] the court declared that the previous exoneration of the defendants based on the application of the 'Due Obedience Law' did not permit a successful *res judicata* defence in a new trial. After characterizing the crimes under investigation – disappearances, tortures and abductions – as 'crimes against humanity', the Federal Court of Appeals declared that the principle of *res judicata* does not apply when the state has failed to fulfil its duty of fully investigating and punishing those responsible for gross violations of human

---

[34] See section 12 of Justice Petracchi's concurring opinion in La Ley, above note 28, at 120.
[35] See La Ley, Suplemento de Jurisprudencia Penal y Procesal Penal, 30 July 2004 issue, at 1, with note of Alejandro Carrió.
[36] See art. VII of this Convention. Its full text in LV-E A.D.L.A. 5862 (1995).
[37] Actually, the second one had not even been signed at that time.
[38] Decided on 13 July 2004. La Ley, 4 August 2004 issue, at 12, case No. 107869.

rights. In its most recent decision concerning the effects of international law on Argentine law, the Supreme Court held on 24 August 2004 that a statute of limitations could not stand in the way of the trial of Arancibia Clavel, accused of a range of offences, including conspiracy to commit murder as part of a political assassination plot, in violation of international humanitarian law.[39]

4. Forcing victims to face DNA tests

One of the most dramatic consequences of the 'disappearances' that took place in Argentina during the 1970s relates to the legal battles undertaken by the families of the 'disappeared' who have attempted to locate children born while their mothers were in captivity. Organizations composed of relatives of those who disappeared were formed.[40] With patience and the help of other human rights groups, they have been able to locate over the years many children who could then renew their ties with their blood family.

In the course of these pursuits, some criminal courts ordered blood tests on those defendants charged with having appropriated these missing children, in order to rebut their defence that they – the defendants – were the real parents of the suspected victims. Courts have determined that tests that require the extraction of blood for DNA analysis can be forcefully imposed on the defendants.[41] A much more serious problem arose in cases where the test was ordered on victims of the alleged abduction, who refused to take the test, claiming that that they will not submit to a test that may result in the conviction of those they consider their real parents and responsible for their raising. In some cases currently being litigated, the alleged victims are no longer minors, and their refusal of the DNA test as adults is more difficult to reject than that of minor children.

The case of Vázquez Ferrá, recently decided by the Argentine Supreme Court,[42] presents the competing values surrounding this problem. Evelin Vázquez Ferrá was already over twenty-one years old, when a blood test was ordered by a criminal court in the prosecution brought against those who raised her. In the course of the investigation the defendants confessed that their daughter was given to them by persons connected to the military during the 1970s, although they had raised her as their own daughter using a

[39] Arancibia Clavel, Supreme Court of Argentina, 24 August 2004 (unpublished, copy on file with the authors).
[40] The most notorious one is the so-called 'Abuelas de la Plaza de Mayo', an organization formed by elderly women trying to locate their grandchildren.
[41] The leading case, decided by the Argentine Supreme Court, is 'H.G.S.' 318 Fallos CSN 2518 (1995). In that case a unanimous Court held that a defendant suspected of having appropriated a child that he tried to pass as his own, cannot oppose a blood test that can be used to disprove his false allegations. The Court found that neither the privilege against self-incrimination nor the due process clause are violated by this investigative step.
[42] 30 September 2003. La Ley, 6 October 2003 issue, at 4.

false birth certificate. In order to corroborate the confession the criminal court ordered a DNA test at the request of those who claimed to be her blood relatives. Evelin Vázquez Ferrá objected to the test and the case reached the Supreme Court.

In a majority decision the Court agreed with her. Some of the Justices found the right to privacy so compelling that it could overcome an invasive investigative technique that violates privacy surrounding the family. These Justices also opined that the same rationale that prohibits forcing an individual to give testimony against those with direct family ties applies in the present case.[43] Most Justices also found that the fact that Vázquez Ferrá was an adult at the time of objecting to the test made this case distinguishable from the H.G.S. case.[44] In H.G.S. the Court had primarily relied on portions of the International Convention for the protection of children's rights, not applicable in the case at issue.

II. International terrorism in the 1990s

On 17 March 1992, a tremendous explosion destroyed the Israeli Embassy in downtown Buenos Aires, killing 28 people and injuring more than 300. Immediately an investigation was opened under the supervision of the Supreme Court of Argentina, which has jurisdiction in all cases concerning diplomats and members of Foreign Services.[45] The most accepted theory is that a truck loaded with explosives was parked directly in front of the Embassy.

On 18 July 1994, an entire building which served as the educational and recreational centre for two important Jewish organizations, Asociación Mutual Israelita Argentina (AMIA), and Delegación de Asociaciones Israelitas Argentinas (DAIA) was also the target of a terrible attack. This time a large van filled with explosives was detonated, killing 86 people and injuring more than 300. This time the investigation was left at the hands of a Federal Court of first instance, according to the Argentine rules that mandate that the investigation of crimes be directed by a magistrate.

A. Two unsuccessful investigations

Those responsible for the two bombings have not been apprehended. For more than a decade different theories have been advanced to explain the unsuccessful investigations. A written presentation made by representatives of AMIA and DAIA to the acting criminal court[46] found many common

---

[43] See the opinion of Justices Belluscio and López. Justices Petracchi, Moliné O'Connor, Fayt and Vázquez concurred with this line of reasoning.
[44] See above note 41 and accompanying text.   [45] Arg. Const. art. 117.
[46] See AMIA – DAIA, 'La Denuncia,' published by Editorial Planeta, 1997.

failings in basic police work in the two investigations. In neither investigation was the zone surrounding the explosions carefully preserved. In their efforts to rescue possible victims, many bystanders made alterations to the crime scene that were later impossible to correct. In addition, in both cases the government agency in charge of identifying those leaving the country immediately after the attacks failed to provide crucial information, claiming a lack of resources.

The AMIA investigation did reveal some connections between individuals trafficking with stolen cars – the van used in the attack among them – and members of the police force of Buenos Aires province.[47] Even though some members of this branch of the police were charged as accessories to the main crime of bombing the building, many observers believe that the case will at most prove the links between those police officers and one particular defendant, charged with having prepared the van to carry the explosives. It has not been proven that those police officers knew that the van would be used in a terrorist attack.[48]

The AMIA and DAIA report also shows a lack of professionalism on the part of the special investigative force within the Federal Police responsible for helping with the investigation: the so-called 'Departamento de Protección del Orden Constitucional'. When requested by the Federal Court to submit all tapes containing telephone conversations recorded at the house of the defendant charged with preparing the van used in the attack, this unit replied that many of those tapes were missing.[49] Photographs and a notebook seized during one of the several searches conducted by the police were also reported missing.[50]

B. Legal tools, illegal practices

In 1994, by Executive Decree 2023/94[51] a Federal Fund for the Protection against terrorism was established, aimed at providing rewards for those who would advance information or agree to give testimony helpful to determine who was responsible for the terrorist attack on the AMIA-DAIA building. In July 1996 the Judge in charge of the AMIA investigation began negotiating with one of the defendants toward obtaining a link between the defendant and the police forces of Buenos Aires province, concerning the delivery of the van later used for the attack. These negotiations were kept secret from all the other defendants. Testimony involving some police officers was finally

---

[47] Ibid. at 49/50.   [48] See the report included in 'Revista Textual,' Nª 70, 16 July 2004.
[49] Ibid. at 64.   [50] Ibid. at 66 and 77.
[51] Signed on 16 November 1994. This Decree was later complemented with Act No. 25.241 passed by Congress, LX-B ADLA 1409 (2000), defining 'acts of terrorism' and reducing penalties for those cooperating with the investigation of terrorist acts.

obtained, and became part of the official record of the case. This testimony also became the main evidence against the police officers held in custody, pursuant to a pre-trial detention decree. At that time, it was not revealed that the Judge had paid to the confessing defendant – allegedly from the Federal Fund mentioned above – the sum of $400,000. The whole story broke some time later, when a videotape of that secret negotiation mysteriously appeared.[52] The Judge and two prosecutors who conducted the secret interviews and arranged for the illegal payments were later removed from the case.[53]

Before the illegal payments scandal, the investigating judge made apparent headway in the case. In 2003, the judge released testimony by a defector from Iran's intelligence service, who fled Iran to Germany in 1996. In 1998 and 2000 depositions, Abdolghassem Mesbahi said that senior Iranian officials ordered the 1994 AMIA bombing and then paid former Argentine President Menem $10 million to deny Iranian involvement in the bombing. Although Iran and Menem denied the charges, Argentine prosecutors claimed that the Meshabi statements are consistent with elements of their investigation.[54] Based on the Meshabi testimony, the judge asked Interpol to arrest four Iranians – the head of Iranian intelligence in 1994, a former Iranian cultural attaché at the Argentine Embassy, a diplomatic courier, and a former education minister. Meshabi also claimed that the 1992 and 1994 attacks were ordered by Ayatollah Ali Khamenei, Iran's supreme leader, and other senior Iranian officials.[55]

President Nestor Kirchner also signed an executive decree opening secret intelligence documents and ordered intelligence agents to testify concerning their knowledge of the 1992 and 1994 bombings, to aid in the investigation of the attacks.[56] The government has had no success trying to extradite the Iranian officials. Britain refused to extradite a former Iranian ambassador to Argentina who was indicted in Buenos Aires in 2003. Argentina also claims that Switzerland has failed to cooperate in an investigation of how the attacks were financed.[57] In the midst of the continuing investigation, a trial has been ongoing of the local police officers and car thieves believed to have supplied the vehicle used in the 1994 bombing. With the removal of the investigative

---

[52] See Claudio A. Lifschitz, 'AMIA,' ed. Marcelo Soriano et al. (Buenos Aires, Departamento Editorial, 2000). The writer of this book was an official of the federal court in charge of the investigation. According to the writer, he became a witness to the congressional investigation that took place when some irregularities of the case started to be revealed.
[53] Above note 48.   [54] 'Judgment in Argentina', Boston Globe, A18, 12 March 2003.
[55] Ibid.
[56] Kevin Gray, 'Argentinean president calls probe of '94 JCC bombing a "disgrace"', Jerusalem Post, 20 July 2003, at 3.
[57] Larry Rohter, 'Argentines Criticize Investigation of '94 Attack', New York Times, 19 July 2004, at A6.

judge for the illegal payments, a new judge has been appointed, but he has a backlog of other work and little resources to conduct a broader investigation.[58] Recent developments in the case have included discussions of having the accused Iranians stand trial in a third country, although Iran has shown no interest in this proposal, and requests by Jewish groups for a belated investigation into a Syrian link to the 1994 attack. Menem is of Syrian descent, and it is alleged that he permitted Syrians under surveillance in Argentina to leave Argentina after the bombing, including a cousin of the president of Syria.[59]

III. Conclusions: common threads

A recurring theme appears in the two parts above. In the late 1960s and 1970s, Argentina became a playground for domestic terrorism fomented by guerrilla groups. The presence of military governments both contributed to and facilitated the operations of these groups. What later appeared as the 'official' response by the government, namely terrorism sponsored by the state directed inward at Argentine citizens, only made matters worse. 'Disappearances' and secret interrogations and torture of anybody suspected of having links with terrorists became an everyday reality. Appropriation of infants of those held in captivity added a final insult to the unprecedented levels of state-sponsored terrorism.

State complicity in terrorism has not been merely a province of the executive in Argentina. For the most part, the Argentine judiciary has been unwilling to confront executive abuses of power during states of siege. For example, the Constitution declares that the executive 'shall not convict or apply punishment upon [its] own authority'.[60] During the 'Dirty War', the *junta* interrogated those it detained, engaged in indefinite detention and torture, and, after summary proceedings before military tribunals, the suspects were in thousands of instances 'disappeared'.[61] The *junta* was not 'convicting' or 'punishing' Argentine citizens – the people were being tortured and killed. After the 'Dirty War' was over, some courts began to assert a stronger role. By and large, however, judges reviewed for 'reasonableness' the detentions in light of the purposes of Article 23 of the Constitution, and sided with the government after executive assertions that the detainee had 'subversive connections'.[62] Ironically, then, the civilian and military leaders in

---

[58] Larry Rohter, 'Justice Elusive in 1994 Attack on Argentine Jews', *New York Times*, 30 May 2004, at 4.
[59] Rohter, 'Argentines Criticize'.   [60] Arg. Const. art. 23.
[61] Martin Edwin Anderson, *Dossier Secreto: Argentina's Desaparecidos and the Myth of the 'Dirty War'* (New York, Westview Press, 1993), 223–94.
[62] Garro, 'Argentine Judiciary'.

Argentina employed the courts and an apparently rational discourse of law to legitimate what were lawless actions.[63]

Similarly, the Menem pardons were accompanied by the colour of law but were not lawful. The Constitution permits Congress to 'grant general amnesties', and it permits the president to 'pardon or commute penalties for crimes subject to federal jurisdiction, with a previous report from a competent tribunal'.[64] The Menem pardons were effectively an amnesty, did not eliminate any penalties that had been imposed, and usurped the congressional role. In addition, after the pardons the Argentine criminal law could not then be applied to the conduct charged of the officers, and the allegations of torture could not be assessed in light of the International Convention on Torture and Cruel Treatment, ratified by Argentina in 1987.[65] Instead of confronting the pardons on their merits, the Argentine Supreme Court responded to a challenge by the families of the disappeared persons by ruling that the victims' families lacked standing to sue.[66] After a prosecutor then disobeyed instructions from the Ministry of Justice and joined as a party with families of the disappeared persons to challenge the pardons of military officials, the Court found standing to sue based on the prosecutor's challenge, but concluded that the prospective pardons could be justified under the Constitution.[67]

Under President Kirchner, the government has pursued greater transparency and its willingness to reopen old wounds has been followed by some judges. Despite the stalled efforts to track down those responsible for the 1992 and 1994 bombings, and the allegations that President Menem actively or passively obstructed the investigations, the current government publicly lamented the disgraceful conduct of the investigation during its first decade and remains committed to pursuing the cases to their conclusion. Finally, the willingness of the Supreme Court and other judges to recognize and then incorporate international humanitarian law principles as part of the fabric of the laws of Argentina has also been a welcome respite from the tradition of deferring to executive branch interpretations of expansive executive powers.

---

[63] Banks and Carrió, 'Presidential Systems', at 34.   [64] Arg. Const. arts. 75 (20); 99 (5).
[65] Act 23.338, XLVII A.D.L.A. 1481 (1987).
[66] Riveros, Omar S. y otrol, [1991-I] J.A. 306 (1991).
[67] Judgment of 14 October 1992 (Aquino), Corté Supreme de Justicia de la Nación, [1993-I] J.A. 45 (1993).

28

Postscript: some recent developments

VICTOR V. RAMRAJ, MICHAEL HOR AND KENT ROACH

Anti-terrorism law and policy is a rapidly evolving field, and since the chapters in this book were last revised, between September and November 2004, there have been numerous developments in the various jurisdictions and areas of law covered in this book. We could not, in the late stages of production, provide a comprehensive update of all of these developments, but some of them were sufficiently important and relevant to the chapters in this book as to warrant a brief mention in a postscript.

I. United Kingdom: the House of Lords rules on indefinite detention of non-nationals

On 16 December 2004, the House of Lords released its landmark decision in *A. v. Secretary of State for the Home Department.*[1] The question in this case was whether the provisions in Part 4 of the Anti-terrorism, Crime and Security Act 2001 (ATCSA), which effectively permitted the indefinite detention of non-nationals of the United Kingdom who were suspected of being involved with international terrorism but who could not be deported, since they might be tortured in the receiving country, were inconsistent with the UK's obligations under the European Convention on Human Rights. The UK had formally derogated from Article 5(1)(f) of the Convention, which permitted the detention of foreign citizens only when 'action is being taken with a view to deportation'. However, under Article 15 of the Convention, measures derogating from Convention obligations in 'time of war or other public emergency threatening the life of the nation' were permitted only 'to the extent strictly required by the exigencies of the situation, provided that such measures are not inconsistent with its other obligations under international law'. So the question before the House of Lords was whether there

---

We are grateful to Paul Tan for his superb research assistance, and to William C. Banks, Kevin Davis, Helen Fenwick, Colin Harvey, Gavin Phillipson, C. H. Powell, Alan Khee-Jin Tan and V. Vijayakumar, for their helpful suggestions regarding this postscript.
[1] [2004] UKHL 56.

was a public emergency threatening the life of the nation and whether the measures in ATCSA were strictly required and consistent with the UK's obligations under international law. The majority of the House of Lords were prepared to defer to the determination of the executive or to assume provisionally that there was, post-9/11, a public emergency that threatened the life of the nation; however, they held, in view of the fact that British citizens similarly suspected of involvement in international terrorism were not subject to indefinite detention, that the detention measures aimed at non-nationals were not 'strictly required' and disproportionate, and so did not constitute a valid derogation.[2] A majority of the Law Lords also found that in derogating only from their right to liberty, the differential treatment of non-nationals was discriminatory and thus in breach of the UK's obligations under Article 14 of the European Convention. The House of Lords quashed the Order derogating from the Convention and issued a declaration of incompatibility in respect of the s. 23 detention provision in ATCSA.

In light of this ruling, the government tabled new legislation in Parliament to deal with suspected international terrorists within the parameters established in *A v. Secretary of State for the Home Department*. The proposed legislation allowed the Home Secretary to impose on suspected terrorists a range of derogating control orders, including house arrest, and non-derogating orders, including restrictions on movement, association and the use of various telecommunication devices. Crucially, the Bill applied to both non-national and British, who could neither be deported nor put on trial. The Bill faced considerable opposition, particularly in the House of Lords. Among the concerns was that the control orders ought to be imposed not by politicians or the executive, but by judges. The House of Lords eventually forced concessions from the government, including a greater judicial role in and an increase in the burden of proof for the imposition of derogating control orders. No derogation has yet been sought, and therefore derogating control orders cannot yet be activated. The Bill has now come into force as the Prevention of Terrorism Act 2005,[3] but is subject to three-month reviews and expiry in a year's time unless it is renewed.

The concerns expressed in *A v. Secretary of State for the Home Department* and the legislative controversy and eventual response, were largely anticipated by the contributors to this book. For instance, Colin Harvey (in Chapter 8) stressed the importance of keeping the asylum system and national security separate, a

---

[2] Lord Hoffmann, in contrast, found that there was no public emergency threatening the life of the nation in the first place: 'This is a nation which has been tested by adversity, which has survived physical destruction and catastrophic loss of life. I do not underestimate the ability of fanatical groups or terrorists to kill and destroy, but they do not threaten the life of the nation' (at para 96).

[3] 2005 c. 2.

point implicitly acknowledged by some of the Law Lords in holding that the right of the government to control immigration and distinguish between non-nationals and nationals in the immigration sphere was not decisive of the discrimination issue relating to indefinite detention, 'as this was not at its heart an immigration issue'.[4] Similarly, Helen Fenwick and Gavin Phillipson recognized that the UK's counter-terrorism scheme is 'open to the criticism that it fails the test of proportionality'.[5]

Yet in the wake of *A v. Secretary of State for the Home Department* and the Prevention of Terrorism Act, concerns persist about the ruling.[6] Harvey remains cautious in his assessment of the ruling, observing that the ruling 'is significant but its precise impact will need to be assessed carefully'.[7] Fenwick and Phillipson observe that derogating orders may still not achieve Convention compliance, assessment of which 'will depend on the security situation at the time when the derogation order was sought and the derogating orders activated'.[8] They also express concern that the House of Commons was unable to defeat the Government on the 2005 Act (the concessions, they point out, were forced by the unelected Lords), and that the legislation is again 'immensely overbroad'.[9] Fenwick and Phillipson express their concern in these terms:

> Most notably, in what is meant to be a response to the lapse of Part 4 of the 2001 Act, which applied only to international terrorism and was only used against al Qaeda, the 2005 Act applies to all terrorists, including, for example, animal rights extremists, etc., and thus for the first time brings *all* these groups within a scheme outside the criminal justice system, that allows for punishment (in effect) without trial. Once again, we will be dependent upon executive restraint in exercising the powers, and, to an extent, upon judicial review, to keep them within reasonable and proportionate limits, though the terms of the legislation itself will in many instances, render this difficult to achieve.[10]

The dialogue between the government and the judiciary concerning the appropriate legislative response to international terrorism seems destined to continue indefinitely. There is perhaps good reason to remain sceptical of the merits of this dialogue. Yet this institutional exchange may be what it takes to encourage the government, perhaps incrementally, 'to tailor

---

[4] Lord Scott of Foscote at para 134. [5] Chapter 21, in this volume, at 459.
[6] See, for example, David Dyzenhaus, 'An Unfortunate Outburst of Anglo-Saxon Parochialism' (2005) 68 *Modern Law Review* 673, criticizing Lord Hoffmann's speech for what Dyzenhaus describes as his 'equation of human rights with the values of the common law constitution' (at 674). See also, in the same volume of the *Modern Law Review* (654–680), other commentaries on *A v. Secretary of State for the Home Department* [2004] UKHL 56 by Tom R. Hickman, Stephen Tierney and Janet L. Hiebert respectively.
[7] Personal correspondence with the editors, 21 June 2005.
[8] Personal correspondence with the editors, 9 June 2005.   [9] Ibid.   [10] Ibid.

provisions more precisely to the particular emergency in order to avoid unnecessary impairments of human rights'.[11] The dialogue also reaffirms the need, noted in the introduction to the book, for students of global anti-terrorism law and policy to be familiar with the multiple instruments available to combat terrorism. The House of Lords' decision concerning the use of immigration law resulted in Parliament enacting new quasi-criminal law legislation that applies to citizens and non-citizens alike. The results of this dialogue will be subject to continued judicial review both in the United Kingdom and, potentially, in the European Court of Human Rights.

II. The treatment of non-national terrorist suspects in Canada and New Zealand

The House of Lord's decision in *A v. Secretary of State for the Home Department* can be contrasted with *Charkaoui v. Canada*, a decision made by Canada's Federal Court of Appeal in December 2004 upholding, under the Canadian Charter of Rights and Freedoms, a security certificate process available for non-nationals suspected of involvement with terrorism. As discussed in Chapter 23, this process allows the executive to declare and detain non-nationals as security risks subject to a special judicial review procedure before a single judge to determine whether the executive acted reasonably. The Court of Appeal recognized that the process, which allows the government to present national security information to the judge without the non-national being present and in some cases without even obtaining a full summary of the information, 'derogates in a significant way from the adversarial process normally adhered to in criminal and civil matters'.[12] Nevertheless, the Court of Appeal upheld the process by asserting that 'the threat of terrorism or a threat to national security does not represent or reflect a situation of normality, at least not in our country'.[13] This judgment seems to recognize an emergency that has not been formally declared in Canada and one that may never end.

The Court of Appeal noted that the British had devised an alternative institutional arrangement, one that allows national security information not disclosed to non-national detainees to be subject to adversarial challenge by a security-cleared special advocate. Nevertheless, the Court of Appeal concluded that the introduction of the special advocate procedure was a matter for the legislature and not the judiciary. A few months after his failed Charter challenge, however, Adil Charkaoui was released on strict conditions with the presiding judge determining that after 21 months' detention, 'the danger has

---

[11] Fenwick and Phillipson, Chapter 21, in this volume, at 459.
[12] *Charkaoui* v. *Canada* 2004 FCA 421 at para 75.   [13] Ibid. at para 84.

been neutralized'.[14] Nevertheless, four other non-national terrorist suspects are still detained in Canada under security certificates.

Similar issues about the detention of non-nationals found by the executive to be a security risk have also occurred in New Zealand in relation to the case of Ahmed Zaoui, who, as discussed in Chapter 24, was detained for security reasons under immigration law despite having been granted refugee status. In an important judgment, the Supreme Court of New Zealand in late November 2004 interpreted the immigration legislation to allow the grant of bail and detention in a place other than a penal institution. It stressed presumptions of respect for the 'ancient and important jurisdiction' of the courts to grant bail and of respect for international law with respect to refugees.[15] Mr Zaoui, like Mr Charkaoui in Canada, was subsequently released subject to strict conditions, with the courts emphasizing the delays of the security risk process and the difference between the standard for removal of non-nationals as security risks and whether they presented a present threat that required detention as opposed to court-supervised conditions.[16] Nevertheless, the conditional release of both Mr Zaoui in Auckland and Mr Charkaoui in Montreal raise questions about the original determinations by the executive that they constituted security threats and the ability of governments to deprive non-nationals of liberty on standards that are much less demanding of the state and less protective of liberty than those used in criminal law. These somewhat similar stories at opposite ends of the world also underline the convergence that sometimes occurs in global anti-terrorism law and policy.

At the same time, there is evidence of divergence between the approaches taken by the Supreme Courts of Canada and New Zealand as to whether a suspected terrorist could ever be lawfully deported to torture. As discussed in Chapter 23, the Supreme Court of Canada indicated in 2002 that it would generally be unconstitutional to deport a non-national to torture, but that there might be 'exceptional circumstances'[17] that could justify such actions. In June 2005, the New Zealand Supreme Court, in litigation brought by Mr Zaoui, rejected the exceptional circumstances approach as inconsistent with both international law and the New Zealand Bill of Rights.[18] It also held that the responsible ministers and Cabinet, and not an Inspector General of the Security Services who reviews the security risk certificate, would have the responsibility to determine whether there was a substantial risk of torture, subject to rules of natural justice and requirements for reasons.[19] It remains to be seen whether the New Zealand Supreme Court will follow or depart

---

[14] *Re Charkaoui* [2005] F. C. 248 at para 75.
[15] *Zaoui* v. *The Attorney General* SC CIV 13/2004 at paras 37, 44. [16] Ibid. at para 68.
[17] *Suresh* v. *Canada* [2002] 1 S.C.R. 3 at para 78.
[18] *Zaoui* v. *The Attorney General* [2005] NZSC 38 at paras 16, 90. [19] Ibid. at para 92.

from the Supreme Court of Canada in deferring to executive determinations about the risk of torture unless they are patently unreasonable.[20] As with so many topics discussed in this book, much will depend on the balance and relation between executive and judicial power.

The high standards of proof required in the criminal law were reaffirmed in Canada when in March 2005 a judge acquitted two men accused of conspiracy to commit murder in relation to the bombing of an Air India flight in 1985 that killed 329 people. The trial judge had heard the evidence without a jury in a complex sixteen-month trial. He concluded that although the state had proven beyond a reasonable that a bomb had been placed on the plane in Canada, it had not proven that the two men were part of the conspiracy. Evidence of political and religious motive was considered in the case, but the trial judge concluded that such motives were 'shared by countless other Sikhs throughout the world and by an unknown number in British Columbia'.[21] In reaching what was a very unpopular verdict, the trial judge stressed that the requirement of proof beyond a reasonable doubt 'is the essence of the Rule of Law and cannot be applied any less vigorously in cases of horrific crimes than it is with respect to any other offence under the *Criminal Code*.'[22] This case underlines the different treatment received in Canada by those accused of criminal acts of terrorism and those subject to immigration security procedures.

III. Further developments: South Africa, the United States, India and Southeast Asia

The South African anti-terrorism bill, discussed by C. H. Powell in Chapter 25, has now been enacted and proclaimed into force as a law, styled the Protection of Constitutional Democracy against Terrorism and Related Activities Act 2004.[23] Although it exempts armed struggles for national liberation, self-determination and independence against colonialism or occupation by foreign forces that are conducted in accordance with the principles of international law from its definition of terrorism,[24] it contains a broad definition of terrorism that applies to politically motivated acts of property damage and other economic harms.[25] As in Australia, Canada, Hong Kong and New Zealand, South Africa's broad definition of terrorism was in part inspired by the broad definition of terrorism in the United Kingdom's Terrorism Act 2000.[26] This suggests that national legislation, as well as international and regional directives, can influence the development of anti-terrorism laws throughout the world. As discussed in

---

[20] *Suresh v. Canada* at para 41.   [21] *R v. Malik and Bagri* 2005 BCSC 350 at para 1238.
[22] Ibid. at para 662.   [23] Act No. 33 of 2004.   [24] Ibid. s.1(4).   [25] Ibid. s.1 (xxv).
[26] K. Roach 'The Post 9/11 Migration of the Terrorism Act 2000' in Sujit Choudhry (ed.), *The Migration of Constitutional Ideas* (Cambridge University Press, forthcoming).

Chapter 25, South Africa's broad definition of terrorism, as well as other features of its law, are likely to be subject to constitutional challenge and judicial interpretation.

In the United States, Congress enacted an Intelligence Reform and Terrorism Prevention Act[27] in December 2004 that reorganizes the American intelligence community, establishing a Director of National Intelligence, a National Counterterrorism Centre and improved intelligence capabilities within the Federal Bureau of Investigation. It also addresses aviation[28] and maritime security, border and immigration controls, and the prevention of terrorist access to weapons of mass destruction. The new legislation also provides for a Privacy and Civil Liberties Oversight Board. This law continues the trend recognized by William C. Banks in Chapter 22 of 'the largest overhaul of government structure since World War II' in response to terrorism,[29] as well as a comprehensive approach to the risks of terrorism. It remains to be seen how effective the massive reorganization of American government around counter-terrorism will be in preventing acts of terrorism in the United States.

This law also revisits some laws made immediately after 9/11 in the USA Patriot Act. As Kevin Davis offers in an update of his commentary in Chapter 9:

> The legislation clarified the mental elements of the offence of providing material support to a foreign terrorist organization. It is now clear that under this provision a defendant must have knowledge either that the organization has been designated as a foreign terrorist organization or that it engages or has engaged in specified activities. This provision has also been amended to indicate that it is to be construed in a fashion that does not abridge rights granted under the First Amendment to the United States Constitution. On another front, the new legislation also amended the procedure for designation of foreign terrorist organizations. Specifically, it added procedures allowing an organization to petition for revocation of a designation and requiring a review of an existing designation after five years if no petitions for review have been made.[30]

It will be interesting to see if other countries revisit aspects of laws enacted in response to 9/11 and Security Council Resolution 1373.

American counter-terrorism efforts are, of course, not limited to the home front. In May 2005, Congress attached a rider that supplemental funds for the

---

[27] Pub. Law. No. 108–458.

[28] Additionally, on the aviation security front, Alan Khee-Jin Tan advises us in an update to Chapter 11 (in personal correspondence with the editors, 27 June 2005) that the United States has extended the date for the implementation of biometric passports for 27 countries in the Visa Waiver Program to 26 October 2006: see http://www.dhs.gov/dhspublic/display?content=4542.

[29] At 490.   [30] Personal correspondence with the editors, 28 June 2005.

global war on terror should not be used for 'torture or cruel, inhuman, or degrading treatment or punishment that is prohibited by the Constitution, laws, or treaties of the United States'.[31] Despite this, reports continue to surface with disturbing regularity about the abuse of those detained at Guantanamo Bay and elsewhere. Reports of abuse of the Quran and humiliation of prisoners also fuelled widespread animosity. Concerns have also been raised that the American-led occupation of Iraq has helped re-vitalize al Qaeda with almost daily bombings by insurgents in Iraq. These events underscore some of the difficulties discussed in the first Part of this book in distinguishing terrorism and counter-terrorism and between legal and extra-legal approaches to combat terrorism.

In India, whatever euphoria there was over the repeal of the Prevention of Terrorism Act (POTA) by the incoming Congress-controlled government in late 2004[32] has been considerably dampened by the institutionalization of what critics say are very similar provisions in the Unlawful Activities (Prevention) Amendment Ordinance 2004[33] and subsequently, the Unlawful Activities (Prevention) Amendment Act 2004.[34] Meanwhile, existing POTA prosecutions are still making their way through the judicial system, with the Supreme Court in two notable cases upholding the denial of bail.[35]

Attention in Indonesia has continued to focus on the outcome of the latest round in the prosecution against the alleged Bali bombing mastermind, Abu Bakar Bashir, who was sentenced to 30 months' imprisonment on 3 March 2005 for having 'approved' of the bombing.[36] This has been upheld on appeal and is expected to be argued before the Supreme Court shortly. He was, however, acquitted of more serious charges. The relatively short term of imprisonment has sparked off an intense controversy between critics who say that this is evidence of the law malfunctioning in favour of terrorism, and those who argue that this merely shows that genuine due process prevails in Indonesia.

Without a doubt, the single most significant development in Southeast Asia has been the flare-up of the insurgency in the south of Thailand, a jurisdiction not specifically covered in this book. An escalation of violence has been met with measures ranging from a declaration of martial law in early 2004, to the setting up of an Independent Commission for National

---

[31] Pub. L. No. 109–13.

[32] By the Prevention of Terrorism (Repeal) Ordinance 2004 (Ordinance 1 of 2004), and subsequently, the Prevention of Terrorism (Repeal) Act, 2004 (Act 24 of 2004).

[33] Ordinance 2 of 2004.   [34] Act 29 of 2004.

[35] *Maulavi Hussain Haji Abraham Umarji* v. *State of Gujarat* (2004) 6 SCC 672 and *State of Tamil Nadu* v. *R. R. Gopal* (2003) 12 SCC 237.

[36] 'Cleric Bashir appeals to Indonesian supreme court', Reuters 21 June 2005, http://www.alertnet.org/thenews/newsdesk/JAK63311.htm.

Reconciliation.[37] The government appears receptive to a proposal by the Commission that martial law should be lifted in favour of a new security law. An analysis of the extent to which this possible development might make a difference must remain the subject of a future work.

It is impossible to do justice in this short postscript to all the recent developments that have affected global anti-terrorism law and policy, but we hope that this brief account will provide a sense of the dynamic, complex and interconnected nature of a subject that will continue to command much public and scholarly attention for the foreseeable future.

Singapore and Toronto
30 June 2005

---

[37] 'Not yet reconciled', *The Economist* 2 June 2005, http://www.economist.com/displayStory.cfm?Story_id=4033992.

INDEX

.